The Afro-American Novel
and Its Tradition

BERNARD W. BELL

The Afro-American Novel
and Its Tradition

THE UNIVERSITY OF MASSACHUSETTS PRESS

AMHERST

In memory of
my mother, Theresa Bell,
and
my cousin, Bernice Hammond,

and for
my wife, Carrie,
sons, Byron, Christopher, and Douglass,
and mentor,
Sterling A. Brown

Copyright © 1987 by The University of Massachusetts Press
All rights reserved
Printed in the United States of America
Set in Linotron Palatino at Rainsford Type

Library of Congress Cataloging-in-Publication Data
Bell, Bernard W.
The Afro-American novel and its tradition.

Bibliography: p.
Includes index.
1. American fiction—Afro-American authors—History and criticism. 2. Afro-Americans
in literature.
I. Title.
PS 153.N5B43   1987   813'.009'896   86-25070
ISBN 0-87023-568-0 (alk. paper; cloth)

British Library Cataloging-in-Publication Data are available.

This publication has been supported by the National Endowment for the Humanities,
a federal agency which supports the study of such fields as
history, philosophy, literature, and language.

What I mean to suggest by this catalogue is the necessity, at the present time, of setting investigations of works of literature and verbal art in a framework that I call the "anthropology of art." The phrase expresses for me the notion that art must be studied with an attention to the methods and findings of disciplines which enable one to address such concerns as the status of the artistic object, the relationship of art to other cultural systems, and the nature and function of artistic creation and perception in a given society.

HOUSTON A. BAKER, JR.
The Journey Back

Contents

Contents

Contents

Introduction

GOT one mind fuh white folk to see, 'nother fuh what I know's me," my paternal grandfather used to say. Like Ellison's nameless protagonist in *Invisible Man*, it was not until many years later, while tracing the history of the Afro-American novel from its sociopsychological and folk roots to its contemporary branches, that I began fully to understand and appreciate his socially symbolic act. This book was initially conceived as a folkloristic and generic doctoral dissertation in the tradition of Daniel Hoffman's *Fable and Form* and Richard Chase's *American Novel and Its Tradition*, but over the past fifteen years I have radically expanded, reorganized, and rewritten it in the light of recent developments in linguistics and critical theory and in an effort to provide a more useful interdisciplinary reference work for general readers as well as specialists in American and Afro-American studies.[1] The historical debates by specialists about the relationship of black American culture and character to white American society and about the differences between the nature and function of the novel, with its allegiance to reality, and romance, with its allegiance to the ideal, provide the sociocultural and literary matrices of this book.[2] "If," as Fredric R. Jameson states in his neo-Marxist rewriting of Kenneth Burke's theory of symbolic action, " . . . narrative is one of the basic categorical forms through which we apprehend realities in time and under which synchronic and analytic thinking is itself subsumed and put in perspective, then we no longer have to be defensive about the role of culture and the importance of its study and analysis."[3] But because the narrative or storytelling tradition is an ancient sub-Saharan African as well as a Greco-Roman means for symbolically expressing both a personal and a collective relationship to a social and metaphysical universe, I believe that approaches to the Afro-American novel that reduce the rich complexities, paradoxes, and ambivalences of different human experiences, especially creativity, to economics, politics, psychology, or linguistics are, at best, incomplete.

This book, then, is a comprehensive sociopsychological, sociocultural interpretive history of the Afro-American novel. It seeks to unearth, iden-

Introduction

tify, describe, and analyze some of the major thematic, stylistic, and structural characteristics of the Afro-American novel from its beginnings in 1853 to 1983, the year that marks the culmination of the achievement of black female novelists with Alice Walker's Pulitzer Prize–winning *The Color Purple* and of the revitalizing power of an Afrocentric aesthetic for black male novelists with John Wideman's highly acclaimed Homewood trilogy. By discussing major texts in their historical, cultural, and literary contexts, I seek primarily to explain the richness of the Afro-American novel as a hybrid narrative whose distinctive tradition and vitality are derived basically from the sedimented indigenous roots of black American folklore and literary genres of the Western world. My basic interpretive strategy is to approach the novel holistically as a socially symbolic act, examining the formal text as a rewriting of the survival strategies, especially the use of the vernacular, music, and religion, by which black Americans as an ethnic group came to consciousness of themselves and celebrated their quest for personal and social freedom, literacy, and wholeness.

Underlying my interdisciplinary approach are three basic assumptions. First, I have assumed that there has always been a cultural and social boundary in America beyond which the black American could not go. As a major contemporary black writer and social critic has stated:

> at some point always, he could not participate in the dominant tenor of the white man's culture, yet he came to understand that culture as well as the white man. It was at this juncture that he had to make use of other resources, whether African, sub-cultural or hermetic. And it was this boundary, this no-man's land, that provided the logic and beauty of his music.[4]

It was also from this position as the prototypical outsiders and marginal people of American culture and society that representative black American novelists began exploring the literary possibilities of their residual oral Afro-American folk forms and Western literary tradition (their dual African and Western cultural heritages) for appropriate structures and language to construct their visions of the human condition as filtered through the prism of their particular time, place, and ethnic group. Social and cultural boundaries are therefore as important as social and cultural change in shaping the form and content of the Afro-American novel. The second basic assumption of this study is that the inadequate attention by readers and critics to such literary matters as genre, structure, style, characterization, and point of view has led to misunderstandings about the merits of individual Afro-American novelists as artists and about their use of the narrative tradition.[5]

Introduction

Third, assuming that the Afro-American novel is not merely a branch of the Euro-American novel but also a development of the Afro-American oral tradition, I raise such questions as: How are its historical and cultural roots, which produce the consciousness and aesthetic choices of the artists, different from those of the Euro-American? How have sociocultural differences shaped the double-consciousness, socialized ambivalence, and double vision considered by some social scientists and artists to be characteristic of Afro-Americans?[6] What are the most distinctive thematic, stylistic, and structural patterns produced in the Afro-American novel as a result of this difference? What is the representative image of its hero? How is the story told in representative novels? Where does the author stand in relation to the narrator, characters, and reader in major novels? How are novels by black women different from those by black men? What values are celebrated in these novels? What, in short, is distinctive about the Afro-American novel?

Discussing more than 150 novels by approximately one hundred representative novelists, giving close attention to forty-one—most of whom have published at least two novels and all of whom are historically and aesthetically important to my theory—I will attempt to answer these questions. I will also attempt to provide the essentials for a "thick description"[7] of the integrally related cultural and social contexts (the symbolic universe of values, cognitive principles, linguistic codes, interaction rituals and roles, and motor behavior) in which the individual and collective artistic achievement of black American novelists can be more meaningfully understood and appreciated. The narrative categories and subgenres that I employ for the different authors are fluid, variable classifications derived from the texts of the author and are intended to suggest the appropriate form and conventions for interpreting the experience mediated in a particular narrative.

To enhance the clarity and coherence of the subsequent chapters on the dialectic relationship between literary texts and anthropological context, the definitions of a few additional terms are essential. The phrase *Afro-American novel*, for example, refers to any extended prose narrative written by an American of African ancestry that illuminates the experience of black Americans in a formal, imaginatively distinctive manner—thematically, structurally, or stylistically—and whose intrinsic linguistic properties do not wholly explain its interpretation, reception, and reputation. By narrative I mean those texts that are distinguished by a story and storyteller in the ancient traditions of sub-Saharan Africa and Europe, both contributors to the cultural legacy of Afro-Americans. In the broadest sense, tradition signifies the customs, beliefs, and conventions inherited from the past. On the distinction between oral and written narrative conventions, classicist Milman Perry writes: "Literature falls into two great parts not so much because there are two kinds of culture, but because there are two kinds of form: one part of literature is oral, the other written."[8] In other words, oral and written narratives are interrelated, continuous socially established structures of meaning. As the composers of oral narrative came into contact with the authors of written narrative in Africa and Europe, a reciprocal influence developed. Islamic and Judeo-Christian literary conventions ultimately dominated among the cultural elite of much of the literate world as a result of cultural imperialism. Transcultural influences are therefore a significant, though ambiguous and ambivalent, force in the development of the Afro-American novel.

More specifically, every black American novelist works within and against a narrative tradition, oral and literary, that each inherits as part of one's cultural legacy and in which each participates, however marginally, in the elusive quest for authority, autonomy, and originality. The contribution and significance of each novelist, in other words, are influenced by his or her relationship to past and present novelists as well as by the relationship of his or her narrative to others in the tradition, both in the narrow literary sense of T. S. Eliot and in the broader cultural sense.[9] As Richard Wright states in "Blueprint for Negro Writing":

> Eliot, Stein, Joyce, Proust, Hemingway, and Anderson; Gorky, Barbusse, Nexo, and Jack London no less than the folklore of the Negro himself should form the heritage of the Negro writer. Every iota of gain in human thought and sensibility should be ready grist for his mill, no matter how far-fetched they may seem in their immediate implications.[10]

The point here is not that black literary texts are self-reflexive, self-justifying intertextual sign systems, but that they are sign systems whose referents are nonliterary as well as literary texts or subtexts.

Rather than merely catalog black novelists and trace what Harold Bloom, in his neo-Freudian theory of nineteenth-century white male poetic influences, calls the anxiety of influence, I will attempt to discover and explain the manner in which representative novelists use their bicultural tradition—oral and literary, Eurocentric and Afrocentric—to create their individual visions of reality.[11] My close reading of selected texts will attempt to reveal how race, class, and sex compound the anxiety of black men and women in search of a distinctive voice beyond the domination of literary forefathers and foremothers, both black and white. The first Afro-Amer-

Introduction

ican novelist, William W. Brown, was certainly aware of his debt, for instance, to the abolitionist tradition, oral and written, as his allusions in the first chapter, epigraphs, and conclusion of *Clotel* reveal. But his use of the tragic mulatto and quest for freedom motifs is different from that of his white contemporaries. Similarly, Paul L. Dunbar and Charles W. Chesnutt continue some of the conventions of the local-color tradition while simultaneously changing others, like the authority of conjuring, to provide more complex truths about nineteenth-century black America. In the twentieth century, Zora N. Hurston's rewriting of the sentimental romance celebrates the liberating possibilities of love, storytelling, and autonomy for black women; Richard Wright's rewriting of the myth of the "bad nigger" continues to stun readers by the power of its naturalistic truth; and Ishmael Reed's rediscovery and revitalization of such traditional forms as the Western, detective novel, and slave narrative intrigue us by their bold experimentation and articulation of an Afrocentric aesthetic.

Whereas an awareness of the oral and literary traditions is helpful for novelists and readers, it is the novelist's reconstruction of the world or reality from a particular vantage point or point of view that constitutes the special meaning of imaginative narrative. Meaning in narrative, in short, is a product of certain shared systems of signification that attempt to make sense of reality; it is the result of the relationship between two worlds: the storyteller's and the audience's, the author's and the reader's. In ancient cultures the storyteller and the audience generally shared the same insular, organic relationship to the story and the world; and the meaning of the story was inseparable from its dramatic performance before a particular audience at a particular time in a particular place. In contrast, in modern and contemporary print and technological cultures the relationship is radically altered by the capacity of the written story to travel to other times, places, and peoples. This means that the modern and contemporary author's language and assumptions about man, nature, God, and the art of storytelling may also differ from those of his intended primary readers. Whether the primary readers are white or nonwhite, male or female, may further influence the author's choice and use of narrative forms and conventions. Thus contemporary readers of novels from earlier or different cultures will find an informed discussion of relevant social and cultural contexts and conventions important in better understanding the author's world or symbolic universe and where the author stands in relationship to his or her audience.

The key terms—*double-consciousness, socialized ambivalence, double vision,* and *folklore*—that I will focus on to explain the distinctive sociopsychological roots of the Afro-American novel are not, except for *folklore*, mutually exclusive in signification. Because they will be defined fully in the first chapter, it is enough to say here that *double-consciousness* signifies the biracial and bicultural identities of Afro-Americans, not a psychotic or schizophrenic way of being-in-the-world;[12] *socialized ambivalence*, the dancing of attitudes of Americans of African ancestry between integration and separation, a shifting identification between the values of the dominant white and subordinate black cultural systems as a result of institutionalized racism; and *double vision*, an ambivalent, laughing-to-keep-from-crying perspective toward life as expressed in the use of irony and parody in Afro-American folklore and formal art. Generally speaking, I use *folklore* in the contemporary sense of the artistic forms and communicative process, especially oral, by which the wisdom and values of a people are transmitted among members of the same reference group: national, ethnic, regional, sexual, age, or professional. The importance of these four terms to the tradition of the Afro-American novel was determined primarily by their centrality, first, to the complex of values, beliefs, and rituals that constitute the matrix of the experiences of black Americans that is encoded in Afro-American folklore and embedded in early Afro-American romances and novels; and second, to the meaning and achievement of the three most highly acclaimed Afro-American romances and novels: *Their Eyes Were Watching God*, *Native Son*, and *Invisible Man*.

While acknowledging the reciprocal relationship between literature and society, the chapters ahead will also be concerned with the generic tensions between the romance and novel. Although the meaning of these genres is contingent upon the context in which they are used over time and space, it is not my intention to rehearse here their often contradictory and confusing definitions from Clara Reeves, Richard Chase and others.[13] Much of this confusion, it seems to me, is the result of associating these literary genres with the larger philosophical meanings of romanticism and romantic on the one hand and realism and realistic on the other, compounded by their use in either a descriptive or evaluative sense. I use the terms in a descriptive sense. Also, generally speaking, while romanticism signifies a transcendent, idealistic concept of reality, realism is grounded in historical, ordinary, empirical experience. More specifically, for modern critics like René Wellek and Austin Warren the literary development of the romance and novel is primarily a difference in style and structure: from the quest for metaphysical truth through the fictive modes of fable, symbolism, and allegory in the former case to the quest for empirical truth through the mimetic modes of nonfictive documents such as letters and chronicles in the latter.[14] For Northrop Frye, in contrast, the essential difference between the two genres is in their conception of character: the romancer primarily creates stylized, archetypal characters, and the novelist, conventional social personalities.[15] Despite the tidal wave of postmodern antigeneric critical theory that has swept the academies, the strategic value of generic concepts, as Jameson states, "clearly lies in the mediatory function of the notion of genre, which allows the coordination of immanent formal analysis of the individual text with the twin diachronic perspective of the history of forms and the evolution of social life."[16]

Although recent critics remind us that the postmodern mixture of fiction and fact is hardly new, and although it is clear that romantic elements are important to major British novels and realistic elements are important to major Euro-American novels, it is still highly problematic why and how these different elements and forms combine and are employed in distinctive ways in the tradition of the Afro-American novel.[17] The difference between the Euro-American and Afro-American novel, in other words, is not to be found merely in the different historical circumstances that fostered them but also in the dynamics of the individual and collective formal use of the narrative tradition by Afro-Americans to illuminate both the limitations and possibilities of the human condition from their perspective. Furthermore, it is the tension between the conventions of the romance and novel in the storytelling practice of representative black Americans in the nineteenth and twentieth centuries, as well as the tension between their texts and their sociopsychological and cultural contexts that generate the subgenres of their narrative tradition.

In order to provide a coherent theoretical and anthropological context in which the problematics of Afro-American canonical stories and the achievements of black American novelists can be more clearly understood and evaluated, the first chapter identifies and describes the sociopsychological and folk roots, residual oral forms, and literary sources from which the narratives of William Wells Brown, Frank J. Webb, Harriet E. Wilson, and Martin Robison Delany derive their distinctive character. Chapter 2 focuses on the distinctive use of language, music, and religion by Frances Ellen Watkins Harper, Sutton Elbert Griggs, Charles Waddell Chesnutt, and Paul Laurence Dunbar in their move toward and beyond social realism in the antebellum (1853–65) and postbellum (1865–1902) periods. Chapter 3 examines the early stirrings of naturalism in W. E. B. Du Bois and James Weldon Johnson during the pre–World War I period (1902–17), and chapter 4 traces the search for new narrative modes in the novels and romances of the Harlem Renaissance (1917–36). The latter chapter

Introduction

examines the poetic realism of Nathan Eugene Toomer, the genteel realism of Jessie Redmon Fauset and Nella Larsen, the folk romances of Zora Neale Hurston and Claude McKay, the folk realism of Langston Hughes and Countee Cullen, the satiric realism of Rudolph Fisher, George Schuyler, and Wallace Thurman, and the historical romance of Arna Bontemps. Chapter 5 takes a close look at Richard Wright's naturalism during the Depression and his influence on novelists of the forties (1936–52): William Attaway, Chester Himes, William Smith, and Ann Petry. The sixth chapter focuses on the movement away from naturalism after World War II (1952–62) by Willard Motley, William Demby, and Gwendolyn Brooks toward the rediscovery of myth, legend, and ritual by Ralph Ellison and James Baldwin. The final two chapters examine the contemporary Afro-American novel (1962–83) in the context of the black arts and women's rights movements, from the neorealism of representative authors like John O. Killens, John A. Williams, and Alice Walker, to an experimentation with poetic and Gothic realism by Gayl Jones, Toni C. Bambara, and Toni Morrison; as well as with modern and postmodern hybrid forms of romance, legend, and fable by Margaret Walker, Ernest Gaines, William Kelley, Ronald Fair, Charles Wright, Clarence Major, John Wideman, Hal Bennett, and Ishmael Reed.

In explaining the formal relations of parts of the text to the whole and the manner in which the language of the text mediates between the author's vision of reality and the reader's, I am indebted to Wayne C. Booth's *Rhetoric of Fiction*.[18] More important than whether the story is told from a first-person or third-person point of view are whether the narrator is dramatized in his own right and whether his values are shared by the author. Dramatized narrators, both male and female, are generally as fully drawn characters as those they tell about, and their characteristics and beliefs are often very different from those of the "implied author" who creates them. The implied author, who should not be confused with the actual author, is the implicit picture the reader gets of an author who stands behind the scenes manipulating narrative elements when the narrator is undramatized. Unless this author is explicitly identified, there will be no difference between his characteristics and those of the undramatized narrator. In such cases the term *author-narrator* is generally used. In discussing the various kinds of involvement or detachment between author, narrator, characters, and reader, most of our attention will be directed to the moral and intellectual qualities of the narrator, for the reliability or unreliability of the narrator is of vital importance to the integrity of the text. A reliable narrator is trustworthy and speaks for or acts in accord with the implied

Introduction

author's norms; an unreliable narrator is untrustworthy and does not. By proceeding, then, from significant historical events that produced the culture and consciousness of black Americans to the manner in which they have symbolically reenacted and illumined the paradoxes and ambivalences of their experience in romances and novels, I am attempting to provide a literary history that affirms a respect for the complex, reciprocal relationship between the principles of narrative form and social reality.

During the many years this book has been in progress, I have been inspired and aided by a host of friends and colleagues. Sterling A. Brown, my mentor, started me on formal training in Afro-American studies and has been my guiding spirit as a scholar. Sidney Kaplan, the principal adviser on my doctoral committee, kept me on track in clearing the thicket of my dissertation. At different stages of subsequent revisions, parts or chapters of this book have been read by Herman Jenkins and Leone Stein, as well as by Arthur P. Davis, Houston A. Baker, Jr., Theodore Hudson, George Kent, Berndt Ostendorf, Michel Fabre, William Strickland, Portia Elliott, Arthur Kinney, John Clayton, David Porter, and Stephen Oates. The candor and generosity of their criticism have been invaluable. Librarians at Fisk University (Jesse C. Smith and Ann Shockley), Howard University (Dorothy A. Porter, Ethel Ellis, Cornelia Stokes, and James Johnson), Yale University (Arna Bontemps), the Schomburg Public Library (Ernest Kaiser), and the Library of Congress have also been generous and supportive in assisting my research, particularly in the special collections. In the early stages of research I was assisted by grants from the University of Massachusetts and the National Endowment for the Humanities. I also wish to thank my diligent research assistant, Andrea Rushing, and typists Mary Coty and Barbara Gould. From beginning to end, from the valleys to the peaks, I have been most profoundly sustained in every way by my multitalented wife, Carrie. Finally, I wish to thank *Black World, CLA Journal*, and the University of Indiana Press for permission to reprint material which first appeared in a slightly different form in their publications.

*The Afro-American Novel
and Its Tradition*

1 / The Roots of the
Early Afro-American Novel

*The history of the American Negro is the history of this strife—this
longing to attain self-conscious manhood, to merge his double self into a
better and truer self. In this merging he wishes neither of the older
selves to be lost. He would not Africanize America, for America has too
much to teach the world and Africa. He would not bleach his Negro
soul in a flood of white Americanism, for he knows that Negro blood has
a message for the world. He simply wishes to make it possible for a man
to be both a Negro and an American, without being cursed and spit
upon by his fellows, without having the doors of Opportunity
closed roughly in his face.*

W. E. B. DU BOIS
The Souls of Black Folk

THE subtitle of *Contending Forces—A Romance Illustrative of Negro Life
North and South;* indicates that it is a romance, but in its preface
Pauline E. Hopkins actually calls, at the dawn of the twentieth
century, for the novel of social and psychological realism, one that
faithfully and passionately illuminates the customs, consciousness, and relationships of the Afro-American in society.[1] In other words, for Hopkins,
as for other representative early Afro-American romancers and novelists,
the distinction between romance and novel was blurred. Because, as she
suggests, the quest of early Afro-American novelists to define, chronicle,
and celebrate the experiences of black people in the United States was influenced by the impact of societal and ideological racism on the development of their distinctive culture and consciousness, this chapter will
examine the sociopsychological and folk roots of the Afro-American novel.

Sociopsychological Roots: Double-Consciousness, Double Vision, and Socialized Ambivalence

Is "the Negro only an American and nothing else" with "no values and
culture to guard and protect"?[2] If he is not, what are the sources of black
American culture and character? To what degree are they a product of

3

Africa? Of American racism? Of poverty or economic marginality? Of the will to be black? The notion that black Americans have no culture or that black culture is merely a colorful variety of the culture of poverty is refuted by recent scholarship in Afro-American studies.[3] Although culture and society are closely related, the fallacious assumption of a direct correlation between them is the source of much confusion about the relationship of black American culture to white American society and of Euro-American culture to Afro-American character. Much of this confusion, it seems to me, is a result of the historical development of the idea of culture, first, as a process of natural growth or human training; next, as a general state or habit of mind; then, as the general state of intellectual development in a society; later, as the general body of arts; and, finally, in this century, as a whole way of life.[4] Some of this confusion can be cleared up if we follow anthropologist Sidney Mintz's reinterpretation of culture "as a kind of resource, and society as a kind of arena—the distinction between sets of historically available alternatives or forms on the one hand, and the societal circumstances or settings within which these forms may be employed, on the other."[5] The emphasis is on culture as a dynamic, complex process in which organized groups in particular contexts use symbolic and material forms to "confirm, reinforce, maintain, change, or deny particular arrangements of status, power, and identity."

"The cultural patterns that shape the behavior of people in groups," as sociologist Charles A. Valentine reminds us, "should not be confused with the structure of institutions or social systems, even though each is obviously dependent on the other."[6] Cultural codes such as interaction rituals and language behavior, for example, have their genesis in society but are neither lost nor acquired overnight, whether their ostensible loss is the result of the oppressive conditions imposed by the slave system or in the urban ghettos. For these codes are an integral part of a symbolic system of shared associations that has an inner coherence and logic quite different, though not completely divorced, from social or economic realities. As historian Herbert G. Gutman notes, "even in periods of radical economic and social change powerful cultural continuities and adaptations continue to shape the historical behavior of diverse working class populations."[7] Whether it be "puttin' on massa," singing sorrow songs, wailing the blues, shouting the gospel, spinning Brer Rabbit tales, rapping about the Signifying Monkey, or writing an apocalyptic novel, the meaning of these cultural forms or socially symbolic acts will be more or less apparent to those who belong to the social or ethnic group that habitually practices, acquires, or invents them. For, as Mintz writes, "appropriate practice

The Roots of the Early Afro-American Novel

confirms a network of understanding, or symbolic accord, corresponding to the networks of social relations within which persons define themselves, act and interact."[8]

The network of understandings that defines black American culture and informs black American consciousness has evolved from the unique pattern of experiences of black people in North America, experiences, as sociologist Robert Blauner acutely observes, "that no other national or racial minority or lower class group shared."[9] These experiences—of Africa, the transatlantic or Middle Passage, slavery, Southern plantation tradition, emancipation, Reconstruction, post-Reconstruction, Northern migration, urbanization, and racism—have produced a residue of shared memories and frames of reference for black Americans. Although there is no valid scientific evidence of a biological relationship between culture and race, the perception of physical differences by the white majority served as the principal basis for the social exclusion and subjugation of African captives and Afro-Americans. Because Afro-Americans are neither biologically homogeneous nor necessarily identifiable by racial features in individual cases as having African ancestry, they are not completely deprived of social mobility and do not suffer total isolation in ghetto communities. Yet the systematic barriers of exclusion and discrimination based on perceivable and socially defined racial differences are more important in the distinctive history of the black American experience than slavery, emancipation, and the long march to the urban North. Few, if any, black Americans would therefore take issue with Ralph Ellison's view that

> being a Negro American has to do with the memory of slavery and the hope of emancipation and the betrayal by allies and the revenge and contempt inflicted by our former masters after the Reconstruction, and the myths, both Northern and Southern, which are propagated in justification of that betrayal. It involves, too, a special attitude toward the waves of immigrants who have come later and passed us by. It has to do with a special perspective on the national ideals and national conduct, and with a tragicomic attitude toward the universe. . . . It involves a rugged initiation into the mysteries and rites of color. . . . It imposes the uneasy burden and occasional joy of a complex double vision, a fluid, ambivalent response to men and events which represents, at its finest, a profoundly civilized adjustment to the cost of being human in this modern world.[10]

Thus, the historical pattern of contradictions between the ideals of white America and the reality of black America has resulted in what I prefer to call ethnically rather than racially different cultural heritages and a complex double-consciousness, socialized ambivalence, and double vision which are a healthful rather than pathological adjustment by blacks to the rigors of the New World.

This healthful, normal adjustment of Africans, their acculturation, in the English colonies of North America is generally acknowledged as beginning in 1619 when twenty captives were brought to Jamestown, Virginia, in a Dutch man-of-war and sold as servants. Although they were called "neegars" by the white colonists, they actually came from heterogeneous West African ethnic groups, and their acculturation began before reaching North America. Anthropologists Sidney Mintz and Richard Price reveal that new social ties and cultural patterns began to develop with the earliest interactions of captive Africans in the slave coffles and factories in Africa, as well as during the Middle Passage or transatlantic slave trade. After pointing out that "most West African religions seem to have shared certain fundamental assumptions about the nature of causality and the ability of divination to reveal specific causes, about the role of the dead in the lives of the living, about the responsiveness of (most) deities to human actions, about the close relationship between social conflict and illness or misfortune, and many others," Mintz and Price conclude that "we can probably date the beginnings of any new Afro-American religion from the moment that one person in need received ritual assistance from another who belonged to a different cultural group. Once such people had 'exchanged' ritual assistance in this fashion, there would already exist a microcommunity with a nascent religion that was in a real sense, its own."[11] In other words, as historian John Hope Franklin states:

> Despite the heterogeneity characteristic of many aspects of African life, the Negroes still had sufficient common experiences to enable them to cooperate in the New World in fashioning new customs and traditions which reflected their African background. To be sure, there were at least two acculturative processes going on side by side in the New World. As Africans of different experiences lived together, there was the interaction of the various African cultures. This produced a somewhat different set of customs and practices, but these were still manifestly rooted deep in the African experience. This was especially true where large numbers of Africans resided in the same place, as in the Sea Island, where they could preserve certain religious practices and even language patterns. At the same time, there was the inter-

action of African and Western cultures, which doubtless changed the culture patterns of both groups.[12]

Unlike the first white immigrants and indentured servants, the Africans were the only group to be systematically deprived of their Old World cultural links and social support systems in order to transform them into slaves for life. This development, which began as early as 1640, was the result of the interplay of the economics of slavery and the psychology of racism, for the increasing demand for cheap labor led to political acts in the late seventeenth century and a social ideology by the late nineteenth century that imposed severe restrictions on the civil rights of blacks and denied their human rights.[13]

By 1638 slaves were introduced into Massachusetts, and in 1641 slavery was given legal sanction in that colony by the "Body of Liberties," statutes prohibiting human bondage "unless it be lawfull Captives taken in just warres, and such strangers as willingly sell themselves or are sold to us."[14] In 1661 Virginia reinforced the system of slavery by legal statute, imposed a fine for interracial fornication in 1662, banned interracial marriages in 1691, defined slaves explicitly as real estate in 1705, and deprived freed blacks of the right to vote in 1723. According to a Maryland law of 1663, "All negroes or other slaves within the province, and all negroes and other slaves to be hereafter imported into the province, shall serve *durante vita;* and all children born of any negro or other slave, shall be slaves as their fathers were for the term of their lives."[15] Because many slaves were fathered by whites, the law was soon changed so that the mother's status determined the children's. Subsequent eighteenth-and nineteenth-century statutes and jurisprudence concerning everything from literacy to politics institutionalized the racist ideology that blacks, bondsmen and freedmen alike, were biologically and culturally inferior, possessing no rights that whites were obliged to recognize.

Despite the struggle of blacks for freedom during the War for Independence and the Industrial Revolution, the economic, political, and psychological compulsion of whites to transform them into docile Christians and subhumans is a matter of record. Cotton Mather's *Rules for the Societies of Negroes* (1693) is typical of the general attitude of the Puritan and Anglican divines, whose interest in Christianizing blacks was primarily to make them obedient, honest, useful servants. That all references to slavery and the slave trade were deleted from the final draft of the Declaration of Independence because of the strong objections of some Southern and a few Northern delegates is one of several illustrations of the class and color interests of members of the Second Continental Congress.[16] Although manumission and antislavery societies increased after the war, the provisions of the Constitutional Convention of 1787 that sanctioned the importation of slaves until 1808 and mandated the return by the states of fugitive slaves to their owners are additional illustrations.[17] If it is true, therefore, that the framers of the Constitution were dedicated to the principle of freedom, it is no less true, as John Hope Franklin points out, that they were equally, if not even more, dedicated to the ethnocentric, socioeconomic proposition that "government should rest upon the domination of property."[18]

Even though the antislavery movement was apparently set back by the moral and political repudiation of the inalienable rights of blacks at the Constitutional Convention, many Afro-Americans still felt that the Declaration of Independence confirmed their own convictions of equality before God and held out the promise of "Life, Liberty and the Pursuit of Happiness" for them as well as for whites. Aware of the painful paradox of their status and struggle, many slaves futilely petitioned legislative bodies for their freedom; others fought with greater success for theirs in the War for Independence, which for blacks was more a matter of freedom from physical bondage than a matter of freedom to participate fully in the political and economic structure of the emerging nation. After the war, the invention of the cotton gin revitalized the slave trade, and the missionary view that Africans were heathens in need of the Christianizing influence of Western civilization became the popular rationalization for zealously exploiting them. In short, the economic exploitation of early black Americans, together with the political and religious justification for it by the founding fathers and the Puritan divines, provides a vivid illustration of the different frames of reference from which black abolitionist novelists like William Wells Brown and Martin Delany on one hand, and white novelists like the proslavery John Pendleton Kennedy and the antislavery Harriet Beecher Stowe on the other, were to perceive and reconstruct the reality of life in the antebellum South.

Reconstruction and the rampant growth of industrial capitalism in the New South and the nation came. But on the heels of the Civil War and abolition of slavery the legendary promise of forty acres and a mule—the economic opportunity that was imperative in order for former slaves to compete equally with whites and to realize the American Dream of the times as independent farmers—was never fulfilled.[19] And the power of the black ballot was short-lived. The post-Reconstruction caste system with its Jim Crowism, disfranchisement, white terrorism, and Black Codes soon relegated the majority of the more than four million landless, illiterate freedmen to such a debased social status that they were little more than slaves. Thousands were lured to the cities or fled North for security. At the same time, an emerging urban black middle class, based on fair complexion, formal education, and puritan values (patriarchy, thrift, temperance, piety, and industry), continued developing separate economic, social, and cultural institutions while simultaneously accelerating its fight for equality with the national white majority. It is not surprising, then, that early Afro-American novelists attempted to understand and reconcile the tensions in their consciousness that resulted from these color, class, and gender conflicts between white American society and black American culture on the one hand, and the descendants of the relatively privileged class of house slaves and the unprivileged field slaves on the other.

The popular notion of black Americans as people with no past is, for the most part, derived from the sociological theories of Gunnar Myrdal, a distinguished Swedish economist, and E. Franklin Frazier, an eminent black American sociologist. Based on the fallacious assumptions of a direct correspondence between culture and society, of culture passing in one direction from Euro-American masters to African slaves, and of white middle-class values as the norm for black Americans, Myrdal's *American Dilemma* and Frazier's *Negro in the United States* conclude that the Afro-American was "an exaggerated American" whose values were pathological elaborations of general American values.[20] As stated earlier, recent research in anthropology, sociology, history, folklore, musicology, and linguistics not only challenges these conclusions but convincingly supports the beliefs long held by many Afro-Americans that the conflicts between black culture and white society have resulted in creative as well as destructive tensions in black people and their communities.

Slave narratives and black autobiographies provide dramatic personal testimonies of the discovery of racism in the process of secondary acculturation, a process that at some point frustrates individuals in their efforts to realize their potential wholeness, unity, or balance as black people and American citizens, compelling them to turn primarily to their ethnic group for protection and direction. Within the ethnic group blacks are disciplined to internalize these tensions or to transform the aborted social energy into cultural energy and expression. Over a long period, this process of acculturation has settled in the deep consciousness of the individuals who went through it as both self-protective and compensatory cultural behavior, the double-consciousness that Afro-American novelists, sometimes self-consciously but often unconsciously, illumine for readers. According to social scientists Peter Berger and Thomas Luckman, "as this experience is designated and transmitted linguistically . . . it becomes accessible and, perhaps, strongly relevant to individuals who have never gone through it."[21] Thus, as Robert Blauner notes, "the black cultural experience more resembles an alternating current than it does a direct current. The movement toward ethnicity and distinctive consciousness has been paralleled by one inducing more 'Americanization' in action and identity."[22] At the same time, of course, white American culture was becoming first African-ized and then Afro-Americanized, especially by music.

A brief examination of the historical debate between Melville J. Her-skovits and E. Franklin Frazier sheds further light on the relationship of black culture to white society and of Euro-American culture to Afro-Amer-ican consciousness. Until the black cultural movement of the 1960s, many social scientists, taking their cue from Frazier, had strong objections to Herskovits's interdisciplinary approach and radical theories about African cultural and social continuities. In their apparent eagerness to join ideo-logical ranks against a study that stressed cultural differences between white and black Americans at a time when the nation was on the threshold of World War II, they blinded themselves to Frazier's inclination, like Herskovits's, to blur cultural and social concepts in overstating his case concerning African survivals in the United States. Whereas social structure was an aspect of culture for anthropologist Herskovits, culture was a product of social organization for sociologist Frazier.

In 1937, in a sociopsychological context similar to Du Bois's nineteenth-century coining of the metaphor *double-consciousness,* which I will discuss shortly, Herskovits described the adjustment of Haitians to the socio-psychological conflict resulting from the contradictory imperatives of Eu-ropean and African cultural traditions as "socialized ambivalence." This process "is responsible for the many shifts in allegiance that continually take place, as it is for the change in attitudes in everyday association" and "is seen to be one of selection, of working over, of revamping and recom-bining the elements of the contributing cultures, with the result that the ensuing combinations, though of recognizable derivation, differ from their aboriginal forms." By proposing socialized ambivalence as "a more realistic understanding of the individuals in other cultures who have likewise fallen heir to conflicting traditions," Herskovits anthropologically reinterprets and extends the sociopsychological process that Du Bois in 1897 developed as a metaphor to describe the bicultural identity of black Americans.[23] Relying on this psychological model, analogical reasoning, comparative historical analysis, and vague, new anthropological concepts, Herskovits,

The Roots of the Early Afro-American Novel

in *The Myth of the Negro Past,* boldly challenged the prevailing ideology of his day concerning black Americans as a socially disorganized people without a past. He advanced the theory that through the processes of retention (the continuity of some African interpretations of phenomena), reinterpretation (the interpretation of white cultural patterns according to African principles), and syncretism (the amalgamation of African and American cultural patterns and sign systems) the African heritage—i.e., the culture of African peoples south of the Sahara, especially the Yoruba and Dahomeans—was a continuing force in black American life.

Frazier disagreed, arguing in *The Negro in the United States* that over the years African social institutions like the extended family system, the primary institution of cultural transmission, were destroyed by slavery. Although on its surface this seems plausible, on a deeper symbolic level many slave narratives and nineteenth-century novels, like *Clotel, Blake,* and *Iola Leroy,* reveal a unique blend of extended and nuclear family systems whose ruptured yet still vital filial ties prompted countless postbellum freedmen to undertake long, arduous searches to reunite their dispersed families. The treatment of surrogate black families in *Many Thousand Gone* (1965), *Jubilee* (1966), and *The Autobiography of Miss Jane Pittman* (1971) provide additional support for Herskovits's concept of the reinterpretation of African kinship networks. In any event, when Frazier, whose primary interest was in the social structures rather than in the cultural forms, concludes that "Negroes acquired new habits and modes of thought, and whatever elements of African culture were retained lost their original meaning in becoming fused with their experiences in the New World," he is on firm ground; but when he jumps from the premise of an early fusion of African culture with New World experiences to the hasty conclusion that in the "process of adjusting themselves to American civilization, the majority of the Negroes have sloughed off completely the African heritage," he misses the mark. The most persuasive contemporary evidence in art history identifying specific Yoruba, Kongo, Dahomean, Mande, and Ejagham influences on the art and philosophies of black people throughout the Americas is Robert F. Thompson's landmark, *Flash of the Spirit* (1984).[24]

Whereas it is true that the radical shift in their social arenas from Africa to West Indian and Southern plantations, and from sharecropping fields to urban factories and ghettos, resulted in black Americans adopting, adapting, or rejecting the material cultural resources of the larger white society, their symbolic universe (linguistic patterns, cognitive system, interaction rituals, and motor behavior) had its own evolutionary logic and enabled them to develop strategies to cope with their oppression. "The intersubjective context of shared meaning," as literary critic Ostendorf persuasively argues, "is a coherent play world which provides cognitive and emotive alternatives to an oppressive social arena, both therapy for incipient pathology and emancipation of the senses."[25] This, in part, explains the uniqueness of the double-consciousness the majority of black Americans experiences.

As stated earlier, Du Bois, a brilliant Afro-American historian and sociologist, was the first to describe tropologically the sociopsychological experience of black Americans as double-consciousness:

> After the Egyptian and Indian, the Greek and Roman, the Teuton and Mongolian, the Negro is a sort of seventh son, born with a veil, and gifted with second-sight in this American world,—a world which yields him no true self-consciousness, but only lets him see himself through the revelation of the other world. It is a peculiar sensation, this double-consciousness, this sense of always looking at one's self through the eyes of others, of measuring one's soul by the tape of a world that looks on in amused contempt and pity. One ever feels his twoness,—an American, a Negro; two souls, two thoughts, two unreconciled strivings; two warring ideals in one dark body, whose dogged strength alone keeps it from being torn asunder.

This double vision and double-consciousness, as we have seen, is a product of the historical dialectic in American society between black and white cultures. The end of the black American's striving, writes Du Bois, is "to make it possible for a man to be both a Negro and an American without being cursed and spit upon by his fellows, without having the doors of Opportunity closed in his face . . . to be a co-worker in the kingdom of culture, to escape both death and isolation, to husband and use his best powers and his latent genius."[26] The historical quest of black Americans, their principal canonical story, in short, is for life, liberty, and wholeness— the full development and unity of self and the black community—as a biracial, bicultural people, as Americans of African descent.

The ideological dispute between Du Bois and Booker T. Washington, the black intellectuals who dominated the national scene and influenced the themes and characterization of novels after the death of Frederick Douglass in 1895, crystallized the political, cultural, and economic dichotomy within the black community. After the Atlanta Cotton Exposition speech of 1895 in which Washington compromised the civil rights of blacks to facilitate their economic growth through industrial training, he, the favorite of white industrial magnates and philanthropists, became the chief black architect of social accommodationism during the rise of industrialism in the New South. Opposition to Washington's policies and iron-fisted control was led by Du Bois, the principal spokesman of that band of militant middle-class blacks who in 1905 founded the Niagara Movement, the forerunner of the predominantly white-founded National Association for the Advancement of Colored People (NAACP). Although the conflict between Washington, a former slave from the Old Dominion, and Du Bois, a New England Brahmin, as to whether industrial training or higher education was the better means for black people to pursue their major objectives seems irreconcilable, the difference between these two leaders was at bottom more a matter of personality and strategy than of principle and genealogy. Both aspired to move their race up from slavery to economic, cultural, and political freedom, literacy, and unity. But whereas Washington chose the rural Southern strategy of conciliation and benevolent despotism, inspired by the gospel of menial labor, property ownership, and the tooth brush preached by his New England school teachers, Du Bois opted for the urban, aristocratic concept of a "Talented Tenth," his cosmopolitan-inspired term for the exceptionally qualified men and women of the race, the cultural elite, to lead the masses in the struggle for full American citizenship. At times Du Bois's militancy was nationalistic, and toward the end of his life, in part out of frustration with the betrayal of his countrymen and country, black as well as white, he joined the American Communist party, renounced his citizenship, and became a citizen of Ghana. But in his more than twenty years of service to blacks through the NAACP, his clarion call was for the "New Negro" to close ranks to achieve integration and social reform within the American system.

Clearly relative in meaning, the term *New Negro* was introduced into the Afro-American novel by Sutton Griggs, a member of the Niagara Movement. As a student at one of the many missionary-founded black institutions in the South, the hero of Griggs's first novel, *Imperium in Imperio* (1899), leads a militant demonstration against the white administration to dramatize that "the cringing, fawning, sniffling, cowardly Negro which slavery left, had disappeared, and a new Negro, self-respecting, fearless, and determined in the assertion of his rights was at hand."[27] Still struggling against racial stereotypes in 1916, William Pickens, a black writer and NAACP officer, published a collection of essays entitled *The New Negro* in which he urged that "every few years should see a book up to date on the general subject of 'The Renaissance of the Negro Race' or 'The New Negro,' " the titles of the first and final essays in his own book.[28] Nine years later Alain Locke, the first black Rhodes Scholar and a Howard University philosophy professor, edited a special Harlem issue of *Survey Graphic*, which he subsequently revised and published as *The New Negro* (1925). This anthology heralded the coming-of-age of a new generation of black artists and galvanized support for the spirit of independence and race consciousness that animated the New Negro movement, also known as the Harlem Renaissance, of the 1920s.[29]

The political, economic, and cultural tensions within the race which culminated in the dispute between Washington and Du Bois and in the New Negro movement actually found their way into the early novel in many forms. In theme and character they are most clearly symbolized in the line commonly drawn between radicalism and conservatism, which, contrary to popular opinion, does not follow rigid color and caste lines. In Griggs's five novels, for example, the mulatto character is typically more militant and confrontational than his darker brother, but it is the relative conservatism of the latter, the Washington strategy of conciliatory politics, that is underscored as the wiser course of action. (Light-complexioned Du Bois took great pride in his mixed racial and cultural heritage; dark-complexioned Washington was ostensibly less proud of his.) Pauline Hopkins's *Contending Forces* deals with the same intraracial tensions, and again the voice of moderation we hear is that of a black intellectual: " 'Brute force will not accomplish anything. We must *agitate*. . . . Appeal for the justice of our cause to every civilized nation under the heavens.' "[30]

However reprehensible some readers might in retrospect consider Griggs and Hopkins's bourgeois predilections for accommodationism in the face of political terrorism and social exploitation when compared to the revolutionary values of such contemporary novels as *Many Thousand Gone* or *The Spook Who Sat by the Door*, the ideology of the Talented Tenth—a reflection of shifting emotions and allegiances fostered by the absurdity of color discrimination and the reality of class distinctions both in the larger society and within the black community—is most lucidly expressed by one of the characters in Griggs's *Pointing the Way* (1908): "Years of development since emancipation have produced a group of cleanly, cultured, aspiring people in the Colored race. The first step in the solution of the race problem is for this group to take charge of and guide the racial thought and life."[31] In other words, to cope with the complexities of their socialized ambivalence, to reconcile the tensions of their double-consciousness, the most intellectually capable and economically fortunate middle-class blacks borrowed Eurocentric forms of culture to develop their potential and to lead the masses in their common struggle for self-determination and dignity as a people. In contrast, the black majority, especially the lower class of marginally employed, underemployed, and unemployed, by virtue of their exclusion from full participation in the systems of the larger society, were more inclined toward the alternative of the continuation and revitalization of residually oral Afrocentric forms of culture.

It is certainly no secret that from the birth of the Peculiar Institution to the premature death of the Great Society, black Americans have been restricted in their exposure to the written word, the chief mode of acculturation in Euro-American society. In the antebellum South, for example, it was a violation of custom and law to teach blacks to read and write; and in the postbellum South nine of ten freedmen were illiterate.[32] "In white America," as cultural historian Charles Keil writes in *Urban Blues,* "the printed word—the literary tradition—and its attendant values are revered. In the Negro Community, more power resides in the spoken word and the oral tradition—good talkers abound, and the best gain power and prestige. . . ."[33] This is not to imply that Afro-Americans are unique in having historically relied on the oral tradition for narrative models to make sense of their world, but as Richard Dorson, the doyen of Euro-American folklorists, has observed: "Only the Negro, as a distinct element of the English-speaking population, maintained a full-blown storytelling tradition. A separate Negro subculture formed within the shell of American life, missing the bounties of general education and material progress, remaining a largely oral, self-contained society with its own unwritten history and literature."[34]

African Oral Narratives

Insofar as Afro-American novelists are the cultural heirs of Western and African narrative traditions, we can more clearly and coherently understand the folk roots of the Afro-American novel by looking first at some of the ancient forms and functions of oral narrative in Africa. Although, as literary historian Emmanuel Obiechina states, "the novel . . . has no strict equivalent in the oral tradition of West Africa," its rise and definition are mainly the result of social factors that mark the change of traditional, agrarian, oral cultures to modern, industrial, literate cultures.[35]

Since the pseudo-independence of Afro-Americans in the late nineteenth century, missionaries, linguists, anthropologists, and folklorists have been collecting and publishing African stories. Oral narratives, which anthropologist William Bascom calls "verbal art" and Dorson "folklore,"[36] are an important means of maintaining the continuity and stability of traditional

African cultures. For the anthropologist, myths, legends, folktales, and other forms of verbal art have four principal functions. They transmit knowledge, value, and attitudes from one generation to another, enforce conformity to social norms, validate social institutions and religious rituals, and provide a psychological release from the restrictions of society.[37] In *Oral Literature in Africa*, Ruth Finnegan stresses the flexibility of African narratives and the difficulty of establishing clear typologies.[38] For example, myth and legend, the sacred and the profane, are mixed in the story Yoruba kings tell justifying their political authority by claiming direct descent from Odudwa—the creator of the earth in Yoruba tradition. Yoruba diviners also used myth to reinforce belief in the need for making the ritual sacrifices they prescribed to maintain the harmony of the individual and the nation with the rhythms of nature. Instead of clear-cut categories, the same story may be told in one society about a god or deity, in another about a trickster figure, and in yet another about a legendary hero; by one people it may be considered sacred and by another entertainment. Despite this frequent mixing of forms and shifting of the same tale from sacred to profane, depending on the ethnic society and specific context in which the tale is told, most West African societies make some distinction between sacred narratives, which they regard as true, and less serious tales of an entertaining and educational nature.

In addition to their pedagogical, anthropological, psychological, and political functions, African oral narratives provided the fertile soil and roots for a written indigenous literature. "Most translations of African literature," writes literary critic Ulli Beier, "are in fact collections of myths, legends and fables."[39] Because of the domination of the structural-functional approach to the study of the oral tradition, however, it is only in recent years that Westerners, particularly folklorists and literary critics, have turned their attention to the relationship of African folklore (i.e., verbal art) to written literature.[40] This is not to say that the folk ideology of Johann Gottfried von Herder—critic, philosopher, and folklorist—did not have a significant impact on the thinking of nineteenth-century European writers in their quest for a national literature. On the contrary, Herder's theory of folk art as the base for a national formal art and of folksongs as the spontaneous, indigenous expression of the collective soul of a people inspired many creative nationalistic writers, including the American romantics Ralph Waldo Emerson and Walt Whitman.[41] In the case of West Africans, however, it was not Herderian folk theory so much as the dialectic influence of the oral and literary traditions in societies struggling for independence and industrialization that probably inspired them to draw on their traditional narratives, proverbs, songs, and rituals for themes, structure, and style. Camara Laye's *Dark Child* (1955), James Ngugi's *Weep Not, Child* (1964), Chinua Achebe's *Things Fall Apart* (1959), and Amos Tutola's *Palm-Wine Drinkard* (1953) are only a few of the modern novels that have their roots in the fertile soil of African folklore. They represent the sophisticated continuation of African storytelling conventions in dialectic tension with the most popular Western form of narrative, the novel.

As for the continuation of the African storytelling tradition by black Americans, Dorson, after a close examination of the tale type and motif indices of black American folktales, concludes that "American Negro tales owed little to Africa and much to Europe and the New World."[42] Although the question of African origins and retentions remains a moot issue, most recent scholarship on the question is consistent with historian John Blassingame's conclusion that "however oppressive or dehumanizing the plantation was, the struggle for survival was not severe enough to crush all of the slave's creative instincts."[43] In short, residual elements of the oral tradition of Africa, each fulfilling a psychological and social need in the lives of the slaves, fused with white American culture and created a new system of shared symbols that, even though complementary, was different in pattern and emphases from both its European and African antecedents. This was particularly true in the slave communities of the Old South.

Afro-American Folk Roots

Digging into the slave past of people of African ancestry in the United States, we discover that the roots of Afro-American folklore, the unique blend of a significant number of African survivals with elements of white American culture, are embedded in the Old South, especially the Georgia Sea Islands and the Mississippi Delta. And they bloom perennially in the verbal, musical, and ritualistic expressions—the socially symbolic acts—of rural and urban black Americans. In 1790 when the first census was taken in the colonies, 91 percent of the black population lived in the South. As late as 1910, 89 percent still lived there. With the outbreak of World War I blacks began pouring into Northern cities: Chicago, New York, Detroit, Philadelphia, Pittsburgh, and Boston.[44] They fled the South for the North, the fields and farms for the shops and factories. They came searching for Canaan. They found Babylon.

It is not surprising that the early Afro-American novel reflects this great demographic shift from rural to urban America. Such different novels and

The Roots of the Early Afro-American Novel

romances as Frank Webb's *The Garies and Their Friends* (1857), Pauline Hopkins's *Contending Forces* (1900), and Dunbar's *Sport of the Gods* (1902)—in which the basic storylines unfold in Philadelphia, Boston, and New York respectively—draw on the romantic machinery of the feudal South as their heroes and heroines search for a place to be somebody and come to grips with the myth of their Afro-American past.

More important in the history of the black experience than the long march to Northern cities are the systematic barriers of exclusion and discrimination based on perceivable and socially defined racial differences. Racism prevented the full participation of blacks in the dominant culture so that their need for symbols and values had to be filled by the ethnic subculture. This process encouraged the retention and reinterpretation of Africanisms (e.g., hoodoo, conjuring or magic, dance, field holler, work song, and folktale) which would enable eighteenth-century blacks to cope with the demands of their new life and to express the will of the group to survive. Developed mainly during the slaves' "leisure" time, these modified African cultural resources and the creation of new forms, such as the spirituals, Brer Rabbit fables, and blues, increased in-group cohesion and cultural solidarity. The need to survive the master-slave relationship occasionally led to behavior that symbolically enacted a deep-seated, irrational desire to be white. Most frequently, however, the struggle for survival led to a surface identification with the master's values and a subservient behavior pattern that exploited the disparity between white ideology and black reality. This double-consciousness is revealed in the folk saying I quoted in my introduction: "Got one mind fuh white folk see, 'nother fuh what I know's me." In addition, to bridge the many different African languages and to communicate with or "put on" the master, eighteenth- and nineteenth-century blacks combined aspects of English grammar with distinctive physical gestures, semantics, syntax, pitch, and rhythm: the process called creolization by sociolinguists Stewart and Dillard.[45] Thus from the nineteenth century on we have concurrent intraracial and interracial lines of behavioral and linguistic development. By the twentieth century, as black novels of the Harlem Renaissance illustrate, the repertoire of survival strategies and rituals continued to evolve: from Tomming, shucking and jiving, and copping a plea to signifying, sounding, playing the dozens, talking trash, and rapping.[46] Rather than stress the alleged pathological implications of these linguistic and behavioral survival strategies or symbolic acts, Ralph Ellison more appropriately and astutely interprets them as a growing sophistication in overcoming oppressive social circumstances and symbolically expressing "a complex double vision" through the cultural resources of language, music, and dissimulation.[47]

But what is the legacy of Afro-American folk culture to the twentieth century? What values does it affirm and reject? What rituals and customs does it seek to preserve? Who are its heroes and heroines? Ellison addresses these questions in general terms when he states that folklore

> offers the first drawings of any group's character. It preserves mainly those situations which have repeated themselves again and again in the history of any given group. It describes those rites, manners, customs, and so forth, which insure the good life, or destroy it; and it describes those boundaries of feeling, thought and action which that particular group has found to be the limitation of the human condition. It projects this wisdom in symbols which express the group's will to survive; it embodies those values by which the group lives and dies. These drawings may be crude but they are nonetheless profound in that they represent the group's attempt to humanize the world.[48]

In her seminal studies of Euro-American culture, Constance Rourke reveals the complex relationship of the first popular indigenous folk characters: the Yankee, the Backwoodsman, and the Negro. Rourke alludes to the popularity of black-face minstrelsy in the 1830s as an example of how "the comic trio tended to merge into a single generic figure," but she carefully points out that "each of the trio remained distinct."[49] Similarly, a close examination of the legends and ballads of Brother Jonathan, Davy Crockett, Daniel Boone, and Paul Bunyan reveals that these narratives derive from a different frame of reference, a different sociocultural context, than those about the legendary black Preacher; John, the trickster slave; Harriet Tubman, the Moses of her people; and John Henry, the steel-driving man.

Drawing on Afro-American folklore for inspiration and material, postbellum black novelists such as Dunbar and Chesnutt were strongly influenced in style by Southern white local colorists like Irwin Russell, Thomas Nelson Page, and Joel Chandler Harris. But the values affirmed by Page's and Harris's fictive uncles are not identical to those affirmed by Chesnutt's, and the white planter's pastoral vision in *Red Rock* (1898) lacks the double-edged irony of the black house servant's vision in *The Sport of the Gods*. Because the difference in consciousness between white American folklore and black American folklore is a difference in response to the New World and the evolution of institutionalized racism, it is not, as some historians argue, the same for all hyphenated ethnic Americans.[50] For the total response of Africans to their experience in an alien and hostile environment included the new modes of interaction and communication, especially language, music, and religion, they developed among themselves along with those forged in the crucible of their experience with whites.

Forged, however, in a society based on the pragmatism of American capitalism and the idealism of the American Creed, both Euro-American and Afro-American folklore are marked by contradictions. Insofar as both at some level champion the values of the Protestant ethic and are inspired by the American Dream, they are similar. But insofar as one is the lore of the oppressor, the white majority, and the other the lore of the victims of oppression, the black minority, they are antithetical. Simply stated, traditional white American values emanate from a providential vision of history and of Euro-Americans as a chosen people, a vision that sanctions their individual and collective freedom in the pursuit of property, profit, and happiness. Radical Protestantism, Constitutional democracy, and industrial capitalism are the white American trinity of values. In contrast, black American values emanate from a cyclical, Judeo-Christian vision of history and of Afro-Americans as a disinherited, colonized people, a vision that sanctions their resilience of spirit and pursuit of social justice. A tragicomic vision of life, a tough-minded grip on reality, an extraordinary faith in the redemptive power of suffering and patience, a highly developed talent for dissimulation, a vigorous zest for life, a wry sense of humor, and an acute sense of timing are basic black American values.[51] These values, mainly the product of the resiliency of African cultural survivals and the resistance to class, color, and gender domination, are the major sources of tension in the themes, characters, and forms of the Afro-American novel.

Residually Oral Forms: Oratory, Myth, Legend, Tale, and Song

Cultures in which oral forms compete with print, as in the case of the black American subculture, may be classified as residually or largely oral cultures.[52] "The residual," Raymond Williams explains, " . . . has been effectively formed in the past, but it is still active in the cultural process, not only and often not at all as an element of the past, but as an effective element of the present. Thus certain experiences, meanings, and values which cannot be expressed or substantially verified in terms of the dominant culture, are nevertheless lived and practised on the basis of the residue—cultural as well as social—of some previous social and cultural institution or formation."[53] In contrast to literate cultures, residually oral cultures are basically aural, functional, collective, and direct. Like oral cultures, they stress performance, mnemonics, and improvisational skills. The tendency is to focus on the here and now, to employ some kind of formulaic mode of expression, and to subordinate the individual to the group or type. Whereas an oral culture relies primarily on sound, the spoken word, and a literate culture primarily on sight, the written word, residually oral cultures rely on the interplay or dialectic between the two. Several residually oral forms may be identified in the Afro-American novel: oratory, myth, legend, tale, and song.

"Oratory," writes literary critic F. O. Matthiessen, "moving with the Revolution from the pulpit to the political forum, was . . . the one branch of literature in which America then had a formed tradition."[54] In other words, when the first Afro-American novel appeared seventeen years after Ralph Emerson's call for a national literature, public addresses by both blacks and whites were among the chief means of education and diversion. The political conventions of free blacks, the Fourth of July verbal fireworks, the soul-stirring revival meetings, the radical abolitionist forum, the refined literary societies, the bombastic declamation contests—all of these in one form or another left their mark on the Afro-American novel. For in addition to having their sensibilities shaped by the black dialect or vernacular of their family and friends, their primary speech community, Afro-American romancers and novelists were influenced by the impassioned formal appeals of David Walker, Henry Highland Garnet, and Frederick Douglass, as well as by the grandiloquent speeches of John Q. Adams, Daniel Webster, and William Lloyd Garrison. In these contrasting modes of discourse they found rhetorical models highly suited for their own moral, social, and aesthetic purpose.

In addition to black dialect and formal public addresses, Afro-American novelists employed ritualized black vernacular contests, especially in narratives of the 1920s and 1960s, to establish ethnic atmosphere, delineate character, and advance plot. Folklorist Roger D. Abrahams provides helpful insights into the use of narrative forms by modern black men to cope with the pressures of life in their community in South Philadelphia.[55] Through the ritual of such verbal contests as toasts, sounding, signifying, and playing the dozens, young blacks in the cities, like their forefathers in rural towns, who had used storytelling or "lying," learn to sublimate their white-provoked feelings of aggression to achieve mastery of words and their world. Whereas black men acquire much of their verbal skill from the street corners, pool rooms, and barber shops, black women pick up much of theirs in their mothers' kitchens, at church gatherings and the beauty parlor. The Afro-American narrative most analogous to the Euro-

American epic formulaic mode is the modern toast, which is a kind of mock heroic epic, composed "of some sort of picaresque or exciting introduction, action alternating with dialogue . . . and a twist ending of some sort, either a quip, and ironic comment, or a brag."[56] As in "Stackolee," "The Signifying Monkey," and *"The Titanic,"* its language is highly self-conscious, artful, and profane; and though highly improvisational, its dominant structure is a long sequence of balanced, four-stress line couplets. Sounding is direct taunting or boastful insult; signifying is a more elaborate, indirect form of goading or insult generally making use of profanity; and playing the dozens is the explicit sexual insult of another person's parents, particularly the mother.[57] Rhyme, repetition, poly-rhythm, and wit are the chief conventions of these ethnic forms of oratory, the black vernacular, which is first developed by boys in play to assert masculinity among themselves and then to achieve a sense of security in their contact with the hostility of the larger society. In the chapters ahead we will see the distinctive manner in which these ethnic forms of speech are used by such different black novelists as Rudolph Fisher, Zora N. Hurston, Ralph Ellison, John O. Killens, and Ishmael Reed.

A blend of oratory, oral narrative, and song, chanted sermons, developed primarily by Southern black fundamentalist preachers, also contribute to the distinctive character of some black American novels. "The sermons almost never rhyme," writes Bruce A. Rosenberg in *The Art of the American Folk Preacher;* "they seldom alliterate, the imagery is meager, yet they are poetic. The lines are metrical, the language is ordered, and the effect is often pleasing." Unlike the characteristics of conventional oratory and preaching, in the chanted sermon "the verses are preponderantly formulaic (in the Parry-Lord sense), there are extended passages with parallel syntax, and the constructions are direct with almost no periodicity." It is important to note that the preachers interviewed by Rosenberg rejected, as I suspect most blacks raised in the Baptist, Methodist, and Holiness faiths would reject, his formulaic theory and would hardly agree with his observation about the meager imagery of the sermons. Nevertheless, his definition of the chanted sermon as "groups of words, which, when recited, are metrically and semantically consistent, related in form by the repetition and identical relative placement of at least half the words in the group" is supported by evidence that "the techniques of composition appear to be similar."[58]

More important, as black theologian and preacher Henry H. Mitchell confirms in *Black Preaching*, the major convention of chanted sermons—a highly dramatic, imaginative, improvisational rendering of the Word of God—is the call-and-response.[59] Derived from the African musical practice of alternating improvised lines with fixed refrains, call-and-response in chanted sermons is the spirited, spontaneous antiphonal exchange between the preacher and his congregation as they participate in a profoundly intimate fellowship. Dunbar's "An Ante-Bellum Sermon" and James Weldon Johnson's *God's Trombones,* as well as Hurston's "The Wounds of Jesus Sermon" in *Jonah's Gourd Vine,* Ellison's incomparable fusion of the "Let My People Go Sermon" and the "Train Sermon" in *Invisible Man,* Baldwin's "Uncleanness Sermon" in *Go Tell It on the Mountain,* and Wright's parody of the "Train Sermon" in *Lawd Today* are among the major testimonials to the influence of the chanted sermon on black novelists.

Symbolic representations of crucial life situations that are shared by a people, residually oral Afro-American myths are moral as well as speculative stories that are archetypal in pattern and ethnic in cultural content. They explain the origins of things, activities of gods, and historical human dilemmas. They are therefore generally combined forms of myth and legend that are concerned with the founders of an ethnic group or lineage and that justify the taboos and authority of the group or lineage. The two principal myth-legends that inform the early novel are a messianic delivery from oppression and an eschatological overthrow of white supremacy, rewritten from the oral tradition and the King James Bible.[60] Mainly self-educated and missionary school trained preachers and teachers fired with a passion for justice and social reform, the first generation of black novelists were frequently concerned with how sanctification and sin, virtue and vice, in this world related to the ultimate destiny of man. And because injustice was the rule rather than the exception for blacks, the hope of future rewards for the racially oppressed and punishment for their oppressors was appealing to many, especially the older generation. Pious, self-effacing types like the Lockleys in George Pryor's *Neither Bond Nor Free (A Plea)* (1902) believed "that in the world about them all things worked together for good."[61] Even though for many blacks the hand of Providence assured the triumph of the good eventually, it moved too slowly for some. Rejecting his father-in-law's pious counsel, Delany's young hero in *Blake* (1859) declares:

> "It is not wickedness, Daddy Joe; you don't understand these things at all. If a thousand years with us is but a day with God, do you think that I am required to wait all that time?"

"Don't, Henry, don't! De wud say 'stan still an' see de salbation.' "
"That's no talk for me, Daddy Joe; I've been 'standing still' long
enough—I'll 'stand still' no longer."[62]

Sermons, prayers, spirituals, hymns, and sayings are the residual oral
forms employed in Afro-American novels to reinterpret, reenact or reject
this Judeo-Christian redemptive view of history.

Whereas in her romance Pauline Hopkins writes: "Surely the Negro race
must be productive of some valuable specimens, if only from the infusion
which amalgamation with a superior race must eventually bring," Martin
Delany ends his with the ominous line: "Woe be unto those devils of
whites, I say."[63] Hopkins and Delany illustrate the socialized ambivalence
caused by the myth of white supremacy and by the social rituals and color
symbolism that justify and perpetuate it. One of the functions of the artist,
as Ellison states, is to recognize these social rituals and illumine their deep
psychological meanings.[64] It is not surprising, therefore, to discover that
the themes, plots, and characterization of the early novels in particular
are frequently concerned with the myth and rituals of white supremacy
and the omnipresent reality of evil perpetrated by whites. In many cases
white and black characters are idealized, but even in these, as well as the
more realistic novels, the attitude of the author and narrator is ambivalence, and irony and parody are frequently at work. "God made us all,"
says the heroine in Chesnutt's *House Behind the Cedars* (1900), "and for
some good purpose, though we may not always see it. He made some
people white, and strong, and masterful, and—heartless. He made others
black and homely, and poor and weak—."[65]

Legends justifying or protesting the relative social position of ethnic
groups, classes, and lineages (e.g., blacks and whites; refined people of
color and unrefined black laborers; house servants and field hands, Baptists and Methodists, mulattoes and "pure" blacks) are also integral to the
tradition of the Afro-American novel. *Clotel*, for example, is a formal rewriting of the apocryphal legend about Thomas Jefferson's illegitimate
daughter by Sally Hemings, his alleged slave mistress. The legends of
black heroes and heroines such as Toussaint L'Ouverture, Cinqué, Nat
Turner, Denmark Vesey, Gabriel Prosser, Harriet Tubman, John Henry,
and Booker T. Washington are common leitmotifs in the early novels. But
Arna Bontemps's *Black Thunder* (1936) was the first sustained formal retelling of a traditional story by an Afro-American novelist of the self-
assertion of black slaves for their freedom. Ironically, this historical romance is not about the messianic revolt of Nat Turner in 1831, the most

historically important slave revolt in America, but about the abortive large-scale plot of Gabriel Prosser in 1800.[66]

Like legends, tales or "lies," as the pre–World War II generation of black folk called them, about tricksters; about the ubiquitous, sometimes moral, sometimes amoral, black preacher; about the "bad nigger"; and about the "super-bad" hustler have been used in various ways with varying degrees of sophistication by Afro-American novelists. For example, Brown employs several black trickster tales in *Clotel* to illustrate the ingenious strategies and disguises used to escape from slavery. In *Imperium in Imperio* Griggs draws on the traditional tale of the chicken-eating preacher for comic relief. Supernatural and realistic tales are major influences on the themes, style, and structure of the short stories in Dunbar's *Folks from Dixie* and Chesnutt's *Conjure Woman*. Modern novelists also reveal the continuity of traditional folktales. Hurston empowers Janie Crawford to liberate herself and her friend Pheoby through storytelling; Wright combines tales about "bad niggers" for his delineation of Bigger Thomas; Ellison endows Trueblood with the gifts of the traditional storyteller; and John O. Killens, William Melvin Kelley, Ronald Fair, Charles Wright, Ernest Gaines, John E. Wideman, and Ishmael Reed experiment with the conventions of legend, tale, and fable.

In addition to oratory, myth, legend, and tale, song or music is a clearly identifiable residual oral form in the tradition of the Afro-American novel. Spirituals, hymns, work songs, patriotic songs, abolitionist songs, ragtime, blues, gospel, and jazz—all, especially the latter three, contribute in different degrees of intensity to the thematic and structural concerns of individual novels, from Brown's *Clotel* to Baldwin's *If Beale Street Could Talk* (1974) and *Just Above My Head* (1979). In *Blake*, for example, Aunt Rachel sings:

> "In eighteen hundred and twenty-three
> They said their people should be free
>   It is wrote in Jeremiah,
>   Come and go along with me!
>   It is wrote in Jeremiah
>   Go sound the Jubilee!"[67]

More recently in *Jubilee*, we hear Vyry often unburdening her soul with song:

> "I been buked and I been scorned,
> Lord, I been buked and I been scorned,

Lord, I been buked and I been scorned,
I been talked about sho's you borned."[68]

Whether used in an organic or ornamental manner by black novelists, these songs of sorrow and joy invariably retained their authentic purpose of decrying oppression and celebrating the possibilities of the human spirit. It is apparently because of these qualities that modern Afro-American music like jazz, which is itself a classical tradition, is rooted in the collective black unconsciousness and symbolically expressed in the spirituals, gospel songs, and blues.

The spirituals, like chanted sermons, are inspired by the Bible, informed by the group experience, and characterized by occasional rhyme, improvised graphic phrases, and dramatic lines delivered in a call-and-response manner. In contrast to the spirituals, gospel songs are formal compositions by individuals. But they are also inspired by that old-time religion, especially the emotional fervor of the Holiness church. Gospels are the sacred modern continuation in song of the story of the black experience in the city, paradoxically characterized by features of both the spirituals and blues. The strong beat, ambiguous imagery, and wide tonal range of gospel songs were significantly influenced by the pioneer compositions of Thomas A. Dorsey, a convert from the blues tradition. Ellison defines the blues as "an impulse to keep the painful details and episodes of a brutal experience alive in one's aching consciousness, to finger its jagged grain, and to transcend it, not by consolation of philosophy, but by squeezing from it a near-tragic, near-comic lyricism."[69] Structurally, the blues generally takes the form of three-line stanzas rhyming *a a b* with four beats in each line. But because the blues has few absolute features, there are many variations on this form. Stylistically, the blues singer employs formulaic imagistic phrases like "Oh, Baby" and "Yes, Lord"—used in the call-and-response mode with accompanying instrumental improvisation—repetition, and occasional ideophonic moans, growls, and shouts. When performed for non-members of the ethnic group or for those with little or no intimacy with the music, it is generally considered mere entertainment; but when performed among black Americans, especially members of the working class, it is a social ritual: a ceremonial, residual oral form whose recurring performance reinforces a sense of order in life and preserves the shared wisdom of the group. As in the themes and style of Baldwin's *If Beale Street Could Talk* and *Just Above My Head*, the blues and gospels are secular and sacred lyrical expressions of hard times and the possibility of overcoming personal misery through toughness of spirit.

Structurally and philosophically, in other words, most contemporary Afro-American music is strongly influenced by the blues. Like the blues, for example, jazz uses the call-and-response pattern with the antiphonal relationship occurring between two solo instruments or between solo and ensemble. And in jazz as in blues a traditional melody or harmonic framework serves as the base or point of takeoff for improvisational flights— either solo or collective. Whereas some black novelists recognized the literary potential of these residually oral folk forms as an extension of their social reality, others became aware of their potential as an act of literary discovery. In either case they were still faced with the challenge of developing and mastering a suitable written narrative form in which to express their particular vision of truth and beauty.

Literary Sources

Nineteenth-century Afro-American novelists were moved by the dual impulse to stress representative detail and the supernatural. The social conditions and cultural exigencies outlined in the beginning of this chapter compelled most of them to attempt a synthesis of the contrary tendencies toward the novel and romance. "In giving this little romance expression in print," Hopkins writes in her preface, "I am not actuated by a desire for notoriety or for profit, but to do all that I can in a humble way to raise the stigma of degradation from my race."[70] Much of this color stigma was reinforced and perpetuated in the narratives of John P. Kennedy, George Tucker, William G. Simms, Thomas N. Page, and Thomas N. Dixon—to whom I shall return shortly as examples of the plantation tradition school of writing—as well as in James F. Cooper's *Spy*, Edgar A. Poe's "Narrative of Arthur Gordon Pym," and Herman Melville's "Benito Cereno," where one finds a gallery of Caesars and Babos, black characters who run the gamut from loyal lackeys to diabolic savages. In responding to these white visions of black character and in creating their own images, Hopkins and her fellow novelists were significantly influenced by contemporary literary sources, especially abolitionist literature, the Bible, and popular fiction.

ABOLITIONIST LITERATURE

Abolitionist literature—letters, newspapers, periodicals, journals, pamphlets, verse, and fiction—was by far the most useful tradition for the didactic purposes of black novelists. The formal diction, rhythmic cadences, balanced syntax, stark metaphors, and elevated tone of works like Harriet Beecher Stowe's *Uncle Tom's Cabin* (1852) provided the stylistic blend of matter-of-factness and sentimentality necessary for their initial moral and political appeals primarily to white readers. By their adaptation of the conventions of abolitionist literature, William W. Brown, Martin Delany, James Howard, Frances E. W. Harper, and others exploited the opportunity to strike a blow at American racism while simultaneously demonstrating their adjustment to Euro-American culture.

More important than *Uncle Tom's Cabin* to the neophyte black novelist, however, were the slave narratives, for they provided a natural bridge between the oral and literary traditions. Those pioneers of the Afro-American novel who were neither preachers nor teachers were either former slaves and abolitionist lecturers or the children of free parents and able spokespersons in the civil rights movement. In one way or another, they were all familiar with the techniques of the lecture platform and the process for translating this oral performance into literary narratives. Most knew that antislavery meetings would generally begin with introductory remarks by a local abolitionist in preparation for the appearance of a seasoned guest lecturer like Garrison or a fugitive slave like Douglass to provide a dramatic account of life in bondage. This performance would be followed by an impassioned, critical analysis of the evils of the Peculiar Institution and, on occasion, either a few songs or poems. Finally, a collection for the cause would be taken up, abolition publications sold, and the meeting adjourned.[71]

The transformation of personal narrative into romance is a matter of literary history. Slave narratives are the personal accounts of physical and psychological bondage and freedom. Some, like *Narratives of the Sufferings of Lewis and Milton Clarke* (1846) and *The Life of Josiah Henson* (1849), were dictated to white amanuenses, but most were written by the fugitive slaves themselves, who had already told their stories dozens of times from the antislavery platform. The pattern of the written narratives by Frederick Douglass, William W. Brown, J. W. C. Pennington, Solomon Northup, and William and Ellen Craft begin with the fugitive slave's realization of the evils of the institution, his first attempts at resistance and flight, his cunning victories over oppression, and detailed descriptions of different phases of bondage; they end with a successful flight North and an activist role in the "true" religion and abolitionist politics.[72] Most of the autobiographies are characterized by moral purpose, Christian values, and emotional fervor. Many read like moral and political allegories. Their style is largely derived from the pulpit, the lectern, and the soapbox, from Scripture and antislavery materials. Even though most of the characters are ostensibly Christian, the narrators carefully distinguish between "true" Christianity and the religion their masters used to justify slavery. And though by and large the narrators' appeals are to the moral conscience of whites, they clearly express a resolute faith in the humanity of blacks and the righteousness of their struggle for freedom, literacy, and fulfillment.

One of the most popular features of the slave narratives was the melodrama and romance of the perilous journey north to freedom. The ingenuity of the escape stratagems and the bold manner in which they were carried out—incidents first passed on by word of mouth in the form of tales and legends among the slaves and then retold from the abolitionist platform—gradually became the stock conventions of the form. Some light-skinned slaves passed for white in their flight north, occasionally stopping at the best restaurants and hotels along the way. Some disguised themselves as master and slave, as did the well-known fugitives William and Ellen Craft. Others, like Henry "Box" Brown, employed more elaborate devices, such as shipping themselves north in packing crates or barrels. The courage and imagination of the fugitives won the respect of white abolitionists. "They are among the heroes of our age," wrote Massachusetts Senator Charles Sumner. "Romance has no stories of more thrilling interest than theirs. Classical antiquity has preserved no examples of adventurous trial more worthy of renown."[73]

The heroism of men and women of unusual ability and integrity looms large in the slave narratives. Most of the heroes were skilled, trusted servants (e.g., artisans, drivers, and exhorters) with ambivalent feelings toward whites and blacks alike, particularly the masses. Some were political in character like Frederick Douglass and Harriet Tubman, some intensely religious like Nat Turner and Sojourner Truth, and others self-serving, faithful individualists like Josiah Henson. Regardless of political and personal differences, they were generally articulate activists committed to the struggle for justice and freedom. And the ideals they represent— an indomitable will to be free, unshakable faith in the justice of their cause, extraordinary genius, and irrepressible bravery—are thematically important in the tradition of the Afro-American novel.

THE BIBLE

Equally as important as abolitionist literature in the tradition of the Afro-American novel is the Bible. Through sayings, sermons, songs, and stories, its moral lessons were passed on by word of mouth and the printed page from generation to generation. Jean Toomer's *Cane* (1923), Countee Cullen's *One Way to Heaven* (1932), Zora Hurston's *Jonah's Gourd Vine* (1934), Waters Turpin's *O Canaan* (1939), Ralph Ellison's *Invisible Man* (1952), James Baldwin's *Go Tell It on the Mountain* (1953) and *Just Above My Head* (1979),

Margaret Walker's *Jubilee* (1966), and Hal Bennett's *Lord of Dark Places* (1970), among others, draw heavily on the Bible for plot and character. Traditionally, blacks have recognized and creatively utilized the parallels between their oppression and that of the Jews. Aside from allusions to the Hebrew patriarchs and prophets, the most frequent biblical adaptations are of the myth-legends, the hybrid narratives, of Moses and the Second Coming of Christ. "Weevils and wars are pest that God sends against the sinful," says Lewis, one of the central characters in *Cane*. "People are too weak to correct themselves: the Redeemer is coming back. Get ready, ye sinners, for the advent of Our Lord."[74] In the wake of the Civil War, Vyry Brown, the heroine of *Jubilee*, sings joyously of both her earthly salvation and the divine judgment to come. In *Moses, Man of the Mountain* (1939) Hurston rewrites the legend of Moses from the black perspective, fore-grounding black dialect, conjuring, and hoodoo. Seth Stanley, the messiah figure in *Appointed* (1894), is white; but Henry Holland in *Blake*, Tucker Caliban in *A Different Drummer* (1962), Jesse Jacobs in *Many Thousand Gone* (1965), Chuck Chaney in *'Sippi* (1967), Dan Freeman in *The Spook Who Sat by the Door*, and most modern-day messiahs in the Afro-American novel are black.

Because of this messianic leitmotif in the tradition of the Afro-American novel, a word or two about the differences between the eschatology of Jews and black Christians is appropriate here.[75] As derived from the Old Testament, the Judaic outlook closely links the coming of the anointed of God with the restoration of the dispersed House of Israel and the peace of Paradise. Early black American converts to Christianity, on the other hand, seem to have derived their eschatological vision mainly from the New Testament, where the end of the world precedes the Second Coming of Christ and the Last Judgment, with its concomitant salvation for the righteous, the just, and damnation for the wicked, the unjust. What was looked for in both redemptive views of history, however, was not an escape from the world, time, and history, but a new world rising out of the ruins of the first. "For, behold," says Is. 65: 17–18, "I create new heavens and a new earth: and the former shall not be remembered, nor come into mind. But be ye glad and rejoice for ever *in that* which I create: for, behold, I create Jerusalem a rejoicing, and her people a joy." The mediator for this salvation is, of course, the Messiah and his appointed Old Testament messenger, Moses.

In the tradition of the Afro-American novel there is also a significant difference between Pharisaic orthodoxy and apocalyptic visionaries. Converted and educated mainly by white Baptist and Methodist missionaries, the vast majority of early black exhorters, like the Pharisees, preached the gospel of piety and humility in the present age while waiting with hope for the advent of the Messiah, the Day of Judgment, and the Age-to-Come. In contrast, the apocalyptics, like the biblical Daniel and historical Nat, wrote off the present age as irredeemably evil, saw the new age as abruptly replacing, not redeeming, this age, and claimed to have a revealed scheme of things. As will be illustrated later in this chapter, these ideological and strategic tensions became an important leitmotif in the Afro-American novel with the publication of *Blake,* whose protagonist is hailed by his people as the "messenger of light and destruction."

The influence of the Bible is also seen in the tensions between the most common major characters in the Afro-American novel: the preacher and the hustler. Andy, a slave exhorter, is one of the principal organizers of the rebels in *Blake;* and Brother Belden, the folk preacher in James Howard's *Bond and Free* (1886), is a gifted man:

> he was blessed or gifted with a stentorian pair of lungs, a very active and original imagination, and could read the Bible with the lids closed, with as much satisfaction to himself as he could when open, because Brother Belden could not read at all. He had, however, been called to preach and . . . he responded. . . . They were all equally deprived, both the called and the uncalled. . . . In him confided; him they honored; in him they saw the messenger of the Lord bearing the only consolation which was like balm to their deepest sufferings.[76]

Like the preacher, the hustler is another gifted man who lives by his wits and rap, the power of his oratorical ability. He might be a confidence man, like Sadness in *The Sport of the Gods,* and belong to that "set which lives, like the leech, upon the blood of others, —that draws its life from the veins of foolish men and immoral women, that prides itself upon its well-dressed idleness and has no shame in its voluntary pauperism."[77] He might be like Mr. Coffin in *Daddy Was a Number Runner,* storyteller, number runner, poker player, and good-hearted family man who deserts his family. Or he might be like Rinehart in *Invisible Man* and become at will "Rine the runner and Rine the Gambler and Rine the briber and Rine the lover and Rinehart the Reverend."[78] The list of hustlers in the black American novel—including many musicians and preachers as well as criminals— and the masks they wear to manipulate the ironies and ambivalence of their lives are legion.

In addition to the dynamic interplay between preacher and hustler types, the tradition of the Afro-American novel reveals a conflict between the stories and supernatural forces of the Bible and the reinterpretations or syncretism of African deities, root doctors, and religious beliefs. Faith in dreams, divine providence, the mysterious powers of the Lord, and a New Jerusalem contend with conjuration, root doctors, hoodoo, and other residual African forces. Having lost the sanctions of religious and social institutions they formally held in Africa, conjuring and hoodoo (the syncretistic blend of Christian and sub-Saharan African, primarily Yoruba, religious traditions in the United States) mingled in time with the witchcraft and ghost lore of European whites and the rituals of the aboriginal peoples.[79] This belief in the mystery, magic, myth, and ritual of residual African religions complements and contends with the paradoxical rationalistic yet Judeo-Christian mode of Western consciousness. That the power of hoodoo, considered mere superstition by most of the literate class, is well established among the black masses can be traced in the Afro-American novel from Brown's *Clotel* to Reed's *Mumbo Jumbo* (1972), Bambara's *Salt Eaters* (1980), and Wideman's *Hiding Place* (1981).

POPULAR FICTION

Whereas abolitionist literature and the Bible provided many of their most distinctive plots, motifs, symbols, and archetypes, early black novelists also found the popular fiction of nineteenth-century America stylistically useful. Beginning in 1833, the Yankee humor of Seba Smith, the creator of the letters of Jack Downing, and his many followers flourished among the reading public. The popularity of Yankee rustics commenting on political affairs in racy, idiomatic language and awkwardly apt metaphors was not lost on blacks in search of appropriate vehicles for their own satirical commentary on American democracy, Christianity, and racism. Nor were the early novelists beyond the influence of the Southwestern frontier humor of Augustus Longstreet's *Georgia Scenes* (1835) and Joseph Baldwin's *Flush Times in Alabama and Mississippi* (1853). Like the crackerbox philosophy of Yankee types, the sketches of Longstreet and Baldwin were provincial but honest attempts at recording native American humor. Frequently given to caricature and burlesque, their emphasis was on the common man, oral tale, colloquial speech, local mores, and regional character types. In *Clotel* we see how Brown combines this vein of frontier humor with slave anecdotes when he disguises his fugitive heroine as an Italian gentleman and manipulates her identity with puns on politics and temperance in a burlesqued dialogue among Cincinnati stagecoach passengers.[80] In another episode we overhear a satirical exchange on politics and slavery between Southern and Northern character types that is representative of ironic regional differences. Most critics generally neglect this satirical dimension of the Afro-American novel.[81]

They point instead to the more common influence of the plantation tradition school of writers. Antebellum writers like George Tucker, William A. Caruthers, John P. Kennedy, and Caroline H. Ingraham created idyllic pictures of plantation life and the peculiar endowments of black people. Postbellum local colorists and regionalists such as Harris, Page, and Dixon— the classic literary apologists for slavery—glorified the antebellum Old South even more. Harris's *Uncle Remus: His Songs and Sayings* (1880), a rewriting of black folklore, and *Gabriel Tolliver* (1902), Page's *In Old Virginia* (1887), and *Red Rock*, and Dixon's *Leopard's Spots* (1902) and *The Clansmen* (1905) celebrated the beauty of an orderly, feudal, agrarian society and lamented its destruction by rapacious Unionists and blacks. Although Harris's and Page's extensive use of monologues and tall tales within a framework suggests their debt to the frontier humorists, romance and melodrama were the dominant forms used by the plantation school of writers. The melodramatic conflict was regional, economic, and racial. The "good guys" in this conflict were the chivalrous, white Bourbon aristocrats; their chaste, dazzlingly beautiful belles; and their devoted, contented slaves and freedmen. The "bad guys" were the malevolent white Union Lea- guers, carpetbaggers, scalawags, and free black advocates of civil rights. In retrospect, the moral absolutism of melodrama was highly effective in recording the postbellum schism in the national consciousness and con- science over safeguarding the newly gained rights of black Americans and in contributing to the tide, some might say backlash, of white nationalism that swept the country after Reconstruction.

But melodrama also served the dualism of early black novelist's psy- chological, social, and aesthetic needs. According to culture historian David Grimstead, melodrama was basically religious drama, "wherein surface detail, psychological, or social, was firmly subordinated to a world view" and "the 'real' truth had to be that which affirmed the optimism of to- morrow over the frequent bleakness of today."[82] The last-minute rescues, numerous reunions of long separated families or lovers, and projected ultimate triumphs of justice over injustice in the early black novels were natural events to those who believed in a universe governed by cosmic yet moral laws. At the same time, viewed from their subjugated economic and political circumstances, the basic goodness of providence, man, na- ture, and society was being perverted on a grand scale by white devils.

In addition, the dime romances with domestic felicity and female chastity at their matrix seemed heaven sent for the treatment of illicit relations between black women and white men. Refined heroes and heroines involved in elaborate disguise, mistaken identity, passwords, and violent episodes were keys to the formulaic packaged Beadle dime novels. In developing their forbidden fruit sexual themes, nineteenth-century black novelists found these melodramatic conventions irresistible. Contrary to popular belief, however, the mulatto heroines of *Clotel* and *Iola Leroy* are not mere carbon copies of Victorian white purity and prudery. True, as Ellen Morton's suicide in *Iola Leroy* indicates, death before sexual dishonor was also the unwritten code for black writers. But—as in the case of Clotel and Althesa—virtue, when frustrated by man-made laws prohibiting interracial marriage, could be satisfied by "a marriage sanctioned by heaven." That both women die before the end of the novel is less important to the plot than their sexual and racial exploitation—Horatio's infidelity and Henry's failure to manumit Althesa—by a perverse, unjust society. In contrast, blue-eyed, near-white Iola survives triumphantly as she reportedly rejects a persistent aristocratic white suitor and selflessly dedicates her life to family and race.

Loyalty to race or region often clashes with loyalty to country in the melodrama of the Afro-American novel, for patriotism was another cardinal virtue of melodrama. "Faith in the goodness of the United States, its government, and its destiny," Grimstead notes, "was modulated only by association with principles of liberty, justice, and equality, which were assumed to be the birthright of all men."[83] Whereas Belton Piedmont, the protagonist in *Imperium in Imperio,* has faith in white people and chooses patriotism over black nationalism when it comes to armed revolution, Dan Freeman in *The Spook Who Sat by the Door* acts on the principle that blacks must use guerrilla warfare to attain their rights. By and large, the emphasis in the tradition of the Afro-American novel is not on my country right or wrong but, as in *Invisible Man,* on ambivalence toward all men and events, ethnic and national. Moreover, when national values are affirmed over ethnic, it is generally because, despite economic, political, and moral perversions, they are based on principles and ideals common to all: liberty, justice, and equality.

An ostensible ambivalence toward these principles influenced characterization and plot. Convinced that the cause of justice and equality was not served when the birthrights, patriotism, and civil rights of blacks were subordinated to those of poor whites, immigrants, and anarchists, postbellum black novelists depicted this travesty with righteous indignation, parody, and irony. "The Negro is not plotting in beer-saloons against the peace and order of society," we hear a character protesting in *Iola Leroy.*

"His fingers are not dripping with dynamite, neither is he spitting upon your flag, nor flaunting the red banner of anarchy in your face."[84] In contrast, Iola is characterized as a black woman whose education and self-respect move her to insist on being self-reliant and gainfully employed in the business world. Understandably, as members of a group that was barred from equal participation in their society during an age when industrialization ran rampant, many black novelists saw middle-class values as the most realistic guarantors of racial justice and equality. Sobriety, piety, thrift, honesty, hard work, property ownership, and education are portrayed as the keys to freedom, literacy, and fulfillment in a puritan, capitalistic system. "Greater industry, skill, the sticking quality, honesty and reliability will open the way . . ." writes Pryor. "If we will only cultivate the saving spirit, cut loose from extravagant habits, work the year round, encourage and assist one another in business, we will acquire wealth, and this will effectively dissipate race prejudice."[85] Among other things, the shifting allegiance of early Afro-American novelists was symbolic of the unfulfilled promise of the nation and the unrelenting desire of black Americans for economic, political, and cultural self-determination.

On the other hand, the double-consciousness of Afro-American novelists produced a corresponding ambivalence toward the literary traditions of the day. Influenced by popular fiction and a predominantly white audience, for example, most early novelists included at least one farcical episode and ostensibly minstrel character in their novels. Brown's Sam, the "Black Doctor" with a flair for wearing ruffled shirts and a half pound of butter in his hair, and Griggs's church member, who flings her white charge across the room and swings on the preacher's neck in religious ecstasy, fall into this category. But even here the humor is double-edged, for beneath the minstrel mask is a satirical treatment of color and caste prejudice and practice. The folk, in short, are not simply portrayed from the white perspective of minstrelsy. Indeed, some, like Griggs's Hannah Piedmont, are self-sacrificing black matriarchs; others, like Dunbar's Sadness, are surrogate fathers; and still others, like Chesnutt's Josh Green, are black avengers.

From its inception, then, the Afro-American novel has been concerned with illuminating the meaning of the black American experience and the complex double-consciousness, socialized ambivalence, and double vision which is the special burden and blessing of Afro-American identity. Contributing to the complexity and diversity of the Afro-American novel is the fact that the first generation of novelists did not rely solely on folklore for creative inspiration and form, but drew heavily on abolitionist literature—in particular slave narratives—the Bible, and popular fiction. Although such diverse extrinsic and intrinsic sociocultural influences suggest the difficulty of describing its tradition, I have discovered that from William Wells Brown to Ishmael Reed the primary unifying principle in the Afro-American novel is the quest for dignity as a free people of African ancestry and the fulfillment of individual potential by merging a divided, alienated self into a truer and better unified, literate self. This quest, derived from the collective experience of black Americans and usually projected with messianic and apocalyptic overtones, begins with bondage, physical or psychological, and leads to some form of deliverance or vision of a new world: moral or political awakening, flight, rebellion, or social reform. Highly rhetorical elements and historical documentation, idealization of character and representative types contended with each other in the novels of the nineteenth and early twentieth centuries as black novelists sought to achieve the appropriate blend of romance and mimesis for projecting their aesthetic view that true art is moral as well as social. Born in a perversely intransigent social arena where color, class, and gender struggle are the major determinants of consciousness, they are generally ambivalent in their attitude toward both Euro-American and Afro-American values. Their view of history is usually cyclical, but occasionally shifts between progressive and apocalyptic. In short, the shifting emphasis in the Afro-American tradition from romance to novel corresponds to the ever-changing social reality of blacks in America and to the symbolic and folkloristic patterns of narrative that each novelist appropriates to structure his or her particular vision of reality.

2 / The Early Afro-American
Novel: Historical Romance, Social Realism
and Beyond

*Fiction is of great value to any people as a preserver of manners
and customs—religious, political and social. It is a record of growth and
development from generation to generation.* No one will do
this for us; we must ourselves, develop the men and women who will
faithfully portray the inmost thoughts and feelings of the Negro
with all the fire and romance which lie dormant in
our history, *and, as yet, unrecognized by writers of the
Anglo-Saxon race.*
PAULINE E. HOPKINS
Contending Forces

I N tracing the movement of the early Afro-American novel toward
social realism and beyond, I have discovered that its history conveniently divides into three periods: Antebellum Novels (1853–65), Postbellum Novels (1865–1902), and Pre–World War I Novels of the Old
Guard (1902–17). With the exception of the novels by Webb and Wilson,
and the three American editions of *Clotel*, the periods designated also
suggest the major thematic shift from slavery to caste, a corresponding
shift in setting from rural to urban, and the first experiments with naturalism.

Antebellum Novels

Prior to the Civil War only four novels by Americans of African ancestry
were published, all of them during the 1850s after the Fugitive Slave Act
and the appearance of *Uncle Tom's Cabin*. Education, temperance, women's
rights, abolitionism, and commercialism were the burning social issues of
the decade. Despite the laws against teaching blacks, for example, some
slaves were receiving education in various parts of the South. Memoirs,
diaries, and slave narratives tell of some whites, especially women and
children with mixed motives, teaching slaves the rudiments of reading
and writing. The cases of Frederick Douglass and William Wells Brown,
even though they were largely self-educated, are perhaps the most widely

37

known. If literacy was a rare pearl that grew slowly among antebellum blacks, books published by blacks were rarer still. The first two novels, Brown's *Clotel; or The President's Daughter: A Narrative of Slave Life in the United States* (1853) and Frank Webb's *The Garies and Their Friends* (1857), were published in London. The second two, Martin R. Delany's *Blake; or The Huts of America: A Tale of the Mississippi Valley, the Southern United States and Cuba* (1859), and Harriet E. Wilson's *Our Nig; or Sketches from the Life of a Free Black, In a Two-Story White House, North. Showing That Slavery's Shadows Fall Even There* (1859), are the first novels published by black Americans in the United States. Delany's appeared serially, and Wilson's was printed privately. Brown's American editions of *Clotel* appeared serially in 1860–61 and in book form in 1864 and 1867.[1]

WILLIAM WELLS BROWN (1814–84)

Clotel is clearly abolitionist in theme and tone. In the preface Brown exposes the institutional entrenchment of slavery in the United States and focuses on the ownership of slaves by persons in high places, especially professed Christians, as the principal reason for the perpetuation of the peculiar institution. Revealing the political nature and primary audience of his narrative, which is essentially a historical romance, he then appeals to the British to use their influence to hasten the abolition of American slavery.

The structure and point of view of the narrative are consistent with its thematic purpose. The first section of the book is Brown's personal memoir, entitled "Narrative of the Life and Escape of William Wells Brown." At its center is what the abolitionists considered the cardinal sin of slavery: the destruction of the black family. The memoir seeks to establish the unimpeachable historicity of most of the details in the narrative proper by using a third-person rather than a first-person narrator. The moral and political significance of the subsequent episodes in which a mother is cruelly torn from her child, which in one case drives the desperate mother to suicide, is expanded and deepened by the third-person editorializing narrator's account of his own flight to freedom.

Born in 1814 in Lexington, Kentucky, Brown, the first Afro-American novelist and playwright, was the son of a white aristocratic slaveholder and a mulatto slave. His sisters were taken away and sold by the proverbial improvident owner, in this case, Dr. John Young. After an unsuccessful escape attempt with her teenage son, the mother is sold down South, and Brown is sold to a merchant who hires him out to work. During his twenty years in slavery, he worked for a cross-section of whites, including an innkeeper, the abolitionist newspaper editor Elijah P. Lovejoy (who was

The Early Afro-American Novel

subsequently killed by a proslavery mob in St. Louis), and a steamboat captain. He finally escapes in 1834 with the aid of a Quaker, Wells Brown, whose name he gratefully adopts. In the years that follow, the fugitive slave educates himself, marries and has three children, and becomes a conductor of the Underground Railroad in Cleveland. He also achieves success as a steward on Lake Erie steamers, as an activist in the temperance movement, and as a lecturer for antislavery societies in New York in 1843 and in Massachusetts in 1847. Brown's trip to Europe in 1849 as a delegate of the American Peace Society to the Paris Peace Congress was extended to 1852 because of the Fugitive Slave Act. Before returning to the United States to be, in his words, "a soldier in the moral warfare against the most cruel system of oppression that ever blackened the character or hardened the heart of man," Brown had earned international respect as an abolitionist lecturer, journalist, and writer.[2] His major publications before his death in 1884 include an autobiography, a songbook, a play, two travelogues, four histories, and a novel or, as I intend to illustrate, a historical romance.

The two major modes of expression that most strikingly influenced Brown's writing after his escape from slavery in 1834 are abolitionist oratory and slave narratives. During his activism in the abolitionist and temperance movements he developed the moral didacticism and perception of the ironies of American slavery that characterized his first published speech for the Massachusetts Anti-Slavery Society in 1847 and his first book, *Narrative of William W. Brown, a Fugitive Slave*, also published in 1847. In addition to irony, the techniques from these oral and literary forms that frequently appear in *Clotel* are documentation from newspapers and borrowed sentimental verse.

Most of the chapters in *Clotel* begin with an epigraph underscoring the romance's urgent message: "chattel slavery in America undermines the entire social condition of man." The injustice of miscegenation and the plight of female mulattoes are the major moral imperatives for abolishing slavery. Juxtaposing factual with fictional narrative, the romance proper opens with a dramatic illustration of the precarious fate of light-skinned black women, Brown's spiritual soul sisters. Currer, the former housekeeper and mistress of Thomas Jefferson, and her two daughters, Clotel, sixteen, and Althesa, fourteen, are sold at a Richmond slave market.[3] Unprotected by the institution of marriage, the young girls are destined to fall victim to the lust of white males. After much suffering, Clotel escapes from the slave pens in the shadow of the White House and jumps into the Potomac River to her death rather than submit to recapture.

The Early Afro-American Novel

As the subtitle of the London edition suggests, the tradition of the Afro-American novel begins with the method and materials of the slave narratives, the residually oral hybrid narratives of realism and romance. Although the point of view is third-person limited omniscient rather than the first person, the narrator is nevertheless morally didactic and consistently ironic. The structure is episodic, the style elevated, and the subject matter rooted in the legends, myths, music, and concrete eye-witness accounts of the fugitive slaves themselves. At the same time, *Clotel* draws on antislavery lectures and techniques: abolitionist verse and fiction, newspaper stories and ads, legislative reports, public addresses, private letters, and personal anecdotes. More specifically, the main plot is essentially a rewrite of Lydia Maria Child's sentimental abolitionist short story "The Quadroons." The romantic elements in *Clotel* are thus derived from a conception of art that is social and historical as well as moral.

The ironic tone of the narrative grows out of the disparity between the humanistic values (i.e., freedom, marriage, and justice) of the omniscient narrator and the moral hypocrisy of white Christians and public officials like Jefferson, who legend says fathered several children by Sally Hemings, his slave housekeeper.[4] Currer is Sally's fictional counterpart. But Brown is sketchy in his treatment of her, for after she is sold to the Reverend Peck, a Connecticut minister turned wealthy Mississippi slaveholder, we learn little about her other than that she dies in a yellow fever epidemic. Actually, Brown is more concerned with Jefferson and Currer's illegitimate daughter Clotel.

Consistent with the conventions of the romance and melodrama, plot overrides character throughout the narrative. Clotel is not carefully delineated as an individual, but as the archetype of the beautiful heroine whose mixed blood, noble spirit, and poetic nature make her a tragic figure. By the use of idealized types, irony, and direct appeals to the Christian conscience of the reader, the author solicits sympathy and help for his race. For example, before becoming mistress to Horatio Green, the son of a Richmond aristocrat, the chaste Clotel insists on a marriage sanctioned by God. But after the birth of a daughter, she is abandoned by her god of clay feet, thrown out of their bower of bliss, and sold down South where she is compelled to rely on her ingenuity and courage to survive the lechery of white males and the jealousy of their insecure, unfulfilled wives. On one occasion, in the manner of fugitive slaves William and Ellen Craft, Clotel disguises herself as a white man and escapes with a fellow slave acting as her servant. Determined to find her own daughter, the fearless heroine then returns to Richmond disguised as an Italian gentleman but is caught in the dragnet to capture Nat Turner. As in the slave narratives, the pattern of movement is from bondage to freedom.

The only differences between Clotel and her daughter Mary are name and ultimate fate. Like her mother, Mary has no peer in beauty, fearlessness, or effective use of male disguises. Of the several tragic octoroons in the narrative, she is as important to the erratic story line as Clotel, and the only one for whom poetic justice prevails in the end. In this sense the closing chapters dealing with her fate are an obligatory feature of the narrative. Impulsively acting to save the life of George Green, a leader in Nat Turner's revolt and her secret lover, she exchanges clothes with him and takes his place in jail while he escapes. Justice triumphs years later when the lovers are reunited and married in France.

Just as Clotel and her many sisters represent virtue in distress, the perversion of true Christianity looms as the arch villainy in the narrative. Georgiana Peck, the minister's daughter and the defender of the true faith, sees the Bible as the bulwark of both Christianity and liberty. Taking issue with her father's sophistry on the question of slavery, she argues that "true Christian love is of an enlarged disinterested nature. It loves all who love the Lord Jesus Christ in sincerity, without regard to colour or condition" (p. 68). True to her Christian principles and the conventions of melodrama, Georgiana, on her deathbed, emancipates her slaves and provides land for them in Ohio.

Those who are untrue to the principle "that all men are by nature equal" and "endowed by the Creator with certain rights, which are irrefragable" come under attack by Brown. Although Jefferson is not actually portrayed, the legend of his mulatto mistress and the nobility of his words reverberate through the narrative. With caustic irony, Brown quotes the ideals expressed in the Declaration of Independence and in Jefferson's antislavery speeches in the Virginia legislature. The symbolic father of the nation, Jefferson is also symbolic of the historical moral hypocrisy of the nation. White ministers who pervert the Bible, favorite targets of abolitionists, are also satirized. The Reverend Peck's piety, refinement, and humanitarianism are undercut by his slave hunting, droll minstrel verse, and the joy of the slaves at his death. Hontz Snyder, his fellow minister, is depicted as a migrant New York missionary who piously distorts the Bible and history as he urges Peck's slaves to be faithful and obedient. But most of the slaves are not impressed by Snyder's sermon. They prefer the folk preaching of Uncle Simon, who knows "thars more in de Bible . . . den what Snyder lets us hear" and "can beat dat sermon all to pieces" (p. 75).

Aside from the problem of narrative authority and ironic distance between the author and most of his white characters, perhaps the most striking feature of *Clotel* is Brown's informed use of folklore. The narrative provides an insider's view of how formal Negro dances were used by white planters to secure mulatto mistresses, of the "doctoring" of the slaves for market, of color and caste prejudice among the slaves, and of the ingenious escape stratagems of fugitive slaves. Like the major characters, the common folk are depicted as types rather than individuals. Some are heroic, as illustrated in the anecdotes about fugitive slaves "puttin' on ole massa" with the "runaway pig" and the "ride and tie" escape stratagems. Others are humorous, like the anecdote of the fugitive slave who insists on paying freight rates because he is compelled to ride in the baggage car. And still others, revealing the author's ethnic ambivalence and appeal to his white audience, are in the minstrel tradition. For example, Brown portrays Peck's servant Sam as a doctor who not only extracts the wrong tooth from a patient but, as mentioned earlier, in his urge to identify with whites dresses for a party with a half pound of butter in his hair and "ruffles extending five or six inches from his breast" (pp. 99–102). In this farcical episode and several others, Brown draws on the eye dialect popularized by frontier humorists and regional writers as well as by minstrel performers as he resorts to caricature and the use of cacography and malapropisms. "Pass dem pancakes and molasses up this way, Mr. Alf, and none of your insinawaysion her," says Sam (p. 100). Brown's socialized ambivalence thus influences the manner in which he uses the oral and popular literary conventions of his era to expose the evils of American slavery and to appeal to whites to affirm the common salvation of enslaved blacks. It remained for Webb, Wilson, Chesnutt, Johnson, and other novelists to develop more deeply and fully the tragic mulatto theme and character that Brown romantically introduced in the Afro-American novel.

FRANK J. WEBB

Unlike *Clotel,* in *The Garies and Their Friends* we do not find a direct attack on slavery anywhere. Even Webb's allusions to abolition, as critic Arthur P. Davis points out in the introduction, are timid and ambivalent.[5] All that literary historians and critics know for certain about Frank Webb is that he was born and reared in Philadelphia. His novel demonstrates, however, that he writes dramatically and persuasively about the problems of growing up as a free black in the City of Brotherly Love and about the tragedy that overcomes an interracial couple who moves North. *The Garies and Their Friends* contrasts the fortunes of two transplanted Southern families.

The dark-skinned, lower middle-class Ellises and their three children are contrasted with the interracial Garies: a wealthy white Georgian, his mulatto wife, and their two children. Prejudice and discrimination in jobs, education, housing, public transportation, the media, and public officials culminate in terrorism by Irish immigrants and members of the white working class. By the end of the novel, the Ellis family is crippled but undefeated by the virulence of Northern race prejudice, whereas the Garies, except for young Emily, are completely destroyed by it. The author-narrator's sympathies are clearly with the strivings of black morticians, realtors, and doctors like the Grants and Whistons, who also figure in the narrative.

Instead of Christian charity or black power, Webb's answer to racial discrimination is green power. " 'I tell you what....' " says attorney George Stevens, the bigoted mastermind of the terrorism, " 'if I was a black living in a country like this, I'd sacrifice conscience and everything else to the acquisition of wealth' " (p. 127). Through success in their small confectioneries, funeral homes, grocery stores, and used clothing shops black characters in the novel strive to achieve power and prestige. They realize that their white contemporaries respected the power of money and property more than democratic and Christian principles. And like Mr. Walters, the "jet-black" millionaire realtor who buys the white hotel in which he is refused dinner in order to evict the offending owner, they are determined that whites will respect their class if not their color. " 'It is impossible,' " says the pragmatic Mr. Walters, " 'to have the same respect for the man who cleans your boots, that you have for the man who plans and builds your house.' " He therefore advises the Ellises to follow the practice of white middle-class families—whose color gives them an "incalcuable advantage"—and start their son Charlie out selling something instead of hiring him out as a servant. For " 'the boy that learns to sell matches soon learns to sell other things; he learns to make bargains; he becomes a small trader, then a merchant, then a millionaire' " (p. 63).

Blind faith in the American Dream and puritan ethic is the salvation, the prerequisite for social mobility but not equality, for most of the black characters in the novel. Webb dramatically illustrates this in the rags-to-riches metamorphoses of Charlie Ellis, the young protagonist, and Kinch De Younge, his buddy. Spurred on by Kinch, whose unorthodox dress and behavior are not cramped by the inhibiting influence of an educated father or of women in his household, the boys enjoy a carefree youth of adventure, marble-shooting, and pranks. After the Ellis family's misfortune—their friends (the Garies) are killed, Mr. Ellis is beaten, mutilated, and thrown off a rooftop, and their home is destroyed by a white mob—Charlie puts aside his youthful ways in order to find a decent job and help support his family. Responding to Kinch's fear that his sudden concern for manners and appearance will destroy their friendship, Charlie assures him that this could never happen but explains " 'that any one who wants to get on must be particular in little things as well as great, and I must try and be a man now'." Through the jobs provided by benevolent whites and adherence to the work ethic, Charlie achieves social status as a responsible young engraver and as the husband of wealthy young Emily Garie, while Kinch, who inherits thousands of dollars from his father, turns into "a full-blown dandy" and marries Caroline "Caddy" Ellis. Class values thus displace color in Webb's narrative.

In contrast to *Clotel*, *The Garies and Their Friends* is more mimetic than historical and more didactic than romantic. The emphasis is on the characters speaking and acting for themselves, and authorial intrusions are limited in the early chapters to descriptions and explanations of character and scene. After the first twelve chapters the commentary of the omniscient author-narrator, which is generally brief and most obvious at the beginning and ending of the chapters, is used more frequently to establish shifts in time and place, to introduce or reintroduce characters, and to reinforce the themes. The intellectual and moral tone of the author-narrator is consistent with the story, and there is very little distance between the class and racial norms of the implied author and the norms of his apparent white British and American readers.

The vicious attacks on black Philadelphians, however factual, are no less colored by Webb's didactic purpose to expose Northern racial hypocrisy than is his depiction of the Garie plantation as a virtual paradise. Even the use of such stilted diction as "worst inexpressibles" and "dilapidated unmentionables" does not seem inconsistent with the manners and condition of the rising black bourgeoisie the author portrays. There is, of course, the inevitable triumph of virtue over villainy, but it is a costly victory; and neither Charlie nor Kinch is the conventional one-dimensional melodramatic hero. Unlike Horatio Alger's Ragged Dick, who was not created until 1867, both are realistic portrayals of characters with a healthy mix of human traits. Their impulsive behavior and unorthodox appearance are in contrast to the basic goodness of their hearts. Similarly, although McCloskey comes close to being another stereotype of the Irish brawler and allows himself to be blackmailed into leading the violence, he has neither the will to kill Garie nor the conscience to die without naming Stevens as the man who fired the fatal shot.

The Early Afro-American Novel

To enhance the credibility of his characters and the theme of Northern hypocrisy, Webb carefully manipulates the moral and temporal distance between the characters themselves and between the reader and the white characters. Looking back on the slave past of Emily Garie's cousin, George Winston, we are told briefly in a summary about a nameless cruel overseer but are allowed in a flashback to see Mr. Moyese, the kind master, cultivating his young mulatto slave's intelligence and ultimately making him "a present of himself." Northern scenes in which liberals like Mr. Twining and radicals like the abolitionist Mr. Blatchford compromise their principles to rebellious white employees and refuse to employ qualified young black apprentices like Charlie are vividly dramatized rather than summarized. In mitigation of Blatchford's moral failure, we are offered the usual economic rationalizations by his friend George Burrell that business debts and the difficulty of finding more workers made him powerless. With the urging of his wife and the approval of his own employees, however, Burrell himself hires young Charlie, thereby morally redeeming himself for readers. The conflicting moral behavior of the white characters fosters socialized ambivalence in the black characters. Caddy Ellis, for example, sees the rioters as "white devils" and feels that God hates them as much as she does, while her sister Esther absolves Blatchford of all blame and assures the Burrells that God will reward them for their uncommon sympathy and kindness (pp. 267, 307).

HARRIET E. WILSON

Although she is our third black American novelist, Harriet E. Wilson is the first to publish a novel in the United States rather than England. *Our Nig*, based on her life as an indentured servant in New England, was published in Boston in 1859. Thanks to the preface, the three authenticating documents in the appendix, and the fine detective work of literary historians, we know more, although not much more, about her life than we know about Frank Webb's. In the preface, Wilson identifies her economic motives for publication as the maintenance of herself and child, her major autobiographical theme as Northern white racism and hypocrisy, and herself as a deserted "sister" and mother in failing health who appeals "to my colored brethren universally for patronage."[6]

The letters in the appendix confirm the author's racial identity and the autobiographical nature of the novel. The most revealing letter about her youth, signed Margaretta Thorn and addressed to "The Friends of Our Dark-Complexioned Brethren and Sisters," attests to the author's identity as an orphaned black who was placed while young with "people calling themselves Christians, (the good Lord deliver me from such,) and they likewise ruined her health by hard work, both in the field and house. She was indeed a slave, in every sense of the word; and a lonely one, too" (p. 139). Thorn also reveals that Wilson had been in poor health since she was eighteen years old, had been married, and had a son whom the county briefly supported when she was physically and financially unable to do so. The long, informative letter from Allida, a pseudonym for "aunt J— —," containing an excerpt from a Wilson letter with a poem to friends in Massachusetts is equally informative about the author's later years. It confirms Wilson's racial identity as " 'black, but comely' " and establishes her residence in New England around 1842. "Through the instrumentality of an itinerant colored lecturer," Allida writes, "she was brought to W— —, Mass . . . an ancient town, where the mothers and daughters seek, not 'wool and flax,' but *straw*—working willingly with their hands! Here she was introduced to the family of Mrs. Walker, who kindly consented to receive her as an inmate of her household, and immediately succeeded in procuring work for her as a 'straw sewer' " (p. 133). Allida also reveals that in 1842 Wilson met a very handsome, gentlemanly fugitive slave who married her, moved her to New Hampshire, "embarked for sea" while she was pregnant, returned after the birth of the baby in the "County House," and later apparently abandoned her again to poverty and sickness, necessitating the child's being taken in by a kind family. Too sick to do domestic work, "she has felt herself obliged to resort to another method of procuring her bread—that of writing an Autobiography" (p. 137). As for the subtext of Wilson's excerpted letter and poem, they are similar in tone and style to the novel, thereby indirectly further attesting to its authenticity. Although very brief, the third and final letter dated "Milfor, July 20th, 1859" and signed "C.D.S." (possibly the accepted abbreviation for Colored Indentured Servant) also confirms Wilson's racial identity by referring to her as one whose "complexion is a little darker than my own" (p. 140).

In his introduction to the reprinted edition of *Our Nig,* literary critic Henry L. Gates, Jr., provides us with the available facts about Harriet Wilson's life. Even though her place and dates of birth and death remain unknown, Gates discovered that the New Hampshire federal census of 1850 lists a twenty-two-year-old, black Harriet Adams as living in Milford, New Hampshire. Other public records reveal that Harriet Adams married Thomas Wilson in 1851 and that she registered the copyright of *Our Nig* in Boston in 1859. Finally, the 1860 New Hampshire death certificate of

George Mason Wilson, who was born in 1852 and died of fever in 1860, establishes that he was the black son of Thomas and Harriet E. Wilson.

Wilson's double-consciousness and double vision are apparent in the title, epigraphs, theme, and protagonist of *Our Nig*. The title and author's pseudonym, "By 'Our Nig'," are an ironic play on the paternalistic identity imposed on some black family servants by the master class. As Wilson's use of quotation marks indicates, she does not accept uncritically her white-ascribed identity. She does not perceive herself in the same demeaning, powerless, dependent manner implicit in the use of "Nig" and "Our Nig" by whites. The subtlety of the verbal irony here is reinforced by the dramatic situation that her primary audience is black and that the term is coined in the novel by Jack, one of the most sympathetic children in the household of the white antagonists, Mrs. Bellmont and Mary, her daughter. The quotations introducing each of the twelve chapters—quotations that range from Byron and the popular romantic writers of the period, both English and American, to the Bible—suggest the surprisingly wide scope of her reading habits as a self-educated, free black woman in the antebellum North.

Indeed, *Our Nig* is an intriguing synthesis of the sentimental novel and the slave narrative, of fiction and fact, of romance and autobiography. After the death of her black father, the mulatto protagonist Frado is deserted by her white mother and, like the author, is indentured to a nineteenth-century white Massachusetts family that abuses her like a slave for several years. Similar to the author's experience, the severe physical illness and spiritual desolation resulting from Frado's abuse by Northern white Christian hypocrites is made more acute by her marriage to a fugitive slave and his apparent desertion during her pregnancy. Frado's first significant step toward independence comes with the assertion of her rights in resisting the beatings of Mrs. Bellmont. Later, this spiritual independence and self-realization are reinforced by her increasing maturity and literacy: "Her school-books were her constant companions, and every leisure moment was applied to them. . . . She had her book always fastened open near her, where she could glance from toil to soul refreshment" (pp. 115–16). After completing her term of indenture, the invalid Frado is assisted by "a plain, poor, simple woman," who provided her with foster care and taught her the art of the needle and the value of useful books: "She felt herself capable of elevation; she felt that this book information supplied an undefined dissatisfaction she had long felt, but could not express. Every leisure moment was carefully applied to self-improvement, and a devout and Christian exterior invited confidence from the villagers" (pp. 124–25). Thus, the principal theme of *Our Nig* is that Northern blacks must also struggle for liberation and literacy against the "Southern principles" of racist oppression and Christian hypocrisy practiced by many Northern whites.

The point of view, narrative structure, and style also reveal the double-vision characterstic of the black American experience and the Afro-American novel. Although the story is told primarily by an omniscient, third-person, editorializing narrator, the titles of the first three chapters ("Mag Smith, My Mother," "My Father's Death," and "A New Home for Me") employ the first-person pronoun. The titles of the subsequent eight chapters do not continue this pattern, but the tension in aesthetic distance, suggesting the close identification on all levels of the author-narrator with her protagonist, returns in the opening sentence of chapter 12: "A few years ago, within the compass of my narrative, there appeared often in some of our New England villages, professed fugitives from slavery, who recounted their personal experience in homely phrase, and awakened the indignation of non-slaveholders against brother Pro" (p. 126). The ambivalence and irony here are that Wilson's narrative also recounts her personal experience with "slavery," which she fears will awaken "severe criticism" of her even though, as she tells us in the preface, she has "purposely omitted what would most provoke shame in our good anti-slavery friends at home" (p. 3).

Addressed primarily to her "colored brethren," the narrative of twelve chapters is a hybrid form of the sentimental woman's novel and the slave narrative. It moves from the oppressive indentureship of the abandoned child of a white mother, Mag, and black father to the heroic assertion of the protagonist's will to self-respect and self-reliance. Gates points out that even though *Our Nig* shares many of the elements of the overplot of nineteenth-century women's fiction given in Nina Baym's *Women's Fiction: A Guide to Novels by and about Women in America, 1820–1870*, it significantly inverts the plot structure of the "white woman's novel" to create the black woman's novel. One major departure in *Our Nig*, Gates observes, is the open-ended conclusion in which the narrator places "the burden of closure, upon her readers, who must purchase her book if the author-protagonist is to become self-sufficient" (p. xlvii). Despite Mag's unfaithful white lover in chapter 1 and Frado's apparent abandonment by her fugitive-slave husband in the brief account of their relationship in chapter 12, the oppression and infidelity of lovers and husbands are less important in *Our Nig* than "the complex interaction of race-*and*-class relationships, depicted in Frado's relation to Mrs. Bellmont, as inextricably intertwined," which dominates the other ten chapters (p. xliv).

Because the author and protagonist lived in New England communities where "people of color were rare," the style of the narrative, like its structure, reveals more familiarity with Euro-American culture than with Afro-American. Both, however, are viewed by the author and her characters with mixed emotions. This is apparent in the erudition of the epigraphs, which are all by white authors, and such romantic diction and tropes as "she was left to guide her tiny boat over life's surges alone and inexperienced" (p. 5). For dramatic effect, Wilson also draws on such sentimental conventions as direct appeals to the reader. After Jim, "a kind-hearted African," prevailed on Mag to marry him, for example, the author-narrator encourages us to understand the utter desperation of her minor character's circumstance as a penniless, moral outcast and to sympathize with her: "You can philosophize, gentle reader, upon the impropriety of such unions, and preach dozens of sermons on the evils of amalgamation. Want is a more powerful philosopher and preacher. Poor Mag. She has sundered another bond which held her to her fellows. She has descended another step down the ladder of infamy" (p. 13). Wilson's ambivalence about the racial and sexual taboos of black and white Americans suggested here is more forcefully dramatized in the dialect, inverted trope, and pun of Jim's proposal of marriage: " 'You's had trial of white folks, any how. They run off and left ye, and now none of 'em come near ye to see if you's dead or alive. I's black outside, I know, but I's got a white heart inside. Which you rather have, a black heart in a white skin, or a white heart in a black one?' " (p. 12). Jim's diction, grammar, and syntax as well as his playful inversion of skin color and human compassion reveal not only his identity as a Northern black but also both his and the author-narrator's socialized ambivalence. The pejorative tropes and wry tone of Wilson's explanation that Frado's husband, an abolitionist lecturer, "left her to her fate . . . with the disclosure that he had never seen the South, and that his illiterate harangues were humbugs for hungry abolitionists" further illustrates this ambivalence (p. 128).

The ambivalence of the author-narrator and protagonist culminates in the most explicit indictment in the novel of the treatment of blacks in New England by Northern white abolitionists: "Watched by kidnappers, maltreated by professed abolitionists, who didn't want slaves at the South, nor niggers in their own houses, North. Faugh! to lodge one; to eat with one; to admit one through the front door; to sit next one; awful!" (p. 129) This rhetorical strategy of a series of verbal forms, which shift abruptly without quotation marks from the descriptive mode of participial phrases to the dramatic with infinitive phrases enclosed by exclamations, underscores the anomaly of the protagonist's situation and the illuminating power of the author's double vision.

As important to the traditions of the Afro-American novel and feminist literature as the illuminating power of Wilson's double vision and her historical significance is her unique treatment of the theme and character of the tragic mulatto. Harriet Wilson not only introduces into American fiction the first interracial marriage in which the wife is white and husband African, but also develops the character of her mulatto protagonist, the couple's daughter, as an individual rather than a type. Frado's story is not about virtue in distress because of mixed blood and male oppression, but about the violation of human rights because of the hypocrisy of New England Christians and of the racial and class exploitation by some white middle-class women. Also, because Wilson was influenced more by the sophistication and sentimentality of the Euro-American literary tradition than by the Afro-American oral tradition and slave narratives, *Our Nig* clearly and convincingly illustrates that the conventions of both traditions contributed to the development of the early Afro-American novel.

MARTIN ROBISON DELANY (1812–85)

Blake is in part the fictionalized adventures of the author, a political activist.[7] Martin R. Delany was born in Charles Town, Virginia, May 6, 1812, the son of a free mother and a slave father. A proud black man, he firmly believed that he was a descendant of African royalty on both sides of his family tree. Although a trained physician, he spent most of the antebellum years in reform activities and newspaper work. Like many of his contemporaries, Delany was an abolitionist, but his radical brand of black nationalism led to criticism from many of his fellow abolitionists. "I thank God for making me a man simply," said Frederick Douglass, "but Delany always thanks Him for making him a black man."[8] A leading spokesman for black independence and self-determination, he attacked the racist practices within the abolitionist movement itself. To investigate the emigration possibilities for free blacks to the then independent Republic of Texas, he took a long, perilous trip down through Mississippi, Louisiana, Texas, and Arkansas in 1839. Much of this trip is fictionalized in *Blake*.

From 1843 to 1847 Delany edited *The Mystery*, one of the few black newspapers of the period, and from 1847 to 1849 was associated with Douglass on *The North Star*. His early writings criticized colonization schemes and expressed the view that the colored people of the United States were a "nation within a nation," a theme subsequently developed by Sutton Griggs in *Imperium in Imperio*. But Delany further provoked the anger of his fellow abolitionists by shifting his ideological position from anti-emigration to advocating the establishment of a nation in Central America or Africa. His nationalist and emigrationist activities culminated in 1859–60 with an expedition to Africa and the serialization of *Blake* in two black periodicals: the *Anglo-African Magazine* and the *Weekly Anglo-African*. Commissioned as a major of infantry during the Civil War, Delany served as a recruiter of blacks in Charleston, South Carolina. After the war he settled there as a powerful Reconstruction politician and post-Reconstruction trial justice, ultimately moving north and dying in Xenia, Ohio, in 1885.

In characterization and theme *Blake* is the most radical black novel of the nineteenth century. Although abolitionist in theme, it is the antithesis of *Uncle Tom's Cabin* and not, as literary historian Vernon Loggins states, "among the numerous analogues" of Stowe's controversial book.[9] Delany's book is intended primarily for a black rather than a white audience, and his hero is a young black Cuban revolutionary, not an American mulatto or a pious old slave. He is scornful of organized religion, not other-worldly; he preaches war against the tyranny of white rule, not Christian charity; he puts his trust in black self-reliance, not in white benevolence; and he advocates emigration to Cuba, not a mass exodus to Liberia.

Divided into two major parts, *Blake* is the story of Carolus Henrich Blacus, alias Henry Blake, alias Henry Holland, alias Gilbert Hopewell: the daring "pure Negro" organizer of an underground revolutionary force that plans to liberate blacks in the United States and Cuba. Part 1 begins in medias res and traces the adventures of the fugitive slave hero as he searches for his wife and organizes fellow slaves in the Deep South, while Part 2 exposes the political intrigue and nature of slavery in Cuba during the 1840s and, through retrospective narrative summary, the Cuban identity of the hero. Delany thus expands the thematic and structural concerns of the slave narratives from the break-up, flight, and reunification of a single family to an international plot of general rebellion and solidarity. The author-narrator's sympathy for his black characters is apparent even in the delineation of minor characters like Ailcey, the gossipy but shrewd house servant to the Franks, and Andy, the folk preacher who becomes Blake's confident and first recruited local organizer. Not far removed in tone from the black nationalist sentiments of the 1960s is the militant portrayal of Blake and his reference to whites as "devils," "white oppressor," and "alabasters."

As in *The Garies and Their Friends,* the emphasis in *Blake* is on showing rather than telling. The presence of the omniscient author-narrator is hardly noticeable in Part 1, which gains in dramatic force from the heavy use of direct speech and surface realism. But in Part 2 where the action shifts to Cuba, lectures, prayers, poems, and songs by the characters are liberally supplemented by the voice of the author introducing the reader to a foreign culture and the seditious activities of Southern expansionists and Cuban exiles. On occasion, Delany even resorts to footnotes for moralizing comments and unessential background information. Although the political, moral, class, and racial norms of the author-narrator and central characters are very similar, those of the emigrationist author-narrator and the abolitionist but anti-emigrationist black readers of the *Weekly Anglo-African* were probably not. This ideological difference between author-narrator and many readers as well as the political tensions and economic priorities of the impending Civil War in part explain why the narrative seems to have been generally ignored and did not appear as a book until the twentieth century.

In addition to its radical racial and political views, Delany's efforts to transcend the conventional comic use of eye dialect to achieve a more realistic depiction of character are only moderately successful. As an intelligent, educated servant, Blake is as proficient in the use of standard English as his genteel white master Colonel Frank. But Mammy Judy and Daddy Joe, his in-laws, speak the regional dialect of illiterate poor whites and blacks. " 'Den yeh 'fen' God case man 'fen' yeh,' " says Daddy Joe. " 'Take cah, Henry, tak cah! mine wat yeh 'bout; God is lookin' at yeh, an' if yeh no' willin' trus' 'im, yeh need'n call on 'im in time o' trouble'."[10] A similar difference is apparent in the delineation of Indians. Whereas the educated young Indian chief uses the idioms and allusions of standard formal English, the old chief's observations on the blood bond between Indians and blacks are embellished by figures of speech from nature: " 'The squaws of the great men among the Indians in Florida were black women, and the squaws of the black men were Indian women. You see the vine that winds around and holds us together. Don't cut it, but let it grow till bimeby, it git so stout and strong, with many, very many little branches attached, that you can't separate them' " (p. 87). Aside from being a sympathetic attempt to portray the vitality of the everyday speech of frontier types, Delany's use of dialect suggests the manner in which not only language but also region, class, color, sex, and age mediate people's perception, interpretation, and assessment of reality.

The use of music, poetry, and prayers in *Blake* also transcends its sociohistorical functions by revealing Delany's aesthetic kinship with William Wells Brown in drawing on folklore, the Bible, and abolitionist literature to shape his narrative. Biblical poems by Mrs. Stowe introduce each of the two major sections of the novel and foreshadow the messianic role of the central character in righting the wrongs of the weak when "Christ the God, is Christ the Man." Whenever a crisis arises or a meeting is held, the ritual of prayer and song expresses the faith of the people in God and collective action. Spirituals and work songs reinforce the theme of group solidarity, while the prowess of Pino Golias, Seraphina Blacus, and Ambrosina Cordora in playing both the African banjo and the Spanish guitar symbolizes their bicultural identity. The pithy abolitionist verse, parodies of patriotic songs, biting satirical lines, and long solemn prayers affirm the fugitive slave's moral resolve to keep the faith necessary to overcome the perversion made by whites of the Bible and human freedom.

Straddling the religious and political worlds of the novel is the messianic Henry Blake. As though in answer to his in-laws' cry, " 'How long! How long! O Laud how long!' " when they hear that their "daughter" Maggie is to be sold and taken to Cuba, Blake disembarks at sunrise from a Mississippi steamboat. The son of a wealthy black Cuban tobacco manufacturer, Blake ran away from home at seventeen, served as an apprentice on a slave ship, was sold under protest to Colonel Franks (one of the largest, most powerful slave traders in the Mississippi Valley), married his owner's mulatto daughter Maggie, fathered a son, and waited for the opportunity to declare his independence. At the news of his wife's fate, Blake bitterly renounces his "oppressor's religion" and Christian hypocrites like the Franks. He is careful, however, to make a distinction between the actual Word of God and false preaching, whether by self-serving whites or self-effacing blacks. Interpreting Daddy Joe's injunction to " 'stan' still an' see de salbation' " as the Bible's message for a different people and different generation, Blake acts out of the conviction that " 'now is the accepted time, today is the day of salvation' " (p. 20). Realizing that on this side of the River Jordan it will take money to organize a nationwide slave revolt, he escapes with a large sum of cash and gives himself two years to carry out his mission.

The author-narrator's ambivalence toward American character and values is apparent in Blake's advice to his fellow rebels. Self-reliance, faith in the "true" religion, and the power of the almighty dollar are for him the keys to black liberation. He tells his followers that their oppressors " 'use the Scriptures to make you submit . . . and we must now begin to understand the Bible so as to make it of interest to us' " (p. 41). They must also understand the strategic importance of money. " 'God told the Egyptian slaves to "borrow from their neighbors"—meaning their oppressors—"all their jewels"; meaning to take their money and wealth wherever they could lay hands upon it, and depart from Egypt. So,' " Blake instructs his organizers, " 'you must teach them to take all the money they can get from their masters, to enable them to make the strike without a failure . . . it is your certain passport through the white gap. . . .' " (p. 43). More practical than Brown's heroine and more romantic than Webb's, Delany's hero understands the nature and function of cultural and economic as well as political power in effecting radical social change.

Although he protests that he is not a spiritual leader, Blake is hailed as "Heaven sent," the "Lord's Avenger," the "Arm of the Lord" and a "messenger of light and destruction." He repeatedly defers to others to lead the prayers and songs that open and close their secret meetings:

> "I am not fit, brother, for a spiritual leader, my warfare is not Heavenly, but earthly; I have not to do with angels, but with men; not with righteousness, but wickedness. Call upon some brother who has more of the grace of God than I. If I ever were a Christian, slavery has made me a sinner; if I had been an angel, it would have made me a devil! I feel more like cursing than praying—may God forgive me! Pray for me brethren!" (P. 103)

Anointed as a high priest in the Order of High Conjurors by the surviving followers of the legendary Nat Turner, Denmark "Veezie," and "General Gabriel," Blake rejects their faith in conjuration as merely another form of false preaching and psychological bondage. He believes only in the true faith and in practical strategies for freedom. Thus when prayer and bribery fail, he uses force to escape from Indiana townspeople and continue his flight to Canada.

The Cuban section of the novel is analogous to Delany's commitment to liberation and self-determination on an international scale, especially his support of the Afro-Cuban struggle for independence.[11] This commitment is implicit in the author-narrator's political identification with Blake and the appeal for the reader's sympathy. Accompanying Blake as he finds his wife, reunites with his family, and executes his plan to free his people, the reader sees that slavery was as brutal in Cuba and during the Middle Passage as it was in the United States. In contrast to the enslaved American blacks, the Afro-Cubans are ready to rebel against exploitation by Spain and the United States. Blake's plan is to recruit Placido, the Cuban mulatto poet and nationalist, to organize the Cubans, while he proceeds to capture a slave ship—a contrived opportunity for the author-narrator to moralize about the horrors of the slave trade. Joining the ranks of the revolutionaries are middle-class mulattoes, field slaves, domestic servants, and fugitive Africans like Mendi, the captive chief whose courage, discipline, and self-reliance mark him as a leader. The principal leaders, however, are Blake, commander-in-chief of the Army of Emancipation, and Placido, director of civil government. Their eloquence persuades the revolutionary council that religious and class differences must be subordinated to the common struggle for liberation. Among the psychological and political advantages for mulattoes in affirming their African heritage are the expected emergence of a wealthy, powerful new Africa and the equality of African people among the great nations of the world. For Blake and the author-narrator, the realization of black nationalism in the Americas and Africa represented not only the end of white control over the land, lives, and livelihood of nonwhites but also the dawn of a new era of peace and prosperity.

Of the four narratives published between 1853 and 1865, *Blake* is by far the most politically radical, *Clotel* the most romantic, *The Garies and Their Friends* the most novelistic, and *Our Nig* the most original. Whereas *Blake* is messianic in theme and characterization, the protagonist a symbolic response to the calls to rebellion and self-reliance of black abolitionist orators such as David Walker in 1829 and Henry Highland Garnet in 1843,[12] *Clotel* employs realistic details, slave narrative anecdotes, and romantic subplots in the service of historical romance. In verisimilitude, coherence of plot, and delineation of character, *The Garies and Their Friends* reflects the major concerns of the emerging middle-class novel; *Our Nig* individualizes the character and theme of the tragic mulatto. Both *Blake* and *Clotel* end melodramatically with the protagonists or their children finding a haven in another country. Webb's characters also travel to Europe, but their unshakable faith in the American Dream dictates their eventual return to Philadelphia. Wilson's protagonist settles in Massachusetts. More important, the structure and movement of all four narratives are in the tradition of the slave narratives and sentimental romance. Families and lovers are separated and reunited; anecdotes about the evils of slavery and race prejudice are sensationally cataloged; tales of seduction of octoroons are sentimentally related; and the villain receives his just retribution while the hero marries the heroine and lives happily ever after, except in *Our Nig*. Again, *Our Nig* and *Blake* are different. *Our Nig* closes ambiguously with the author-narrator's appeal for the sympathy and aid of the reader for the invalid yet heroically struggling protagonist. The truncated version of

Blake presently available to us closes on an apocalyptic note that is prophetically in tune with the black nationalism of narratives of the late 1960s. In any event, by the end of the Civil War, the tradition of the Afro-American novel clearly revealed a preoccupation with the struggle of black Americans for freedom from color and caste discrimination as they affirmed their humanity in the process of defining and developing themselves as an ethnic community and as individuals. This quest was symbolically expressed in a mixed narrative form in which romantic elements often dominated social realism.

Postbellum Novels

The period from the end of the Civil War to the turn of the century saw the rise of American nationalism, industrialism, and imperialism. For white America it was an age of technology, commerce, and finance, while for black America it was an age of short-lived political freedom and long-term peonage, repressive laws, convict labor, and lynchings. In the scramble for wealth and power, Indians, blacks, the poor, and the land were unscrupulously exploited by the captains of industry. Greed and corruption were cloaked under the gospel of progress, and the blessings of civilization were self-righteously imposed on the colored peoples of China, Cuba, and the Philippines. At the same time, social realism was on the rise. In the hands of Bret Harte, Edward Eggleston, Joel C. Harris, Thomas N. Page, George W. Cable, James W. Riley, Mark Twain, and others, folk material, frontier humor, and nostalgia for the days before the war were being popularized in the form of local color and regional writing. With its surface fidelity to regional setting, character, and dialect, local-color writing was the literary bridge between American romanticism and realism.

Aside from a fourth version of Brown's novel entitled *Clotelle; or, The Colored Heroine: A Tale of the Southern States* (1867), no new Afro-American novel was published after the Civil War until James Howard's *Bond and Free* (1886). Between 1886 and the publication of *The Sport of the Gods* in 1902, the major literary dilemma of Afro-American novelists was how to be true to their vision of reality and still reach their predominantly white readers. Before exploring this dilemma and the anxiety of influence in the novels of Harper, Griggs, Chesnutt, and Dunbar, it is important to note that even in the preface to *Bond and Free* we discover the author seeking indulgence for whatever errors his antiplantation tradition novel may contain, affirming the truth of its incidents, and confessing that he has "endeavored to suppress all rancorous feeling" to avoid offending anyone.[13]

This may be interpreted as a literary adaptation of the pseudo-apology introduced into black oratory by Frederick Douglass,[14] but, in fact, it would be more than fifty years before such conciliatory attitudes toward predominantly white audiences are radically reversed by Richard Wright.

Meanwhile, because they wished to be published, the novelists of the period were compelled to print their own works or make compromises. Except for Griggs, whose audience was largely black, they all chose to compromise, which usually involved a moderation of militancy while persevering in the artistic attempt to counter the white literary distortions of reality and the black experience. The moral vision of novels like Sanda's *Appointed* (1894) and J. McHenry Jones's *Hearts of Gold* (1896), for instance, was unrelentingly shaped by faith in the Christian and constitutional principles of brotherhood and equality. Whereas this humanism and egalitarianism were reinforced by satirical attacks on the corrupt institutions charged with the responsibility of guaranteeing these rights to every man, they were undercut by the paradox that by virtue of color and class some men were more equal than others. According to one of the major characters in *Appointed*, " 'the poorer and more ignorant the people—North or South— the deeper rooted are their prejudices.' "[15] In contrast, the more refined and better educated among both races—i.e., the quality folks—were generally believed to possess the capacity to alleviate racism. Thus the hope and fight for a better world in the novels of Harper, Griggs, Chesnutt, and Dunbar are influenced as much by the material fortunes of man as by the providence of God. And as their novels illustrate, the first task in moving toward social realism in the Afro-American novel was to clear the ground of the lore of white racism and sow the seeds for a more faithful portrayal of the complexities of black character and culture.

FRANCES ELLEN WATKINS HARPER (1825–1911)

Contrary to William Still's prediction in the introduction to *Iola Leroy; or, Shadows Uplifted* (1892), Frances Harper's only novel has not eclipsed her achievements as a reformer and poet. The daughter of free parents, Frances Ellen Watkins was born in 1825 in Baltimore, Maryland. Moving to Ohio in 1850, she taught at Union Seminary in Columbus and began her long association with the abolitionist and temperance movements. Between 1853 and 1860, when she married Fenton Harper, she worked with the Underground Railroad in Pennsylvania and lectured for the Anti-Slavery Society in Maine. After the war, the Women's Christian Temperance Union appointed her "Superintendent of Colored Work," and she lectured widely on education, temperance, thrift, and morality. One of the most well-known Afro-American reformers and lecturers of her time, Harper was also extremely popular as a poet. Her poems, as Benjamin Brawley notes, "were the ornaments of her public addresses."[16] She frequently printed them in booklets which she sold for a quarter or less after her speeches; over the years she sold thousands of copies. Following her death in 1911, Harper was memorialized by the World's Women's Christian Temperance Union.

A melodramatic study of the color line, *Iola Leroy*, like William Dean Howell's *Imperative Duty* (1892), stresses the moral duty of mulattoes to repress the urge to pass for white and to inspire others by their selfless dedication to social reform and service to their race. Combining the sentimentality and rhetoric of romance with the psychological and sociological truth of mimesis, it is the first Afro-American novel to treat the heroism of blacks during and after the Civil War. The major characters reflect the author's deep involvement in the abolitionist, temperance, and women's rights movements. During the war Iola serves as a nurse in a field hospital, and her brother Harry enlists in a black regiment. Afterward, both commit themselves to the education and moral uplift of the freedman. In addition, both Aunt Linda, an enterprising matriarchial figure, and Iola, whose courage and independence are a departure from the traditional image of the tragic mulatto, are outspoken, self-reliant women. Acting on the belief "that every woman ought to know how to earn her own living," Iola joins "the great rank of bread winners" (p. 205). The color prejudice of white female co-workers gets her fired from her first job as a salesclerk but fails to shake her conviction that " 'the best blood in my veins is African blood' " (p. 208). Robert Johnson, Iola and Harry's uncle, serves as a lieutenant in a black company and as an agent for the temperance movement. Like Delany's Blake, he believes in "the real, genuine religion" but he doesn't "take much stock in white folks' religion," and although light-skinned, he considers it "treason, not only to the race, but to humanity" for a black man to pass for white (pp. 47, 208). As a transitional novel depicting the role of blacks during the Civil War and the struggles for personal and group social mobility during the Reconstruction era, *Iola Leroy* provides a panoramic view of the courage and commitment of mulattoes to freedom, justice, race, and family, especially motherhood.

In the tradition of abolitionist novels, the narrative centers on the breakup of slave families. The novel can be coherently divided into five major parts: the breakup of the Johnson and Leroy families during the Civil War in North Carolina (chaps. 1–8), a flashback of twenty years to Iola's interracial parents and "white" childhood (chaps. 9–12), the search for the central characters' mothers and the reunification of their families (chaps. 13–23), the Northern experiences of Robert and Iola (chaps. 24–32), and the return of the families to the South (chap. 33).

The episodic movement and mixed third-person and dramatic point of view of the novel grow naturally out of Robert's and Iola's search for their mothers. As they move about the country, the third-person omniscient narrator and major characters indict those whites and blacks who exploit the uneducated, inexperienced members of the black community. For example, in order to get elected to the state legislature John Anderson " 'make out he'd got 'ligion, an' war called to preach' " (p. 161). Because much of the narrative is in dialogue and black dialect, its pace is quick. Neither the injustices of the North—the housing discrimination Robert experiences in Pennsylvania is the same problem Iola faces at a Christian boarding house in New England—nor the "complexioned prejudices" within the race are glossed over. And at a forum on the general welfare of the race, the most pressing issues for blacks of the postbellum period (emigration, white terrorism, the power of the black ballot, the education of women, and moral improvement) are discussed by a distinguished group of speakers, including Iola, who delivers a paper on the "Education of Mothers."

If *Iola Leroy* repeats situations from Brown's *Clotel*, as Sterling Brown and Hugh Gloster have noted,[17] such borrowings are most meaningfully interpreted in the context that Harper was a late contemporary of Brown and Delany, and an important abolitionist in her own right. Like them, she was drawing on the abolitionist literary tradition and a common reservoir of oral folklore. Character and plot hinge on music and religious confession, for a folk hymn, birth mark, and testifying are the deus ex machina by which Robert and Iola recognize their kinship and by which Robert is reunited with his mother. After the predictable melodramatic round of marriages—Iola spurns a white suitor to wed a mulatto doctor who dedicates himself to his race, and Harry weds an equally dedicated black woman who founds a school for freedmen—the text of the novel closes with the subtexts of the author's note and verse to the reader reinforcing her faith in God's justice, black intelligence, and white Christians. Whereas the author's note and poem appeal to God for justice and to whites for a more Christian humanity, the characters, especially the protagonist with whom the narrator morally identifies, dramatically encourage blacks to take advantage of their God-given powers, to make a total commitment to the advancement of the race, and to prepare for the coming of a brighter day. With its fidelity to race, satirical thrust, and surface realism, *Iola Leroy* continues the pattern of abolitionist novels but introduces a more complex though melodramatic image of mulatto women, the black family, and the roles blacks played in liberating themselves.

SUTTON ELBERT GRIGGS (1872–1933)

In spite of the renaissance of black art in the 1960s Griggs remains one of the most neglected, controversial black novelists of the early twentieth century.[18] Born on June 19, 1872, in Chatfield, Texas, Sutton Griggs, the son of a prominent Texas minister, was educated at Bishop College in Marshall, Texas, and at Virginia Union Theological Seminary in Richmond. An eloquent speaker and influential Baptist preacher, he was ordained in 1893 and devoted his life to the church and the civil rights movement. Along with Du Bois, Trotter, and McGhee, Griggs helped to launch the Niagara Movement in order to confront white America with black demands for immediate political and social reforms.

Before his death January 3, 1933, Griggs wrote more than thirty works, including novels, pamphlets, a biography, and an autobiography. Committed to the the the doctrine of self-reliance, he began privately publishing his own novels in 1899. And in 1914 he founded the Public Welfare League in order to encourage the development of black talent, to support black business and professionals, to foster cooperation among blacks, to influence public opinion toward the race, and to safeguard black interests and provide help whenever necessary. Most of his racial tracts were published by the League and, unlike the novels, were addressed primarily to whites.

In a very real sense these tracts were a logical extension of the five novels he published between 1899 and 1908. The first, *Imperium in Imperio*, announced to the world that blacks would no longer tolerate the denial of their rightful voice in government. Because of its low sales among blacks, who were his intended audience and market, Griggs felt that he had not delivered the right message. Still hoping to win the support of his race, he wrote *Overshadowed* (1901) in a more conciliatory tone. The "proem" to this novel expresses its theme in the parable of a grain of corn, representing the Negro, struggling for existence with the roots of an oak tree, symbolizing Anglo-Saxon culture. As the novel closes, the hero, Astral Herndon, renounces both America and Africa as being "overshadowed" with intolerable handicaps for blacks, and in frustration declares himself "A Citizen of the Ocean." But his son, the author-narrator tells us with high seriousness, is destined to return, and through him " 'the Negro shall emerge from his centuries of gloom, with a hope-emblazoned brow, a heart freighted with courage, and a chisel in his hand to carve . . . his name in the hall of fame.' "[19] When *Overshadowed* met the same fate as *Imperium*

in Imperio, Griggs was badly shaken but wrote *Unfettered* (1902) to determine whether, in his words, "I was wrong in expecting support from the
race, did not deserve it, or else the race was doing wrong to withhold
support."[20] More than the others, this novel and its appended sequel are
well-meaning yet ineffectual attempts to explore black aspirations. The
sequel, "Dorlan's Plan," is a formal proposal to solve American racial
problems by transferring the standard of character measurement from color
to culture and by establishing a representative racial organization to foster
cooperation both within the group and with "broad-minded," patriotic
white Southerners. The financial failure of this third novel, despite favorable reviews, convinced Griggs to abandon fiction for other pursuits.
However, when the National Baptist Convention persuaded him to answer
Thomas Dixon's scurrilous attacks on the race in *The Leopard's Spots,* he
retaliated with *The Hindered Hand* (1905) and *Pointing the Way* (1908)—
impassioned indictments of political repression and color prejudice.

Imperium in Imperio vies with *Blake* as the most thematically radical Afro-
American novel of the nineteenth century. One modern white critic, unable to find a contemporary review of the book, suggests that it was too
treasonous to be evaluated.[21] Another considers it "blatantly black nationalist." In contrast, black critics argue that it "chronicled the passing of the
servile black man and hailed the advent of the intellectually emancipated
Negro" and that it provides "ideological paradigms for the 'New Negro'
. . . a framework upon which later novelists might build."[22]

A comparative account of the lives of a black and a mulatto boy growing
up in the postbellum South, the novel divides into three major parts with
an author's note to the reader and a framing prefatory declaration and
conclusion (chap. 20) by a first-person observer. The first part (chaps. 1–
8) contrasts the formal education of the central characters; the second
(chaps. 9–14), their professional, political, and personal experiences; and
the third (chaps. 15–19), their loyalty to race and country. Like the authenticating documents in slave narratives, Griggs's note to the public is
an imaginative attempt to provide a historical, authoritative basis for the
story. It establishes the narrator's credibility by identifying the source of
the manuscript (Berl Trout, secretary of state of the underground black
nation); by describing the character and background of the person providing the documents on which the narrative is based (a personal friend
of both central characters and a man whose "strict veracity" and high
moral conscience are vouched for by Griggs himself); and by referring to
the author's possession of additional supportive documents. In "Berl Trout's
Dying Declaration" and the conclusion of the novel, the first-person nar-

rator proclaims himself a patriot to the human family but a traitor to his race.

Instead of continuing with the first-person observer as narrator, the three major parts are narrated by an editorializing third-person omniscient narrator. As the plot unfolds, we discover no significant moral, racial, or political distance between the implied author, the narrator, and the protagonist. The first two parts portray the radicalization of blacks by color and class discrimination. Racial pride, scholarship, oratory, and a white benefactor enable Belton Piedmont, the black protagonist, to rise above poverty, prejudice, and discrimination to become president of a black college. In contrast, Bernard Belgrave's fair complexion and his white father's money and influence are largely responsible for his status as a Virginia legislator and Supreme Court lawyer. Belton is destined for martyrdom as a patriot because he subordinates racial consciousness to love of country, while Bernard's vanity, bitterness at white malice and terrorism, and commitment to separatism lead him to propose a revolutionary alliance with foreign powers. Although the political and moral dichotomy is clear, evil is neither absolute nor exclusively racial. Rather, as illustrated by Dr. Lovejoy's sermon on "the Kingdom of God is within us" and Belton's militant integrationist position, it is a matter of the quality of one's character. Neither the weakness of the good nor the machinations of the bad is solely determined by the color of one's skin. The militancy in the novel therefore finds its impulse in Griggs's faith in a moral universe and the realization by Americans of the principles of liberty, justice, and equality—not, as one critic asserts, in "a fanatical Negro nationalism."[23]

Like Delany, Griggs stresses the need for a black political organization. The last part of the novel outlines an exclusively black secret nation. Bernard is recruited and initiated into the nation by Belton, and the two climb to the top of this organization by different paths. Founded "to unite all Negroes in a body to do that which the whimpering government childishly but truthfully says it cannot do," the Imperium is an underground government dedicated to the protection of the lives, rights, and privileges of black Americans. White terrorism and Bernard's political cunning provoke the Imperium into endorsing a plan of open revolt and the seizure of two Southern states. Aside from its prophetic foreshadowing of organizations of the 1960s like the Republic of New Africa, the romanticism of this political strategy is, of course, more in tune with the melodrama of the novel than with historical reality. On the other hand, Belton's repudiation of this plan and the subsequent confession of Berl Trout to the author-narrator underscore Griggs's implicit endorsement of his hero's more moderate solution to the racial problem.

The Early Afro-American Novel

Gloster's judgment that the novel "exhibits the racial outlook that produced the National Association for the Advancement of Colored People" is essentially correct.[24] The hero is a militant integrationist who recommends separation of the races only as a last resort. His rationalizations, in the tradition of Booker T. Washington, are representative of the shrewd old-fashioned Southerner who relies on his ability to manipulate the white paternalism of men like Mr. King, young Belton's benefactor, to advance the interests of both the races and the nation. In response to Bernard's "Ballot or Bullet" speech, Belton offers a third alternative: the pen. Along with Du Bois and other radical spokesmen of the period, Griggs believed in moral suasion. Their faith in humanity fostered the conviction that the pen could prove mightier than the sword in the battle for equal rights.[25] " 'Before we make a forward move,' " Belton pleads, " 'let us pull the veil from before the eyes of the Anglo-Saxon that he may see the New Negro standing before him humbly, but firmly demanding every right granted him by his maker and wrested from him by man. . . . But be prepared, if he deems us unfit for so great a boon, to buckle on our swords and go forth to win our freedom with the sword just as has been done by all other nations of men.' "[26] These political sentiments, as the plot and delineation of the major characters illustrate, are clearly consistent with the author-narrator's.

In characterization *Imperium in Imperio* is another ambitious step toward social realism as it extends the limits of black romance and melodrama. Like *Blake,* it glorifies black character and attacks the myth of white supremacy. Its prefatory and concluding sections are imaginative appendages that seek to distill Belton into "the spirit of conservatism in the Negro" and Bernard into his diabolical counterpart. As rendered in the novel proper, however, their double-consciousness as black Americans is not so simple. Loyalty to color clashes with loyalty to country, conservatism with progressivism, and social reform with revolution. And whereas Griggs's use of dialect reveals a less acute ear for language than Delany's, his reliance on set formal speeches, oratorical contests, sermons, and political debates to delineate character and pace the action of the narrative reflects a more polemical literary use of the oral tradition than employed by black abolitionist novelists and a move away from one-dimensional characters to a more complex double vision.

CHARLES WADDELL CHESNUTT (1858–1932)

William Wells Brown published the first black American novel, but Charles Chesnutt is generally considered the first major Afro-American fiction writer. Born on June 20, 1858, in Cleveland, Ohio, he spent his formative years in Fayetteville, North Carolina, during the Reconstruction period.[27] Ambitious, largely self-educated, middle class, and light enough to pass for white, he responded with ambivalence and creative genius to the lore of his race and region. He was motivated to collect folk material for a book by the commercial success in 1880 of Albion Tourgée's *Fools Errand,* a sympathetic portrayal of blacks in contemporary North Carolina. Much of his collecting was a product of clerking in his father's general store, where he frequently overheard old timers swapping antebellum tales which, along with anecdotes about his teaching experience in Fayetteville, he jotted down in the journal he kept. After marriage in 1878, he had two daughters and became a court stenographer, a lawyer, and a man of letters. Returning to the North in 1883, he worked during the day as a Wall Street reporter for Dow, Jones and Company and wrote fiction at night. The folklore collected during his years in the South provided a rich supply of raw materials for his first narratives.

Influenced by such local colorists and regionalists as Lowell, Harris, Page, Cable, and Tourgée, Chesnutt was guided in his writings by a "high holy purpose." In the journal entry for May 29, 1880, he declares:

> The object of my writings would be not so much the elevation of colored people as the elevation of the whites—for I consider the unjust spirit of caste which is so insidious as to pervade a whole nation, and so powerful as to subject a whole race and all connected with it to scorn and social ostracism—I consider this a barrier to the moral progress of the American people; and I would be one of the first to head a determined, organized crusade against it. Not a fierce indiscriminate onset, not an appeal to force, for this is something that force can but slightly affect, but a moral revolution which must be brought about in a different manner. The subtle almost indefinable feeling of repulsion toward the Negro, which is common to most Americans cannot be stormed and taken by assault; the garrison will not capitulate, so their position must be mined, and we will find ourselves in their midst before they think it.[28]

Chesnutt's faith in God, the puritan ethic, and white Northern liberals fostered his belief that if blacks would prepare themselves for recognition and equality, literature could promote acceptance of the idea. But as he pursues these romantic moral assumptions in his two collections of short stories and three novels, we witness, especially in *The Colonel's Dream* (1905), his waning faith in the capacity of whites to advance the cause of democracy by dismantling the color bar.

Chesnutt won the acclaim of the white literary world with the publication of *The Conjure Woman, and Other Stories* (1899) and *The Wife of His Youth and Other Stories of the Color Line* (1899). On the surface, the style of the first collection resembles that of Harris and Page. But in tone and fidelity to Afro-American character, the conjure tales of Uncle Julius are a far cry from those told by Page's Uncle Sam and Harris's Aunt Fountain. Instead of being a mere mouthpiece for the glorification of the Old South, Uncle Julius, a shrewd old ex-slave whose colorful imagination and mother wit enable him to outsmart a transplanted white Northerner, spins off a series of wry wonder tales that exploit the ignorance of whites about the ways of black folk while simultaneously affirming the humanity of both. Believing that the double-consciousness of mulattoes offered him a greater challenge as an artist, Chesnutt in his second volume of short stories and three novels turned to the theme of color and caste. The main character in the title story of *The Wife of His Youth* outlines the most pressing problem of mulattoes. " 'I have no race prejudice,' " says Mr. Ryder, " 'but we people of mixed blood are ground between the upper and nether millstone. Our fate lies between absorption by the white race and extinction in the black. The one doesn't want us yet, but may take us in time. The other would welcome us, but it would be for us a backward step.' "[29] A proud, conservative member of the Blue Vein society, whose membership is restricted to those of free birth whose skin is so light that their veins appear blue, Mr. Ryder wrestles with the moral dilemma of acknowledging the wife of his youth: an illiterate, toothless black woman who has selflessly helped him escape from slavery and faithfully searched for him for twenty-five years. Ryder's ultimate acknowledgment of his mate suggests the implied author's position on color and class lines within the race.

Less popular than Dunbar, Chesnutt was nevertheless the better craftsman in fiction. His stories satisfied the critical taste of subscribers to the *Atlantic Monthly*, while Dunbar's appealed to the less demanding readers of *Lippincott's*. Howells compared the "quiet and force" of Chesnutt's art to that of "Maupassant, or Tourgeunief, or Mr. James, or Miss Jewett, or Miss Wilkins."[30] And another critic found Chesnutt's imagination and sentiment more profound than Dunbar's.[31] When his first novel, *The House Behind the Cedars* (1900), a tragic romance on "passing," was published, it also received highly favorable reviews.

But *The Marrow of Tradition* (1901), based on the lynchings that occurred during the 1898 elections in Wilmington, North Carolina, and *The Colonel's Dream*, an attack on the peonage and convict lease labor system, ran into heavy negative criticism. Howells and Paul Elmer More headed the list of reviewers who found *The Marrow of Tradition* humiliatingly bitter.[32] "Mr. Chesnutt," Howells wrote paternalistically in *North American Review*, " . . . has lost literary quality in acquiring literary quantity, and though his book, *The Marrow of Tradition*, is of the same strong material as his earlier books, it is less simple throughout, and therefore less excellent in manner."[33] Preferring that realism restrict itself to the more genteel aspects of life, the Dean of American Letters went on the say that Chesnutt "stands up for his own people with a courage which has more justice than mercy in it. The book is, in fact, bitter, bitter. There is no reason in history why it should not be so, if wrong is to be repaid with hate and yet it would be better if it was not so bitter." In contrast, Chesnutt considered the novel the best he had written.

Set in Wellington, North Carolina, during the Reconstruction era, the plot of *The Marrow of Tradition* is simple enough. At its center are the reactionaryism of the white aristocratic Carterets and the liberalism of the half-white middle-class Millers. The conflict between these two families, heightened by Major Carteret's belief in "the divine right of white men" and the enmity of Olivia Carteret for her half-sister Janet Miller, is dramatized in a series of confrontations in which the life of either the Carteret or the Miller child hangs in the balance. The novel reaches its climax with the death of the Miller child in a riot incited by Major Carteret's race-baiting editorials. But when the Carterets beg Dr. Miller to save their dying son's life, the Millers overcome the impulse of an eye for an eye and achieve a moral victory by agreeing to help the child. The message is clear: racial harmony depends on whether the next generation of whites will perpetuate the racist values of the Old South or create a more democratic and humanistic social order.

It is this theme that informs the novel, from the melodramatic use of names to the delineation of characters. Stressing the relative status of the children to each other and to the plot, the Carteret child is ceremoniously christened Theodore Felix but called "Dodie," while the Miller child remains nameless. Through the characters we also discover that the major cause of racial conflict in Wellington is white chauvinism. At the heart of the Southern tradition is a rigid code of social etiquette based on color and class. On one side of the color line are members of old Southern families like the Carterets, poor whites like McBane, and ineffectual intellectuals like Lee Ellis, a Quaker. On the other side are the Millers and Attorney Watson, members of the black middle class, and Mammy Jane, Jerry Letlow, Sandy Campbell, and Josh Green, poor, working-class blacks.

Arousing his white readers' interest by employing an old family retainer's trusted memory to provide retrospective narrative (a convention of Southern local color and regional writers), Chesnutt begins the novel with Mammy Jane's chronicle of the black-white love affair involving Sam Merkell, Olivia's father, Polly Ochiltree, his sister, and Julia Brown, his mulatto housekeeper and mistress. " 'Eve'ybody s'posed Mars Sam would give her a house an' lot, er leave her somethin' in his will,' " says Jane, as she recalls the Carteret family history. " 'But he died suddenly, and didn' leave no will, an' Mis' Polly got herse'f 'pinted gyardeen ter young Mis' 'Livy, an' driv Julia an' her young un out er de house, an' lived here in dis house wid Mis' 'Livy till Mis' 'Livy ma'ied Majah Carteret.' "[34] The abuse and rejection of Julia and her daughter Janet, first by Polly and then by the Carterets, symbolize the historical relationship between white and black America. Such relations, the omniscient author-narrator interjects, "had been all too common in the old slavery days, and not a few of them had been projected into the new era. Sins, like snakes, die hard. The habits and customs of a people were not to be changed in a day, nor by the stroke of a pen" (p. 7). The dramatic irony here is that this reference to the Emancipation Proclamation and the Thirteenth, Fourteenth, and Fifteenth amendments of the Constitution also applies, the reader realizes, to Chesnutt's novels. Even though social realism is probably more likely to influence attitudes than laws, neither necessarily achieves this humanistic objective. This is particularly true, as Chesnutt reveals, when the lore of white racism is the marrow of the American tradition. And the most diseased aspect of this tradition for him was the prejudice and discrimination suffered by interracial middle-class families.

Plot and characterization reveal that the ethical, social, and political distance between the author-narrator and the minor characters is greater than that between him and the central character, Dr. Miller. Torn between his allegiance to color and class, the author-narrator is pessimistic about the pernicious influence of racism. Belatedly acknowledged after the tragic death of her son and the destruction of her husband's hospital, Janet bitterly rejects Olivia's sisterly recognition as coming too late and costing too much. Her warring passions and ringing rejection indicate Chesnutt's insightful displacement of the traditional stereotype of the tragic mulatto. Dr. Miller, Janet's husband, agonizes over the fact that even though he has submitted to the puritan ritual of becoming well scrubbed, well educated, and well mannered, he still suffers racial discrimination and social abuse. Nothing was more absurd to the refined doctor than the practice of Jim Crow. " 'Surely,' " he says, " 'if a classification of passengers on trains was at all desirable, it might be made upon some more logical and considerate basis than a mere arbitrary, tactless and . . . brutal drawing of a color line' " (p. 60). Character, culture, and class would, in his judgment, provide such a basis. Meanwhile, in the apocalyptic closing of the novel, black politicians and professionals are chased out of town; black townsmen are intimidated and murdered in the streets; and black militants are shot down defending themselves and their community from a white mob. Only in the Pyrrhic victory of the Millers is there any glimmer of hope for racial harmony in the future.

Chesnutt's aesthetics were in one respect clearly shaped by the demands of his white audience. After Richard Gilder, editor of *Century Magazine*, had rejected one of his short stories, Chesnutt expressed his disappointment in a letter to George W. Cable:

> Pardon my earnestness. I write *de plein coeur*—as I feel Mr. Gilder finds that I either lack humor or that my characters have a "brutality, a lack of mellowness, lack of spontaneous imaginative life, lack of outlook that makes them uninteresting." I fear, alas, that those are the things that do characterize them, and just about the things that might have been expected to characterize people of that kind, the only qualities which the government and society had for 300 years labored faithfully, zealously, and successfully to produce, the only qualities which would have rendered their life at all endurable in the 19th century. I suppose I shall have to drop the attempt at realism and try to make them like other folks.[35]

In order to be published he at least had to appear to satisfy the prejudices of his white readers.

To achieve this end Chesnutt developed a highly sophisticated ironic voice. On one level, then, Mammy Jane and her grandson Jerry Letlow—whose surname symbolizes his obsequious nature—are characterized by a "doglike fidelity" to their white employers. Ancient in years and wearing a colorful frock with a red head rag, Jane exudes an undying, syrupy loyalty to her white mistress. But this image, like Chesnutt's brief yet unsympathetic portrayals of the "chip-on the-shoulder" new black generation, is a satirical slap at white interpretations of black character. Upset by the self-assertiveness of a young black nurse who rejects "old-time negroes" and considers her relationship to the Carterets as nothing more than business, Jane fumes about education spoiling young blacks: " 'I's fetch' my gran'son' Jerry up ter be 'umble, an' keep in 'is place. An' I tells dese other niggers dat ef dey'd do de same, an' not crowd de w'ite folks, dey'd git ernuff ter eat, an' live out deir days in peace an' comfo't. But dey don' min' me—dey don' min' me!' " (p. 44). In addition to capturing the authentic speech of a poor black North Carolinian,[36] Chesnutt here effectively sets up the dramatic irony of Jane's tragic death. While hurrying to aid her white folks, she is killed by those she trusts most to protect her. Jerry, who also depended on white benevolence for his personal identity and security, is another ironic victim of the white mob.

The realistic portrayals of Sandy Campbell and Josh Green also reveal the sharp eye of an intimate observer of black character and the caste system. Sandy is subtly satirized as a self-important body servant to old Mr. Delamere and a back-sliding Methodist who considers himself better than a Baptist of any degree of sanctity. Less convincingly developed is Josh Green, a militant laborer who has pledged to kill the Klansman who killed his father and drove his mother insane. As a dock worker and symbol of the revolutionary potential of the black masses, he refuses to participate in Jim Crow rituals and puts " 'one of dem dagoes' " in the hospital for calling him a " 'damn' low-down nigger.' " When Dr. Miller and Attorney Watson refuse to lead the resistance against the white mob, Josh assumes command and shouts: " 'Come along boys! Dese gentlemen may have somethin' ter live fer: but ez fer my pa't, I'd ruther be a dead nigger any day dan a live dog!' " (p. 284).

Actually, Chesnutt's black characters go beyond the demythologizing of white lore as they honestly struggle with their ambivalence as black Americans. Even though he sympathizes with the plight of the masses, Chesnutt, like Griggs, criticizes both the slavish imitation of white mores and the use of violence as a solution to racial differences. At the same time, he recognizes the responsibilities of the black middle class to the black masses. Dr. Miller, for example, is willing to devote his medical skills to the cause of his people, but he is neither ready nor willing to sacrifice his life foolishly for them. As he watches Josh and the others march off, "while entirely convinced that he had acted wisely in declining to accompany them [he] was yet conscious of a distinct feeling of shame and envy that he, too, did not feel impelled to throw away his life in a hopeless struggle" (p. 285).

As a member of the black bourgeoisie himself, Chesnutt realized that the vested interests of black intellectuals, professionals, and businessmen not only discouraged them from becoming revolutionaries but also frequently compromised their effectiveness as leaders in the struggle for liberation of the masses. Thus Dr. Miller's manner of resolving his double-consciousness is dictated more by class values than by ethnic solidarity or race consciousness. Social reform, not revolution, is his choice. In the last line of the novel, Chesnutt cautiously yet optimistically allows this vision of social reality to speak for itself. As Dr. Miller finally gains entry to the Carteret home, the symbol of social acceptance, to operate on the Carterets' child, he is urged: " 'Come on up. . . . There's time enough, but none to spare' " (p. 329).

In its realistic illustration of the blood and cultural ties that bind black and white Americans together, its moral purpose of unmasking white terrorism and lore, and its ironic, more persuasive treatment of the complex influence of color and class on black character, *The Marrow of Tradition* enriches the tradition of the Afro-American novel and moves it further on the road toward social realism.

PAUL LAURENCE DUNBAR (1872–1906)

Chesnutt's chief rival for the distinction of being the first of his race to achieve national fame for popularizing black folklore in American literature was Paul Laurence Dunbar. Born in 1872 in Dayton, Ohio, he was the son of fugitive slaves. Whereas his mother fed young Paul sugar-coated tales about plantation life, his father stressed the grim realities of slavery. As the nostalgia of *Oak and Ivy* (1893) and *Folks from Dixie* (1898) suggests, his mother's view made the stronger impression on him. Gradually, however, his talks with other ex-slaves and his own trips South deepened his understanding of racial injustice and his literary use of black dialect. The irony and social criticism of *The Strength of Gideon and Other Stories* (1900) and *The Sport of the Gods* (1902) are the high-water marks of this new perspective.

In addition to the influence of his mother, the younger Dunbar subscribed to the agrarian values of the Midwest and, with increasing authority and originality, the literary techniques of James Whitcomb Riley, Irwin Russell, Joel C. Harris, and Bret Harte. His early efforts at Western and plantation tales are informed by a naive faith in the virtues of the natural environment and the evils of the metropolis. "The Tenderfoot" (1891) and *The Love of Landry* (1900), whose setting and plot reflect the fact that Dunbar wrote the book while in Colorado for his health, fall into the first group, whereas the sentiments and use of dialect in *Oak and Ivy* and *Folks from Dixie* reveal his debt to Russell and Harris. His purpose in writing was, he says, "to be able to interpret my own people through song and story, and to prove to the many that after all we are more human than African."[37] This view is representative of the socialized ambivalence of blacks of Dunbar's era when Africa was associated with savagery, and blackness was a badge of shame. As indicated by his own reliance on white patrons and the saccharine themes of stories like "One Man's Fortune,"[38] the younger Dunbar was firmly convinced that the protection, progress, and prosperity of Africans in the Edenic garden of America was dependent on the humanity, however flawed, of white aristocrats. More to the point, perhaps, the tension between a realistic and romantic image of American society in his fiction is the result of these social and aesthetic ideas.

In contrast to the success of his three collections of short stories, Dunbar's novels were not favorably received. In part this was because *The Uncalled* (1898), an attack on religious bigotry, *The Love of Landry*, a Western romance, and *The Fanatics* (1901), a subtle indictment of sectional chauvinism, either ignore or merely exploit Afro-American character as atmosphere. But in *The Sport of the Gods* Dunbar achieves a high degree of racial and artistic integrity. Like Chesnutt's *Marrow of Tradition*, *The Sport of the Gods* debunks the myths, stereotypes, and rituals that perpetuate racial conflict and warp the national character. Drawing on Afro-American music (ragtime and blues) as a leitmotif, the book as social realism moves beyond a mere reiteration of the plantation-school thesis to an indictment of the Southern tradition of noblesse oblige and Northern commercialism. Of greater significance in Dunbar's spiritual and aesthetic coming-of-age is the creation of Sadness, the first blues figure in the Afro-American novel.

The Sport of the Gods, in other words, might be meaningfully read as a black American pastoral, an ironic inversion of the values of the pastoral romance and the plantation tradition, or a naturalistic romance. The narrative questions the illusion of innocence, simplicity, and harmony of life for blacks on the plantation and the popular myth of the North as a land of milk and honey. Structurally, the novel is a story within a story. The minor plot line (chaps. 1–6) relates the events leading to Berry Hamilton's five-year imprisonment in the rural South, and the major line of action (chaps. 7–18) deals with the alienation and romances of the members of his family in the urban North. As in *The Garies and Their Friends*, the depiction of urban life in *The Sport of the Gods* is more mimetic than historical and more didactic than romantic as the Hamiltons are destroyed by social and cosmic forces.

Disarming his reader, the omniscient author-narrator begins ostensibly in the manner of Harris and Russell by establishing the Hamiltons, a family of loyal emancipated slaves who cast their lot with the New South, in a virtual postbellum paradise. Twenty years of domestic service to the Oakleys have rewarded Berry and his wife Fannie with a neat little cottage in their white employer's backyard. The mutual affection and interdepend-

72

The Early Afro-American Novel

ence of white Southern aristocracy and black menials is dramatized in their "bower of peace and comfort" and the encouragement of their children, Joe and Kitty, to imitate the ways of their quality white folks. With uncommon subtlety, however, Dunbar undercuts the Southern code of chivalry and the legendary paternalism of master to servant. Although Berry has been known by whites "as an honest, sensible negro, and the pink of good servants," he is falsely accused by his employer and convicted of theft. When Fannie insists on her husband's innocence, she and the children are evicted by the Oakleys. White sentiment ranges from the paternalism that blacks were irresponsible, primitive creatures to the racism that they were naturally depraved and beyond redemption. Even when Maurice Oakley discovers that his brother has lied about the stolen money, Southern honor is valued over truth, justice, and Berry's life; for the fact, in the words of one Southern aristocrat, " 'would be sure to hurt Oakley's feelings, and he is one of our best families' " (p. 227).

Bearing the burden of socialized ambivalence, the black community also turns its back on the accused. " 'Tell me, tell me,' " says one black on hearing the news, " 'you needn't tell me dat a bird din fly so high dat he don' have to come down some time. An' w'en he do light, honey, my Lawd, how he flop!' " (pp. 50–51). Berry's lodge members request an immediate audit of the books he kept as treasurer, his church drops him from membership, and his friends offer him no support. The cruelest blow comes after his wife and children are evicted: neither white nor black townspeople will employ them or rent them a place to live. This is hardly the conventional idealistic picture of the South.

The reality of Northern hypocrisy and big business interests is also attacked in the novel. Focusing on the yellow journalistic practices of the *Universe*, a New York newspaper, the author-narrator demonstrates that "a corporation . . . had no soul and therefore no conscience" (p. 235). Skaggs, a reporter for the *Universe*, follows a lead on the Hamilton story which ultimately proves Berry's innocence. But the author-narrator's attitude toward Skaggs, a self-righteous, unscrupulous New Englander, is critical. Skaggs and the *Universe* represent the moral duplicity of Northern businessmen whose humanitarian gestures mask their own regional and racial prejudices. That Berry is released from prison as a result of the newspaper's crusade seems less important to the implied author than unmasking the practice of yellow journalism and the exploitation of black Southerners by white Northern philanthropists.

Structurally, the novel ends where it began. The ironic tension between a realistic and romantic image of black American experience is resolved in the Hamiltons' return and resignation to their fate in the South. In the final vignette we see a dispirited Berry and Fannie sitting calmly in their cottage on the Oakley estate, clasping each other's hand and listening to the shrieks of Maurice Oakley, who has gone mad from a morbid fear that his dishonorable act will be discovered. Reflecting on the disintegration of their family, the Hamiltons "knew they were powerless against some Will infinitely stronger than their own" (p. 255). In a deterministic world where whites have arrogated to themselves the power of gods, this means either that the social problems of blacks will ultimately be resolved in the South or that the evils of the Southern plantation and its paternalism are preferable to those of the urban North. In either case, the implied author sees no hope for blacks to prevail against the social and economic power of whites.

As for social and cultural modes of survival in the urban North, Dunbar, making use of his background as a songwriter and local colorist, innovatively employs the blues and ragtime as narrative devices.[39] One of the great American paradoxes he reveals in the use of these devices is the puritan and Victorian attitude of many blacks toward these forms of folk music.[40] To pre–World War I rural black Southerners, especially those with middle-class ambitions, there were basically two kinds of ethnic music: the Lord's (spirituals) and the devil's (blues, ragtime, and jazz). Consequently, when Thomas, "a dashing back-area-way Don Juan," introduces the Hamiltons to ragtime music and urban night life, he is, in effect, functioning as the devil's agent. As Mrs. Hamilton succumbs to the luring excitement of the music and the colorfully dressed black singers and dancers, she loses faith in her rural folk values. Reinforcing his diabolical urban role, Thomas also takes young Joe Hamilton to the Banner Club, "a social cesspool," where he falls under the spell of a chorus girl. Impressed by the crowd of drunks, prostitutes, politicians, hustlers, artists, and reporters that hang out in the club, Joe turns to heavy drinking and then to murder when his girlfriend Hattie throws him out. His sister Kitty's moral decline is symbolized by her substitution of "the detestable coon ditties which the stage demanded" for simple old songs she used to sing down South. Kitty eventually finds a future on the stage as a chorus girl and rejects her family and past, a rejection of black folk values that the implied author views with ambivalence.

Ironically, the most unique outsider in *The Sport of the Gods* is Sadness, the living embodiment of the blues. Instead of turning to the Bible, the bullet, or the bottle to cope with the searing experience of racism, Sadness survives by plumbing the depths of his soul and affirming the resiliency of the human spirit. With a wry sense of humor, he recalls how his father was lynched:

> "Oh, yes, but it was done with a very good rope and by the best citizens of Texas, so it seems that I really ought to be very grateful to them for the distinction they conferred upon my family, but I am not. I am ungratefully sad. A man must be very high or low to take the sensible view of life that keeps him from being sad. I must confess that I have aspired to the depths without ever being fully able to reach them." (Pp. 146–47)

In order to maintain some control of reality and some measure of dignity, Sadness has developed a tragicomic vision of life, which in the Afro-American tradition affirms the redemptive power of suffering and humor.

Sadness also belongs to the tradition of the confidence man or hustler. A graduate of the school of hard knocks, he has a degree in streetology and the rap of a natural born game-runner. " 'Thomas, let me fall on your bosom and weep,' " he says after hearing that Joe has money and would be a pushover for a con game. " 'This is what I've been looking for for a month' " (p. 111). Sadness moves in to run his game on Joe the first night they meet. But after getting to know him, he becomes the boy's surrogate father and shrewdly tries to steer him away from the life of those who live " 'like the leech, upon the blood of others,—that draws its life from the veins of foolish men and immoral women, that prides itself upon its well-dressed idleness and has no shame in its voluntary pauperism' " (p. 150).

Judging by its satiric tone, especially the dramatic irony of the closing scene, and by the fact that "the gods" in the title of the book symbolize white power as well as cosmic fate, *The Sport of the Gods* is certainly more than a reiteration of the plantation-school thesis.[41] Caught up in the white nationalist and agrarian ideological snares of his time, Dunbar was at best ambivalent about the rural South and the migration of blacks to the cities. In his artistic vision, the black American was the butt of a cosmic, sardonic joke, and his only salvation was in the redemptive power of suffering and a symbiotic relationship with whites. Viewed in this light, the social realism, satire, and double-consciousness of *The Sport of the Gods* signal both a break with the plantation tradition and the culmination of a constantly shifting but discernible movement of black novelists toward a less simple form of realism that is more compatible with their distinctive experiences and aesthetic vision.

The Early Afro-American Novel

As twentieth-century readers, we are inclined to forget the tenacity of the tradition of white supremacy with which postbellum black novelists had to contend and the gravity of their dilemma. Confronted by a gallery of mid-nineteenth-century stereotypes of Afro-American character and a deeply prejudiced white audience, Harper, Griggs, Chesnutt, and Dunbar were understandably constrained and ambivalent in their use of folklore and romance. Only one generation removed from slavery, they felt obliged to put forward the best foot or class of the race to reveal that black Americans were "more human than African." This ambivalence is reflected in their vision of the Tragic Mulatto, Bad Nigger, Contented Servant, Comic Black, and the American Dream. The interplay between romance and realism in their narratives thus derives from a conception of narrative art that is social and moral. Like their antebellum predecessors, postbellum black novelists generally acknowledged a dual responsibility: to their race and their craft. Among other things, this means that the early Afro-American novel was employed as a vehicle for counterattacking white literary distortions of the black experience and as romances whose characters symbolize the survival strategies and values of Afro-American culture. Frequently, the demands of the white marketplace and the subordination of craftsmanship to moral and social reform resulted in the displacement of Bad Niggers and Sambos by Respectable Mulattoes and Black Messiahs. As the romantic and realistic modes continued to contend for dominance, it was left to future generations to create the social climate in which black novelists could explore the American color, class, and gender conflicts more honestly and powerfully.

3 / The Pre–World War I Novels of the Old Guard: Romance, Realism, and Naturalism

The cultural memory of Africa informs the Negro's life in America,
but it is impossible to separate it from its American transformation. Thus,
the Negro writer if he wanted to tap his legitimate cultural tradition
should have done it by utilizing the entire spectrum of the American
experience from the point of view of the emotional history of the black man
in this country: as its victim and its chronicler.

LEROI JONES
"the myth of a 'negro literature' "

THE years 1903–17, according to cultural historian Vernon L. Parrington, were "a time of extraordinary ferment, when America was seeking to readjust her ideals and institutions to a revolutionary economic order that had come upon her . . . the old America had been intensely conservative, naively provincial and self-satisfied, compassed by complacence founded on optimism—the gospel of the business man. The new America was eager and hopeful, impatient to square institutions to the new conditions."[1] Whether progressive, moderate, or conservative, those over thirty years old, the Old Guard, were optimistic about the future development of the nation. A major distinction, in addition to that of their ages, between the Old Guard and the New Negro is the shift from their focus on transforming folk culture into "high" culture as the standard of moral and spiritual humanistic achievement to their validation of the moral authority and spiritual wisdom of folk culture itself. As in the past, however, the movement away from cultural elitism to industrial capitalism and political democracy was primarily for whites. Frustrated by their efforts to participate in the development of white businesses and moved by the desperate plight of millions of black Southerners, black leaders urged their followers to achieve economic independence by organizing their own businesses. In 1899 W. E. B. Du Bois, while director of the Atlanta University Studies Program, convened a conference on "The Negro in Business" which ratified the call for a national league of Negro

76

businessmen. In 1900 Booker T. Washington organized the National Negro Business League, and by 1907 more than 300 local branches were formed.[2]

Along with their economic development, black Americans were hopeful that the reign of terror against them would come to an end. But before the outbreak of World War I over 1,100 blacks across the land were lynched. And as thousands of blacks began their long march to the cities, an epidemic of racial terrorism began to spread. White mobs would attack black communities for the largely imaginary or exaggerated offenses of one or two individuals. Contrary to popular opinion, most lynch victims were not accused of rape or attempted rape, but of homicide, robbery, insulting whites, and other violations of the ethics of Jim Crow. In 1904 several blacks were burned alive and their communities terrorized in Statesboro, Georgia; in 1906 several more blacks were massacred in Atlanta, their homes and businesses looted and put to the torch. In November of the same year President Theodore Roosevelt dishonorably discharged three companies of black soldiers for their alleged involvement in the death of a white citizen during the Brownsville, Texas, riot.

The denial of civil rights and the pattern of white violence were equally widespread in the North. Among the most infamous were the Illinois lynchings that occurred in 1908 near Abraham Lincoln's home. In reaction to white atrocities, customarily committed with impunity, some progressive black members of the Old Guard, including W. E. B. Du Bois, Monroe Trotter, and Sutton Griggs, organized in 1905 the Niagara Movement. Some joined later with concerned white liberals to found the NAACP in 1910 and the Urban League in 1911. Their purpose was to protect the person and rights of black citizens. In 1913 eighty-six people were lynched in the United States. Eighty-five were black. Beginning with the Dyer Bill in 1919, the NAACP lobbied vigorously but vainly for many years for a federal antilynching law.[3] In the election of 1912, Woodrow Wilson won many black votes by expressing the desire to have "justice done to the colored people in every matter" and by assurances that should he become president, blacks could count on him "for absolute fair dealing, for everything by which I could assist in advancing the interests of their race in the United States."[4] The death of Booker T. Washington in 1915 and the failure of Wilson's peace gestures in 1917 marked the end of the nation's strained official policy of neutrality toward blacks at home and Germans abroad. In March 1917 the United States joined France in her war against Germany, and the call went out to blacks from Du Bois and other leaders to close ranks and join the crusade to make the world safe for democracy.

Romance, Realism, and Naturalism

The predominance of romance, realism, or naturalism in the narratives of
the Old Guard, the third generation of black novelists, is closely related
to the prevailing hope or despair of blacks of ever fully realizing their
racial and national identities in America. In Henry Downing's *American
Cavalryman* (1917), a melodramatic interracial love story of mistaken identity that examines the social ties between black America and Liberia, this
means escape to Africa; and in F. Grant Gilmore's *Problem* (1915), another
mistaken racial identity love story which, for the first time, celebrates the
exploits of the black soldier in the Spanish-American War, it means finding
a solution to the color problem in Cuba. But in Oscar Micheaux's *Conquest*
(1913), a success story about a prosperous black homesteader, and *Forged
Note* (1915), a semi-autobiographical tale of the frustration of a black novelist who is unsuccessful in selling his book to Southern blacks, the refuge
is South Dakota. And whereas in Otis Shackelford's *Lillian Simmons* (1915)
the solution to the thwarted will of blacks is Booker T. Washington's brand
of black capitalism in Chicago, in F. W. Grant's *Out of the Darkness* (1909) the
author-narrator prefers Du Bois's program to Washington's. Thus, most of the
Old Guard novelists employed stock interracial love plots involving the theme
of racial passing and solidarity to stress the strategy of either Washington or
Du Bois as the solution to the problem of the color line.

Sentimentality, sensationalism, seduction, and suicide—psychological,
emotional, or physical—these are the general characteristics of popular
romance in eighteenth- and nineteenth-century Britain and America. In
Love and Death in the American Novel, Leslie A. Fiedler more narrowly defines
the American romance as "a gothic fiction, nonrealistic and negative, sadist
and melodramatic—a literature of darkness and the grotesque in a land
of light and affirmation."[5] But the range of Euro-American romances and
romancers is actually much broader than this and their influence on Afro-
American romances and romancers more complex than this definition
suggests. For in the Euro-American domestic romances or sentimental
novels of William H. Brown, Suzanna Rowson, Susan Warner, and E. D.
E. N. Southworth, the Gothic romances of Charles Brockden Brown, the
historical romances of James Fenimore Cooper, and the symbolic romances
of Hawthorne and Melville we discover several subgenres in the tradition.[6]
In *The American Novel and Its Tradition*, Richard Chase reduces these
subgenres into two streams.[7] Cooper and William Gilmore Simms began
these two streams of romance, according to Chase, when they adapted
European and British narrative conventions to suit the contradictory na-

tional culture and the penchant for melodrama of nineteenth-century America. The Cooper stream of romance cultivates the allegorical and moral potential of the form and includes such major authors as Hawthorne, Melville, Twain, and Faulkner. The Simms stream tells a good story, usually stressing the dramatic aspects of the form, but swerves away from the truth of the human heart to escapism, fantasy, and sentimentality. The history of the Euro-American novel for Chase is therefore not only the history of the rise of realism since the Civil War but also the recurring discovery of the power of romance. "Our fiction," writes Fiedler, "is essentially and at its best nonrealistic, even anti-realistic, long before *symbolisme* had been invented in France and exported to America, there was a full-fledged native tradition of symbolism. That tradition was born of the profound contradictions of our national life and sustained by the inheritance from Puritanism of a 'typical' (even allegorical) way of regarding the sensible world—not as an ultimate reality but as a system of signs to be deciphered."[8]

In contrast, as illustrated in the antebellum and postbellum narratives of Brown, Wilson, Webb, Delany, Harper, Griggs, Chesnutt, and Dunbar, the distinctiveness of the early subgenres in the tradition of the Afro-American novel is derived from their frequent, systematic, and consistent use of the conventions of oratory, including the vernacular, music, and religion. The epistemological and moral authority of these conventions was determined by the shared sociohistorical and sociopsychological ethnic experiences of the authors and the anxiety and ambivalence that characterizes their use of such literary paradigms as slave narratives, the Bible, and popular fiction. The Afro-American subgenres also combine the themes of love, marriage, and success with the protagonist's struggle for freedom from color and caste discrimination in a cyclical quest to fully realize his or her rights and potential for growth as a person of biracial and bicultural identity. The uniqueness of the Afro-American novel, in short, derives from both the double-consciousness of its sociocultural and sociopsychological content and the double vision immanent in the pattern of oral and literary conventions of Afro-American and Euro-American sign systems that structure that content.

Realism, as in Cervantes's *Don Quixote* and Twain's *Adventures of Huckleberry Finn*, defines itself against the excesses of romanticism and romance. It displaces metaphysical reality with social reality and substitutes historical, humanistic truth for ahistorical, transcendental truth. Responding to the antireferential bias of modern criticism and the deconstructionist theory of the indeterminant meaning of texts, critic George Levine defines literary realism "as a self-conscious effort, usually in the name of some moral enterprise of truth telling and extending the limits of human sympathy, to make literature appear to be describing directly not some other language but reality itself (whatever that may be taken to be); in this effort, the writer must self-contradictorily dismiss previous conventions of representation while, in effect, establishing new ones." In this regard, nineteenth-century realism was not "a solidly self-satisfied vision based in a misguided objectivity and faith in representation, but a highly self-conscious attempt to explore or create a new reality." The realistic novel therefore persistently questions "not only the nature of artificially imposed social relations, but the nature of nature, and the nature of the novel."[9] As illustrated by the early Twain, Howells, Chesnutt, and Dunbar, who all became less sanguine and more skeptical in their later careers, American realists believed in an empirically shareable world, were generally sympathetic toward democratic principles, and employed the dramatic method as their chief technique. Other major characteristics of nineteenth-century social realism include an analytical observation of ordinary life, a criticism of social problems and the disparity between the practices and principles of democracy, and a psychological exploration of middle- and lower-class characters.

Naturalism, according to critic George Becker, is in essence and in origin . . . no more than an emphatic and explicit philosophical position taken by some realists, showing man caught in a net from which there can be no escape and degenerating under those circumstances; that is, it is pessimistic materialistic determinism."[10] In *American Literary Naturalism: A Divided Stream*, Charles C. Walcutt describes naturalism as two streams, "partly defying Nature and partly submitting to it," which assumes protean forms (clinical, panoramic, slice-of-life, stream of consciousness, and chronicle of despair) and styles (documentary, satire, impressionistic, and sensational).[11] In other words, as illustrated in the novels of Zola and Flaubert, naturalism applies the principles of scientific determinism to fiction, portraying man as circumscribed or victimized primarily by either external forces (economic determinism) or internal drives (biological determinism). The first of these tendencies generally results in sociological studies of the background of many characters; the second fosters psychological studies of individual characters. "The extraordinariness of character and event in the naturalistic novel," as critic Donald Pizer acutely observes, "creates a potential for symbolism and allegory, since the combination of the concrete and the exceptional immediately implies meanings beyond the surface. Naturalism is thus closely related to the romance in its reliance on a sensationalistic symbolism and allegory." Allegorical representations of "how little we are or know, despite our capacity to be and our desire to know" in Euro-American naturalistic novels of the turn of the century are often circular in structure. "The effect of this symbolic structure," Pizer reminds us, "is to suggest that not only are human beings flawed and unfulfilled but that experience itself does not guide, instruct, or judge human nature."[12] During the 1890s while Howells was promoting a literary fidelity to the sunnier details of everyday life, these naturalistic tendencies began to appear in the novels of Stephen Crane (*Maggie,* 1893), Frank Norris (*McTeague,* 1899, and *The Octopus,* 1901), and Theodore Dreiser (*Sister Carrie,* 1900).

They also began to appear in Afro-American novels. When refracted through the double-consciousness and double vision of black American novelists, however, the dual tendencies of naturalism are often suspended in dialectic tension. The sociohistorical source of this tension is the deep-rooted romantic belief of nineteenth-century black Americans in moral responsibility and free will, in a world of purpose and meaning, which contradicted deterministic philosophy and mechanistic despair. As a result, we usually discover a tragicomic vision at the end of Afro-American novels or an ambiguous glimmer of hope beyond despair that concedes life's limitations while celebrating its possibilities. Although we first experience this tragicomic, naturalistic vision in Chesnutt's *Marrow of Tradition* and Dunbar's *Sport of the Gods,* the novels of Du Bois and Johnson are better examples of these dual tendencies and tensions.

WILLIAM EDWARD BURGHARDT DU BOIS (1868–1963)

Du Bois was born in 1868 in Great Barrington, Massachusetts. Educated at Fisk, Harvard, and the University of Berlin, he was a distinguished man of letters and one of the intellectual giants of his age. In a career of more than seventy years as humanist, educator, and writer, he was an unrelenting foe of Western racism and imperialism. He was one of the chief architects of modern Pan-Africanism and became the first editor of *The Crisis* (1910–34) after serving as the principal editor of *Atlanta University Publications* (1897–1910), the pioneering scholarly project in black studies modeled after his *Philadelphia Negro* (1896), the first in-depth scientific study of urban blacks. Du Bois's many publications include a book of verse and five novels: *The Quest of the Silver Fleece* (1911), *Dark Princess* (1928), and "The Black Flame Trilogy," i.e., *The Ordeal of Mansart* (1957), *Mansart Builds a School* (1959), and *Worlds of Color* (1961). He died an expatriate in Ghana in 1963.

More documentary than meditative, more appealing as historical romance than social realism, Du Bois's novels reflect his critical view of American society and the stylistic flexibility of the beginnings of naturalism in the Afro-American novel. Understanding the economic underpinnings of Western racism and imperialism, Du Bois explores the values of American democracy, affirming them in principle while attacking those social institutions and types that perverted them. What, he asks in effect, shall honesty do in the face of deception, decency in the face of insult, integrity in the face of oppression? The answers he gives in *Dark Princess* and "The Black Flame Trilogy" are complex and contradictory, involving force and love, freedom and law. More than anything else these four novels are a chronicle of despair in which the only hope for the world is the rise of an independent, industrialized Africa and Asia under the banner of socialism and the leadership of the Talented Tenth of nonwhite nations.

Du Bois is acutely aware of the victimization of nonwhites by an acquisitive, multinational white hegemony and the conflicting loyalties of the tragic African, Asian, and Afro-American elite, but he is unsuccessful in translating the dynamics of these unrelenting social and psychological forces into credible fiction that engages our modern sensibility. The basic problem is that of philosophical and technical synthesis. Intellectually, Du Bois, who was sympathetic to socialism and became a Marxist and member of the American Communist party before his expatriation and death in Ghana,[13] was an economic determinist, but emotionally he could not convince himself that socioeconomic influences would inevitably overwhelm the human will. As the ideological tensions and melodramatic endings of his novels indicate, he never completely synthesized naturalistic determinism and romantic idealism. Perhaps we can better understand the scope and depth of the philosophical and technical problems that mar these later novels by a close examination of his first and most satisfactory extended narrative.

Straddling the romantic and naturalistic traditions, *The Quest of the Silver Fleece* interprets the black experience from a socialist perspective and employs the myth of Jason and the Argonauts to give the narrative wider meaning. Through Miss Taylor, the New England school teacher, and Blessed Alwyn, her prize student, Du Bois alludes to the classical Eurocentric myth in the early chapters and outlines correspondences between Jason's theft of the golden fleece and Colonel Creswell's exploitation of the land and black labor to corner the market in cotton. Other parallels are drawn between the evil powers of Medea and Elspeth, the mother of Zora Creswell, the female protagonist, and between the Black Sea and the black community of Tooms County, Alabama. The economic symbol that dominates the book and informs its structure is cotton—the Silver Fleece.

The quest of the Silver Fleece is the allegorical symbol of the novel's principal structure and theme: the journey to socialism and personal redemption. In an economic system whose power is built on cheap cotton and in a region where "cotton was currency; cotton was merchandise; cotton was conversation,"[14] the way to salvation for blacks was not through the benevolence of the Southern white aristocracy supported by Northern philanthropy. Nor was it through a coalition of the quality folks of both races. To free themselves from the economic and moral power of white planters and the cotton combine, the characters in the novel must acquire an education and marketable resources, for, as the founder of Smith's School tells one of her black students, " 'without intelligence and training and some capital it is the wildest nonsense to think you can lead your people out of slavery' " (p. 137). And in Tooms County, cotton was the only source of capital available to escape from poverty, ignorance, and injustice. Ultimately, black sharecroppers and white millhands, as an overworked white woman and Zora agree, " 'had ought ter git together.' " At present, however, the struggle for survival centers on cotton, the source of hope and despair in the book.

The movement of the novel parallels the three-stage development of Zora's mission to redeem herself and her community. "Out of protection of womanhood as the central thought," the omniscient narrator informs us, "she must build ramparts against cruelty, poverty and crime" (p. 359). In the first stage (chaps. 1–18) Zora is the innocent victim of evil external forces. She is an amoral child of the swamp, steeped in wood-lore and visionary tenderness. Her dream is to build a castle on an island in the swamp and live in freedom. To escape the evil of the plantation system and a Medea-like mother who subjects her and other girls to the lust of the Creswells, Zora and Bles plan secretly to grow enough cotton on her hidden fertile island in the swamp to pay for Zora's education. As the major seed sown by Elspeth and cultivated with love by Zora and Bles comes to flower into the Silver Fleece, a corresponding growth is experienced by the two characters. Zora "still ran and romped in the woods and dreamed her dreams; she still was passionately independent and 'queer.' Tendencies merely had become manifest, some dominant. She would, unhindered, develop to a brilliant, sumptuous womanhood; proud, conquering, full-blooded, and deep bosomed—a passionate mother of men" (p. 125). Meanwhile, Northern cotton brokers and Southern landowners conspire to corner the market on cotton and internationalize the exploitation of farmers and workers. Early victims of these economic forces include the protagonists. Their love is blighted by Bles's discovery that Zora is not a virgin; the fruit of their labor of love—two bales of exceptionally beautiful cotton—is stolen by the Creswells; and the forces that threaten Zora's spiritual innocence appear even more ominous with Elspeth's death.

The next stage of her quest for the "answer to the puzzle of life" (chaps. 19–29) is experience. "She sought the Way," says the sympathetic but Victorian narrator, "but what way and whither she did not know, she dared not dream" (p. 215). Only the importance of the Silver Fleece remained. "When it came back to her," she thinks, " . . . it would bring happiness; not the great Happiness—that was gone forever—but illumination, atonement, and something of the power and the glory" (p. 215). In the meantime both characters had to be educated in the way of the world. For Zora the most immediate salvation from the path of Hell taken by motherless girls in the community like Bertie meant becoming a personal maid and traveling companion to the wealthy Mrs. Vanderpool. With the Silver Fleece, her stolen dream, returned to her in the form of cloth to be woven into a wedding dress for Helen Creswell, Zora is launched into the world of beauty, books, and politics; but it is in a little Washington church that she discovers the true way. " 'The good of others is our true good,' " says the preacher, reinforcing the norms of the narrator and implied author; " 'work for others; not for *your* salvation, but the salvation of the world' " (p. 295). Zora's call is to return to the South to help free her people. And when her faith in Mrs. Vanderpool is betrayed and her efforts to advance Bles's political fortune fail, she acknowledges the call.

Redemption (chaps. 30–38) is the third and final stage of Zora's development. She now looks on the world about her with new eyes. Cruelty, poverty, and crime she saw, and it burdened her heart. But it was not until she saw Bertie's innocent young daughter in the company of a white child molester that the paramount mission of her life began to come clearly in focus. "She would protect this girl; she would protect *all* black girls," she resolves. "It was her duty, her heritage. She must offer this unsullied soul up unto God in mighty atonement—but how?" (p. 359). Her answer was to buy the swamp land with the money Mrs. Vanderpool had given her and to develop it into a self-sustaining black community. The cleared rich swamp land would support a home for orphaned girls, a school with a model farm, industries, and other agencies to make life better for blacks. In addition, a hundred acres would be set aside for the public good, and each man, woman, and child was expected to help work the land a reasonable number of days a year. Zora "did not anticipate any immediate understanding with the laboring whites, but she knew that eventually it would be inevitable. Meantime the Negro must strengthen himself and bring to the alliance as much independent economic strength as possible" (398). She asks Bles to be her co-worker in developing this black, quasi-socialist plan, and after redeeming herself in his eyes, asks him to marry her.

In this overview of the structure and movement of the novel, the contradictory impulses that the implied author never completely resolves are obvious. Classical myth clashes with black folk beliefs, economic determinism with spiritual freedom, Marxist theory with African cultural survivals, and allegory with realism. The implied author would have us see the unscrupulous Creswells as modern-day Jasons, the conjuring Elspeth as Medea, and the elfish Zora as the victim of collusion between a diabolical mother and the Creswells. But the Eurocentric analogies are strained and unpersuasive, and the Afro-American characters are burdened by unreconciled dual roles and identities. As an allegorical sower of the seeds of hope and despair, Elspeth is appropriately mysterious and vague. But as the daughter of a king's son and her own daughter's procuress, she is unconvincing. Equally unconvincing and unresolved is the conflicting portrayal of Zora as a "heathen hoyden," an uninhibited country girl, and "a born leader wedded to a cause." On one hand, she symbolizes the shortcomings of a primitive people in an advanced, exploitative, capitalist society, and on the other, the spiritual zeal of a social reformer. She was "so old and again so much a child, an eager questioning child, that there seemed about her innocence something holy" (p. 98).

The dialectic between African retentions and Christian myth-legend also informs Zora's quest. The mysterious mighty black man with white hair and deathly eyes who appears at the hour of Elspeth's death and of Zora's greatest need is both God's messenger and an African swamp deity. Zora's quest is simultaneously for personal moral redemption, with the Silver Fleece representing purity, and the social redemption of her race, with the Silver Fleece representing economic power. Zora is visionary and worker, intellectual and activist, madonna and whore. Yet the omniscient narrator tells us that she knew little about the "strange faith" of her people: "She herself had been brought up almost without religion save some few mystic remnants of a half-forgotten heathen cult. The little she had seen of religious observance had not moved her greatly, save once yonder in Washington. There she found God after searching that had searched her soul; but He had simply pointed the Way, and the way was human" (p. 372). Although African retentions and black evangelism have combined in a kind of Christian humanism to awaken her faith, it is the interaction between her will and her environment that enables Zora to realize her human potential and move toward the creation of a new social order. Thus, Du Bois's intellectual sophistication, moral pieties, and cultural nationalism (" 'We black folks,' " says Zora confidently, " 'is got the *spirit*. We'se lighter and cunninger; we fly right through them; we go and come again just as we wants to. Black folks is wonderful' " [p. 46]) are the shifting sands on which the economic superstructure of *The Quest of the Silver Fleece* is precariously perched.

The bizarre union of nineteenth-century Victorian diction and socioeconomic determinism, and the abrupt shifts from allegorical abstractions like "the Way," "the Vision Splendid," and "Truth and Goodness and Love" to dispassionate matter-of-fact observations like "the Black Belt is primitive and the landlord wields the power" are clear illustrations of the unresolved tensions between Du Bois's double-consciousness and the dual tendencies of naturalism. Consequently, *The Quest of the Silver Fleece*, among other things, is a striking example of the difficulty of imposing Eurocentric myth and a mechanistic sociological perspective on the black experience and of the continuous search for appropriate syntheses of narrative techniques to render the pleasure and pain of that experience.

JAMES WELDON JOHNSON (1871–1938)

Whereas Du Bois's novels follow the sociological tendencies of naturalism, James Weldon Johnson's single novel follows the psychological. When it was first published anonymously in 1912, *The Autobiography of an Ex-Coloured Man* was paradoxically so realistic that it was accepted by readers as autobiography and so psychoanalytical that it was hailed in the introduction to the 1927 edition by Carl Van Vechten, a white novelist and controversial publicist of 1920s black artists, as "an invaluable sourcebook for the study of Negro psychology."[15] On one hand, Johnson's professional background sharpened his analysis of color and class differences in the United States; and on the other hand, it reinforced his conservative middle-class prejudices.

Born in Jacksonville, Florida, in 1871 to middle-class, musically talented parents (his Bahamian mother was a fine singer and the first black public school teacher in Florida; his Afro-American father played the guitar and was the headwaiter at a big hotel), James Johnson was nursed by a "white mammy" and was "reared free from undue fear of or esteem for white people as a race." While attending Atlanta University, he taught one summer in rural Hampton, Georgia, boarding with a local black family who helped him to realize how song and laughter were used by the black community as survival techniques. After graduating in 1894, he achieved early distinction as a poet and lyricist. His first literary criticism and encouragement had come from Dr. T. O. Summers, a prominent white Florida surgeon who had been his summer employer and friend. In 1899 Johnson published his first dialect poem, "Sence You Went Away," in *Century Magazine.* In the same year he and his brother Rosamond collaborated in writing "Lift Every Voice and Sing" in commemoration of Abraham Lincoln's birthday. This song later became famous as "The Negro National Anthem." In 1900 James, Rosamond, and Bob Cole, a friend, formed a partnership which over a period of seven years produced more than two hundred popular show songs.[16]

In part, Johnson's success as a poet and songwriter was due to his belief that "a demonstration of intellectual parity by the Negro through the production of literature and art" would help to eliminate white racism.[17] This conviction was shared by both black conservatives and militant integrationists of the period. *The Autobiography,* which he began writing in 1905 while attending Columbia University, was also a product of this impulse. Because of the many demands on his time as school principal, lawyer, poet, lyricist, diplomat, and secretary of the NAACP, he did not complete the novel until seven years later.

Episodic in structure, the novel unfolds in retrospective narrative with the narrator, moved by the imp of the perverse and "a vague feeling of unsatisfaction," clinically relating the principal trauma of his life. From the pinnacle of success as a "white" businessman, he recalls his travels around the United States and Europe, providing a panoramic view of black society while at the same time rationalizing the moral cowardice of his decision to pass for white.

To win the reader's sympathy and belief, Johnson filters the narrative through the consciousness of a first-person, nameless musician-narrator. The child of an "unsanctioned love" between a Southern white aristocrat and a black servant, the narrator-hero recalls a variety of early childhood experiences that have left an indelible imprint on his memory. At the center of the novel is the narrator's ambivalence about his ethnic identity and desire "to be a great coloured man." Sent to Connecticut with his mother so that his father could marry a Southern belle, the young mulatto narrator not only believes he is white but leads his classmates in the racial harassment of black students. A teacher's disclosure in class that he is black is so traumatic that it causes him to withdraw from the world into his books and music. Analyzing the change that came into his life "after that fateful day in school," the narrator recalls:

> From that time I looked out through other eyes, my thoughts were coloured, my words dictated, my actions limited by one dominating, all-pervading idea which constantly increased in force and weight until I finally realized it in a great, tangible fact. And this is the dwarfing, warping, distorting influence which operated upon each and every coloured man in the United States. He is forced to take his outlook on all things, not from the view-point of a citizen, or a man, or even a human being, but from the view-point of a *coloured* man. (P. 21)

Reinforcing the prototypical significance of Du Bois's trope of double-consciousness, Johnson's narrator had long suspected that black people, including intelligent students like the classmate he called "Shiny," were treated as inferiors, but it is not until he reads *Uncle Tom's Cabin* that he becomes fully aware of the paradoxical hate-love feelings between whites and blacks. As a result of this traumatic awakening to socialized ambivalence, the narrator fluctuates between feelings of shame and pride in his racial identity.[18]

Shiny, a symbol of the emerging black middle class, is the focus of these ambivalent feelings. Struck by the student's dark complexion, sparkling eyes, and bright teeth, the narrator names him "Shiny" even though he respects his intelligence, which gives an ironic dimension to the name, and is inspired by him to take pride in his racial heritage. Shiny's valedictorian speech on the Haitian revolutionary leader Toussaint L'Ouverture stirs the ambitions of the narrator to bring glory and honor to himself and the Negro race. Late in the novel after his white fiancée accepts Shiny, who has realized his potential and become a college professor, the narrator summons enough courage to reveal his own racial identity.

Most of the episodes in the South reveal the narrator's acceptance of the puritan ethic of thrift, cleanliness, industry, and sobriety. In Atlanta, Georgia, he is repelled by "the unkempt appearance, the shambling, slouching gait and loud talk and laughter" of working-class blacks (p. 60); but he is proud of the refinement and cultural activities of black high society in Jacksonville, Florida. In describing the structure of this society, the narrator, with the prevailing prejudices of his day and the tacit agreement of the implied author, divides it into three classes based on the economic relationship of its members to white society. On the lowest rung is the desperate class of common laborers: "the men who work in the lumber and turpentine camps, the ex-convicts, the barroom loafers are all in this class." In the next class are the domestic servants, who are characterized as "simple, kind-hearted, and faithful." And the upper class is composed of businessmen and professionals who have "money, education and culture" and "live in a little world of their own" (pp. 76–79).

The implied author's sympathy for the rising black middle class is most apparent in his ironic portrayal of the mulatto narrator-hero. The ironic distance between implied author and narrator-hero is neither intellectual nor social; it is moral. The implied author subtly divorces himself from his narrator's decision to resolve his double-consciousness and socialized ambivalence by repressing his black American identity, his essential self, and permanently adopting a white American identity. Rationalizing his choice, the narrator explains: "I would neither disclaim the black race nor claim the white race: but that I would change my name, raise a moustache, and let the world take me for what it would" (p. 190). It was not "fear or search for a larger field of action and opportunity" that was driving him, he says, but "shame at being identified with a people that could with impunity be treated worse than animals" (pp. 190–91). Actually, this psychological motive is reinforced by the narrator's determination to avail himself of, in his words, "every possible opportunity to make a white man's success," which, in effect, means acquiring personal wealth as well as a problematic pride in the power and privilege of the white majority. While analyzing his earlier desire to achieve distinction as a black composer, he admits that his motives "were very largely mixed with selfishness" (p. 147). In fact, until he decides to marry across the color line, he viewed his passing for white and achieving success as a businessman as a practical joke on the white world. The narrator's motives, in short, are complex and contradictory, yet credible and tragicomic.

Appealing directly to whites and conservative middle-class blacks, the narrator confesses his social bias: "the fact that the whites of the South despise and ill-treat the desperate class of blacks is not only explainable according to the ancient laws of human nature, but it is not nearly so serious or important as the fact that as the progressive coloured people advance, they constantly widen the gulf between themselves and their white neighbors" (pp. 79–80). This honest but nevertheless tragically reactionary expression of class prejudice, compounded by informative but intrusively didactic speeches on race relations and gratuitous remarks on black culture, weakens the integrity of the narrator and the novel's structure. Some of the material, such as the solemn, eight-page discussion of the revival meeting, is, as the narrator confesses, "better suited to a book on social phenomena than to a narrative of my life" (p. 109).

On balance, most of the depiction of urban black life is integral to the development of plot and character. Particularly educational for the narrator-hero are the Harlem clubs, where he enjoys ragtime music, meets the bohemian crowd, and develops into the best ragtime pianist in New York. So impressed is one wealthy white patron by the gifted musician-narrator that he hires him as a personal companion for a European trip.

Actually, the thematic importance of music is established early in the novel. For music is the vehicle for the narrator's realization of a fusion of his dual cultural heritage. Even as a child, he was deeply influenced by the old folksongs and hymns passed on to him by his mother. And before his seventh birthday he learned to play the piano "by trying to reproduce the quaint songs . . . with all their pathetic turns and cadences." Then at twelve he won acclaim as a prodigy for his superb performance of Beethoven's "Sonata Pathetique." But it is not until his European trip that the narrator's youthful ambition to become a famous composer is reawakened by a German musician who demonstrates how ragtime can be transformed into classical music: "I made up my mind to go back into the very heart of the South, to live among the people, and drink in my inspiration firsthand. I gloated over the immense amount of material I had to work with, not only modern rag-time, but also the old slave songs—material which no one had yet touched" (pp. 142–43). Once again, however, this sense of commitment and ethnic pride, informed by his need to elevate and transform folk art into high art, disappears in the face of the brutal reality of hostile environmental forces. While collecting sermons and spirituals in the South, the narrator is so terrified by the ritual of a black man's being burned alive by whites that he sacrifices his musical genius and moral integrity on the altar of whiteness. Ultimately, the mild regret he suffers for having sold his "birthright for a mess of pottage" is carefully balanced by the rationalization that "my love for my children makes me glad that I am what I am and keeps me from desiring to be otherwise" (p. 211). But this achievement of personal wholeness is at best an ambiguous, Pyrrhic victory.

In contrast to the economic determinism of *The Quest of the Silver Fleece*, *The Autobiography* emphasizes biological and psychological determinism. Johnson's vision of the mulatto American artist is particularly tragic, for it moves beyond social realism to a psychological explanation of how color and class prejudices alienate the mulatto artist as individual from the darker, poorer members of his ethnic community and warp the natural impulse to affirm his worth and identity as a black American. The pity and fear we feel as readers grow out of our awareness that the narrator's unheroic choice is a result of social and psychological circumstances that threaten to diminish the humanity of blacks and whites alike.

Legacy of the Old Guard

As in the postbellum period, the novels appearing between 1902 and 1917, when the United States entered World War I, continued to explore the tragicomic vision and heroic struggle of black Americans. In contrast to the melodramatic terror and pity of the antebellum novels and those by their less well-known contemporaries, however, the vision of Dunbar, Chesnutt, Du Bois, and Johnson is more ironic, especially when reconstructing the experience of passing for white. And the depiction of the double-consciousness of their protagonists, although usually members of the black bourgeoisie, reflects the major internal and external conflicts of blacks during the turbulent years when they were stiffening their resistance to terror and their determination to realize at all costs their full rights as American citizens. Whether teacher, preacher, porter, or domestic, class lines in the black community were divisive but much less rigid than those in the white community. That many of the protagonists, such as Chesnutt's Dr. Miller and Johnson's nameless musician-narrator, chose the less noble course of action when confronted by conflicting racial and class interests is, from an aesthetic point of view, salutary. For it reveals that even the most conservative Old Guard novelists were above denying historical fact and psychological truth—however neurotic the parade of pretentious colored folk and their paternal white folks—in order to repudiate the stereotypes of Dixon and Page. Whatever their formal shortcomings as craftsmen, the most popular and successful novelists of the Old Guard were exceptionally honest and perceptive social critics whose contributions to the tradition of the Afro-American novel have only been receiving the serious, sustained study they deserve since the 1960s.

Ostensibly, in addition to affirming the possibilities of the romantic vision of black American character, F. W. Grant, Oscar Micheaux, Otis Shackelford, F. Grant Gilmore, and Henry Downing extended the thematic range of the Afro-American novel. Aside from the stark reality and symbolism of ritual lynchings, obligatory Jim Crow episodes, and international intrigue, the most enduring characters to be passed on to novelists of the

The Pre–World War I Novels of the Old Guard

Harlem Renaissance were the musician and the orator. Also significant intertextually is the use of black church meetings, political councils, public lectures, literary forums, graduation exercises, and cabarets for strengthening group solidarity, expressing ambivalence toward black folklore, and celebrating the unique vernacular gifts of major and minor characters.

4 / The Harlem Renaissance and the Search for New Modes of Narrative

*We younger Negro artists who create now intend to express our
individual dark-skinned selves without fear or shame. If white people are
pleased we are glad. If they are not, it doesn't matter. We know
we are beautiful. And ugly too. The tom-tom cries and the tom-tom laughs.
If colored people are pleased we are glad. If they are not, their
displeasure doesn't matter either. We build our temples for tomorrow, strong
as we know how, and we stand on top of the mountain, free
within ourselves.*

LANGSTON HUGHES
"The Negro and the Racial Mountain"

IN 1918 the war to make the world safe for democracy ended, but
returning black American soldiers soon discovered that their struggle
had not. Of the more than seventy blacks lynched during the first
year of the postwar period, ten were black soldiers in uniform. Eleven
were buried alive. And from June 1919 to the end of the year approximately
twenty-five race riots erupted. Bitterly disappointed by the efforts of whites
to deprive them of gains in jobs and housing made during the war, urban
black migrants and war veterans across the nation resisted. Thus the first
major period of urban unrest and racial war began in what James Weldon
Johnson called the "Red Summer."

The post–World War I years also marked an unprecedented upsurge of
world and national interest in Harlem and black culture. European artists—
Pablo Picasso, André Gide, Guillaume Apollinaire, and Darius Milhaud,
to name a few—reacted to the radical changes resulting from modern
industrialism and science by turning to the traditional beauty of African
and Afro-American art and incorporating it into their experiments in modernism. Native-born writers like Ezra Pound, T. S. Eliot, Gertrude Stein,
Ernest Hemingway, e. e. cummings, Sherwood Anderson, Eugene O'Neill,
and Waldo Frank, in revolt abroad and at home against the sterility and
philistinism of industrial America, led the search for new American values
and modes of expression. In the popularization of psychoanalytic theory,
especially Freud's concept of the libidinal self, and the European theories

of African and Afro-American culture as evidence of the simplicity and beauty of preindustrial, precivilized culture, they found the new vision and direction for white America's salvation. In Stein's "Melanctha" (1909), Vachel Lindsay's "Congo: A Study of the Negro Race" (1914), O'Neill's *Dreamy Kid* (1919) and *Emperor Jones* (1920), Frank's *Holiday* (1923), Anderson's *Dark Laughter* (1925), and Carl Van Vechten's *Nigger Heaven* (1926), we find the nation's vision of the black American and his alleged primitivism. An oversimplification of the resiliency and vitality of black character and culture, literary primitivism exalted instinct over intellect, simple forms of social organization over more complex forms, and nature over art. In their flight from the problems of modern industrialism, many white Americans turned to home-grown varieties of the noble savage for salvation.

At the same time, the reaction of "practically an entire generation of young Negro writers . . . to Toomer's *Cane*," in the words of Arna Bontemps, "marked an awakening that soon thereafter began to be called a Negro renaissance."[1] The Negro renaissance, better known as the Harlem Renaissance or the New Negro movement, was the period of the meteoric rise of such talents as Claude McKay, Jean Toomer, Countee Cullen, Langston Hughes, Bill Robinson, Florence Mills, Josephine Baker, Ethel Waters, Paul Robeson, Roland Hayes, Aaron Douglass, Louis Armstrong, Bessie Smith, and Duke Ellington; it was the second birth of Afro-American culture, highlighting black music, dance, and literature.

By and large, the New Negro turned to Africa and Afro-American folklore for a usable past. The nineteenth-century image of Africa as a primitive land, a source of shame and self-hatred for many black Americans, was transformed into a symbol of pride by many developments. In addition to the influence of modern science and white artists, there were the four Pan-African Congresses convened between 1919 and 1927 by Du Bois,[2] the pioneer studies on Africa and Afro-American history by Du Bois and Carter G. Woodson,[3] the Back-to-Africa movement of Marcus Garvey, a charismatic Jamaican black nationalist who fired the imagination of the masses with his grand design for the redemption of black people, and the flowering of Afro-American art. On the other hand, the frustration of coping with an alien urban environment and industrial society encouraged many transplanted black Southerners to cling tenaciously to their folk roots. Seeking to identify with the folk, race-conscious intellectuals and writers began to tap the roots of their ethnic heritage with varying degrees of ambivalence. In the vanguard of the New Negro artists who began their literary careers by looking to Africa for inspiration were Langston Hughes and Countee Cullen. Hughes's "The Negro Speaks of Rivers" and Cullen's "Heritage" are excellent examples of the function and meaning of Africa to black American writers of the twenties. Both poems reveal the romantic attraction of a place remote in time and space, a place the artists had been taught to reject, a place whose landscape and rhythms of life evoked primitive images and ambivalent passions. In much of their later work, including their novels—Hughes's *Not Without Laughter* (1930) and Cullen's *One Way Ticket to Heaven* (1932)—both artists shift their concern to the everyday lives of ordinary black folk and the church-centered culture that represents the marrow of the Afro-American tradition.

From the beginning, the thrust of the writers, as Robert Hayden has stated, was "more aesthetic and philosophical—more metaphysical . . . than political."[4] Hughes captured the feeling of aesthetic freedom and ancestralism,[5] the expression and affirmation of the race spirit in black art (which will be discussed more fully later in the chapter) that characterized the Harlem upsurge in his well-known essay "The Negro and the Racial Mountain."[6] Literary contests and awards sponsored by *The Crisis* and *Opportunity*, the journals of the NAACP and Urban League, supplemented by the patronage of liberal white publishers like Charles Boni and Negrophiles like Carl Van Vechten were important sources of encouragement for struggling young black artists.

But the most widely known midwife for the literary birth of the gifted young blacks was Alain Locke, a Howard University professor of philosophy, chronicler of the period, and editor of the *New Negro*. Containing essays by established black and white men of letters as well as representative selections of creative writing by the younger generation, the *New Negro* celebrates what Locke optimistically viewed as "the attainment of a significant and satisfying new phase of group development" by Americans of African descent. Rejoicing in the new spirit and race consciousness of the age, Locke declares that:

> The Younger Generation comes, bringing its gifts. They are the first fruits of the Negro Renaissance. Youth speaks, and the voice of the New Negro is heard. What stirs inarticulately in the masses is already vocal upon the lips of the talented few, and the future listens, however the present may shut its ears. Here we have Negro youth, with arresting visions and vibrant prophecies; forecasting in the mirror of art what we must see and recognize in the streets of reality tomorrow, foretelling in new notes and accents the maturing speech of full racial utterance.

Writing out of the depths of their group and personal experience, the talented few, Locke was convinced, spoke with a particular representativeness. For "all classes of a people under social pressure are permeated with a common experience; they are emotionally welded as others cannot be. With them, even ordinary living has epic depth and lyric intensity, and this, their material handicap, is their spiritual advantage."[7] In his enthusiastic efforts to create a wider reception for the New Negro artists, Locke oversimplified the artistic results of sociopsychological tensions and individual expressions of black American double-consciousness. For when the New Negro novelist reconstructed the experience of blacks in America, he invariably highlighted those elements of the racial and national past that defined his personal identity and social vision. The result was a wide range of narrative forms and techniques: poetic realism, historical romance, genteel realism, folk romance, folk realism, and satire.

Poetic Realism and Historical Romance

Jean Toomer's *Cane* and Arna Bontemps's *Black Thunder* represent the chronological boundaries and wide spectrum of narrative forms that characterize the flowering of the Harlem Renaissance in the early twenties and its decline in the the early thirties. The search for identity, a usable past, and literary form led to poetic realism in *Cane* and to historical romance in *Black Thunder*. The first is essentially a psychological study of a modern black writer in an experimental mode, and the other, unlike the apocryphal legend about Jefferson's mulatto daughter in Brown's *Clotel*, is a retelling of a heroic legend in the traditional mode. None of the New Negro writers was more preoccupied with Freudian themes of the repressed self or more innovative in the use of language and form than Toomer. More than any of his contemporaries, he represents a synthesis of the concerns of writers of the Lost Generation and the Harlem Renaissance, and his work embodies the tensions of modern science and folk tradition, of psychoanalytic technique and Afro-American music, of mysticism and Afro-American spirituality.

NATHAN EUGENE TOOMER (1894–1967)

Born in Washington, D. C., in 1894, Jean Toomer grew into a handsome, introspective young man who, because of his light complexion, was frequently mistaken for a foreigner while in college. Between 1914 and 1920, while attending colleges in Wisconsin, Massachusetts, Illinois, and New York, he became convinced that he was neither white nor black, but simply an American. His dislike of being called a Negro and his marriages to white women in 1931 and 1934 were consistent with this conviction. Later, in "The First American," an early draft of the long Whitmanesque poem

"Blue Meridian," he developed the idea that a new race was evolving in America and that he was one of its first conscious members. Until his death in a nursing home in 1967, he, like Whitman, saw this nation as a crucible for the fusion of various nationalities and races into a new order of man—the American. Failure to understand the metaphysical as well as the sociopsychological nature of Toomer's socialized ambivalence and belief in the myth of America as a melting pot of ethnic groups has been one of the major causes of the misinterpretation of the man and his work.[8]

"I am not a romanticist," Toomer declares in an early draft of his autobiography. "I am not a classicist or a realist, in the usual sense of these terms. I am an essentialist. Or, to put it in other words, I am a spiritualizer, a poetic realist."[9] Basically, this means two things. First, it means that Toomer believed in the transcendency of the soul and the attainment of spiritual truth through intuition. Convinced that "the parts of man—his mind, emotions, and body—were radically out of harmony with each other,"[10] Toomer in 1923 found the way to reestablish harmonious human development in the teachings of Georges I. Gurdjieff, a Russian spiritualist of Greek and Armenian ancestry. Among other things, the Gurdjieffian method, a fusion of Eastern mysticism and Western science, involved sacred exercises, dances, contemplation, and psychic feats. Second, Toomer's declaration means that as a writer, he tried, in his words, "to lift facts, things, happenings to the planes of rhythm, feeling, and significance. . . . to clothe and give body to potentialities."[11]

Cane is an intricately structured, incantational collection of thematically related writings. Divided into three major parts, it progresses from a highly poetic to a heavily dramatic form. "Karintha," the opening impressionistic sketch of Part 1, is barely five pages in length and depends on the refrains of a song for its haunting effects, while "Blood-Burning Moon," the sixteen-page concluding sketch of the same section, achieves unity and force in its narrative structure. Similarly, the striking metaphorical style of the first brief sketch in Part 2, "Seventh Street," culminates in the symbolism and dramatic internal monologue of "Bona and Paul." "Kabnis," the single sketch comprising all of Part 3, is cast in the form of an allegorical play. Because of its hybrid nature, *Cane* defies categorical classification but is most rewardingly interpreted as a poetic *kunstleroman,* the quest of a modern black artist for sociopsychological wholeness and creative authority.

The three major divisions of the book can be meaningfully compared to the Freudian theory of personality and the Gurdjieffian theory of triadic psychic centers, i.e., intellectual, emotional, and instinctive. Part 1, with its focus on the Southern past and the libido, presents the rural thesis,

while Part 2, with its emphasis on the centers of commerce and the superego, offers the urban antithesis. Part 3 then functions as a synthesis
of the earlier sections with Kabnis representing the black writer whose
difficulty in resolving the tension of his double-consciousness prevents
him from tapping the creative reservoir of his soul.

Toomer attempts to overwhelm the reader with the truth of his mystical
vision of life through images and symbols whose appeal is more to our
powers of intuition and perception than to cognition. Neither the characters nor the plot is developed sufficiently to sustain the reader's interest.
The meaning of the book is implicit in the arabesque pattern of imagery,
the subtle movement of symbolic actions and objects, the shifting rhythm
of syntax and diction, and the intensity of the narrator's tortured sensibility. Approached as a poetic novel, the disparate elements and illusive
meanings of the book coalesce into an integral whole and provide a poign-
ant insight into the sensibility of a modern black artist.

On the surface, *Cane* is a pastoral work contrasting the values of uninhibited, unlettered black folk with those of the educated, puritanically
inhibited black bourgeoisie. On this level Toomer draws on the Afro-
American tradition of music as a major structural device. The melancholic
fragments of spirituals and work songs woven into the sketches create a
flowing rhythm and delicate pattern of Gothic images that fuse the dis-
similar Christian and non-Christian elements of the book. While in Georgia, the home state of his father and grandfather, Toomer was deeply
moved by the beauty of the folksongs he heard and saddened by the belief
that the industrialization of the South would soon make them relics.
Adapting pastoral conventions to his purpose, he therefore uses the songs
as symbols of the spiritual resiliency of rural black Americans and, by
extension, of the souls of a new order of man.

Equally important as a symbol of rural life is sugar cane itself. Purple
in color, pungently sweet in odor, mysteriously musical in sound, and
deep rooted in growth, cane represents the beauty and pain of living close
to nature. It also represents the Gothic qualities of the black American's
African and Southern past, especially his ambivalent attitude toward this
heritage. Additional symbols of the natural agents whose mysterious beauty
and cyclical life strike a responsive chord in the soul of man are the soil,
pine trees, sunset, smoke, cotton, corn, and moon. In contrast, the symbols
of city life include alleys, vestibules, theaters, box seats, and night clubs:
artificial objects and spaces which confine or distort the expression of
natural instincts. But *Cane* is not a traditional pastoral; neither country nor
city folk live simple, virtuous lives. "Back to nature," Toomer noted, "even
if desirable, was no longer possible, because industry had taken nature

into itself."[12] Consequently, only those characters who aspire to a higher level of consciousness of self succeed in moving beyond the limitations of their finite social circumstances.

On its lower frequencies, then, *Cane* is the story of a metaphysical quest: a search for the truth about man, God, and America that takes its nameless poet-narrator on a circular journey of self-discovery. In the early sections of the book the poet-narrator is the unnamed first-person observer through whose sensibility the spiritual anguish and transformation of Karintha, Becky, and the other characters are rendered. His journey carries him from the Deep South to the Midwest and back again to the soil of his ancestors. Throughout his odyssey, Kabnis, the poet-teacher in Part 3, seeks, like Toomer himself, to know the spiritual truth of life, to reconcile the beauty and pain of his Afro-American heritage, and to express his new consciousness in the magic of the word.

In Part 1 the reader is alerted to the unity of life and the imminence of spiritual rebirth by the Gothic imagery of ten poems and six impressionistic sketches of Southern women. Each of the women is involved in a bizarre incident; each is dominated by a divine sexual impulse; and each sketch reveals a contrast between personal desires and social conventions. Although the setting of Part 2 moves from the Georgian countryside to the District of Columbia and Chicago, its seven sketches and five poems continue the poet-narrator's quest to reconcile himself to his heritage as a black American artist. Part 2 focuses on the perversion of the will and emotions when they are enslaved by the genteel mores of society. When freely and fully realized, the mind and body function as a spiritual unit. Spirituals, folk songs, jazz, poetry, and dance are Toomer's symbols for the attainment of this goal.

Shifting to a third-person omniscient narrative voice, Part 3 dramatizes the inability of Ralph Kabnis to reconcile himself to the blood and soil that symbolize his ethnic and national identities. Kabnis and Lewis are the implied author's dramatic projection of the double-consciousness of Afro-Americans. Referring to Kabnis, Lewis states: "Life had already told him more than he is capable of knowing. It had given him in excess of what he can receive. I have been offered. Stuff in his stomach curdled, and he vomited me."[13] Kabnis is a neurotic, thin-haired, lemon-faced poet-teacher from the North who considers himself an American. He is a descendant of Southern blue bloods. Lewis, his counterpart, is a tall, copper-colored man whose "mouth and eyes suggest purpose guided by an adequate intelligence. He is what a stronger Kabnis might have been, and in an odd faint way resembles him" (p. 189).

Kabnis cannot cope with the legacy of American racism and slavery.

Life in Georgia is an intimidating, shameful experience; "the whole white South weighs down upon him." Even the night wind whistling through the cracks of his cabin seems to create a threatening song:

> White-man's land,
> Niggers, sing.
> Burn, bear black children
> Till poor rivers bring
> Rest, and sweet glory
> In Camp Ground. (P. 157)

And as he watches the courthouse tower in the moonlight, "he sees himself yanked beneath that tower. He sees white minds, with indolent assumption, juggle justice and a nigger" (p. 163). Because Kabnis fears being lynched and identified with the praying and shouting of a "preacher-ridden race," he cowardly submits to the accommodationism of school principal Hanby and rejects his slave past as symbolized by Father John, the old ex-slave who lives in the cellar of Halsey's wagon shop. Toomer's hero is only "a promise of soil-soaked beauty; uprooted, thinning out. Suspended a few feet above the soil whose touch would resurrect him" (p. 191). Peering into Kabnis's soul, Lewis says: "Cant hold them, can you? Master; slave. Soil and the overreaching heavens. Dusk; dawn. They fight and bastardize you. The sun tint of your cheeks, flame of the great season's multicolored leaves, tarnished, burned. Split, shredded; easily burned. No use. . . . " (p. 218). A tragic figure, Kabnis cannot cope with the paradoxical truth of his Afro-American heritage.

As artists, Kabnis and Lewis are also strikingly contrasting characters. Because of his tortured soul, Kabnis is incapable of expressing in writing the quintessential experience of the South. " 'Those words I was tellin y about,' " Kabnis confesses in the end, " 'they wont fit int th mold thats branded on m soul. . . . Th form thats burned int my soul is some twisted awful thing that crept in from a dream, godam nightmare, an wont stay still unless I feed it' " (p. 224). Lewis, on the other hand, is in complete control of his creative powers and his external world. In order to capture the truth of the region, he asks questions and goes " 'pokin round and notin somethin,' " says the Rev. Layman. " 'Noted what I said th other day, and that werent for notin down' " (p. 177).

Symbolically, the minor characters in "Kabnis" represent various ways of adjusting to the bitter-sweet life of the South. Father John, for example, represents the indomitable spirit of the black American's past and is, in effect, a black nemesis in the tradition of Nat Turner. In contrast, Carrie

Kate, the wagon-shop owner's younger sister, represents the racial hope of the future. "She is lovely in her fresh energy of the morning, in the calm untested confidence and nascent maternity which rise from the purpose of her present mission" (p. 233). Her mission includes being a bridge between the past and present, between Father John and Kabnis. Thus, at the end of the allegory, she reaches out and touches Kabnis's soul, and he sinks to his knees before her. She then goes to Father John, kneels before him and whispers, "Jesus, come." In the final scene of *Cane*, as the sun rises symbolically, "Light streaks through the iron-barred cellar window. Within its soft circle, the figures of Carrie and Father John" (p. 239). With this tableau of youth and age, time past and time to come, the spiritual odyssey ends, leaving us with the glimmer of hope that Carrie, unlike Kabnis, will be able to attain higher consciousness and fulfill her redemptive mission in life.

Like his white literary peers who published in such little magazines as *Broom*, the *Liberator*, and the *Little Review*, Toomer was deeply involved in experimenting with new forms and themes. In pursuing this goal he confesses being strongly influenced by two approaches to literature. First, he was attracted to those Euro-American writers and works that used regional matter in a poetic manner, especially Robert Frost's poems and Sherwood Anderson's *Winesburg, Ohio*. Second, he was impressed by the self-conscious art of the Imagists. "Their insistence on fresh vision and on the perfect clean economical line," Toomer writes, "was just what I had been looking for. I began feeling that I had in my hands the tools for my own creation."[14] The artistic fusion in *Cane* of Christian myth and elements of the African and Afro-American experience, especially the tradition of black music, bears witness to these influences and establishes the book as a unique contribution to the tradition of the Afro-American novel.

ARNA WENDELL BONTEMPS (1902–73)

Arna Bontemps makes use of history and folklore in a more traditional manner than Toomer. Born in 1902 in Alexandria, Louisiana, Bontemps grew up in California and graduated from Pacific Union College and the University of Chicago. He arrived in Harlem in 1923 and soon became an important member of the chorus of new black voices of the age. Influenced by Toomer, Hughes, and Cullen's discovery of a usable past and his own dim memories of his folk heritage, he began publishing poems in *The Crisis* in 1924; and in "The Return," which won the 1927 *Opportunity* poetry contest, "the dance of rain" becomes the metaphorical vehicle for a return from the urban present to ancestral Africa. In 1935 Bontemps moved his family to Chicago where he eventually enrolled in the university, joined the South Side Writers' Group, founded by Richard Wright in 1936, and, after the publication of *Black Thunder*, was added to the staff of the Illinois Writers Project. After the Depression, Bontemps was a teacher, lecturer, and, from 1943 to 1965, librarian at Fisk University. Before his death in 1973 he published a wide range of books, including children's stories, biographies, histories, anthologies, poetry, and three novels: *God Sends Sunday* (1931), *Black Thunder* (1936), and *Drums at Dusk* (1939).

In Bontemps's three novels we see a shift from urban folklore to revolutionary history. *God Sends Sunday* uses a blues motif to introduce the red-light districts of New Orleans and St. Louis and a new picaresque character into the tradition of the Afro-American novel. The narrative traces the fortunes and misfortunes of Little Augie, a pint-sized orphan whose success as a jockey catapults him into profligacy. Because he was born with a caul over his face, Augie believes he is "unfailingly lucky" and "bound to wander all his natural days" until his luck runs out. His love of riding horses enables him to escape from the dull life of the Red River plantation where he was born to become one of the top jockeys in the Mississippi Valley. The more successful he becomes as a jockey, the more insatiable becomes his appetite for drinking, gambling, sex, and the blues. Catering to the popular taste of the time, Bontemps transforms his hero into Little Poison: a flamboyantly dressed "sugar daddy" with gold eyeteeth, distorted folk idiom, and a reputation for beating up prostitutes. Unfortunately, Augie and his crowd are more caricatures than realistic portrayals of street people. Sensational shoot-outs and gratuitous violence are highlights of the church picnics, brothels, and boogie-houses of Bontemps's New Orleans and St. Louis. After fulfilling his passion for Florence Dessau, the mulatto ex-mistress of his white employer, Augie has a streak of bad luck; his woman deserts him; and he rapidly declines in the second half of the narrative. His migration to California, second murder of passion, and flight to Tijuana, Mexico, are crudely melodramatic and anticlimactic.

Unlike the sensationalism of *God Sends Sunday*, both *Black Thunder* and *Drums at Dusk* are stories of revolution and the will to freedom that depend on tradition for authority and dramatic interest. The first turns to the slave narratives and court records for the legendary efforts of blacks to liberate themselves, while the second relies more heavily on historical documents. One is the tragic story of the abortive Virginian revolt of Gabriel Prosser in 1800, and the other the intriguing adventures of Les Amis des Noirs, Boukman (the voodoo priest), and Toussaint L'Ouverture in the successful Haitian revolution of 1791–1803. Stylistically, *Black Thunder* is the better of the two historical romances.

The preparation for *Black Thunder* began in 1933 when the eyes of the world were shifted from the failure of Wall Street to the political demonstrations of Ghandi in India and the second Scottsboro trial in Decatur, Alabama. Whereas the nonviolent Indian resistance to British tyranny won the sympathy of many, the unjust conviction of nine black boys for the alleged rape of two hoboing white girls stirred black and white progressives to heated protest. Living about thirty miles from Decatur at the time, Bontemps and his family became anxious because of the mood of their community and took the opportunity to visit James Weldon Johnson, Charles S. Johnson, and Arthur Schomburg in Nashville, Tennessee. "Discovering in the Fisk Library a larger collection of slave narratives then I knew existed," Bontemps writes, "I began to read almost frantically. . . . I knew instantly that one of them would be the subject of my next novel."[15] Intrigued by the legends of Denmark Vesey, Nat Turner, and Gabriel Prosser, he felt that the latter most accurately reflected the impulse to freedom of most slaves. After further research, Bontemps moved his family to Watts, California, and began his second novel.

With the radical slogans of the French Revolution and the example of the slave revolt in San Domingo as leitmotifs, *Black Thunder* focuses on the pent-up will of oppressed people to be free. In anger and fear, white Virginians in the book blame slave unrest on the seeds of discontent sown by foreigners like Creuzot, the French painter, and Biddenhurst, the radical young English lawyer. The Virginians refuse to acknowledge the humanity of the slaves and fail to recognize the natural impulse of the slaves to freedom and the reinforcement of that impulse by their own interpretation of the Bible. Gabriel believes that the Day of Judgment is at hand and that " 'God's going to fight them because they oppresses the poor.' " But thunder and torrential rains on the night the revolt begins lead to its postponement and ultimate betrayal by two old house servants. The slaves ascribe the failure to bad weather and bad luck. They had not heeded the signs nor ritualistically protected themselves against evil forces in the manner of the followers of Toussaint L'Ouverture. Freedom, in short, was a dream whose time had not come for Gabriel Prosser and his rebel band, except in death by hanging.

The influence of the slave narratives is apparent in the theme of *Black Thunder;* more subtle and instructive is Bontemps's skillful adaptation of the conventions of the tradition. The narrative is organized in five books: plan of revolt, abortive execution and betrayal of plan, white retribution, Gabriel's surrender and resolution to die with dignity, and Gabriel's trial and hanging. Although Gabriel is the hero, the emphasis is on the revolt of 1,100 slaves, not, as in the traditional slave narrative, on the escape of one or two individuals. In addition, Bontemps's tone is more dispassionate and his style more inventive. Court records, newspapers, journals, and letters are used as documentary sources of narrative authority, and the omniscient narrator initially speaks in a collective historical voice. But these narrative conventions are less prominent than Bontemps's extensive experiment with multiple points of view and interior monologue. Probing into the minds of both minor and major characters, black and white, the author-narrator effectively mixes third-person objective with first-and third-person subjective techniques. The frequent omission of quotation marks and other editorial cues to introduce the direct thoughts of characters achieves the same time perspective for internal states of being as for external behavior and heightens the dramatic force of the brief character portrayals.

Whereas the desire for freedom is the most significant and natural motive for the revolt, it is neither uncomplicated by other motives nor simplistically rendered in the consciousness of the different characters. The two betrayers of the revolt, for example, are deeply divided in loyalty to their white masters and their ethnic group. Pharoah, the more obsequious of the two, betrays the revolution out of personal vindictiveness, fear of white retribution, and hope of reward. Ben, the self-debasing, convincingly delineated servant to Mosely Sheppard, has internalized the ethics of paternalism and confesses out of a deep sense of concern for his master's good will and safety. In some cases sexual desire also adds complexity to character motivation. Thus Criddle, hog-killer on the Prosser plantation, is charged with the task of preventing a poor white farmer and his daughter from giving warning of the attack, but he has mixed emotions, colored by sexual desire, about killing Grisselda, the daughter. Repressing his fleeting desire, he resolves to be firm: "Us ain't sparing nothing, nothing what raises its hand. The good and the bad goes together this night, the pretty and the ugly. We's going to be as hard as God his self."[16] However, Grisselda escapes while her father is being killed and reappears during the hangings as a kind of white nemesis. The implied author's moral distance from these characters is revealed in such subtle ways as Ben's interior self-condemnation for his perverted loyalty. Although Ben lives under the threat of reprisal from fellow blacks at the close of the novel, he survives the physical death of those he betrayed.

Bontemps uses history to express his imaginative vision of the nature and function of revolution. By manipulating the facts of the Gabriel Prosser revolt, he reveals the timeless problems man has in overpowering color and class oppression to achieve freedom and social equality.[17] But unlike

William Styron's *Confessions of Nat Turner,* Bontemps's imaginative treatment of an important historical figure violates neither our understanding of the integrity of the man nor our knowledge of the complex interpersonal relations resulting from American racism. Rather than rely exclusively on traditional white historiography and journalism, which generally view slave revolts and their leaders as criminal, Bontemps provides us with an enduring literary version of the heroic Gabriel Prosser of Afro-American legend.

Genteel Realism: Assimilationism, Nationalism, or Biculturalism

Harlem was the major base of operation for Marcus Garvey's Universal Negro Improvement Association (UNIA), the largest mass movement of blacks ever developed in this country.[18] Founded in Jamaica in 1914, the UNIA was brought here at a time when the betrayed promises of Reconstruction, World War I, and urbanization had plummeted the faith of the black masses in themselves and the future to a new low. A spiritual disciple of Booker T. Washington, Garvey came to the United States in 1916 with the intent of meeting the founder of Tuskegee Institute, raising funds for the UNIA, and returning to Jamaica to build an institution similar to Tuskegee. Unfortunately, Washington died before Garvey arrived. But Washington's ideas about self-determination lived on in the more radical dream of Garvey's black nationalism.

With fiery eloquence and colorful splendor, Garvey advocated the return of Africa to Africans, resurrected the "lost" civilizations of Africa, proclaimed himself provisional president of the continent he had never visited, and organized several ill-fated business enterprises, including a steamship company to transport American blacks to Africa, the motherland, according to modern archeological research, of the human race.[19] (In this sense, whether black, white, or brown, we are all of African descent.) Romantic, flamboyant, and grandiloquent, Garvey combined the style of the political demagogue and folk preacher to rekindle the pride and win the loyalty of the masses with the message that they were the black and beautiful descendants of a noble race of people. At the same time, Garvey's frequent attacks on middle-class, fair-complexioned leaders like Du Bois, Johnson, and White exacerbated class and color tensions within the black community. From its peak of over a million members between 1920 and 1925, Garvey's movement declined with his imprisonment for mail fraud in 1925 and deportation in 1927.

Although Locke believed that Garveyism was "a transient, if spectacular, phenomenon," he, too, envisioned the New Negro as "the advance-guard of the African peoples in their contact with Twentieth Century civilization" and the younger generation's principal mission as the reestablishment of the pride and prestige of the race in the eyes of the world. And when he stated that the "racialism of the Negro is no limitation or reservation with respect to American life; it is only a constructive effort to build the obstructions in the stream of his progress into an efficient dam of social energy and power,"[20] he was announcing that the major thrust of the artists and intelligentsia was toward cultural dualism, not assimilationism.

As a social concept, assimilationism is the process by which different ethnic groups are absorbed into the larger community. It projects the image of America as a melting pot of nationalities, a myth popularized in 1908 through the Broadway production of Israel Zangwill's *Melting Pot*. But as history and social critics reveal, the myth was and is remote from reality. The reality, as social historian Charles Silberman has noted, is that "American politics and American social life are still dominated by the existence of sharply-defined ethnic groups. . . . The WASPs (White Anglo-Saxon Protestants), the Irish-Americans, the Italian-Americans, the Jewish-Americans do differ from each other in essential ways. They vote differently, raise their children differently, have different ideas about sex education, religion, death, etc."[21] On the other side of the tracks, black psychologist Kenneth Clark reminds us, most Afro-Americans still come into the world, live, learn, work, play, pray, and die in ghettos.[22] Thus, with each ethnic group contributing a distinctive flavor to the whole, America is more like a tossed salad or gumbo than a melting pot.

This is not to say that the form and content of the Afro-American novel were not influenced by the conflict between nationalism and assimilationism. By family background and education, the New Negro novelists were mainly second-generation members of the middle-class black intelligentsia, a group whose color and class ambivalence was more intense and complex than that of the first generation of lower middle-class novelists.[23] Even though Walter White, Jessie Fauset, and Nella Larsen continued to explore the theme of passing, they placed more emphasis on class than color. By focusing on the morals and manners of well-educated members of black high society, they introduced the novel of manners and genteel realism into the tradition of the Afro-American novel. Fauset and Larsen also provided the important perspective of twentieth-century black women toward traditional white middle-class values. Once their characters succeeded in repressing the duality of their identities in order to cross the color line, they would reassess their judgment of the spiritual and cultural virtues of the black experience that transcended the perversity of racial restrictions.

JESSIE REDMON FAUSET (1882–1961)

The daughter of an African Methodist Episcopal minister, Jessie Fauset was born in Camden County, New Jersey, near Philadelphia in 1882. Educated at Cornell (Phi Beta Kappa), the University of Pennsylvania, and the Sorbonne, she became a high school teacher, poet, editor, novelist, and midwife of the Harlem Renaissance.[24] Attracted by her poetry, Du Bois invited her to join his editorial staff on *The Crisis*, where she championed the literary nationalism of the young writers of the day. Before her death in 1961, she published more novels during the Harlem Renaissance than any of her contemporaries: *There Is Confusion* (1924), *Plum Bun* (1929), *The Chinaberry Tree* (1931), and *Comedy: American Style* (1933). Like Jane Austen, Jessie Fauset is concerned with the commonplace details of domestic life, and at her best, as black critic Sterling A. Brown has observed, "succeeds in a realism of the sort sponsored by William Dean Howells."[25]

In the foreword to *The Chinaberry Tree* Fauset reveals her social and artistic preference for depicting "something of the homelife of the colored American who is not being pressed too hard by the Furies of Prejudice, Ignorance, and Economic Injustice," and who as " . . . naturally as his white compatriots . . . speaks of his 'old' Boston families, 'old Philadelphians,' 'old Charlestonians.' And he has a wholesome respect for family and education and labor and the fruits of labor. He is still sufficiently conservative to lay a slightly greater stress on the first two of these four."[26] By stressing the genteel tradition and everyday rituals of the urban black elite, Fauset limits her presentation of truth and reality to the class of people she knew best.

Unfortunately, her depiction of the prejudices and foibles of this narrow segment of society is more sentimental than satirical. The moral of her novels is that the respectable, genteel black American "is not so vastly different from any other American, just distinctive."[27] In *There Is Confusion* dark-skinned Joanna Marshall and light-skinned Peter Bye overcome color prejudice and achieve success by confronting the truth of their family backgrounds and committing themselves to education, hard work, respectability, and each other. Even so, neither the characters nor the author-narrator has much sympathy for commonplace minds or people. In *The Chinaberry Tree* adultery and illegitimacy overshadow the lives of three black women in a small New Jersey town. Fauset is more concerned with the realistic details of Aunt Sal and Laurentine's daily routine and their ability to rise above the ostracism of their community than she is the narrowness of small-town notions of respectability. As the central unifying metaphor, the chinaberry tree is a sentimentally contrived symbol of the illicit love of Aunt Sal and Colonel Halloway and of the shadowy past that unites Sal with her illegitimate daughter, Laurentine, and illegitimate niece, Melissa. Unlike Howells, Fauset does not shrink from the unpleasant aspects of the black bourgeoisie as she approvingly reveals that their morals and manners are not appreciably different in kind from those of the white bourgeoisie.

Fauset's other two novels are antiromantic exposures of the tradition of passing. The nursery rhyme epigraph, title, and five-part romantic structure of *Plum Bun* suggest the mixture of tragic and comic elements in Mattie's and her daughter Angela Murray's indulging their desire for excitement and freedom by passing for white. The ideological distance between the author-narrator and Angela, an amateur painter who initially rejects race and family because she believes that "being coloured in America is . . . nothing short of a curse," is apparent in the characterization of Angela's darker sister Virginia, in much of the serious dialogue, and in the melodramatic reversal of Angela's fate after she confesses her black identity. In the end Angela chooses a life of poverty and self-respect with mulatto suitor Anthony Cross after rejecting a life of wealth with racist, sexist white Roger Fielding. In short, a close examination of the plot development and characterization reveals a sexual, class, and moral kinship between the author-narrator and heroine that subtly undercuts a romantic urge to whiteness. The well-received speech by a leading black spokesman on racial sacrifice crystallizes the nature of this kinship:

"Our case is unique . . . those of us who have forged forward, who have gained the front ranks in money and training, will not, are not able as yet to go our separate ways apart from the unwashed, untutored herd. We must still look back and render service to our less fortunate, weaker brethren. And the first step toward making this a workable attitude is the acquisition not so much of a racial love as a racial pride. A pride that enables us to find our own beautiful and praiseworthy, an intense chauvinism that is content with its own types, that finds completeness within its own group; that loves its own as the French love their country, because it is their own. Such a pride can accomplish the impossible."[28]

After turning down a belated marriage proposal from Roger and winning a prize to study painting in Paris, Angela is melodramatically reunited at the close of the novel with Anthony, who had also been passing for white in the United States.

Tragic and comic elements also inform six chapters of *Comedy: American Style*, which is actually a domestic tragedy dramatizing the results of Olivia Cary's pathological urge to whiteness. Olivia, who deeply resented her parents for having "made her colored," grew up in New England passing as an Italian, and married Christopher Cary because of his potential status as a medical doctor and as the father of white children. As an adult, she drives her daughter Teresa into a loveless marriage to a Frenchman, her dark-skinned son Oliver to suicide, and her indulgent husband to depression and bankruptcy. As the curtain falls in the final chapter, Olivia is a dispirited, lonely woman marooned in a Paris pension. In these "absurdly truthful" novels about the problems of passing and self-determination, Fauset too often alienates the contemporary reader by her precious sensibility and narrow concern for the cultural dilemma of middle-class mulatto women.

NELLA LARSEN (1893–1963)

The problems of identity for black middle-class women are also at the center of the private and public worlds of Nella Larsen. The daughter of a Danish mother and West Indian father, Larsen was born in Chicago in 1893. After her father died and her mother remarried a white man who apparently resented his stepdaughter's African ancestry, she grew up in a home with little love and less kindness. Educated at Fisk University, the University of Copenhagen, and Lincoln Hospital Training School for Nurses, Larsen sought personal fulfillment in Europe, marriage to a black scholar, and careers as a nurse, librarian, and novelist before her death in 1963. On the basis of her two successful novels—*Quicksand* and *Passing*—she was awarded the Harmon Medal in 1929, and in 1930 she became the first black woman to receive a Guggenheim Fellowship for creative writing. Although flawed, the narrative structure and characterization of both novels are better controlled than that in *Plum Bun*, Fauset's best novel.

In *Quicksand* and *Passing* the characters are convincing in their obsession with fashion, decorum, marriage, and housekeeping. In *Quicksand* some characters are praised by the heroine, Helga Crane, for their "impeccably fastidious taste in clothes," and others are scorned by the omniscient narrator for wearing "five-years-behind-the-mode garments." Helga's quest is not for money but for "the things which money could give, leisure, attention, beautiful surroundings. Things. Things. Things."[29] The daughter of a black gambler father and a white immigrant mother, she also seeks acceptance as an individual. But in black high society, the undramatized omniscient narrator states reproachfully, "if you couldn't prove your ancestry and connections, you were tolerated, but you didn't 'belong' " (p. 34). In *Passing*, Irene Redfield, the heroine who occasionally passes for convenience, is equally tragic in her misguided sense of values. " 'I am wrapped up in my boys and the running of my house,' " she primly tells her old acquaintance Clare Kendry. " 'I can't help it.' "[30] Irene, like most middle-class women of pre–Depression America, accepted the conventional morality that held the security of marriage to be more important than love and happiness. The superficialty of her domestic and social tranquility, which she imagines threatened by Clare, reflects the distorted values of her class and the larger, white male-dominated society. Her desire to kill Clare in the dramatic last scene of the novel further underscores the depth of her insecurity.

Structurally, *Quicksand* is the better of the two novels. The narrative movement in *Passing* is static and, as Hoyt Fuller observes, not unlike the banal scene-setting and dialogue of a magazine story for women.[31] In contrast, the movement of *Quicksand* is vertical on its psychological axis and circular in its spatial pattern. The heroine begins each new experience in high spirits, goes through a period of restiveness and withdrawal, sinks into deep disgust and despair, and then, except for her final adventure, escapes to a new experience. From South to North, America to Europe, and back again, the circular and vertical movements are from entrapment to escape and ultimate engulfment.

A lonely, sexually repressed, intelligent black woman with no family, Helga Crane escapes from "an unchildlike childhood among hostile white folk in Chicago" and from the "trivial hypocrisies and careless cruelties" of snobbish blacks at Naxos, the small Southern college where she taught, to the "peace and contentment" of Harlem:

> Her existence was bounded by Central Park, Fifth Avenue, St. Nicholas Park, and One Hundred and Forty-fifth Street. Not at all a narrow life, as Negroes live it, as Helga Crane knew it. Everything was there, vice and goodness, sadness and gaiety, ignorance and wisdom, ugliness and beauty, poverty and richness. And it seemed to her that somehow of goodness, gaiety, wisdom and beauty always there was a little more than of vice, sadness, ignorance, and ugliness. It was only riches that did not quite transcend poverty. (Pp. 88–89)

In a short time, however, Harlem lost its charm for her, and she recoiled in aversion from its sights and sounds and people. She even began to dislike upper-class friends like Anne Grey, who passionately hated white people yet "aped their clothes, their manners, and their gracious ways of living." With a check and advice from her mother's brother, she escapes from the "desperate black folk" of Harlem to visit her Aunt Katrina Dahl in Copenhagen.

Elated and then depressed by her Danish aunt and uncle's exploitation of the repressed sensual aspects of her black identity for their own social advancement, Helga rejects a conceited Danish suitor, Axel Olsen, and returns to New York. The memory of her unhappy subjection as a child to her mother's shame and hatred of blacks had reinforced Helga's dread of mixed marriages and children. Most decisively, after two years in Denmark, she had become homesick for blacks:

> For the first time Helga Crane felt sympathy rather than contempt and hatred for that father, who so often and so angrily she had blamed for his desertion of her mother. She understood, now, his rejection, his repudiation, of the formal calm her mother had represented. She understood his yearning, his intolerable need for the inexhaustible humor and the incessant hope of his own kind, his need for those things, not material, indigenous to all Negro environments. She understood and could sympathize with his facile surrender to the irresistible ties of race now that they dragged at her own heart. (P. 158)

But color and class restrictions in America also reinforced her feelings of ambivalence and "a fine contempt for the blatantly patriotic black Americans."

Helga found it increasingly difficult to repress her desire for Dr. Anderson, the urbane black intellectual and former principal at Naxos. Personal insecurity had contributed to her rejection of James Vayle, her snobbish fiancé from Naxos, Axel Olsen, and the courtship of Robert Anderson, whose marriage to Anne Grey created conflict between the two friends. Anderson's casual kiss at a party rekindles Helga's passion, but his sober middle-class values prevent him from responding. This plunges her into self-loathing and the arms of God and of the Reverend Green, a fundamentalist preacher. In desperation, Helga seeks salvation through submission to deep-rooted religious and sexual urges, and returns to Alabama as Green's wife. Her missionary resolve to uplift the black poor in her husband's flock is soon suffocated in the quagmire of too many children, too much harsh reality, and too much passion. Unlike her experiences in Naxos, New York, and Copenhagen, she was incapable of escaping "the oppression, the degradation, that her life had become" in Alabama.

*

In their novels, as I have illustrated, Nella Larsen and Jessie Fauset reject the romantic extremes of nationalism and assimilation in favor of cultural dualism. The color fantasies of Angela Murray, Olivia Cary, and Clare Kendry are satirized; Anne Grey's hatred of whites is treated unsympathetically; and the snobbery, pretentiousness, and hypocrisy of the black bourgeoisie are uniformly condemned. Although marriage, husbands, and children are contributing agents to the tragedies of Olivia, Irene, and Helga, Fauset and Larsen clearly stress color anxieties and class ambitions over sexual oppression in their heroines' quests for personal wholeness. As portrayed in Laurentine Halloway's and Helga Crane's quests, for example, Fauset and Larsen see the substance, not the shadow, of middle-class American values as the goal of black women. Thus, in the genteel world of their novels, racial pride, family background, and formal education are important, but they must be complemented by respect for individualism, economic security, and social advancement.

Contrary to popular opinion, Nella Larsen and Jessie Fauset, like their contemporaries, were in revolt against the assimilationist assumption that blacks had to deny their color and culture, had to become white in mental outlook if not in physical appearance, in order to become first-class American citizens. For Langston Hughes "this urge within the race toward whiteness, the desire to pour racial individuality into the mold of American standardization, and to be as little Negro and as much American as possible" was the mountain standing in the way of true Afro-American art.[32] The path for the serious artist to the top of the mountain, to the establishment of racial forms of art, was rocky, and the mountain was high. And because black American nationalism was in part an emotional and intellectual reaction to white racism, it generated different forms of social action and artistic expression to achieve self-determination, group solidarity, ethnic pride, and human dignity.

Folk Romance: Pastoralism, Primitivism, and Ancestralism

Carl Van Vechten played a major role in influencing the literary interpretation of black Harlem life as primitive. As portrayed in his controversial but commercially successful *Nigger Heaven*, the spirit and life style of black Americans was not only atavistic but, in the words of Du Bois, "one damned orgy after another, with hate, hurt, gin and sadism."[33] The self-analysis of his middle-class heroine reveals the major thrust of the novel:

Savages! Savages at heart! And she had lost or forfeited her birthright, this primitive birthright which was so valuable and important an asset, a birthright that all the civilized races were struggling to get back to— this fact explained the art of a Picasso or a Stravinsky. To be sure, she, too, felt this African beat—it completely aroused her emotionally—but she was conscious of feeling it. This love of drums, of exciting rhythms, this naive delight in glowing colour—the colour that exists only in cloudless, tropical climes—this warm, sexual emotion, all these were hers only through a mental understanding. With Olive these qualities were instinctive. . . . Why, Mary asked herself, is this denied me?

The dominant setting of this spirit is Harlem cabaret life: "The music shivered and broke, cracked and smashed. Jungle land. Hottentots and Bantus swaying under the amber moon. Love, sex, passion . . . hate."[34] Van Vechten reduced his black characters to tortured, often grotesque, amoral souls who inhabited a jungle of joy in which the good life was symbolized by barbaric orgies, bloodletting fights, and jive talk that required a "Glossary of Negro Words and Phrases" to decipher.

Rather than pursue Van Vechten's notion of primitivism, it is more illuminating to describe this romantic phase of development in the tradition of the Afro-American novel as a form of pastoralism or, more distinctively, ancestralism. It would be absurd to argue that New Negro artists were not influenced by Freudian theory and white literary interpretations of the Afro-American experience. Some even succumbed on occasion to the commercial temptation to glorify sexuality and violence for the sake of a white benefactor or audience. In the main, however, the intention of the more committed New Negro artists was to project their vision as honestly as they could: to discover a usable past, to define and explore their culture, not exploit it. Their purpose was to express the historical struggle of black Americans to achieve a dynamic synthesis of their individual and collective double-consciousness. Their passion was to reconcile the urban present and future with the rural, occasionally distant and strange, past. And their immediate dilemma was to free themselves from the well-meaning but pernicious influence of whites encouraging them to emphasize the exotic aspects of Harlem life, and from the equally well-meaning but misguided counsel of the black elite criticizing them for literary pandering and for not using their talents to portray the intellectual and social parity of the race.[35]

The term *Afro-American pastoral* draws attention to this historical synthesis of African and Western narrative traditions of which the New Negro novelist was heir. This was no simple fusion of oral and written literature, as German critic Janheinz Jahn points out, but a confluence of styles, patterns of expression, and attitudes.[36] Thus the term stresses continuity and change: a reinterpretation of the past in the light of new experiences and a dialectically evolving consciousness. Based on an implicit contrast between country and city life, the pastoral tradition is rich in thematic and stylistic variety:[37] from the classical realism of Theocritus's Sicilian rustics and the allegorical Arcadia of Vergil's ecologues to the modern romantic defenses of a feudal society by the plantation tradition movement and the Southern agrarians; from the Judeo-Christian Edenic myths and West African myth-legends of a past Golden Age to the contrasting urban and rural black havens of McKay and Hurston. Breaking with the traditional distinctions between agrarian and industrial landscapes, the Afro-American pastoral focused on the near rather than remote past for paradigms of the good life, celebrated urban as well as rural settings, elevated social outcasts and plain folk to heroic stature, and attacked the repressive forces of Western civilization, especially social conformity and racism.

The celebration of race consciousness in the novels by New Negroes may also be conveyed by the concept of ancestralism. Out of a sense of loss, a feeling that the times were out of joint and the soul was under siege by destructive forces, a romantic longing for a freer, more innocent time and place was born: a time and place where the rhythms of life were closely linked to nature and one's essential humanity was unquestioned; a time and place that fostered a feeling of harmony and peace with one's ancestors, one's self, and one's progeny. In the crucible of the creative imagination a dimly remembered or romanticized past fused with the realities of a demanding present to produce an organic vision of a new, more promising social order. More often than not the realization of this vision in the novels of the period proved abortive, but its impulse toward social justice and racial progress was triggered by the fact of institutional racism and reinforced by an ambivalence to Afro-American spirituality, Christian myth, and the American Dream. Whether the subject was the pretentiousness and idealism of Fauset's and Larsen's high-brow, Northern city folk, the sensationalism and atavism of McKay's Harlem laborers and street people, or the provincialism and pragmatism of Hurston's down-home low-brows; whether the conflict was largely with white ancestors as in *There Is Confusion* and *Quicksand* or with black, as in *Home to Harlem* and *Jonah's Gourd Vine*, the quest in the novels of the New Negro was for the resolution of the psychological and social dilemma of the modern black American, for an affirmation of the human spirit over the forces that threatened its integrity and development.

The international scope of the concept of ancestralism is apparent in the Négritude movement of Caribbean and Francophone West African writers. Coined in 1939 by Aimé Césaire in "Journal of a Return to My Native Country," a long narrative poem, and popularized in 1948 by Léopold Senghor in *New Anthology of Black and Malagasian Poetry*, the term *Négritude* involves more than antiracist racism. Only the most doctrinaire ideologues refuse to concede that peoples of African descent have historically suffered discrimination and oppression because of their color as well as their class. Consequently, Négritude writers not only refused to continue their deference to the white gods of European culture but also sought to destroy the myth of white supremacy and to resurrect the beauty of blackness in order to foster self-pride and to win respect for cultural pluralism and human equality. Regarding the relationship between the New Negro movement and the concept of Négritude, Senghor, the former poet-president of Senegal, has said:

> we owe a great deal to the United States. Indeed, with regard to our Négritude, we have depended largely on the teachings of our professors of ethnology, anthropology on the subject of Black African civilizations. But, was it not the "New Negro" movement, the movement of the "Negro Renaissance," with Alain Locke and the others, was it not they who stimulated us to do as they did, to write poetry! In this way, and at this moment, I want to give America that which is due her, that is to say to have been, in a way, the initiator of Négritude.[38]

A common African past and experience with racism and Western economic exploitation were therefore initially a more pragmatic and logical basis for cultural solidarity than political struggle; and rather than being provincial, the character of New Negro art stimulated and encouraged corresponding impulses in Caribbean and Francophone West African literary traditions. The shift toward a biracial, working-class approach to the problems of black Americans during the Great Depression was short-lived; but with the emergence and development of independent African nations in the 1960s and the realization that black regimes can be as oppressive as white, a racial analysis of the plight of oppressed peoples is being increasingly challenged in primacy by economic and feminist analyses. Neither analysis in isolation, however, adequately explains the protracted and complex political, economic, and cultural struggle of blacks for self-determination and social parity.

FESTUS CLAUDIUS MC KAY (1899–1948)

A transplanted Jamaican and social radical, Claude McKay transcended the primitivism of Van Vechten by drawing on his authentic racial past and intellectual independence. Born in 1889 in Clarendon, Jamaica, he traced his ethnic roots to the Ashanti and his love of nature to the Clarendon hills of his youth. Tutored in philosophy and religious skepticism by an agnostic brother and a white Englishman, Walter Jekyl, who also encouraged him to write dialect poetry, he won popularity in 1912 as a native Bobbie Burns for his first two volumes of verse: *Songs of Jamaica* and *Constab Ballads*. In the same year McKay came to the United States to continue his education at Tuskegee Institute and Kansas State College, but he dropped out after two years to pursue his love of poetry and life. Through Max Eastman, he was introduced in 1919 to the cause of the political Left, spent 1920 in London coediting the *Workers' Dreadnought* and preparing his third book of poetry for publication, and in 1922 became associate editor of the *Liberator*. During the next twelve years, which were spent in Europe and Spain, he published a fourth book of poetry, a collection of short stories, *Gingertown* (1932), and three novels, *Home to Harlem* (1928), *Banjo* (1929), and *Banana Bottom* (1933).

McKay's denials notwithstanding, *Home to Harlem*, on one level, exploits the literary primitivism of his white peers. Relying more heavily on black idiom, slang, sex, animal imagery, gratuitous violence, and a noble-savage motif than its apparent model, "*Home to Harlem*," as a contemporary reviewer wrote, "is *Nigger Heaven* in a larger and more violent dose."[39] Vividly dramatized, the book is conveniently divided into three major sections. In the first, Jake, the protagonist, who has deserted from an army work battalion and spent the war years abroad, returns to Harlem and picks up a seductive brown prostitute who pleases him so much that he resolves to find her again. The search for Felice, the symbol of the sensual, joyous side of Harlem life, provides the loose, episodic structure of the narrative. In the second part, we follow the adventures of Jake and his Haitian friend Ray as cook and waiter on a Pullman train. The third section returns again to Harlem where Ray, in frustration with the evils of American civilization, ships out on a freighter for Europe, and Jake, reunited with Felice and attempting to avoid arrest for desertion, departs for Chicago.

By focusing on the urban black worker and penetrating the surface vitality of his struggle to survive, *Home to Harlem* moves beyond the primitivism of *Nigger Heaven*. Knowing the life of the unskilled black city worker first-hand, McKay demonstrates a keen ear for the language as he explores Jake's consciousness and behavior. " 'I've never been a sweetman yet,' " says Jake. " 'Never lived off no woman and never will. I always works.' " On the surface, Jake is a free spirit who "nourished a perfect contempt for place" and a marriage of spirits with "the infectious joy" of Harlem and Felice. Ray, who envies Jake's elemental simplicity and yearns occasionally to lose himself in "some savage culture in the jungles of Africa," is an aspiring black writer whose education, sensibility, and dreams foster racial and cultural ambivalence. The dramatic conflict, however, is not between Jake, the man of instinct, and Ray, the man of intellect, but between the capacity of both men to realize their dreams for economic security and human dignity in a parasitic, modern urban society. For on a deeper level, Jake is also a dreamer:

> "Ef I was edjucated, I could understand things better and be proper-speaking like you is. . . . And I mighta helped mah li'l sister to get edjucated, too (she must be a li'l woman, now), and she would be nice-speaking like you' sweet brown, good enough foh you to hitch up with. Then we could all settle down and make money like edjucated people do, instead a you gwine off to throw you'self away on some lousy dinghy and me chasing around all the time lak a hungry dawg."[40]

Just as the exploitative life of a pimp would violate Jack's sense of righteous living, the bourgeois life of a married man would mean the death of Ray's dream of giving artistic form to the fertile reality around him. Although the unlettered Jake is in closer cultural and spiritual contact with his ethnic past than Ray, the deracinated Caribbean artist, the survival of both characters as modern black men demands their coping with the decay and death which are also integral parts of black Harlem.

Both Jake and Ray reappear in *Banjo,* a big plotless book extolling what the omniscient narrator calls "the irrepressible exuberance and legendary vitality of the black race." Neither, however, is the protagonist. This role falls on Lincoln Agrippa Daily, better known as Banjo, the leader of five "beach boys" who bum around together in the old port of Marseilles. Insofar as the book relates the adventures and misadventures of an international group of black vagabonds on the European continent, it is picaresque in form. Outcasts from America, the West Indies, and Senegal,

Banjo, Malty, Ginger, Dengel, and Bugsy loaf on the beach and in bars; steal wine from casks on the docks or panhandle to buy it in bars; sing and play Dixieland jazz in the streets and bars; beg food from ships in port; dance the Charleston and Black Bottom; fight over black and white prostitutes; and when they must, work on the docks and in the neighboring vineyards.

Less dramatic and more expository than *Home to Harlem, Banjo* is as much a rejection of the black bourgeoisie and white civilization as it is a celebration of black folk values and cultural pluralism. By virtue of his itinerant life style, his talent as a folk musician—symbolized by the protagonist's nickname and ubiquitous instrument—and his instinctive joy, Banjo is a romantic prototype of the rootlessness, creativity, and spiritual resilience of the common people of the race. "Close association with the Jakes and Banjoes had been like participating in a common primitive birthright," thinks Ray, a fledgling writer who "wanted to hold on to his intellectual acquirements without losing his instinctive . . . black gifts of laughter and melody and simple sensuous feelings and responses." Whereas Ray loved "their rich reservoir of niggerisms" and "their natural gusto for living down the past . . . to go on gaily grinning in the present," he hated civilization for making black people, especially members of the middle class, ashamed and guilty about their warm human instincts. "Civilization," says the editorializing narrator, "had gone out among these native, earthy people, had despoiled them of their primitive soil, had uprooted, enchained, transported, and transformed them to labor under its laws, and yet lacked the spirit to tolerate them within its walls."[41] The twin cancerous growths of civilization are thus unsurprisingly identified as racism and commercialism. This incredibly oversimplistic contrast between black primitivism and white civilization (the apparent influence of popularized distortions of Freud and Marx) and the less than persuasive rhetorical projection of Ray as a synthesis of the two cultural extremes reveal the implied author's cultural ambivalence and predilection for folk romance.

The rural Jamaican setting, village characters, colorful dialogue, and tranquil mood of *Banana Bottom* make it the most conventional and successful of McKay's pastoral romances. Like Ray, Bita Plant, the heroine, is alienated from her ancestral roots by Western education and Christian values. Malcom and Priscilla Craig, white Protestant missionaries, respond to Bita's rape when she is twelve years old by a retarded village musician. They seek to redeem her from her past by adopting and sending her to England for the elite education that would qualify her to continue their work at Jubilee Mission. But upon her return, Bita finds the rigorous Christian life at the mission unnatural, and Harold Newton, the young theological student who was being assiduously groomed to be her husband, suddenly goes crazy and defiles himself with a goat. It is mainly the influence of a friendly white folklorist, Squire Gensir, that enables her to overcome the alienation of color, caste, and culture. " 'You're intolerant because of your education,' " he informs Bita. " 'Obeah is a part of your folklore, like your Anancy tales and your digging jammas. And your folklore is the spiritual link between you and your ancestral origin. You ought to learn to appreciate it as I do mine.' "[41] Squire Gensir also enables McKay to integrate much of the music, dance, speech, and religious custom of his native Jamaica into the structure of the narrative. Despite such weaknesses in plot and mood as Bita's melodramatic seduction in the wagon carrying her father's corpse, the assertion of her independence as a woman and the resolution of her cultural ambivalence by marriage to Jubban, a hardworking, humble farmer, are more insightful and successful than the static delineation of Ray: "She had no craving for Jubban to be other than what he was. . . . He accepted with natural grace the fact that she should excel in things to which she had been educated as he should in the work to which he had been trained. Her music, her reading, her thinking were the flowers of her intelligence and he the root in the earth upon which she was grafted, both nourished by the same soil."[42] In rewriting his pastoral Jamaican experience, McKay thus introduces into the tradition of the Afro-American novel a Caribbean male's romantic resolution of the socialized ambivalence and double-consciousness of deracinated black artists and intellectuals like Ray, with whom McKay closely identifies.

ZORA NEALE HURSTON (1891–1960)

Although Zora Neale Hurston's folk romances are set in the Deep South, they also emphasize the pastoral aspects of rural black life with which the author was familiar. By birth, personality, hard work, and academic training, Hurston was destined to achieve distinction for her imaginative use of ethnic folklore. Delivered by a white family friend while her father was on the road, she was born on January 7, 1891, instead of the usually cited January 1, 1901,[43] in the black town of Eatonville, Florida. Her father, a former Alabama sharecropper, was an itinerant preacher and self-employed carpenter who served three terms as mayor of Eatonville. He was disappointed that she was not a boy and resented her assertive, stubborn nature. In her relationship with whites, however, she seems, by her own admission and to some black friends, to have been cleverly ingratiating and accommodating. But, to biographer Robert Hemenway, "a more likely interpretation is that she refused to repudiate the folk origins that were such a rich part of her total identity."[44] Orphaned at nine by her mother and apparently unloved by her stepmother, she lived with relatives and friends until at sixteen she left Eatonville to work as a maid for a white singer in a traveling theatrical company. Aided by several white patrons and domestic jobs, she was educated at Howard University, Barnard College, where she became a protégée of Dr. Franz Boaz, and Columbia University, to which she received a fellowship to do advanced work in folklore and anthropology. Drawing on her unique folk and formal background for materials, Hurston won acclaim for her short stories and articles in *Opportunity* and other magazines during the close of the Harlem Renaissance and the Depression. She died in poverty and anonymity in St. Lucie County, Florida, in 1960. The superb biography by Robert Hemenway and the feminist movement's reassessment of her literary significance, spearheaded by Alice Walker, has led to the retrieval from obscurity of Hurston's two books of folklore; her three romances, *Jonah's Gourd Vine* (1934), *Their Eyes Were Watching God* (1937), and *Moses: Man of the Mountain* (1939); and her novel, *Seraph on the Suwanee* 1948).[45]

Jonah's Gourd Vine, as black critic Darwin Turner has observed, demonstrates Hurston's strengths and weaknesses as a novelist.[46] Her complete identification with folk values, her ear for language, and her lively imagination contribute to the vivid impressions and dramatic appeal of the narrative but distort its structure, characters, and mood. Using her womanizing father as a model for the antiheroic protagonist and the Bible to give symbolic significance to the plot, Hurston subordinates plot and character to the illustration of black folklore. The title of the book and its theme are an imaginative rewriting of Jon. 4:1–11. The biblical parable stresses God's mercy for the repentant sinners of Nineveh, whereas Hurston's narrative emphasizes God's judgment on the Reverend Pearson for his unregenerate lechery.

Set in Alabama and all-black Eatonville, the narrative divides into three movements. The first (chaps. 1–16) traces the rise of John Buddy Pearson from poverty as an illiterate field hand living on the wrong side of the creek to success as a lecherous preacher and wife-made tradesman-politician. The second (chaps. 17–23) follows his fall into disgrace at the hands of a vengeful, hoodoo-practicing second wife and envious friend. And the third (chaps. 24–25) is an abruptly rising and falling movement that focuses on his redemption by a wealthy third wife and death in a car accident after proving himself a contrite but incorrigible adulterer. In addition to

The Harlem Renaissance and the Search for New Modes of Narrative

the disproportionate length of these major parts, the narrative time is compressed or expanded at the expense of the logical development of plot and character. For example, John's return with his mother and brothers to Pearson's plantation to pick cotton is relegated to a subordinate clause, whereas the description of the barbecue following the harvest extends through five pages of dialogue, music, and dance. Mechanical shifts in time and melodramatic episodes also weaken the realistic characterization of Lucy Potts, the heroic first wife, and Hattie Tyson, the malicious second wife whom John divorces after discovering that she was conjuring him.

The language sparkles with colorful invective, metaphors, and folksayings. " 'You know Ahm uh fightin' dawg and muh hide is worth money,' " Amy taunts her husband. " 'Hit me if you dare! Ah'll wash yo' tub up 'gator guts and dat quick.' "[47] As illustrated in the opening sentence of the first chapter, even the omniscient author-narrator speaks in vivid folk metaphors: "God was grumbling his thunder and playing the zig-zag lightning thru his fingers." This usage is functional insofar as it contributes to the pastoral atmosphere of the narrative and reveals the author-narrator's intimacy and sympathy with her subject. Particularly effective is the Reverend Pearson's ten-page sermon, which vividly dramatizes the poetic gifts of the Southern black preacher. But frequently the use of metaphor, invective, and folksayings are inappropriate and improbable for the dramatic mood, indicating either a lack of control of the aesthetic distance between author-narrator and material or the exploitation of the language as an end in itself. This is particularly true of the beginning of several chapters and of Lucy's and John's dialogue, in which Hurston integrates lexical, idiomatic, and syntactical features in a credible Southern black dialect. In addition, because the Reverend Pearson's death is summarized rather than dramatized, the reader is detached from this tragic event and does not share the author-narrator's apparent sympathy for the protagonist. *Jonah's Gourd Vine* is therefore more successful as a celebration of the poetry of the Southern black folk preacher and of the moral strength and folk wisdom of a Southern black woman than it is as a realistic tragedy.

Their Eyes Were Watching God is Zora Neale Hurston's best romance. Its language is poetic without being folksy, its structure loose without being disjointed, its characters stylized without being exotic, and its theme of personal wholeness centered on egalitarianism in living and loving, especially in heterosexual relationships. As in *Jonah's Gourd Vine*, the third-person omniscient narrator and characters frequently speak in folk metaphors and evoke colorful nature images. The narrator's most vivid metaphors appear in descriptions of sunrise and sunset, such as "The sun was gone, but he had left his footprints in the sky" and "Every morning the world flung itself over and exposed the town."[48] Physical and human nature are organically related thematic signs.

The metaphorical style gives poetic intensity to the theme of sexual politics, which is expressed in the opening paragraphs of the narrative:

> Ships at a distance have every man's wish on board. For some they come in with the tide. For others they sail forever on the horizon, never out of sight, never landing until the Watcher turns his eyes away in resignation, his dreams mocked to death by Time. That is the life of men.
>
> Now, women forget all those things they don't want to remember, and remember everything they don't want to forget. The dream is the truth. Then they act and do things accordingly. (P. 5)

The inner forces that control the lives of men and women are different; some are driven by the need to possess things; others are moved by the need for a mutual relationship of sharing with people. Thus the dramatic tension in the narrative occurs between the efforts of Janie Mae Crawford, the heroine, to fulfill her dreams as a "coffee-and-cream" complexioned rural woman, and the conventions of a male-dominated, lower middle-class society that frustrate the realization of her romantic vision of love and fulfillment until she meets Vergible "Tea Cake" Woods.

The central episodes of the primary narrative, which is framed by Janie's passing on her story to her friend Pheoby and the fusion of symbols of natural and personal harmony, focus on the three men who challenge Janie's youthful concept of love and personal fulfillment. The first is Logan Killicks, an older man with property whom her plantation-born grandmother compels her to marry at sixteen so that men would not make "a work-ox," "a brood-sow," or "a spit cup" of her. With her unattractive, unromantic first husband, Janie learned that "marriage did not make love." The second is adventurous Joe Starks, who "did not represent sun-up and pollen and blooming trees, but he spoke for far horizon. He spoke for change and chance" (p. 28). Charmed into bigamy by Joe's dream of becoming "a big voice" in all-black Eatonville and by his whirlwind courtship, Janie is gradually robbed of her own dream by her second husband's authoritarianism, vanity, and abuse. With the death of Joe Starks and her youth, Tea Cake comes into her life, and her dream is fulfilled. A fun-loving, guitar-playing, crap-shooting, knife-carrying handsome young migrant, "he looked like the love thoughts of women. He could be a bee to a blossom—a pear tree blossom in the spring. . . . He was a glance from

God" (p. 90). Janie and Tea Cake marry and move to the Everglades, where they share the intense joy of working, playing, and living among black migrant workers. But in "the meanest moment of eternity," Janie kills her rabies-mad third husband in self-defense after the gun he aims at her misfires three times.

The major problems in the narrative are the awkward handling of point of view, especially the moral and emotional distance between the protagonist and her grandmother, and of time structure. Choosing to mix third-person omniscient, dramatic, and first-person modes of presentation, the implied author begins the frame story in the first chapter with the omniscient narrator metaphorically setting the mood, introducing the theme, and dramatizing the conflict between her enlightened, independent central character and the inhibiting conventions of her folk community. Grounded in the oral tradition of Southern blacks, from the gossip about Janie by the "mouthy" Eatonville community to the tales about Big John the Conqueror by "the great flame-throwers" in the Everglades, the plot begins nearly twenty-four years after the events to be narrated have taken place. With Janie's confident, content return after a year and a half to the curious, gossipy community of Eatonville, the stage is set for her to tell her close friend Pheoby, with whom she has "been kissin' friends for twenty years," about the events leading to her return. " 'To start off wid,' " Janie says, " 'people like dem wastes up too much time puttin' they mouf on things they don't know nothin' about. Now they got to look into me loving Tea Cake and see whether it was done right or not! They don't know if life is a mess of cornmeal dumplings, and if love is a bed-quilt!' " (pp. 9–10). Rather than Janie's first-person narration taking over from this point, the implied author switches half-way into the second chapter to the point of view of Janie's grandmother Nanny, and in the third and subsequent chapters the omniscient narrator controls the flow of past events. Although this heightens the dramatic impact of Nanny's character, it diminishes the reader's emotional involvement with and moral sympathy for Janie, who boldly asserts the power to speak in a signifying confrontation with Joe Starks in chapters six and seven, but whose first-person narration resumes only in the close of the frame in the final two pages of the story. On the other hand, Hurston's mixture of points of view and time gives her more latitude to introduce farce, a mock-heroic funeral, and folktales into the narrative, especially in the sixth chapter.

A closer look at the relationship between Nanny and Janie reveals that the implied author philosophically and emotionally identifies with her protagonist's rejection of her family as she pursues love and adventure.

Raised until six in the backyard of "the quality white folks" for whom her grandmother worked, Janie awakened to the possibilities of love and life at sixteen. After spending a spring afternoon watching bees pollinating a blossoming pear tree—the symbol of love, marriage, and procreation— Janie is seen by her grandmother allowing a boy to kiss her. This episode reminds Nanny of her experience during slavery of being impregnated by her master, of her seventeen-year-old daughter's rape, impregnation, and dissolution, and of her own imminent death, and reinforces her moral imperative to protect her granddaughter. Nanny is determined that before she dies Janie will marry Logan Killicks, thereby, in the narrator's words, "desecrating" Janie's pear-tree vision. Nanny assures Janie of her love and passes on to her the ancient lessons about racial, sexual, and class politics that she has learned:

> "Honey, de white man is de ruler of everything as fur as Ah been able tuh find out. Maybe it's some place way off in de ocean where de black man is in power, but we don't know nothin' but what we see. So de white man throw down de load and tell de nigger man tuh pick it up. He hand it to his womenfolks. De nigger woman is de mule uh de world so fur as Ah can see. Ah been prayin' fuh it tuh be different wid you. Lawd, Lawd, Lawd. . . . You ain't got nobody but me. . . . Ah got tuh try and do for you befo' mah head is cold."
> (Pp. 16–17)

Whereas the implied author seems here to share philosophically in Nanny's ancient wisdom, she is closer emotionally and morally, as we shall see, to her protagonist's desire " 'tuh utilize mahself all over' " (p. 94).

Because she was born in slavery, Nanny tells Janie, " 'it wasn't for me to fulfill my dreams of whut a woman oughta be and do. . . . But nothing can't stop you from wishin'. You can't beat nobody down so low till you can rob 'em of they will' " (p. 17). Nanny's dream was " 'to preach a great sermon about colored women sittin' on high, but they wasn't no pulpit for me' " (p. 18). In coping with slavery and unwed motherhood, she sacrificed her own dreams of economic security and moral respectability for the benefit of a daughter who " 'would expound what Ah felt.' " When her daughter Leafy " 'got lost offa de highway,' " however, Nanny " 'save de text' " for Janie, believing that her sacrifices were not too much if Janie " 'just take a stand on high ground lak Ah dreamed' " (p. 18). After passing on the text of her dream of self-realization as a woman—of developing self-esteem, security, and status in marriage—Nanny begs Janie: " 'Have

---

some sympathy fuh me. Put me down easy, Janie, Ah'm a cracked plate' "
(p. 21). However, Janie and the implied author reject not only Nanny's
dream of what a woman ought to be and do, but also—and this is a major
flaw in the tradition of female friendship and shared understanding that
feminist readings of the text celebrate[49]—never really understand or share
the "ancient power" of her love and sacrifice to provide a better life for
her family.

Janie is more faithful to her symbolic significance as a Bodacious
Woman—an individualist who audaciously rebels against social conventions and rejects family in pursuit of her romantic personal interests,
dreams, and development—than to traditional poor black women who
respect the sturdy bridges of kinship, male and female, that helped them
to survive the pitfalls of life. Janie is alienated from both the legitimate
and the spurious middle-class values of the black community. Rejecting
the economic security that Nanny and most black women dream of as a
cornerstone of marriage, a youthful Janie " 'wants things sweet wid mah
marriage lak when you sit under a pear tree and think' " (p. 24). She later
confuses Joe Starks's line that she was " 'made to sit on de front porch' "
with her pious grandmother's dream that she " 'just take a stand on high
ground,' " scornfully accusing her grandmother of wanting her to " 'Git
up on uh high chair' " and to sit " 'on porches lak de white madam' " (p.
96). In contrast to Janie's personal feeling that lower middle-class black
life is unexciting and unfulfilling, her friend Pheoby says: " 'Maybe so,
Janie. Still and all Ah'd love tuh experience it for just one year. It look lak
heben tuh me from where Ah'm at' " (p. 96). For Janie romance is more
important than finance in marriage and common folk less inhibited and
pretentious than middle-class people. Rebelling against the class that Tea
Cake calls "high muckty mucks" and Joe's his-and-hers gold-looking spit-
toons to remarry and go down "on the muck" with someone both poorer
and younger than herself, Janie states: " 'Dis ain't no business proposition,
and no race after property and titles. Dis is uh love game. Ah done lived
Grandma's way, now Ah means tuh live mine' " (p. 96). Of the envious,
more often ambivalent, lower middle-class community of Eatonville,
where she endured, even if she did not enjoy, power and privilege for
twenty years as Mrs. Mayor Starks, and to which she returns an autonomous new woman, Janie feels: " 'If God don't think no mo' 'bout 'em
then Ah do, they's a lost ball in de high grass' " (p. 9).

After her husband Joe Starks's death, which she symbolically helped to
precipitate by attacking his male vanity in front of his peers with the power

of her verbal wit (" 'When you pull down yo' britches, you look lak de change uh life' " [p. 69]), Janie, at thirty-nine, takes stock of her life by reflecting on her mother and grandmother:

> Digging around inside of herself like that she found that she had no interest in that seldom-seen mother at all. She hated her grandmother and had hidden it from herself all these years under a cloak of pity. She had been getting ready for her great journey to the horizons in search of *people;* it was important to all the world that she should find them and they find her. But she had been whipped like a cur dog, and run off down a back road after *things.* It was all according to the way you see things. Some people could look at a mud-puddle and see an ocean with ships. But Nanny belonged to that other kind that love to deal in scraps.

Nanny had taken the biggest thing God ever made,

> the horizon—for no matter how far a person can go the horizon is still way beyond you—and pinched it in to such a little bit of a thing that she could tie it about her granddaughter's neck tight enough to choke her. She hated the old woman who had twisted her so in the name of love. Most humans didn't love one another nohow, and this mis-love was so strong that even common blood couldn't overcome it all the time. (Pp. 76–77)

What are we to make of Janie's inability and unwillingness to identify with her mother and grandmother, especially in light of the high price they paid for their and her survival?

If Janie does not identify with the historic slavery and sexual exploitation of her female ancestors, can she realistically represent a tradition of female friendship, understanding, and support? Are Janie's security, respectability, and individuality determined only by her sexual ties to Joe Starks? Is the grandmother's dream for Janie to " 'take a stand on high ground' " really reducing life to the pursuit of material things? Although the symbol of the horizon is a poetically effective expression of the possibilities of life, is it just, compassionate, or responsible for Janie to despise the love and dreams of parents whose historical circumstances and consciousness influence them to interpret the possibilities of life within the context of traditional strategies of survival? Is it possible, in short, to cut oneself off completely from one's parents and past and fully realize one's identity as an individual? For Janie, the love of Tea Cake, idealized life of folk on the "muck," and friendship with Pheoby are the only human relationships she needs to attain and sustain personal wholeness, however problematic this may seem for some readers.

In closing the frame of what Alice Walker, her literary daughter, calls "one of the sexiest, most 'healthily' rendered heterosexual love stories in our literature,"[50] Hurston returns to her thematic metaphors. " 'Ah done ben tuh de horizon and back,' " Janie tells Pheoby, " 'and now Ah kin set heah in mah house and live by comparisons.' " The memory of the love she shared with Tea Cake, especially in the upstairs bedroom, not only sustains her in his death but also, by the allegorical manner that she passes it on, inspires Pheoby: " 'Ah done growed ten feet higher from jus' listenin' tuh you, Janie. Ah ain't satisfied wid mahself no mo'. Ah means tuh make Sam take me fishin' wid him after this' " (p. 158). Reinforcing the centrality of Janie's love of Tea Cake to her fulfillment as a woman, Hurston tells us in the closing lines of the narrative that Tea Cake "wasn't dead. He could never be dead until she herself had finished feeling and thinking. The kiss of his memory made pictures of love and light against the wall. Here was peace. She pulled in her horizon like a great fish-net. Pulled it from around the waist of the world and draped it over her shoulder. So much of life in its meshes! She called in her soul to come and see" (p. 159). The tragic irony here is that Janie is probably dying from Tea Cake's biting her as she cradled him in her arms after shooting him. The implied author and heroine of *Their Eyes Were Watching God* therefore suggest that genuine love between a man and a woman is an exhilarating, fulfilling relationship of mutual respect, sharing, and sacrifice. Rather than exclusively female, however, the tradition that Hurston passes on through Janie is black, oral, and Southern. It was acquired by listening to and participating in the telling of "lies" by men in Florida as well as by the storytelling of her grandmother. The theme, symbolism, style, structure, and characterization of the narrative combine to impress the reader with the validity and power of this romantic folk vision of what a woman ought to be and do.

Hurston's final two long narratives are strikingly different in form and style. *Moses: Man of the Mountain* turns the Old Testament legend of Moses into a satiric tale of racial oppression, the vices of modern-day blacks, and the virtues of a great messiah. The emphasis is on the ingratitude of the oppressed and on the heroic character and mystic powers (the hoodoo) of a great leader. Because the style relies more on black idiom than on slang, quaint spelling, and folksayings, the dialogue here, unlike earlier books, does not attract attention to itself but complements Hurston's adaptation of biblical language and standard English. The indirect satirical portrayal of the vices and folly of the Hebrew slaves as those of modern-day oppressed blacks unfortunately borders on low comedy. In contrast, *Seraph on the Suwanee* is neither comic, nor folkloristic, nor about blacks. It is a psychological study of Arvay Henson, a neurotic, poor white Floridian whose prejudices and insecurity lead to the tragic disintegration of her family. Although it is Zora Neale Hurston's most ambitious and most mimetic long narrative, its focus on whites places it outside the scope of this study. In retrospect, Hurston's legacy to other novelists and romancers is the most compelling modern feminist vision of an autonomous woman and inspirational love story in the tradition of the Afro-American novel.

Except for *Home to Harlem*, the romances and novels of Claude McKay and Zora Neale Hurston were published after the Harlem Renaissance had peaked. With the crash of the stock market in 1929 and the beginning of economic depression in 1930, the Harlem vogue began its rapid decline. The immediate literary reaction of Hurston and several other novelists was a more intense personal search for modern forms of ancestralism, of continuity of the folk tradition. George Henderson's *Ollie Miss* (1935) and George Lee's *River George* (1937), for example, also expose the legendary lives of common people who live on the economic and political margins of society. Although the thematic scope of the folk romances of McKay, Hurston (except for *Their Eyes Were Watching God*), Henderson, and Lee is narrow, their unaffected language, bold explorations of the economic, spiritual, and sexual drives behind the violence of black male-female relationships, and emphasis on the color and caste problems of black lovers reveal undercurrents of folk realism and the continuing search for a usable past on which to build a more viable, humanistic future.

Folk Realism: Religion, Music, Humor, and Language

Unlike the narratives of McKay and Hurston, in which realistic details are used in the service of romance, the novels of Langston Hughes and Countee Cullen focus on the everyday life of ordinary churchgoing black folk. The allegiance of these authors is more to a rendering of representative than marginal or allegorical types. Whether in the big city or a small town, their characters are less idealized, their settings less exotic, and their plots less melodramatic. Their novels strive for the truth of a particular environment and the social rituals of common folk rather than for the truth of the world at large and the life-style of street people and migrants. Although each truth has some validity, neither in isolation tells the whole truth of the myriad faces of the black experience in America during the 1920s and 1930s.

During the 1920s Harlem reigned supreme as the cultural capital of the New Negro movement. Between 1900 and 1925 the white neighborhood in the heart of Manhattan—roughly from 125th Street to 145th Street, south to north, and from the Harlem River to 8th Avenue, east to west—was transformed into a black metropolis. From all points on the globe people flocked to the city within a city, searching for shelter or stardom or swinging times: emigrants from Africa and the West Indies as well as migrants from the South; young, gifted, and black artists from across the land; white blue-collar workers and blue bloods from Europe; and white publishers, dilettantes, and bohemians from downtown Manhattan. Harlem was the cosmopolitan black showcase of the nation, a "Promised Land" for some and "Playland" for others.

But for thousands of transplanted cotton pickers, tobacco choppers, and cane cutters, adjustment to the complexity of an exploitative, industrialized urban environment made the big city a spurious paradise. Exploited as cheap labor and barred by color from full participation in their society, including some of the night clubs (e.g., the Cotton Club) in their own community, the black masses spooled out their lives in an arabesque pattern of hard work and synthetic joy: "going to meet the man," "slaving for Miss Ann," or "running a game on lames"; attending a house party or gin joint with jumping music on Saturday nights; and taking their troubles to the Lord in prayer and song on Sunday. These were the rituals of survival for the plain folk of Harlem and, with less intensity and sophistication, Kansas. "The ordinary Negroes," Hughes tells us in *The Big Sea*, "hadn't heard of the Negro Renaissance. And if they had, it hadn't raised their wages any."[51] With the possible exception of Zora Neale Hurston and Rudolph Fisher, Hughes and Cullen were more successful in providing a realistic portrayal of the ways in which ordinary black folk used religion, music, humor, and language to cope with adversity than their counterparts.

JAMES LANGSTON HUGHES (1902–67)

Born in Joplin, Missouri, in 1902, Langston Hughes was raised in Lawrence, Kansas, and Cleveland, Ohio, by his grandmother and mother. His father, James Hughes, deserted the family while Langston was still in diapers. Upon completing high school, Langston visited his father in Mexico before matriculating at Columbia University in 1921. The sights and sounds of a burgeoning Harlem distracted him from his studies and, to his father's disgust, deepened his love for the spirit, rhythms, and colors of his people. Settling in Harlem, he worked at odd jobs until economic discrimination, racial prejudice, and family problems drove him to ship out to sea on a cargo vessel in 1923. After traveling to West Africa and Europe, Hughes returned to Harlem in 1924 and the following year entered Lincoln University in Pennsylvania with the help of an elderly white patron, Mrs. Rufus Osgood Mason, who subsidized Hurston and other black artists at various times. This time he was determined to attain both a degree and a livelihood as a writer.

A highly prolific and versatile artist, Hughes was widely regarded as the poet of his people. He took the world for his audience but the lives of ordinary black people for his principal subject. His first volumes of verse, *The Weary Blues* (1926) and *Fine Clothes to the Jew* (1927), introduced jazz and blues into poetry and, in their sympathetic portraits of street people and the working class, reveal an exquisite sense of the ironic and melodramatic nature of the black American experience. The music of his poetry was the sound of Lenox Avenue, Seventh Street, and South State Street; and his language has been appropriately called Harlemese: vibrant, rhythmic, direct, and racy. During his more than forty years of literary creativity and his reign as the poet laureate of black America, Hughes published seventeen volumes of verse, eleven plays, three collections of short stories, four collections of the folk wisdom of Jesse B. Semple,[52] several anthologies, librettos, and radio scripts, numerous books for children, and articles, as well as two novels: *Not Without Laughter* (1930) and *Tambourines to Glory* (1958).

Not Without Laughter is the story of a black boy growing up in Stanton, a small Kansas town, in the 1920s. With fidelity to time and place, Hughes uses the education of Sandy Williams, the protagonist, to illuminate the importance of religion, music, humor, and language in the lives of ordinary black folk. These cultural forms enable blacks to repress and sublimate hardships as they pursue a better life for themselves and future generations. The plot traces the influence of Sandy's family on his emerging values. With more than twenty of the thirty chapters devoted to the role of his grandmother, Aunt Hager Williams, and her youngest daughter, Aunt Harriett, in shaping Sandy's identity, Hughes reveals the strengths and weaknesses of a matrifocal black family. Aunt Hager is delineated as a hardworking, pious black widow who supports her family by taking in washing and who teaches her grandson that despite racial injustice " 'there ain't no room in this world fo' nothin' but love.' " Feeling that she has failed in raising her three daughters, her goal in life is to see Sandy get a good education and become a great leader like Booker T. Washington. Although her religiosity inhibits the family's capacity to laugh at life, she teaches Sandy the meaning of love and sacrifice.

Less convincingly drawn than the grandmother but no less interesting as characters are Aunt Hager's three daughters: the biggest disappointment in her life. Seared by racism, Harriett is an embittered, rebellious youth who rejects her mother's narrow religiosity, hates whites and class bigotry. Harriett's talent as a singer and determination to live an independent, rich life enable her to rise from prostitution to become the princess of the blues. Annjee, Sandy's mother, is a dark, heavy-set domestic who considers herself lucky to be married to "a light, strong, good-looking young husband," even though, as her mother constantly reminds her, he is rarely home and seldom works. Tempy, the oldest daughter, is the "stuckup and dicty" imitator of the ways of white folks. The pretentious, class-conscious wife of a mail-clerk and owner of several houses, she becomes an Episcopal convert and avoids her mother and sisters out of shame of their "niggerish" ways.

Whereas Aunt Hager is the symbol of Christian love and charity in the family, Jimboy, Sandy's father, is the symbol of laughter and song. Unlike McKay's Banjo and Hurston's Tea Cake, his delineation reveals more than the alleged rootless freedom and instinctive joy of the race. A guitar-playing, blues-singing, traveling man, Jimboy and the other black men in town could not find steady, well-paying work in Stanton. " 'The white folks,' " says Jimboy with cutting irony, " 'are like farmers that own all the cows and let the niggers take care of 'em. Then they make you pay a sweet price for skimmed milk and keep the cream for themselves—but I reckon cream's too rich for rusty kneed niggers anyhow!' "[53] When Jimboy was home, "all the neighborhood could hear his rich low baritone voice giving birth to the blues." He was so good at it as a young man that W. C. Handy had once advised him to turn professional, but he was too restless and adventurous to heed the advice. Older and still restless, he amuses himself in Stanton by teaching Harriett to sing "the old Southern songs, the popular rag-time ditties, and the hundreds of varying verses of the blues that he would pick up in the big dirty cities of the South" (p. 50). In time Harriett also becomes a consummate artist at sublimating personal pain and suffering through song and dance. Thus from his father and young aunt, Sandy learns that music, dancing, and laughter are as important as religion in coping with racial injustice and economic insecurity.

The omniscient author-narrator's ear for language is most vividly demonstrated in "the rambling talk of old colored folks." The dialogue of Aunt Hager and her elderly neighbors, Sister Whiteside and Madam de Carter, sparkles with the lexical and syntactical features of black English. Commenting on the cyclone that has just carried off Aunt Hager's porch, Madam de Carter says sympathetically: " 'But praise God for sparing our lives! It might've been worse, Sister Williams! It might've been much more calamitouser! As it is, I lost nothin' more'n a chimney and two washtubs which was settin' in the back yard. A few trees broke down don't 'mount to nothin'. We's livin' ain't we? And we's more important than trees is any day!' " (p. 7). More important for Sandy's introduction to language is Cudge Wilson's pool hall, the center for educating young black males in the oral tradition and compensatory laughter. Because the local YMCA was segregated, black youth went to the pool hall to play billiards, shoot dice, watch passing girls, and talk. Deepening our understanding of the relationship of the oral tradition to Sandy's character, the author-narrator informs us that often

> arguments would begin—boastings, proving and fending; or telling of exploits with guns, knives, and razors, with cops and detectives, with evil women and wicked men; out-bragging and out-lying one another, all talking at once. . . . No matter how belligerent or lewd their talk was, or how sordid the tales they told—of dangerous pleasures and strange perversities—these black men laughed . . . because to them, no matter how hard life might be, it was not without laughter. (Pp. 250–51)

This sympathetic portrayal of the common folk and Sandy's kinship with Cudge Wilson rather than Tempy's refined friends are clear indications of the implied author's message.

Through Sandy, Hughes affirms what in his judgment are the best values of black American character and culture, glossing over the sexism of the oral tradition that Hurston foregrounds. At the end of the novel Sandy resolves to emulate the most progressive and creative values of his race and family. He rejects his grandmother's Christian fundamentalism, but promises to fulfill her dream for him to become a great man. He disapproves of his father's irresponsibility and aimlessness, but embraces Harriett's vibrant spirit and independence. He dislikes Tempy's dull friends and urge to whiteness, but aspires to buy his own home. He refuses his Uncle Siles's notion that blacks never have anything because they are " 'clowns, jazzers, just a band of dancers,' " for the more valid explanation that they are "dancers because of their poverty; singers because they suffered; laughing all the time because they must forget" (p. 293). And he disregards invidious distinctions among historical black leaders by choosing Booker T. Washington, W. E. B. Du Bois, and Frederick Douglass for his heroes. For these reasons, *Not Without Laughter* is an illuminating, realistic portrayal of how black boys have historically carved their identities out of the combined paradoxes of their ethnic and national heritage, of how generations have helped to enslave or liberate future generations.

More melodramatic and ironic than his first novel, *Tambourines to Glory* is a comic novel about the attitude of simple black urban folk toward religion. The narrative structure grows out of the contrasting motives and joint efforts of two Harlem women who exploit that "religious jive" by founding a sanctified church. In dramatizing the rise of their church from street-corner meetings with Bible and tambourines to the majestic Tambourine Temple with its chorus and orchestra, the undramatized omniscient author-narrator, who is morally and intellectually superior to his characters, contrasts Essie Belle Johnson's indolence, compassion, and blind faith with Laura Reed's unscrupulous pursuit of "Men, wine and something fine." Preying on the desperation and gullibility of the poor, Laura and her boyfriend Buddy sell counterfeit "holy" water and lucky lottery numbers in the church until Buddy's infidelity drives Laura to murder him and frame Essie for the crime. "Religion has got no business being made into a gyp game," Essie finally realizes in her interior monologue just before the denouement. "Whatever part of God is in anybody is not to be played with—and everybody has got a part of God in them."[54] This theme takes a different turn in Countee Cullen's *One Way to Heaven.*

COUNTEE PORTER CULLEN (1903–46)

Despite the cloud of mystery fostered by Countee Cullen about his early life, it is generally accepted that he was born in New York on May 30, 1903, adopted by the Rev. and Mrs. Frederick Cullen, the founder of Salem Methodist Episcopal Church in Harlem, and raised in the conservative atmosphere of the parsonage. The most highly educated and technically proficient traditional lyricist of the Harlem Renaissance, Cullen saw his first poetry in print while he was still a student at De Witt Clinton High School. Before graduating from New York University with Phi Beta Kappa honors in 1925, he published his first widely acclaimed volume of verse, *Color.* By 1926, when he received his master of arts degree from Harvard and was appointed associate editor of *Opportunity,* he had won first- or second-place prize in several nationwide poetry contests. In technique his verse is strongly influenced by Keats and Shelley, and in theme, by racial ambivalence that vacillates between African ancestralism and Western classicism. This ambivalence is apparent in the moral paradoxes and use of irony in his six volumes of verse, two children's books, anthology, and single novel—*One Way to Heaven*.

Divided into two major parts, *One Way to Heaven*, like Hughes's *Tambourines to Glory*, is a sympathetic exposure of the gullibility and superstition of unsophisticated lower-class urban blacks. It is the love story of Sam Lucas, a one-armed confidence man who fakes religious conversion at black churches up and down the Eastern seaboard to satisfy his immediate physical needs, and Mattie Johnson, an attractive but desperate young domestic whose religious zeal Sam awakens with his con game. At revival meetings and watch-night services, Sam goes into his act at a dramatic moment during testimonials. Walking from the rear of the church to the mourner's bench, he would throw down a greasy deck of cards and polished razor, fall on his knees in tears, and sob for salvation. To devout Methodists and Baptists, Sam's last-minute conversion was "mystery and miracle and the confirmation of faith." As they came forward to shake hands with the converts and show their gratitude, many of the faithful would secretly slip him money, and "he had never joined church yet but it had led to an affair." In Part 1 (chap. 1–7) Sam's act in a Harlem church becomes the catalyst for Mattie's salvation, and in blind faith she marries him. In Part 2 (chaps. 8–15) her religiosity drives him into the arms of another woman. But a fatal case of double pneumonia brings them together again, and for her sake he fakes a deathbed conversion.

The author-narrator's mild ridicule of the superstitious practices of his lower-class characters is in sharp contrast to his sardonic treatment of the pretentious customs of the black bourgeoisie. Sam, for example, uses his cards and razor for both good and evil, and though an indolent, irreligious vagabond, his excessive pragmatism evokes our sympathetic laughter. Equally humorous and realistic is Mattie's Aunt Mandy, whom the third-person omniscient author-narrator describes in the sympathetic manner that characterizes the frequent commentaries on the beliefs and rituals of the lower class: "Though she was not averse to trusting serenely to the ways of Providence, she often attempted by reading tea leaves and coffee dregs, and by consulting her cards, to speed the blessings of Heaven or to ward off, if possible, some celestial chastisement."[55] In contrast, the language used in chapters 8, 9, and 10 to describe Constancia Brandon, Mattie's well-bred but patronizing black employer, and her high-society crowd is characterized by biting wit, repartee, and hyperbole.

A Boston-born Baptist, Constancia Brandon changed her name at sixteen and rejected "the religious ecstasies of the Baptist and Methodist faiths . . . to scale the heavenly ramparts by way of the less rugged paths of the Episcopalian persuasion" (p. 91). Constancia's "tongue was her chief attraction, ornament, and deterrent." At Radcliffe she was called Lady Macbeth, not because she was unsexed and shrewd in the pursuit of her ambition, but because she never spoke in a monosyllable when she could use a polysyllable. Her monthly soirees were pompous, gala occasions. Although these innumerable gatherings were held "under the uninviting and prosaic auspices of the Booklovers' Society," it was widely known and admitted by more than half of the group itself that they never read books. Now and then, however, "they might under pressure, purchase the latest opus of some Negro novelist or poet" (p. 147). The core of this polyglot group of booklovers, friends, and social parasites includes Sarah Desverney, a local librarian for whom "no Negro had written anything of import since Dunbar and Chesnutt"; Bradley Norris, a radical poet "to whom everything not New Negro was anathema"; Samuel Weinstein, a caustic self-appointed Negrophile and authority on Negro life; and Mrs. Harold De Peyster Johnson, a race-conscious public school teacher on whom the author-narrator heaps more than four pages of blistering scorn: "She had, as it were, midwifed at the New Negro's birth, and had groaned in spirit with the travail and suffering of Ethiopia in delivering herself to this black *enfant terrible*, born capped and gowned, singing, "The Negro National Anthem" and clutching in one hand a pen, in the other a paintbrush" (p. 150). Whether humorous or witty, amused or contemptuous, Cullen's satire is generally indirect, and his motives are most clearly revealed in Constancia's explanation for inviting the Negrophobic Professor Calhoun to address the Booklovers' Society on "The Menace of the Negro to Our American Civilization." " 'An irrefutable evidence of a sense of humor . . . is the ability to laugh at oneself, as well as at one's tormentors and defamers,' " she says, " 'If we haven't learned that in these three hundred years, we have made sorry progress' " (p. 167).

Even though the chapters depicting black high society sparkle with wit, farce, caricature, and repartee, they have at best a tenuous connection to the moral theme of the narrative, which is symbolized in the bond between Sam and Aunt Mandy. For them and the ministers, Johnson and Drummond, life is ambiguous; the ways of God mysterious; and "there were more ways to Heaven than one" (p. 226). The moral ambiguity of Sam's life is apparent in the use of his cards and razor. In response to his question about whether cards were evil, Aunt Mandy, the moral center of the novel, replies, " 'It all depends on the kind of cards you have and what you do with them' " (p. 58). Although a staunch Methodist, Aunt Mandy relies on the power of conjuration as well as on the songs and emotionalism of her church to affirm her faith in love and life. During prayer service, she was as fervent in her singing, rocking back and forth, and moaning as the other "aging handmaidens of the Lord." She felt that it was all right to be lost in the inner life, "but there were things in this other life which were more important. And loving was one." When Mattie was losing Sam to another woman, Aunt Mandy advises her that " 'sometimes when the angels is too busy to help you, you have to fight the devil with his own tools' " (p. 239). After sleeping three nights on the cards and razor which were baptized in Madam Samantha's magic water, Mattie is suddenly reunited with Sam. Thus, the plot, characters, and style of *One Way to Heaven* point with wry humor to more than one way to heaven.

In addition to the convincing portrayals of commonplace church-going people, the novels of Cullen and Hughes provide interesting contrasts in narrative technique and the handling of time. In *Not Without Laughter*, a *bildungsroman*, and *Tambourines to Glory*, a low comedy, the emphasis is on dramatizing events in order to heighten immediacy and verisimilitude; represented and representational time are frequently congruent; and showing predominates over telling. In contrast, *One Way to Heaven*, a mixture of satiric comedy and comedy of manners, relies heavily on the author-narrator's commentary on plot, character, and theme to make explicit and to expand the ironic pattern of the narrative; the time-ratio is manipulated to facilitate analysis of character; and telling predominates over showing. There is little emotional but considerable moral and intellectual distance between the author-narrators and their protagonists. The relationship of the reader to the protagonists, however, is less simple. Because the authors permit Sandy and Sam to tell only part of their stories and then only in the third person, much of the reader's sympathy for them is sacrificed, which is a more serious weakness in *Not Without Laughter* than in *One Way to Heaven*. Because in *Tambourines to Glory* Essie tells much of her inherently comic story in the first-person, our emotional attachment to her is stronger. Finally, because Cullen exploits irony, ambiguity, and symbolism more self-consciously than Hughes, he appeals to the reader's intellectual interests but risks more serious flaws in structure and character as he moves from the realistic to the satiric mode.

Satiric Realism: The Vices and Follies of the Folk and Black Bourgeoisie

The conventions of satire, particularly irony, as illustrated in chapter 1, were employed by early Afro-American novelists, but it was not until the decline of the Harlem Renaissance that satiric realism fully emerged in the tradition of the Afro-American novel.[56] Stripping away the disguise of romantic characters (white knights, fair damsels, black buffoons, and savages), oratory (set speeches and stylized conversations), and situations (white paternalism and male domination as eternal laws of nature), several black writers of the Harlem Renaissance turned to comedy and satire for models to depict the ordinary experience of blacks. Whereas comedy, as in Hughes's *Tambourines to Glory*, is basically a humorous representation of the everyday life of lowbrow characters for its own sake, satire, as in Cullen's *One Way to Heaven*, has a clear moral aim. But because the black American experience has historically been a mixture of the comic and the tragic, and because the black novelist's audience has been largely white and middle class, Hurston, Hughes, and Cullen as well as the most talented black satirists of the period—Rudolph Fisher, George Schuyler, and Wallace Thurman—generally combined the conventions of both forms in their narratives. Although the era gave license to authors to parade the follies and vices of marginal types as ethnic virtues and cultural truths, the black satirists assumed the role of moralists revealing the truth beneath the mask of surface reality.

Satire has historically been defended as a moral weapon, and the satirist as a defender of truth, justice, and reason. In *The Power of Satire* Robert C. Elliott traces the development of satire from its ancient origins in magic, myth, and ritual to sophisticated modern literary forms in western Europe and England.[57] Beginning with the improvised invective in Greek phallic songs, Elliott moves quickly to other times and places to describe the use of magical words and ritual phrases by satirical poets in Arabia, Ireland, Africa, and Alaska. These poets use satire to destroy the honor, wealth, health, or lives of personal and public enemies. Although satirists in pre-literate cultures relied on the belief of their victims in the efficacy of their apparent preternatural power, the power itself was not derived so much from secret incantations and the mechanics of sympathetic magic as from the satirist's command over the word.[58] Legends, tales, and sagas in the different cultures reveal the pervasive ancient belief that people actually died from the attacks of satirists. As Janie Crawford's destruction of her husband with razor sharp wit and words in *Their Eyes Were Watching God* illustrates, verbal abuse and ridicule, depending on the valuation placed on the opinion of others, are potent weapons for social control or liberation.

Using the guilt-shame anthropological model,[59] Elliott describes not only the potency of criticism, shame, and rejection in societies that rely on external sanctions to govern behavior, but also the therapeutic function of ritualized ridicule in releasing pent-up aggressive impulses. Ritualized ridicule, as I explained in the first chapter, takes several forms in black American culture, including signifying, sounding, and playing the dozens. Because satire always contains an implicit or explicit set of normative values, and because the satirist generally represents himself as a responsible critic of men and manners, as a writer who prefers to expose vice and folly through indirection, it is not surprising that the chief device of black satirists is irony. Basically, narrative irony is the result of a disparity of viewpoints among characters, narrator, and reader, and, in more sophisticated works of structural irony, between narrator and author. The uses of satire and irony in the Afro-American novel range from the simple effects of Rudolph Fisher, George Schuyler, and Wallace Thurman during the Harlem Renaissance to the extraordinary complexity of modern and contemporary novelists.

RUDOLPH FISHER (1897–1934)

One of the most witty, talented, and admired Harlem Renaissance artists, Rudolph Fisher successfully combined careers in literature and medicine. The son of a minister, he was born in 1897 in Washington, D.C., but grew up in Providence, Rhode Island, and graduated from Brown University with Phi Beta Kappa honors in 1919. Returning to Washington, he attended medical school at Howard University and graduated with highest honors in 1924. After marriage and an internship at Freedman's Hospital, he moved to New York to specialize in roentgenology at Columbia University and to pursue his interest in writing fiction. Perhaps his best and most representative story is "City of Refuge," a satirical treatment of the urbanization of a black Southern migrant. It first appeared in the *Atlantic Monthly* in 1925. Additional stories appeared in such magazines as *The Crisis, Opportunity, McClure's, American Mercury,* and *Story*. At the same time, Fisher was publishing medical articles in the *Journal of Infectious Diseases*. Before his death in 1934, he also published two novels: *The Walls of Jericho* (1928) and *The Conjure-Man Dies* (1932). The latter was produced as a folk play at the Layfayette Theatre in Harlem in 1936.

The Walls of Jericho is a satirical treatment of prejudice and self-delusion.

The Harlem Renaissance and the Search for New Modes of Narrative

Structured around a remote, incongruous analogy between the biblical legend of Joshua and the legendary Joshua Jones, a black furniture mover, the novel reveals Fisher's ironic view of the walls people build around their neighborhoods and themselves. In its modern context the legend signifies the external reality of the color line that encircled the growing Harlem colony during the 1920s and the disparity between the surface behavior and deeper self of the characters. The main theme is dramatically introduced early in the first of the six major sections of the novel. Fred Merrit, a fair-skinned lawyer, assaults the color line when he buys a house on Court Avenue, the most exclusive white residential street adjacent to black Harlem. A racial chauvinist, Merrit confesses that though " 'I'd enjoy this house, if they let me alone, purely as an individual, just the same I'm entering it as a Negro. I hate fays. Always have. Always will. Chief joy in life is making them uncomfortable. And if this doesn't do it—I'll quit the bar.' "[60] Color and class prejudice are therefore the chief objects of Fisher's satire. Because white resistance to black neighbors had resulted in riots and terrorism, Merrit hires the toughest furniture movers in Harlem to move him into the hostile white neighborhood. The moving crew is Jinx Jenkins and Bubber Brown, minor comic characters, and is supervised by big, strong Joshua Jones, a legendary piano mover and the main character, whose surface toughness conceals a compassionate heart, which is sympathetically revealed through the agency of his girlfriend, Linda Young.

Midway through the novel the legend of Joshua and its modern interpretation are explained, first in the black vernacular of Joshua and then in the formal words of Tod Bruce, an Episcopal minister. Joshua's folk version of the formal sermon actually serves a double function for the omniscient author-narrator. First, it establishes the intellectual distance between author-narrator and main character, and second, it reveals the author-narrator's sympathy for the working class by burlesquing the pomp and ceremony of middle-class religious rituals. In colorful, irreverent dialect, Joshua tells about " 'a bird named Joshua' " who " 'thought he was the owl's bowels, till one day he run up against a town named Jericho' " (p. 181). Fisher undercuts his hero's intelligence by pointing out that although Joshua knew the story, its "meaning was a little too deep" for him. In contrast, the Rev. Tod Bruce, aware of the continuing struggle for literacy of many in his congregation, explains the modern lesson of the Jewish legend in plain, standard English: " 'Self-revelation is the supreme experience, the chief victory, of a man's life. In all the realm of the spirit, in all the Canaan of the soul, no conquest yields so miraculous a reward' "

(p. 186). Two battles are clearly being fought in the novel: one for living space and the other for self-revelation.

As a friend and guide, the author-narrator cultivates the exotic appeal of Harlem for his white readers. This is apparent in the minstrel antics and coarse wit of Jinx and Bubber, the burlesque description of the General Improvement Association's annual costume ball—a transparent criticism of the NAACP and UNIA—and the showy display of varieties of black speech, from jiving to playing the dozens. The heated comic arguments between Jinx and Bubber provide the levity that buoys the serious themes of housing discrimination, intraracial prejudice, and race war. Slang, idiom, syntax, physical gestures, and the dozens all contribute to the surface realism and satirical effect of their dialogue on the anticipated race war triggered by Merrit's move to a white neighborhood. But instead of allowing their dialogue to stand on its own, Fisher proceeds to explain its sociopsychological significance to his mainly white readers. By interpreting the verbal insults and aggression between Jinx and Bubber as an effort to suppress the mutual affection that their class considers unmanly and unnatural, Fisher reinforces the ironic thrust of the plot and characters while simultaneously revealing his ambivalence toward the comic pair. An uneven blend of biblical legend, satire, and comedy, *The Walls of Jericho* reveals the bitter-sweet truths of color and class prejudice beneath the surface reality of Harlem.

The Conjure-Man Dies, the second detective novel by a black American, is also a hybrid work.[61] A mystery tale of black Harlem, its clever plot, gallery of urban characters, and tragicomic style combine the classical mode of S. S. Van Dine, the creator of the complex Philo Vance stories of the 1920s, and the realistic mode of Dashiell Hammett, the creator of the hardboiled, idiomatic Sam Spade stories of the 1930s.[62] Unlike *The Walls of Jericho, The Conjure-Man Dies* is more entertaining than satirical.

The plot involves the puzzling death and resurrection of N. Frimbo, who was an African king, a Harvard graduate, a student of philosophy, and a popular Harlem psychic. The plot begins with the emergency house call of Dr. Archer, an erudite physician with a penchant for detective work, to examine Frimbo, who has been mysteriously murdered by a handkerchief stuffed down his throat. Dr. Archer was called by Jinx and Bubber, the comic characters from *The Walls of Jericho,* who are on the scene when Frimbo is murdered and are thus prime suspects. As black Detective Perry Dart and Dr. Archer team up to solve the murder, the chain of events becomes increasingly bizarre. Male sex glands are discovered in the psychic's laboratory; a dental bridge, turban, and thigh bone are found at the

The Harlem Renaissance and the Search for New Modes of Narrative

scene of the crime; Frimbo's assistant and the corpse mysteriously disappear; and finally, Frimbo reappears alive, only to become a suspect in his own murder along with the people who had been waiting to see him that night. After Jinx is charged with murder, the truth slowly unfolds in selective flashbacks, dramatic monologues, and the logical deductions of Dr. Archer. By an ingenious use of these standard devices, Fisher controls the suspense while gradually informing the reader that the murdered man was actually Frimbo's assistant. He belonged to the same African clan as the psychic and thus had the same surname. To fulfill the traditional obligations of a subject to protect the life of his king, N'ogo Frimbo, the assistant, had changed roles with N'gana Frimbo and was murdered by Stanley Crouch, the landlord and jealous husband of the psychic's lover. In turn, N'gana reconstructs the crime and sacrifices his own life to entrap the murderer of his faithful subject and servant.

In addition to the erudite Frimbo and Dr. Archer and the comic Jinx and Bubber, the gallery of characters include Detective Dart and several Harlem types. Perry Dart was one of the first of the few black members of the Harlem police force to be promoted to detective. A Manhattanite by birth, he is dark skinned, intelligent, alert, practical, and knows Harlem "from lowest dive to loftiest temple." Like his white fictional detective prototypes, he is also self-effacing and shrewd. " 'I'm going to need some of your brains,' " he tells Dr. Archer. " 'I'm not one of these bright ones that can do all the answers in my head. I'm just a poor boy trying to make a living, and this kind of a riddle hasn't been popped often enough in my life to be easy yet.' "[63] Among the murder suspects are Spider Webb, "a number-runner who worked for Harlem's well-known policy-king, Si Brandon;" Doty Hicks, a notorious drug addict and pusher; and Easley Jones, a mysterious railroad porter. Also on the scene at the time of the crime was Mrs. Martha Crouch, the attractive wife of the landlord, and Mrs. Aramintha Snead, a devoted church worker who was seeking Frimbo's help to cure her husband's drinking problem. " 'Everybody know 'bout this man Frimbo,' " she explains to Detective Dart. " '—say he can conjure on down. And I figger I been takin' it to the Lord in prayer long enough. Now I'm goin' take it to the devil' " (p. 81). All the characters therefore have one thing in common: a belief in the supernatural, especially the mystical powers of the conjure-man.

Structurally and stylistically, *The Conjure-Man Dies* is an incongruous combination of mystery and low comedy. The novel begins and ends with a stanza from a popular blues song of the period that establishes the tragicomic mood and provides a motive for the murder:

I'll be glad when you're dead, you rascal you,
I'll be glad when you're dead, you rascal you.
What is it that you've got
Makes my wife think you so hot?
Oh you dog—I'll be glad when you're gone! (Pp. 3, 316)

Suspecting his wife of unfaithfulness with the conjure-man, the landlord kills the "rascal." Stylistically, the incongruity is apparent in the dialogue and the author-narrator's exposition and descriptions. The comic exchanges between Jinx and Bubber, for example, contrast sharply with Dr. Archer's pedantic dialogue with Frimbo. More important, although the average Harlemite believes Frimbo is a "caster of spells," Frimbo himself ironically rejects such beliefs as superstitious nonsense. " 'I am no caster of spells,' " he declares pompously. " 'I am a psychist—a kind of psychologist' " (p. 114). Like *The Walls of Jericho*, then, *The Conjure-Man Dies* reflects Fisher's ambivalence about the black bourgeoisie and his wry vision of the capacity of black Americans to laugh at life and themselves as the key to their survival and the triumph of their humanity. The celebration of black humor and experimentation with it in the detective novel are Fisher's major contributions to the tradition of the Afro-American novel.

GEORGE SAMUEL SCHUYLER (1895–1977)

For George Schuyler, one time left-wing radical and long time archconservative black journalist, the key to survival for Afro-Americans was assimilation. Born on February 25, 1895, in Providence, Rhode Island, he was reared in Syracuse, New York, by a wise old puritanical grandmother who passed on to him her rigorous Protestant ethic. From his free-born New York parents and predominantly white community, he acquired a scorn for black culture and racial chauvinism. He also learned at an early age that racial discrimination meant there was no future for him in his hometown; he therefore left school in 1912 to join the army. While stationed in Honolulu in 1916, he began writing satirical skits for *The Service*, a weekly magazine edited by civilians for the military. At the end of the war, he returned to Syracuse and in 1921 became an active member of the Socialist party. The following year he launched his career in journalism by moving to New York and working with A. Philip Randolph on the *Messenger*, a black socialist journal, and publishing articles in such varied magazines as the *World Tomorrow*, the *Nation*, and *American Mercury*. In "Shafts and Darts: A Page of Calumny and Satire," his column in the *Messenger*, he began his irreverent attacks on the social leaders and issues of his day. In 1924 he began his nearly forty-year association with the *Pittsburgh Courier* newspaper as columnist and editorial writer. And in 1931 he reached his peak as a satirist in two novels: *Black No More* and *Slaves Today*.

Like Fisher's *Walls of Jericho*, *Black No More* is a satirical treatment of the irrationality of color prejudice. But Schuyler, unlike Fisher, is more concerned with action than character, and the structure and style of his novel are more ironic than mimetic. His author-narrator addresses the reader from outside the flow of action with sarcastic and hyperbolic commentary that magnifies the absurd contradictions of racial chauvinism, especially the myths of white purity and supremacy. The novel begins with a black doctor's discovery of what he naively believes to be the solution to the color problem: an electrical process for turning black people white. The immediate popularity of Dr. Crookman's Black-No-More treatment results in private wealth for himself and his black sponsors, but chaos for the nation. Black leaders lose their followers, black organizations their members and contributors, black businessmen their customers, and black politicians their constituents. The white supremacist organization (the Knights of Nordica) is taken over by Matthew Fisher, the hero with a "slightly satanic cast," and his Nordicized black sidekick, Bunny Brown; an alarming number of white women begin giving birth to black babies; and researchers for the most snobbish white organization (the Anglo-Saxon Association of America) discover that millions of white families have black ancestry, including that of Mr. Snobbcraft, the president of the association, and that of the Reverend Givens, the Imperial Grand Wizard of the Knights of Nordica and Democratic candidate for president of the United States. With the discovery at the end of the novel that the Nordicized blacks are whiter than the born Nordics, the obsession to avoid identification as having black ancestry reverses itself with the help of an enterprising former black beautician who invents a skin stain that turns white skin light-brown and Zulu tan. "A white face became startlingly rare," says the author-narrator. "America was definitely, enthusiastically mulatto-minded."[64] In the bizarre world of *Black No More* brown was beautiful, not black.

Because the tension between the themes of assimilation and radical economic reform is not structurally reconciled, the novel ends ambiguously. The root of the color problem in the novel is the free enterprise system, the target of the young black writers and economic radicals of the 1930s,[65] for it is the businessmen who are most opposed to Dr. Crookman's efforts to achieve "chromatic democracy" in the nation. For black capitalists, "the refrain was that Negro business—always anemic—was about to pass out entirely through lack of patronage" (p. 96). It is also the an-tihero's realization "that so long as the ignorant white masses could be kept thinking of the menace of the Negro to Caucasian race purity and political control, they would give little thought to labor organization" that influences him to exploit the money-making possibilities of maintaining the racial status quo by becoming the Grand Exalted Giraw of the Ancient and Honorable Order of the Knights of Nordica. Soliciting contributions from Southern white capitalists, he explains the difference between the KKK and the KN: "While both were interested in public morals, racial integrity and the threatened invasion of America by the Pope, his organization glimpsed its larger duty, the perpetuation of Southern prosperity by the stabilization of industrial relations" (p. 108). Although the industry and ingenuity of Dr. Crookman and the other characters are debunked by the author-narrator's commentary and descriptions, the narrative action dramatizes the successful manipulation of color prejudice and capitalism by the Mephistophelian hero and his unscrupulous followers. In short, while the ideological and moral disparity between the author-narrator and his characters underscores Schuyler's sardonic rejection of racism and capitalism, and implicitly prescribes socialism as the panacea for these ills, the plot reveals his ambivalence toward the American Dream and gives an unintentional ambiguity to the novel.

A subdued attack on the vices of the Liberian aristocracy, *Slaves Today* is less ambiguous but no less ironic than *Black No More*. The omniscient author-narrator is clear about the class nature of the tyranny he sees in Liberia. President Johnson, District Commissioner Jackson, and Captain Burns "were but slightly less dark than the natives over whom they ruled but they felt no kinship with the aborigines for that reason. It was no more difficult for them to oppress and exploit fellow black men than it usually is for powerful whites to do the same thing to fellow white men. Color did not enter here—it was class that counted."[66] Most Liberians were contemptuous of farming, preferring, instead, the prestige and profiteering of law and politics. The most powerful and wealthy were the unscrupulous "grandsons of Negro freedmen" who were engaged in the slave traffic to Fernando Po where laborers were in demand for the Spanish cocoa plantations. "Each man sent meant fifty dollars split three ways between the recruiter, the agent and His Excellency" (p. 14). The characters, but not the author-narrator and reader, are blind to the ironic situation: "Their forefathers had come here to this expanse of jungle to found a haven for the oppressed of the Black race but their descendants were now guilty of the same cruelties from which they had fled" (pp. 100–01). Thus, whereas *Black No More* is an outrageously irreverent satire of color prejudice in the United States, *Slaves Today* is a sober unmasking of the romance of black power in Africa.

WALLACE THURMAN (1902–34)

His contemporaries generally agreed that Wallace Thurman was one of the most talented, well-read, neurotic writers of his era. Born in 1902 in Salt Lake City, Utah, into a family with Indian and Jewish forebears on his mother's side, he was made extremely self-conscious about his dark complexion by his family and community. He attended the University of Utah as a premedical student between 1920 and 1922, when he withdrew because of a nervous breakdown. After his recovery, he studied for two more years at the University of Southern California. In 1925 he migrated to Harlem in search of literary fame. Like Schuyler, he was associated with the *Messenger*, where his critical mind and speed-reading talents combined to make him a highly fastidious managing editor. Torn between the ambition to be a great writer and the demands of the commercial market, he was a reader for the Macaulay Publishing Company, a ghost writer for novels and magazines like *True Story*, founding editor of two short-lived magazines (*Harlem* and *Fire*), a film writer, co-author with William J. Rapp of the Broadway play *Harlem*, and author of two caustic satires: *The Blacker the Berry* and *Infants of the Spring*.

The title and theme of Thurman's first novel are derived from the folk saying, "the blacker the berry, the sweeter the juice." Thurman gives this saying a wry twist as he examines the impact of intraracial prejudice on his heroine, Emma Lou Morgan. The tragedy of her life was that she was not only very dark-complexioned, but also a poor, undistinguished young woman. "She should have been a boy," she laments to herself, "then color of skin wouldn't have mattered so much, for wasn't her mother always saying that a Black boy could get along, but that a Black girl would never know anything but sorrow and disappointment?"[67] Ridicule and rejection by the semi-white, male-dominated world of her mother's family and the all-white Boise, Idaho, community in which she was raised helped to make this a self-fulfilling prophecy by teaching her to hate her blackness and her self. Hoping that the "whiter and whiter, every generation" credo of her mother's family and friends was characteristic only of provincial minds and cities, she set out for college, seeking in vain for acceptance by a larger community. Ostracism by fellow students, discrimination by

Harlem employers and co-workers, and exploitation by her light-skinned lover all confirm that it was not merely Emma Lou's hypersensitivity about her dark complexion that made her life tragic. The truth, as expressed by Truman Walter, an obvious surrogate for the author-narrator's views, was that " 'in an environment where there are so many color-prejudiced whites, there are bound to be a number of color-prejudiced blacks' " (p. 147). Emma Lou's tragic quest for love and respect ends with her realization that "what she needed to do now was to accept her black skin as being real and unchangeable, to realize that certain things were, had been, and would be, and with this in mind begin life anew, always fighting, not so much for acceptance by people, but for acceptance of herself by herself" (pp. 226–27). The biographical parallels between Thurman and Emma Lou are striking; more important, they too frequently reflect the confusion of psychological distance between the author-narrator and the heroine.

In the role of defender of truth and reason, the author-narrator relies more heavily on dialogue and dramatic irony than on ridicule to distance himself intellectually and morally from his confused heroine and to explain the cause of color prejudice among blacks. " 'Ridicule will do no good, nor mere laughing at them,' " says Truman. " 'I admit those weapons are about the only ones an intelligent person would use, but one must also admit that they are rather futile . . . because, well, these people cannot help being like they are—their environment has made them that way' " (p. 142). Rather than a justification for discrimination between light- and dark-skinned Afro-Americans, Truman and the author-narrator seem to offer this simplistic sociopsychological explanation of the effects of racism primarily for the benefit of white and middle-class readers. For even though the excursions into a Harlem cabaret and rent party in the middle of the novel reflect the heroine's social entrapment and moral decline as a result of color prejudice and feelings of inferiority, they also reveal Thurman playing the fashionable role of guide to Harlem and expressing his criticism of the decadent quality of the Harlem Renaissance. Because of the innocence and "rather polished manners and exteriors" of outstanding personalities of the period, it is Emma Lou's dissolute mulatto and Filipino lover, Alva, who is ironically recruited to escort them to the house party. The chief irony, however, is that Emma Lou internalizes the snobbery and prejudice of those who reject her. She not only considered black Hazel Mason a barbarian but "resented being approached by any one so flagrantly inferior, any one so noticeably a typical southern darky, who had no business obtruding into the more refined scheme of things" (pp. 26–27). Emma Lou's tragedy, then, is that she considered herself "too black" and, like Thurman, lacked the will and community support to explore the cultural alternatives of her shame. Unlike Thurman, however, Emma Lou is trapped by her sex as well as her class and color.

Several characters in *Infants of the Spring* are also entrapped by their personal insecurities and environment, suffering from racial discrimination, little or no talent, and profligacy. But *Infants of the Spring* is far more bitter and tragic than *The Blacker the Berry*. A scathing indictment of the excesses of the Harlem Renaissance and its leading personalities, Thurman's second novel, with its title and theme of blighted youth taken from *Hamlet* (1.3.36), shifts away from character study and extensive exposition to action and dramatized narrative, which is largely witty or brooding dialogue. The focus is on Niggeratti Manor, a house in Harlem that is managed by a black patron of the arts, Euphoria Blake, for the benefit of young black artists and writers. Among them are Raymond Taylor, a talented, highly neurotic writer and cynical commentator on the Harlem scene of the 1920s; Stephen Jorgenson, a white college student, camp follower and friend of Ray's; Paul Arbian, a bizarre painter and Oscar Wilde devotee; Eustace Savory, a pretentious Victorian singer of classical music; and Pelham Gaylord, a pathetic, talentless "natural born menial" who aspires to become an artist.

As the plot unfolds to reveal the blighting effects of bohemianism and Negrophiles on budding black artists, the omniscient author provides inside views of only the main character, Raymond. By doing this, Thurman attempts to win our sympathy for this character, whose self-criticism intensifies his brooding egoism and feelings of inferiority. A highly ambitious and sensitive writer, Ray is torn by color consciousness and self-doubt:

> He wanted to write, but he had made little progress. He wanted to become a Prometheus, to break the chains which held him to a racial rack and carry a blazing beacon to the top of Mount Olympus so that those possessed of Alpine stocks could follow in his wake. He wanted to do something memorable in literature, something that could stay afloat on the contemporary sea of weighted ballast, something which could transcend and survive the transitional age in which he was living. He wanted to accomplish these things, but he was becoming less and less confident that he was possessed of the necessary genius.[68]

He has intelligence, wit, and talent, but these are either insufficient to surmount the barriers of race or are being perverted by the commercialism and decadence of the age. Consequently, Ray broods in shame to himself:

The struggle to free himself from race consciousness had been hailed before actually accomplished. The effort to formulate a new attitude toward life had become a seeking for the red badge of courage. That which might have emerged normally, if given time, had been forcibly and prematurely exposed to the light. It now seemed as if the Caesarian operation was going to prove fatal to both the parent and to the child. (P. 147)

The problem here, as with much of the novel, is that the sympathy of the reader is tempered by the narrator's neuroticism and by the lack of adequate psychological and intellectual distance between the author-narrator and his main character. Frustrated at being patronized by philanthropists, social workers, and Negrophiles, Ray frequently tells us that he and some of his fellow artists seek to lose their race consciousness and be acclaimed for their achievements. On an emotional level, then, the reader cautiously sympathizes with the neurotic protagonist.

But philosophically and morally, many modern black readers will be alienated by the deep-seated shame of the protagonist and the norms of the novel. These norms, as expressed by Ray, the center of consciousness of the narrative, are " 'that the average Negro intellectual and artist had no goal, no standards, no elasticity, no pregnant plasm' " (p. 146). Symbolic of the dissolute norms of the bohemian intellectuals and artists of the era is Niggeratti Manor, which is converted at the end of the novel into a dormitory for young black working women after Euphoria becomes disillusioned with her artist tenants and evicts them. Because of his "chaotic and deranged" mind, however, Ray is hardly a reliable narrator. In addition, because there is no discernible intellectual and moral distance between the omniscient narrator and the protagonist, most black readers are likely to challenge and reject descriptions of themselves as a slave race whose only viable solution to racism is assimilation. " 'Negroes are a slave race,' " says Ray, " 'and a slave race they'll remain until assimilated. Individuals will arise and escape on the ascending ladder of their own individuality. The others will remain what they are. Their superficial progress means nothing. Instinctively they are still the servile progeny of servile ancestors' " (pp. 141–42). The unintentional irony of the situation and the malice of this bitter attack on blacks of his era are compounded by a warped, elitist consciousness. " 'Eventually only the Babbitt and the artist will be able to break the chains. The rest must wait until the inevitable day of complete assimilation' " (p. 217). Thurman's prediction through Ray that blacks will criticize his books and him severely because he has no race pride is only half of the truth. The other half is that Thurman was unable to distance himself adequately from his subject and protagonist in *Infants of the Spring* to enable his satire to transcend the age it denounces.

Because realism was a means to an end for the satirists and not an end in itself, we find Fisher, Schuyler, and Thurman widely different in their manner of criticizing the people, customs, and institutions of the Harlem Renaissance. Fisher views color prejudice with amusement, whereas Schuyler and Thurman lash out at it with bitter anger. As blacks they realize that color prejudice was not only the cardinal vice of white American society but also the source of much of the tragicomic nature of the Afro-American experience within the black community itself. Moreover, because black folk humor had traditionally been a form of masked aggression, when turned inward on the race it became a form of self-aggression and compensatory relief from discrimination through laughter. It affirmed the humanity of blacks in the face of white society's efforts to deny or destroy that humanity. Consequently, burlesque, sarcasm, exaggeration, invective, and irony were all used in the service of satiric comment on intraracial discrimination and racial chauvinism, sparing neither the man on the street nor the leaders of the race. But whereas the satirists were successful in unmasking the hypocrisy and self-righteousness of the leaders of the race and rejecting idealized images of the race, they were less successful in avoiding scorn for lower-class urban blacks and their evolving culture. Although they presumed to speak for the lower class, they were actually spokesmen for the black intelligentsia. Their goal was a form of humanism that sought to lift lower-class blacks out of their ethnic community to the spurious perfection of assimilation into the larger white community. Whereas this had long been the goal of the majority of the black middle class, what was advocated now was an alliance with the white working class. But the status, wealth, and power offered by white America and radical black intellectuals before the economic disaster of 1929 were more shadow than substance. As a result, then, of the precipitous decline of the Harlem Renaissance and the onset of the Depression, a more sobering vision of the urban black American experience began to appear in the naturalistic works of Afro-American novelists.

5 / Richard Wright and the
Triumph of Naturalism

The history of the Negro in America is the history of America written in
vivid and bloody terms; it is the history of Western Man writ small.
It is the history of men who tried to adjust themselves to a world whose
laws, customs, and instruments of force were leveled against
them. The Negro is America's metaphor.

RICHARD WRIGHT
"The Literature of the Negro in the
United States"

I
T was the sociological imagination that was to have its day in the
1930's," writes social historian S. P. Fullinwider, "as the social scientists moved into the position of potential leadership, and as the
blues writers, pushed by the logic of the depression, turned to social
protest in the tradition of economic radicalism."[1] Although the sociological
imagination called for assimilation and personal adjustment, it wanted
neither within an exploitative social structure. Influenced by white and
black social scientists of the "Chicago School" and by the activities of the
Communist party, Richard Wright and other black novelists of the thirties
and forties saw the Great Depression as strong evidence that American
society was on the verge of economic collapse. With varying degrees of
commitment, they envisioned the solution in terms of biracial working-
class solidarity and a restructuring of the American economic system. The
cry for reform had fallen on deaf ears. Although in 1941 President Roosevelt, anticipating our entry in World War II against fascist imperialism
and racial genocide in Europe, issued Executive Order 8802 banning discrimination in defense industries and government, racial violence erupted
in Detroit, New York, Los Angeles, Chicago, and in the South. These
events reinforced the radical belief that only the organized power of the
masses could prevail over the power of the wealthy few and the intransigent racism of their middle-class allies. In 1947 President Truman's Committee on Civil Rights issued a report, "To Secure These Rights,"
recommending improvement in the administration of federal laws pro-
tecting the rights of minorities; and in 1948 a similar committee recom-

mended a policy of integration for the armed services. The stark reality of the exploitation of the urban black masses and of the devastating sociopsychological impact of urbanization and institutional racism as well as World War II led to the triumph of a disquieting new naturalistic vision in the Afro-American novel between 1937 and 1952.

The "Chicago School" of Sociology

In the introduction to *Black Metropolis,* Wright states that "it was from the scientific findings of men like the late Robert E. Park, Robert Redfield, and Louis Wirth that I drew the meanings for my documentary book *Twelve Million Black Voices;* for my novel, *Native Son.'*[2] Park, Redfield, and Wirth were University of Chicago social scientists who broke new ground in the field of urban sociology and race relations with their pioneer studies on the impact of industrialization, urbanization, and social differentiation on "primitive peoples" and ethnic minorities.[3] The "Chicago School" of sociology strongly influenced the thinking and research of many social scientists, including such well-known black sociologists as Charles S. Johnson, E. Franklin Frazier, Horace Cayton, and Oliver C. Cox.

This was especially true of Park's theories on race relations and the city. (Park had spent several years at Tuskegee as a ghost writer for Booker T. Washington.) Park's theories on "social disorganization" and the "marginal man," even though the latter was defined as a racial and cultural hybrid, a mulatto, seem to be the basis of their major studies as well as of Wright's conception of Afro-American character and culture in his writings of the 1940s. Although Wright was not a student at the university, he was influenced through Professor Wirth and his research assistant, Horace Cayton, whom he first met in 1933. Unable to find work, Wright and his mother were on welfare at the time, and their social worker, Mrs. Mary Wirth, sent him to seek her husband's help in becoming a writer.[4] Over the years, Cayton and Wright became fast friends. More important, drawing on the studies done by Park's students and associates in an attempt to give structure to their own urban experiences with the ethics of Jim Crow during the Great Depression, Wright developed the theory of race relations and black personality that appears in *Lawd Today* and *Native Son.*

The Great Depression and the Communist Party

Wright's hunger for a life that would be freer and fuller than the one he had known in the South led him to Chicago in 1927, but the Depression prolonged his hunger, driving him into the ranks of the underemployed and the unemployed. The Department of Agriculture and Federal Reserve Board reported that between 1929 and 1933 agricultural prices fell more than 60 percent and industrial production plummeted from an index figure of 120 in 1929 to 57 in 1933. The gross national product declined from $104 billion to $75 billion and, according to the Bureau of Labor Statistics, more than 12 million workers were unemployed in March 1933.[5] While banks and businesses closed in the city and thousands of people stood in bread and soup lines for handouts, the government paid farmers, especially large landowners and planters, millions of dollars to plow under or temporarily not raise wheat, corn, barley, peanuts, hogs, dairy cattle, and beef.

The most disadvantaged and desperate major group during the Great Depression was black landless farmers and workers. "Negro sharecroppers were found to have an average income of $295 per year as compared with $417 for white sharecroppers; the Negro cash renter averaged $307, the white $568; the Negro wage hand averaged $175, the white $232." The unemployment figures for blacks, according to Urban League reports, were 30 to 60 percent greater than for whites. Not only were whites generally given preference for available jobs, but in some areas blacks were dismissed as elevator operators, bellboys, cooks, waiters, and delivery boys, and replaced by whites. Because of flagrant discrimination by leaders of the Agricultural Adjustment Administration and the National Recovery Administration, as well as the powerlessness of black organizations, "most of the AAA and NRA benefits did not trickle down to the masses of black workers and farmers."[6]

For the intellectuals and black writers of Wright's generation, some of the activities and programs of the Communist party of the USA that seemed to meet the social and cultural needs of blacks had strong appeal. Prior to 1928, as Wilson Record points out in *The Negro and the Communist Party*, the Party's efforts to recruit blacks as members or sympathizers were less than successful.[7] Despite their economic exploitation and political disorganization, most black workers of the 1920s were ignorant and frightened of the Communists, and most black intellectuals and writers were skeptical at best of the Party view that racial oppression was simply an expression of economic bondage and that the solution of the "Negro problem" was in the unity of Negroes with all class-conscious workers. After all, there were no guarantees that socialism would provide any more racial equality than a capitalist democracy. But the Party's redefinition in 1928 of the "Negro problem" in the United States as a problem of an oppressed nation, an aspect of the general pattern of imperialism, whose solution—

self-determination for the Black Belt—would be the same as any other oppressed colonial nation, offered hope of an ally to black nationalists. Because the Party's active support of their self-determination doctrine vacillated after 1934, however, in response to the needs of the Soviet Union's foreign policy, black intellectuals and writers who were sympathetic to the program became increasingly disillusioned. Earlier in the 1930s many had been impressed by the Party's opposition to fascism, and some still supported the activities in behalf of blacks by such front organizations as the industrial unions affiliated with the Trade Union Unity League; the committees and councils of the League of Struggle for Negro Rights, with Langston Hughes, a "fellow traveler," as its elected president; and the International Labor Defense, which played a prominent role in the Scottsboro trials. Some black people saw hope in the Party's running of a black candidate for vice president in the national elections of 1932 and 1936. Of greater interest to black writers were the John Reed clubs and the opportunities their journals provided for publication. But most saw their hopes and their race betrayed in 1939 with the signing of the Stalin-Hitler non-aggression pact and the Party's subordination of the struggle against racial discrimination to the struggle of the Soviet Union for world power.

In 1933 Wright joined the John Reed Club in Chicago and made a full commitment to the Party.[8] "It was not the economics of Communism," he states in *The God That Failed*, "nor the great power of trade unions, nor the excitement of underground politics that claimed me; my attention was caught by the similarity of the experiences of workers in other lands, by the possibility of uniting scattered but kindred peoples into a whole. It seemed to me that here at last, in the realm of revolutionary expression, Negro experience could find a home, a functioning value and role." As for his own role, he writes:

> The Communists, I felt, had oversimplified the experience of those whom they sought to lead. In their efforts to recruit masses, they had missed the meaning of the lives of the masses, had conceived of people in too abstract a manner. I would try to put some of that meaning back. I would tell Communists how common people felt, and I would tell common people of the self-sacrifice of Communists who strove for unity among them.[9]

Thus, for the first time in his life Wright felt accepted and needed by the white world, and began to articulate his mission as a writer. To his alarm, members of the Party considered him, a junior high school graduate and self-educated man, a black intellectual. Though they entrusted him with many important duties, his writings were under constant scrutiny for bourgeois consciousness and violations of the Party line. Mutual distrust and Wright's irrepressible individualism finally led to an official break with the Party in 1944, the year before the United States ended World War II by dropping the atomic bomb on Hiroshima and Nagasaki.

The Federal Writers' Project

The New Deal agency that was most beneficial to unemployed black writers was the Federal Writers' Project (FWP). Established in 1935 as a subdivision of the Works Progress Administration (WPA) and a distinct agency within the Federal Arts Project (FAP), which included art, music, and theater, the FWP supported more than six thousand writers of various degrees of talent. Among these were several who were destined to become well-known black novelists: Richard Wright, Claude McKay, Chester Himes, Ralph Ellison, Frank Yerby, Arna Bontemps, William Attaway, Willard Motley, Zora Neale Hurston, and Margaret Walker. The primary task of the FWP was to prepare the *American Guide*, a comprehensive, multivolume guide to the United States. To insure that blacks were not neglected in research and publications sponsored by the agency, Sterling A. Brown, with the support of the black leadership, was appointed editor for Negro Affairs. In addition to compiling 378 regional books and pamphlets between 1935 and 1939, white and black writers collected black folk materials, and the most serious and talented of the group were provided with the inspiration and security to continue their own private creative projects.[10] Many of the short pieces written by FWP writers during their spare time, including Richard Wright's "Ethics of Living Jim Crow," appeared in *American Stuff* (1937), a voluminous anthology prepared by directors of the project and published commercially.

RICHARD NATHANIEL WRIGHT (1908–60)

A member of both the Illinois and New York FWP, Richard Wright was a man with a mission and a message: his mission was to overwhelm the sensibilities of the white world with the truth of his naturalistic vision and the power of his craftmanship; his message was that the Afro-American was America's metaphor. Born in 1908 on a farm near Natchez, Mississippi, Wright survived an emotionally and physically starved childhood to become the most celebrated black American writer of all time. But his survival, as revealed in the bleak account of his youth in *Black Boy* (1945) and *American Hunger* (1977), had its price. It left deep scars on his personality

Richard Wright and the Triumph of Naturalism

and fostered the sense of alienation and rebellion that came to pervade his real and imaginary worlds.

In sheer drama, his life reads like one of his short stories or novels. Before reaching his seventeenth birthday, Wright was deserted by his father, made a drunkard by Memphis bar flies, placed in an orphanage by his poverty-stricken mother, forced to flee Arkansas after the lynching of his uncle, reared under the religious tyranny of his grandmother and aunts, terrified by the suffering of his mother brought on by poverty and a paralytic stroke, bullied and beaten by white bigots, and involved in petty thefts with his friends. It was not because of the American Dream that he achieved success as a writer, but in spite of it. In *Black Boy* Wright sums up life in the South for a black man as a choice between militancy, submissiveness, projection of self-hatred, or escape through sex and alcohol. Not included among these various ways of reacting to what Wright has elsewhere called the ethics of living Jim Crow is the course of action he finally chose: sublimation of his frustration through writing and flight from the South in 1927 and from America with his second white wife in 1947.

Despite the militancy of most of his early black characters and his classification of Bigger Thomas's hatred of whites as black nationalism, Wright intellectually rejects both the concept of black consciousness and the values of Afro-American culture. This is clearly evidenced in the thematic and structural concerns of *Lawd Today*, a novel that was completed before 1937 but not published until 1963, and *Native Son*. But perhaps the most explicit expression of Wright's feelings on this subject appears in his nonfiction works. In *Black Boy*, for example, Wright states:

(After I had outlived the shocks of childhood, after the habit of reflection had been born in me, I used to mull over the strange absence of real kindness in Negroes, how unstable was our tenderness, how lacking in genuine passion we were, how void of great hope, how timid our joy, how bare our traditions, how hollow our memories, how lacking we were in those intangible sentiments that bind man to man, and how shallow was even our despair. After I had learned other ways of life I used to brood upon the unconscious irony of those who felt that Negroes led so passional an existence! I saw that what had been taken for our emotional strength was our negative confusions, our flights, our fears, our frenzy under pressure.

(Whenever I thought of the essential bleakness of black life in America, I knew that Negroes had never been allowed to catch the full spirit of Western civilization, that they lived somehow in it but not of it. And when I brooded upon the cultural barrenness of black life, I wondered if clean, positive tenderness, love, honor, loyalty and the capacity to remember were native with man. I asked myself if these human qualities were not fostered, won, struggled and suffered for, preserved in ritual from one generation to another.[11]

As though this complete alienation from black culture, in which Ralph Ellison rightly perceives a degree of literary posturing, were not unfortunate enough, Wright goes on to reinforce it in subsequent works.[12] His publications, many of which antedate *Black Boy*, include numerous articles and poems, a play, two autobiographies, two collections of short stories, a collection of essays, a folk history, three journalistic books on Third World countries, and five novels, of which the most important is *Native Son*.

In part, the tension perceived in *Native Son* between Wright's dual role as artist and spokesman for his people is the result of his early commitment to literature and Marxism. By craftiness and dissimulation, Wright managed as a young boy to circumvent the legal and extralegal methods the South uses to keep blacks ignorant of the world around them, and began stuffing himself on a steady diet of books and magazines. The biting social and literary criticism of H. L. Mencken, the debunking of Babbittry in the fiction of Sinclair Lewis, the naturalistic explorations of character and culture by Theodore Dreiser, the effective use of stream-of-consciousness techniques by Gertrude Stein to reveal the black psyche, the psychoanalytic theory of personality advanced by Sigmund Freud, and the pragmatic behavioral theories of William James—from these widely varied sources Wright derived his early aesthetic and philosophical views on literature and life. And when he moved North he immersed himself in the sociological theories of the "Chicago School" and the socioeconomic interpretation of history advanced by Marx and Lenin. The latter influences are apparent in the short story "Bright and Morning Star," first published in 1938 and included in the 1940 edition of *Uncle Tom's Children*.

Wright's greatest literary achievement after *Uncle Tom's Children*, the outstanding collection of four short stories that in 1938 launched him on his career in fiction and reportedly brought tears to Eleanor Roosevelt's eyes, is *Native Son*. In this widely acclaimed naturalistic work, Wright focuses on the South Side slums of Chicago during the Great Depression, analyzes the character of Bigger Thomas, and projects him as a representative product of the insidious values of American society. In the course of the novel, Bigger is controlled by social and psychological forces that drive him to self-hatred, a rejection of his family and race, a knife attack on his closest friend, the murder and mutilation of his employer's daughter, and the rape and murder of his girlfriend. With stunning power, Wright's naturalistic vision affirms the myth of the Bad Nigger and attempts to develop it into a kind of modern Everyman.

Divided into three books ("Fear, "Flight," and "Fate"), *Native Son* explores the impact of oppression on the black psyche. It reveals how racial segregation is inextricably linked with white and black myths of the Bad Nigger in shaping Bigger's attitudes and actions. "Fear" begins with a dramatic episode that is symbolic of the relationship between those who fear and those who cause fear. Bigger shares a run-down, rat-trap of a kitchenette with his mother, younger brother, and sister, and they are endangered in the opening scene by a huge, fang-baring black rat that is both a physical and psychological threat. Mrs. Thomas and her daughter's fear borders on hysteria as they call Bigger to kill the rat. When Bigger corners it, the "rat's belly pulsed with fear," and it leaps at Bigger and sinks its fangs in his trousers in an act of desperation and defiance. After stunning it with a skillet, "Bigger took a shoe and pounded the rat's head, crushing it, cursing hysterically."[13] Two aspects of this episode are of vital significance to the theme and structure of the novel. First, for the rat and Bigger, fear evokes increasing aggression, and only murderous violence overcomes the fear. Second, the deadly confrontation is a metaphor for Bigger's relationship to white society in much the same manner that Wright's vision of the Afro-American is a metaphor for America and modern man. Bigger and his family are the oppressed victims of the white, exploitative, industrialized world. Because of their color, their poverty, and the white myth of the Bad Nigger, they are confined to the Black Belt of Chicago and prevented from developing their human potential for growth. The full consciousness of the shame and misery of the way they are forced to live threatens to engulf the protagonist in fear and despair. "He knew that the moment he allowed what his life meant to enter fully into his consciousness," says the limited omniscient narrator, "he would either kill himself or someone else" (p. 14).

Fear and freedom, then, are the central themes of the first book, and they are filtered through Bigger's consciousness, which is the source of both the major strength and weakness of the novel. On one hand, Wright gives dramatic intensity and intimacy to the narrative by restricting the focus to Bigger's mind. Although much of the narrative comes to us through the consciousness of Bigger Thomas, it is a consciousness rendered in the language of Richard Wright. Thus we understand more than Bigger does. On the other hand, Wright sacrifices verisimilitude and the intellectual integrity of his protagonist in his effort to universalize the psychological and sociological message of the book. " 'Why they make us live in one corner of the city?' " Bigger asks his friend Gus. " 'Why don't they let us fly planes and run ships . . . ' " (p. 23). As in the initial rat episode, Wright heightens and objectifies Bigger's inner feelings by the use of metaphor. It is a high-flying sky-writer, for instance, that triggers Bigger's thoughts about the power and freedom of white boys who can acquire the technical skills that enable them to fulfill their material needs in the modern mechanized world. And it is through the ritual of white role-playing, an ambivalent imitation of the ways of white folks, that he seeks to reconcile the truth of the military, economic, and political impotence of blacks with the power of whites. In the climax of this scene, the narrator drives home the point of Bigger's deep-seated impulse toward freedom and flight:

> a slate-colored pigeon swooped down to the middle of the steel car tracks and began strutting to and fro with ruffled feathers, its fat neck bobbing with regal pride. A street car rumbled forward and the pigeon rose swiftly through the air on wings stretched so taut and sheer that Bigger could see the gold of the sun through their translucent tips. He tilted his head and watched the slate-colored bird flap and wheel out of sight over the edge of a high roof.
> "Now, if I could only do that," Bigger said.
> Gus laughed.
> "Nigger, you nuts."
> "I reckon we the only things in this city that can't go where we want to go and do what we want to do." (Pp. 23–24)

The dramatic impact of the bird metaphor and dialogue in this passage gives sharp relief and poignancy to Bigger's contrasting feeling of entrapment in a hostile world.

Fear of confronting the white world responsible for his confinement and exploitation, for his socialized ambivalence, pushes Bigger into becoming a Bad Nigger. In an attempt to conceal his fear of robbing a white storekeeper, Bigger turns on Gus in the pool room and transfers his fear to him. But Gus knows his friend too well and boldly unmasks him in front of his gang. The antithetical settings and themes of *The Gay-Woman* and *Trader Horn*, the double-feature movie in which the stereotypical characters "were adjusted to their soil and at home in their world, secure from fear and hysteria," symbolize the dilemma of Bigger's socialization as an Afro-

American. He belongs to neither of the worlds portrayed on the screen; for rather than accommodate himself to the duality of his cultural identity, he consciously rejects the black world, and the white world systematically excludes him. Bigger, in other words, is a man precariously dangling between two worlds. And his vicious attack on Gus after the movie is a pathological expression of his fear and hatred of both.

The pathological nature of Bigger's double-consciousness and the defense mechanism of relieving his anxiety by deliberately assaulting and denigrating members of his own race are hardly compatible with the ideology of black nationalism some critics see in the novel.[14] Actually, Wright's portrayal of Bigger resurrects the white American myth of the depraved, emancipated black Southerner. As popularized in the post-Reconstruction fiction of Thomas Nelson Page and Thomas Dixon, the Bad Nigger is bestial and criminal in nature. Wright revitalizes this white myth of black character, which subconsciously influences the behavior of many whites, and attempts to elevate it to the level of the archetype of the rebel in an irrational, exploitative society. Informing this vision is the fact that white society has lived in fear of those it oppresses, fearing that they will sooner or later successfully rise against it. Deprived of the opportunity to live free and full lives because they are black and poor, some radical black individuals who heroically defy the power of whites, ambivalently called Bad Niggers by fellow blacks, use rebellion as an act of self-affirmation. "The Bigger Thomases," says Wright in "How 'Bigger' Was Born," "were the only Negroes I know of who consistently violated the Jim Crow laws of the South and got away with it, at least for a sweet brief spell."[15] Through Bigger, then, Wright explores the limits of individual responsibility for rebellion and crime. Rather than inferior blood, Bigger's fate involves a complex pattern of emotional and urban environmental forces with which Bigger must come to terms within himself.

The major catalysts in Bigger's character development are not his immediate family and friends, but the Daltons. Mr. Dalton is a rich white slum landlord who refuses to rent property outside of the ghetto to blacks, yet prides himself on giving disadvantaged colored folks a chance. His philanthropy takes the form of hiring uneducated blacks as chauffeurs and giving millions of dollars to the NAACP and black schools, but he refuses to employ the youths his money helps to educate, thereby intensifying their frustration and compounding his complicity in their plight. Unlike her husband, Mrs. Dalton is physically as well as morally blind. Thus her failure to see that decent housing and a good job are as vital in the struggle of black people for social adjustment and a better life as education is even more ironic. Mary, their daughter, is a spoiled rich girl whose radical political posturing blinds her and Jan Erlone, her Communist boyfriend, to their selfish motives, as well as to the shame and hatred their condescension evokes from Bigger. After carrying Mary to her bedroom because she is too drunk to walk, Bigger, dreading being caught in a white woman's bedroom, accidentally suffocates her, and later beheads the body and stuffs it into a roaring furnace.

"Flight," Book 2, is concerned with the themes of freedom and rebirth. Paradoxically, the act of murder becomes an act of creation for Bigger. It temporarily ends his sense of fear and shame:

> The thought of what he had done, the awful horror of it, the daring associated with such actions, formed for him for the first time in his fear-ridden life a barrier of protection between him and a world he feared. He had murdered and had created a new life for himself. It was something that was all his own, and it was the first time in his life he had had anything that others could not take from him. (P. 101)

Wright's portrayal of Bigger thus seeks to move beyond a reincarnation of the white myth of the Bad Nigger. After killing Mary, Bigger convinces himself that the circumstances of his fear and hatred militate against accommodation to social conventions and structures if he is to achieve a meaningful sense of self. By willfully confronting and accepting the hidden meaning of his life of anxiety and violence, his repressed fear and hatred of whites for controlling his life, Bigger is reborn. He accepts the ascribed white definition of the Bad Nigger, transvalued by Wright's imagination, as a rebel against social conventions and the status quo. At the same time, his sense of self, the psychological distance between him and others as dramatized through imagery (Bigger is repeatedly shown standing alone in the middle of a confined space),[16] symbolism (he rejects the cross and the Party), and indirect interior monologue (the author's presence is apparent in the exposition of Bigger's consciousness), is that of an outsider or marginal man, a person living apart from the values of both black and white cultures. Given his obsession with fear and the consuming hatred that isolated him from other people, the crucial question is not whether Bigger succeeds as a realistic character, but is how valid and effective he is as the representative black American and a symbol of modern man.

As Book 2 unfolds, the answer to this question seems clear in Bigger's increasing pathological violence and self-destruction. His decision to take advantage of the need of people to cling to conventional social beliefs, values, and institutions while blinding themselves to anything that does not fit their preconceived ideas animates him with a new sense of power and confidence. Freedom for him then becomes the license to exploit others, both black and white. Bessie Mears, his alcoholic girlfriend, is the most tragic victim of his newly discovered freedom. Forcing her to join him in his plan to blackmail the Daltons, Bigger takes his reluctant accomplice to a vacant tenement on the South Side where he rapes her, and then beats her head in with a brick before tossing her body down an airshaft. His reason: he decided that she was worthlessly blind and too dangerous to leave behind. In a house-to-house search, the police ultimately trap and capture him in a manner foreshadowed by the rat episode that opened the novel. Thus, in Book 2 Bigger the bully and pool-room thug becomes Bigger the monster created by a racist, capitalist social system. Whether the monster Wright re-creates actually exists or is a mythic character is, for many readers, not particularly important, for, as Baldwin states, "we believe he exists."[17]

Explaining the genesis of Bigger's character, Wright tells us "that the civilization which had given birth to Bigger contained no spiritual sustenance, had created no culture which could hold and claim his allegiance and faith, had sensitized him and had left him stranded, a free agent to roam the streets of our cities, a hot and whirling vortex of undisciplined and unchannelized impulses."[18] Whereas Wright's interpretation of the double-consciousness and socialized ambivalence of Afro-Americans explains in part the core of Bigger's character, the principal question remains: Is Bigger's reaction to urban modern America more representative than the accommodation strategies of the members of his family? Baldwin was among the first to point out the profound implications of this question:

> If, as I believe, no American Negro exists who does not have his private Bigger Thomas living in the skull, then what most significantly fails to be illuminated here is the paradoxical adjustment which is perpetually made, the Negro being compelled to accept the fact that this dark and dangerous and unloved stranger is part of himself forever. Only this recognition sets him in any wise free and it is this, this necessary ability to contain and even, in the most honorable sense of the word, to exploit the "nigger," which lends to Negro life its high element of the ironic and which causes the most well-meaning of their American critics to make such exhilarating errors when attempting to understand them.[19]

In short, Wright's image of black character is consciously more mythic than mimetic. Unlike other members of his family, whom we see only through his jaundiced eyes, Bigger fails to achieve a viable adjustment to his environment and to come to grips with his double-consciousness as a black American. Rather than affirming his mixed emotions about the duality of his identity, he rejects all culture, all tradition, all values, and chooses extreme asocial behavior. Striking out perversely against black and white alike in his quest for personal freedom, Bigger, in Book 2, is a psychopath who evokes more fear than mercy and more pity than guilt from the reader.

Book 3 underscores Bigger's quasi-tragic fate as an American product. His fate as an outsider is determined by the unrelenting pressure of social and psychological problems fostered by the moral and economic paradoxes of the modern American system. These paradoxes are dramatized in the lurid newspaper accounts of his trial, the other-worldly counsel of the Rev. Hammond and Mrs. Thomas, the friendship and aid of the Communists Jan and Max, the mock justice of the deputy coroner and the state prosecutor, the mob of howling white urban racists, and the perverse philanthrophy of the Daltons. Born black and poor, Bigger was unable to realize his fundamental rights and human potential in a social system that excluded him as a person and denied him the opportunities for their expression that is the heritage of white Americans. Bigger, in fact, is the dispossessed and disinherited American who rebels against the system that stunts and warps his humanity. He is a native son, but through the force of his individual will he seeks to become more than a product of his environment.

As in Books 1 and 2, the tension in Book 3 is largely psychological, and the dynamics of Bigger's personality are more Freudian than Marxist. Wright not only titles Book 1 "Fear," but also draws on Freud in "How 'Bigger' Was Born":

> There seems to hover somewhere in that dark part of all our lives, in some more than in others, an objectless, timeless, spaceless element of primal fear and dread, stemming, perhaps, from our birth (depending upon whether one's outlook upon personality is Freudian or non-Freudian!), a fear and dread which exercises an impelling influence upon our lives all out of proportion to its obscurity. And, accompanying this *first fear*, is, for want of a better name, a reflex urge toward ecstasy, complete submission, and trust. The springs of religion are here, and also the origins of rebellion.[20]

What is fear? And what is its antithesis? Fear can be defined as the anticipation of pain; and trust, its emotional opposite, as the anticipation of pleasure. According to Freud, there are three types of anxiety or fear:

Richard Wright and the Triumph of Naturalism

reality anxiety, neurotic anxiety, and moral anxiety. The source of the first is in the external world, and its prototype is the traumatic moment of birth. Neurotic anxiety has its origins in the id; it is a constant dread of being overwhelmed by an uncontrollable urge to think or act in a way that will bring harm to the self. In moral anxiety the source of the threat is the conscience of the superego system.[21] The prototypical trauma is a reaction to the loss of the object of pleasure and security, the mother's womb. Wright is concerned primarily with the second type of fear: fear of the id. The superego, according to Freud's theoretical models, is achieved by the identification of the individual with parents, family, and society (i.e., acknowledging their authority) and represents the social conscience that restrains the various drives of the id. Bigger's fear is the subjective reaction to his alienation from urban American capitalism and racism. Because he is alienated from his family, ethnic group, and white society, his basic drives are uncontrolled by any kind of moral or social conscience. Bigger's problem, which becomes acute after his sentence to die in the electric chair, is to decide whether his life as a black American provides the basis for hope or despair. "To fall between them," he feels, "would mean living and dying in a fog of fear." How will the cycle of hope and despair end? This is the tension in Book 3.

Stylistically, the tension in Book 3 is more dialectic than dramatic. It is in Bigger's indirect interior monologues, his dialogue with Max, and Max's long-winded, seventeen-page courtroom speech that the reader senses Bigger's dilemma. One of the major weaknesses of the novel, particularly in Book 3, is the implied author's alienation of the reader by the excessive, sometimes awkward, use of indirect interior monologue to explain and intensify feelings and thoughts that have already been forcefully dramatized. Immediately after his capture, for example, the uneducated, inarticulate protagonist contemplates death:

And regulating his attitude toward death was the fact that he was black, unequal, and despised. Passively, he hungered for another orbit between two poles that would let him live again; for a new mode of life that would catch him up with the tension of hate and love. There would have to hover above him, like the stars in a full sky, a vast configuration of images and symbols whose magic and power could lift him up and make him live so intensely that the dread of being black and unequal would be forgotten; that even death would not matter, that it would be a victory. This would happen before he could look them in the face again: a new pride and a new humility would have to be born in him, a humility springing from a new identification, with some part of the world in which he lived, and this identification forming the basis for a new hope that would function in him as pride and dignity. (P. 256)

Vacillating between hope and despair, Bigger thinks:

Maybe they were right when they said that a black skin was bad, the covering of an apelike animal. Maybe he was just unlucky, a man born for dark doom, an obscene joke happening amid a colossal din of siren screams and white faces and circling lances of light under a cold and silken sky. (P. 256)

By this point in the narrative, the reader is already convinced that Bigger has completely internalized the white myth of the Bad Nigger. He not only identifies with the hatred of whites for blacks, but also feels that by killing Mary and Bessie he has fully taken upon himself the ascribed crime and stigma of being black. Furthermore, having rejected the rituals and values of black culture, he feels the need for a new identification with others if he is to overcome his sense of shame.

It is to Jan and Max, the Communists, but not to their Marxist vision, that Bigger turns for a new sense of communion with others and for hope. When Jan shows compassion for him and proves his friendship by bringing Max to defend him, it is the first time in Bigger's life that a white person acts like a human being toward him. Bigger wanted to believe in Max, to trust him, but was afraid it would end just as all other commitments of faith had ended. He insists on interpreting his problems from a racial and existential, rather than class, perspective. With the exception of Jan and Max, whites to Bigger were "a looming mountain of white hate." When asked if he ever hoped for anything, he mumbles, " 'What for? I couldn't get it. I'm black.' " Rather than communion with other humans, the best he can hope for is life in prison. As a projection of the dehumanized image of black character that many whites carry around in their minds, however, he inspires fear and revenge in others rather than mercy and justice.

Nevertheless, Max's emotional defense argument is a plea for white mercy. The basis for the plea is Bigger's mental and emotional attitude and the responsibility of white Americans in shaping those attitudes. " 'This Negro boy's entire attitude toward life is a crime!' " Max argues. " 'The hate and fear which we have inspired in him, woven by our civilization into the very structure of his consciousness, into his blood and bones, into the hourly functioning of his personality, have become the justification of

Richard Wright and the Triumph of Naturalism

his existence' " (p. 367). Wright's implicit propositions that men can and do murder for self-realization, and that Bigger is such a man, are effectively dramatized. But Bigger is not effective as either a black nationalist or the representative of twelve million black Americans. Pitiable and shocking, his problem is a particular case, a clinical case, that is given extended meaning through symbolism and the myth of the Bad Nigger. " 'I didn't want to kill!' " Bigger shouts to Max at the end of the novel. " 'But what I killed for, I *am*! It must've been pretty deep in me to make me kill!' " (pp. 391–92). Max is terrified at Bigger's tragic self-understanding and the decision to die in hatred, an unrepentant killer. Having internalized the white myth of the Bad Nigger and rejected the folk culture that has traditionally strengthened the will of black Americans to endure, Bigger resolves his ambivalence with a vengeance. By closing the novel with Bigger's self-isolation and inability to develop meaningful relationships with others, Wright drives home the message that this is not merely Bigger's tragedy, but the American tragedy.

Aside from the one-dimensional characterization of the Thomas family, the soapbox tone of the courtroom speech, and the occasional heavy-handed use of symbolism and lapse into clichés and turgidity, the most serious flaw in *Native Son* is the imaginative conception of black Americans as pathological social deviants and the distance between the implied author's essential norms and those of enlightened middle-class readers, especially blacks. Wright's unqualified rejection of the viability of black folk culture as a way of maintaining or changing arrangements of status, power, and identity in a hostile environment is intellectually, politically, and morally untenable for many. Baldwin was not merely being petulant and self-serving when he complained of the absence of "any sense of Negro life as a continuing and complex group reality" in *Native Son*.[22] He, like many other readers, apparently knew that white oppression, even during slavery, was never absolute in its control over the intragroup lives of black Americans, who, from the slave quarters to the urban ghettos, have carried with them a system of values and rituals that has enabled them to sustain their humanity. Granted that white violence, both physical and psychological, and economic exploitation have caused many black Americans like Bigger to question their worth as human beings and to hate their white oppressors, neither the white nor the black myth of the Bad Nigger was ever as totally destructive of Afro-American character as Wright would have us believe. Nor did the black folklore so perceptively dramatized in *Uncle Tom's Children* become abruptly extinct in an urban setting as Wright reveals in *Lawd Today*.

Richard Wright and the Triumph of Naturalism

The violent, stunted life of Jake Jackson in *Lawd Today* is an early re-flection of Wright's experiment with point of view and his belief in the ineffectuality of the Southern black migrant's values and traditions in the big city. Unlike Bigger, Jake, a caricature of the black urban worker, em-braces the rituals and values of the black world. But, as in *Native Son*, Wright again treats all black folklore as derivative of the lust for trash of the larger society or as irrational, backward encumbrances that restrict human freedom and distort personality development. "When he went to the movies," says the editorializing narrator,

> he always wanted to see Negroes, if there were any in the play, shown against the background of urban conditions, not rural ones. Anything which smacked of farms, chain gangs, lynchings, hunger or the South in general was repugnant to him. These things had so hurt him once that he wanted to forget them forever; to see them again merely served to bring back the deep pain for which he knew no salve.[23]

Thus, whereas Wright morally and intellectually distances himself from his protagonist, one of the most pathetic antiheroes in Afro-American fiction, he emotionally sympathizes with him. The ironic tone of scene after scene emphasizes Wright's profound rejection of the traditions of black culture, his Afro-American heritage, as useless baggage from the rural Southern past. As "The Ethics of Living Jim Crow," *Black Boy*, and *American Hunger* reveal, the psychological and emotional scars inflicted on Wright during his childhood in the South prevented him as a writer from affirming those qualities of Afro-American religion, language, music, and humor that have proved their vitality and viability in a modern, indus-trialized urban society.

The major achievement of *Native Son*, then, is its stark, naturalistic vision of the social paradoxes that bind white and black Americans. As the prod-uct of dual cultural tensions of the pre–World War II era, Bigger Thomas was and is a symbol of America's failure to provide the freedom and security necessary for all individuals, regardless of race, creed, or sex, to fulfill their basic psychological and physical needs, their potential for growth, while in pursuit of the promise of a better and fuller life. In this sense, Bigger may also be viewed as modern man struggling in the most instinc-tive manner for a sense of identity and community in an urban society whose impersonalization and disorganization destroys his humanity. Wright's most significant contributions to the tradition of the Afro-Amer-ican novel thus are threefold: his complex and controversial naturalistic vision of urban black characters and culture, his creation of the best-known character in black fiction by a synthesis of white and black myths of the

Bad Nigger, and his projection of the Afro-American as the metaphor for America and modern man. "All my life," he states in *Black Boy*, "had shaped me for the realism, the naturalism of the modern novel. . . ."[24] By realism Wright is probably referring to the Marxist concepts of critical and socialist realism, which depict the oppressive aspects of bourgeois society and, in the latter case, foreshadow the evolution of a socialist society.

The Triumph of Naturalism

Although earlier novels by Dunbar, Du Bois, and Johnson had dealt with the conflict between determinism and the human will, it was the interplay between Freudian psychology and Marxist social analysis in *Native Son* that established the naturalistic model for many black novelists of the forties. Unlike the novels of the New Negro, those influenced by the example of *Native Son* are informed by the belief that the character and history of man can be completely explained by biological and socioeconomic facts. The Wright paradigm of naturalism stresses the violence and pathological personalities that result from racial oppression and economic exploitation. Novelists generally identified as being strongly influenced by Wright include William Attaway (*Blood on the Forge*, 1941); Carl Offord (*The White Face*, 1943); Chester Himes (*If He Hollers Let Him Go*, 1945, and *Lonely Crusade*, 1947); Curtis Lucas (*Third Ward Newark*, 1946); Ann Petry (*The Street*, 1946); Alden Bland (*Behold a Cry*, 1947); Willard Motley (*Knock on Any Door*, 1947); William Gardner Smith (*Last of the Conquerors*, 1948); and Willard Savoy (*Alien Land*, 1949). As the analysis that follows of selected novels by Attaway, Himes, Petry, and Smith will demonstrate, however, the naturalistic vision of these novelists takes such different forms that the concept of a "Wright School" is at best misleading. Attaway's *Blood on the Forge*, for example, is a panoramic study of the destruction of a family and a way of life, whereas Himes's *If He Hollers Let Him Go*, Petry's *Street*, and Smith's *Last of the Conquerors* have more in common with case studies of alienated individuals. In style these narratives combine objectivity with satire, impressionism, or sensationalism; in point of view, they range from omniscient to first-person narrators with varying degrees of reliability. Their salient themes are color and class violence, and their protagonists are generally victims of forces beyond their control or full understanding.

WILLIAM ATTAWAY (1912–)

Like Richard Wright, William Attaway was a migrant from Mississippi. The son of a physician, he was born in Mississippi in 1912 and migrated to Chicago with his family while he was very young. He attended the University of Illinois, where he began writing plays and short stories. His father's death during the Depression set him adrift. Answering the call of the sea and the open road, he became a seaman, labor organizer, salesman, and hobo before returning to finish college. His publications in such periodicals as *Challenge* (1934–37) qualified him for the Illinois Federal Writers' Project in 1935, where he met Wright. He is primarily remembered for his two novels: *Let Me Breathe Thunder* (1939) and *Blood on the Forge* (1941).

In contrast to *Let Me Breathe Thunder*, which reveals the influence of John Steinbeck and is the first-person narrative of the adventures of two white hoboes and a Mexican boy on the West Coast, *Blood on the Forge* is influenced by Wright and employs an omniscient narrator to tell the story of the Southern black migrants who found the Northern steel mills more deadly than the share-cropping system from which they sought to escape. Emphasizing class rather than color warfare, Attaway dramatizes both the humanistic and mythic significance of his theme. On one level we sympathize with the personal struggle of the three Moss half-brothers—Chinatown, Melody, and Big Mat—for the basic human needs of food, shelter, jobs, and dignity. On another we see their experience as the archetype of the exodus from the South of many thousands of blacks who began moving North in waves in the 1890s. In flight from Jim Crow laws, the boll weevil, and Mississippi floods, they sought the land of promise and a new life. But racism and the folk culture of Southern migrants poorly prepared them for the impact of the industrialized North and for casting their lot with European immigrants against the industrial magnates.

Divided into five parts, *Blood on the Forge* moves swiftly and dialectically from the exploitation of the Moss brothers on a dying Kentucky farm to their exploitation as strike-breakers in Pennsylvania steel mills. Attaway's interweaving of interpretive commentary by the omniscient narrator with Southern black dialogue dramatically establishes the folk thesis in Part 1. "Nineteen-nineteen, early spring: the last time, there among the red clay hills, he was to reach down his guitar."[25] The bond between the Moss family and the land is broken by the landowner's abuse of the land for profit and the riding boss's contempt for Big Mat's dead mother. Fearing that the riding boss would lead a lynch mob after him for the beating he gave him, Big Mat and his brothers seize the opportunity offered by a field agent for the mills and are sent North in sealed boxcars. Big Mat's monologue in the rural black dialect of the period signals the end of a way of life:

Ain't nothin' make me leave the land if it good land. The hills bigger
'n any white man, I reckon. Take more 'n jest trouble to run me off
the hills. I been in trouble. I been born into trouble. Shareworked
these hills from the bad land clean to the mines at Madison. The old
folks make crop here afore we was born. Now the land done got tired.
. . . Somehow it seem like I know why the land git tired. And it jest
seem like it come time to get off. The land has jest give up, and I
guess it's good for things to come out like this. Now us got to give
up too. (Pp. 36–37)

Like Wright, Attaway has an acute ear for the distinctive phonological and
syntactic patterns of black speech.

In addition, the compactness of Part 2, and its symbolic description of
the trip North in sealed boxcar trains, reveal Attaway's mythic vision of
the black experience as he conjures up the helplessness, darkness, stench,
congestion, misery, and fear of the Middle Passage from Africa to the New
World. Part 3 provides a panoramic view of the steel community and
contrasts the remembered Southern landscape and peasants' attitude toward nature with the actual Northern landscape and the mill owners'
attitude. "To us niggers," says the reliable narrator in the collective voice
of the migrants, "who are seeing the red-clay hills with our minds this
Allegheny Country is an ugly, smoking hell out of a backwoods preacher's
sermon" (p. 45). In Part 4 the industrial environment alienates the brothers
from each other, and nature exacts its price for the abuse it suffers when
a furnace explodes, killing fourteen men and blinding Chinatown; and in
Part 5 Big Mat, while envisioning himself as a black riding boss and leading
strike-breaking deputies in a night raid on the union's headquarters, is
killed by a union sympathizer. Crippled in body and spirit, Chinatown
and Melody head for Pittsburgh at the end of the novel.

The author-narrator's omniscience and dispassionate tone seek to reduce
our moral and emotional identification with the characters and events
while increasing our political sympathy with them. We see the life of the
steel community from a distance, ranging widely from the desperate Slavic
families in their rows of frame shacks to the loveless whores of Mexican
Town in their one-room shanties. For thematic and structural unity, the
fornication and incest of the European children are portrayed with somewhat greater detachment than the prostitution and hopelessness of Anna,
the fifteen-year-old Mexican child/woman whose sexuality drives a wedge
between Big Mat and Melody. Attaway's delineation of Anna reinforces
the theme that is most powerfully expressed in the empty life of the Moss

170

Richard Wright and the Triumph of Naturalism

brothers: the exploitative combination of capitalism and modern industrialization mangles the bodies and distorts the personalities of peoples of the soil. For Chinatown, the youngest brother, delight in the senses and a gold tooth that makes him feel like somebody enables him to cope with his harsh life in the South, but in the North life becomes completely empty when the mill explosion blinds him. For Melody, who down South "never had a craving in him that he couldn't slick away on his guitar," the new environment and hunger for Anna called for a new music, the urban blues, which intensified rather than relieved his craving and drove him to smash his right hand "so never again would he be able to hold a pick."

Attaway dispassionately demonstrates that the folk values of European immigrants and North American migrants, who cling tenaciously to emotional responses to life, do not adequately prepare them to cope with the social and psychological problems endemic to post–World War I industrial communities. Although Zanski and other European immigrants see the wisdom of black and white workers joining together in a union, Mat's experience as a black sharecropper has not encouraged him to trust whites, and his rejection by Anna unleashes the pent-up hatred and violence that lead to his death. The moral and political distance between the author-narrator and his main character are most vividly dramatized in Part 5, where Big Mat, after choking an old Ukrainian to death and "laughing crazily" in exaltation of his power, is clubbed to death by a young Ukrainian worker. In a vision just before his death, the truth belatedly and implausibly comes to him: "Maybe somewhere in these mills a new Mr. Johnston [the Kentucky landowner] was creating riding bosses, making a difference where none existed" (p. 233).

With an uncommon understanding of the dynamics of the Southern black folk personality and control of aesthetic distance, Attaway portrays Big Mat, the main character and oldest brother, as the victim of both biological and socioeconomic forces that he does not fully understand. In Part 1 he is driven by the fundamental urges of hunger, fear, and sex, especially dread of God's curse on him for being illegitimate. A huge, strong, brooding, deeply religious man, he attributes his wife Hattie's six miscarriages to the curse. " 'The Lawd don't love no child of sin. That's why he don't love me. That's why he put the curse on me' " (p. 24). To expiate his sin and lift the curse, he reads the Bible daily and abstains from drinking liquor. But when in Part 3 he receives a letter from Hattie telling him of her seventh miscarriage, he turns in vain to Anna and to violence for affirmation of his manhood and humanity. Finally, in Parts 4 and 5 it is the curse of the land as expressed by Smothers, the old, crippled, black prophet of doom, rather than the curse of blood that distorts Big Mat's personality and leads to his destruction. Thus, the obsessions and blindness of the Moss brothers are as responsible for their defeat as the impact of the industrial environment.

Attaway shares with Wright a pessimistic attitude toward the viability of folk culture in a modern industrial world and a concern for the psychological subtleties of his characters as well as their harsh social realities. More significantly, although Attaway was not a Marxist, his analysis in *Blood on the Forge* of the dynamics of capitalism as its alienates men from the land and themselves is the best Marxist interpretation of society in the tradition of the Afro-American novel and anticipates the critical realism of John O. Killens.

CHESTER BOMAR HIMES (1909–84)

The roots of Chester Himes's personal double-consciousness are revealed in his three semi-autobiographical novels—*Cast the First Stone* (1952), *The Third Generation* (1954), and *The Primitive* (1955)—and two autobiographies: *The Quality of Hurt* (1972) and *My Life of Absurdity* (1976). The youngest of three sons, he was born on July 29, 1909, in Jefferson City, Missouri. His childhood was filled with the turbulence of a querulous, neurotic light-complexioned mother and a psychologically emasculated, dark-skinned father, whose marriage disintegrated under the stress of his wife's contempt for black people and the frustrations of Northern Jim Crow and unemployment. When he was fourteen, Himes, in an accident that he held himself partly responsible for and that left him guilt-ridden for many years, saw his younger brother Joe blinded in a chemistry demonstration. After graduation from high school in 1926, Chester himself was in a serious accident, permanently injuring his back after falling down an elevator shaft on his hotel job. He recovered sufficiently from this accident by September, however, to matriculate with the help of a disability pension at Ohio State University in Columbus. Depressed by the white environment, he dropped out in 1927 and became a bellhop and hustler. In 1928 he was arrested for armed robbery and sentenced to twenty to twenty-five years in the Ohio State Penitentiary.

While in prison, which was incredibly free of racial conflict but rampant with homosexuality and violence, he became a professional gambler and writer. His apprenticeship stories were published in such black weekly newspapers and magazines as the *Atlanta World*, the *Pittsburgh Courier*, the *Afro-American*, and *Abbott's Monthly*; and his first professional story, "Crazy in the Stir," was sold to *Esquire* in 1934. In 1936 he was released on parole, and he married the following year. In 1953, after the publication of his two most important novels, *If He Hollers Let Him Go* (1945) and *Lonely Crusade* (1947), and the failure in 1951 of his first marriage, and then, in 1952, of a torrid, ambivalent affair with a white woman, he became an expatriate in Europe, frustrated and embittered by his futile struggle with the absurdity of American racism. Driven by the absurdity and ambivalence of his experience as a black American, he sought desperately to reconcile his hope and despair, love and hatred, by turning to interracial sex, including two marriages to white women, and to writing. Of the more than eighteen books he published before his death in Spain in 1984, fifteen are novels, including the eight black detective novels featuring Coffin Ed Johnson and Grave Digger Jones.

Although the detective novels he published in France did not bring Himes his first significant literary award—in 1944 he won a Julius Rosenwald Fellowship—they did introduce him to a larger audience than he had in America.[26] In 1958 he was awarded the Grand Prix de Littérature policière for the French translation of the first Coffin Ed and Grave Digger detective novel, *For Love of Imabelle* (1957). In an interview with John A. Williams, Himes explains that he turned to detective novels primarily for the money. "The *Serie Noire* was the best paid series in France. So they started off paying me a thousand-dollar advance, which was the same as the Americans were paying, and they went up to fifteen hundred dollars, which was more."[29] With no illusions about the tradition of the detective novel as a literary form, Himes candidly expresses his views on the relationship of life and black writers to that tradition:

> American violence is public life, it's a public way of life, it becomes a form, a detective story form. So I would think that any number of black writers should go into the detective story form. As a matter of fact, I feel that they could be very competent. Anyway, I would like to see a lot of them do so. They would not be imitating me because when I went into it, into the detective story field, I was just imitating all the other American detective story writers, other than the fact that I introduced various new angles which were my own. But on the whole, I mean the detective story originally in the plain narrative form—straightforward violence—is an American product. So I haven't created anything whatsoever; I just made the faces black, that's all.[27]

As a friend of the pioneer black detective novelist Rudolph Fisher, the creator of the Coffin Ed–Grave Digger series, and the writer who taught Ishmael Reed "the essential difference between a black detective and Sher-

Richard Wright and the Triumph of Naturalism

lock Holmes," Himes underestimates his importance in the tradition of the detective novel.[28]

Set in Harlem, the eight detective novels published between 1957 and 1969 introduced two black precinct detectives to the hard-boiled tradition of Dashiell Hammett's Sam Spade and Raymond Chandler's Philip Marlowe.[29] Fantasy and realism clash in the violent, colorful Harlem of Coffin Ed and Grave Digger, tough cops Himes patterned after two black Los Angeles detectives.[30] In the first novel in the series, *For Love of Imabelle*, the narrator establishes the appearance and pattern of behavior of the famous Harlem detective team: "Both were tall, loose-jointed, sloppily dressed, ordinary-looking dark-brown colored men. But there was nothing ordinary about their pistols. They carried specially made long-barreled nickel-plated .38 calibre revolvers. . . . Folks in Harlem believed that Grave Digger Jones and Coffin Ed Johnson would shoot a man stone dead for not standing straight in a line."[31] The only difference in appearance between the two is that Coffin Ed's face is permanently disfigured by acid thrown in his eyes in a fight with hoodlums. Tough, with violent tempers, Himes's detectives are unlike the ratiocinators of Poe, Arthur Conan Doyle, and Rudolph Fisher. Those detectives are men of thought in an essentially ordered society; Himes's are men of action in an essentially chaotic, violent world. They have a reputation for pistol-whipping and shooting suspects and hoodlums in order to protect the innocent. Despite their excessive violence and simplistic moral judgments, however, Coffin Ed and Grave Digger are heroes to many readers. "If they lived in the real world," Stephen F. Milliken perceptively writes in his critical study of Himes, "it might be more accurate to call them fascists, thugs, or vigilantes, but they live instead in the very special world of literary heroes, a world of the imagination, in which the forces of right and the forces of evil finally have it out, tooth and claw, and the forces of right, represented by the heroes, inevitably triumph."[32]

Although the success of Himes's detective novels is primarily due to the characterization of Coffin Ed and Grave Digger, the narrative technique used in the series also heightens the dramatic intensity and immediacy of setting, character, and action. The stories are told mainly in dialogue with the occasionally disembodied voice of a third-person omniscient narrator introducing relevant and functional descriptions of the setting and characters. The language crackles with the energy of the Harlem idiom and the slang of street people: hustlers, pimps, whores, gamblers, pushers, and con artists. The plot line is simple yet suspenseful: either the good guys are searching for a murderer; or the bad guys are searching desperately for a mysterious object, killing anyone who gets in their way until the good guys become involved in the search, either for the mysterious object itself or for a suspect or witness who is one of the searchers. After a series of fantastic incidents, the good guys capture the murderers or the mysterious object, clear themselves of charges of brutality, and go home to their families on Long Island. The plot unfolds at a rapid pace with frequent shifts in narrative time to keep the spotlight on outrageously funny or violent incidents and characters.[33] The narrative technique of the detective novels contrasts sharply with Himes's first and most powerful novel.

If He Hollers Let Him Go is a tightly structured naturalistic book with a psychological and satirical thrust. The title comes from a play song that black children use to exclude individuals from games.[34] The setting is Los Angeles, the year, 1944, and the protagonist, Bob Jones, an assistant foreman (leaderman) in a World War II shipyard. The theme and structure of the novel derive their resonance and coherence from a series of nightmares. Nightmares of impotency begin each of the five days of the novel, establishing a mood of fear and despair that increasingly pervades the protagonist's daily consciousness. The novel opens with a set of nightmares that includes a helpless black dog that nobody but the protagonist wanted, a search for a murder suspect whom the police presume is a crippled black, and the protagonist's humiliating rejection for a job by two laughing white men. The metaphorical condensation and displacement of images of racial rejection, persecution, humiliation, and impotence are symbolic of Bob Jones's repressed desire for personal and political equality. The novel closes with the nightmare of a Marine sergeant about to kill the protagonist, not because he confesses raping a white woman and killing a white man for calling him a "nigger," but simply because the Marine "ain't killed a nigger yet." The close correlation between Bob's nightmares and social reality reinforces the central theme: racial hatred and bigotry during World War II turned the American Dream into a nightmare of fear and despair for many educated black men who, like Bob Jones, sought to free themselves from color and class labels and realize their human and civil rights. Falsely accused of rape and completely disillusioned, Bob accepts the judge's offer to join the army rather than go to trial.

Despite surface similarities, *If He Hollers Let Him Go* is more a reaction to *Native Son* than an imitation of it. Both are detailed studies of the effects of racism on the personality of a black man, are filtered through the consciousness of the protagonist, and are critical of Marxism and the black bourgeoisie. Commenting on Bigger Thomas as a product of American

Richard Wright and the Triumph of Naturalism

racism, Bob states: " 'Well, you couldn't pick a better person than Bigger Thomas to prove the point. But after you prove it, then what? Most white people I know are quite proud of having made Negroes into Bigger Thomases.' "[35] Although Bob, like Bigger, is controlled by a fear and hatred of whites, his solution for the problem and his fate as a college-educated black man are seen as more tragic than Bigger's by the implied author. Driven to nightmares, sexual insecurity, and compulsive, self-destructive acts, Bob, with whom Himes seems to identify on all levels, believes that " 'the only solution to the Negro problem is a revolution. We've got to make white people respect us and the only thing white people have ever respected is force' " (p. 84). This political awareness is inconsistent, however, with Bob's contempt for both working-class and middle-class blacks, as well as with the denouement of the novel. Unable to resolve his ambivalence about being black and to resist a white co-worker's challenge to his manhood, Bob does not compel the respect of the other characters or the reader. Instead, he compels our ambivalence as he indicts himself as "a black son of a bitch destroying himself because of a no-good white slut from Texas," and we see his nightmares of impotency become his waking reality.

By allowing his protagonist to tell the story in the first person, Himes apparently wants the reader to identify emotionally and morally with Bob and to experience his ambivalence toward blacks and whites. But the protagonist-narrator's contempt for a black ethos, combined with his naive American idealism and masculinity, actually frustrates a healthy balance in his double-consciousness and alienates many readers. "Anyone who wanted to could be nigger-rich, nigger-important, have their Jim Crow religion, and go to nigger heaven," says Bob in self-analysis. "I'd settle for a leaderman job at Atlas Shipyard—if I could be a man, defined by Webster as a male human being. That's all I'd ever wanted—just to be accepted as a man—without ambition, without distinction, either of race, creed, or color; just a simple Joe walking down an American street, going my simple way, without any other identifying characteristic but weight, height and gender" (p. 144). Implicit here is Himes's view that it is the black American's manhood that the myths and rituals of white society are determined to deny or destroy.[36] After Japan's attack on Pearl Harbor, his promotion to leaderman, and the confinement of Japanese-Americans, Bob's fear of whites and negative identification with nonwhites increase. "It was thinking about if they ever did that to me, Robert Jones, Mrs. Jones's dark son, that started me to getting scared. . . . I was the same color as the Japanese and I couldn't tell the difference. 'A yeller-bellied Jap' coulda meant me too. I could always feel race trouble, serious trouble, never more than two feet off. Nobody bothered me. Nobody said a word. But I was tensed every moment to spring" (pp. 7–8). Personal rather than historical awareness of the color and class contradictions in the theory and practice of American egalitarianism thus intensifies Bob's ambivalence toward people and events.

Himes dramatizes Bob's ambivalence toward white people by his conflicting desires to run over them with his car and to seek their acceptance. But it is dramatized most effectively in his relationship to Madge Perkins, the mythic American White Bitch, who acts as if she were a naked virgin and he were King Kong whenever they meet. Caught up in this bizarre sexual and political ritual, Bob responds with lust and loathing. The root of his ambivalence is his resistance to actual and imagined threats to his manhood, which he narrowly defines according to the white American myth of maleness. "Bob's supreme aspiration, his thwarted ideal," as Milliken rightly observes, "is to live out the American myth of maleness, with all its folklorish components: heroic fighter, dauntless leader of men, and tender lover. But this is the one role that racism denies to the black man."[37]

In setting and theme *Lonely Crusade*, Himes's second novel, is similar to *If He Hollers Let Him Go*, but its plot and characters are more complex and contrived. Set in Los Angeles in the spring of 1943, *Lonely Crusade* is a novel of ideas illustrating the belief that modern black American men are engaged in a lonely, agonizing struggle to attain the ideal of American manhood that the nation has historically and systematically denied them because of their color. It is the episodic journey of Lee Gordon, a black union organizer, to spiritual rebirth and heroic action through embracing and then subordinating racial consciousness to class consciousness. Dialogues, interior monologues, and editorializing comments on unionism, racism, and Communism are key stages in the protagonist's rite of passage, and the several subplots that intertwine with the main plot introduce minor characters whose personalities, briefly but compellingly outlined, give direction to the protagonist's tortuous crusade and are agents in his transformation. Smitty and Joe Ptak, the sentimental white union secretary and the battle-scarred union organizer from national headquarters, provide the lessons in unionism. Ruth Gordon, the black wife whose economic independence Lee resents and whose body he violates as therapy for his spiritual emasculation by whites; Luther McGregor, the street-wise, treacherous black Communist who "knows how to be a nigger and make it pay"; Lester McKinley, the former professor of Latin and black psychotic who

Richard Wright and the Triumph of Naturalism

has a compulsion to kill white men; and Jackie Forks, Lee's white Communist lover who not only "thought herself inviolable within the party, but sacrosanct within the world"—all educate him to the different yet inevitable effects of racial consciousness. Bart, the black Communist leader whose "Protestant, puritanical, Negro inheritance" clashed occasionally with the ruthlessness of Party tactics, provides the key lesson in Communism; and Abbie Rosenberg, the Jewish Communist whose eclectic progressive philosophy becomes the catalyst for Lee's spiritual rebirth, offers the guidance by word and example that enables him to embrace his own reality and transcend the daily fear of living and dying. Unfortunately, Himes's handling of Lee Gordon's deep-seated conviction of the basic inferiority of black people and the abrupt, spiritual transformation that results in his redemptive heroic death for the cause of unionism at the end of the novel violate the formal integrity of the narrative, and are more melodramatic than naturalistic.

In response to the criticism of his imaginative vision of the personalities of black Americans as pathological and even psychotic, Himes writes in "Dilemma of the Negro Novelist in the United States":

There can be no understanding of Negro life, of Negroes' compulsions, reactions, and actions; there can be no understanding of the sexual impulses, of Negro crime, of Negro marital relations, of our spiritual entreaties, our ambitions and our defeats, until this fear has been revealed at work behind the false-fronted facades of our ghettoes; until others have experienced with us to the same extent the impact of fear upon our personalities. It is no longer enough to say the Negro is a victim of a stupid myth. We must know the truth and what it does to us.

If this plumbing for the truth reveals within the Negro personality, homicidal mania, lust for white women, a pathetic sense of inferiority, paradoxical anti-Semitism, arrogance, uncle-tomism, hate and fear of self-hate, this then is the effect of oppression on the human personality. These are the daily horrors, the daily realities, the daily experiences of an oppressed minority.[38]

All his novels reveal this "plumbing for the truth." Although middle class and better educated, Himes's characters are at least as much the victims of racial and cultural oppression as Richard Wright's; and his sociopsychological vision of black Americans, which is like Wright's even though explicitly at odds with Bigger's characterization, reduces the complexity and paradoxes of elements of the Afro-American tradition to fear, hatred, powerlessness, and rage, especially sexual, in the black male. The melodramatic socialist vision of *Lonely Crusade* is his most ambitious, imaginative treatment of the complex theme of Afro-American double-consciousness. Aside from Coffin Ed Johnson, Grave Digger Jones, and his better educated, less violent Bigger Thomases, Himes's most significant contributions to the tradition of the Afro-American novel are, in short, his naturalistic exploration of black male rage and rebellion and his masculine celebration of sex and unionism as the personal and communal purification rituals for transcending racism.

ANN LANE PETRY (1911–)

The setting and themes of Ann Petry's novels are a natural outgrowth of her intimacy with the black inner-city life of New York and the white small-town life of New England. Born in 1911 in Old Saybrook, Connecticut, Ann Petry grew up in a predominantly white environment and, in the family tradition, graduated in 1934 with a degree in pharmacy from the University of Connecticut. After working in the family drugstores in Old Saybrook and the nearby town of Lyme, she married in 1938 and moved to New York to work and pursue her childhood interests in writing. From 1938 to 1944 she worked as a journalist for two Harlem newspapers: *Amsterdam News* and *People's Voice*. In 1943 her short stories began appearing in *The Crisis* and *Phylon*. The early chapters of *The Street* won her the Houghton Mifflin Literary Fellowship in 1945. In 1948 she returned to Connecticut to raise her family and continue writing. Her publications include four children's books, a collection of short stories, and three novels: *The Street, Country Place,* and *The Narrows*. The novels reveal her movement from a naturalistic vision of the big city to a demythologizing of black and white relations in small-town America.

The Street is a conventional novel of economic determinism in which the environment is the dominant force against which the characters must struggle to survive. The novel opens symbolically in November 1944 with the wind, cold, dirt, and filth of 116th Street overpowering the hurried Harlem pedestrians, including the apartment-hunting protagonist, Lutie Johnson. It closes with Lutie's leaving the city by train after killing the man who assaults her, the snow falling symbolically, "gently obscuring the grime and garbage and the ugliness" of the street. As the plot progresses episodically, we see that it was "streets like 116th Street or being colored, or a combination of both with all it implied" that drove the protagonist's father to drink, her mother to an early grave, and the neighbors to various forms of desperation and death.[39] Lutie Johnson was determined

Richard Wright and the Triumph of Naturalism

that none of these things would happen to her, but her will to succeed is ineffectual against relentless economic, racist, and sexist forces that had walled her in an ever-narrowing space since birth. Far from being an accident, we learn through the narrator's probing into Lutie's mind, these forces "were the North's mob ... the method the big cities used to keep Negroes in their place" (p. 200).

Unlike Wright's and Himes's male protagonists, Lutie Johnson is neither psychologically tormented nor driven by a fear of white people. Raised by her tale-telling, puritan-minded grandmother, she is a respectable, married woman, driven by hunger for a better life and a place to be somebody. She seeks to satisfy this hunger by naively subscribing to the Protestant ethic and the American Dream as expressed by the Chandlers, a wealthy white New England family for whom she worked for two years as a live-in maid, and as embodied in Benjamin Franklin, with whom she compares herself. Ignoring her own social reality—she is a working-class black woman with an eight-year-old son to support; separated from her unfaithful, unemployed husband; living in Harlem during World War II; struggling to maintain her moral principles and to share equally in the wealth of the nation—she fantasizes "that if Ben Franklin could live on a little bit of money and could prosper, then so could she" (p. 44). In blind pursuit of the American Dream, Lutie loses her family and her hope for happiness, but not her self-respect. When she fails to get the singing job she had counted on to move off 116th Street and up the ladder of success, social reality begins to displace her dream world. "The trouble was with her," she concludes. "She had built up a fantastic structure made from the soft, nebulous, cloudy stuff of dream. There hadn't been a solid, practical brick in it, not even a foundation. She had built it up of air and vapor and moved right in. So of course it had collapsed. It had never existed anywhere but in her mind" (p. 191). Ann Petry's naturalistic delineation of her protagonist and use of symbols of confinement, as well as contrasting images of the white world of Lyme, Connecticut, and the black world of Harlem thus demythologize both American culture and Afro-American character.

The story is told by a disembodied third-person omniscient narrator, but Petry allows Lutie's consciousness to dominate the narrative and generally avoids moralizing. The action and setting are subordinated to Lutie's impression of their impact on black women, who unrepresentatively have no contact with the black church. Except for the denouement, whose sensationalism some critics consider a serious weakness,[40] the author-narrator explores the social evils of segregated communities, white and black,

Richard Wright and the Triumph of Naturalism

with restraint and objectivity. But it is clear that neither Petry nor her protagonist simplistically blames black men for the broken homes, poverty, and hopelessness that characterizes too many urban black communties. Although they share some of the responsibility, the root of these social problems is not black men like her alcoholic father and adulterous husband, nor black women like Mrs. Hedges, the whorehouse madam, but white people like Junto, the vice lord, and the Chandlers, whose power and privilege are based on the economic and racial exploitation of blacks. If it is impossible to escape the agony and desperation of the black inner city, it is equally impossible, as the Chandlers reveal, to escape the delusions and degeneracy of small white towns.

In *Country Place* Petry moves beyond economic and racial determinism to explore the realities beneath the myths of rural, small-town communities. In contrast to traditional stories and images of the beneficence, continuity, integrity, and homogeneity of values in small, rural communities, her narrative reveals the hypocrisy, violence, prejudice, and stagnation of Lennox, Connecticut, shortly after World War II. *Country Place* is a first-person, retrospective narrative with the town druggist as an on-the-scene chronicler of the "untoward events" in the lives of the Grambys and Roanes. Because the major characters are white, and because time and place are more important thematically than color and class, it is not as relevant, however, to our theory of a distinctive Afro-American narrative tradition as *The Street* and *The Narrows*, her third and best-wrought novel.

In *The Narrows* Petry moves even further beyond economic determinism as she continues to explore the impact of time and place on the shaping of character. This time the setting is the black community in Monmouth, Connecticut, another small, typically provincial, white New England town, during the era of Senator Joseph McCarthy's witch hunt for Communists in the State Department. The red neon signs on Dumble Street tell the story of its change; we learn through septuagenarian Abigail Church's reverie that

it was now, despite its spurious early-morning beauty, a street so famous, or so infamous, that the people who lived in Monmouth rarely ever referred to it, or the streets near it, by name; it had become an area, a section, known variously as The Narrows, Eye of the Needle, The Bottom, Little Harlem, Dark Town, Niggertown—because Negroes had replaced those other earlier immigrants, the Irish, the Italians and the Poles.[41]

181

Petry's fine craftsmanship is immediately apparent in the compelling manner that the structure, style, and theme of the narrative fuse as Abbie reflects on what in addition to the color and class hatred in the world has brutalized her adopted son Lincoln "Link" Williams, the protagonist. "In Link's case—well, if they hadn't lived on Dumble Street, if the Major had lived longer, if Link had been their own child instead of an adopted child, if she hadn't forgotten about him when he was eight, simply forgotten his existence, if she hadn't had to figure so closely with the little money that she had . . . and eke it out with the small sums she earned by sewing, embroidering, making jelly. If" (pp. 13–14).

The theme, simply stated, is that our lives are shaped as much by contingency as they are by time and place. "On how peculiar, and accidental, a foundation rests all of one's attitudes toward a people. . . . " Abbie thinks. "Frances hears the word Irish and thinks of a cathedral and the quiet of it, the flickering light of the votive candles, the magnificence of the altar, and I see Irishwomen, strong in their faith, holding a family together. Accident? Coincidence? It all depended on what happened in the past. We carry it around with us. We're never rid of it" (pp. 253–56). This theme is developed in the main plot—the love affair between Link, a black orphan and Dartmouth graduate, and Camilio Williams, the internationally known heiress to the wealth and power of Monmouth's most prominent white family, the Treadways—and the several tributary subplots. The movement of the main plot is more psychological than chronological, for its pace is frequently interrupted by digressions and flashbacks to Link's childhood. The meeting of the couple in the Narrows, their falling in love, the discovery that she is rich and married, his rejection of her for betraying his trust and using him as a black stud, her revenge by claiming he attempted to rape her and thus appealing to traditional color and class prejudice—all are influenced by chance and the historical past. The weight of the contingency of their lives and the history of American racism and New England hypocrisy are too heavy a burden for Link and Camilio's love to survive. For breaking the American tribal taboo, Link is murdered by Camilio's mother and husband.

Link, as his name suggests, is the major connection between the past and the present, the white world and the black, the rich and the poor; and it is his consciousness that dominates the third-person omniscient point of view that shifts from character to character. Adopted when he was eight by Abbie and Major Crunch, and having grown up in Monmouth, Link, at twenty-six, has lost faith in himself, other people, and his control over life. Most of the plot unfolds in his and Abbie's minds.

Richard Wright and the Triumph of Naturalism

His interior monologues, reveries, and flashbacks and those of the other characters weave a gossamer, impressionistic pattern of events that illuminate his double-consciousness and suggest why he is content to be a bartender at the Last Chance although he was a star athlete and Phi Beta Kappa student at Dartmouth, where he majored in history. Kidnapped at the end of the novel by Camilio's mother and husband, Link remembers the sensational front-page pictures of a drunk Camilio and an escaped black convict in the Narrows under headlines that inflamed historical color and class hatred by luridly portraying the black community as the breeding ground for crime and criminals: "So it was Jubine Lautrec's Harlot and The Convict by Anonymous that got me in this black Packard. That is one-quarter of the explanation. The other three-quarters reaches back to that Dutch man of Warre that landed in Jamestown in 1619" (p. 399).

The frequency, length, and occasional remoteness to the events at hand of the digressions and flashbacks give complexity to the characters but annoyingly impede the progress of the plot, and emotionally and psychologically distance the reader from the tragedy of the central character. This is most apparent in the denouement when Link is kidnapped and murdered. Equally passive but more strikingly individualized are Abbie and some of the minor characters. Abbie, a black New England puritan, is an old widow who is driven by an ambivalence about black people and an obsession with aristocratic values. Major, her dead husband, was a robust, sensitive mountain of a man who used to tell stories about the legendary members of his family, whom he affectionately called "swamp niggers." Jubine, the "recording angel" of Monmouth, is a man with a deep compassion for "the poor peons" like himself, a man "who spent a lifetime photographing a river, and thus recorded the life of man in the twentieth century. For the first time" (pp. 43–44). Malcolm Powther, a black Judas, is a pompous, worshipful servant to rich white people, whose values he embraces, and to his sensual, promiscuous wife, whom he fears will leave him for another man. And Peter Bullock, the unprincipled owner and publisher of the *Monmouth Chronicle,* which has been transformed over the years from an antislavery newspaper into an antiblack tool of the white ruling class, is a slave to custom, to a house, to a car, to ulcers, and to the major advertisers in his paper, especially the Treadwell family. Petry's use of symbolic characters like Cesar the Writing Man, the wandering poet who scribbles biblical verses on the sidewalk of Monmouth, is also dramatically effective. Early in the novel Cesar gives philosophical resonance to the characters, plot, and theme when he writes the following passage from Eccles. 1:10 in front of the cafe where Camilio and Link rendezvous:

Richard Wright and the Triumph of Naturalism

"Is there anything where of it may be said, See this is new? It hath been already of old time, which was before us" (p. 91).

Petry, like Himes and Wright, is adept at character delineation, but her protagonists are cut from a different cloth than those of her major contemporaries. In contrast to the pathology of a Bigger Thomas or Bob Jones or Lee Gordon, Lutie Johnson and Link Williams are intelligent, commonplace, middle-class aspiring blacks, who, despite the socialized ambivalence resulting from racism and economic exploitation, are not consumed by fear, hatred, and rage. Petry's vision of black personality is not only different from that of Himes and Wright, it is also more faithful to the complexities and varieties of black women, whether they are big city characters like Mrs. Hedges in *The Street* or small-town characters like Abbie Crunch in *The Narrows*. Ann Petry thus moves beyond the naturalistic vision of Himes and Wright to a demythologizing of American culture and Afro-American character. This is her most invaluable achievement in the tradition of the Afro-American novel.

WILLIAM GARDNER SMITH (1926–74)

Born in 1926 in Philadelphia, William Gardner Smith discovered at an early age that he had a flair for writing. He became a local reporter for the Pittsburgh *Courier* when he was eighteen and finished his first novel two years later. Drafted into the army in 1945, he served a year in Germany before returning to become a student at Temple University and continuing his career as a journalist and novelist. In 1951 he returned to Europe and became a member of the black expatriate community in Paris, where he died in 1974. Smith published four novels: *Last of the Conquerors,* an interracial love story in which black soldiers ironically discover more freedom in Germany than they found in the United States; *Anger at Innocence* (1950), a nonblack love story between a middle-aged married man and a pickpocket half his age; *South Street* (1954), a melodramatic tale of black militancy and interracial love; and *The Stone Face* (1963), an impressionistic story of the political awakening of a black expatriate to racial oppression in France. The best of these is the last.

The respect and freedom that black American soldiers in *Last of the Conquerors* find in Europe are also stressed in *The Stone Face.* But in his fourth and final novel Smith reveals a more mature command of his craft and a deeper, more political understanding of the nature and function of racism in the world. Divided into three major parts ("The Fugitive," "The White Man," and "The Brother"), the novel effectively traces a black expatriate's discovery that racial oppression not only exists in France, but that it is just as virulent as it is in the United States; only in France the primary victims are Algerians rather than black Americans. The theme is that wherever oppression exists, it dehumanizes the oppressor as well as the victim; and anybody who lives complacently in its shadow is guilty of social and moral blindness and irresponsibility.

The plot movement is episodic and rather conventional, but the recurring, contrasting images of the stone face of white hatred and of ostensibly unmolested interracial couples in Paris heighten the dramatic intensity of the narrative. The symbolic use of vision also enhances the development of character and theme. The situation in "The Fugitive" is that Simeon Brown, a black reporter and amateur painter, leaves the United States in 1960 to escape the pathology of American racism and to avoid killing the next person who racially abuses him. Stabbed in the eye as a youth by a teenage Polish gang leader, Simeon cannot forget his attacker's face, which becomes the symbol of white hatred and the subject of his unfinished portrait of "an inhuman face, the face of *un-man,* the face of discord, the face of destruction."[42] His love affair with Maria, a Jewish refugee from Poland who is going blind and seeks to forget her terrible past by becoming a Hollywood actress, is a melodramatic counterpoint to the protagonist's situation. The climax is triggered in "The White Man" by two events that prick Simeon's conscience about living comfortably in Paris and leaving the struggle against oppression to others. First, he sees a front-page picture in the *Herald Tribune* of black children in Little Rock, walking bravely to school through lines of soldiers and howling white mobs; and second, his Algerian friend Ahmed decides to join the Algerian liberation movement (FLN) and return to his homeland to fight against French colonialism. In "The Brother" Maria and Simeon take contrasting roads after her successful eye operation. She pursues her escapist dream of Hollywood, but Simeon seals his bond of brotherhood with the Algerians by getting involved in an FLN street demonstration and buying a ticket to return to fight the stone face in the United States.

Smith effectively uses a combination of direct observer and third-person omniscience to introduce the reader to the new Lost Generation, modern-day black intellectuals and artists who sought to escape the prejudice and violence of American racism by becoming permanent expatriates in the major cities of Europe. Like Hemingway's disillusioned, dissolute characters in *The Sun Also Rises,* most of Smith's characters are journalists, novelists, and musicians who drift from café to café and bed to bed in a vain effort to assuage their guilt for not being involved in the human and civil rights struggles in their native countries:

Clyde drank at the Monaco to forget about Jinx, Jinx drank at the Select to forget about herself, Doug made love to his State Department girl, Babe belched after a gigantic meal and joked off a feeling of guilt, Benson lay drunk and bitter in bed with his mistress, and Ahmed lay dead, his head battered to a pulp by police clubs, on the corner of rue du Bac and the Boulevard Saint-Germain. (P. 202)

Avoiding intrusive editorial comments, Smith makes extensive use of dialogues and symbols of distorted vision, encouraging identification with the moral and political awakening of his central character by generally restricting the focus to his double-consciousness.

Smith's protagonists are more like Petry's than like those of Himes, Attaway, and Wright. They are bright young men who are products of Philadelphia's inner city, but who, with the exception of the Bower brothers in *South Street*, seek to repress if not resolve their brooding sense of double-consciousness and potential for violence in foreign lands. Neither as adept at character delineation nor as experimental with language as Petry, Smith achieves his place in the tradition of the Afro-American novel by his plain style and exploration of the socialized ambivalence of black male expatriates in Europe as they desperately seek personal wholeness in interracial love and a separate peace.

Continuity and Change in the Novel of the Forties

Of the twenty-eight novels published by black Americans in the forties, excluding the nine by Oscar Micheaux and Frank Yerby,[43] more than a dozen bear traces of the influence of *Native Son* and mark the triumph of naturalism. The best of these—*Native Son, Blood on the Forge, If He Hollers Let Him Go*, and *The Street*—have been the primary focus of this chapter, which has attempted to demonstrate that sociological approaches that reduce their naturalistic vision to protest literature are inclined to oversimplify and misrepresent the individuality of the novelists' vision of life and aesthetic achievement. This individuality is most apparent in their conceptions and delineations of the dynamics of Afro-American character, which foster ambivalence toward blacks as well as whites, and in their resolutions of the problems of racism and economic exploitation that they portray.

At the same time, the Afro-American novel in the decade from Wright's *Native Son* to Smith's *Anger at Innocence* (1950) reveals both continuity and change. The theme of color and class conflict remains dominant, whether in the triumph of the naturalists or the satirists like Dorothy West, whose *The Living Is Easy* (1948) exposes the counterfeit black Brahmins of Boston, and Saunders Redding, whose *Strangers and Alone* attacks the inferiority syndrome of Southern black colleges. West and Redding, like Griggs, Chesnutt, Fisher, Thurman, and Schuyler, reveal that the conflict of color and class is intraracial as well as interracial. Whereas emphasis on external social reality with the conventional closed plot continues, with more documentation of acts of prejudice and discrimination than of black folklore, there is a corresponding shift, as the novels of Wright and Himes illustrate, to an exploration of the impact of oppression on the feelings and thoughts of the major characters. Although the general tone of naturalistic fiction is objective, pessimistic, and amoral, the black naturalism of the 1940s does not preclude the possibility of an implicit, albeit ironic, reaffirmation of faith in a moral universe and the sanctity of the individual by the implied author. On one level, for example, Bigger's confession to Max at the end of *Native Son* that he has instinctively rebelled against the morality of a social system that violated his humanity and individuality makes this point: " 'I ain't trying to forgive nobody and I ain't asking for nobody to forgive me. I ain't going to cry. They wouldn't let me live and I killed. Maybe it ain't fair to kill, and I reckon I really didn't want to kill. But when I think of why all the killing was. I begin to feel what I wanted, what I am. . . . ' " (p. 391). Implicit also is the traditional call for social change. By documenting the inherent weaknesses in the social system, what the novels of the forties actually demand, as critic Carl Milton Hughes has pointed out, "is not fundamental change in the social structure; rather they insist on making the letter and spirit of our Constitution and the Declaration of Independence indispensable to American social structure a reality."[44] This is in sharp contrast to some of the revolutionary novels of the 1960s and 1970s, which are more apocalyptic.

Two momentous changes were introduced in the Afro-American novel of the forties. The most obvious and controversial was Wright's creation of Bigger Thomas as the prototypical urban black American, obsessed by a fear and hatred of white people and driven to violence in rebellion against and, paradoxically, in affirmation of his dehumanization. Rejecting the traditional survival strategies offered by black music, the black church, and the extended black family, Wright, influenced by the work of Freud, Marx, Park, and Dreiser, depicted the black American as the victim of modern America and as the Bad Nigger incarnate. For novelists like Himes, who tailored Wright's pathological model of Afro-American personality to fit his own better educated protagonists, violence in the form of personal rebellion was the only therapeutic solution to oppression. But for Attaway, Petry, Smith, and those novelists whose vision of Afro-American character affirmed its double-consciousness and its multidimensional nature, personal rage and rebellion were not the only nor necessarily the most politically correct or humanistic mode of response to racial oppression and economic exploitation. The other change that occurred in the post–World War II period was an increase in the number of writers who published novels in which the protagonists and the majority of characters were white. In addition to Frank Yerby's white historical romances, these include Ann Petry's *Country Place,* Willard Motley's *Knock on Any Door* and *We Fished All Night,* Zora Neale Hurston's *Seraph on the Sewanee,* and William Gardner Smith's *Anger at Innocence.* Nick Romano in *Knock on Any Door* is perhaps the most sympathetically drawn and memorable of the white protagonists of the decade. As the tradition of the Afro-American novel continued into the fifties, the novelists moved significantly beyond naturalism to the rediscovery of the viability of myth, legend, and ritual as well as modern cultural codes and literary constructs.

6 / Myth, Legend, and Ritual in the Novel of the Fifties

People rationalize what they shun or are incapable of dealing with; these superstitions and their rationalizations become ritual as they govern behavior. The rituals become social forms, and it is one of the functions of the artist to recognize them and raise them to the level of art.

RALPH ELLISON
"The Art of Fiction"

THE integration that had been inaugurated in the closing years of World War II," as historian John Hope Franklin notes, "was greatly accelerated in the postwar years."[1] One of the dubious honors for black Americans as a result of the climate fostered by the recommendations of President Truman's interracial committees on civil rights and integration is that blacks constituted 30 percent of the United States forces in the Korean war (1950–51) but were only 10 percent of the general population. In 1954 the Supreme Court announced its landmark desegregation decision that the doctrine of "separate but equal" in public education was inherently contradictory and unconstitutional. A year later, blacks in Montgomery, Alabama, led by the Reverend Martin Luther King, Jr., boycotted the city bus lines to resist racial discrimination and abuse, launching the first postwar direct action movement of the masses, organized and led by blacks themselves. In 1957 Congress passed the first civil rights bill since 1875. It created the Civil Rights Commission, whose hearings in several cities on black voting disclosed that Southern white registrars were denying blacks the right to vote. "By 1962 more than thirty cases had been brought by the attorney general," according to Franklin, "to protect blacks in their efforts to vote in Mississippi, Louisiana, Alabama, Tennessee, and Georgia."[2] Also in 1957, President Eisenhower sent federal troops to Little Rock, Arkansas, to protect black school children from the violence of howling white mobs. The winds of social change were also blowing in West Africa, where Ghana achieved independence in the same year. In 1960 four black college students in Greensboro, North Carolina, sat-in at a downtown lunch counter in an effort to desegregate the facility, setting off a chain of nonviolent direct action sit-ins, freedom rides, wade-ins, and freedom marches across the country. The Congress of Racial Equality (CORE) and the Student Nonviolent Coordinating Committee (SNCC) spearheaded this phase of direct action, but they were soon joined by the Southern Christian Leadership Conference (SCLC) and the National Association for the Advancement of Colored People (NAACP), who began using the motto "Free by '63." In 1961 political and military intrigue by imperialist countries, following the independence of the Congo, resulted in the execution of Premier Patrice Lumumba. Rounding out this thumbnail sketch of 1952–62, we note another small yet significant step in the deinstitutionalization of racism by President Kennedy, who, with a stroke of his pen in 1962, ended discrimination in federally supported housing.

Beyond Naturalism

From 1952 to 1962 two parallel movements in the tradition of the Afro-American novel can be observed: a movement away from naturalism and nonracial themes, and a movement toward the rediscovery and revitalization of myth, legend, and ritual as appropriate sign systems for expressing the double-consciousness, socialized ambivalence, and double vision of the modern black experience. Black novelists of the forties, as Carl Milton Hughes illustrates, broadened their perspectives and began experimenting with nonracial themes and white protagonists.[3] This experimenting continued into the fifties with Smith's *Anger At Innocence* (1950), Demby's *Beetlecreek* (1950), Motley's *We Fished All Night* (1951), and *Let No Man Write My Epitaph* (1958), Himes's *Cast the First Stone* (1952), Petry's *Narrows* (1953), Wright's *Savage Holiday* (1954), and Baldwin's *Giovanni's Room* (1956). Most of these have nonwhite minor characters and a third-person undramatized narrator who is sympathetic toward the white protagonist, who, significantly, is a social misfit or outsider.

Baldwin's *Giovanni's Room*, a lyrical story of American and French homosexuality, and Himes's *Cast the First Stone*, a prison novel with homosexual overtones, are largely autobiographical narratives in which the implied authors closely identify with the major events and the first-person narrators. More typical are Wright's *Savage Holiday*, a melodramatic Freudian tale of the repressed sexuality of Erskine Fowler, "a Mason, a Rotarian, a Sunday School Superintendent, a man of parts"; Petry's *Narrows*, whose protagonist, as discussed in chapter 5, is black, but whose theme stresses the impact of chance and the historical past on the development of character; and Motley's *We Fished All Night*, the story of three Chicagoans who return from World War II as psychological and moral cripples, and *Let No*

Myth, Legend, and Ritual in the Novel of the Fifties

Man Write My Epitaph, a sequel to *Knock on Any Door* that traces the crim-
inality and salvation of Nick Romano's youngest brother and illegitimate
son. Motley, Smith, and Demby border on sentimentalism in depicting
the essential goodness of their white characters.

Theodore Hall, in *Anger at Innocence,* a naturalistic treatment of good
and evil, is, for example, a quiet, poetry-loving night watchman with
"strange ideas" and "a lot of taboos." Thirty-nine years old, he abruptly
leaves his wife of eighteen years and takes up with a nineteen-year-old
tramp he wants to marry, but who kills him and herself after he refuses
to adopt completely her life of degeneracy. Warned by her neo-Calvinist
mother that "Rodina was born evil," Hall, a "good" man, believes just
the opposite, but he is unable to redeem her. "She could not change," we
learn in Rodina's monologue, "neither could Theodore change. Even if he
wanted to. He was what he was. . . . He was good, she was evil."[4]

Bill Trapp, the tragic white victim in *Beetlecreek,* is as much the central
character in William Demby's first novel as is Johnny Johnson, the lonely
black fourteen-year-old Pittsburgh boy who resettles in Beetlecreek, West
Virginia, with his aunt and uncle. David Diggs, Johnny's frustrated, college-educated uncle succumbs to "good-timing" in his efforts to escape
the death-grip feeling of being black and trapped in Beetlecreek. Scapegoat
for the provinciality, prejudice, and fears of the townspeople, black and
white, Trapp, who has lived between the black and white sections of town
as a recluse for fifteen years, seeks spiritual regeneration and sociability
by reaching out to the black community, especially to Johnny and David,
who identified with the old man's feelings of neglect and loneliness. Even
when he worked in the carnival, "he felt close to them," Trapp reflects.
"Watching them secretly as he did he could see that they were always
dodging something, were ashamed of something, just as he was; they
were the same breed as he."[5] Critical of what he sees as the philistinism
and provincialism of blacks, Demby, an expatriate in Italy from 1949 to
the 1960s, is emotionally and morally sympathetic toward Trapp, whose
well-meaning but naive effort "to reach out and touch people, to love,"
by giving a picnic in his yard for black and white children results in the
malicious rumors that he was a child molester and fiend. Demby is also
sympathetic toward Johnny, whose initiation into the Nightriders, a black
youth gang, required him to violate his compassion for Trapp by adopting
the community's narrow-minded values and burning down Trapp's house;
and toward David, who by leaving Beetlecreek at the end of the novel
with an old college flame, "had stepped outside himself by going with
the girl, bringing life to himself when the village had already killed

him. . . . ."[6] Thus we see that the experiment with nonracial themes and protagonists which began in the forties continued in the fifties, when the prevailing political sentiments were integrationist. Contrary to Hughes's contention, however, the parallel tendency of a "break with naturalism and the accompanying philosophy of determinism" did not significantly manifest itself until the fifties.

The gradual movement away from naturalism is apparent in the novels of Lloyd Brown and Frank L. Brown. Lloyd Brown's *Iron City* (1951) is a prison novel that uses black folk history and spirituals to delineate the character of two members of the Communist party and newspaper clippings to advance a plot that attacks the legal lynching of Lonnie James, the protagonist, and promotes a Marxist vision of the weaknesses of American society. Frank Brown's *Trumbull Park* (1959), the first-person story of a black airplane factory worker's courage in resettling his family in a white public housing project in Chicago, also draws on black folklore, especially the songs "We Shall Not Be Moved" and "Every Day I Got the Blues." These conventional narratives celebrate the emerging spiritual as well as political heroism of the working class, a type of critical realism that culminates in the novels of John O. Killens.

The break with naturalism is more pronounced in Wright's *Outsider* (1953) and Gwendolyn Brooks's *Maud Martha* (1953). In *The Outsider* Wright rejects facile color and class explanations of the dilemma of modern man to develop the existential theme that in a godless, meaningless world man must achieve meaning and purpose in the process of creating his own standards and himself. Employing a third-person intimate narrator to probe the consciousness of his protagonist, Cross Damon, Wright relies heavily on indirect interior monologue and Cross's dialogue with Ely Houston, the physically deformed but mentally acute district attorney, to argue that by accident of race or birth or chance some men, especially blacks, are outsiders, gifted with a double vision by being inside and outside of American society at the same time and terrified by the psychological knowledge that "man may be just anything at all."[7]

Maud Martha is one of the missing links between the poetic realism of *Cane* in the 1920s and *The Bluest Eye* and *Sula* in the 1960s. Gwendolyn Brooks, a Pulitzer Prize–winning poet, breaks with conventional plot structure and divides her novel into thirty-four impressionistic vignettes or slices-of-life. They outline the growth of Maud Martha from a seven-year-old who found "it hard to believe that a thing of ordinary allurements . . . was as easy to love as a thing of heart-catching beauty" to a post–World War II married woman awaiting her second child. She is doubtful that "the ridiculousness of man would ever completely succeed in destroying the world—or, in fact, the basic equanimity of the least and commonest flower"; and she is thankful that "while people did live they would be grand, would be glorious and brave, would have nimble hearts that would beat and beat."[8] Focusing on Maud, an ordinary black woman whose coming-of-age involves an agonizing struggle with color prejudice, a chauvinistic husband, and an "everydayness" in appearance that she compares to a dandelion, the third-person narrator is intimately involved with the feelings and thoughts of the self-effacing, sensitive protagonist. Her "dearest wish" in life was "to be cherished" by those she loved, especially her husband, whom she criticizes for his insensitivity to her needs and desires. The power of Brooks's lyricism gives poignancy and beauty to the ordinariness of Maud's story, and her use of a commonplace flower as a metaphor for black women was adopted by women novelists of the 1970s like Toni Morrison and Alice Walker.

Myth, Legend, and Ritual

The most dramatic break with naturalism occurs in the rediscovery of myth, legend, and ritual by Ralph Ellison and James Baldwin. Because myth, legend, and ritual were discussed at length in the first chapter, here I need only summarize briefly some earlier observations in order to stress the continuing importance of Afro-American folklore in the modern black American novel. By and large black novelists of the fifties rejected the ahistorical universality of Greco-Roman myth and ritual for a mixture of Christian and social myths and rituals rooted in the particularity of the black American experience. For example, the myth of white supremacy and the rituals that reinforce and perpetuate the Manichean black and white, evil and good, significations of Western mythology with its overtones of an apocalyptic clash are still a major source for themes, symbols, and images in the novels of the fifties. "It took me a long time to learn how to adapt such examples of myth into my work—also ritual," writes Ellison. "The use of ritual is equally a vital part of the creative process. I learned a few things from Eliot, Joyce and Hemingway, but not how to adapt them. When I started writing, I knew that in both *The Waste Land* and *Ulysses* ancient myth and ritual were used to give form and significance to the material; but it took me a few years to realize that the myths and rites which we find functioning in our everyday lives could be used in the same way. . . . In any society there are many rituals of situation which, for the most part, go unquestioned. They can be simple or elaborate, but they are the connective tissue between the work of art and the audience."[9] Because myth, legend, and rituals are cultural codes for communally sanctioned attitudes, beliefs, and behavior, they are ideally suited for novelists in search of appropriate signs and forms to reconstruct the socialized ambivalence—the shifting, conflicting emotions of love and hate, shame and pride fostered by social oppression—of black American life.

RALPH WALDO ELLISON (1914–)

Ralph Waldo Ellison stands alone in the tradition of the Afro-American novel. On the strength of a single novel, a collection of essays, and several uncollected short stories, he has been acclaimed a major contemporary American author. Born in Oklahoma City, Oklahoma, in 1914, Ellison grew up in a frontier community during the era of Southwestern jazz. Oklahoma, which achieved statehood only seven years before Ellison's birth, "had no tradition of slavery, and while it was segregated, relationships between the races were more fluid and thus more human than in the old slave states." The death of his father in 1917 and the frontier atmosphere of post–World War I Oklahoma encouraged Ellison to think of himself as a renaissance man. With a romantic sense of freedom and adventure, he and his friends created their own heroes and ideals. "Gamblers and scholars, jazz musicians and scientists, Negro cowboys and soldiers from the Spanish-American and First World Wars, movie stars and stunt men, figures from the Italian Renaissance and literature, both classical and popular," Ellison tells us, "were combined with the special virtues of some local boot-legger, the eloquence of some Negro preacher, the strength and grace of some local athlete, the ruthlessness of some businessman-physician, the elegance in dress and manners of some headwaiter or hotel doorman."[10]

As a young boy, Ellison wanted to become a symphonic composer. He attended a school in which harmony was taught from the ninth through the twelfth grades, but the study of jazz, now more appropriately classified as Afro-American classical music by some of its devotees, was considered disreputable because of its apparent low-class origins. Because this music was all around him, he nevertheless came to know and admire it, and its artists, especially musicians like Jimmy Rushing, the blues singer, Walter Page, the bassist, and Icky Lawrence, the trumpeter. Ellison's ideal was to emulate such men as Page and Lawrence in mastering and synthesizing the conventions of the Euro-American and Afro-American classical traditions. In 1933 he entered Tuskegee Institute to study Euro-American classical music under William Dawson. In his sophomore year he discovered Eliot's *Waste Land*, and his interest in writing was awakened. In 1936 after the eclipse of the Harlem Renaissance, he went to New York to work and study sculpture, but after meeting Richard Wright, who was then editing *New Challenge*, Ellison found his interest in writing quickening. Wright invited him to do a book review for the magazine and encouraged him to study the techniques of Conrad, Joyce, Dostoyevsky, and James.

During the recession of 1937 Ellison spent his nights writing and studying the literary theory and technique of Eliot, Joyce, Dostoyevsky, James, Pound, Stein, Hemingway, Malraux, Faulkner, Hughes, and Wright. He learned from all of them, adapting those things that suited his purposes and rejecting the rest. "When I began writing in earnest," Ellison says, "I was forced . . . to relate myself consciously and imaginatively to my mixed background as American, as Negro American, and as a Negro from what in its own belated way was a pioneer background. More important and inseparable from this particular effort, was the necessity of determining my true relationship to that body of American literature to which I was most attracted and through which . . . I would find my own voice, and to which I was challenged, by way of achieving myself, to make some small contribution, and to whose composite picture of reality I was obligated to offer some necessary modifications."[11] Thus Ellison reveals that his major concerns as a writer are with the relationship of Afro-American to Euro-American culture and the responsibility of the black artist to his people and his craft.

His novel, *Invisible Man*, is a monumental book of extraordinary intensity and richness. In a poll of the literary establishment by *Book Week*, it was judged "the most distinguished single work" published in America between 1945 and 1965. Its complex time structure, spacious setting, anonymous ethnic hero, allegorical and legendary characters, ironic theme, and ceremonial use of varieties of language all suggest that Ellison has drawn on Afro-American folklore, as Melville draws on Euro-American folklore in *Moby Dick*, and the epic tradition to render his double vision of America. Like Johnson's *Autobiography of an Ex-Coloured Man*, Toomer's *Cane*, and Wright's *Native Son*, *Invisible Man* is a spiritual odyssey, but in imaginative scale and epic power it surpasses these earlier works. In fact, more than any other black novel, *Invisible Man* has just claim to being considered an incomparable modern black epic.

Divided into twenty-five chapters with a prologue and epilogue, *Invisible Man* traces a nameless black youth's journey from naive faith in the American Dream to an enlightened affirmation of self and society. The novel begins in medias res with the hero looking back some twenty years on

Myth, Legend, and Ritual in the Novel of the Fifties

the lesson of his life, invoking the spirit and music of Louis Armstrong for the epic question: "What Did I Do to Be So Black and Blue?" "I am an invisible man," he declares in the first line of the prologue, and as he elaborates on this theme the flow of the narrative begins moving simultaneously and paradoxically in a linear, vertical, and circular direction— from South to North, ignorance to enlightenment, the illuminated basement in the prologue to the illuminated basement in the epilogue. As he contemplates his situation and response in the prologue, the hero states sardonically:

> The point now is that I found a home—or a hole in the ground, as you will. Now don't jump to the conclusion that because I call my home a "hole" it is damp and cold like a grave; there are cold holes and warm holes. Mine is a warm hole. And remember, a bear retires to his hole for the winter and lives until spring; then he comes strolling out like the Easter chick breaking from its shell. I say all this to assure you that it is incorrect to assume that, because I'm invisible and live in a hole, I am dead. I am neither dead nor in a state of suspended animation. Call me Jack-the-Bear, for I am in a state of hibernation. My hole is warm and full of light. Yes, *full* of light. I doubt if there is a brighter spot in all New York than this hole of mine, and I do not exclude Broadway. Or the Empire State Building on a photographer's dream night. But that is taking advantage of you. Those two spots are among the darkest of our whole civilization—pardon me, our whole *culture* (an important distinction, I've heard)—which might sound like a hoax, or a contradiction, but that (by contradiction, I mean) is how the world moves: Not like an arrow, but a boomerang. (Beware of those who speak of the *spiral* of history; they are preparing a boomerang. Keep a steel helmet handy.) I know; I have been boomeranged across my head so much that I now can see the darkness of lightness. And I love light. (Pp. 9–10)

This lengthy, representative passage immediately establishes the tone, tempo, and texture of the narrative: its blues mood, jazz beat, wry humor, satirical density, mythic death and rebirth motif, and paradoxical affirmation and rejection of American values.

Born and educated in the South, the invisible hero, we learn, in the narrative proper, is so thoroughly conditioned by the values, rituals, and taboos of white America that he learns "to repress not only his emotions but his humanity" (p. 86). In order to assert his humanity he must acknowledge his Afro-American folk heritage and reject the pervasive racism, boundless optimism, compulsive individualism, and rampant commercialism of American culture.[12] The seed for this change of character is planted in the death-bed advice of the hero's grandfather and the dream that concludes the first chapter. In the dream, the grandfather tells the hero to read a gold engraved letter in the briefcase he has won. The letter says: "To Whom It May Concern/Keep this Nigger-Boy Running." This letter and other pieces of paper that define the hero's social role and say essentially the same thing mark the different sections of the novel, chart the invisible hero's quest for self-realization, signify why he is so black and blue, and allegorize the odyssey of black Americans.

After receiving his high school diploma and participating in a Jim Crow ceremony for the most important white men in his hometown, the hero wins a scholarship to the local black college. At college, he is expelled in his junior year by the dean, Dr. Bledsoe, for his rebellious spirit and is sent to New York with "introductory letters" to trustees of the school. The letter addressed to Mr. Emerson indirectly leads to a job in a paint factory where the naive hero is seriously injured and summarily discharged with papers absolving the factory of responsibility for his condition. He is then recruited by Jack, a white official of the Brotherhood, a quasi-Communist organization, and given a bit of paper that assigns him a new name and role as political organizer in Harlem. In Harlem the hero clashes with Ras the Exhorter-Destroyer, a black nationalist, over who is "the true interpreter of the people." When he becomes too independent in his new role, the hero receives an anonymous letter reminding him that he lives in a "white man's world" and warning him to stay in his place. After witnessing the tragic death of Tod Clifton, a young black organizer for the Brotherhood who is killed while selling Sambo dolls on a street corner, the hero picks up one of the grinning "orange-and-black tissue paper" dolls and puts it in his pocket. In the final chapter of the novel, the enlightened hero decides to trust his own sense of reality and burns all the papers representing his earlier uncritical, passive attitude toward life. "Before he could have some voice in his own destiny," Ellison explains, "he had to discard these old identities and illusions; his enlightenment couldn't come until then."[13]

The hero's failure to understand his grandfather's advice "to overcome 'em with yesses, undermine 'em with grins, agree 'em to death and de-struction" paves the way for the tragicomic, often ambiguous rituals and sustained irony of the novel. Seeing himself as a nascent Booker T. Washington, the hero, for example, accepts an invitation from the white su-perintendent of colored schools to repeat his graduation speech on the

Myth, Legend, and Ritual in the Novel of the Fifties

theme of humility as the black American's key to progress for the town's "leading white citizens." When he arrives to give the speech, however, he finds himself the feature attraction at a stag party of cursing, howling drunks. In the ritual that follows he and eight of his classmates are compelled to watch a nude blonde belly dancer, to fight each other blindfolded in a battle royal, and to scramble for fake gold coins tossed on an electrified rug. This ritual introduces the black youth to the false gods of American culture: sex, violence, and money. Specifically, it dramatizes the thoughtless acceptance by blacks of a pattern of behavior designed by whites to emasculate and humiliate black men: reinforcing the taboo against sexual contact between black men and white women, duping young blacks into fighting each other rather than their primary oppressors, and encouraging them to sacrifice moral values for material gain. Guilt ridden about the actual political suppression of black people and anxiety ridden about their imagined sexual powers, white Americans have established these rituals to reinforce caste lines and perpetuate the myth of white supremacy.

The "battle royal" ritual also signifies that the heroic figure at the center of the novel is a modern-day reincarnation of the legendary Booker T. Washington. With apparent gusto, Ellison parodies Washington's Atlanta Cotton Exposition Speech of 1895 and reveals the absurdity of blind faith in the value of humility as a way of life. " 'We of the younger generation extol the wisdom of that great leader and educator,' " the hero shouts above the din of his audience,

"who first spoke these flaming words of wisdom: 'A ship lost at sea for many days suddenly sighted a friendly vessel. From the mast of the unfortunate vessel was seen a signal: "Water, water, we die of thirst!" The answer from the friendly vessel came back: "Cast down your bucket where you are." The captain of the distressed vessel, at last heeding the injunction, cast down his bucket, and it came up full of fresh sparkling water from the mouth of the Amazon River.' And like him I say, and in his words, 'To those of my race who depend upon bettering their condition in a foreign land, or who underestimate the importance of cultivating friendly relations with the Southern white man, who is his next door neighbor, I would say: 'Cast down your bucket where you are'—cast it down in making friends in every manly way of the people of all races by whom we are surrounded....' " (Pp. 31–32)

But the men ignore the youth's efforts to be seen and heard; and his "belief in the rightness of things" makes him pathetically unresponsive to the humiliation and debasement he suffers. For knowing his place and staying in it, the narrator is launched on his journey in life by the white super-intendent, who gives him a briefcase containing a scholarship to the state college for Negroes.

Insofar as he is a white-appointed black spokesman and Southern ed-ucator, Dean Bledsoe—like Redding's Dr. Wimbush in *Stranger and Alone*—is a bearer of the Washington tradition. As the legend goes, Bledsoe, like Washington, began "college, a barefoot boy who in his fervor for education had trudged with his bundle of ragged clothing across two states."[14] Testily admitting, " 'I had to wait and plan and lick around. . . . Yes, I had to act the nigger' " (p. 128) to get this position, Bledsoe is a modern-day Uncle Tom, an unscrupulous betrayer of his people's trust, and a self-advancing conspirator in the myth of white supremacy. Regardless of how he got his office, he tells the hero, the important thing is that he controls the school:

> "Negroes don't control this school or much of anything else—haven't you learned even that? No, sir, they don't control this school, nor white folk either. True they *support* it, but I control it. I's big and black and I say 'Yes, suh' as loudly as any burr-head when it's convenient, but I'm still the king down here. I don't care how much it appears otherwise. Power doesn't have to show off. Power is confident, self-assuring, self-starting and self-stopping, self-warming and self-justi-fying. When you have it, you know it. Let the Negroes snicker and the crackers laugh! Those are the facts, son. The only ones I ever pretend to please are *big* white folk, and even those I control more than they control me. You think about that. When you buck against me, you're bucking against power, rich white folk's power, the na-tion's power—which means góvernment power!" (P. 127)

This, Ellison implies, is the danger of compulsive individualism in a laissez-faire social system based on the conflicting principles of egalitarianism and racism. Not unlike Washington in *Up From Slavery*, Bledsoe is blind to the larger moral and political issues involved in his paradoxical position of power and powerlessness in a racist society. He not only confuses the shadow for the substance of power, but also ironically sees himself as a black Horatio Alger and boasts of his achievements being compatible with the American Dream. " 'And I'll tell you something your sociology teach-ers are afraid to tell you,' " Bledsoe continues. " 'If there weren't men like me running schools like this, there'd be no South. Nor North, either. No, and there'd be no country—not as it is today. You think about that, son' "

(p. 127). Later, if not at this point, we are tacitly encouraged by the implied author to conclude with the hero: " 'Bledsoe, you're a shameless chitterling eater!' " (p. 230).

To render the insidious influence of those American values that distort and subvert the humanity of whites as well as blacks, Ellison, like the romantic writer after whom he was named, Ralph Waldo Emerson, ingeniously employed the symbol of the eye in many forms to give thematic resonance to the tension between visibility and invisibility. First suggested in the title of the novel, the symbol appears early in the prologue where the sense and sound of the fusion of the first-person pronoun with the physical eye emphasizes the significance of personal consciousness in harmonizing one's achieved and ascribed identities. The individual must first look inside himself to find the core of his being, a product of the legacy of his history and achievements, before looking outside to others and the identity they ascribe to him. Throughout the novel the stress is on words, incidents, and characters that suggest the clarity, distortion, obstruction, or absence of this double vision of Afro-American character. For example, as the hero reflects on the past, he sees in his mind's eye:

> the bronze statue of the college Founder, the cold Father symbol, his hands outstretched in the breathtaking gesture of lifting a veil that flutters in the hard, metallic folds above the face of a kneeling slave; and I am standing puzzled, unable to decide whether the veil is really being lifted, or lowered more firmly in place; whether I am witnessing a revelation or a more efficient blinding. And as I gaze, there is a rustle of wings and I see a flock of starlings flighting before me and, when I look again the bronze face, whose empty eyes look upon a world I have never seen, runs with liquid chalk—creating another ambiguity to puzzle my groping mind: Why is a bird soiled statue more commanding than one that is clean? (Pp. 37–38)

Here Ellison continues to weave the two major structural devices or signs of the text—the legend or subtext of Washington and the symbol of sight or vision—into an intricate pattern, foregrounding the various kinds and degrees of blindness to spiritual and social truths.

Those leaders who present themselves to the hero as beacons of light and bearers of the American tradition are blind. In chapel, the Reverend Homer Barbee intones a moving sermon on the epic deeds of the founder and of Bledsoe. But after invoking his vision of "the history of the race" and exhorting the black college students to follow in the footsteps of their leaders, Barbee, a blind shepherd, trips over Bledsoe's legs and falls. In

New York, as Brother Jack bitterly tells the hero that he must be loyal to the Brotherhood and accept the views of the Party leadership, one of Jack's eyes erupts out of his face. The "short-changing-dialectical deacon," who lost his eye in the line of duty to the Brotherhood, is blind in one eye and, as his mechanistic view of history indicates, cannot see well out of the other.

Norton is another bearer of the American tradition whose leadership black Americans must contend with in their quest for self-determination. " 'I am a New Englander, like Emerson,' " Norton tells the hero, who serves as chauffeur during the trustee's visit to the college campus. " 'You must learn about him, for he was important to your people. He had a hand in your destiny' " (p. 42). Norton, as his name suggests, bears the legacy of New England abolitionism, philanthropy, and paternalism. Outlining his role during Reconstruction as one of the original founders of the college, he claims to have been so close to the founder and believed so intensely in his vision for the destiny of black people that he could not recall whether it was the founder's vision or his own. The founder's vision, like Booker T. Washington's, was to establish an industrial school that would train former slaves how to lift themselves up by their bootstraps, ostensibly a Southern black adaptation of Emerson's theory of self-reliance. Once trained to believe in the dignity of labor and transformed into skilled craftsmen, according to this theory, the former slaves could then acquire the necessary wealth and property to qualify as American citizens. Or as Washington himself expressed his social vision:

> The wisest among my race understand that the agitation of questions of social quality is the extremest folly, and that progress in the enjoyment of all the privileges that will come to us must be the result of severe and constant struggle rather than of artificial forcing. No race that has anything to contribute to the markets of the world is long in any degree ostracized. It is important and right that all privileges of the law be ours, but it is vastly more important that we be prepared for the exercises of these privileges. The opportunity to earn a dollar in a factory just now is worth infinitely more than the opportunity to spend a dollar in an opera-house.[15]

Like Washington's system of values, Norton's are well meaning but politically naive and morally reprehensible.

In explaining how his fate is inextricably linked to that of the invisible hero, Norton says: "Through you and your fellow students I become . . .

three hundred teachers, seven hundred trained mechanics, eight hundred skilled farmers, and so on. That way I can observe in terms of living personalities to what extent my money, my time and my hopes have been fruitfully invested. I also construct a living memorial to my daughter" (pp. 45–46). A product of American puritanism and industrial capitalism, "forty years a bearer of the white man's burden, and for sixty a symbol of the Great Traditions," Norton is guilt-ridden and blind to moral values. His philanthropy and paternalism cloak his warped humanity.

The Jim Trueblood episode reveals the depth of Norton's sense of guilt and Ellison's sophisticated fusion of the myth of Oedipus and the Afro-American folk tradition. Jim Trueblood is a black sharecropper and pariah to the nearby black college community. He is more symbolic and legendary than realistic as a folk character. In addition to being a spinner of yarns and singer of spirituals and blues, he is a hard-working family man. As a link with their slave past, he was tolerated by the aspiring middle-class college community, who sought to help him become socially respectable, until he disgraced himself and his ethnic group.

Like Oedipus, Trueblood is guilty of incest. When the millionaire hears that the sharecropper is the father of both his expectant wife's and daughter's children, Norton becomes so anxious to speak to Trueblood that he nearly runs across the yard, stammering:

"Is it true . . . I mean did you?"

"Suh?" Trueblood asked, as I looked away.

"You have survived," he blurted. "But is it true.....?"

"Suh?" the farmer said, his brow wrinkled with bewilderment.

"I'm sorry sir," I said, "but I don't think he understands you."

He ignored me, staring into Trueblood's face as though reading a message there which I could not perceive.

"You did and are unharmed!" he shouted, his blue eyes blazing into the black face with something like envy and indignation. Trueblood looked helplessly at me. I looked away. I understood no more than he.

"You have looked upon chaos and are not destroyed!"

"No suh! I feels all right."

"You do? You feel no inner turmoil, no need to cast out the offending eye?"

"Suh?"

"Answer me!"

"I'm all right, suh," Trueblood said uneasily. "My eyes is all right too. And when I feels po'ly in my gut I takes a little soda and it goes away." (Pp. 50–51)

In this witty "puttin' on massa" performance, with its parallels to humorous Southwestern-traveler dialogues, Ellison juxtaposes Northern and Southern dialects to dramatize the cultural difference between the puritan sensibility of Norton and the folk sensibility of Trueblood. But Ellison avoids facile stereotypes of American regional and ethnic character. For despite Norton's apparent Calvinistic horror at Trueblood's sin, we sense that he is a secret sharer in the sharecropper's incest. The ecstasy with which Norton describes his daughter, who died while accompanying him on a tour of the world, surely signifies the Oedipal level on which he unconsciously identifies with Trueblood. This level of signification is brilliantly reinforced when Norton takes a hundred dollar bill out of a wallet containing the platinum-framed picture of his daughter and gives it to the sharecropper to "buy the children some toys."

Like many epic characters, Trueblood's name is symbolic. "Trueblood (pur song)," according to one critic's misreading of the text, "is the full-blooded, half-assimilated African in whom historic circumstances of the past three centuries have neither encouraged nor indeed permitted the civilized amenities to develop."[16] As Freud theorizes and Trueblood's name suggests, incest, the consummation of an instinctive sexual attraction to blood relatives, is being true to one's blood. Only the social taboos and laws of a community influence individuals to repress and sublimate such basic drives and dreams.[17] On this mythic level, then, Trueblood and Norton, despite racial and cultural differences, are sharers in the human condition. Furthermore, Kate's handiness with the axe and Trueblood's willingness to be punished for his act, which was actually the reenactment of a dream while he slept between his wife and daughter, reveal that black American folk values are probably more intolerant of incest than middle-class white values. In fact, in looking at the dispassionate, punitive reaction of the black college community and the prurient, delighted response of the white community in the episode, it is the reaction of Trueblood and his wife that seems more normal. Like Oedipus, after discovering he had committed incest, Trueblood leaves home. But unlike Oedipus, who physically blinds himself and becomes a wanderer to atone for his guilt, and Norton, who allows his sense of hidden sin and guilt to blind him to the humanity of blacks, Trueblood turns to the blues tradition for the vision and strength to put his guilt and responsibility in perspective:

One night, way early in the mornin', I looks up and sees the stars and I starts singin'. I don't mean to, I didn't think 'bout it, just start

Myth, Legend, and Ritual in the Novel of the Fifties

singin'. I don't know what it was, some kinda church song, I guess. All I know is I *ends up* singin' the blues. I sings me some blues that night ain't never been sang before, and while I'm singin' them blues I makes up my mind that I ain't nobody but myself and ain't nothin' I can do but let whatever is gonna happen, happen. I made up my mind that I was goin' back home and face Kate; yeah, and face Matty Lou too. (P. 63)

The courage and discipline that Trueblood discovers in the blues are essential values that the hero must learn by acknowledging his folk heritage.

As a boy Ellison also learned the lesson of his heritage. But in an exchange between him and Stanley Hyman over the use of folklore in *Invisible Man*, he argues that it was Eliot and Joyce who made him aware of the literary value of his folk heritage. "My point," he explains,

... is that the Negro American writer is also an heir of the human experience which is literature, and this might well be more important to him than his living folk tradition. For me, at least, in the discontinuous, swiftly changing and diverse American culture, the stability of the Negro American folk tradition became precious as a result of an act of literary discovery. Taken as a whole, its spirituals along with its blues, jazz and folk tales, it has ... much to tell us of the faith, humor and adaptability to reality necessary to live in a world which has taken on much of the insecurity and blues-like absurdity known to those who brought it into being. For those who are able to translate its meaning into wider, more precise vocabularies it has much to offer indeed.[18]

On a larger scale, then, *Invisible Man* portrays the historical quest of black Americans for identity in a society whose traditions simultaneously inspire and inhibit their impulse toward freedom and self-realization.

Insofar as the blues is a lyrical expression of "both the agony of life and the possibility of conquering it through sheer toughness of spirit," the mood of *Invisible Man* is bluesy. "I'd like to hear five recordings of Louis Armstrong playing and singing 'What Did I Do to Be so Black and Blue'— all at the same time," says the hero in the prologue:

Sometimes now I listen to Louis while I have my favorite dessert of vanilla ice cream and sloe gin. I pour the red liquid over the white mound, watching it glisten and vapor rising as Louis bends that military instrument into a beam of lyrical sound. Perhaps I like Louis Armstrong because he'd made poetry out of being invisible. I think it must be because he's unaware that he *is* invisible. And my own grasp of invisibility aids me to understand. . . . Invisibility, let me explain, gives one a slightly different sense of time, you're never quite on the beat. Sometimes you're ahead and sometimes behind. Instead of the swift and imperceptible flowing of time, you are aware of its nodes, those points where time stands still or from which it leaps ahead. And you slip into the breaks and look around. That's what you hear vaguely in Louis' music. (P. 11)

Here the theme of the novel is given resonance by the complex connotation of the stock blues phrase, the striking color imagery with its subtle, wry allusion to pain and violence, the ambiguous use of Louis Armstrong (whose minstrel mask frequently cast a shadow over the splendor of his music) as the archetypal black musician who has successfully synthesized two cultural traditions, and the technical allusion to modal improvisations in jazz and blues notes (that is, the blues feeling derived from the flatting or bending of thirds, sevenths, and fifths into quarter tones). The recurrence of the numbers three and seven (blue notes), fragments of blues lyrics ("She's got feet like a monkey / Legs like a frog—Lawd, Lawd! / But when she starts to loving me / I holler Whooo, God-dog! / Cause I loves my baabay, / Better than I do myself. . . . "), and allusions to the cathartic effect of the blues in the Trueblood and Junkman episodes, further reinforce the jazz-blues motif of the novel.

Ellison sees the blues singer and jazz musician as paradigms of the American experience. Both are products of the interaction between the limitations and possibilities of the American experience. Both are creators of an indigenous form of American culture, Afro-American music. More important, both achieve their personal identities against the background of tradition. Drawing on the blues tradition of twelve-bar stanzas divided into three call-and-response sections with the rhyme scheme *a a b*, the blues singer achieves his or her individuality by an improvisational use of stanzas (eight, ten, or sixteen), stock imagistic phrases, moans, groans, cries, and shouts, along with idiosyncratic physical movements and gestures. In this manner the blues singer explores the full range of the art, constantly expanding its possibilities through creative resourcefulness and mastery of traditional conventions.

The jazz musician also asserts individuality through the mastery of traditional conventions. From the jazz musicians he knew in Oklahoma, Ellison learned the discipline required of the artist. "These jazzmen," he writes in "Living with Music,"

. . . many of them now world-famous, lived for and with music intensely. Their driving motivation was neither money nor fame, but the will to achieve the most eloquent expression of idea-emotions through the technical mastery of their instruments (which, incidentally, some of them wore as a priest wears the cross) and the give and take, the subtle rhythmical shaping and blending of idea, tone and imagination demanded of group improvisation. The delicate balance struck between strong individual personality and the group during those early jam sessions was a marvel of social organization. I had learned too that the end of all this discipline and technical mastery was the desire to express an affirmative way of life through its musical tradition and that this tradition insisted that each artist achieve his creativity within its frame. He must learn the best of the past, and add to it his personal vision. Life could be harsh, loud and wrong if it wished, but they lived it fully, and when they expressed their attitude toward the world it was with a fluid style that reduced the chaos of living to form.[19]

Thus the jazz group is a microcosm of society with initiation rites and ceremonies that challenge the individual musician to define himself through improvisational solo flights upon traditional materials. In the ordeal of the jam session the soloist seizes the cut or break in the melodic line, plays off the basic beat of the drummer, bassist, or pianist, and expresses his own unique voice, his soul, before cutting back to the melodic line and beat of the group. This is the complex fate of the hero of *Invisible Man*. He must assert his individuality in the midst of the chaos and discordant beat of history, acknowledging the limitations of life while at the same time affirming its infinite possibilities.

The jazz motif is also evidenced in Ellison's exuberant, improvisational use of language. Beginning with the folktale on boxing in the prologue, Ellison delights in cutting into the tempo of the narrative to play variations on the theme of invisibility by organically incorporating in *Invisible Man* the litany of a down-home chanted church sermon, a parody of Washington's Atlanta speech, a Southwestern tall tale, a classic Southern sermon, a jive spiel, a sidewalk speech, a radical political speech, a black nationalist dialectic, and a funeral sermon. The tempo, nuance, imagery, passion, and range of the varieties of Afro-American speech are overpowering and integral to the development through repetition of plot, theme, and character.[20] Perhaps the most striking example of this use of language occurs in the ritualistic jive of the blues-singing junkman whom the hero meets in Harlem:

"Well, daddy-o, it's been good talking with a youngster from the old country but I got to leave you now. This here's one of them good

206

Myth, Legend, and Ritual in the Novel of the Fifties

ole downhill streets. I can coast a while and won't be worn out at the end of the day. Damn if I'm-a let 'em run *me* into my grave. I be seeing you again sometimes—And you know something?"

"What's that?"

"I thought you was trying to deny me at first, but now be pretty glad to see you. . . . "

"I hope so," I said. "And you take it easy."

"Oh, I'll do that. All it takes to get along in this here man's town is a little shit, grit and mother-wit. And man, I was bawn with all three. In fact, I'maseventhsonofaseventhsonbawnwithacauloverboth-eyesandraisedonblackcatboneshighjohntheconquerorandgreasy-greens—" he spieled with twinkling eyes, his lips working rapidly. "You dig me, daddy?"

"You're going too fast," I said, beginning to laugh.

"Okay, I'm slowing down. I'll verse you but I won't curse you— My name is Peter Wheatstraw, I'm the Devil's only son-in-law, so roll 'em! You a southern boy, ain't you?" he said, his head to one side like a bear's.

"Yes," I said.

"Well, git with it! My name's Blue and I'm coming at you with a pitchfork. Fe Fi Fo Fum. Who want to shoot the Devil one, Lord God Stingeroy!"

He had me grinning despite myself. I liked his words though I didn't know the answer. I'd known the stuff from childhood, but had forgotten it; had learned it back of school.. . . .

"You digging me, daddy?" he laughed. "How, but look me up sometimes, I'm a piano player and a rounder, a whiskey drinker and a pavement pounder. I'll teach you some good habits. You'll need some good bad habits. You'll need 'em. Good luck," he said. (P. 155)

This performance not only illustrates the richness and vitality of Afro-American speech, but also, in contrast with his earlier rejection of True-blood as a shameful symbol of the past, dramatizes the hero's progress toward self-realization through an affirmation of his heritage as embodied in the junkman.

In his personal quest for wholeness the hero also bears witness to the historic odyssey of his people in search of freedom and self-fulfillment. Through retrospective narrative, philosophically charged by the ironic distance between the formerly innocent and presently experienced narrator-

Myth, Legend, and Ritual in the Novel of the Fifties

protagonist, we learn that in his yea-saying days he was ashamed of the slave heritage of his grandparents and the sharecropper legacy of True-blood. In the post–Reconstruction period his forebears were told by a black spokesman that "they were free, united with others and our country in everything pertaining to the common good, and, in everything social, separate like the fingers of the hand. And they believed it" (p. 19). And in violent rituals like the battle royal, the caste system of the unrecon-structed New South had conditioned him to believe that it was dangerous to open his heart to anyone ever. The modern sense of insecurity and fear is dramatized in the nightmarish episode at the Golden Day, "a kind of sporting-and-gambling house" visited by black, mentally ill, shell-shocked Veterans of World War I, patients at a nearby veterans' hospital.

In order to revive Norton from the shock he suffers after hearing True-blood's tale of incest, the narrator takes him to the Golden Day for a stimulant. The mere presence of the white trustee ignites the powder keg of emotions sealed up in the veterans and explodes in chaos and violence. One of the "patients" immediately greets Norton as his grandfather, Thomas Jefferson:

> "Gentlemen, this man is my grandfather!"
>
> "But he's *white*, his name's Norton."
>
> "I should know my grandfather! He's Thomas Jefferson and I'm his grandson—on the field-nigger side," the tall man said.
>
> "Sylvester, I do believe that you're right. I certainly do," he said, staring at Mr. Norton. "Look at those features. Exactly like yours—from the identical mold. Are you sure he didn't spit you upon the earth, fully clothed?" (P. 73)

The satire in this passage, as throughout the novel, is double edged. While reconstructing the legend that one of the fathers of the country, the prin-cipal author of the Declaration of Independence, also fathered three or more children by his slave mistress, Sally Hemings, Ellison simultaneously deconstructs the myth of white purity and the fear of miscegenation by illustrating that since the founding of the nation white men have been violating black women and fathering children by them.[21] Another patient, symbolically enacting the release of repressed violent resistance to white oppression, then hits Norton on the chin as though he were jabbing a punching bag.

When Supercargo, the towering black surrogate of the white ruling class in charge of the patients, appears at the top of the stairs in white shorts demanding absolute order, the martial atmosphere of the Golden Day erupts in violence and Norton passes out. Anxious over Norton's safety, the hero is overcome with hysteria:

> Then some of the milling men pushed me up against him and suddenly a mass of whiteness was looming two inches from my eyes; it was only his face but I felt a shudder of nameless horror. I had never been so close to a white person before. In a panic I struggled to get away. With his eyes closed he seemed more threatening than with them open. He was like a formless white death which had been there all the time and which had now revealed itself in the madness of the Golden Day. (Pp. 79–80)

The hero at this stage of events is incapable of relating to himself and others as autonomous beings. He acts like a robot or "walking zombie" and conceives of Norton as "a God, a force." For this reason, he is disturbed by the irreverent freedom with which Norton is treated by the men at the Golden Day, especially the former brain specialist who helps Norton regain consciousness.

Most of the patients had been members of the black bourgeoisie—lawyers, teachers, and preachers—before the war. Believing in the American Creed, they had voluntarily served in the European war to make the world safe for democracy only to return to the undemocratic circumstances of their own country. The institutionalized brain surgeon symbolizes the disillusioned black victims of this travesty of the American Creed. Educated at the same college as the hero, the anonymous inmate became a successful brain surgeon and served in France during World War I. When he returned to the South to practice his profession and serve humanity, he was brutally beaten by members of the Ku Klux Klan. "Ten men in masks drove me out from the city at midnight," he recalls with bitterness, "and beat me with whips for saving a human life. And I was forced to the utmost degradation because I possessed skilled hands and the belief that my knowledge could bring me dignity—not wealth, only dignity— and other men health!" (p. 86). As a result of this ironic and tragic experience, he achieves the power and wisdom that enable him to penetrate the terrifying madness of American society and to recall those fundamentals that "most peasants and folk peoples almost always know through experience though seldom through conscious thought" (p. 84).

Alluding to the invasion of the South during Reconstruction by Northern industrialists, the neurosurgeon tells Norton: "To some you are the great white father, to others the lynchers of souls, but for all, you are confusion come even into the Golden Day." Later, on the bus North, the sage inmate, whose conversation with Norton has resulted in his sudden transfer to the major mental institution in Washington, D.C., advises the hero: " 'Come out of the fog, young man. And remember you don't have to be a complete fool in order to succeed. Play the game, but don't believe in it—that much you owe yourself. Even if it lands you in a strait jacket or a padded cell. Play the game, but raise the ante, my boy. Learn how it operates, learn how *you* operate. . . .' " (p. 137). In keeping with the improvisational quality of the novel, its repetitious but ever innovative and complex modal variations on the theme of Afro-American double-consciousness, this scene contrasts with the hero being launched off to college and eternal dependence on the paternalism of whites for his identity. Here he is launched off to the North and independence (like the mass migration North of black Americans in the post–World War I period) with the neurosurgeon's farewell advice: " 'Be your own father, young man. And remember, the world is possibility if only you'll discover it. Last of all, leave the Mr. Nortons alone, and if you don't know what I mean, think about it. Farewell' " (p. 139).

In the North the variations on the theme of the hero's invisibility continue. A subway ride becomes another test of faith and the narrator's rite of passage to a new urban life, as he plunges downhill in the crowded subway and is regurgitated on the platform like a modern-day Jonah, a reluctant prophet, from the belly of a frantic whale. The moral perversions of American culture take a more subtle form in the North. On Wall Street men move like robots controlled by the power of money and industry. The ominous threat of industrial capitalism to human values is dramatized in the Big-Brother-Is-Watching feeling of the hero as he walks down Wall Street, and the emasculating influence of technology is dramatically felt in his sex organs by a rapidly ascending elevator ride.

In chapter 9 the hero begins to establish a precarious adjustment to his past and to define himself. First, he acknowledges his relationship to the blues-singing junk man, whose personal and social insight was like one of the men from the Golden Day: " 'Man, this Harlem ain't nothing but a bear's den. But I tell you one thing,' he said with swiftly sobering face, 'it's the best place in the world for you and me, and if times don't get better soon I'm going to grab that bear and turn him every way but loose!' " (p. 154). In confined, crowded neighborhoods the black migrants become victims of social parasites and the impersonal forces of urban life. The homosexual son of Mr. Emerson signifies one of these forces, the limitations or excesses of Emersonian optimism and individualism. He befriends the hero but offers him the dubious freedom and identity of becoming his valet and joining his party at the Club Calamus. The hero's rejection of this role is a further step toward self-reliance.

In the Liberty Paint Company episode Ellison re-creates the exploitation of the black migrant by American industry and labor. Using Emerson's name without his permission, the hero is hired as a union scab in a paint factory that advertises in neon lights: "Keep America Pure With Liberty Paints." The trademark of the company, a major supplier of paint to the government, is a screaming eagle: a sign for strength, speed, gracefulness, predacity, and acute vision. The company takes pride in making the purest white paint in the nation—"Optic White." But the hero discovers that this paint is actually made by mixing ten drops of black graduate with white paint. This was his job. The irony of his unacknowledged role in the development of American industrial capitalism and culture is reinforced when buckets of paint that he ruins with concentrate remover and mischievously added drops of black graduate are declared Optic White even though to him they appear to have a gray tinge. Thus Ellison continues wryly to play with the theme of vision, employing the ambiguity and paradox of social rituals and symbols to satirize modern American myths of racial and cultural purity.

Reassigned to work with Lucius Brockway, the narrator again finds himself the object of suspicion and hostility. He is looked upon by the pro-union employees as an informer for the boss and by the anti-union Lucius Brockway as a threat to his job. Lucius, an old uneducated black boiler man, represents the hidden key to the success of the Liberty Paint Company. Because of his common sense, his more than twenty-five years experience of working with the machinery, and his help in creating the slogan, "If it's Optic White, It's the Right White"—a reference to his collusion in the myth of white supremacy—he misguidedly feels that he is inexpendable. "They got all this machinery," he says with unconscious irony, "but that ain't everything; *we are the machines inside the machine*" (p. 190). Fearful that the college-educated hero is a union man after his job, Lucius, during a fierce brawl signifying the destructive aspects of socialized ambivalence, nearly kills him by deceiving him into overpressurizing one of the boilers until it explodes. Symbolically, the hero's personal odyssey retraces the pattern of his people's collective odyssey, from slavery to freedom: ontogeny recapitulates phylogeny. Ellison, in other words, continues to reconstruct the complex, sometimes symbiotic but more often parasitic, relationship between the two cultures in the growth of the nation, and between the individual and the community in the development of personal wholeness.

During his painful recovery from the boiler explosion, the hero experiences another rebirth. This time he is placed in a hospital machine and given a prefrontal lobotomy, reinforcing the leitmotif of the dehumanizing power of technology and the resiliency of the folk imagination. After a series of electrical shock treatments that disorients him but fails to destroy his personality, the hero reorients and reaffirms himself by recalling his childhood identities as Buckeye the Rabbit and Brer Rabbit. Finally, when he is considered pacified, he is released from the machine:

> I felt a tug at my belly and looked down to see one of the physicians pull the cord which was attached to the stomach node, jerking me forward.
> "What is this?" I said.
> "Get the shears," he said.
> "Sure," the other said. "Let's not waste time."
> I recoiled inwardly as though the cord were part of me. Then they had it free and the nurse clipped through the belly band and removed the heavy node. I opened my mouth to speak but one of the physicians shook his head. They worked swiftly. Then I was told to climb out of the case. (P. 213)

After this transforming experience with industry, labor unions, and technology, the narrator discovers the invigorating folk spirit of Harlem in the maternal care of the blues-singing Mary Rambo. " 'Don't let this Harlem git you,' " she encourages him. " 'I'm in New York but New York ain't in me, understand what I mean? Don't get corrupted' " (p. 222). Immersed in the sights, sounds, and smells of Harlem, he begins to achieve a new sense of freedom and reconciliation with his folk past through the simple urban ritual of buying a baked yam from a street vender and eating it with delight in public. Earlier he had rejected an ethnic breakfast of pork chops and grits; now he willfully and joyously affirms the symbolic nurturing significance of soul food. "They're my birthmark," he confesses to the vendor in a wry parody of God's declaration to Moses. "I yam what I am!"[22] The hero also defines himself up North through his efforts to help prevent two old transplanted black Southerners, "ground up by industrial conditions" and slum landlords, from being "thrown on the dump heaps and cast aside."

The hero's speech to help the dispossessed old couple incites a riot and leads to yet another new identity. Instead of a womb symbol like the subway ride, Ellison brilliantly combines the musical technique of counterpointing with the cinematic technique of foregrounding to reveal the narrator's rebirth. Running away from the police, the hero first cuts through a block in which a funeral procession is underway in the background; then in the next block he encounters a doctor hurrying to deliver a baby. When Jack catches up with the hero and proceeds to recruit him to be "the new Booker T. Washington," Jack dismisses the humanity of agrarian types like the dispossessed old couple. But the hero refuses to deny their humanity or his relationship to them. " 'I like them,' " he says, " 'they reminded me of folks I know down South. It's taken me a long time to feel it, but they're folks just like me, except that I've been to school a few years' " (p. 253). Later, during the climax of his first formal speech for the Brotherhood, the hero endangers his usefulness to the organization by revealing his soul and identifying too closely with the dispossessed and disinherited. " 'I feel, I feel suddenly that I have become more human,' " he says in a subdued voice:

> Do you understand? More human. Not that I have become a man, for I was born a man. But that I am more human. I feel strong, I feel able to get things done! I feel that I can see sharp and clear and far down the dim corridor of history and in it I can hear the footsteps of militant fraternity! No, wait, let me confess . . . I feel the urge to affirm my feelings . . . I feel that here, after a long and desperate and uncommonly blind journey, I have come home . . . Home! With your eyes upon me I feel that I've found my true family! My true people! My true country! I am a new citizen of the country of your vision, a native of your fraternal land. I feel that here tonight, in this old arena, the new is being born and the vital old revived. In each of you, in me, in us all. (P. 300)

The confessional conflation of personal and public tropes (family and home with militant fraternity, true country, new citizen, and fraternal land) also signify the emotional, moral, and political identification of the implied author with his protagonist and the wretched of the American system.

In addition, most of the martial atmosphere in the novel is generated in Harlem by the clash between the Brotherhood and the black nationalists over who will control and lead the black community. Both Tod Clifton and the narrator are black organizers for the white political organization, and both are slow to realize that the Brotherhood, like American Communists during the 1920s and 1930s, were well-meaning but doctrinaire ideologues determined to exploit the disillusionment of black people for the geopolitical advancement of the working class and the Party.

In contrast, Ras the Exhorter is a black nationalist leader. A Garveyite,

Myth, Legend, and Ritual in the Novel of the Fifties

Ras advocates black pride, solidarity, and autonomy. He passionately loves black people and hates white tyranny. In a street battle with the heavy-handed symbolism of a neon sign in the background flashing "Red Checks Cashed Here," Ras pulls a knife on Tod Clifton, but rather than kill his black brother he breaks down at the last minute in tears and curses. " 'When the black man going to tire of this childish perfidy?' " he shouts angrily:

> "He got you so you don't trust you black intelligence? You young, don't play you'self cheap, mahn. Don't deny you'self! It took a billion gallons of black blood to make you. Recognize you'self inside and you wan the kings among men! A mahn knows he's a mahn when he got not'ing, when he's naked—nobody have to tell him that. You six foot tall, mahn. You young and intelligent. You black and beautiful—don't let 'em tell you different! You wasn't them t'ings you be dead, mahn. Dead! I'd have killed you, mahn. Ras the Exhorter raised up his knife and tried to do it, but he could not do it. . . . Ras recognized your black possibilities, mahn. Ras would not sahcrifice his black brother to the white enslaver. Instead he *cry*. So why don't you recognize your black duty, mahn, and come jine us?" (P. 324)

Ras persuades the hero, who remembers a similar experience in the battle royal, of the insanity of blacks fighting blacks. But neither the hero nor Tod is ready to join Ras in building a black nation. The implied author also politically distances himself from Ras.

With revolutionary fervor Ras believes that his hate for the "white mahn's civilization" cannot be "wiped out" by "some blahsted lies in some bloody books written by the white mahn." It must be wiped out by the white man's payment in blood for the "three hundred years of black blood" that was spilled to build this country. " 'And remember that I am not like you,' " he tells Tod and the hero. " 'Ras recognizes the true issues and he is not afraid to be black. Nor is he a traitor for white man. Remember that. I am no black traitor to the black people for the white people' " (p. 326). Although Tod and the hero take issue with his apocalyptic vision, if not his view that Harlem is "the black mahn's territory," both later learn the bitter truth of their manipulation like Sambo dolls by the Brotherhood. By this time, Ras the Exhorter, "dressed in the costume of an Abyssinian chieftain" and mounted on a great black horse, has become Ras the Destroyer, the leader of a Harlem rebellion.

As the novel reaches its climax, the nameless hero continues to negotiate his way through the chaos of history, affirming his folk past and achieving a precarious adjustment to the socialized ambivalence fostered by the paradoxical values of white America. He rejects the strategy of Ras's violence (during the riot he spears Ras in self-defense); accepts Brother Tarp's filed leg chain (a token of Southern injustice that contrasts with Bledsoe's smooth chain link); assumes some moral responsibility for Tod's death (another death and rebirth cycle for the equally manipulated hero); and wryly pokes fun at Sybil's obsession to be brutalized and raped by a black man. He also temporarily assumes the guise of Rinehart, a hustler (confidence man). But because the hustler not only discovers the possibilities of living in chaos but also uses his awareness to exploit others for personal gain, the hero rejects the role. At this stage of his development, the hero, chased by white terrorists, falls into a coal cellar where he gradually resolves to become neither a social parasite like Bledsoe, Norton, and Rinehart, nor the blind follower of men and ideologies represented by Booker T. Washington, Emerson, Jack, and Ras. This is the answer to the epic question of the novel and to his blues.

In the epilogue, Ellison closely identifies with the narrator's conviction that withdrawal from the world is neither a permanent nor a responsible manner of asserting personal or national identity. Symbolically, the narrator's withdrawal to the coal cellar, illuminated by 1,369 bulbs, is a meditative retreat inward to the source of light, the wellspring of the understanding heart and soul, where, according to Emersonian transcendentalism, the individual discovers intuitively that he is a part of the divine universe and the divine universe is a part of him. Ellison's allusion to the power of instinct is similar to Emerson's ideas in "Self Reliance." "There is, by the way, an area in which man's feelings are more rational than his mind," says the hero, "and it is precisely in that area that his will is pulled in several directions at the same time" (p. 496). Because of his mind, the hero is restless and dissatisfied with his hibernation. "The fact is," he continues, "that you carry part of your sickness within you, at least I do as an invisible man" (p. 497). We all bear a share of the guilt for the failure of the American Dream, the narrator and implied author encourage us to believe: most out of blind racism, many out of blind individualism, and others out of blind chauvinism. Once the hero becomes fully aware that "life is to be lived, not controlled; and humanity is won by continuing to play in the face of certain defeat"—this is the moral lesson of his grandfather's enigmatic deathbed advice—he must reenter the world and act on this hard won self-awareness. Telling his story, passing on the spirit and wisdom of the Afro-American experience, is his personal and social act of faith.

Myth, Legend, and Ritual in the Novel of the Fifties

Like Faulkner and Wright, Ellison employs the black American as the metaphor of America and the modern human condition. In Ellison's words, the Afro-American "experience is that of America and the West, and is as rich a body of experience as one would find anywhere. We can view it narrowly as something exotic, folksy or 'low-down,' or we may identify ourselves with it and recognize it as an important segment of the larger American experience—not lying at the bottom of it, but intertwined, diffused in its very texture."[23] This modern odyssey of a nameless black American is Ellison's legacy to the tradition of the Afro-American novel, an incomparable tour de force that brilliantly celebrates the richness, ambiguity, and vitality of Afro-American culture and character.

JAMES ARTHUR BALDWIN (1924–)

"Mr. Ellison," Baldwin wrote in 1955, " . . . is the first Negro novelist I have ever read to utilize in language, and brilliantly, some of the ambiguity and irony of Negro life."[24] In capturing the poetic and dramatic power of the black church in prose, however, Baldwin surpasses Ellison. Born on August 2, 1924, during the early days of the Harlem Renaissance and the Jazz Age, James Baldwin, unlike Wright and Ellison, is a poor Northern boy from the cultural capital of black America. A manchild in the Promised Land, he grew up in the bosom of Harlem and the church. Small, frail, big-eyed, and the oldest of nine children, he spent his formative years in the Pentecostal church under the stern eye of his stepfather, David, "a dour clergyman who indicted the entire white world for oppressing the black." His stepfather's hatred taught him the meaning of hate and love, of socialized ambivalence. Driven by the fury of David Baldwin's Old Testament example, young James steeped himself in the lore of the black evangelical church and was called to preach at fourteen. Although he was a successful child preacher, neither his stepfather nor the church was his first love. In fact, he grew to hate the tyranny of both, leaving the church at seventeen and his stepfather's house the following year.[25] In 1948 he fled from the tyranny of American racism and puritanism to Paris.

The only real communication Baldwin recalls, in *Notes of a Native Son*, having with his stepfather is when he told him that he preferred the pen over the pulpit.[26] " 'For me,' " Baldwin says, " 'writing was an act of love. It was an attempt—not to get the world's attention—it was an attempt to be loved. It seemed a way to save myself and to save my family. It came out of despair. And it seemed the only way to another world.' " He had been at it since he was ten, writing songs and plays in elementary school, publishing his first story in a church newspaper when he was twelve, and serving as editor of both his junior and senior high school magazines. It was during this period that he was influenced by Countee Cullen, a major poet of the Harlem Renaissance, who at Frederick Douglass Junior High School taught him French and was adviser to the literary club in which Baldwin was a prominent member. Earlier, when he was around nine or ten, "a young midwestern substitute" drama teacher gave him books and took him to see his first play, thereby introducing him to a world beyond Harlem and his stepfather's religiosity. Flattered by his teachers and both admired and bullied by his classmates, he began commuting to the library three or four times a week, reading everything he could and translating his feelings of hatred, fear, and loneliness into plays, poetry, and short stories. The first book he read, according to his mother, was *Uncle Tom's Cabin*. He was about eight and "just read it over and over again."[27] Later in high school, he discovered Richard Wright and made him his idol and literary father. "In *Uncle Tom's Children*, in *Native Son*, and above all, in *Black Boy*, I found expressed, for the first time in my life, the sorrow, the rage, and the murderous bitterness which was eating up my life and the lives of those around me," Baldwin confessed after Wright's death. "His work was an immense liberation and revelation for me. He became my ally and my witness, and alas! my father."[28]

Like his literary father, Baldwin is certainly no black revolutionary or romantic celebrator of Afro-American culture. But whereas Wright coldly and categorically rejected the black American's African past and urban present as unnecessary cultural baggage for modern man, Baldwin agonizes over his dual heritage as an Afro-American. In "Autobiographical Notes," he says:

> I know . . . that the most crucial time in my own development came when I was forced to recognize that I was a kind of bastard of the West; when I followed the line of my past and I did not find myself in Europe but in Africa. And this meant that in some subtle way, in a really profound way, I brought to Shakespeare, Bach, Rembrandt, to the stones of Paris, to the cathedral at Chartres, and to the Empire State Building, a special attitude. These were not really my creations, they did not contain my history; I might search in them in vain forever for any reflection of myself. I was an interloper; this was not my heritage. At the same time I had no other heritage which I could possibly hope to use—I had certainly been unfitted for the jungle or the tribe. I would have to appropriate these white centuries, I would have to make them mine—I would have to accept my special attitude,

my special place in this scheme—otherwise I would have no place in *any* scheme. What was the most difficult was the fact that I was forced to admit something I had always hidden from myself, which the American Negro has to hide from himself as the price of his public progress; that I hated and feared white people. This did not mean that I loved black people; on the contrary, I despised them, possibly because they failed to produce Rembrandt. In effect, I hated and feared the world.

These mixed emotions about himself and others, about men and events, are the result of seeing himself through the eyes of a world that sees him as the barbarous antithesis of civilized man.

In "Stranger in the Village" Baldwin describes in theological terms the special attitude—Du Bois called it double-consciousness and Herskovits called it socialized ambivalance—he brings to the cathedral of Chartres:

I am terrified by the slippery bottomless well to be found in the crypt, down which heretics were hurled to death, and by the obscene, ines-capable gargoyles jutting out of the stone and seeming to say that God and the devil can never be divorced. I doubt that the villagers think of the devil when they face a cathedral because they have never been identified with the devil. But I must accept the status which myth, if nothing else, gives me in the West before I can hope to change the myth.[29]

Baldwin seems perilously close here in sociopsychological terms to Bigger Thomas in resolving his sense of double-consciousness and socialized ambivalence. Although, unlike Bigger, he may not have internalized the white myth of the Bad Nigger, his assumption that he must accept the myth before he can possibly change it has the same warping effect on his personality: shame, fear, and self-hatred.

Some of Baldwin's early interviews and essays paint a similarly bleak picture of African and Afro-American character and culture. In his youthful mind Africans were invariably associated with primitiveness and barba-rism. As a schoolboy he associated his father (actually his stepfather), and the members of his church with Africa. "I compared the people in my father's church to African savages," he told an interviewer. "This was because of my relation to my father. . . . I was ten or twelve. The church and my father were synonymous. Music and dancing, again sweat, out of the jungle. It was contemptible because it appeared to be savage. But this was also my image of my father. I guess I was hipped on being

American and the things they did seemed so common, so vulgar. My image of myself was of not having anything to do with my father or anything my father represented."[30] Describing his stepfather in "Notes of a Native Son," he states that "he looked to me . . . like pictures I had seen of African tribal chieftains: he really should have been naked, with war-paint on and barbaric mementos, standing among spears."[31] Baldwin's alienation from himself and his people, which he subsequently came to believe was an American and not just on Afro-American identity problem, is further illustrated in his essay "The Discovery of What It Means to Be an American," in which he states: "I had never listened to Bessie Smith in America (in the same way that, for years, I would not touch water-melon), but in Europe she helped to reconcile me to being a 'nigger.' "[32] Yet in "The Harlem Ghetto," an essay written years earlier, he stated that "it is simply impossible not to sing the blues, audibly or not, when the lives lived by Negroes are so inescapably harsh and stunted."[33] What does this all reveal? Well, it reveals first that Baldwin's socialization by the dominant Euro-American culture and black fundamentalist subculture taught him to love and hate, to be proud and ashamed, of his dual identity as an Afro-American, and second that, like Wright, his early exposure to blues and jazz was strongly influenced by similar mixed emotions.

Before he could be free as a writer, Baldwin felt compelled to rebel against his literary father. Wright had given him encouragement in the early stages of *Go Tell It on the Mountain*, helped him to win a Eugene F. Saxton Fellowship, and tolerated him as an admirer if not as a protégé.[34] But as in his relationship to his stepfather, Baldwin was awed by Wright's personality and saw his work as a roadblock to his own independence as an artist. In "Everybody's Protest Novel" he therefore relegates *Native Son* to the same class of protest novels as *Uncle Tom's Cabin* and concludes that "the failure of the protest novel lies in its rejection of life, the human being, the denial of his beauty, dread, power, in its insistence that it is his categorization alone which is real and which cannot be transcended." In "Many Thousands Gone" he delivers what seems to be the cruelest cut of all. Actually, the major thrust of this essay is a valid criticism of Wright for filtering the entire novel exclusively through Bigger Thomas. "What this means for the novel," Baldwin rightly observes, "is that a necessary dimension has been cut away; this dimension being the relationship that Negroes bear to one another, that depth of involvement and unspoken recognition of shared experience which creates a way of life."[35] With the ostensible Brutus thrust of these essays, Baldwin not only killed the re-lationship between Wright and himself but also implied that his own novels would provide a more faithful, comprehensive portrayal of the richness and vitality of Afro-American character and culture.

In truth, the way of life reconstructed in most of Baldwin's novels is informed by a biblical imagination that is almost as bleak as that in *Native Son*. In *Go Tell It on the Mountain* (1953) the Grimes family has only a tenuous grip on reality due to the religiosity of the storefront Pentecostal church. In *Giovanni's Room* (1956) the subject of black culture is displaced by the moral and social problems of white homosexuals in Europe. In *Another Country* (1962) a tortuous series of racial and sexual encounters— white vs. black, homosexual vs. heterosexual, North vs. South, European vs. American—drives jazz musician Rufus Scott to suicide but becomes the rite of passage to self-understanding for his jazz-singing sister Ida and the social rebels of modern America who affirm bisexuality as the highest form of love. In *Tell Me How Long the Train's Been Gone* (1968) Leo Proudhammer contends with his private and public demons—heart condition, white mistress, black militant lover, racism, and the stultifying influence of his family—as he claws his way to salvation as a black actor. In *If Beale Street Could Talk* (1974) Tish and Fonny, the blues protagonists, are able to endure and transcend the agony of harassment in the ghetto and prison through love (personal and familial) and art (black music and sculpture). And in *Just Above My Head*, Hall Montana, the first-person narrator-witness and older brother of the gospel-singing protagonist, testifies about the agonizing realities of human suffering and the ecstatic possibilities of love in the lives of those touched by his brother's journey on the gospel road.

As fascinating and ambitious as these novels are, only *Go Tell It on the Mountain*, *If Beale Street Could Talk*, and *Just Above My Head* illuminate the matrix of shared experience of black Americans. But like Wright, Baldwin focuses sharply on a single dimension of black culture. His emphasis, however, is not political but spiritual and sexual, not the terrifying possibilities of hatred, but the terrifying possibilities of love. In contrast to Wright's unrelenting narrative drive, Baldwin's short stories and novels are memorable for the soul-stirring eloquence and resonance of their pulpit oratory and black music as they plumb the depths of our suffering and the possibilities of our salvation. His use of the rhetoric, lore, and music of the black church show to their best advantage in his four collections of essays and in *Go Tell It on the Mountain*. But they are also organically significant in *If Beale Street Could Talk* and *Just Above My Head*.

Like the mood of the sorrow songs, *If Beale Street Could Talk* is informed by the blues world of everyday social myths and rituals derived from the impact of contemporary inner New York City life on young black men and women. In this blues environment the myth of black men as rapists and the rituals of police harassment continue to threaten the freedom and manhood of young blacks and the survival of strong, supportive black families. Baldwin, in short, is again testifying about suffering and love in the black family, but, as in *Another Country* and *Tell Me How Long the Train's Been Gone*, he tries with uneven success to be more political in his fifth novel.

Set in Harlem, Greenwich Village, Puerto Rico, and the Tombs (New York City's infamous jail), the book is divided into two disproportionate sections: "Trouble About My Soul," which is more than one hundred pages, and "Zion," which is only twenty pages long. The story begins with Tish Fisher, the nineteen-year-old central character who is three-months pregnant by her fiancé, Fonny Hunt, looking back on the growth of her love for this twenty-two-year-old sculptor, who is in the Tombs awaiting trial on a rape charge. Told in the first-person, except for the awkward shift to third-person in the Zion section, the plot unfolds loosely and slowly through flashbacks and interior monologues as the narrator and we bear witness to the reactions of the Fisher and Hunt families to Fonny's trouble with the police and to the news of Tish's pregnancy. Tish's family is supportive. Her mother even goes to Puerto Rico to confront Fonny's accuser, and her sister pays for his legal defense against the racist cop primarily responsible for the false charges. But Fonny's family, except for his father, Frank, is unsupportive. In their loyalty to the extreme sacred and secular polarities of Afro-American culture, his sanctified mother and bourgeois sisters denounce Tish, Fonny, and the unborn baby. Because of the many postponements of his trial and the necessity of having to fight to avoid his own mental and physical rape, Fonny is spiritually toughened and transformed by his jail experience. He redefines himself as an artisan rather than an artist. Working at a downtown store, visiting Fonny daily, and sharing her strength and love with him as she witnesses his transformation and the "dreadful price" he must pay for his manhood, Tish survives her rite of passage into womanhood. The book ends somewhat triumphantly and melodramatically with Tish going into labor just as Fonny is giving life to a sculptured bust of her.

Bordering perilously on sentimentality in his affirmation of heterosexual and familial love as traditional values for black survival, especially for young black men, in the inner cities of contemporary America, Baldwin occasionally violates the integrity of his narrator's blues character and experience. His failure, for example, to provide details that explain the first-person narrator's knowledge of the events that occur during Attorney

Hayward's briefing of Mrs. Fisher for her trip to Puerto Rico, during her adventures there, and during Fonny's imprisonment stand out among the minor weaknesses in the handling of point of view. More serious is the intellectual, emotional, and sexual distance between the implied author and his female protagonist-narrator. The description of neither her sexual initiation nor her pregnancy is particularly revealing of the complexity of these crucial aspects of a young black woman's sexuality. And such thoughts by the protagonist as "The truth is that dealing with the reality of men leaves a woman very little time, or need, for imagination," and "Each of these men would gladly go to jail, blow away a pig, or blow up a city, to save their progeny from the laws of this democratic hell"[36] are not consistent with the blues dynamics of the novel. Credulity is also strained by Fonny's abrupt transformation into a vaguely politicized artisan as a result of his identification with other black prisoners, some of whom he must fight to avoid being raped. In his continuing attempt to reconcile the cry of the soul, the tradition of the spirituals and gospel, with the call of the flesh, the tradition of the blues, Baldwin, unlike the consummate success of the short story "Sonny's Blues," has labored with uneven success in *If Beale Street Could Talk* to communicate the truth of the blues dynamics of antagonistic cooperation: adverse forces that, as Albert Murray states in *The Hero and the Blues,* cooperate with the hero "not only by generating the necessity for heroism in the first place, but also by contesting its development at every stage and by furnishing the occasion for its fulfillment."[37]

In contrast to the secular blues texture of personal experience in *If Beale Street Could Talk, Just Above My Head* examines the emotional texture of black personal relationships rooted in the black church and developed on the gospel road. The narrative journey is divided into five major sections ("Have Mercy," "Twelve Gates to the City," "The Gospel Singer," "Stepchild," and "The Gates of Hell"), each prefaced by epigraphs from traditional sacred black music and interwoven with similar songs of sorrow and joy. But the plot movement is not linear but spiraling as we bear witness with the narrator to his memory of the long, narrow, winding road of his gospel-singing brother Arthur Montana, the Soul Emperor, to love, stardom, and death at thirty-nine. Two years after Arthur's death from a stroke in the toilet of a London pub, Hall Montana, Arthur's forty-eight-year-old brother and manager, tells the story in retrospect. The discontinuous narrative weaves variations on the theme of the agony and ecstasy of Arthur's quest for love in the improvisational manner of the songs of sorrow and the songs of joy. As one critic perceptively observes, Hall "hears his brother's life as one melodic theme off which he riffs the personal history of those whose rhythms lend that theme both assonance and dissonance."[38] Addressing us intimately as "friend," Hall invites us in the opening section to see and hear with him the solid foundations of the Montana family provided by Florence, the unpretentiously compassionate mother, and Paul, the blues and jazz piano-playing father. We also bear witness to the spiritual death and incestuous violation of Julia, the child evangelist, and her rebirth through the love of Hall and an African diplomat; to the premature despair, dissolution and death of three members of The Trumpets of Zion gospel quartet (Crunch, Red, and Peanut) before Arthur becomes a star; and to the agony of Arthur's sense of dread over his inability to live the song he sings as well as the ecstasy he finds in the love of Julia's younger brother Jimmy.

Intimately addressing us again in the final section of the novel, Hall confesses what we had already realized from the passion of the language and music. The narrative is far more his story than he had intended, for "it is a love song to my brother. It is an attempt to face both love and death":[39]

> "Oh. Oh. Oh. Arthur. Speak. Speak. Speak. I know, I know. I wasn't always nice to you, I yelled when I shouldn't have yelled, I was often absent when I should have been present, I know, I know; and sometimes you bored the shit out of me, and I heard your stories too often, and I knew all your fucking little ways, man, and how you jived the people—but that's not true, you didn't jive the people, you sang, you sang, and if there was any jiving done, the people jived you, my brother, because they didn't know that *they* were the song and the price of the song and the glory of the song: you sang. Oh, my God my God my God my God my God, oh my God my God my God oh no no no, my God my God my God my God, forsake me if you will and I don't give a shit but give me back my brother, my God my God my God my God my God!" (Pp. 14–15)

Hall sings variations on the theme of this song throughout the novel, not only for Arthur and us, the readers, but also for his teenage children, Tony and Odessa, who are "the beacon on this dark plain" and for whom he is "their key to their uncle, the vessel which contains, for them, his legacy" (p. 498).

As for his wife, Ruth, she is the first real commitment he has made outside of his commitment to Arthur, but, he tells us, "this commitment was possible only because, loving me, she knew how much I loved my brother, and, loving me, she loved Arthur, too" (pp. 21–22). And though time took its toll on Arthur,

> Time could not attack the song. Time was allied with the song, amen'd in the amen corner with the song, inconceivably filled Arthur as Arthur sang, bringing Arthur, and many thousands, over. Time was proud of Arthur, so I dared whisper to myself, in the deepest and deadliest of the midnight hours; a mighty work was being worked, in time, through the vessel of my brother, who, then, was no longer my brother, belonging to me no longer, and who was yet, and more than ever, forever, my brother, my brother still. (P. 30)

Baldwin thus comes full circle in *Just Above My Head* in his passionate, perceptive treatment of the possibilities of love in the context of the black church and the black family.

Although *Just Above My Head* has passion, purpose, and perception, it lacks the coherence and sustained power of *Go Tell It on the Mountain*, his first and most carefully wrought novel. Exploring the theme of salvation for poor urban blacks, it reveals how the dogma and rituals of the storefront Pentecostal church exploit the black Southern migrant's sense of sin, shame, and sorrow in the "promised land"—the Northern ghetto—and force him to choose between salvation and damnation. Although the major focus of the novel is on John Grimes's initiation into manhood, Baldwin uses a third-person omniscient narrator and a series of flashbacks to explore the lives of the other members of the Grimes family and to reveal the historical and cultural ties that bind them to one another. In this sense, *Go Tell It on the Mountain* is a more sociopsychologically balanced reconstruction of life in the ghetto than *Native Son*.

The novel is divided into three major sections. Part One, "The Seventh Day," centers on the provincial world of fourteen-year-old John Grimes. John is a manchild in the Promised Land: a product of the ghetto, "where the houses did not rise, piercing as it seemed, the unchanging clouds, but huddled, flat, ignoble, close to the filthy ground, where the streets and the hallways and the rooms were dark, and where the unconquerable odor was of dust, and sweat, and urine, and homemade gin."[40] Cut off from the bustling white world of Broadway and bombarded with sermons on the Calvinist doctrine of original sin, John is an intelligent but highly insecure youngster. The time and place of the central action is a Saturday, March 1935, in Harlem: John's birthday and day of salvation. When the novel opens, John is troubled by the thought that nobody remembers his birthday and that he has committed a dreadful sin by masturbating. He also struggles with the sense of guilt that his hatred for Gabriel, his step-father and God's minister, has caused him to harden his heart against God. Later, after helping his brother Roy clean the house, John takes the change his mother gives him for a birthday gift and goes to a Broadway movie. When he returns home, he finds his family in a heated argument over Roy, who has been stabbed by a white boy. That evening John and Elisha, a boy preacher from Georgia, open the Temple of the Fire Baptized, a storefront Pentecostal church and prepare it for "tarry" (prayer) service.

By the end of the first section, the reader realizes that Baldwin is not only exploring the personal dilemma of his protagonist but also exposing the moral foundations of the institutional pillars of the black community. As major institutions in the black community, the family and the church are both at the center of Baldwin's vision of Harlem. And because the Grimes family worships at the Temple of the Fire Baptized, the role that its dogma and rituals play in their lives is held up to scrutiny. Popular among many first-generation migrants from the rural South, the black storefront church generally portrays itself as an oasis in the desert of perdition. The ritual of Old Testament sermons accompanied by the ec-static singing and clapping of the Saints (the sanctified women members) serve to convince young members like John Grimes that though their church may not be the biggest in Harlem it was surely "the holiest and best." Stock sermons on the wages of sin and the wickedness of the world also serve to distort the values of church members, encouraging them to be otherworldly and fearful of normal relationships with others. The Sunday before John's birthday, for instance, Elisha is singled out by the minister and preached at for "walking disorderly" with Ella Mae, a young girl. Taught with neo-Calvinist zeal that they are the carnal children of Adam, the young members of the Temple of the Fire Baptized become frustrated in their struggle for healthy social and sexual freedom, for full personal and social development, for wholeness. As a result of this Christian fundamentalism, the legacy of evangelical eighteenth-century New England puritanism and nineteenth-century Southern Methodism, the mere act of growing up becomes terrifying. More disturbing to John than the thought that nobody remembers his birthday is the burden of guilt and fear he suffers over masturbation. He cannot even look at a photograph of himself as a naked infant without feeling shame and anger.

Baldwin uses conventional color symbolism which correlates darkness with damnation and light with salvation to reinforce John's obsession with sin and uncleanness. The family name of Grimes itself signifies the ambivalent feelings of many black Americans about the color of their skin. Is it a stigma of sin or a badge of glory? Should it inspire self-hatred or self-glorification? For John there is no compromise "between the way that led to life ever-lasting and the way that ended in the pit. . . . He could not claim, as African savages might be able to claim, that no one had brought him the gospel" (p. 45). Consequently, he looks with "shame and horror" on the dirt that permeates his kitchen and makes him feel unclean; and while sweeping the living room carpet, he dreads the sight of dust all around him and the feeling that he cannot get rid of the dirt or, symbolically, wash himself clean of sin. By making sex and sin synonymous, the black storefront church, like its evangelical Calvinist antecedents, terrifies its members into turning to it as a refuge from the wickedness of the world.

Part 2, "The Prayers of the Saints," is a series of flashbacks and indirect interior monologues probing into the thoughts and feelings of John's Aunt Florence, his father, Gabriel, and his mother, Elizabeth. "Florence's Prayer" retraces the path that has led her to the Temple of the Fire Baptized. She is dying of cancer and fearful of meeting her God without being saved. Florence's thoughts therefore focus on the people from whom she seeks forgiveness: the mother she had left down home on her deathbed, the brother and sister-in-law she had scorned and mocked, and the husband she loved but had lost because of her middle-class obsessions. "Gabriel's Prayer" reveals how he was driven to the ministry by his desire for power and his fear of Hell. Buried in his past is an unfruitful marriage to Deborah, whose barrenness resulted from an assault by white rapists; an adulterous relationship with Esther, the unacknowledged mother of his illegitimate son; and a loveless marriage to Elizabeth, whose son John was born out of wedlock. "Elizabeth's Prayer" recalls her tortured path to salvation. She trembles with fear of God at the trials she must yet endure for the hatred she bore for her aunt, the illicit love she shared with Richard, the illegitimate child she brought into the world, and the security she craved in her marriage to Gabriel. The unreliability of each narrator is corrected by the prayerful narration of the other and further corrected by the undramatized omniscient narrator whose norms, as suggested by structure, symbol, ritual, and language, are close to those of the implied author.

As the length and title of the second section suggests, the ritual of prayer is a key element in the otherworldly doctrine of the storefront church. In both the rural and urban Pentecostal church, God is depicted as a stern father who answers the prayers of his obedient children, delivering those who heed his commands and punishing those who do not. Baldwin draws on this lore of the Old Testament and achieves aesthetic distance from his narrative by employing prayers both as a structural device and as a symbol in the novel. From the prayers whispered at the breakfast table to those intoned during tarry services, the Grimes family dramatizes the tradition of black folks taking their troubles to the Lord in prayer and bearing witness to the spiritual imperative of being born again. On the one hand, prayers are used to establish and reinforce a common ethnic bond by tracing the history of black Americans from the plantation to the ghetto; and on the other, they are used as a symbol of blind faith in a religion of social oppression and emotional desperation.

Before beginning her prayer, Florence sings "Standing in the Need of Prayer" along with the Saints. After kneeling, she recalls her mother, who was born in slavery and indoctrinated by her enslavers to believe that the emancipation of slaves "was in answer to the prayers of the faithful, who had never ceased, both day and night, to cry out for deliverance" (p. 86). Florence also remembers that the first prayer she heard was during the post–Reconstruction period of white terrorism. After Deborah's father was beaten nearly to death for threatening the men who had raped his daughter, the black community, fearful that the angry whites would burn down their homes and believing that it was better to look to Heaven for salvation, merely prayed and waited. Florence then recalls the moment at the turn of the century when she told her dying mother that she was moving North, and her mother prayed for the Lord to stretch out his "hand and hold her back from the lake that burns forever." Whether wrathful or merciful, the image of God imposed on the slaves by whites, in contrast to their own image of him, was a tool of social oppression. In New York, Florence soon sheds her rural Southern folk ways and begins to embrace urban bourgeois values. After marrying a city fellow who sang the blues and drank alcohol, she drives him away from her side by complaining about his "common nigger" ways and forcing him to go with her to "Uplift meetings" to hear speeches "about the future and duties of the Negro race." Florence even learns to pray in silence instead of expressing the deepest truths of her being by crying out and shouting like the folks down home and the members of the Temple of the Fire Baptized. But the price of Florence's urge to whiteness and bourgeois urban respectability with its concomitant repression of ethnicity and violation of the integrity of her being is "to die, alone and in poverty, in a dirty, furnished room" (p. 115).

In Gabriel's prayer Baldwin exposes the gnarled roots of the Calvinist dogma and evangelical practices of the Pentecostal church. Baptized at a camp meeting when he was twelve, Gabriel, in his mother's eyes, is a manchild destined for the Promised Land. His introduction to prayer and the word of God comes from his mother, who passes on her slave-inherited Christian faith through biblical stories about the suffering and deliverance of the Hebrew children. To keep Gabriel on the narrow path of right-eousness, his mother would pray over him after each whipping she gave him. But neither prayer nor paddle kept Gabriel from enjoying the pleas-ures of life. Before he is called to preach, he violates every taboo of the church, from dancing and card playing to gambling and whoring. Unlike Florence, who hated him for being a "big, black prancing tomcat of a nigger," Gabriel's mother and Deborah direct their hate at the sin rather than the sinnerman and continue to pray for him. Finally, gripped by the terror of going "down into the grave, unwashed, unforgiven," Gabriel gets religion and is called to the pulpit.

In addition to casting a shadow over Gabriel's qualifications for the ministry, Baldwin depicts the elders of the Pentecostal church as sleek cats who prey on the ignorance and blind faith of black people. Invited to participate in the Twenty-Four Elders Revival Meeting, a huge twenty-four day revival meeting with sermons by different preachers each day, Gabriel prays and fasts to prepare himself for the occasion. But, to his surprise, he finds himself questioning the integrity of his brothers of the cloth:

> They seemed to him so lax, so nearly worldly; they were not like those holy prophets of old who grew thin and naked in the service of the Lord. These, God's ministers, had indeed grown fat, and their dress was rich and various. They had been in the field so long that they did not tremble before God any more. . . . They each had, it seemed, a bagful of sermons often preached; and knew, in the careless lifting of an eye, which sermon to bring to which congregation. Though they preached with great authority, and brought souls low before the altar . . . they did not give God the glory, nor count it as glory at all; they might as easily have been . . . highly paid circus-performers, each with his own special gift . . . they [also] spoke, jokingly, of the comparative number of souls each of them had saved, as though they were keeping score in a poolroom. (Pp. 138–39)

The dramatic irony is that even though the church elders are charlatans, Gabriel, who sees himself as an Old Testament prophet through whom God will work some miracle, is hardly more exemplary as a Christian leader.

In portraying Gabriel's conversion, sermons, and visions, Baldwin draws on his own experience as a child preacher and student of the Bible. Poetry and prose are intertwined as he paints a graphic picture of Judgment Day, liberally incorporating eschatological symbols from the New Testament in his vignette: a lone tree on a hill, the awesome silence of God's judgment, the tearful prayers of a sinner, the sound of singing voices, the vision of a new heaven and earth, and the rejoicing of nature at a new beginning. Equally impressive in its use of biblical imagery and black church rhetoric is Gabriel's sermon on the text of uncleanness. " 'For let us remember,' " Gabriel says, his voice rising and the tempo increasing,

> "that the wages of sin is death; that it is written, and cannot fail, the soul that sinneth, it shall die. Let us remember that we are born in sin, in sin our mothers conceive us—sin reigns in all our members, sin is the foul heart's natural liquid, sin looks out of the eye, amen, and leads to lust, sin is in the hearing of the ear, and leads to folly, sin sits on the tongue, and leads to murder. Yes! Sin is the only heritage of the natural man, sin bequeathed us by our natural father, that fallen Adam, whose apple sickens and will sicken all generations living, and generations yet unborn! It was sin that drove the son of the morning out of Heaven, sin that drove Adam out of Eden, sin that caused Cain to slay his brother, sin that built the tower of Babel, sin that caused the fire to fall on Sodom—sin from the very foundations of the world, living and breathing in the heart of man, that causes women to bring forth their children in agony and darkness, bows down the backs of men with terrible labor, keeps the empty belly empty, keeps the table bare, sends our children, dressed in rags, out into the whorehouses and dance halls of the world." (Pp. 134–35)

Sermons like these, with their improvisational, rhythmic mixture of biblical metaphor, folk images, colloquialisms, and repetitions, gave black Americans a religious explanation for their rejection by and isolation from white America, encouraging blacks to believe that, like the Jews, they, too, were a chosen people whom God would, in his own time, deliver from oppression and exploitation. Equally important, the subject and fervent delivery of this sermon suggests Gabriel's obsession with sin and his own vindictive character.

After his spiritual conversion, Gabriel awakens from a wet dream with the thought: "Out of the house of David, the son of Abraham" (p. 145). He then has a second dream in which he climbs to the top of a high rugged mountain. Dressed in white robes and bathed in the blazing sun, he looks down the steep mountain. "And now up this mountain in white robes, singing, the elect came. 'Touch them not,' the voice said, 'my seal is on them.' And Gabriel turned and fell on his face, and the voice said again: 'So shall thy be.' Then he awoke" (p. 187). Gabriel, who in the Old Testament is the interpreter of visions and prophecies, translates this dream as a sign from God to choose Deborah as "his holy helpmeet" and as a promise from God that he would have a son "who would work until the day of the second coming to bring about His Father's Kingdom" (p. 151). The texts of Gabriel's sermon—Isa. 6:5 and 2 Sam. 18:19–30—also allude to David and the coming of Christ. The analogue of God's promise to Abraham and David gives a mythic dimension to Gabriel's vision and the relationship he has with his son.

Both Abraham and David, like Gabriel, were involved in bastardy and adultery. Abraham had a son, Ishmael, by Hagar, bondwoman to his wife Sarah; and David had a son, Solomon, by Bathsheba, the wife of Uriah. Baldwin uses Ishmael and Absalom, David's legitimate son by Maacah, as symbols of the rebellious outcast. Both Ishmael and Absalom were disinherited and alienated by their fathers. Similarly, Gabriel disowns Royal, his bastard son by Esther. With the money Gabriel steals from his wife, Esther goes to Chicago to have her son. After Esther's death, her body and her son came home. And though a day does not pass in which he does not see "his lost, his disinherited son, or heard of him," he will not acknowledge Royal. Instead, Gabriel prays for him and "watched him run headlong, like David's headlong son, towards the disaster that had been waiting for him from the moment he had been conceived" (p. 185). Only after the news of Royal's death in a Chicago barroom reaches him does Gabriel break down and confess his guilt to Deborah, who tells him from her dying bed, "Honey . . . you better pray God to forgive you. You better not let go until He makes you *know* you been forgiven" (p. 200). Here again Baldwin points out the reliance on prayer by the black masses as a key to salvation, while simultaneously suggesting that the gravity of Gabriel's sin requires more than prayer. After Deborah's death, Gabriel moves North, meets Elizabeth and receives her and her bastard son, John, as a sign from God. Richard, Elizabeth's lover and John's father, is also a fatherless child. Baldwin, in short, is highly resourceful in using bastardy as a metaphor for the estranged relationship between blacks and white America.

The theme of estrangement runs through the novel. A few months after his birth, Gabriel is deserted by his father. He in turn disowns his son by

Esther. After marrying Elizabeth, he alienates his stepson John and his natural son Roy. When Gabriel slaps Elizabeth during an argument, Roy curses him, " 'You slap her again, you black bastard, and I swear to God I'll kill you' " (p. 57). During tarry service, Gabriel is embittered by the fact that neither of his sons is there crying "on the threshing-floor" and that "Only the son of the bondwoman stood where the rightful heir should stand" (p. 149). Gabriel also feels bitter toward Elizabeth, who refuses to recognize any difference between John and his half-brother Roy. "But how could there not be a difference between the son of a weak, proud woman and some careless boy" Gabriel feels, "and the son that God had promised him, who would carry down the joyful line his father's name" (p. 151). He thinks of John as a "presumptuous bastard boy" and of the members of his race as "a bastard people, far from God, singing and crying in the wilderness." At the end of his prayer, Gabriel's hypocrisy and moral insecurity are apparent to John.

Elizabeth's prayer reinforces the theme of black Americans' feelings of alienation and disinheritance in their father's land. While she prays for John's deliverance, Elizabeth's thoughts fly back over her life. Her own estrangement begins with a hypochondriac mother, who read spiritualist pamphlets and never tired of telling Elizabeth that she was "an unnatural child." Although Elizabeth loved her father, she was separated from him at her mother's death. Raised in Maryland by an oppressively religious aunt, she grew up hating her and felt alienated from her father for not coming to free her from a loveless house. Elizabeth also feels estranged from God. This feeling results from the "pride, hatred, bitterness and lust . . . of which her son was heir." Even while praying, Elizabeth realizes that she is not prepared to deny her love for Richard, John's father. Once before she had turned away from God for Richard. He too was proud, sensitive, and fatherless. Convincing her aunt that she wanted to move North where the opportunities for a good job and education were better, Elizabeth follows Richard to Harlem where they planned to marry. But they found it difficult to save much out of their incomes as chambermaid and elevator boy. Free from the puritan zeal of her aunt, Elizabeth surrenders to Richard and begins to think of herself as a fallen woman. When she mentions Jesus to Richard and his friends, their reaction is bitter. The harsh reality of ghetto life has taught them, like the realities of plantation life taught their slave ancestors, the hyprocrisy of institutionalized Christianity. Like Richard and the many thousands of migrants before him, Elizabeth gradually discovers that the only difference between the North and South is that the North promised more. Sadly enough, "what it promised it did not give, and what it gave, at length and grudgingly with one hand it took back with the other" (p. 200).

Through the loss of Richard and discovery of Gabriel, Elizabeth bears witness to this belief. Picked up as a robbery suspect by the police and viciously beaten for insisting on his innocence, Richard tells Elizabeth that she ought to pray to that Jesus of hers and get him to come down and tell these white men something. And with vengeance in her heart for the whole white world, she prays. Ignorant of Elizabeth's pregnancy and broken in spirit, Richard commits suicide after the police release him. A year later, Florence, who works with Elizabeth as a cleaning woman on Wall Street (a situation that symbolically suggests the continuing capitalistic exploitation of black labor in general and black women in particular), introduces Elizabeth to Gabriel. Alienated from her family and God by her sense of sin, Elizabeth desperately reaches out for the security she sees in Gabriel and his faith. "She had believed him when he said that God had sent him to her for a sign," she recalls. "He had said that he would cherish her until the grave, and that he would love her nameless son as though he were his own flesh. And he had kept the letter of his promise: he had fed him and clothed him and taught him the Bible—but the spirit was not there. And he cherished—if he cherished her—only because she was the mother of his son, Roy" (p. 237). All this Elizabeth divines over the years. Prayer is the only thing she has left. And as she comes to the end of her prayer for John's salvation, she hears his cry and sees him on the threshing floor under the spell of the Lord.

Part Three, "The Threshing Floor," is a detailed account of John's spiritual rebirth and its immediate impact on his family. On the floor in front of the church altar, John, with whom the narrator closely identifies, is possessed by an overpowering force that cleanses his heart and soul of the darkness of sin and despair. As they watch John on the threshing floor, Elizabeth is tearfully proud and Gabriel piously reserved. Florence, on the other hand, is happy that John gets religion, but scornful of Gabriel's false piety. In the end, John is overjoyed that the Lord has touched him; he is fearful however of the many faces of the Devil—his hatred for Gabriel and love for Elisha—and asks Elisha to pray for him and remember to go tell it on the mountain that no matter what happens to him he had been saved. More than anything else, the implied author makes clear through the point of view and characterization, it is their religion and desperate faith in the power of prayer that binds the Grimes family together.

John's initiation rite is characterized by an intense struggle with the doctrines of the Pentecostal church that black is the color of damnation and that sex and sin are identical. To attain sanctification, he must pray to God and follow Jesus "up the steep side of the mountain," as Elisha reminds him. To achieve his identity John must accept the legacy of his people—the people that walk in darkness; he must go down into the valley of the shadow of death and discover that inner light and strength that comes only through suffering. He must make his peace with the reality of socialized ambivalence in white America—of being simultaneously a native son and a stranger in his father's house and his own land—and be neither enslaved nor dehumanized by it. Rather, he must be strengthened by the grace of God to go tell it on the mountain.

Early in the novel, when it is expected that he would walk in Gabriel's footsteps, John believes that his salvation will resolve the estrangement between him and his father. "Then he would no longer be the son of his father," he thinks, "but the son of his Heavenly Father, the King. Then he need no longer fear his father, for he could take, as it were, their quarrel over his father's head to Heaven—to the Father who loved him. . . . Then he and his father would be equals, in the sight, and the sound, and the love of God" (p. 194). But while praying on the threshing floor he is torn by the sin of his "yearning tenderness for holy Elisha" and of "having looked on his father's nakedness and mocked and cursed him in his heart." John must define himself against the antithetical forces of love and hate implicit in Noah's curse on his youngest son, Canaan. He must adjust to the lore of Christianity, for it is both his cross and his curse. Without the hope found in the ritual of prayer, life would be unbearable for John.

Feeling himself in the company of "the despised and rejected, the wretched and the spat upon, the earth's offscouring," John cries out for help and hears Elisha's voice—not Gabriel's—telling him to call on Jesus. It is Elisha's prayers that strengthen him in his struggle with the armies of darkness; Elisha's voice that fills him with sweetness; and Elisha's hand that stretches out to lift him up from the floor. Finally, it is to Elisha that John turns for a "holy kiss," which further reinforces the homosexual leitmotif of the novel.

It is symbolically as well as thematically significant that Elisha not his family, is the intercessor in John's salvation. Elizabeth, Florence, and Gabriel have been drained of moral energy and hope. They are doomed to a life of wretchedness and despair. But as the symbol of youthful passion sacrificing itself for the church, however repressive its dogma, Elisha offers John a ray of hope for the future. In this sense, he is a Christ-figure. By turning to Elisha, John also reconciles himself, however precariously, to the pain of his warring passion for life, for wholeness, and the bitterness of his heritage as a black American. At the end of the novel, the beginning of a new life is symbolized by the rising sun that "fell over Elisha like a golden robe, and struck John's forehead, where Elisha had kissed him, like a seal ineffaceable forever" (p. 302). The sensuality of this tableau suggests the need for love and communion in the black Pentecostal church, where, according to the implied author, the guiding principles are Blindness, Loneliness, and Terror rather than Faith, Hope, and Charity.

Baldwin's major achievement in *Go Tell It on the Mountain* is his lyrical treatment of the doctrines and rituals of the inner-city black Pentecostal church and the witness he bears to the high price many blacks, collectively and individually, have paid for their moral victory over social oppression. In a deftly controlled series of flashbacks, shifting points of view, interior monologues, pulpit oratory, and biblical symbols, Baldwin strikes a delicate balance between private anguish and public tragedy in his vision of a Northern black teenager's initiation into manhood and the life of the urban storefront church. *Go Tell It on the Mountain* thus heightens the messianic tone of the Afro-American novel, introduces a more compassionate treatment of homosexuality, and establishes Baldwin's chief thematic concerns as the American perversion of Christian principles, especially the redemptive power of love, and the reconciliation of personal sexual freedom with traditional black moral values.

In retrospect, then, the most significant development in the tradition of the Afro-American novel between 1952 and 1962 was the rediscovery of myth, legend, and ritual by Ralph Ellison and James Baldwin. Although Petry's *Narrows*, Wright's *Outsider*, and Brooks's *Maud Martha* move beyond naturalism in exploration of new themes, forms, or styles, it is Ellison's *Invisible Man* and Baldwin's *Go Tell It on the Mountain* that most dramatically remind us of the continuity of traditional narrative forms in appropriately modern black contexts. Ellison and Baldwin were both influenced by the achievement in naturalism of Richard Wright, but each chose a different and distinctive approach to the novel. Each became aware of the literary possibilities of his folk tradition as a result of his own personal experiences and his own study of literature. As in the black American novels of the nineteenth century, however, history and myth, illustrative and representational character types, traditional and personal sign systems are juxtaposed or integrated with each other as Ellison and Baldwin seek the appropriate interplay of realism and modernism for their aesthetic and social purpose. Shaped by the Depression, the Harlem Renaissance, his college background, and his writing apprenticeship, Ellison,

Myth, Legend, and Ritual in the Novel of the Fifties

the older of the two writers, reveals a more modern sensibility in the literary and folkloristic patterns of *Invisible Man* than Baldwin, whose sensibility is poignantly more unconventional, does in *Go Tell It on the Mountain*. As products of institutional racism and the integrationist movements of the 1940s, however, both novelists reveal their own socialized ambivalence and double vision in their themes, plots, characterization, and point of view. The novels of both also reveal the qualities of realism and modernism that were to become more pronounced and dichotomous in the 1960s and 1970s.

7 / The Contemporary Afro-American Novel, 1: Neorealism

When Black women's books are dealt with at all, it is usually in the
context of Black literature, which largely ignores the implications of
sexual politics. When white women look at Black women's words they
are of course ill-equipped to deal with the subtleties of racial politics.
A Black feminist approach to literature that embodies the realization that
the politics of sex as well as the politics of race and class are crucially
interlocking factors in the works of Black women writers
is an absolute necessity.

BARBARA SMITH

"Toward a Black Feminist Criticism"

REBELLION or revolution—that was the burning question of the 1960s. Whether the cry was "We Shall Overcome" or "Burn, baby, burn!" black and white voices were raised in protest against racism, poverty, war, corruption, and sexism. Americans were deeply disillusioned by the moral bankruptcy of their political and economic system and took radical action to correct or to escape the social injustice of the decade in myriad forms of movements and cults. These radical movements and cults ranged from the bombing of buildings identified as part of the military-industrial complex by the Weathermen, a white revolutionary splinter group of Students for a Democratic Society (SDS), and the burying of cars as menaces to the ecology by college students, to the emergence of the drop-out and turn-on followers of Timothy Leary, the guru of the drug culture and former Harvard professor, and the ritual murders by the Charles Manson cult. Eclipsing the first manned United States landing on the moon in 1969, a revolution in moral conscience and social consciousness was underway. Spearheading these radical changes and most significant for their impact on the Afro-American novel from 1963 to 1983 were the black power movement and, toward the end of the 1960s, the women's rights movement.

The Black Power and Black Arts Movements

The slogan *Black Power* was popularized by Stokely Carmichael and Willie Ricks during SNCC's continuation of James Meredith's protest march through the South in 1966. But the phrase is more than a slogan and has a meaning as large as the history of the struggle of black people against racism in the United States. As a concept *black power* expresses the determination of black people to define and liberate themselves. The concept rests on the fundamental premise "that group solidarity is necessary before a group can operate effectively from a bargaining position of strength in a pluralistic society." As Stokely Carmichael and Charles V. Hamilton explain:

> The adoption of the concept of Black Power is one of the most legitimate and healthy developments in American politics and race relations in our time. . . . It is a call for black people in this country to unite, to recognize their heritage, to build a sense of community. It is a call for black people to begin to define their own goals, to lead their own organizations and to support those organizations. It is a call to reject the racist institutions and values of this society.[1]

Black power thus has a wide range of meanings, from the development of economic and political solidarity and the attainment of full equality as American citizens to the radical reform or, if necessary, revolutionary overthrow of old political and economic structures.

The concept also has a long history. In 1954 Richard Wright titled his book about Ghana *Black Power*, but as the essays in Floyd Barbour's *Black Power Revolt* reveal, the concept can be traced back to Benjamin Banneker's letter to Thomas Jefferson in 1791. The most passionate early statement on black power is David Walker's "Appeal to the Colored Citizens of the World" in 1829. On the international level the concept was promoted by the six Pan-African meetings convened between 1900 and 1945. "From the end of World War II through the early 1960's," historian John H. Bracey, Jr., writes, "integration was the dominant ideology among Negro protest movements. A few nationalist groups, such as the UNIA splinter groups and the Nation of Islam, persisted but could arouse little mass support."[2] Among the many legal actions, sit-ins, marches, freedom rides, boycotts, demonstrations, and voter registration drives, the most salient civil rights events of the period were the 1954 Supreme Court school desegregation decision, the 1963 March on Washington, and the 1964 Civil Rights Act. The two dominant yet vastly different black leaders of the period were Malcolm X, the charismatic, militant Minister of the Nation of Islam and its chief spokesman until 1964, when Malcolm broke with his leader Elijah Muhammad over irreconcilable doctrinal differences; and Martin Luther King, Jr., the equally charismatic, nonviolent Southern Baptist preacher who rose to national prominence as the moving spirit of the Montgomery bus boycott in 1955, of the passive resistance tactics of the Southern Christian Leadership Conference (SCLC), a major civil rights organization, and of the March on Washington in 1963. Assassinated for their activism, Malcolm in 1965 and King in 1968, both men became martyrs of the black power movement and paradigms of heroism in the black arts movement, most compellingly re-created in the tradition of the Afro-American novel in John A. Williams's *Man Who Cried I Am.*

In the early 1960s the example of the emerging free African nations and the Cuban Revolution kindled the latent revolutionary nationalism of many black Americans and spurred the development of black studies programs in colleges across the nation. Black power advocates redefined the liberation struggle of black Americans as part of the larger struggle of oppressed peoples against Western imperialism. Frustrated by the snail's pace of integration efforts and the tactics of passive resistance, they revived indigenous theories of the colonial relationship of blacks to the dominant culture of the United States. In a cogent explanation of the theory of black Americans as subjects of domestic colonialism, social critic Harold Cruse writes:

> The American Negro shares with colonial peoples many of the socioeconomic factors which form the material basis for present day revolutionary nationalism. Like the peoples of the underdeveloped countries, the Negro suffers in varying degree from hunger, illiteracy, disease, ties to the land, urban and semi-urban slums, cultural starvation, and the psychological reactions to being ruled over by others not of his kind. He experiences the tyranny imposed upon the lives of those who inhabit underdeveloped countries.... From the beginning, the American Negro has existed as a colonial being. His enslavement coincided with the colonial expansion of European powers and was nothing more or less than a condition of domestic colonialism. Instead of the United States establishing a colonial empire in Africa, it brought the colonial system home and installed it in the Southern states. When the Civil War broke up the slave system and the Negro was emancipated, he gained only partial freedom. Emancipation elevated him only to the position of a semi-independent man, not to that of an equal or independent being.... As a wage laborer or tenant

farmer, the Negro is discriminated against and exploited. Those in the educated, professional, and intellectual classes suffer a similar fate. Except for a very small percentage of the Negro intelligentsia, the Negro functions in a subcultural world made up, usually of necessity, of his own race only. . . . The only factor which differentiates the Negro's status from that of a pure colonial status is that his position is maintained in the "home" country in close proximity to the dominant racial group. It is not at all remarkable then that the semi-colonial status of the Negro has given rise to nationalist movements. It would be surprising if it had not.[3]

In the revolt against historical exploitation and the many beatings, jailings, and killings of civil rights activists, blacks in the communities across the nation began striking out in rage: in Harlem in 1964, Watts in 1965, Newark and Detroit in 1967, and nearly every city in the nation in 1968 after the assassination of Martin Luther King, Jr. Responding to the needs of the black lower class, some groups, such as US, promoted the development of an indigenous African-based cultural value system, ritualized in the ceremony of Kwanzaa, a holiday celebrated from December 26 through January 1 to reinforce the spiritual ties of black Americans to Africa. Others, such as the Black Panther Party, the Revolutionary Action Movement (RAM), the Republic of New Africa, and the League of Revolutionary Black Workers, adopted the ideology and strategy of achieving black self-determination by any means necessary, including armed struggle.

"Black Art is the aesthetic and spiritual sister of the Black Power concept," writes Larry Neal, a major proponent of the black arts movement. "As such, it envisions an art that speaks directly to the needs and aspirations of Black America. In order to perform this task, the Black Arts Movement proposes a radical reordering of the western cultural aesthetic. It proposes a separate symbolism, mythology, critique and iconology."[4] It was launched in the spring of 1964 when LeRoi Jones, whose play *Dutchman* had stunned the theater world, and other black artists opened the Black Arts Repertory Theatre-School in Harlem and took their plays, poetry readings, and concerts into the streets of the black community. Before the end of the summer the Harlem school was forced to close because of internal problems, but black art groups soon sprang up on campuses and in cities across the nation. At the same time, black musicians like Little Richard, Chuck Berry, B. B. King, Muddy Waters, Otis Redding, Aretha Franklin, John Coltrane, Stevie Wonder, Jimi Hendrix, Isaac Hayes, and the Supremes became national and international style setters. Black actors and actresses such as Sidney Poitier, James Earl Jones, Cicely Tyson, Ossie Davis, Ruby Dee, Harry Belafonte, Clarence Williams, and Bill Cosby became more highly visible in major roles in the movies and on television. And mass periodicals such as *Essence, Encore, Black Collegian, Black Enterprise,* and *Black World;* small presses like Broadside and Third World; and journals like *Umbra, Black Dialogue, Liberator, Journal of Black Poetry,* and *Black Scholar* were born and, in some cases, died early, untimely deaths due to financial difficulties.

Because the black arts and black power concepts both relate broadly to the Afro-American's desire for self-determination and nationhood, both are nationalistic. "One is concerned with the relationship between art and politics; and other with the art of politics."[5] Nevertheless, most black writing of the 1960s, Neal contends, was aimed at the destruction of the double-consciousness described by Du Bois in *The Souls of Black Folk.* "It has been aimed at consolidating the African-American personality. And it has not been essentially a literature of protest. It has, instead, turned its attention inward to the internal problems of the group.... It is a literature primarily directed at the conscience of black people."[6]

The Women's Rights Movement

Just as the nineteenth-century struggle for equal rights for women was fired by the struggle to free the slaves, the women's rights movements of the 1960s were fired by the civil rights and black power movements. "The call to that first Woman's Rights Convention came about," as feminist Betty Friedan explains, "because an educated woman, who had already participated in shaping society as an abolitionist, came face to face with the realities of a housewife's drudgery and isolation in a small town."[7] Similarly, participation in the civil rights movement, ambivalence about the black power movement, especially its male chauvinism, and boredom with their actual or expected lives as suburban housewives spurred many American women more than a century later to renewed activism for women's rights. Most of the leading feminists, of course, were and are middle-class white women. Consequently, the question arises: How relevant are the experiences, truths, and priorities of white women to black women? Subject to all the restrictions against blacks as well as those against women, the black woman is for many people, as black folk wisdom teaches, "de mule uh de world." Her experience and truths are generally glossed over or ignored when references are made to women and blacks. Even so, as Gerda Lerner documents in *Black Women in White America,* "black women, speaking with many voices and expressing many individual opinions, have been nearly unanimous in their insistence that their own emancipation cannot be separated from the emancipation of their men. Their liberation depends on the liberation of the race and the improvement of the life of the black community."[8] Thus, as the public interest began to shift in the late 1960s from the rights of blacks to the rights of women, publishers became more receptive to the voices of black women writers, and novels by Margaret Walker, Rosa Guy, Mary Vroman, Louise Meriwether, Paule Marshall, Kristin Hunter, Caroline Polite, Sarah Wright, Alice Walker, Alice Childress, Ellease Southerland, Gloria Naylor, Toni Morrison, Gayl Jones, and Toni Cade Bambara, among the better known, were all published before the end of 1983.

Facile generalizations about the parallels between the struggle of blacks and women for status ignore the complexity and distinctiveness of the history of black women, a history that reaches from the legacy of their African past and slave experience to their experience with industrialization and modern corporate America. "There is nothing to indicate," as political analyst Toni Cade astutely reminds us, "that the African woman, who ran the marketplace, who built dams, who engaged in international commerce and diplomacy, who sat on thrones, who donned armor to wage battle against the European invaders and the corrupt chieftains who engaged in the slave trade, who were consulted as equals in the affairs of state—nothing to indicate that they were turning their men into faggots, were victims of penis envy, or any such nonsense. There is nothing to indicate that the Sioux, Seminole, Iroquois or other 'Indian' nations felt oppressed or threatened by their women, who had mobility, privileges, a voice in governing of the commune. There is evidence, however, that the European white was confused and alarmed by the egalitarian system of these societies and did much to wreck it, creating wedges between the men and women."[9] In the late sixties, therefore, many Afro-Americans were encouraged by historical circumstances to continue resisting or rejecting Eurocentric models and interpretations of manhood and womanhood. They turned instead to non-Western, nonwhite communities and Afrocentric models to discover or create possibilities for autonomous selves and communities through a commitment to the development of a more just, egalitarian social order.

This means, then, that the reality of black womanhood is not dependent on black males first defining their manhood. "Above all else," stresses "The Black Feminist Statement" of the Combahee River Collective, "our politics initially sprang from the shared belief that Black women are inherently valuable, that our liberation is a necessity not as an adjunct to somebody else's but because of our need as human persons for autonomy."[10] Although drafted in 1977 by a radical group of primarily New York black feminists and lesbians, this statement nevertheless crystallizes the alienation of many black women from the Euro-American feminist movement:

> We believe that sexual politics under patriarchy is as pervasive in Black women's lives as are the politics of class and race. We also often find it difficult to separate race from class from sex oppression because in our lives they are most often experienced simultaneously. We know that there is such a thing as racial-sexual oppression which is neither solely racial nor solely sexual, e.g., the history of rape of Black women by white men as a weapon of political repression.
>
> Although we are feminists and lesbians, we feel solidarity with progressive Black men and do not advocate the fractionalization that white women who are separatists demand. Our situation as Black people necessitates that we have solidarity around the fact of race, which white women of course do not need to have with white men, unless it is their negative solidarity as racial oppressors. We struggle together with Black men against racism, while we also struggle with Black men about sexism.[11]

In *Black Women Writers at Work* Bambara in 1983 told an interviewer:

> What has changed about the women's movement is the way we perceive it, the way black women define the term, the phenomena and our participation in it. White bourgeois feminist organizations captured the arena, media attention, and the country's imagination. . . . Black women and other women of color have come around to recognizing that the movement is much more than a few organizations. The movement is exactly what the word suggests, a motion of the mind. . . . We're more inclined now, women of color, to speak of black midwives and the medicine women of the various communities when we talk of health care rather than assume we have to set up women's health collectives on the same order as non-colored women have. In organizing, collectivizing, researching, strategizing, we're much less antsy than we were a decade ago. We are more inclined to trust our own traditions, whatever name we gave and now give those impulses, those groups, those agendas, and are less inclined to think we have to sound like, build like, non-colored groups that iden-

tify themselves as feminist or as women's rights groups, or so it seems to me.[12]

This not only gets to the heart of the differences that many black women have about the priorities and objectives of the women's rights movement, but also explains in part why Alice Walker adapted the term *womanist* from black folk expression to signify a black feminist or feminist of color, a woman who, among other things, is audaciously committed to the survival and wholeness of entire people, male and female. More to the point of my readings of contemporary Afro-American novels by black women, the comments above provide the necessary context or subtext for a better understanding of why black women are primarily concerned with how racism, sexism, and classism have influenced the development of love, power, autonomy, creativity, manhood, and womanhood in the black family and community.

In pursuing these themes black women novelists provide a much neglected perspective and chorus of voices on the human experience, but, contrary to the assumptions of some critics, this does not necessarily mean that their works constitute a distinctive literary tradition. The absence, silence, or misrepresentation of black women in literary and nonliterary texts or contexts by black men as well as white men and women is now commonplace knowledge. "Except for Gwendolyn Brooks, and perhaps Margaret Walker," as Calvin Hernton reminds us in an extremely rare and perceptive black feminist essay by a black male, "the name of not one black woman writer and not one female protagonist was accorded a worthy status in the black literary world prior to the 1970's."[13] Black feminist critics, such as Mary Helen Washington in her introduction to *Black-Eyed Susans* and Barbara Christian in *Black Women Novelists,* applaud the displacement of stereotypic with realistic images by black women writers like Morrison, Meriwether, Marshall, and Bambara. In her essays Andrea Benton Rushing convincingly illustrates that Eurocentric qualities and categories of stereotypic white women such as passivity, compliancy, the submissive wife, and the woman on a pedestal are inappropriately applied in analyses of black women characters, whose historical experiences and cultural imperatives are different from white women.[14] As illustrated in their fiction, interviews in *Black Women Writers at Work,* and the pioneer essays on black feminst criticism by Barbara Smith and Deborah E. McDowell, many black women novelists employ to a greater or lesser degree the following signs and structures: (1) motifs of interlocking racist, sexist, and classist oppression; (2) black female protagonists; (3) spiritual journeys from victimization to the realization of personal autonomy or creativity; (4) a centrality of female bonding or networking; (5) a sharp focus on personal relationships in the family and community; (6) deeper, more detailed exploration and validation of the epistemological power of the emotions; (7) iconography of women's clothing; and (8) black female language.[15] While agreeing with Smith that feminist criticism is "a valid and necessary cultural and political enterprise," McDowell questions the impreciseness of current definitions of lesbianism by black feminists, the possible reductiveness of a lesbian aesthetic, and the vagueness of Smith's analysis in "Toward a Black Feminist Criticism." McDowell advocates that black feminist critics combine a contextual approach with rigorous textual analysis, including a concern for the issue of gender-specific uses of language.[16]

But many black women writers, including feminists, who acknowledge the influence of male as well as female literary foreparents, underscore the problematics of a separate black female literary tradition. Bambara, for example, says:

> Women are less likely to skirt the feeling place, to finesse with language, to camouflage emotions. But a lot of male writers knock that argument out... one of the crucial differences that strikes me immediately among poets, dramatists, novelists, storytellers is in the handling of children. I can't nail it down, but the attachment to children and to two-plus-two reality is simply stronger in women's writings; but there are exceptions. And finally, there isn't nearly as large a bulk of gynocentric writing as there is phallic-obsessive writings. I'd love to read/hear a really good discussion of just this issue by someone who's at home with close textual reading—cups, bowls and other motifs in women's writings. We've only just begun... to fashion a woman's vocabulary to deal with the "silences" of our lives.[17]

Mary Helen Washington agrees, as she argues for a black female literary tradition in her introduction to *Midnight Birds:* "Black women are searching for a specific language, specific symbols, specific images with which to record their lives, and, even though they can claim a rightful place in the Afro-American tradition and the feminist tradition of women writers, it is also clear that, for purposes of liberation, black women writers will first insist on their own name, their own space."[18] Because there are many intertextual parallels between black male and female novelists, readers should examine these parallels to determine the distinctiveness, consistency, and frequency of their appearance and use in narratives by black women in deciding for themselves whether a separate black female literary tradition exists.

Toward Modernism

Because the novel is a synthetic literary form, the product of a complex blend of the social and cultural forces that shape the novelist's attitude toward life and language, especially the imaginative use of narrative conventions, it is not surprising that from 1962 to 1983 the Afro-American novel has been characterized by continuity and change. During this period, black novelists sought structures and styles appropriate for the imaginative reconstruction of their sense of the double-consciousness of black people as refracted through their particular vision of a rapidly changing experience of social reality and art. The eruption of the Vietnam and Arab-Israel wars, the assassinations of major political leaders and civil rights workers, the profiteering of multinational corporations, the launching of the first manned flight to the moon, the emergence of the black power movement, the exposure of the Watergate scandal involving "high crimes and misdemeanors" by President Nixon, and the influence of the pill in radicalizing the women's rights movement swept away most of the vestiges of the traditional grounds for confidence in a stable universe, a democratic society, and a mimetic approach to art. Ambivalence toward authority (father, president, God, family, nation, Kingdom of God) with its conflicting attitudes of acceptance and rejection, deepened and spread to all aspects of life and to all fields, resulting often in a crisis of belief for many novelists and readers.

In the past, fact was often stranger than fiction, but in the modern and contemporary worlds the line between fantasy and reality is nearly invisible. To protect the rights of the Vietnamese people the American military machine destroys their villages, crops, and countryside with thousands of tons of bombs and deadly toxic chemicals. To preserve law and order the police use clubs, water hoses, electric cattle prods, and snarling dogs on praying, singing civil rights demonstrators. To save the souls of his flock of followers, a contemporary shepherd, the Reverend James Jones, encouraged hundreds to drink poison Kool-Aid. Challenging the authority and purpose of literature, cultural theorists and literary critics celebrate it as a nondiscursive, nonconceptual mode of discourse that has no authority or purpose beyond its symbols, signs, and structure. How do contemporary novelists respond to this moral breakdown, social absurdity, and discrediting of the moral authority of art? More in despair than in hope, more concerned with problems of language than with problems of life, postmodernist Euro-American novelists such as John Barth, William Gass, Donald Barthelme, Kurt Vonnegut, Jr., Ronald Sukenick, and Richard Brautigan turn to fantasy and black or gallows humor. Other contemporary novelists such as Bernard Malamud, Saul Bellow, and Flannery O'Connor use more traditional techniques to portray more conventional visions and values. In contrast, as contemporary Afro-American novelists attempt to displace personal ambivalence and social absurdity with a new order of thinking, feeling, and sharing based on self-determination, a sense of community, and a respect for human rights, most, like John O. Killens, John A. Williams, and Alice Walker continue the tradition of realism; while some, like Toni Morrison, explore poetic realism. Others, like Margaret Walker, Ernest Gaines, William Melvin Kelley, Ronald Fair, Hal Bennett, Charles Wright, Clarence Major, John Wideman, and Ishmael Reed, experiment with modern forms of slave narrative, romance, fable, and satire.

Literary Neorealism: Critical and Poetic

Despite the modern formalist view that separates the literary work from objective reality, the appeal of several types of traditional realism is seen in first novels by the majority of black novelists of the sixties. Many of these, such as Gordon Park's *Learning Tree* (1963), Kristin Hunter's *God Bless the Child* (1967), Rosa Guy's *Bird at My Window* (1966), Barry Beckham's *My Main Mother* (1969), Louise Meriwether's *Daddy Was a Number Runner* (1970), and Al Young's *Snakes* (1970), are *bildungsromans*, stories about growing up black in Kansas, Harlem, Maine, and Detroit. Some, such as Nathan A. Heard's *Howard Street* (1968), Robert Dean Pharr's *Book of Numbers* (1969), and George Cain's *Blueschild Baby* (1970), are graphic, naturalistic accounts of the sporting life of hustlers, whores, and addicts. Others, like Cecil Brown's *Life and Loves of Mr. Jiveass Nigger* (1969) and Clarence Major's *All Night Visitors* (1969) are clinically detailed studies of black expatriate and domestic existential stud types. All are essentially mimetic in their tacit common-sense assumption of an intelligible though problematic reality and in their efforts to achieve a close correspondence between their symbolic act of representation and aspects of objective reality. As realists the authors, with Major the most striking exception, are generally more pragmatic than idealistic in their quest for truth and their concern for the effect of their work on the reader. Because limitations of space preclude discussing all of these by no means mutually exclusive types of neorealism, I will focus on two that represent the polarities of the continuing tradition of realism—critical and poetic—and ambivalence of Afro-American novelists toward their dual cultural heritage.

But first we should be clear about the meaning of neorealism. Like earlier types of realism in the Afro-American novel, which used the conventional linear, closed plot and combined elements of the slave narratives, historical romance, and genteel realism, and which attacked racial discrimination while embracing middle-class values, neorealism is not only a literary method, but also a philosophical and political attitude toward the human condition. It is in sharp contrast to the implicit nihilism and explicit antimimesis of Alain Robbe-Grillet and Ronald Sukenick, who reject conventional approaches to plot and characterization as inadequate for expressing their perceptions of cultural disintegration and the indeterminacy of language. They prefer to experiment with fantasy and self-reflexional linguistic signs in reconstituting both the novel and reality as fictions. But Afro-American neorealists, like earlier black realists, assume that man is a social being who ought not to be separated from the social and historical context, no matter how alienating and discontinuous, in which he finds his significance and develops his potential as an individual. In short, there is more hope for humanity and the world expressed in Afro-American neorealism and, as the next chapter will illustrate, modernism and postmodernism than in European and Euro-American postmodernism. However, in contrast to traditional social realism such as Frank Webb's *The Garies and Their Friends* and Jessie Fauset's *Chinaberry Tree*, which are essentially bourgeois in the truth they express in a documentary, linear manner, neorealism, as John O. Killens's *Youngblood* illustrates, is generally alienated from the old racist, sexist, socioeconomic order and seeks to displace it with new terms of order. Aside from the neoslave narratives of Margaret Walker and Ernest Gaines, which will be examined more appropriately in the next chapter, the most fascinating types of neorealism in the contemporary Afro-American novel are critical realism, which is related to socialist realism, and poetic realism, which uses regional and racial matter in a poetic manner.

Critical Realism

Influenced by the radical struggles of the age for social change, especially the black power, black arts, and women's rights movements, some contemporary Afro-American novelists explored the flexibility and appropriateness of critical realism for their color, sex, and class approach to reality. Unlike social realism, a non-Marxist term referring to the generally middle-class life, manners, and truth treated in nineteenth-century realism, critical realism is a Marxist literary concept that is illustrated in the work of Balzac and Flaubert as well as Turgenev and Tolstoy. It is most meaningfully explained by its relationship to socialist realism, which is the antithesis of modernism. The perspective of "socialist realism differs from critical realism," writes Hungarian critic Georg Lukács, "not only in being based on a concrete socialist perspective, but also in using this perspective to describe the forces working towards socialism *from the inside.*" Concreteness involves an awareness of the class and ideological development, structure, and goal of society as a whole. Socialist realism, then, is historical and comprehensive in its description of the totality of society, and seeks to identify the human qualities essential for the creation of a new, progressive social order. In contrast, critical realism is not an outright affirmation of socialism so much as it is a negative attitude toward capitalism and a readiness to respect the perspective of socialism and not condemn it out of hand. Whenever such an affirmation is evident though, it will be somewhat abstract, "for even where a critical realist attempts to describe socialism, his is bound to be a description from the outside." The writer using the "outside" method derives exemplary character types from the individual and his personal conflicts; and from this base he works toward wider social significance. But the writer using "the 'inside' method," Lukács explains, "seeks to discover an Archimedian point in the midst of social contradictions, and then bases its typology on an analysis of these contradictions."[19] Although none of the black neorealists is politically committed to Marxist doctrines, Killens, Williams, and Alice Walker, as I will illustrate, use the indirect, outside method of critical realism as well as other conventions to develop their negative attitude toward capitalism and their positive typologies for a new social order. Aesthetically, they all seem to believe with Georg Lukács that perspective is of major importance, with Henry James that character is the essence of everything, and with Ralph Ellison that contemporary fiction, despite its technical experimentation, is an ethical as well as a linguistic sign system. Because of their historical ambivalence, contemporary Afro-American novelists, have, in short, tailored critical realism and traditional social realism to fit their consciousness of the interrelated dynamics of racism, capitalism, and sexism.

JOHN OLIVER KILLENS (1916–)

If Richard Wright is the spiritual father of critical realism, John O. Killens is its contemporary moving force. Born on January 14, 1916, in Macon, Georgia, he was raised and educated primarily in the South. He also attended Howard, Columbia, and New York universities. A major figure in the Harlem left-wing literary movement of the 1950s, Killens was a founder of the Harlem Writers' Guild and contributor to Paul Robeson's *Freedom* newspaper. In the June 1952 issue of *Freedom* he reveals his belief in a rather inflexible theory of socialist realism by denouncing Ralph Ellison's *Invisible Man* as a "vicious distortion of Negro life."[20] His commitment to the tradition of realism was expressed not only in his writings but also in the creative writing workshops he taught in the 1960s at the New School for Social Research and at Fisk, Howard, and Columbia universities, where he encouraged the creative efforts of black women writers like Sarah Wright.

Although he has written a couple of screenscripts and plays, a collection of essays, and numerous uncollected pieces, Killens is best known for his four novels: *Youngblood* (1954), *And Then We Heard the Thunder* (1963), *'Sippi* (1967), and *The Cotillion* (1971). His declared intention in all his writing is "to change the world, to capture reality, to melt it down and forge it into something entirely different." Politically, the envisioned something different is socialism, and the method is critical realism. The emphasis in his novels is on telling "as much of the truth as he knows the painful truth to be, and let the flak fall where it may."[21] Believing with Du Bois and Wright that the truth will set us free, he focuses on past and present socioeconomic forces and racial prejudices in America that inhibit and distort the development of dignity and unity among black and working-class people. More important, for him and some other black neorealists the concept of "the hero" is still viable. "At a time when the novel throughout the world celebrates the emergence of the anti-hero," writes Addison Gayle, "Killens reasserts the value of the hero, argues, that is, that heroism lay in the attempt to produce a better world for oneself and his people, and that the telling mark of the hero is his love for people."[22]

Youngblood and *The Cotillion* are the best examples of Killens's preoccupation with color and class, for in them he affirms the potential of black people and celebrates their development of black consciousness. In *Youngblood* Killens portrays the life of a black family in a small Southern town during the Depression when thousands of blacks were fleeing the South in search of a better life and vicariously triumphing over the power of whites with Joe Louis. The novel primarily delineates the character of Robert Youngblood, but it also bares the tough roots of the Youngblood family tree. The accounts of Robert's parents, Laurie Lee and Joseph Youngblood, for example, foreshadow the heroic spirit of their son, whose experiences, like those of his parents, convince him that the only way for blacks to live with dignity in America is to unite and fight for their human and civil rights.

The title of the novel, the biblical subtitles, and the verses from black spirituals which introduce its four major divisions, together with its episodic structure and realistically drawn characters, all reinforce the theme that a dynamic, assertive new generation of black Americans is coming of age and continuing the struggle against racial, economic, and sexual exploitation. In documentary fashion, Killens moves from one episode to the next, invariably selecting episodes that reveal the heroic spirit of the Youngbloods while, at the same time, vividly—sometimes melodramatically—depicting the fear, hate, and violence that characterized race relations in the Deep South at the turn of the twentieth century. Laurie's earliest and most indelible impression of white people, for instance, is the terrifying, debasing experience she had at eleven years old with a white man who not only tried to rape her, but also "upped her skirt and peed on her thigh" in utter contempt for her as a black person.

More important than the structure and style of *Youngblood,* however, are its characters, who dramatize the moral and political idea that blacks ought to stay in the South and fight for their rights. As idealized "new Negroes" of the twentieth century, the Youngbloods represent the generation of proud, enlightened people whose sacrifices, unity, and militancy are essential qualities for the progressive society of tomorrow. Laurie, symbolically born in Tipkin, Georgia, at precisely 12:01 AM January 1, 1900, is a heroic Southern black mother who passes on the lessons of her grandmother and teaches her children to "fight em every inch of the way, especially the big rich ones."[23] Her husband, Joe, stands as a strong, fiercely proud working-class black who resolves to die a man rather than live a coward. For his determination to end the practice of short-changing his pay, Joe is shot and killed by the white paymaster. Although the narrator is a disembodied omniscient presence, there is little moral, political, or emotional distance between him and the Youngbloods. He completely embraces their values and encourages our identification with them.

In addition to the parents, there are the Youngblood children, Jenny and Robert, who, in their proud spirit and firm belief in the power of black unity and militancy to achieve economic and social freedom, continue the tradition of their parents. Richard Myles, a black college-educated New Yorker whose tragic love affair motivated him to rebel against his middle-class background and plunge into civil rights work in Georgia, also helps to shape the protagonist's growing black consciousness. More traditional and negative in character are Leroy Jackson and Benjamin Blake, twentieth-century "handkerchief heads": black people who betray their race to the white community for personal gain.

On the other side are such stock white characters as George Cross, Jr., a die-hard conservative Southerner who is irrevocably committed to the exploitative way of life on which his power and privilege are based; Dr. Riley, a Southern liberal who does not live up to his expressed commitment to social equality when a dying black man needs his help; the ministers Culpepper and Poultry, traditional Southern fundamentalist leaders who pervert the Scriptures to terrorize and control their guilt-ridden followers; and Oscar Jefferson, the obligatory "good" poor white Southerner whose gnawing conscience impels him to volunteer his blood in a futile effort to save Joe Youngblood's life.

At the end of the novel, the progressive color and class consciousness of the Youngblood family prevails. Although Joe Youngblood is killed for his courageous refusal to be cheated by the white paymaster, the success of his son Robert in organizing fellow workers into a union and the silent display of unity and militancy at Joe's funeral at the close of the book imply victory for the family and a new social order. Predictably, Killens's answer to the thematic question of the book—"How do you live in a white man's world?"—is dramatically answered by the indomitable fighting spirit of the Youngbloods themselves.

Revealing an increasing use of the black oral tradition, *And Then We Heard the Thunder* and *'Sippi* also focus on the themes of black awareness and unity. The message in *And Then We Heard the Thunder* is that blacks should neither sacrifice their manhood nor compromise their dignity at any time, place, or cost. The Southern setting and dialogue, which sparkles with signifying, folksayings, and ethnic humor, establish the ironic situation and define the characters. The irony of the plot is that black Americans had to wage a double war for freedom during World War II: one overseas against foreign fascism and the other at home against domestic fascism. The third-person narrator traces the evolving black consciousness of Solomon "Solly" Saunders, an ambitious middle-class soldier who attempts to ignore his color in order to achieve success in the white world only to discover in an apocalyptic racial war that "all of his individual solutions and his personal assets—Looks, Personality, Education, Success, Acceptance, Security, the whole damn shooting match, was one great grand illusion, without dignity."[24] Through Solly, Killens predicts the transformation of many Negroes into blacks during the 1960s. "If I'm proud of me," Solly says after reading Wright's *Twelve Million Black Voices*, "I don't need to hate Mister Charlie's people. I don't want to. I don't need to. If I love me, I can also love the whole damn human race. Black, brown, yellow, white" (p. 372). But love is an ideal state derived from social reality. "Perhaps the New World *would* come raging out of Africa and Asia with a new and different dialogue that was people-oriented. What other hope was there?" (p. 499). Meanwhile, the reality was the racial war that ends the novel and the conviction of the black soldiers who died in that war that it was necessary to beat some sense into the heads of white folks to get their respect. The class struggle does not therefore dominate the struggle for racial justice in Killens's consciousness but, as Solly illustrates, it is intertwined with it.

In *'Sippi* Killens explores the human story behind the impact of the Supreme Court school desegregation decision of 1954. With Mississippi and New York as the backdrop of his huge canvas, he outlines the radical changes in attitude and strategy that characterize the increasingly bitter conflict between white power and black power during the 1960s. For the most part, however, the idea that black people must unite and organize their economic and political strength so that they can seize the constitutional rights that whites will not grant them is passionately but less credibly and excitingly rendered in *'Sippi*. At the center of Killens's third novel is the growth of the protagonist into black manhood and an Afro-American version of the tale of two star-crossed lovers of the mid-twentieth century: Carrie Wakefield, the daughter of a wealthy plantation owner and the apotheosis of Southern white womanhood, and Charlie Chaney, the son of Wakefield's faithful black field hand and the prototype of the contemporary militant black prince. A fusion of critical realism and historical romance, the novel opens with a stylized prologue that explains the folkloristic and thematic significance of the book's title. The chain of reactions set off by the Supreme Court school desegregation decision of 1954—beginning with Jesse Chaney's wry announcement that there " 'ain' no more Mississippi. Ain' no more Mississippi. It's jes' 'Sippi from now on' "[25] and concluding the book with the assassination of the leader of the black revolution and the protagonist's grim decision to join the Elders for Protection and Defense of Wakefield County—ushered in a new age of black militancy and self-determination.

In *Youngblood* Killens comes closest to portraying the role that the revolutionary working class plays in the new society; in *The Cotillion*, despite the working-class status of the Lovejoys, this perspective is underdeveloped. In Killens's alienation from the old order, melodramatically illustrated in the apocalyptic battle between white and black American soldiers at the end of *And Then We Heard the Thunder*, class, color, and culture are inextricably linked. But class, for him, becomes a subordinate element in his writing during the black power and black arts movements of the late 1960s when the struggle for racial and cultural identity was at its peak, and the intended primary audience was the black underclass. This is particularly true in the satirical typology of *The Cotillion,* which is self-consciously neither comprehensive in its description of society nor objective in its historical vision.

Set in New York, *The Cotillion* is a "Black black comedy," written in "Afro-Americanese" to satirize debutante balls and "other Bourgeois bullshit . . . pulling Black folks in the opposite direction of peoplehood."[26] The characters, with the exception of the narrator, are flat and one dimensional, the language idiomatic and hyperbolic, the events melodramatic and ironic, the structure loose and freewheeling, and the style vibrant and witty. "White folks invented these debitramp balls," the heroine's father explains, "so that their darling little heifers could git a good shot at the prize bull in the pasture. . . . But colored folks just do these things cause they see white folks doing them" (p. 158). In her quest for identity Yoruba Evelyn Lovejoy, the heroine, is torn between the urge to whiteness of Daphne, her pretentious, Barbadian mother, and the call to black consciousness of her Georgia-born father, Matthew, and her black prince, Ben Ali Lumumba, the jive-talking narrator-writer who turns the Grand Cotillion into a black and beautiful occasion.

Using conventional techniques, Killens is less concerned in his novels with the forces breaking up our society than with those leading toward a new nation, a new social order. Because of his faith in the future and in people, he continues the tradition of conventional plots and of the outsider as hero. But the essential values of the new social order he envisions are found in his love and respect for the dignity, unity, and potential of black people, his primary audience. Because the journey of his characters to self-esteem and social awareness is predictable, and because the characters themselves are more often types than individuals, his novels lack the suspense, complexity, and, except for *The Cotillion,* vibrancy, ambiguity, and ambivalence of contemporary life and major contemporary Afro-American novels. What they provide in the tradition of the Afro-American novel is a simple, clear moral and political reaffirmation of the revolutionary potential of black history, culture, and youth in creating a better tomorrow for all people.

JOHN ALFRED WILLIAMS (1925–)

His parents met and married in Syracuse, New York, but John A. Williams was born on December 5, 1925, in Jackson, Mississippi, his mother's hometown. While he was an infant, the family returned to Syracuse, where he grew up, joined the navy, married, and attended Syracuse University. A childhood interest in reading and early efforts at poetry while in the navy were subsequently cultivated by the discipline acquired in creative writing classes at Syracuse University in 1951. After writing for the *Progressive Herald, Chicago Defender,* and the National Negro Press Association, Williams began his first novel in 1954. "When I began the process of becoming a writer," he says, "it wasn't for the money and it wasn't for fame; it was to keep my sanity and to find some purpose in my life."[27] Although completed in 1956, this first novel, *The Angry Ones,* was not published until 1960. Since then Williams has published more than a dozen books, including several novels.

Clearly in the tradition of realism, Williams's novels nevertheless reveal a growing radical consciousness and preoccupation with form. "I suppose I am a realistic writer," he explains. "I've been called a melodramatic writer," but I think that's only because I think the ending of a novel should be at the ending of the book. . . . In terms of experimenting, I think that I've done some very radical things with form in *The Man Who Cried I Am* and in *Captain Blackman,* which had to be an experimental novel in order to hold the theme of the novel. What I try to do with novels is to deal in forms that are not standard, to improvise as jazz musicians do with their music, so that a standard theme comes out looking brand new."[28] Thematically and structurally, Williams, unlike Killens, is primarily concerned with the struggle of the individual black American to reconcile his present marginal middle-class status with the past experience of his race.

This and an increasing bitterness at capitalism and racism are dramatically evident in the early novels. In *The Angry Ones,* his first and weakest novel, Steve Hill, the protagonist, triumphs over the anger and frustration of economic and sexual exploitation by white liberal friends, renouncing violence and finding a tenuous, unconvincing security in a new job and marriage to his brother's widow. *Night Song* (1961) is the bitter-sweet story of the creative yet self-destructive rage of Eagle, a black jazz musician, and the impotent rage of Keel Robinson, his friend, a "black white man." Because it is a more experimental and successful novel than *The Angry Ones,* it will be discussed more fully, along with *The Man Who Cried I Am,* later in this chapter. *Sissie* (1963) is an exploration of the psychic damage suffered by the modern black family and a demythicizing of black matriarchy. In his fourth novel, *The Man Who Cried I Am* (1967), Williams's radical consciousness culminates in the theme of racial genocide and an experiment with time structure.

The later novels continue to explore the themes of armed violence and

love as alternatives to American racism and to experiment with time structure, but, except for *Captain Blackman* (1972), they are less original and
effective in their fusion of form and content. In *Sons of Darkness, Sons of Light*
(1969) Eugene Browning, a political moderate, triggers a racial Armag-
gedon with his plan to have a white detective killed for his merciless
shooting of a black youth. *Captain Blackman*—Williams's most self-conscious experiment with multiple time shifts, flashbacks, dream sequences,
and interior monologues—retraces through Abraham Blackman the heroic
exploits of black soldiers back down the corridors of American history,
from Vietnam to the Revolutionary War. In *Mothersill and the Foxes* (1975),
Odell Mothersill, a black social worker, is a modern-day Priapus or Legba
and sower of seeds who discovers that love and selfhood involve more
than sex. And through the reminiscences of the multiple narrators in *The
Junior Bachelor Society* (1976), we discover along with Richard "Bubbles"
Wiggins, a frustrated high school third-string halfback and president of
the Junior Bachelor Society, that the nostalgia of thirty-year-old boyhood
friendships disappears in the face of the harsh truths and painful memories
that surface in their reunion.

Looking more closely at *Night Song*, we discover that it is a blues story
in the jazz mode. Set in "a world of cool, of arrogant musicians and
worrying night club owners . . . a world in which the days were really
nights because you lived in the dark and sang your song of life then,"[29]
the novel is antiphonal in structure, stressing the call-and-response relationship between Keel and Eagle with a sharp counterpoint provided by
David Hillary. The traditional blues theme that life and one's humanity
should be affirmed in the face of disappointment, defeat, and even death
is the melodic base for improvisation by the disembodied third-person
omniscient narrator.

Basically, *Night Song* is the tragic story of Richie "Eagle" Stokes, a romantic takeoff on the legendary saxophonist Charles "Bird" Parker, and
those whose lives he touches and renews through the sacrifice of his own:
Keel Robinson, a black Harvard Divinity School graduate and converted
Muslim (Sadik Jamal) whose moral outrage at the hollowness of bourgeois
values, especially institutionalized religion, and at racial prejudice leaves
him incapable of consummating his love for his white girl friend; and
David Hillary, a morally impotent white liberal college instructor, "the
kind who do nothing when it counts for everyone" (p. 140), who is guilt
ridden over killing his wife in a car accident. The source of Eagle's blues
is that everyone uses him, especially the white world. " 'You white,' " he
tells Hillary after taking him in off the street. " 'It's your world. You won't

let me make it in it and you can't. Now ain't that a bitch?' " (p. 67). More viable as a mythic and legendary culture hero than as a conventional realistic character, Eagle is driven by his love-hate feelings and embodies the paradoxes of Afro-American character and culture, its possibilities and limitations. " 'Some people preserve statues and old drawings on cave walls,' " Keel explains to Hillary, " 'but we have to have Eagle. He's us. He's fire and brain; he's stubborn and shabby; proud and without pride; kind and evil. His music is our record: blues. . . . Eagle is our aggressiveness, our sickness, our self-hate, but also our will to live in spite of everything. He symbolizes the rebel in us' " (p. 93).

In addition to his significance as an ethnic cultural symbol, Eagle, his music, and the bohemian world are the agents for spiritual redemption for Keel and Hillary. For both, the experience is "like an immersion . . . a baptism" (p. 90). Keel, supported by the patience, understanding, and love of Della, his girlfriend, responds by publicly and frequently reciprocating Eagle's humanitarianism, an act that enables him to rise gradually above the impotence of racial hatred to a renewed faith in himself and life. In contrast, Hillary, who thinks that he has risen above cowardice and bigotry to become "a new man, changed by the people he'd been living with," betrays his "new-found humanitarianism" and Eagle when he fails to come to Eagle's aid as a cop brutally billy-clubs him senseless. " 'How could we be unworthy of your love yet worthy of your confession?' " Keel asks him after discovering the betrayal. " 'It's not only that you don't know where you are, you don't know where we are. Are you at the top looking down or at the bottom looking up?' " (pp. 142–43).

In the ambiguity and ambivalence of this passage as well as in the thematic structure of the novel, the author-narrator's close philosophical and political identification with Keel Robinson is apparent. Because Keel cannot politically and economically "understand why a white man can't make it in his society" (p. 15), he immediately distrusts and hates Hillary as another white exploiter. The author-narrator's delineation of Hillary as an outsider who knows the surface but not the deeper, ritualistic meaning of jazz foreshadows Hillary's betrayal of Eagle and confirms Keel's suspicion that his friendship for blacks is self-serving and unreliable. Only in "Bohemia, that isolation in time and space which impelled one to act basically" (p. 119), does the author-narrator reveal Hillary cautiously responding to Eagle's charity and acknowledging his potential for moral salvation. For John Williams, then, it was in the apolitical diversity and individualism of Greenwich Village, not the black community, where "people were more like people." It is also in the Village that Keel, like many alienated and talented blacks and whites of the late 1950s, sought salvation from socialized ambivalence. His problem was "resisting reality" and affirming his love for the white woman who loved him. Middle-class family, money, Protestantism, and Islam did not sustain his faith in himself as a black man, so he turned to the interracial world of the Village where Eagle and Della helped him to reconcile the tensions of his double-consciousness. "Della had come, he always said to himself, when he needed her most, almost immediately after he had left the church, and at a time when he felt his obligations to his parents had been paid" (p. 41). But Keel was confused, torn between love and hate, because Della was white, and it is only after Hillary's climactic betrayal of Eagle that Keel is able to express fully and publicly his love for her. Thus racial integration and interracial love, still a radical solution for American racism in 1961, are the cornerstones of Williams's early vision in this underrated novel of a new social and ethical system. But how new, how progressive, is the social system that Williams projects? Actually, the class and color struggles are presented within an apolitical, bourgeois framework with their effects on society being demonstrated indirectly by their personal moral and psychological consequences. Williams explored this vision more deeply and politically in an international historical context in *The Man Who Cried I Am.*

The Man Who Cried I Am, like *Night Song,* is in the realistic tradition, but its plot, which culminates in the discovery of a bold plan of racial genocide and closes ambiguously on an apocalyptic note, is complicated by a shifting temporal and spatial frame and a sardonic use of symbolism. It is the story of the political radicalization and death of Max Reddick, a successful black novelist and former presidential speechwriter, whose faith in the American Dream is betrayed at every level and whose rectal cancer symbolizes the pain and danger that constantly threaten the lives of American blacks. Realizing that he is dying of advanced carcinoma, Max flies to the Paris funeral of his friend and rival literary lion, Harry Ames, and then takes a train to Amsterdam for a final visit with his estranged Dutch wife, Margrit Reddick. He discovers in Leiden the reason for his friend's death in a letter that Harry leaves which contains the details about King Alfred, an elaborate government plan to "terminate, once and for all, the Minority threat to the whole of the American society, and, indeed, the Free World."[30]

Divided into three major parts, *The Man Who Cried I Am* is Williams's most thematically provocative and technically innovative novel. Because of institutionalized racism, the novel intriguingly reveals, the assertion of individuality and independence by black Americans, especially writers, is painful and dangerous. As in the tradition of critical realism, Williams emphasizes the internal contradictions of the characters in an exploitative social system rather than the forces working toward reconciliation and coexistence in a new system. The existential theme suggested by the title is that the survival of mankind depends on the moral commitment of the individual to self and society in the face of irrationality and death. The actual time and place of the action is twenty-four hours in May 1964, in the Netherlands, but Williams skillfully manipulates the time through multiple flashbacks, recollections, dreams, and interior monologues to cover nineteen years, 1945–1964, and three continents: Europe, Africa, and the United States. Part 1 introduces the cannibalistic theme of white against black and black against black as the white publishing establishment pits black writers against each other in a dog fight for the status of king of the black literary mountain; Part 2 explores the problems of black writers and interracial couples in America and Europe; and Part 3 reveals the ultimate treachery of the American government as black CIA agents, who have infiltrated the black American colony of expatriate artists in Paris, systematically assassinate everyone suspected of having knowledge of King Alfred. Max's decision to marry Margrit Westover is the climactic episode of the existential theme of moral courage implicit in the novel's title. The personal commitment of taking a white wife is a prelude to the political commitment to race that he affirms by arming himself for racial war and by calling Minister Q to inform him of King Alfred.

The spirits of the two major black leaders of the sixties and a few of the celebrated modern black male expatriate writers walk the pages of the novel. Minister Q reminds us of Malcolm X; the Reverend Paul Durrell, of the Reverend Martin Luther King, Jr.; and Harry Ames, of Richard Wright. "Where Durrell employed fanciful imagery and rhetoric, Minister Q preached the history, economics and religion of race relations; he preached a message so harsh that it hurt to listen to it" (pp. 209–10). Minister Q and Durrell are one-dimensional characters, but Harry Ames has many of the frailties of the flesh, much of the socialized ambivalence and the dread of conspiracy, of his historical model, who died mysteriously in Paris. In a dialogue with Max about being a writer, Harry rejects the idea of a "tradition of colored writers" and expresses the view that by writing and publishing a book Max, like himself, is a very special person. This is a cause for pride in producing more books, but it " 'also makes you dangerous because they don't burn people anymore, they burn books, and they don't always have bonfires' " (p. 45). In literary achievement and life style Max Reddick embodies the individualistic spirit of Chester Himes and Williams himself.

258

The undramatized third-person omniscient narrator enhances the compelling force of the major characters and events in the novel. We move from an intimate view of an estranged interracial couple to a broad view of racial and political conspiracy. The tone is tragic, ambivalent, and sensational. We get sympathetic internal views of Margrit and Harry, but it is Max's double-consciousness that predominates and represents the norms of the work. By extensive use of the flashback technique to telescope the past into the present and to reenact Max's memories, Williams minimizes the effects of authorial intrusions and dramatizes his hero's double-consciousness and many of the crucial events, both public and private, that led to his radicalization and death. Harry's posthumous letter to Max containing information about King Alfred is a short-fused time bomb that enables Max to reflect on his ambivalent relationship with Harry and that serves as an effective device for Williams to shift between internal and external views of the characters and events. "The one alternative left for Negroes," we read with Max at the end of the novel, "would be not only to seek that democracy withheld from them as quickly and as violently as possible, but to fight for their very survival. King Alfred . . . leaves no choice" (p. 304). The intimate view we get of Margrit and Max overshadows the intense but brief view we get of Lillian Patch, Max's middle-class black fiancée who dies from a botched abortion. "If there had been no Lillian would there be a Margrit?" Max wonders after his momentous decision to marry Margrit (p. 281). Because the story is told predominantly through Max's consciousness, there is little moral, philosophical, and political distance between the omniscient author-narrator and his hero. Williams thus closely identifies with the values of his central character, and encourages the reader to do so as well.

Because of his experiment with technique and form, Williams is a critical realist in only the broadest sense of our definition. His critical attitude toward capitalism and its system of privilege emphasizes the exploitation and exclusion of blacks, which may be interpreted as an implicit respect for the socialist perspective. But his title, theme, and central character are romantically individualistic. Borrowing from Malcolm Lowry's telescoping of time in *Under the Volcano* and from Richard Wright, Chester Himes, and Ralph Ellison, among others, in technique, Williams develops the wider social significance of his critical attitude toward America from the personal conflicts and alienation of members of the black middle class, especially male artists. He therefore combines Eurocentric and Afrocentric techniques in continuing the tradition of realism while simultaneously expanding the form of the novel through a reaffirmation of the symbolic importance of the legends and rituals of black music in Afro-American life and literature. "What I try to do with novels," he tells an interviewer, "is to deal in forms that are not standard, to improvise as jazz musicians do with their music, so that a standard theme comes out looking brand new. This is all I try to do with a novel and, like those musicians, I am trying to do things with form that are not always immediately perceptible to most people."[31]

ALICE WALKER (1944–)

Born on February 9, 1944, to sharecroppers in Eatonton, Georgia, Alice Walker was the youngest of eight children. She was a lonely, solitary child as a result of a disfiguring scar she suffered at eight years of age. Educated in local schools and reacting to the cruel insults of her peers and relatives, she "retreated into solitude," she told an interviewer, "and read stories and began to write poems."[32] In 1961 she entered Spelman College, and in her sophomore year was spiritually reborn as an activist in the Georgia voter registration movement of SNCC. She transferred to Sarah Lawrence in 1963 and received her B.A. in 1965. In the summer of 1965 she traveled to East Africa, returning to college pregnant, sick, alone, and suicidal. It was during this crisis in the winter of 1965 that she completed in one week most of the poems in *Once,* her first book of poetry, which was not published until 1968 when the women's movement began displacing the black power movement in the social arena. Walker has taught at several East Coast colleges and has worked with Head Start in Mississippi and the Department of Welfare in New York City. Her numerous honors and awards include Bread Loaf Writers' Conference Scholar in 1966, Merrill Writing Fellow in 1966–1967, McDowell Colony Fellow in 1967, the Rosenthal Award in 1974 for *In Love and Trouble,* the Lillian Smith Award in 1973 for *Revolutionary Petunias,* and the Pulitzer Prize in 1982 for *The Color Purple.* Walker's publications through 1983 include three volumes of poetry: *Once* (1968), *Revolutionary Petunias* (1973), and *Good Night, Willie Lee, I'll See You in the Morning* (1979); two collections of short stories: *In Love and Trouble* (1973) and *You Can't Keep a Good Woman Down* (1981); and three novels: *The Third Life of Grange Copeland* (1970), *Meridian* (1977), and *The Color Purple* (1982).

"I am preoccupied with the spiritual survival, the survival *whole* of my people," she explains her thematic concerns to an interviewer. "But beyond that, I am committed to exploring the oppressions, the insanities, the loyalties, and the triumphs of black women. . . . For me, black women are the most fascinating creations in the world. Next to them, I place the old people—male and female—who persist in their beauty in spite of everything." Consistent with this professed concern for the wholeness of both males and females and celebration of "outrageous, audacious, courageous or willful" black women, Walker calls herself a womanist rather than feminist. In her fiction as in her life she has an openness to mystery, animism, which she believes is both the one thing that Afro-Americans have retained of their African heritage and the thing that is "deeper than any politics, race, or geographical locations." She therefore admires women writers who are responsive to mystery: Chopin, the Brontës, Simone de Beauvoir, and Doris Lessing. She admires these writers also because they are "well aware of their own oppression," and "their characters can always envision a solution, an evolution to higher consciousness on the part of society even when society itself cannot."[33] In other words, the class and political struggle explored in Walker's novels is primarily sexual. And the higher consciousness she seeks for society is based on her insider's view of the working-class history of blacks in general and the socialized ambivalence of black women in particular as well as her outsider's view of the conflict of white women with capitalism. Among the many writers who influenced her, she lists Russians, Greeks, Africans, Asians, and such Americans, black and white, as Jean Toomer, Zora Neale Hurston, Arna Bontemps, Emily Dickinson, Robert Graves, William Carlos Williams, e. e. cummings, and Flannery O'Connor. Of these, Hurston is the literary precursor, foremother, and spirit-guide that inspires the audacious autonomy that she expresses in her womanist vision.

The Third Life of Grange Copeland, her first novel, is structured like a crazy quilt in that it is disproportionately divided into eleven parts with forty-eight minichapters that outline the three lives of the patriarch of the Copeland clan. Ostensibly about Grange Copeland's rebirth of self-respect after a youth and manhood of dissolution, the novel actually details the social pathology that he passes on to his son, Brownfield. Part 1 briefly outlines the weekly cycles of sweat, fear, and hatred broken on Saturday by the rituals of song, dance, drink, and fighting that characterized the sharecropping life of Grange, and, after years of violent abuse, his wife Margaret. When Grange finally deserts the family, Margaret poisons herself and Brownfield's baby brother, whose "father might have been every one of its mother's many lovers." The pace of the narrative picks up in Parts 2 and 3 as Brownfield follows in his father's footsteps from sharecropper to wife beater. Grange also abruptly and inexplicably reappears to marry Josie, the whore he abandoned but now shares with his son. The eight pages of Part 4 are exclusively reserved for the birth of Ruth, Grange's granddaughter and the agent of his miraculous redemption. Parts 5, 6, and 7 detail Brownfield's malicious treatment of his wife and three daughters with only a brief interlude when his wife, Mem, asserts herself with a shotgun. The novel reaches its violent climax with Brownfield killing Mem and with Ruth going to live on the farm with her grandfather and Josie. In Part 8 Brownfield plots with Josie to take Ruth after his release from prison. Parts 9 and 10 reveal Grange passing on the lessons of his life to Ruth, briefly summarizing his life of hatred in the North. In Part 11 Grange kills Brownfield after he succeeds in getting custody of Ruth, and Grange in turn is killed by the police after returning to Ruth's cottage on their farm.

With more compassion for her female than male characters, with the exception of Grange as an old man, the omniscient author-narrator catalogs episodes in the Copeland family life, especially Brownfield's, to arouse the reader's indignation at the price black women pay as the victims of economic, racial, and sexual exploitation. Margaret Copeland, Brownfield's mother, was like the family dog in some ways. "She didn't have a thing to say that did not in some way show her submission to his father."[34] Grange drives her to drink, degradation, and death. His dreams of escaping the sharecropping system gone, his pride crushed, Brownfield makes his wife quit her teaching job—"Her knowledge reflected badly on a husband who could scarcely read and write," says the editorializing narrator—and begins beating her regularly "because it made him feel, briefly, good. Every Saturday night he beat her, trying to pin the blame for his failure on her by imprinting it on her face. . . . The tender woman he married he set out to destroy" (p. 63). Through violent abuse and forcing the family to move from one sharecropper's shack to another, Brownfield destroys his wife spiritually and physically. Only Ruth's birth is viewed as a miraculous event. " 'Out of all kinds of shit,' " says Grange, " 'comes something clean, soft and sweet smellin' " (p. 79). But Brownfield felt that his three daughters "were not really human children" and gave them only the dregs of his attention when he was half drunk. " 'You nothing but a sonnabit,' " four-year-old Ruth tells her father after he moves them back into sharecropping. Walker's weaving of character, event, and point of view indicates that she fully agrees with this sentiment. Through Ruth's innocence, Grange learns to love and to accept the responsibility of his life before he dies, but his own son Brownfield goes to his grave blaming white folks and others for the failure of his life. "He felt an indescribable worthlessness," says the author-narrator, "a certain ineffectual *smallness*, a pygmy's frustration in a world of giants" (p. 231).

Although more middle class and less physically violent, the black men of the 1960s in Walker's second novel, *Meridian*, are, with the exception of the father, similarly disloyal and despicable in their abuse of women. Meridian's father was a "dreamy, unambitious" history teacher who grieves over crimes committed against native Americans and, who gives as restitution the family's sixty acres containing one of their ancient cemeteries to a local native American. He also "cried as he broke into" his wife's body " . . . as she was to cry later when their children broke out of it."[35] In contrast, Eddie, Meridian's teenaged husband, was "good" because he kept his promise to marry her if she got pregnant and, even though he "cheated" on her and later deserted her and his child, he did not beat her. Truman, her conquering prince, the French-speaking civil rights organizer and painter, impregnated her but betrayed her to marry and then desert a white exchange student and his child. Tommy, a bitter civil rights activist, rapes Truman's wife, Lynne, in revenge for the arm he lost to a white sniper. And Alonzo, the apolitical scrap-yard worker, was so grateful for Lynne's invitation to sleep with her that he "licked her from her earlobes to her toes" (p. 167). Like the omniscient narrator, the implied author thus encourages the reader to see most of her black male characters in the limited moral category of the "low-down dirty dog" in the novel who impregnated the thirteen-year-old tragic Wild Child.

Towering over the low-down dirty dogs and moving like a soul possessed through the thirty-four titled brief chapters of the three-part narrative is the protagonist, Meridian Hill. She shares with her father the legendary peculiar madness of her eccentric paternal great-grandmother, Feather Mae, and is haunted by guilt at her inability to embrace a nurturing role as daughter, wife, and mother. Frail and hallucinatory, Meridian agonizes "for shattering her mother's emerging self," gives away her first child in order to go to college, aborts her second in disillusionment with its unfaithful father, and then, at the suggestion of a callous male gynecologist, has her tubes tied to avoid being further trapped by sex and motherhood while pursuing her commitment in the rural South to community organizing, teaching, and poetry (pp. 40–41). Unlike her mother and grandmothers, we learn from the narrator, Meridian "lived in an age of choice" (p. 123). Despite her unorthodoxy, however, a black Baptist church memorial service for a young civil rights martyr in 1968 lifts her burden of guilt and shame. Affirming the respect she owed her life and the dedication she owed her people, she promises to kill for freedom if necessary, a revolutionary commitment that she had rejected earlier in the novel and that Walker's language implicitly endorses. But the social context and symbolic conclusion resound with personal self-indulgence, for Walker does not describe the revolutionary role of the working class in contemporary society. Nor does the novel end apocalyptically. Instead, Meridian forgives Truman, leaves him in her small religious house, and "returns to the world cleansed of sickness." Wearing her cap and snuggled in her sleeping bag, he wonders if she "knew that the sentence of bearing the conflict in her own soul which she had imposed on herself—and lived through—must now be borne in terror by all the rest of them" (pp. 227–28). The civil rights movement, in short, provided a means of spiritual and moral redemption from a guilty past for individuals like Meridian, not a radical new social order in which all could realize their full potential.

The best but most problematic of Walker's novels is the Pulitzer Prize–winning *The Color Purple*. Less compelling as criticial realism than as folk romance, it is more concerned with the politics of sex and self than with the politics of class and race. Whereas its epistolary form continues the tradition of Samuel Richardson's *Clarissa Harlowe* (1748) and William H. Brown's *Power of Sympathy* (1789) (the sentimental, sensational tales of seduction that initiated the British and Euro-American traditions of the novel), its unrelenting, severe attacks on male hegemony, especially the violent abuse of black women by black men, is offered as a revolutionary leap forward into a new social order based on sexual egalitarianism. Like Hurston's *Their Eyes Were Watching God*, the style of *The Color Purple* is grounded in black folk speech, music, and religion; and its theme is a contemporary rewriting of Janie Crawford's dreams of what a black woman ought to be and do. But rather than heterosexual love, lesbianism is the rite of passage to selfhood, sisterhood, and brotherhood for Celie, Walker's protagonist.

Although rooted in the particularity of the folk experience of some Southern black women, the awakening of the protagonist's consciousness to love, independence, and sisterhood is more romantic than realistic. Rather than portray the growth into womanhood of an average Southern black woman of the 1920s and 1930s, Walker has created a contemporary paradigm of the liberated woman. Covering more than thirty years between the two world wars, the ninety-four letters in which Celie emerges from the brutal domination and abuse of men to a liberated, autonomous self include twenty-three letters to her from Nettie, her younger sister, fourteen from her to Nettie, which came back unopened, and one from Shug Avery, the blues singer who is the moral center of the novel, to Celie. Most of the confusingly undated, often arbitrarily arranged letters are a dramatic monologue to a white, partriarchal God, symbolizing the complexity of metaphysical as well as social oppression for black women in their quest for freedom, literacy, and wholeness. Focused on psychological rather than historical realism, they begin when Celie is fourteen, and they tell more than show her realization of womanist consciousness: from her repeated rape and impregnation by her stepfather; brokered violent marriage to Albert; and rejection of God as a "trifling, forgitful and lowdown" man; to her transforming love for Shug; economic and artistic independence as a seamstress and merchant; and reunion on July 4th with family, friends, and an animistic God that Shug teaches her "ain't a he or she, but a It."[36]

By her handling of the symbolic significance of Shug as a blues singer, of Afro-American religion, and of the black vernacular to develop Celie's long black song of suffering and womanist consciousness, Walker effectively weaves a magic spell that conjures up the socialized ambivalence and double-consciousness of Afro-American culture and character between 1914 and 1945. In the tradition of such blues "bad" women as Bessie Smith, Shug embodies and evokes the moral ambivalence of many black Americans toward music and behavior that they feel make the best of a bad situation by being as raw, mean, and wild as human existence itself frequently is. Worldly black folk flock to concerts and jukejoints to see Shug and hear the devil's music, while less worldly and otherworldly folk scorn her as a sinner and sing the Lord's music. Like her "wild sister" in Memphis and the legendary Bessie, Shug, called the Queen Honeybee of the blues, drinks, fights, and "love mens to death" (p. 104). Telling Celie about her earlier love for Albert and how the black community, including her parents and his, condemned her because she moved beyond liberty to license in "taking other women mens" and having three children out of wedlock, Shug says: "I was so mean, and so wild, Lord. I used to go round saying, I don't care who he married to, I'm gonna fuck him. . . . And I did, too. Us fuck so much in the open us give fucking a bad name" (p. 104). Only Albert, the father of her three children, and Celie, who fantasizes about her, honestly and completely love Shug. This socially forbidden love inspires her to create a "low down dirty" blues that she calls Miss Celie's song, which, of course, is Walker's text, and culminates in their bisexual affair. By living the liberated life she sings about without compromising her integrity, Shug, like Bessie, romantically challenges Albert, Celie, and readers to live with boldness and style in the face of adversity, absurdity, and conventional morality.

Shug teaches Celie not only about the sexual importance of her "little button" and "finger and tongue work," but also about the spiritual necessity of conversion to an animistic idea of God. "Just because I don't harass it like some peoples us know," says Shug, "don't mean I ain't got religion" (p. 164). By sympathetically delineating Shug as a blues heroine with religion, who is estranged from the orthodoxy of the Christian tradition, Walker offers her as a contemporary symbol of the ideal pattern of sexual and spiritual liberation and a rebuke of traditional Afro-American values and institutions.

Walker, in other words, is morally and politically unsympathetic toward what she considers anachronistic, chauvinistic conventions in the black family and the black church. She ascribes Celie's abject shame and passivity to the dominance of patriarchy, hypocrisy, and otherworldliness in the black church and family. By contrasting the stepfather's incest and the daughter-in-law Sofia's temerity with Celie's timidity, she clearly distances herself from Celie's belief in the biblical injunction to "Honor father and mother no matter what" and to suffering in this world, for "This life soon be over. . . . Heaven last for all ways" (p. 39). In the only church scene that is dramatized, however, the implied author is morally and politically close to both Celie and Shug as "even the preacher got his mouth on Shug, now she down. He take her condition for his text. . . . Talk about slut, hussy, heifer and streetcleaner" (p. 40). Intertextually, Walker's text—a rewrite and conflation of the legendary lives of her great-grandmother, "who was raped at twelve by her slaveholding master,"[37] and Bessie Smith, the literary life of Janie Crawford, and both the legendary and literary lives of Zora Neale Hurston—parallels Shug's embedded text of Celie's song and contrasts with the preacher's embedded text. Finally, in Celie's second letter to Nettie in which she renounces God, Walker implicitly supports Shug's belief that people "come to church to *share* God, not find God" and that because "Man corrupt everything," Celie ought to "conjure up flowers, wind, water, a big rock" (pp. 165, 168). Morally and politically, both Celie and Shug are reliable narrators for the womanist norms of the novel. The sign of these norms is the color purple. "I think it pisses God off if you walk by the color purple in a field somewhere and don't notice it," Shug tells Celie and us (p. 167). The color purple signifies a metaphysical, social, and personal rebirth and a celebration of lesbianism as a natural, beautiful experience of love.

Like her treatment of religion and blues, Walker's encoding of black speech and male characters signifies her sexual, moral, and political closeness to the outrageously audacious black women in the narrative. The values and vitality of black American communities, including the socialized ambivalence and quest for wholeness from cradle to grave of its members, are encoded in the sounds, semantics, and syntax of their speech: from "It be more than a notion taking care of children ain't even yourn" (p. 6) to "She look like she ain't long for this world but dressed well for the next" (p. 42). In contrast to the truth of this double vision, the letters in standard Euro-American English from Nettie that tell how the Reverend Samuel and Corrine, the black couple who adopt Celie's kidnapped children and homeless sister, and practice their sanctified religion among the Olinka people as token members of a largely white missionary association, conjure up neither the texture, the tone, nor the truth of the traditional lives of African peoples.

Equally problematic is the implied author and protagonist's hostility toward black men, who are humanized only upon adopting womanist principles of sexual egalitarianism. Except for Odessa's Jack, the black men are depicted as dogs or frogs—a rewriting of feminist fictions of male sexuality in general and Hurston's deadly signifying on Jody Starks in particular—with no hope of becoming princes. Gender role reversal or sharing, however, does foster some redemption for them. For example, Harpo not only acquires a love for housekeeping, especially cooking, but also becomes a househusband while his wife works as a storekeeper. Adam, Celie's son, endures the traditional facial scarification initiation rite of Olinka females to prove his love for Tashi. And Albert, whom Celie calls Mr. ——, learns not only to make quilts, Walker's symbol for the repressed creativity of women, with Celie, but also to acknowledge her independence and integrity as a person. Guided by the spirit and achievement of Hurston, Walker has Shug to express this theme of the book more poetically in the vernacular when she tells Celie: "You have to git man off your eyeball, before you can see anything a'tall" (p. 168).

In her novels, then, Alice Walker provides a contemporary black feminist's vision of the lives of black Southerners. Although she does not promote socialism as the panacea for the ills of capitalist America, she does stress in *The Third Life of Grange Copeland* the need to change a patriarchal economic system that breeds alienation, exploitation, and the destruction of people's lives, especially black women's. Her characters are uneducated, ignoble young working-class types like Grange and Brownfield Copeland who, except for Grange as an old man, lack the "inner sovereignty" and "embedded strength" of educated, heroic women like Mem and Ruth. In *Meridian* she focuses more sharply on the making of a revolutionary and on living up to what is required by history and economics. Correcting the naive belief in the first novel that the mere capacity of people for change and love is sufficient to effect political and economic change, the second novel answers the basic question: "Is there no place in a revolution for a person who *cannot* kill?" (p. 193; Walker's emphasis).

The Contemporary Afro-American Novel, 1: Neorealism

Most strikingly, her protagonist is a naive, guilt-ridden visionary for whom the civil rights movement is the rite of passage to liberation from guilt and rebirth as a committed community organizer and candidate for political sainthood. Even more revolutionary, the sexual politics of *The Color Purple* also reduces the scale of the struggle for social change to the task of creating a new autonomous self: an androgynous self and society. Walker's hope for change in the future rests, then, with the young, old, and outrageously bold black woman. By exploring the oppressions and celebrating the triumphs of Southern black wives, mothers, and daughters as they relate more to each other than to working-class black men, she tailors the tradition of critical realism to fit into folk romance and reinforces the theme of black feminism in the Afro-American novel.

Before comparing Walker to the other critical realists discussed in this chapter, it is important to note in passing that the theme of black feminism is explored by Gayl Jones in *Corregidora* (1975) and *Eva's Man* (1976) with even more mystery and horror, and by Toni Cade Bambara in *The Salt Eaters* (1980) with more political insightfulness and technical brilliance.

Because of a hysterectomy following an accident caused by her domineering, drunk husband, blues singer Ursa Corregidora cannot live up to the legacy of three generations of Corregidora women to procreate and perpetuate the incestuous line of tragic witnesses begun by her slave-breeding, Portuguese ancestor, who fathered his own slaves and prostitutes. To avenge the abuse that she and other black women have suffered, she kills her husband with kindness as the novel closes ambiguously with the act of fellatio. *Eva's Man* continues less ambiguously this castration motif in women's resistance to historical sexual abuse by opening with Eva Medina, the forty-three-year-old, college-educated protagonist, undergoing psychiatric treatment in prison for poisoning and biting off the penis of her weekend lover. The chilling terror of both novels is evoked through flashbacks, reveries, and interior monologues that effectively modulate the tempo, suspense, and horror of these first-person Gothic narratives.

Less sensational but more dialectical in its understanding of the historical forces of progress and reaction, Bambara's *Salt Eaters* affirms the viability of traditional divinatory practices that celebrate the mystery and sacredness of life in the post–civil rights activist period of the 1970s, teaching those in search of personal wholeness "the difference between eating salt as an antidote to snakebite and turning into salt, succumbing to the serpent."[38] After a suicide attempt, Velma Henry—mother, wife, sister, computer analyst, community organizer, civil rights activist, antinuclear activist, women's rights activist, and protagonist—learns through the legendary faith healer of Claiborne, Georgia, Minnie Ransom, and the community healing circle that personal and social wholeness and health are "no trifling matter." Philosophically, the implied author and omniscient narrator share the protagonist's conviction "that the truth was in one's own people, and the key was to be centered in the best of one's own traditions" (p. 169). The retrospective, discontinuous narrative therefore focuses primarily on Velma in the healing session but constantly shifts and probes with clinical precision into the internal and external lives of other characters. Like the ritual of the healing session, the double-edged wit of the black vernacular— e.g., the faith healer was "dressed for days," looking "like a farmer in a Halston, a snuff dipper in a Givenchy" (pp. 4, 8)—brilliantly plumbs the depths of Afro-American double-consciousness and fosters a sympathetic understanding of Velma. At the same time, the banter between Minnie and her spirit-guide Old Wife and among the Seven Sisters of the Grain singing troupe dramatizes the interrelated roles of ancestral intelligence and political activism in attaining and sustaining unity of self and society.

Continuity and change, then, are the chief characteristics of these novels I have loosely grouped here under the rubric *critical realism*. Killens, Williams, and Alice Walker, like William Attaway, employ both an insider's and outsider's view in their use of critical realism, responding in different ways to the problems of the past and the modern winds of social and cultural change. Their novels, except for *The Color Purple*, are generally more historical and mimetic than romantic and didactic. Fidelity to the truth of the actual past and to the truth of the psychology of the present are their common objectives. They also attempt to develop from the inside the psychology and morality of individuals in search of a better future. Killens, however, is more direct in style and characterization than Walker, and is more concerned with historical types than individuals. Killens's creation of members of the working class and their middle-class allies heralds the emergence of a bold new world of proud, heroic types like the Youngbloods, Charlie Chaney, and Ben Ali Lumumba, and illustrates his anticapitalist position and strong, sometimes polemical, support for the perspective of socialism. Alice Walker's men, on the other hand, are traditional black male chauvinists of both the lower and middle class who stereotypically vent their hatred of exploitation by whites on their families, especially the women, and whose only redemptive act is, like Grange Copeland's, to turn from hatred to love and to faith in a new social order based on sexual, economic, and racial equality. In contrast, the struggle—

sometimes violent, usually sensational and tragic—by her women characters to reject traditional roles of motherhood, nurturing, and dependence heralds the emergence of a new generation of radical black heroines in search of selfhood, security, and power.

Perhaps the most experimental in technique and structure in this group, excluding Jones and Bambara as well as Walker's use of quilting and epistles, is John A. Williams, whose underrated *Night Song* and *The Man Who Cried I Am* occupy the outer boundaries of social and critical realism. They probe the socialized ambivalence of the black artist, musician, and writer rather than the proletariat or the social forces responsible for their alienation and exploitation; and *Night Song* experiments with the modalities of black music. By their talented, usually compelling, occasionally brilliant, use of black folklore, especially music, religion, and speech, Killens, Williams, and Walker deepen our understanding of the limitations and possibilities of the lives of black Americans, and the vitality of the tradition of the Afro-American novel, including its poetic and Gothic qualities.

Poetic Realism and the Gothic Fable

By combining a concern for the truth of the lives of men and women in actual situations with a concern for the imaginative power, compression, and lyricism of language, poetic realism calls attention to the problematics of reality and language while simultaneously insisting that reality is shaped more by consciousness than consciousness is by reality. Like Toomer, contemporary black poetic realists strive more for truth of sensation and environment than for truth of fact, focusing on the supernatural ties of the present to the past and on psychological and sociological concepts for their images of ethical conduct in a world of mystery and unnatural events. In other words, the mystery and terror of atmosphere, events, and character are exploited in the Gothic vision of Afro-American poetic realists. In poetic realism the metaphoric and metonymic qualities of the language—the substitution of figurative for literal expressions—as well as deft, bold strokes of color, distilled experiences, and fleeting but sharp and frequently recurring images of the dominant, often eccentric, traits of the characters and their environment are also usually more meaningful to the author than the photographic representation of external reality. Although occasionally such characters are one dimensional, static, and grotesque, they are more frequently, as in Toomer's *Cane*, impressionistic and dynamic, with the poetic sensibility of the author-narrator distilling characters and events. Lyrical passages, of course, appear in the narratives of many black novelists, and many others, including Walker, Jones, and Bambara, explore the Gothic aspects of contemporary Afro-American experience, but Morrison has published two of the best recent examples of this tradition in what I call the Gothic fable: generally short poetic narratives whose celebration of the beauty, truth, and possibilities of life is derived from the exploitation of its magic, mystery, and terror.

CHLOE ANTHONY "TONI" MORRISON (1931–)

Born to a shipyard worker and choir singer on February 18, 1931, in Lorain, Ohio, Chloe Anthony Wofford changed her name to Toni after finishing school in Lorain and going East to Howard in 1949. At Howard she majored in English, taking her B.A. in 1953 and an M.A. from Cornell University in 1955. Having traveled to the Deep South with the Howard University Players, she returned there after college to teach at Texas Southern University from 1955 to 1957 and then moved on to a similar post at Howard University from 1957 to 1964. While teaching at Howard, she married a Jamaican and had two sons. She went on to become an editor in 1964, first at a textbook company in Syracuse and then in 1965 at Random House. By the end of 1983, she had published four novels: *The Bluest Eye* (1970), *Sula* (1973), *Song of Solomon* (1977), and *Tar Baby* (1981).

All four novels continue the poetic and Gothic branches of the Afro-American narrative tradition. Despite its primarily Caribbean setting, occasional Faulknerian sentences, and extended metaphors like the female soldier ant conceit in chapter 10 that reinforces the thematic ambiguity of ensnaring, autonomous black females symbolized in the title, *Tar Baby* is the least poetic and Gothic of the four.

The most ambitious and Gothic is *Song of Solomon*. The two-part novel opens in 1931 in a town near Lake Superior with the mysterious, bizarre suicide flight from a hospital roof of Mr. Robert Smith, a black insurance agent dressed in a blue costume with wide silk wings. On one hand, the symbolic and thematic significance of this leap to death by a commonly named minor character is apparent: it causes the early birth of the uncommonly named black protagonist, Macon "Milkman" Dead, in the historically for-whites-only Mercy Hospital, which blacks sardonically call No Mercy Hospital. On the other hand, the mystery and horror of this event and the fact "that Mr. Smith didn't draw as big a crowd as Lindberg had four years earlier,"[39] despite having announced his suicide plans two days before, are even more richly exploited metaphorically and metonymically by Morrison. The densely woven, arabesque texture of this opening scene includes the trivia of the daily lives of the absent poor ("most of the women were fastening their corsets and getting ready to go see what tails or entrails the butcher might be giving away" [pp. 3–4]); the anecdotal humor of black names (Not Doctor Street, No Mercy Hospital, and Lincoln's Heaven) that wryly reveal cultural and social differences between white and black townspeople; and the mysterious song of the strange black woman wrapped in an old quilt and wearing a knitted cap pulled down over her forehead. We are immediately alerted to the theme that life is precious and that many dead lives and faded memories are buried in the names of places and people in this country: Not Doctor Street, Lincoln's Heaven, Solomon's Leap, Macon Dead, Milkman Dead, Magdalene called Lena Dead, First Corinthians Dead, Pilate Dead and Sing Dead. But we do not discover until chapter 6 that Robert Smith's suicide is the result of pressures he can no longer endure as a member of the Seven Days, a secret black vigilante society that avenges the deaths of black victims of white terror. And it is not until chapter 12 of the fifteen-chapter novel that we learn the legendary meaning of the Song of Solomon that Pilate sings as Smith plunges to his death and that the protagonist sings at the end of the novel before plunging to his. Setting, story, and characters thus create a haunting mood of unknown terror.

We move with Milkman through the compressed thirty-two years of his haunted, self-absorbed life up North in Part 1 and his trip South to his buried family legacy in Part 2. The melodramatic flashbacks and reveries of the characters as well as the digressions of the editorializing, omniscient narrator enable us to discover with Milkman the hidden truth about himself and his strange family, with which he must deal in order to become a whole person. With shifting degrees of delight and disgust, we learn with the protagonist that his mother Ruth continued breast feeding him in a small green room long after he began school; that she was caught by her husband making love to her dead father, whose grave she still secretly visited; that his maternal "grandfather was a high-yellow nigger who loved ether and hated black skin" (pp. 76–77); that his father Macon sold his soul to own things and compelled Ruth to attempt repeatedly to abort Milkman's birth; and that his paternal great-grandfather Solomon was an African slave who fathered twenty-one children in Virginia, where legend and a children's song tell of him flying back home to Africa. We also learn that his Aunt Pilate, who wore a brass box earring containing her name, was an unkempt, bootlegging mystic who was miraculously born without a navel after her mother's death. Pilate spoke with the dead—especially her father—and used her supernatural powers to save Milkman's life before he was born. Our moral sympathies are further manipulated by flashbacks revealing that the top of Milkman's paternal grandfather's head was shot off from the back by white Pennsylvanians who wanted his farm, Lincoln's Heaven; and that his friend Guitar became a vigilante because of his conviction that "white people are unnatural" and his fear that "every one of them is a potential nigger-killer, if not an actual one" (pp. 155–56). Because her supernatural birth and powers mark her as a bridge between the living and the dead, Pilate, who has "acquired a deep concern for and about human relationships" (p. 149), is the moral center of the novel. Her death at the end of the novel while she and Milkman are reburying her father Jake's bones on Solomon's Leap moves Milkman to embrace the whole truth of his life in a suicidal leap down on her assassin, Guitar.

"What is curious to me," Morrison says in her lectures, "is that bestial treatment of human beings never produces a race of beasts." Since her childhood in Lorain, she was fascinated by the uncommon efforts of common black people to cope with socialized ambivalence. How do they deal with the sexist rules and racist absurdities of life in a small town? Drawing on her family's tradition of telling ghost stories and her long-standing commitment to literature, Morrison began attempting to answer this question and expanding her commitment in 1962 by joining a writers' workshop at Howard. The short story she began in this workshop became the nucleus of *The Bluest Eye*.

Less ambitious in scope and length than *Song of Solomon*, both *The Bluest Eye* and *Sula* are novels of poetic realism and Gothic fables about growing up poor, black, and female in a male-dominated, white middle-class society. In *The Bluest Eye* Morrison contrasts the experience and values of two black families, the poor yet proud MacTeers and the poor, ashamed Breedloves, with those of the Shirley Temple of the white Fisher family. The major focus is on eleven-year-old Pecola Breedlove and the MacTeer sisters, ten-year-old Frieda and nine-year-old Claudia, the narrator. The novel is cleverly structured around an opening story from the standard elementary school Dick-and-Jane readers of the 1940s (the time of the action), which insidiously inculcated an inferiority complex in black children of the inner city by promoting the values of the homogenized white suburban middle-class family. The brief children's story, which Morrison repeats in three different styles—from standard to nonstandard English— provides an ironic contrast to the plot, which is further reinforced by the narrator with a marigold-planting analogy that ingeniously and immediately establishes the lyrical style and tragic mood of the narrative. The novel proper is then divided into the four seasons (autumn, winter, spring, and summer) with the Dick-and-Jane story also broken down into seven headnotes for the minichapters, sharpening the contrast between the ideal experience of the white world and the actual experience of blacks portrayed in the minichapters. After being raped by her drunk father, deceived into believing God had miraculously given her the blue eyes she prayed for, suffering a miscarriage, and being ridiculed by other children, Pecola loses her sanity, and the marigold seeds planted by the MacTeer sisters do not grow. Metaphor and metonomy thus complement each other in their signification: it is painfully difficult for little black girls to grow into healthy womanhood with a positive self-image when "all the world had agreed that a blue-eyed, yellow-haired, pink-skinned doll was what every girl child treasures."[40]

Progressing from girlhood to womanhood, *Sula,* the most poetic of Morrison's four novels, focuses on the friendship of two black women and moves into retrospection over a period of forty-six years. Part 1 with six chapters that chronicle the years from 1919 to 1927 distills the legendary qualities of the Bottom, a hilltop black neighborhood in Ohio; of Shadrack, the shell-shocked World War I veteran and founder of National Suicide Day; of Sula Peace, the tough, adventuresome main character and of her girlhood friendship with Nel Wright, whose wedding ruptures the special relationship they shared. The five chapters of Part 2 (1937, 1939, 1940, 1941, and 1965) continue the chronicle with a worldly-wise, independent Sula returning to the Bottom after a ten-year absence, becoming both a pariah and redeemer of her time and place and people.

Morrison's language throughout *Sula* is even more charged with the beauty, wonder, and pain of the poetry of the black experience than it is in *The Bluest Eye.* Our feelings are stirred and our awareness of the characters' ambivalence about people and events deepened by the irony of such place names as the Bottom (a name derived from the legend or "nigger joke" about the white farmer who kept his promise of freedom and a piece of bottom land to his slave by convincing him to accept infertile land up in the hills as the bottom of heaven), Irene's Palace of Cosmetology, Edna Finch's Mellow House, and the Time and a Half Pool Hall. Equally striking are such metaphorical images as "Grass stood blade by blade, shocked into separateness by an ice that held for days"; and "As Reverend Deal moved into his sermon, the hands of the women unfolded like pairs of ravens and flew high above their hats in the air."[41] But the most clever is Sula's use of a spider conceit to express her disappointment with Nel:

Now Nel was one of *them.* One of the spiders whose only thought was the next rung of the web, who dangled in dark dry places suspended by their own spittle, more terrified of the free fall than the snake's breath below. Their eyes so intent on the wayward stranger who trips into their net, they were blind to the cobalt on their own backs, the moonshine fighting to pierce their corners. If they were touched by the snake's breath, however fatal, they were merely victims and knew how to behave in that role (just as Nel knew how to behave as the wronged wife). But the free fall, oh no, that required—demanded—invention: a thing to do with the wings, a way of holding the legs and most of all a full surrender to the downward flight if they wished to taste their tongues or stay alive. But alive was what they, and now Nel, did not want to be. Too dangerous. Now Nel belonged to the town and all of its ways. She had given herself over to them, and the flick of their tongues would drive her back into her little dry corner where she would cling to her spittle high above the breath of the snake and the fall. (P. 120)

Insensitive to Nel's pain at finding her husband, Jude, in bed with her, Sula, as this elaborate analogy reveals, is disappointed at the possessiveness and jealousy of the one person to whom she felt close. No longer, she thinks, is Nel willing to affirm the possibilities of life, to risk rebellion against social conventions and traditional sex roles in order to define herself and assert her independence and vitality.

When they met in 1922, Sula and Nel's friendship was as intense as it was sudden. "Because each had discovered years before that they were neither white nor male, and that all freedom and triumph was forbidden to them, they had set about creating something else to be" (p. 52). Solitary and lonely, they were the only children of distant mothers and incomprehensible fathers—Sula's was dead and Nel's a seaman. Nel's mother, Helene Wright, was attractive, vain, and oppressively class conscious in an effort to escape her Creole mother's wild blood. Resisting her mother's attempts to impose distorted middle-class values on her, Nel declares: " 'I'm me. I'm not their daughter. I'm not Nel. I'm me. Me' " (p. 28). Sula's mother, Hannah Peace, was "a kind and generous woman" with "extraordinary beauty and funky elegance," who, like her own mother, Eva Peace, loved all men. Unlike Eva, however, Hannah was promiscuous. Neither Eva nor Hannah showered her daughter with motherly affection. Eva had little time or energy to provide more than the basic necessities for her children's survival, yet she fiercely and ironically demonstrates the depth of her maternal love by burning her drug-addict son to death and throwing herself out of a two-story window in a futile attempt to save

Hannah from burning to death. Receiving no sustaining affection from Eva, Hannah is unable or unwilling to show affection to Sula. " 'You love her,' " she tells a friend, " 'like I love Sula. I just don't like her. That's the difference' " (p. 57). Feeling unloved and revealing the evil she embodies, Sula emotionlessly watched Hannah burn to death. Although at twelve years old both were "wishbone thin and easy-assed," Nel "seemed stronger and more consistent than Sula, who could hardly be counted on to sustain any emotion for more than three minutes" (p. 53). Thus, Nel and Sula found in each other the intimacy they needed, and they are equally responsible for the drowning of a small boy, Chicken Little, a secret guilt that seals the bond between them and with Shadrack, whom they suspect saw their wicked act.

Morrison intentionally makes Sula an ambitious character who evokes ambivalence from all quarters, including the undramatized author-narrator. On one hand, Sula represents a liberated modern black woman, who, in rejecting marriage, declares: " 'I don't want to be somebody else. I want to make myself', " and defiantly tells her grandmother: " 'Whatever's burning in me is mine. . . . And I'll split this town in two and everything in it before I'll let you put it out' " (pp. 92–93). But Ajax, the handsome, sinister street poet who stirred Sula's girlhood sexual fantasies, becomes her nemesis and the agent for her discovery of the meaning of possessiveness after he responds to her brain as well as her body. On the other hand, Sula represents the actual and imagined force of evil in the black community. When she put her grandmother in a home, they called her a roach; and when she took Jude from Nel and slept with white men, they called her a bitch. The folks of the Bottom, true to their culture, also remembered the "weighty evidence" of Gothic events that proved that Sula was evil: the talk about her watching her mother burn, the plague of robins that announced her return to Medallion, the accidental injury of Teapot and death of Mr. Finley, and the ominous birthmark over her eye.

The voice of the omniscient author-narrator is at once sympathetic toward and critical of the black people of the Bottom. She explains their "full recognition of the legitimacy of forces other than good ones" with the awareness and compassion of an insider, affirming their resolve to survive in the face of hard times and evil. But she is critical of the tradition of inferiority implicit in black women's shame of dark complexion, of broad, flat noses, and of coarse, short hair. Ambivalent about Sula, Morrison ascribes her dangerous behavior to her limited opportunities and alternatives for personal growth as a black woman:

In a way, her strangeness, her naivete, her craving for the other half of her equation was the consequence of an idle imagination. Had she paints, or clay, or knew the discipline of the dance, or strings; had she anything to engage her tremendous curiosity and her gift for metaphor, she might have exchanged the restlessness and preoccupation with whim for an activity that provided her with all she yearned for. And like any artist with no art form, she became dangerous. (P. 121)

Most important, the author-narrator, like the blacks of the Bottom, sees Sula as both a pariah and a redeemer:

> Their conviction of Sula's evil changed them in accountable yet mysterious ways. Once the source of their personal misfortune was identified, they had leave to protect and love one another. They began to cherish their husbands and wives, protect their children, repair their homes and in general band together against the devil in their midst. In their world, aberrations were as much a part of nature as grace. It was not for them to expel or annihilate it. . . . The presence of evil was something to be first recognized, then dealt with, survived, outwitted, triumphed over. (P. 118)

At the end of the novel, Eva, with a tough-minded understanding of life despite her senility, compels Nel to realize that she and Sula were just alike.

In theme and style Toni Morrison's novels are a fine example of vintage wine in new bottles. Her exploration of the impact of sexism and racism on the lives of black women in her Gothic fables provides a more complex and, perhaps, controversial vision of the personalities and bonding of fiercely alive modern black women than the idealized images of most writers of the 1960s. Particularly in *The Bluest Eye* and *Sula* she distills history and fact with the poetic freedom and Gothic vision of modernist and postmodernist writers. Her sharp eye for the concrete details and telltale gestures that evoke a sense of place and character in the fables and *Song of Solomon* are complemented by a wonderful gift for metaphor and metonymy that are as penetrating in their insightfulness as they are arresting in their freshness and suggestiveness. Her characters are eccentric and maimed as a result of their experience as black men and women in an environment that rigidly defines their humanity by economic, sexual, and racial myths, but still they persevere in their efforts to cope with or triumph over the obstacles in their path to self-esteem, freedom, and wholeness. Thus Pecola is destroyed psychologically, Sula dies an outcast among her own, and Milkman follows the path of his African ancestor, but both Claudia and Nel survive the terror and tragedy of their friends' lives, achieving in the process a precarious adjustment to the worlds of Shirley Temple and the Bottom. Pilate's moral victory is even more Pyrrhic. Because Morrison probes the awesome will to live of her characters in order to suggest the truth of their psychic experience and the complexity of their humanity, her Gothic fables, reminiscent of Toomer's *Cane*, are a quintessential blend of realism and poetry, bizarreness and beauty, revelation and lyricism.

Continuity in the Novel of the Sixties and Seventies

Of the more than one hundred novels by fifty black American novelists published between 1962 and 1983 that I have examined for this and the following chapter, most continue the synthesis of traditional forms of realism and romance that characterized the beginning of the Afro-American novel in 1853. In this chapter I have focused on twenty-one novels by six authors that reveal two intriguing trends in realism of the 1960s and 1970s: critical realism and poetic realism. Of the six authors selected on the basis of their contributions both to these trends in the Afro-American novel and to stimulating readers' awareness of the possibilities of life, all are first-generation college-educated individuals who, except for Bambara, have published two or more novels. Bambara's extraordinarily insightful synthesis of traditional and modern conventions in her first novel compelled its brief examination. In general, the six authors are representative of the educational background, literary productivity, and preferred narrative conventions of contemporary Afro-American novelists. The classifications, it should be remembered, indicate narrative conventions that the authors have employed with distinction in one or more novels, and are intended as neither arbitrary nor immutable labels to confine the authors or their novels. Rather, the classifications are intended to foster clarity and coherence in understanding the ambivalence of the authors toward all traditions and the contributions they have made to continuity and change in the tradition of the Afro-American novel.

These authors' conflicting emotions and various literary contributions were influenced in part by the radical political and cultural developments of the 1960s—beginning with the March on Washington in 1963, the black arts movement in 1964, the accelerated use of paperback books in college classrooms in 1965, and with cultural democratization, the cashing-in on the new vogue in black studies and feminism by publishers and reprint houses in 1969. These developments generated a new, often heated debate in academic circles over the purpose of art, the function of the artist, and the death of the novel. There was, of course, less discussion about black American fiction in the media than about Euro-American and African fiction, and, except for *Negro Digest (Black World)*, both the black and white media were more interested in promoting black poetry and drama. Nevertheless, there was more than enough ferment in the literary marketplace and writers' workshops for writers like John O. Killens, John A. Williams, Alice Walker, Gayl Jones, Toni Cade Bambara, and Toni Morrison to fulfill their roles as black artists in defining the complexity of Afro-American life and, to paraphrase Ralph Ellison, to realize that in spite of all its technical experimentation, the autonomy of the novel as a system of artificial signs is qualified by its interrelationship with other cultural systems, especially linguistic and ethical.

In their definition of Afro-American life, these writers therefore continue to tap the roots of Afro-American culture and institutions—black music, speech, religion, and the family—repudiating those codes and conventions that impede individual and collective growth and self-determination, and celebrating those that enhance these humanistic objectives. Consistent with recent social developments, there is more emphasis on the importance of music, speech, and religion as the foundations of contemporary Afro-American culture and the principal modalities for expressing the complex double vision of Afro-American character than on institutionalized Christianity, which is increasingly criticized and even displaced in importance in the works of some novelists by politics, ancestralism, or other Afrocentric beliefs and rituals. Bambara's *Salt Eaters* is exceptional in its quest for a balance of the spiritual and political, of the traditional and modern. In Williams's *Sissie*, Alice Walker's *Third Life of Grange Copeland* and *The Color Purple*, and Morrison's *Bluest Eye* and *Sula*, we see a critical exploration of the strengths and weaknesses of the institutions of the black family and church as well as of the continuing racial and sexual exploitation of black people, especially women. Influenced by the sexual revolution as well as by the continuing color and class struggle in the American social arena, contemporary Afro-American neorealists are still basically inclined toward a redemptive, paradoxically progressive and apocalyptic view of history even when the surface patterns are dialectical, cyclical, and spiral. Ambivalent in their narrative allegiances to a black aesthetic, they have increased the range of their thematic concerns from the religious and political to the economic, psychological, and philosophical aspects of contemporary life.

Because most contemporary black American novelists are college educated, it is not surprising that the literary and nonliterary influences on their use of narrative conventions have been wide-ranging and varied. Many acknowledge the importance of Western and Euro-American writers, some mention Russians, Asians, and Africans, and others include such Afro-Americans as Toomer, Hurston, Wright, Himes, and Ellison. In a national poll of thirty-eight black writers in 1965, more than half named Richard Wright as the most important black American writer of all time; and John A. Williams's *Man Who Cried I Am* and John O. Killens's *And Then We Heard the Thunder* were ranked equally high as the most important novels written by a black American since *Invisible Man*. According to the managing editor of *Negro Digest*, "The writers were asked no questions dealing with style and technique, partly because these considerations— the editors believe—are more the concern of English teachers and creative writing courses than of readers interested in knowing which writers and which ideas the writers think are important. Style and technique are problems for the individual writer to work out for himself, and his attitude toward style and technique will be reflected in his own work and in the work he admires."[42] Viewed from the historical, anthropological, and formalistic perspectives of this study, however, *The Man Who Cried I Am* is the more successful of the two novels. There are, of course, several novels written since 1965 that are better or equally well written, including Ernest Gaines's *Autobiography of Miss Jane Pittman*, Morrison's *Sula*, and Bambara's *Salt Eaters*. In the 1970s Zora Neale Hurston was rediscovered and reassessed as a major voice in the tradition of the Afro-American novel, inspiring the search of many black women writers beyond their mothers' gardens for other literary mothers. Because of the diverse influences, interests, and talents of contemporary black American novelists, we find a corresponding diversity in their attitudes toward and use of realism and modernism. Even among the neorealists examined in this chapter, we find that some—especially Williams, Morrison, and Bambara—are inclined on occasions to move beyond realism. This is not to imply that modernism and postmodernism are more viable modes for constructing the vision of contemporary Afro-American novelists. Nor does it imply that the neo-slave narratives of Margaret Walker and Ernest Gaines that will be examined in the next chapter are necessarily superior on all levels to novels by other neorealists. Readers, like novelists, in short, should be as open minded and responsive to the imperatives of change and the revitalization of earlier forms in the narrative tradition as they are in affirming their identification with historical continuity and enduring ethical values that underlie the distortions and discontinuities of our contemporary culture of narcissism.

8 / The Contemporary Afro-American Novel, 2: Modernism and Postmodernism

They made their own fiction, just like we make our own.
But they can't tell whether our fictions are the real thing or whether
they're merely fictional.

ISHMAEL REED
in *Interviews with Black Writers*

PEAKING at Gettysburg during the centennial year of the Emancipation Proclamation, Vice President Lyndon B. Johnson said, "Until justice is blind, until education is unaware of race, until opportunity is unconcerned with the color of men's skins, emancipation will be a proclamation but not a fact."[1] Two years after his succession to the presidency following the assassination of John F. Kennedy, President Johnson addressed the Howard University commencement audience and expressed a more radical commitment to interracial reform than any other chief executive. "In far too many ways," he stated, "American Negroes have been another nation: deprived of freedom, crippled by hatred, the doors of opportunity closed to hope." After referring to his role in passing the Civil Rights Act of 1964, the first civil rights legislation in almost a century, and his signing of the Voting Rights Act of 1965 as the beginning of freedom, he continued:

> But freedom is not enough. You do not wipe away the scars of centuries by saying: Now, you are free to go where you want, do as you desire, and choose the leaders you please.
>
> You do not take a man who, for years, has been hobbled by chains, liberate him, bring him to the starting line of a race, saying "you are free to compete with all the others," and still justly believe you have been completely fair.
>
> Thus it is not enough to open the gates of opportunity. All our citizens must have the ability to walk through those gates.
>
> This is the next and the more profound stage of the battle for civil rights. We seek not just freedom but opportunity—not just legal equity but human ability—not just equality as a right and a theory, but equality as a fact and a result.[2]

Despite the results of Johnson's Great Society programs in helping Afro-Americans, women, other minorities, and the poor to fulfill their human and civil rights, the modest gains of blacks and the War on Poverty were compromised by the economic and moral drain of the war in Vietnam and reversed by the neoconservative presidencies of Richard Nixon, Gerald Ford, Jimmy Carter, and Ronald Reagan. How these and other experiences between 1963 and 1983 influenced the development of modern and postmodern attitudes and conventions by contemporary Afro-American novelists is our chief concern in this chapter.

Modernism and Postmodernism

If Euro-American modernism challenges or violates traditional assumptions about what is real, true, and therefore meaningful by separating the literary text from the external world and defining it as an autonomous, self-sufficient world, then postmodernism compels us to consider that literature has no meaning, that its meaning exists only in our consciousness, or that its meaning is to be found in the indeterminacy of its language. Theorists of modernism like I. A. Richards, Thomas Cassirer, Suzanne Langer, T. S. Eliot, Carl Jung, Northrop Frye, Roman Jakobson, and Roman Ingarden argue, as Gerald Graff lucidly explains in *Literature Against Itself*, that "literature and art deal with experience only as myth, psychology, or language, not as an object of conceptual understanding." Structuralist critics, those who analyze individual works of literature as signifying systems of hierarchical structures whose meaning is the dynamic relationships of the differences from and oppositions to other elements in the system itself, attempt to demystify the modernist concept of literary autonomy "by showing that literary language, linguistic conventions, and 'textuality,' not the imagination or consciousness of the writer, are the constitutive agents of writing."[3] In "The Fiction of Realism" critic J. Hillis Miller succinctly states the antimimetic, antireferential theory of structuralism:

> One important aspect of current literary criticism is the disintegration of the paradigms of realism under the impact of structural linguistics and the renewal of rhetoric. If meaning in language rises not from the reference of signs to something outside words but from differential relations among the words themselves, if "referent" and "meaning" must always be distinguished, then the notion of a literary text which is validated by its one-to-one correspondence to some social, historical, or psychological reality can no longer be taken for

granted. No language is purely mimetic or referential, not even the most utilitarian speech. The specifically literary form of language, however, may be defined as a structure of words which in one way or another calls attention to this fact, while at the same time allowing for its own inevitable misreading as a "mirroring of reality."[4]

Mimetic readings of texts for Miller and other structuralist critics then are considered misreadings. Most contemporary Afro-American novelists subscribe neither to this old reductive theory of mimesis nor to the new gods of textuality and self-referentiality.

Postmodernism moves beyond modernism of the 1950s in an effort to expand the possibilities of the novel and to reconstruct the liberated lives of the generation of the 1960s. That generation's sensibilities were shaped and misshaped by modern jazz, rock music, drugs, war in Vietnam, political assassinations, black power and women's rights movements, civil rights and antiwar demonstrations, campus sit-ins and building take-overs— all brought to us daily in black and white or living color by the magic of technology and television. To proclaim the death of art's traditional claims to truth and to herald the birth of a new sensibility, postmodernists employ fantasy, parody, burlesque, and irony. Whether by conscious ironic reconstruction of ancient myths and rituals or by self-conscious innovativeness that explores the limits of language and the liberating power of the creative process, white postmodernists like John Barth and Ronald Sukenick expressed the belief that conventional elements of fiction were exhausted and ineffective in expressing the truth of contemporary life and that the basis of a new fictive reality resided either in the individual perceiving mind or in the act of perception, not in the world outside of the novel.[5]

As illustrated primarily by Ellison and Baldwin, modernism in the Afro-American novel from 1952 to 1962 involved concurrent movements: one away from such earlier forms as realism and naturalism and the other back to a reshaping of such traditional narrative modes as myth and legend. Probably for this as well as for other reasons, critics like Jerome Klinkowitz believe that black modernist and postmodernist novelists are not aesthetically unlike such white contemporary novelists as John Hawkes, John Barth, Donald Barthelme, Richard Brautigan, and Ronald Sukenick.[6] Whereas there is apparently some truth to this line of thought, it is not the whole truth. Margaret Walker, Ernest J. Gaines, William M. Kelley, Charles Wright, Ronald Fair, Hal Bennett, John E. Wideman, Clarence Major, Ishmael Reed, Leon Forrest, and Toni C. Bambara—to name a few black modernists and postmodernists—are definitely influenced by the traditions of Western literature and committed to the freedom of hybrid narrative forms. But because the legacy of institutional racism and sexism that shaped and continues to shape their consciousness fosters ambivalence about their culture, and because the struggle for social justice continues, most modern and postmodern Afro-American novelists, like their nineteenth-century predecessors, are not inclined to neglect moral and social issues in their narratives. With the possible exception of Clarence Major (who is a member of a white postmodernist fiction collective), they, unlike white postmodernists of what some critics call the antinovel philosophy, are deeply concerned with fictive visions that focus on the truths of the perversity of American racism and the paradoxes of Afro-American double-consciousness. Unlike their white contemporaries, black American postmodernists are not merely rejecting the arrogance and anachronism of Western forms and conventions, but also rediscovering and reaffirming the power and wisdom of their own folk tradition: Afro-American ways of seeing, knowing, and expressing reality, especially black speech, music, and religion.

Thus, while insisting on their freedom as individual artists to choose their own subjects, form, and style—widening the range of influences on their novels from literature and music to painting, film, and pop culture—Walker, Gaines, Kelley, Fair, Wideman, Wright, Bennett, Reed, and Major achieve their distinctive voices simultaneously within and against a narrative tradition of continuity and change. This they achieve by experimenting with different combinations of myth, ritual, parable, fable, legend, allegory, and satire in a postmodern mode of romance that I join Robert Scholes in calling *fabulation*. Scholes defines fabulation as "a return to a more verbal kind of fiction . . . a less realistic and more artistic kind of narrative; more shapely, more evocative; more concerned with ideas and ideals, less concerned with things."[7] Although an extraordinary delight in form with a concurrent, self-conscious emphasis on the authority of the shaper of the form distinguishes in part the art of the contemporary romanticist or fabulator from that of the conventional novelist or satirist, the continuing power and wisdom of the traditions of spirituals, sermons, blues, and jazz distinguish on a lower register the possibilities of Afro-American form and style from those of Euro-American.

The following classifications, as I stated earlier, are intended neither to be exhaustive nor to pigeonhole authors or novels, for in the final analysis it is the sincerity, sensitivity, and skill of each author that enable him or her to trust the tenor of the times and the subject of each work to dictate its own appropriate form and style. Consequently, over a period of time the novels of a particular author will more likely than not include any number of variations of different forms and styles. I have nevertheless discovered that some novelists and novels are the best examples of a particular combination of tendencies I have borrowed the term *fabulation* to describe. The classifications are therefore not mutually exclusive but basically descriptive of tendencies in at least one, and usually what I consider the best, of the novels by selected representative authors.

Fabulation, Legend, and Neoslave Narrative

Some contemporary black fabulators combine elements of fable, legend, and slave narrative to protest racism and justify the deeds, struggles, migrations, and spirit of black people. Although the use of black folklore—especially music, speech, and religion—is didactic, contemporary black fabulators rely more on the artifice of the storyteller and humorist than on social realism to stimulate our imagination, win our sympathy, and awaken our conscience to moral and social justice. The power of faith, messianic hope, self-reliance or direct action, and the lynching ritual are central motifs of this hybrid form.

MARGARET ABIGAIL WALKER (1915–)

The daughter of a fundamentalist music teacher and a Methodist Episcopal minister who lived in a world of books, Margaret Walker was born on July 7, 1915, in Birmingham, Alabama. "I got my love for books and my desire to write from my father," she explains. "He belonged to a family of people who for generations had been interested in culture, in languages, and religions. Books and music, art—that is what I was formed to."[8] She began reading authors like Langston Hughes and Countee Cullen, and writing poetry when she was about twelve. Her first poem, "Daydreaming," was published in *The Crisis* when she was nineteen. After early education in the South, she completed her B.A. in 1935 at Northwestern University in Evanston, Illinois.[9] In Chicago during the thirties she developed her poetic voice and control of form, publishing her best-known poem, "For My People," in *Poetry* in 1937. She met many writers in Chicago, including Richard Wright, Arna Bontemps, Fenton Johnson, Willard Motley, and Gwendolyn Brooks. Some she met through Langston Hughes, who introduced her to Wright in 1936 at the National Negro Congress. Others, including several radical white writers, she met at writers' conferences or in such organizations as the Writers' Project of Chicago and the South

Side Writers' Group, a black literary circle organized by Wright, which she joined in 1936. In 1939 she completed her first novel, "Gorse Island," and left the WPA to study in the Writers' Workshop at the University of Iowa, receiving her M.A. in 1940 for the collection of poems *For My People*, which was published in 1942 as winner of the Yale Award for Younger Poets.[10] After marrying, raising four children, and teaching at Livingstone, West Virginia State, and Jackson State colleges, she returned to the University of Iowa in 1961 for her Ph.D., which she received for *Jubilee* in 1965. As the author of three books of poetry, Walker is more widely acclaimed as a poet than for her singular achievement as a novelist in *Jubilee*.

"Long before *Jubilee* had a name," Walker says about the genesis of the novel, "I was living with it and imagining its reality. Its genesis coincides with my childhood, its development grows out of a welter of raw experiences and careful research, and its final form emerged exactly one hundred years after its major events took place."[11] The story of Elvira and Randall Ware, Walker's great-grandparents, and of slave life in Georgia was passed on to Walker in enthralling bedtime stories told by her grandmother, who would indignantly defend their truth, declaring "I'm not telling her tales; I'm telling her the naked truth." Walker was influenced most at Iowa by her adviser Paul Engle, in Chicago by her friend Richard Wright, in New York by historian Lawrence Reddick, then curator of the Schomburg Collection of Negro History on 135th Street in Harlem, and throughout her writing career by Langston Hughes. She was also influenced in the technique and form of historical fiction and folk literature by such authors as Chekhov, Tolstoy, Scott, Faulkner, Steinbeck, and Pearl Buck as well as by Vernon Cassell, Joseph Warren Beach, Robert Lively, and Georg Lukács. Explaining her debt to Lukács in philosophy and point of view, she writes: "I have Lukács to thank for an understanding of the popular character of the historical novel; for the recognition that I was among the first dealing with characters looking up from the bottom rather than down from the top; and for an understanding of Abraham Lincoln as a world historical figure who was always a minor character seen through the mind of the major characters."[12] Margaret Walker's task in *Jubilee*, then, was to create fiction from the oral history of her family and the recorded history of the nation.

As its structure and style reveal, *Jubilee* is a neoslave narrative based primarily on folk material and Vyry's quest for freedom. Set in Georgia, the novel has three main divisions of eighteen to twenty-two sections each and moves chronologically from the antebellum years through the early years of Reconstruction. Each minichapter has a title and headnote, usually an excerpt from a spiritual, a folksong, or a folksaying which corresponds to the increasingly jubilant mood of the plot. For instance, the first headnote is from "Swing Low, Sweet Chariot," a sorrow song, and the last from "My Father's House," a joyous song. Most of the section titles are descriptive, like "Cook in the Big House" and "Seventy-five lashes on her naked back," but some are song titles, like "Flee as a bird to your mountain" and "There's a star in the East on Christmas morn." Part 1 begins dramatically during slavery with two-year-old Vyry, John Dutton's last child by his slave mistress, being brought to see her mother, Hetta, who is dying at twenty-nine years of age after giving birth to her fifteenth child. It ends with Vyry's abortive flight to freedom with her young children. Part 2 sags under the weight of the facts about the Civil War years, often introduced by Walker through a catalog of excerpts from speeches, letters, and newspaper articles. Part 3 picks up the pace again as the novel ends during Reconstruction with a free, mature, and pregnant Vyry, whom her daughter overhears feeding and calling her own chickens, content with her decision to stay with Innis Brown, her second husband, and raise their family rather than to reunite with Randall Ware, her first husband, after his twelve-year absence. The main plot thus focuses on Vyry's commitment to freedom as expressed in the sermons about Moses, the legendary President Lincoln, and the indomitable will of black folks themselves.

If it is the function of good realistic art to create character types of general appeal, then *Jubilee* is an impressive novel. In the creation of Vyry, Margaret Walker has given us one of the most memorable women in contemporary Afro-American fiction. A pillar of Christian faith and human dignity, Vyry, the protagonist of the novel, commands our respect first as an individual and then as a symbol of nineteenth-century black womanhood. Shaped by plantation culture, she realistically embodies its strengths and weaknesses. As John Dutton's illegitimate daughter, she could pass as the twin of her master's legitimate daughter, Lillian—"same sandy hair, same gray-blue eyes, same milk-white skin."[13] She thus has a privileged yet precarious status in the caste system of the plantation. Raised in the Quarters of the Big House as a cook, she is neither bitter nor political in her philosophy of life. Her major strengths are integrity, resourcefulness, pragmatism, and songs. Her weaknesses are caste prejudice, fidelity to former white owners, and political naïveté. Torn between loyalty to her first husband and her white family, and loyalty to her second husband and her children, she is guided by her Christian ethics in arriving at a practical rather than radical resolution of the conflict. In contrast to the stereotypic loyal family retainer, she remains on the Dutton plantation after the war because of her promise to Randall Ware that she would wait for him and because of her compassion for her former white mistress. Expanding in the denouement of the novel on the significance of Vyry's character and culture, the author-narrator reveals a close moral and political identification with the protagonist and implicitly invites our similar response:

> In her obvious capacity for love, redemptive and forgiving love, she was alive and standing on the highest peaks of her time and human personality. Peasant and slave, unlettered and untutored, she was nevertheless the best true example of motherhood of her race, an ever present assurance that nothing could destroy a people whose sons had come from her loins. (P. 407)

Vyry thus evolves as a heroic symbol of the black woman whose Christian faith, humanism, courage, resourcefulness, and music are the bedrock of her survival and the survival of her people. But by limiting Vyry's politics to the domestic and familial, Walker's vision celebrates the black woman of yesterday rather than of tomorrow.

The other characters in the novel are also drawn with knowledge of the times and sympathy for the people. The white characters, particularly the Dutton family, are stock representatives of the planter class of the antebellum and postbellum South. John, Salina, and their children, Lillian and John, Jr., were staunch defenders of their privileged color and class position in the plantation tradition. Suffering death or madness but not complete defeat with the collapse of the Confederacy, they foreshadow the rise of white terrorism and intransigence that denied land, education, and the vote to blacks in the New South. The minor black characters are types clearly derived from the oral tradition, revealing Walker's intimate knowledge of black speech and music, and the slave narratives. "Brother Ezekiel," for instance, "was a powerfully built, stovepipe-black man. He was neither young nor old. He was the plantation preacher, at least among the slaves" (p. 9). He was in the tradition of those slave exhorters who were gifted speakers and singers who not only admonished their flocks "to have faith in God and He would send them a Moses, a deliverer to free His people," but who also served as a conductor on the Underground Railroad and as a spy for the Union Army. Because of their different backgrounds, the major black male characters, Randall Ware and Innis Brown, are antithetical types. A member of the artisan class of free black laborers who served in the Union Army and a Reconstruction politician, Randall is the voice of black nationalism and radicalism in the novel. It is he who plants the idea of freedom in Vyry's head, giving concrete social reality to the sermons and prayers that God would send a Moses to free her and her people. He is bitter because whites do not respect his rights as a free citizen, and he resists their efforts to cheat, terrorize, and emasculate him. Born a slave, Innis is hard working and courageous in his protection of Vyry and as naive, conservative, and practical as she is. All he wants in life is a farm of his own where he could raise his own crops and family.

On the problem of verisimilitude and point of view in the novel, Walker explains that her characters "are so real, so intensified, that I become involved with them, so exaggerated that they seem to exact human proportions, and I struggle and suffer with them" (p. 28). The mixture of direct observer and omniscient points of view early in *Jubilee* provides both an opportunity for the reader to participate in the drama of the characters' lives and a wide range of understanding and feeling from a black perspective for the setting and characters. In contrast to the romantic nostalgia of Margaret Mitchell's *Gone With the Wind, Jubilee* is realistic and critical. Though the author-narrator is basically omniscient, she is at one with the Christian values of the protagonist, who at the end of the novel distances herself politically and emotionally from her first husband:

> "Well, all I got to say, Randall Ware, is I can't understand you no more'n I can understand evil white peoples what ain't got no shame and ain't got no God. But I ain't gwine try to beat the white man at his own game with his killing and his hating neither. . . . I knows I'm a child of God and I can pray. Things ain't never gwine get too bad for me to pray. And I knows too, that the Good Lawd's will is gwine be done. I has learned that much. I'm gwine leave all the evil shameless peoples in the world in the hands of the Good Lawd and I'm gwine teach my childrens to hate nobody, don't care what they does."
> (P. 404)

There is Christian faith, hope, and charity in this voice, but no ironic distance here or elsewhere in the novel. In other words, it reveals less of the influence of the critical realism of Lukács than of the social realism of the slave narratives and Afro-American double-consciousness.

In *Jubilee*, then, Margaret Walker gives us our first major neoslave narrative: residually oral, modern narratives of escape from bondage to freedom. (Gaines's *Autobiography of Miss Jane Pittman* would be the second.) As in Brown's *Clotel*, the narrator of *Jubilee* is omniscient and didactic; its structure is episodic; and its subject matter rooted in black folk history and culture. Unlike the slave narratives, which were told in the first person, and *Clotel,* however, the mood of *Jubilee* is not romantic, the author-narrator's voice not ironic, and the plot does not override character. Vyry, although of mixed blood like Clotel, is realistically drawn, yet, at the same time, she has general appeal as a symbol of nineteenth-century black womanhood that challenges historical stereotypes. Although she does not support the political radicalism of Randall Ware, she is nevertheless heroic in her role as nurturer and coprovider of her family. Walker's purpose, unlike Brown's, was not to bring about the abolition of physical slavery but, as she states, "to tell the story that my grandmother had told me, and to set the record straight where Black people are concerned in terms of the Civil War, of slavery, segregation and Reconstruction."[14]

ERNEST J. GAINES (1933–)

The oldest of twelve children, Ernest Gaines was born on January 15, 1933, on River Lake Plantation, Point Coupee Parish, Louisiana. As a child, he chopped sugar cane for fifty cents a day. When he was fifteen, his family moved to Vallejo, California, where he finished school. At sixteen he wrote his first novel, which was unceremoniously rejected by a New York publisher. In 1953 he was drafted into the army for two years and then attended San Francisco State College, receiving his B.A. in 1957. After publishing two stories in the college magazine, he gave himself ten years to become a writer. In 1958 he won a Wallace Stegner Fellowship in Creative Writing for a year of study at Stanford University, and the following year he received the Joseph Henry Jackson Literary Award. By 1980 his major publications included a collection of short stories, *Bloodline* (1968), and four novels: *Catherine Carmier* (1964), *Of Love and Dust* (1967), *The Autobiography of Miss Jane Pittman* (1971), and *In My Father's House* (1978). Because *In My Father's House*—the story of a Southern civil rights leader's sins resurfacing in his vengeful, unacknowledged son to shake his father's faith in himself, his community, and his God—is the least compelling, it will be more fruitful to focus on the other three novels, especially the monumental achievement of *The Autobiography of Miss Jane Pittman.*

Before arriving in California and writing what he confesses was "the worst number of pages that anyone could possibly call a novel," Gaines had read little and written less. "I doubt that I read two novels before I went to California," he told an interviewer. "But I came from a long line of storytellers. I come from a plantation, where people told stories by the fireplace at night, people told stories on the ditch bank.... I think in my immediate family there were tremendous storytellers or liars or whatever you want to call them."[15] He started to read a lot, especially about the rural South, during the summer of 1949 in the Vallejo public library. That summer he also wrote the first draft of *Catherine Carmier*. At San Francisco State he continued to read novelists like Erskine Caldwell, Faulkner, Steinbeck, Willa Cather, Turgenev, and Hemingway. "When I did not find my people in the Southern writers," he says, "I started reading books about the peasantry in other places. I read [about] the John Steinbeck people of the Selinas [sic] Valley, the Chicanos as well as the poor whites. This led me to reading the writers of other countries. Then in some way I went into the Russians and I liked what they were doing with their stories on the peasantry; the peasants were real human beings, whereas in the fiction of American writers, especially Southern writers, they were caricatures of human beings, they were clowns."[16] Thus, rather than George Washington Cable or Kate Chopin, who wrote critically about the complex web of racism and sexism in the Creole communities of old Louisiana, the major literary influences on Gaines's early novels are Turgenev and Faulkner.[17]

Turgenev's sense of nihilism and Faulkner's sense of Southern history inform *Catherine Carmier*. "My *Catherine Carmier* is almost written on the structure of *Fathers and Sons*," Gaines tells us. "As a matter of fact, that was my Bible."[18] Like *Fathers and Sons*, the plot of *Catherine Carmier* treats a young man's return to his rural home and the past from which he and others of his generation have grown alienated in thought, feelings, and values. Unlike Turgenev's nihilistic Bazarov, Jackson Bradley, the black protagonist, is neither as cynical and articulate in his repudiation of the plantation tradition nor as unheroic in his search for truth and dignity in Louisiana. As Jackson's former teacher on the Grover plantation, one of several a few miles outside of Gaines's mythic town of Bayonne, old Madame Bayonne is both the spirit of the old Bayou social order and the narrator on the scene. Her retrospective account of the stubborn pride and brooding guilt of the Creole clan of Raoul Carmier and of the relationship between Jackson and Catherine dominates the omniscient narrative and is reminiscent of the Faulknerian vision of a South doomed to pass on the burden of its sins against God and man from father to son.

In *Of Love and Dust* Faulkner's influence is again apparent. Like *Catherine Carmier*, *Of Love and Dust* is set on a plantation ten or twelve miles from Bayonne, near Baton Rouge, where, even though the year is 1948, the antebellum social order and value system still shape the lives of blacks, whites, and Creoles: a racially mixed people of primarily French or Spanish ancestry. Thus young lovers like Marcus Payne, the citified black convict-lease protagonist, and Louise Bonbon, the Cajun overseer's wife, who rebel against the old order, are doomed to defeat and death. By their defiance of traditional racial taboos, they nevertheless represent the forces for social change.

In contrast to the Euro-American influence on the first two novels, in *The Autobiography of Miss Jane Pittman* Gaines draws heavily on the tradition of the slave narratives for his reconstruction of the life of a venerable old black storyteller whose personal journey from slavery to freedom resonates with the collective struggle of black people for freedom for over a century. Divided into four books ("The War Years," "Reconstruction," "The Plantation," and "The Quarters"), the novel is the story of Miss Jane Pittman's life as told by her and "other people at the house" to the editor, a nameless young history teacher. Over an eight- or nine-month period the teacher interviews and tapes Miss Jane in order to better understand and explain black history to his students. The story unfolds chronologically, from 1864, when Miss Jane (then named Ticey) was a ten- or eleven-year-old slave on a Louisiana plantation, to 1963, when she, now 110 or more, defiantly walks past Robert Samson, the plantation owner, on her way to a civil rights demonstration in Bayonne. In telling her story, Miss Jane, in the traditional manner of storytellers, often digresses as the mood strikes her to elaborate on people and events with acute, frequently colorful, descriptions and mother wit. Late in the novel, for instance, she tells Jimmy, a young civil rights organizer who was born on the plantation but now lives in the city: " 'People and time bring forth leaders. . . . Leaders don't bring forth people.' "[19] She also follows the folk habit of establishing time by reference to natural or social events. Because other black people in the community at times contribute to the narration, "Miss Jane's story," as the editor states in the introduction, "is all of their stories and their stories are Miss Jane's" (p. viii).

Set in Louisiana, Book 1 opens just before the end of the Civil War at the plantation where the protagonist is renamed Jane by a friendly Ohio soldier. Quickly and episodically the story moves to the end of the war. Jane heads North with other freedmen, who are attacked by patrollers and "Secesh soldiers"; and she and Ned, the young son of an older woman who saved her from rape, are the sole survivors. In Book 2 the tempo slows and the texture of the novel loosens as Jane raises Ned and experiences the federal government's betrayal of blacks with the exodus of the Northern troops in 1877 and the return to power of the Confederates. This is effectively dramatized in the take-over by Colonel Dye of the Bone plantation where she had settled and by the white terrorism that drove Ned into Kansas and killed him when he returned to teach and, in emulation of Frederick Douglass, lead his people. Taking Joe Pittman as her common-law husband, Jane moves to a plantation on the Louisiana-Texas border, where Joe becomes chief horse-breaker and is killed by a black stallion as she had dreamed and a conjure woman had prophesied.

Miss Jane continues her story in Book 3 with descriptive and analytic digressions on the customs, people, and values of the region. Now over fifty years old, she moves to the Samson plantation, joins the church, and becomes the cook at the big house. The suicide of young Tee Bob Samson brings Jane and the reader face to face with the role of her generation in perpetuating the racial taboos responsible in part for the tragedy. Finally, in Book 4 the resilience of Afro-American character and the messianic theme of the novel are reinforced when Jimmy, a fatherless child whom Miss Jane helped to midwife and whom the folks down in the quarters had welcomed at birth as "The One," follows in Ned's footsteps. After Jimmy is murdered while leading a civil rights demonstration in Bayonne, the black community, led now by Jane and Alex, a youthful organizer— a partnership that symbolizes the strength of cooperative leadership by individuals from both the old and young generations in the unending struggle for justice—defy white authority by continuing the demonstration.

Like Margaret Walker's Vyry, Miss Jane Pittman is an extraordinarily credible black woman. She is illiterate, sassy, resourceful, and faithful— particularly to Ned, Joe Pittman, the Samsons, and the folks down in the quarters. In contrast to Vyry's traditionalism, however, Miss Jane's in- dependence, loyalty to blacks, and response to the winds of social change prevail over her loyalty to whites and the past. During the forties she says:

> I wanted to move out of the house soon after Tee Bob killed himself, but Robert kept me up there to be with Miss Amma Dean. I stayed five years more and I told them I wanted to get out. Robert told me I got out when he said I got out. I told him at my age I did what I wanted to do. Miss Amma Dean told me she wanted me up there because I needed looking after much more than she did, but, she said, if I wanted to go, go. I told them I wanted to go, I wanted to move down in the quarters. (P. 201)

Rather than a black superwoman, Gaines painstakingly delineates Miss Jane as a complex, dynamic individual. She is barren, yet is surrogate mother to Ned; she claims not to believe in hoodoo, yet consults Madame Gautier about her dreams of Joe's death. She likes fishing, hard work, baseball, and vanilla ice cream. She also "gets religion" late in life, but will give up neither her love of sports nor having the funnies read to her in order to keep her status as mother of the church. Because of her age, her strength, and her wisdom, Miss Jane Pittman towers above her time, bridging past and present—a noble inspiration to all who behold her— just like the oak tree she respects and talks to.

The larger significance of Miss Jane as an individual embodying the basic qualities necessary to bridge the old and new social orders is reinforced by Gaines's delineation of Tee Bob, Joe Pittman, Ned, and Jimmy. Tee Bob, a college student and the plantation owner's only legitimate son, tries to break with the customs of the past by proposing marriage to a Creole. But he finds that historical racist attitudes and myths are too deeply rooted to change overnight or for him to endure alone, so he kills himself as much out of protest as defeat. Although he is weak and ineffectual, Gaines, nevertheless, has sympathy for him as a victim. "There will always be men struggling to change," Gaines explains in *Interviews with Black Writers*, "and there will always be those who are controlled by the past. In many cases, those who are controlled by the past can be just as human and sometimes more human than those who try to change conditions; there must always be those who try to break out of the trap the world keeps going in. Man must keep moving."[20]

All of Gaines's heroes seek to fulfill their natural rights and develop their human potential; but because white people have historically sought to deny black men their manhood, attempts by black men to assert themselves frequently result in violence and death. Joe dies attempting to maintain his pride and position as the chief horse-breaker on the Clyde plantation. " 'Now, little mama,' " he says, " 'man come here to die, didn't he? That's the contract he signed when he was born. . . . Now, all he can do while he's here is do something and do that thing good. The best thing I can do in this world is ride horses' " (p. 89). Ned and Jimmy die because they stand up to whites for their rights as men and citizens. " 'Be Americans,' " Ned preaches to the young in his bold sermon at the river. " 'But first be men' " (p. 110). Knowing that he would be killed, he tells them, " 'You don't own this earth, you're just here for a little while, but while you're here don't let no man tell you the best is for him and you take the scrap' " (p. 108). In seeking the strength and prayers of the old folks on the plantation, the great-aunts and uncles of the black church, Jimmy explains:

> "I can't promise you a thing. . . . But we must go on, and the ones already working will go on. Some of us might be killed, some of us definitely going to jail, and some of us might be crippled the rest of our life. But death and jail don't scare us—and we feel that we crippled

now, and been crippled a long time, and every day we put up with the white man insults they cripple us just a little bit more." (Pp. 226–27)

As a contemporary realist, Gaines thus reveals the traits of the men and women of a new social order in the personal and social commitments of individuals, for the hope of change in the future lies, according to his vision of the peculiarly American human condition, in the courage and pride of the young and the faith and resourcefulness of the old.

Subtly and compellingly, Gaines expresses his social and moral views through the manipulation of the distance between himself, the editor, the characters, and the reader in dramatized situations. Because the narrator looks back on the events she relates from the perspective of many years, the editor and implied author immediately address themselves to possible problems for the reader with the verisimilitude of the story and the reliability of the storyteller. The editor not only establishes the historical background and credibility of the storyteller in the introduction, but, as an outsider to the culture and a history teacher, he also heightens the dramatic and historical truth of the narrative by the intellectual and cultural distance between himself, Miss Jane, and the implied author. We perceive this distance in the editor's exchange with Mary Hodges, Miss Jane's friend and companion; in his initial concern about Miss Jane's rambling, repetitious storytelling style; and in how he has tried "not to write everything, but in essence everything that was said" (p. vii). Listening to the first-person narrator's voice, we are drawn emotionally and psychologically closer to her, absorbed by the truth and strength and complexity of her humanity as we relive her experience and come to better understand the values that have sustained black Americans in their historical struggle for freedom and dignity. The creation of this remarkable character and of the second major neoslave narrative (five years after *Jubilee*, the first, and five years before Ishmael Reed's *Flight to Canada*, the third) are Ernest Gaines's chief contributions to the tradition of realism in the Afro-American novel.

WILLIAM MELVIN KELLEY (1937–)

William Melvin Kelley was born in New York City in 1937. Educated in private schools (Fieldston, and Harvard University), he became one of the most talented and innovative postmodern fabulators. As an undergraduate he studied poetry with Archibald MacLeish and fiction with John Hawkes, an important Euro-American fabulator, and won the Dana Reed Prize for creative writing in 1960. In the following two years, he won fellowships to the New York Writers' Conference and the Bread Loaf Writers' Conference as well as a grant from the John Hay Whitney Foundation to work on his first novel, *A Different Drummer* (1962), for which he won the Richard and Hinda Rosenthal Foundation Award. During 1963–64 he and his wife lived in Rome, and during much of the 1970s, in Paris and Jamaica. He has taught at the State University of New York at Geneseo and the New School for Social Research.

In the 1964 preface to *Dancers on the Shore,* his collection of short stories on the black experience, Kelley wrote: "let me say for the record that I am not a sociologist or a politician or a spokesman. Such people try to give answers. A writer, I think, should ask questions. He should depict people, not symbols or ideas disguised as people."[21] But by 1965 he was convinced that the task of the black writer as artist was to address himself to the Afro-American to help him "to find those things that were robbed from him on the shores of Africa, to help repair the damage done to the soul of the Negro in the past three centuries."[22] Actually, from his first short story, "Spring Planting," which appeared in 1959 in *Accent,* to the stories and essays that appeared before 1962 in the *Urbanite, Harvard Advocate,* and the *New York Times Sunday Magazine,* we see Kelley affirming a dual commitment: to his craft and to black people. And in his collection of short stories and four novels—*A Different Drummer, A Drop of Patience* (1965), *dem* (1967), and *Dunfords Travels Everywheres* (1970)—we see his inventive genius at work exploring the Afro-American oral tradition and the complexity of interracial and intraracial color, sexual, and class relationships.

From *A Different Drummer* to *Dunfords Travels Everywheres* Kelley interweaves the histories of the Dunford and Bedlow families and their heritage as Afro-Americans from Africa and the South. Set in a mythical East South Central State in the Deep South, *A Different Drummer* introduces us to "the African," whose heroic spirit and deeds inform the legend of African blood; to Tucker Caliban, his great-great-grandson, whose personal act of liberation sparks the mass exodus of blacks from the South; and to Wallace Bedlow (in the story "Cry for Me"), whose flight to his brother Carlyle in New York culminates in popular acclaim as an authentic blues man. Of the sixteen stories in *Dancers on the Shore,* six focus on the middle-class Dunfords; five on the working-class Bedlows and their relatives; and one on young Peter Dunford and Mance Bedlow. The other four stories trace the fate of General Dewey Willson's black descendants. In *A Drop of Patience,* a fable on American neglect of the creative gift of black jazz musicians, Ludlow Washington, a blind genius of jazz from the mythical town of New Mersails, cracks up after discovering his exploitation and betrayal by the racism and commercialism of New Yorkers, especially the white woman he loved. After his recovery, he turns his back on their belated recognition and finds a small church in need of a good musician. *dem* is a fable on the soap-opera lives of whites in which the sins of the fathers are visited upon their children. Mitchell Pierce, a white advertising executive, suffers the retribution of nonwhites for centuries of violence, injustice, and rape when he is faced with raising a black child, the surviving fraternal twin that his wife delivers after being impregnated within a short time by both him and her maid's black boyfriend, Calvin Coolidge "Cooley" Johnson. And in *Dunfords Travels Everywheres*, Kelley's imaginative and stylistic tour de force of parody and irony, Chig Dunford's quest to discover his own nature and the nature of the world leads him and the reader on a circular journey from European cities to Harlem and from the present world of his struggle with a deadly white consciousness to an awakening black consciousness of his African and Southern past.

Kelley parodies the characters, structure, and style of James Joyce's *Finnegan's Wake* and the mythology of the Eddas, one of Joyce's Scandinavian sources, in *Dunfords Travels Everywheres*.[23] Similar to the twins Shem and Shaun in *Finnegan's Wake*, Chig and Carlyle, as the fusion of their names to Chiglyle suggests, are blood brothers though they live on different levels of class and color consciousness. Strucfurally, the adventures of the Harvard-miseducated, racially unawakened Chig Dunford in Europe contrasts with the Harlem adventures of his double, the street-educated racially aware Carlyle Bedlow. Kelley's book, like Joyce's, begins its circular pattern with the protagonist asleep and unaware of the personal, historical, and mythic significance of racism and his alma mater, mother Africa. In chapters 1 through 7, set in a mythical European country where by law the people are segregated by the blue-red or yellow-red clothing they wear each day, we are introduced to Chig and his five expatriate traveling companions. Wendy, who is believed to be white and is pursued by Chig, and Lane, Wendy's former lover who resents interracial affairs, stand out as the group discusses the recent assassination of John F. Kennedy and the turbulent race relations in the United States. Thus Kelley displaces Joyce's riddle of the universe with the problem of the color line and interracial sex, experimenting with different combinations of several languages to establish the ambiguity and universality of the problem.

Chapters 8 and 9 introduce us to Chig's sleeping black consciousness, dramatized by a lecture on "the foxnoxious bland stimili, the infortunelessnesses of circusdances which weak to worsen the phistorystemical intrafricanical firmly structure of our distinct coresins: The Blafringo-Arumericans,"[24] presented in the professorial voice of Chig's "hId-self." The Aesopian proverb that a fool will cross a female ox (a European woman) with a male elephant (an African man) reinforces the theme that Afro-Americans should not subscribe to racial stereotypes about integration nor sacrifice their biological and cultural kinship with Africa and each other for integration with Euro-Americans. In chapters 10 through 16 the professorial voice continues its efforts to awaken Chig to his "chiltural rackage," relating the sexual adventures of Carlyle with a Harlem dentist's wife to illustrate that Euro-Americans have "lied about everything" and that it is not enough for middle-class blacks to accumulate money; they ought to affirm a commitment to their race, too.

The odd-numbered chapters 17 through 29 trace Chig's actual and surreal return to New York on a ship he believes is also transporting African slaves, while the even-numbered chapters 18 through 28 trace Carlyle's success at hustling the devil to save his friend Hondo Johnson's soul. In chapter 30, Carlyle, Hondo, and Chig are all in Jack O'Gee's Golden Grouse Bar and Restaurant, but instead of acknowledging kinship with Carlyle and Hondo, Chig falls asleep listening to a radio program that triggers dreams about the adventures of two Afro-American Texas Rangers, C. Turtom and S. Rabisam. Their daring exploits are fused in sound and sense with elements of the fabled African race between the Turtle and the Hare and the Euro-American children's rhyme "Jack and Jill" ("We vphought t'aFoetofinish, n Jackel O'Chill vrain off wi dPrixpost"), suggesting the need for a historical awareness of the greed and deceit of whites, who seek to destroy the unity and bleach the souls of blacks. Because Chig, "dDreamer boy," will not wake up to the lessons of the collective unconsciousness of his race, "Rabbit" and "Turtle" send him around again to "dProfessay's Lecturall" for lesson thirty-one.

Kelley, like Joyce, manipulates language and standard orthography to express the sound and sense of things on several levels of consciousness. The predominantly standard English that opens the novel represents the conscious level; and a highly phoneticized form of neoblack English, "d'Tongue o'Now Afreequerquenne," reflects the semiconscious level of both Chig and Carlyle ("seeing z'Mr. Chacallo vbegin tclose dGap in dOwnderstanding o'dFront o'h Experience n tspy dRelayshinship betwin hId-self n dhat"). Equally intriguing, a comic mixture of pidgin English, Spanish, and French that dramatizes the "Languish" of "The Blafringro-Arumericans," the first generation of Africans transported as slaves to the New World, taps Chig's unconscious mind, the dream realm of the black professor, and "the New Africurekey Univercity Family."

Kelley wryly reconstructs the poetic and prose Eddas—the mythology, ethical conceptions, and heroic lore of the ancient North—to contrast with his reconstruction of African mythology and to "telve int'd Relationship betwine weSelfs n d'cold Glareys o'Stunangle" (p. 89). What the Vedas are for India, and the *Odyssey* and *Iliad* are for Greece, the Eddas signify for Scandinavia. Norse and Greek mythologies embody the deepest truths of pagan peoples. From them comes much of the spiritual, ethical, and intellectual Indo-European heritage of white Americans.[25] Allusions to the treachery and fratricide of Odin, the father of the gods, Balder, his son and the most beloved god, who is killed with mistletoe by his brother Hoder in a plot devised by Loki, Odin's foster brother,[26] link the fall or assassination of a beloved American president to the prophecy of the "Iklanders": "the misaltoetumle of the leader of La Colon y de la Thour Yndia Company, Prestodont Eurchill Balderman, preachful as expected, L. Oki to fry" (p. 49). The northern origins and chilling life-destroying values of Odin and his descendants are symbolically contrasted with the equatorial origins and passionate life-giving values of Africa and her descendants:

> The sun beaming the source of all emcergy hit your big, blrown Mamal's tights and heirs and bolleys and moletains most evory afternoun around the pool at the Lake Vik Hotel. There you got your birthbin. There she dalied, darkened by day, greener dang rain, ho-honnesbig at the rounded buttem, bowed at the bubberia, pinched in the reygion of her tawny stem-buck too. You couldn't wait to get a.m. from school to lay wid-her. You couldn't wait to get the homme to skul so you could run in the strait for her expression in flesh; which deskription inner mind, in contraced to the Momhoo hauting the rocker on the northside of Mudderterrorhanian Aye., N.E.W., bids fire to apall. (Pp. 53–54)

Africans and their descendants, says Chig's dramatized alter ego, should beware that their physical and creative energies not be used for fuel to warm the descendants of "W. Oten-Chiltman," whose legends and lives glorify death and destruction: "Almist since the bin of bawn, he lobbed them to lobe a heart for the frigg of it, unrevel a ball for the yarn of it, burn a barn for the beef of it, but a hut for the strut of it, incise a shoe for the sock of it, heat a sheat for the wick of it. That and Alotoflikkyr and Heshappy, Mr. Chilyle" (p. 54). Unfortunately, many readers will probably find that it takes too much time and effort to understand Kelley's word games and multilevel puns, and will not adequately appreciate the richness of his comic imagination and ironic reconstruction of myth.

More realistic and therefore more accessible, but no less impressive in its fabulation, is *A Different Drummer*, which has a double plot and dual protagonists. The first plot concerns the moral awakening and personal revolt of Tucker Caliban against the control of whites over his life, and the second focuses on the education of whites, especially young Harry Leland and Dewey Willson III, about the nature of racism and the meaning of courage and self-reliance. Divided into eleven chapters, the novel opens in documentary fashion with an excerpt from *The Thumb-Nail Almanac* of 1961, establishing the time of the current action, 1957, and the history of a mythical East South Central State: the home of the Willsons, the most important white aristocrats in the Gulfport area, and the Calibans, their former slaves.

Told predominantly in retrospective narrative and flashbacks through multiple white narrators, the novel proper begins with the ritual gathering of the townsmen of Sutton to hear old Mr. Harper retell the legend of the African as an explanation of Tucker Caliban's radical transformation and the mysterious exodus within three days of most of the blacks in the state. The next two chapters reflect the impact of this development on the consciousness of Harry Leland, a white farmer, and Harold, his eight-year-old son. The fifth chapter, "One Long Ago Autumn Birthday," dramatizes the nature of the modern Caliban-Willson family relationship through the punishment young Tucker unjustly suffers because of the failure of moral courage of his companion Dewey Willson III. The next five chapters then explore the consciousness of the Willsons: Dymphna, the seventeen-year-old daughter who was influenced by the moral example of Tucker's wife, Bethrah; Dewey III, the eighteen-year-old son who grew up with Tucker; Camille, the mother and wife who stood patiently by her husband after his loss of faith and courage; and David, the Southern journalist who lost the courage to continue his struggle against the legacy of racism until Tucker Caliban's methodical destruction of his farm on the old Willson plantation freed them both. The book closes with Mr. Harper consoling Dewey III after his failure to stop the lynching of the Reverend Bradshaw, a West Indian black nationalist leader from the North and his father's former fellow activist against racism. In the final episode young Harold Leland ironically fantasizes that the revelry of the lynching ritual he hears is a party celebrating Tucker Caliban's return to his farm.

A Different Drummer affirms self-reliance and moral courage as the imperatives for social change. The legend of the heroism of Tucker Caliban's African ancestor and the myth of his blood as the explanation for Tucker's personal courage contrast with the failure of courage of the Willsons, whose name is ironic, and society in general to affirm the natural rights of man. The Willson family's story is told primarily through David's diary entries from 1931 to 1957 concerning the Calibans. Tucker's act of conscience in liberating himself and his family from a slave and paternalistic past inspires Dewey and David Willson as well as other blacks to assert their right to dignity and freedom. "Anyone, anyone can break loose from his chains," thinks David, who is morally reawakened after reading how Tucker salted his land, burned down his house, and left for the North with his family. "That courage, no matter how deeply buried, is always waiting to be called out. All it needs is the right coaxing, the right voice to do that coaxing, and it will come roaring like a tiger."[27] The day is coming fast, as the Reverend Bradshaw realizes and his lynching at the end of the novel symbolizes, when the Tuckers of the world will not need leaders to free them, for they will realize that they can and must free themselves.

William Melvin Kelley is clearly less ambivalent toward American individualism than most contemporary black novelists. His most striking theme is that the road to freedom and fulfillment is through self-reliance. For most blacks, as illustrated in *Dunfords Travels Everywheres* and *A Different Drummer*, this means the courage to affirm one's ethnic and personal identity as Afro-American and to trust oneself rather than institutions and organizations to achieve greater independence, growth, and well-being. In giving form to this moral and social vision Kelley is most original in his postmodern adaptation and fusion of traditional narrative modes such as myth, legend, and fable. His skill and sensitivity in filtering Tucker Caliban's story through the consciousness of multiple white narrators, and his dazzling creation of interrelated linguistic and mythological systems in *Dunfords Travels Everywheres* are his chief contributions to the tradition of the Afro-American novel.

RONALD L. FAIR (1932–)

Like Kelley, Ronald Fair is best known for his adaptation of such traditional forms as legend and fable. Born on October 27, 1932, in Chicago to transplanted Mississippi plantation workers who were proud to be black, Fair was educated in the city's public schools. His interest in writing was nurtured by one of his black English teachers. After finishing high school and serving three years as a hospital corpsman in the navy, he returned to Chicago to attend business school and from 1955 to 1966 worked as a court reporter. Influenced by the slave narratives and the example of Richard Wright, he continued to write in his spare time, publishing his first pieces in the *Chicago Daily Defender, Chat Noir Review, Negro Digest,* and *Ebony*. He has taught at Columbia College in Chicago and at Northwestern and Wesleyan universities. His publications include two novels—*Hog Butcher* (1966) and *We Can't Breathe* (1972)—and three novellas: *Many Thousand Gone* (1965) and "Jerome" and "World of Nothing" in *World of Nothing* (1970), for which he won a National Institute of Arts and Letters Award in 1971.

Hog Butcher and *We Can't Breathe* reveal the continuing appeal of traditional realism and naturalism to some contemporary black novelists. Told by a third-person omniscient author-narrator who closely identifies with the vitality and integrity of his ten-year-old protagonist, *Hog Butcher*, which is set in Chicago in 1965, is the story of Wilfred Robinson's courage in testifying against police who mistakenly killed his hero, Cornbread, as a burglar and tried with the collusion of "officialdom" to cover up their mistake. But as the voice of the author-narrator in the intervening critical vignettes that give historical resonance to the novel makes clear, it is also the story of the wave of poor but proud, vibrant black people who migrated to Chicago from the South in the 1940s and 1950s to fulfill their dreams. For Ronald Fair, who borrows the title of his novel from Carl Sandburg's poem "Chicago" and draws heavily on his years as a court reporter to give verisimilitude to his courtroom scene, the white Chicago system is the hog butcher that cuts out the souls of blacks. But the protagonist symbolizes the vitality that the author sees "blossoming among the stone and steel weeds of Chicago. There is, among the young," he says, "among the undeformed, the uncorrupted, the uncompromised, a desire to change the way of life."[28]

Like *Hog Butcher*, *We Can't Breathe*, a semiautobiographical novel, reveals the bitter-sweet memories of growing up black in Chicago. The protagonists of both are young black boys who symbolize the author's faith in the future. In contrast, however, to the four-week time span of the events in *Hog Butcher*—which spotlights the friendship of Earl, Wilfred, and Cornbread, the shooting of Cornbread, and the coroner's inquest into the shooting—the time span in *We Can't Breathe* is five years in the life of nine-year-old Ernest Johnson, with whom the author closely identifies on all levels. The first-person narrative traces Ernie's childhood efforts to survive with self-respect as he moves into a new neighborhood on the South Side where his friends and extended family are trapped by centuries of injustice and destroyed by racism.

Fair's three novellas are more postmodern than his novels. Although *Many Thousand Gone*, his first and most popular book, is not self-consciously innovative in its exploration of the creative process, it is less realistic and more concerned with ideas and ideals than traditional social realism. Designed primarily for a black general audience during the black arts movement, it is explicitly identified in the subtitle as a fable, but the title, borrowed from a black spiritual and folksaying, and internal evidence reveal that it is actually a blend of legend, fable, and slave narrative. Rooted in the historical black experience of slavery and exploitation in the South, it is the brief, simple account of the heroic deeds of Granny Jacobs and Josh Black; its moral and political lessons, ironically dramatized in the closing episode, are that blacks must free themselves. Set entirely in the mythical town of Jacobsville, Mississippi, the plot is melodramatic, episodic, and highly compressed in time, covering the years 1832 to 1963 in fewer than 120 pages. The characters are one-dimensional stock figures with Granny Jacobs, the noble black matriarch, Jesse, the messianic black prince, and Josh Black, the bold black avenger, as the most striking; and the point of view is a mixture of third-person omniscient and dramatic. Although the protagonist is actually the whole black community rather than any single member of that community, the theme and structure of the book, like the slave narratives, are concerned with the journey from bondage to freedom. In Part 1 of the two-part narrative, the emphasis is on the slave past and the legacy of black matriarchy and the hope of being freed by a black messiah like Little Jesse, the last of the "first-borns who were genuinely Negro" and Granny Jacob's great-grandson. In Part 2 the focus shifts to the radical present, the emergence of black unity and militancy among the young, and the false hope of the older black generation in a white emancipator, the president, whose federal investigators are outsmarted and arrested by the local sheriff.

The catalysts for the emergent unity and militancy in the black community are the arrival of a clandestine subscription to *Ebony*, a popular pictorial black Northern magazine that was scheduled to print a story on Jesse's success in Chicago as an author, and the twenty-five-year-old secret the community shares with Granny Jacobs about how she staged a mock funeral for her great-grandson in order to help him to escape to "God's country" so that he could be free and help his people. By its celebration of the achievements of a growing black urban middle class, *Ebony*, which is essentially conservative and integrationist in its politics, fosters a revolutionary sense of group pride and solidarity among the blacks of Jacobs County. Consequently, when three teenage black girls are raped and butchered to death, the town's 3,000 blacks revolt, burning down the town and killing many of the 400 white men who were on their way to "roast Granny and Preacher Harris alive." Fair ends his American fable ironically as well as apocalyptically with Josh watching the jail holding the federal investigators go up in flames before casually unlocking the door "to set his emancipators free."[29]

Of the short works, "Jerome" and "World of Nothing" are the most innovative in design and ideas. Short and pithy, "Jerome" is a parable of the Black Jesus and an allegorical story of the nature of evil in the modern world, especially the Catholic church. Called "Little Jesus," "Black Night of Christ," and "a true son of God" by the entire neighborhood where he spread the word of God, sometimes just by his presence, five-year-old Jerome is the bastard child of thirteen-year-old Lula and Father Jennings, an ironic twist on the parents of Jesus Christ. Driven by Lula's obsession with devils, by their desecration of the church with their lust for each other, and by Father Jennings's coveting the rector's job, they feel accused by Jerome and see him as the devil. Jerome, who is troubled that he "sensed as much evil in his Father's house," sets fire to the church and is killed by a hysterical Lula and Father Jennings. The reverence of Thelma, the old witch, for Jerome in the prologue, story proper, and epilogue reinforces the meaning of her dramatic scream at the end. " 'They've killed the Black Jesus.' "[30]

In "World of Nothing" Fair returns to his basically naturalistic vision of blacks trapped in the South Side ghetto of Chicago. But this time he is much more imaginative and satirical as he creates a kaleidoscope of sixteen vignettes that capture the pathos and wry humor of place and people. He does this chiefly through the effective use of verbal and situational irony. The first-person anonymous narrator-protagonist, who is a sometime writer and most-of-the-time drunk, tells us he lives in the World of Nothing:

> Nothing is a state of black. It's a world where the only white face is an occasional policeman or the peddler or the store owners or those goddamn insurance men. But mostly it's all black. It's even black when the sun beats down on our shiny faces; the rays seem to soak into our world and shatter and form a black cloud that hangs like a gloomy continuation of night symbolic of the segregated quarters wherein we eat and laugh and love and cry and live and die. (P. 65)

In this world he shares a two-room apartment in The Place of Peace Hotel with his buddy and fellow wino, Red Top, with whom he once traveled to the white world, a World of Even Less. "It doesn't seem right," says the narrator, "that a people can have so much and still have nothing. We could show them but they don't want any part of us so we'll just keep it to ourselves and have something of real substance from practically nothing of value" (p. 80).

"World of Nothing" is more playful in tone and more artful in construction than Fair's other narratives. This postmodern artifice is apparent in the colorful, wry names and in the two- to three-page descriptions of the places and people in the narrative. As we accompany the narrator, our guide, on his picaresque journey through the World of Nothing, we meet such fantastic people as Junkie Thaddeus Popcorn Jones, the neighborhood junkie who collects $5,000 in an insurance swindle after being pushed in front of a wealthy, drunk white man's car; Miss Joanne Joanne, the whorehouse madam's beautiful protégée who likes animals but hates junkies so much that she pushes Junkie Jones in front of a car because he asked her for a nickel; Miss Luhester Homan, a happy, unmarried welfare mother of five children by different men and "one of the most highly respected ladies in the neighborhood"; Preacher Robinson and Sister Grace of the fundamentalist tent church; and Johnnie Sweepstakes, a gambling man who "lost at policy, at horses, at blackjack, at poker, and even at matching and pitching pennies with the kids." At the end of the novella, Red Top, the narrator's friendly, popular roommate, finds meaning in his life through "tent church" religion and leaves the World of Nothing, causing the protagonist anxiety over his own loss to the world of work and conformity until he finds a new roommate. "This guy," he tells us, "is just like me: Buy what you want and beg what you need. It's great to meet someone who is alive. Oh God, it feels good to be alive again. To be free to be alive again" (p. 131). Similar to *Many Thousand Gone* and "Jerome," "World of Nothing" closes on a wry note of regeneration.

Fair's novels, in other words, illustrate that although a wide range of earlier narrative modes are always present in the tradition of the Afro-American novel, certain experiments with combinations of these earlier forms and conventions seem most appropriate to the tenor of the changing times. Whereas *Hog Butcher* and *We Can't Breathe* are evidence of the perennial presence of realism and naturalism, the more intriguing *Many Thousand Gone* is clearly related in structure and tone to the Aesopian fable, the legend, and the slave narrative. By their symbolic tendency toward allegory, "Jerome" and "World of Nothing" involve the reader in the postmodern process of fabricating the meaning of reality for oneself. "Jerome" draws on both the sacred and profane traditions of the parables of Jesus and the tales of Boccacio, and "World of Nothing" draws on satiric and picaresque forms.

Fabulation, Romance, and Fantasy

Modern and postmodern blends of romance and fantasy, as in expatriate William Demby's *Catacombs* (1965), stress the artificiality of reality and the reality of artifice. In *The Catacombs,* for example, Demby sets his quasi-autobiographical, nonrepresentational narrative in the tomb and womb of Christianity in Rome and casts himself as an expatriate narrator-writer whose manipulation of diary entries and newspaper clippings, as well as of his allusions to painting, sculpture, and the cinema is designed to make us share in his vision that we are all nothing more than the products of our creative imagination and will to change. Questioning the effectiveness of conventional language and social realism to discover the truth of the apocalyptic tendencies in Western culture and American life, some contemporary black fabulators, in other words, have experimented self-consciously with dream visions, stylized characters, and linguistic forms to illuminate the burden and blessing of Afro-American double-consciousness. Whereas the quest of some protagonists is for a personal and public wholeness that reconciles conflicting values, including lust and love, the quest of others is for a physical or spiritual heaven or hell.

In *There Is a Tree More Ancient Than Eden* (1973) and *The Bloodworth Orphans* (1977), for example, Leon Forrest draws heavily on the symbolic language of the Bible, folk sermon, and black vernacular to reveal the trials and tribulations of bearing witness to the sorrows of life, the pains of death, and the promise of rebirth. Steeled to the challenge of life primarily by the folk wisdom of his Aunt Hattie Breedlove, Nathaniel Witherspoon, the principal narrator in both novels, bears witness to the saga of the Bloodworths, a saga highlighted by nightmarish rituals of rape, miscegenation, bastardy, incest, parricide, abortion, abandonment, and adoption. "We ought to rise above being scandalized and shamefaced because of our past" is the hard-learned lesson of both books. Because "we all orphans of the wreckage," we ought to accept the frailty of the flesh and act on the faith that "you make of your name what you make of your center being and life."[31] The two books, of which the first is the more controlled and engaging, plumb the depths of the surreal lives of their combined cast of more than three dozen characters, several of whom appear in both books, to chart an allegorical journey from hell to heaven, from the Salem Cup-Overflowing Tabernacle to the River Rock of Eden Baptist Church, from Southern Trees Bearing Strange Fruit to the Tree of Knowledge and the Tree of Life. But because Forrest's manipulation of points of view among several apparently unreliable narrators, his overwrought allusive structure, and his rapturous, surrealistic style, like Demby's, overwhelm all but the most patient of serious readers, we will examine more closely the artifice and achievement of two better known black fabulators.

JOHN EDGAR WIDEMAN (1941–)

The lower frequencies of an Afro-American tradition, oral and literary, were significantly muted in the life and work of John Wideman before the black power movement. Neither in largely black Washington, D. C., where he was born on June 14, 1941, nor at white Oxford University, where as a Rhodes Scholar he was formally trained in English literature, did he read Richard Wright and other black writers. His education in black literature came after his graduation in 1963 from the University of Pennsylvania, where he was awarded both a Ben Franklin Fellowship and a Thouron Fellowship for Creative Writing, and after his acceptance in 1966 of a Kent Fellowship for Creative Writing at the University of Iowa. With this formal academic background, it is not surprising that the early influences on Wideman's craftsmanship were James Joyce and T. S. Eliot, whom he first read in high school, and Henry Fielding and Laurence Sterne, whom he studied at New College, Oxford. It was not until 1967, after the publication of his first novel, *A Glance Away*, and after he started teaching black literature courses at the University of Pennsylvania, that he began to read slave narratives, black folklore, the novels of Wright and Ellison as well as Toomer's *Cane*. The vision and experimentation of these writers, he states in an interview, were important in the development of his Afrocentric aesthetic, for it awakened in him "a different sense of self-image and the whole notion of a third world." He also says: "If there is any single book I learned a hell of a lot from, it's *Tristram Shandy*. . . . I hope that I have learned from the nonrepresentational school about fantasy and playing around with different forms. The novel started out with these two tendencies—realism and fantasy."[32]

In part because of the conflict between his ethnic background and his formal training in literature, Wideman's five novels (*A Glance Away* [1967], *Hurry Home* [1970], *The Lynchers* [1973], *Hiding Place* [1981], and *Sent for You Yesterday* [1983]) and his collection of stories (*Damballah* [1981]) reveal a tension between realistic material and experimentation with form and style, especially stream-of-consciousness techniques and black speech. In *A Glance Away*, Wideman says, "I am going to school to various other writers, using other's techniques, but also trying out some things that I hope are original."[33] Eliot's Eurocentric influence is apparent in the mood, style, and characterization of this first novel, which is a quasi-parable on the resurrection of Edward Lawson, the thirty-year-old black protagonist who returns to Philadelphia on Easter Sunday, April 20, from a drug rehabilitation center in the South only to suffer the pain and guilt of his mother's death. The person driven by his own painful memories to get him through the night is Robert Thurley, a fictionalized J. Alfred Prufrock, a middle-aged white homosexual professor of comparative literature who pursues black lovers and for whom "Eliot was . . . the poet of weariness, of old age."[34] Although Eliot's specter hangs over most of the book, in the final ten pages Wideman displaces dialogue with the alternating inner thoughts of Eddie, Robert, and Brother Small, their albino friend, as they sit in spiritual communion around a small fire in a hobo camp.

Equally Prufrockian in characterization but more nonrepresentational and experimental in time structure and point of view is *Hurry Home*. Whereas Thurley, the ineffectual, suffering intellectual in *A Glance Away*, wanders through the streets and after-hours clubs of Philadelphia, Charles Webb, the guilt-ridden white writer and intellectual of *Hurry Home*, wanders through the museums, cafés, and beaches of Spain in a vain search for redemption from the black son he has never seen because he had abandoned his black mistress not knowing she was pregnant. Using interior monologue, letters, journal entries, rapid shifts in time and point of view, surreal vignettes, mythic associations, linguistic puns, and frequent allusions to writers and painters, especially Hieronymus Bosch and his triptych of "The Adoration of the Magi," Wideman is concerned in his second novel with the thin line between reality and fantasy, "between individual and collective experience which permits one to flow into the other."[35] Going to get a haircut for his graduation, Cecil Otis Braithwaite, the protagonist who, aided by the sacrifices of his girlfriend Esther and his scrub-woman mother, is only the second of his race to graduate from the university law school, is symbolically rejected by the black community as a "Humbug magistraitassed uppitty nigger."[36] He, in turn, deserts Esther on their wedding night to go to Spain and Africa, seeking to understand his double-consciousness and to accommodate both the gospels and the Easter song, the "St. John Passion," of Heinrich Schutz. The question that Cecil asks throughout the book is, Why did you do that? As he actually and imaginatively travels back in the past for answers, his personal experience is conflated into the collective history of his race. But after three years of wandering through the corridors of time and foreign countries, reconstructing and reliving the journey of his race from Africa to America, he hurries home in the spring to work in a hair straightening parlor, to rejoin his wife, and to dream. "To go back into one's past," Wideman states, "is in fact dreaming. What is history except people's imaginary recreation."[37] Thus Cecil's actual past and his dream past, like his personal and racial identities, become merged in the course of the novel.

Although the ambiguities of the imagination and of the relationship between blacks and whites in America are common themes in Wideman's first three novels, *The Lynchers* is the most intriguing blend of realism and surrealism. Its primary theme is that the historical social realities of race relations in America are driving blacks and whites to apocalyptic attitudes and actions. At the center of the novel is the destruction of the black Wilkerson family—Orin "Sweetman" and Bernice, the parents, and Thomas, their son—and a plan conceived by Willie "Littleman" Hall to lynch a white cop in order to release black people from a fear of death at the hands of whites and to assert a new vision of reality. Introduced by twenty pages of quotations from documents that immerse the reader in the historical record of the use of lynching as a ritual of brutal racial power, the novel proper is divided into three major parts whose chronological time span is less than a month but whose psychological span is years.

Set in the 1960s on the South Side of Philadelphia, Part 1 plunges the reader into a sea of internal and external events that reveal the debris of Orin's and Bernice's lives and the distress that drives Thomas to risk participating in the lynch plan. In Part 2 Wideman continues to experiment with a wide range of techniques—dream fragments, interior monologue, flashbacks, black vernacular, rapid shifts from third- to first-person narration, and overlapping time frames—to introduce us to the details of the plan, the experiences that led Littleman to conceive it, and the mixture of black history and revolutionary rhetoric he uses to recruit his three irresolute, mutually distrustful accomplices. The plan is to kill a pimping white cop's black whore and to have the community publicly lynch him for her death, symbolically liberating the community from oppression and defining themselves in the process "as fighters, free, violent men who will determine the nature of the reality in which they exist." The "plan's as simple as death," says Littleman. "When one man kills it's murder. When a nation kills murder is called war. If we lynch the cop we will be declaring ourselves a nation."[38] The climax of the external events occurs in Part 2 when Littleman, while making an inflammatory speech on the steps of a black junior high school, is severely beaten by the police, but the internal climax does not come until Part 3 when Wilkerson's consciousness merges with the daughter of the lynchers' intended first victim. Part 3 also reveals how the lynch plan is completely aborted after Wilkerson's father is arrested for killing his best friend; how the protagonist himself is shot in a desperate assertion of independence by Rice, an accomplice; and how Littleman dies in the hospital after a futile effort to recruit a young black hospital orderly, Alonzo, whose confusion and blind rage represent the revolutionary potential of the next generation. More important than the failure of the lynch plan, then, are the social realities that impinge on the consciousness of the characters and influence their existential choices, which are, in a sense, parodies of the revolutionary identities forged in political struggle that Frantz Fanon so brilliantly outlines in *The Wretched of the Earth.*

Wideman, in other words, is primarily concerned with delineating the reciprocal influence of reality on the imagination and the imagination on the reality of his characters. The past and present flow together in the bitter-sweet memories of Wilkerson's parents as they sit across from each other in the kitchen:

> Pocked walls breathing sourly, patient mirrors of everything and if peeled layer by layer paint to paper to paper to paint to paint you would see old lives crowded as saints in the catacombs. Their children's hand prints crawling up the wall. The low border when it was a third leg to hold them up, the grease streaks from the boys' slicked down heads as they leaned back cockily on spindly legged chairs sneaking smokes and trading lies around the kitchen table, up near crease of ceiling and wall, splash of roach where she told Thomas not to squash them even if he could reach that high. Once blue, once yellow, hopelessly white, blue again, now the rosette paper meant for somebody's living room.... She realized how easily it could all disappear. Everywhere in the neighborhood buildings were being torn down. (P. 31)

Of the four avenging angels—Graham Rice, a neurotic, spineless janitor; Leonard Saunders, a street-hardened post office worker; Thomas Wilkerson, an ineffectual dreamer and junior high school teacher; and Littleman, the crippled, silver-tongued messenger of historical truth and the mastermind of the lynching plan—Wilkerson and Littleman are Wideman's symbols of the modern intellectual man. In contrast to Wilkerson, Littleman has strong convictions and faith in his plan to change reality. " 'Are you still so unconvinced?' " he asks Wilkerson. " 'Why is it so much easier for you to doubt than believe?' " (p. 113). But both, as Wideman illustrates by juxtaposing the political and psychological significance of the lynch rope in America, are men of ideas rather than action. Whereas Littleman needs Wilkerson as an intellectual and revolutionary disciple,

Wilkerson needs Littleman as a surrogate for the father he loves and hates because his life seemed so accidental and shapeless.

As the omniscient narrator glides in and out of third- and first-person points of view, Wideman compels us to become intimately involved with the characters, their frustrations and their existential choices. Internal and external events merge in Sweetman's mind in the opening domestic scene:

He would call her but if it is morning she may be asleep and perhaps she slept right through and I can tell her any lie, choose the decent hour I came in just too tired so went to sleep downstairs on the couch. Even as he forms a probable fiction he knows she will be sitting in the kitchen, aware of everything. And she is and she asks why did he bother to come home for the hour he did. He wants more from her. He wants her calling him out of his name, calling him *Sweetman*, treating him like he's still in the street or like she wants him gone. (P. 30).

Wideman then quickly shifts to Bernice's thoughts and feelings about the emptiness in her kitchen and her life, about her husband drinking himself to death, ashamed to face her, and her getting "older, tireder and poorer." Next we see and hear Sweetman on his way before sunup to wrestle garbage cans and chase rats, rapping with other sanitation engineers, including his best friend Childress.

Later, Wideman encourages our sympathy for his protagonist, who is reflecting over the pages of his appointment book:

Were there only two choices? Either cage time in the red lines that marched across the page or like his father in his lost weekends abandon any illusion of control. Littleman believed all men were trapped. No choice existed except to reverse or destroy the particular historical process which at a given time determines the life of individual men. He would see my father and me as equally unredeemable. Perhaps he is right. I believe in his plan. It may free men for an instant, create a limbo between prisons. But can the instant be extended? Can it support life and a society? I don't think Littleman cares. I don't think my father cared when he felt the need to escape. (P. 71)

By the end of the novel the reader's sympathies have shifted several times among the characters. And though he sympathizes with Littleman's historical imperatives and existential choices, Wideman, as the tragic denouement illustrates, identifies more closely with his protagonist's internal changes, especially his moral and political decision to sabotage the plan.

The Homewood trilogy marks the culmination of Wideman's move from a Eurocentric to a fundamentally Afrocentric tradition, his coming home as it were in the form and style of an extended meditation on history: oral and literary, personal and social. *Damballah*, the collection of twelve stories that the author calls long overdue letters to his imprisoned younger brother, Robby, invokes the ancestral gods of Africa in the New World, especially Damballah Wedo, the venerable serpent god of paternity, as the spirit guides for his mythic ancestral journey. To invoke these gods, says Wideman, is "to stretch one's hand back to that time and to gather up all history into a solid contemporary ground beneath one's feet."[39] From the prefacing texts—letter to Robby, brief note on Damballah, and Begat Chart—and the opening legend of the passing on of the spirit of Damballah to Afro-Americans, the generic distinctions between history and fiction, novel and romance, orality and literariness collapse as Wideman blends epistle, legend, myth, fable, biography, and autobiography in a series of interdependent fictive constructs. The book concludes cyclically without closure with "The Beginning of Homewood," another letter to his brother. This letter is metafictional in that it is about the creative act of writing. Wideman explains that it began as a literary retelling of the family legend about how the family tree was planted on Bruston Hill in Homewood, the black community of Pittsburgh, Pennsylvania, with the arrival of Sybela Owens, their great-great-great-grandmother, who ran away from slavery with her white master's son, Charles Bell: "her lover, her liberator, her children's father. . . . " (p. 197). "This woman, this Sybela Owens, our ancestor," Wideman writes reflectively and ambivalently, "bore the surname of her first owner and the Christian name Sybela, which was probably a corruption of Sybil, a priestess pledged to Apollo. . . . On the plantation Sybela Owens was called Belle. Called that by some because it was customary for slaves to disregard the cumbersome, ironic names bestowed by whites, and rechristen one another in a secret, second language, a language whose forms and words gave substance to the captives' need to see themselves as human beings" (p. 195). The story, passed on orally by the women in the family, of her legendary urge for freedom as a runaway slave, her crime, corresponds in the author-narrator's consciousness to that of his imprisoned brother and fosters anxiety and ambivalence about his own freedom and success. Why not me, he asks: "Ask myself if I would have committed the crime of running away or if I would have stayed and tried to make the best of a hopeless situation. Ask if you really had any choice, if anything had changed in the years between her crime and yours" (p. 200).

The two novels, *Hiding Place* and *Sent for You Yesterday*, continue Wideman's meditation on the history of his family, home, and people. Its title borrowed from the black spiritual "There's No Hiding Place Down There," *Hiding Place* expands "Tommy," the imaginative rewriting of the story in *Damballah* that foregrounds Robert Wideman's actual involvement in a robbery attempt and murder, and reweaves it with the story of Mother Bess, the granddaughter of Mother Sybela and the oldest living family member. Through the interweaving of memory, reverie, and interior monologues as well as by the manipulation of black speech, music, and religion, Wideman reveals the sociopsychological process by which the gnarled old roots and wayward young branches of the Owens/Bell family tree strengthen and renew themselves together. Mother Bess, who is hiding from the world in the dilapidated ancestral home on Bruston Hill because of the loss of her only son and blues-singing husband, reluctantly shares her hiding place and spiritual wisdom with her great-grandson Tommy, who is running away from the police because he was an accomplice in a robbery attempt that resulted in murder. Reconciling their mutual ambivalence at the end of the novel, both find the resolve in themselves and each other to come out of hiding and return to confront the blueslike reality of Homewood and the world.

Its title borrowed from the blues song that Jimmy Rushing made popular, and its time structure influenced by Laurence Sterne's *Tristram Shandy*, *Sent for You Yesterday* is the long, sad song of Homewood and the contemporary inheritors of its blues legacy. Dividing the novel into three major sections ("The Return of Albert Wilkes," "The Courting of Lucy Tate," and "Brother"), Wideman, who is emotionally, psychologically, and morally close to the surnameless narrator, dances back and forth in time through dreams, memories, and reveries. He artfully yet ambivalently employs the rhythms of black speech and music, especially train symbolism, to reconstruct the blues legacy of Homewood to present and future generations of the French, Tate, and Lawson families. Spanning the years from 1941 to 1970, the novel begins in 1970 with the first-person narrator, christened "Doot" by his Uncle Carl French's best friend Brother Tate, looking back, like Tristram Shandy, to events before he was born. He remembers and affirms through stories he has heard over the years in Homewood that he is "linked to Brother Tate by stories, by his memories of a dead son, by my own memories of a silent scat-singing albino man who was my uncle's best friend."[40] Just as the untrained Brother Tate mysteriously embodies the blues spirit and piano-playing talent of Albert Wilkes, whose return after seven years to a rapidly declining Homewood results in the police blowing his brains out in the Tate home, the narrator, "In Brother's eyes

. . . grew up living not only my own life, but the one snatched from June-bug," Brother's son of the same age who died in a fire in 1941.

Brother Tate's sixteen-year silence in mourning for his son, his youthful ritual of playing chicken with oncoming trains, and his recurring dreams of trains, as well as Lucy Tate's storytelling quilt and the bone fragment from Albert Wilkes's skull that she saves signify, along with the blues, the keep-on-keeping-on lessons that the old Homewood people taught their young by example. As Lucy tells her lover and the narrator's uncle, Carl French, in the closing pages of the book:

> "They made Homewood. Walking around, doing the things they had to do. Homewood wasn't bricks and boards. Homewood was them singing and loving and getting where they needed to get. They made these streets. That's why Homewood was real once. Cause they were real. And we gave it all up. Us middle people. You and me, Carl. We got scared and gave up too easy and now it's gone. Just sad songs left. And whimpering. Nothing left to give the ones we supposed to be saving Homewood for. Nothing but empty hands and sad stories."
> (P. 198)

Nevertheless, Wideman closes the novel with a ray of hope as his principal narrator, Doot, begins responding to Smokey Robinson's "Tracks of My Tears" on the radio and fantasizing that Brother Tate was signaling to Albert Wilkes to begin playing the piano. Finally, Doot was "learning to stand, to walk, learning to dance" (p. 208).

The major underlying theme, then, in Wideman's novels is that what we think we are is at least as important as what we are. "From the very beginning," he says, "Western civilization has an idea of what black men are, and that idea has come down to us generation after generation, has distorted and made impossible some kinds of very human and basic interaction. The mechanics of that are both very frightening and very fascinating."[41] To explore the interior landscapes of his characters and the conflict between their ascribed and achieved identities as black men, Wideman, who also believes that racial memories exist in the imagination, draws on a wide variety of sources in his shift from a Eurocentric to a basically Afrocentric tradition. As in Demby's *Catacombs*, his innovative use of legend, myth, music, and painting in *A Glance Away, Hurry Home*, and *The Lynchers* gives resonance to the theme of double-consciousness in the tradition of the Afro-American novel. At the same time his use in the Homewood trilogy of Afrocentric terms for order to counterbalance the anxiety of Eurocentric influences in his experiment with time structure and point of view is paradigmatic of black postmodernists' double vision of contemporary black American experiences of reality.

CLARENCE MAJOR (1936–)

Clarence Major marches to a different drummer in the tradition of the Afro-American novel. Born on December 31, 1936, in Atlanta, Georgia, he was raised in Chicago. At twelve years old, "while writing crude little novels in school notebooks,"[42] he began exploring the literary landscape to stake out his claim for a writing career. In high school he read everything by Richard Wright and then turned to other black writers like Chester Himes, Willard Motley, and Frank Brown. While a student at the Armed Forces Institute in Wyoming in 1954, he sold his first story, "Ulysses, Who Slept Across from Me," and published his first collection of poetry, *The Fires That Burn in Heaven*. After military service he accepted a fellowship at the Art Institute of Chicago to pursue an equally serious interest in painting. "I think my experience with painting, the way that I learned to see the physical world of lines, color, and composition," Major told an interviewer, "definitely influenced my writing."[43] Since 1958 his poems, short fiction, and essays, all revealing an increasingly postmodernist concern for experimenting with language and form, have appeared in many literary and popular magazines. *Swallow the Lake*, one of his eight collections of poems, won a National Council of the Arts Award in 1970. Moving to New York City in 1966, he became an editor of *Journal of Black Poetry* from 1967 to 1970 and taught literature and creative writing at the Academy of American Poets in 1968, Brooklyn College in 1968–69, and Sarah Lawrence College in 1972–73. In addition to his eight collections of poetry, Major has edited three anthologies and published a book on Afro-American slang, a collection of essays, and four novels: *All-Night Visitors* (1969), *NO* (1973), *Reflex and Bone Structure* (1975), and *Emergency Exit* (1979).

Even though he has published in black magazines, edited the *Journal of Black Poetry*, and written the frequently anthologized "A Black Criterion," which calls for black poets to destroy the hold of white standards on their minds and work, he claims to have never been a black cultural nationalist.[44] Responding in 1973 to a question about the theme of that 1967 essay, he stated that he now found "repulsive the idea of calling for black writers to do anything other than what they each choose to do. . . . No style or subject should be alien to them. We have to get away from this rigid notion that there are certain topics and methods reserved for black writers. I'm against all that. I'm against coercion from blacks and from whites."[45] Like white Euro-American postmodernists Brautigan, Barthelme, and Sukenick, Major believes that the novel is a linguistic invention that exists on its own terms.[46] He is therefore concerned, he explains to an interviewer, with writing "one that takes on its own reality and is really independent of anything outside itself. . . . You begin with words and you end with words. The content exists in our minds. I don't think that it has to be a reflection of anything. It is a reality that has been created inside of a book. It's put together and exists finally in your mind."[47]

Major's thematic and structural movement beyond racial and political consciousness to a preoccupation with exploring the boundaries of language and imaginative consciousness can be traced in his four novels. Each is told by a first-person, unreliable, dramatized narrator-protagonist; each is more fragmented and discontinuous in structure than its predecessor; and each engages in linguistic play that blurs the line between the worlds of fantasy and social reality. *All-Night Visitors*, divided into two essentially surreal parts called "The Early Warning System" and "The Intricacy of Ruined Landscapes," is the episodic journey of Eli Bolton, a black, neurotic, twenty-eight-year-old Vietnam veteran. Driven to despair and alienation because of his loveless childhood in an orphanage and by witnessing the brutal rape and murder of children and women in Vietnam, Eli seeks to reconstruct his fragmented self and reconcile himself to the bizarre, equally violent reality of life in Chicago and New York. However, Major's impressionistic, occasionally lyrical celebration of sex, especially fellatio, as the primal expression of the narrator-protagonist's selfhood is predictably chauvinistic and provocative. The emphasis on sexual orgasm is less effective as an iconoclastic assault on puritan morality and the inhumanity of the Vietnam war than as a metaphorical expression of the link between sex and death. As a graphic, phenomenological description of sexual exploits with a series of all-night partners it also gives a problematic, existential meaning to Eli Bolton's quest for an integrated, responsible self, culminating in his loving and losing a young white VISTA worker. This climactic episode sets the stage for the symbolic resolution of the novel in which a dispossessed, pregnant Puerto Rican mother and her seven small children awaken Eli's will to translate human compassion into socially responsible action. Whether we believe this transformation, marked by a thunderstorm and Eli's declaration that he "had become firmly a man," depends on the degree to which, first, we interpret his experiences as surreal or real and to which, second, we accept the definition of contemporary black manhood that these experiences and the author imply.

NO, as critic O'Brien states, "moves beyond the first novel in insisting that the self is a phenomenon of language and the imagination rather than of actual experience, time, and place."[48] Divided into three parts whose titles—"influence of the moon," "the witch-burning," and "the mount meru"—suggest the surreal landscape of the novel, it is the retrospective narrative of the narrator-protagonist's growing awareness of his multifaceted, fluid identity, from his first sexual experiences as a child on a farm in Chickamauga, Mississippi, to his full self-awareness as an adult confronting a bull in a bullring in a Latin American country. "I didn't realize," the adult narrator-protagonist states in the opening expository paragraph of the novel, "that I was really trying to crash out of a sort of penal system in which I was born and grew up. Looking back though, I do realize that the activity of my life indicates merely the position of various political, social, and moral incidents."[49] Called such names as Moses Westby, the Boy, Junebug, and Nat Turnips, the protagonist, whom the reader has difficulty distinguishing from the father, Moses Westby, the guard, is not conscious of being on the road to self-determination until after he and other members of the family are shot in a suicidal rage by his father, and after he consummates his marriage to Oni Dunn. Constantly and abruptly shifting nominal, temporal, spatial, and cultural references create a confusing, uninhibited linguistic world that contrasts with the protagonist's personal and social sense of living in a prison.

Liberation comes only in the bullring, where touching the bull's head invested life with essence: "In other words I had to give meaning to it," he reflects; "and it had to contain courage. And at the same time I argued with the shallowness of it. With myself—with being." That this crucial event, including the protagonist's subsequent goring by the bull, actually occurred is called into question by the narrator-protagonist's anticlimactic statement: "When I woke up it was a full hour before I began to put the pieces of myself together again."[50] Whether the Hemingwayesque bullring episode of manly courage and grace in the face of danger and death is an actual or imagined experience is less important to the implied author and narrator-protagonist than the shaping influence it has on the ever-changing sense of self. Thus, in the closing line of the novel the narrator-protagonist is flying back to the United States toward what he ambiguously "believed to be a new beginning." For Major, then, as O'Brien notes, "the self is created by and emerges as the product of an imagination that can give it meaning and direction through language."[51]

Unquestionably, the most radically experimental and aesthetically challenging of Major's four novels are *Reflex and Bone Structure* and *Emergency Exit*. A composite of everything from a catalog of names from a telephone directory and police report to informational graphics and reproductions of abstract paintings, including a picture of the author in a cow pasture, *Emergency Exit* is a dazzling experiment in collage or montage writing. Major introduces us to the black Ingraham family and their largely white liberal neighbors in Inlet, Connecticut, through an elaborately extended metaphor—the juxtaposing and rapid succession of disparate fragments and images whose principal recurring motif is a doorway—which stresses, as the narrator states, that the ultimate *thingness* of our lives operates as a sort of *extended* metaphor.[52]

Less self-indulgent and more satisfying to the average reader's search for a sense of order is *Reflex and Bone Structure*. Divided into two melo-dramatically titled parts, "A Bad Connection" and "Body Heat," it is a metafictional mystery novel in what two critics call the antidetective tra-dition.[53] Major's narrator-protagonist is a fiction writer who discusses the process of constructing a mystery novel while he is simultaneously in-volved as suspect and detective in a murder mystery. "I want this book to be anything it wants to be," the narrator-protagonist tells us near the end of the first part of the novel, suggesting a close relationship between his aesthetic ideas and those of the author. "I want the mystery of the book to be an absolute mystery."[54] Earlier, Cora Hull, a black Greenwich Village actress who is involved in a love quadrangle that results in her murder, tells the nameless narrator-protagonist, "This book you're writing isn't nearly as strange as reality. The only way you're going to make any sense is to stick with the impossible. Any resemblance to the past or present should be purely accidental" (p. 56). From the opening page of the murder mystery, when scattered pieces of bodies are found, to its resolution on the final page when the narrator-protagonist identifies the bodies and himself as the murderer in a burst of short, staccato statements, we are witnesses to and participants in the creative energy of Major's fabulation and linguistic collage.

As the characters are developed in fragments, we are constantly re-minded by the narrator-protagonist that he is the self-conscious creator of this murder mystery and that he is "extending reality, not retelling it" (p. 49). In addition to the elusive, promiscuous Cora, who "needs variety, still a child at heart, still dreaming of the prince who won't ever come" (p. 39), and the narrator-protagonist, who is not only a writer and a suspect in the murder but also a detective paradoxically "trying to solve a murder. No, not a murder. It's a life" (p. 32), the other characters involved in the love quadrangle are Canada Jackson and Dale. Canada collects guns, seeks to improve the world, and "invents and reinvents the world as he wishes it to be." Because he "sometimes . . . can even handle Canada from the inside out" (p. 31), the narrator-protagonist feels emotionally and psychologically close to him. However, he hates Dale, whom he only vaguely delineates and jealously blows to bits with Cora:

> The fact that Dale really has little or no character doesn't help matters. I cannot help him if he refuses to focus. How can I be blamed for his lack of seriousness. And it isn't that he doesn't talk to me. He talks too much to me, really, and he plots too much, has too many secrets, leaves nothing in the open. Whatever it was about him that attracted Cora shall always remain a mystery to me. (P. 42)

Like the protagonist, we are challenged to either solve the mystery of the novel or accept it.

Unlike the structure of traditional detective novels, however, in which the solution of the murder is gradually achieved through the discovery of clues and the construction of a logical, lucid case against a single suspect, *Reflex and Bone Structure* is self-consciously fragmented, bizarre, and ambiguous. Parodying the traditional form of the detective novel and extending its possibilities, Major, like his narrator, is primarily concerned with comparing and contrasting the difficult task of the contemporary novelist and the detective in constructing a meaningful sense of self and others, both private and public, out of fragments. As critics McCaffery and Gregory state, "the detective and the antidetective . . . seek different answers which suggest the differing epistemological assumptions of the ages in which they were produced: One looks to eliminate the temporary description of an ordered universe, the other for an arbitrary fictional pattern that will not explain away mystery but will enable him to live with it."[55] The aesthetic bond between Major and his narrator-protagonist is apparent in the experimental style and form of the narrative as well as in the explicit internal references to the title of this novel and to the progtagonists of Major's first two novels.

In *Reflex and Bone Structure* Major breaks away from the black detective tradition of Rudolph Fisher and Chester Himes, and in each of his novels he does something new with language and form. Although Ralph Ellison's influence can be seen in the depiction of Moses Westby in *NO* and the nameless narrator-protagonist in *Reflex and Bone Structure*, Major, like Demby in *The Catacombs*, is more clearly influenced by the Euro-American postmodernist approach to writing than other contemporary black American novelists. Rejecting social realism and "militant fictionists," he states, with more disdain and dogmatism than understanding and tolerance, that "the deliberate effort, propaganda, has never helped anyone toward a larger sense of self. It has always been the novel or poem that begins from and spreads all across the entire human experience that ends liberating minds."[56] In defense of his own novels, he argues in "Formula or Freedom" that

> the novel *not* deliberately aimed at bringing about human freedom for black people has liberated as many minds as has the propaganda tract, if not more. This does not mean that a wholly human novel by a black writer necessarily becomes assimilable for just anybody. It does mean, though, that a work that takes long root in its author's experience—race being a part of that experience—not only makes sense anywhere in any language but also is likely either to raise hell or to lower heaven.[57]

In other words, Major correctly perceives that he and other black novelists who are committed to modernism and postmodernism can at least depend for support on a small, select readership. This readership does not, however, include many blacks, for whom neither the self nor life can be meaningfully or satisfactorily reduced to the blissful, liberating linguistic constructs of structuralist and poststructuralist theory that is advanced in books like Roland Barthes's *Pleasure of the Text*. Many white readers, as Frank Kermode suggests in *The Sense of an Ending*, also "find that there is an irreducible minimum of geometry—of humanly needed shape or structure—which finally limits our ability to accept the mimesis of pure contingency."[58] Nevertheless, judged on their own terms, all four of Major's novels extend the experimental tradition of the Afro-American novel by their subordination of race to a phenomenological exploration of sex and language as a ritualistic rebirth and affirmation of self. Their attempt to resolve Afro-American double-consciousness by the subordination of social truth and power for blacks to the expressionistic truth and freedom of the artist also extends this tradition.

Fabulation and Satire

Drawing on their sense of the profound ironies and blueslike absurdity of the 1960s and 1970s, some contemporary black novelists employ distinctive combinations of fabulation and satire to spread the news of their tragicomic visions of our times. They have not completely lost faith in the power of satire and laughter as therapy for the ills of the world, but more like Schuyler and Thurman than Fisher, they are much more irreverent and scornful of the hypocrisy of Western civilization, Christian orthodoxy, American principles, and black togetherness.

CHARLES STEVENSON WRIGHT (1932–)

A Southwestern country boy, Charles Wright was born on June 4, 1932, in New Franklin, Missouri, and raised in Sedalia by his grandparents after his mother's death in 1936. An avid reader, he was a regular at the Sedalia Public Library and as a teenager began hitchhiking on weekends to St. Louis and Kansas City to the movies, museums, and libraries. He started writing short pieces in high school, using Hemingway as his model, and for the newspaper, *Kansas City Call*. Drafted into the army shortly after his nineteenth birthday, he served a year in this country and a year in Korea. After his discharge in 1956, he settled in St. Louis to write and, like the protagonist in his autobiographical first novel, soon became "the darling of a heterogeneous group of the arty and the literary."[59] Wright's racial wounds, urge to travel, and profound sense of loss plunged him into the bowels of New York life in 1957. He lived in the Bowery and Greenwich Village while working as a messenger, waiter, dishwasher, and writer. From 1967 to 1973 he wrote a column, "Wright's World," in the *Village Voice*. His publications include two books of poetry, a collection of his journalistic pieces, which are as surreal and ironic as his fiction, and two novels: *The Messenger* (1963) and *The Wig* (1966).

Although he dedicates *The Messenger* to Richard Wright, frequently alludes to other modern novelists in his books, and confesses to having been impressed by Katherine Ann Porter's offbeat style when he was younger, Wright names only Hemingway and Mailer as influences on his writing. Internal evidence in the novels, however, suggests wider influences, including the blues and jazz traditions. As for whether he prefers fantasy or realism, Wright says, "I don't think that one is better than the other. It's whatever suits your purpose."[60] He is disappointed though that most readers of *The Wig* either did not understand or did not appreciate his experiment with form and style.

The Messenger is a picaresque novel which chronicles the desperation and amorality of the protagonist's life in New York's Greenwich Village and the nostalgic memories of his ostensibly peaceful youth in a small town in Missouri. In contrast, *The Wig* is a modern fable whose nonconventional, episodic plot satirizes American racial and cultural myths that delude the protagonist into believing at the beginning of the narrative that a good head of hair is the key to success (" 'The Wig is gonna see me through these troubled times' ")[61] and at the end, that his submission to sterilization will save the nation. (" 'Having children is the greatest sin in this country. . . . ' " [p. 179].) Whereas *The Messenger* overwhelms us with the blues feeling that many if not "most men and women suffer unbearably" (p. 169), *The Wig* is an ironic reflection of the American belief that " 'Everybody's got *something* working for them' " (p. 19).

In spite of these differences, the two novels are similar in several respects. Both are set in New York; both have rogues for protagonists; both are told in the first person; both are episodic in structure; both are wry in tone; and both showcase a variety of street people and eccentrics. Excluding the protagonists, the most sympathetically drawn of these characters are Ruby Stonewall and The Deb. Ruby is the "played-out," blues-singing cousin of Charles Stevenson, the beatnik protagonist in *The Messenger;* her blackness teaches her the humility and compassion she tries to pass on to him. The Deb is the prostitute with short, kinky hair in *The Wig,* whom Lester Jefferson, the protagonist, loves and pursues as "an all-American girl"; her death results in Lester's loss of his curls and his manhood. Several of the characters in *The Messenger* bear striking similarities to those in *The Wig:* Mrs. Lee, "an aging, ageless coquette" who has an insatiable appetite for Puerto Rican gigolos in *The Messenger,* seems to reappear in *The Wig* as Nonnie Swift, a degenerate old Southern belle who wants her baby of unknown racial identity to be born in the "unchained slavery" of Harlem. Claudia the Grand Duchess, "a fabulous Negro drag queen" and friend of the protagonist in *The Messenger* is almost the twin of Miss Sandra Hanover, the Crown Princess, a black homosexual with plucked eyebrows, Chinese-style bangs, and two-inch fake gold-finger-nailed hands who in *The Wig* fantasizes about being old movie queens. In short, both novels are first-person narratives whose amoral protagonists take us on a tour of the underground culture and surreal lives of New Yorkers for whom everyday reality and the American Dream are both nightmares.

In comparing the protagonists in the two novels, we discover that Charles Stevenson, a messenger, writer, and beatnik, is the more sympathetically drawn, but Lester Jefferson, an employed blind pursuer of the American Dream, is the more tragic. Living from day to day in quiet desperation on pot, pills, alcohol, and jazz, Charles, as his memories of his grandparents and his friendships with the neighborhood drug addicts, prostitutes, and homosexuals reveal, is a sensitive, aware individual who "knew and understood loss and loneliness" (p. 68), and who could not "don a mask and suck the c—— of that sweet secure bitch, middle-class American life" (p. 95). Because the author neither undercuts his narrator nor offers an alternative set of values to those he embraces, we sense no significant racial, political, or moral distance between the two. "They make me an outsider," the apparently reliable narrator says,

> A minority within a minority. They called me a dago as a child, before my curls turned to kinks. That sun again! But these kinks form my proud crown. Negro, Negroid, Nigger. Black, brown, and beige. Yellow, shit-colored. Buck, boy. I am the result of generations of bastard Anglo-Saxon, African, Black-creek, and Choctaw Indian blood. Me, the last of the Negro, southwestern, Missouri Stevensons. (P. 144)

Semiautobiographical passages such as this reinforce the fictional nature of reality and the reality of fiction.

Less reliable as a narrator is the protagonist of *The Wig*, Lester Jefferson. As "a minority within a minority" he is racially close to Charles and the author, but his norms are radically different from theirs. A twenty-one-year-old, "slightly schizophrenic" Harlemite, he sees himself as "Walter Mitty's target-colored stepson," has faith in the American Dream, and is convinced that processed hair, The Wig,[62] will be his "acquisitional gimmick" for success. As we accompany him on his quest, we are fascinated by Wright's satirical treatment of the thin line between fantasy and reality in American life, ranging from the Uncle Tom masks and gimmicks for making-it used by movie and rock-and-roll stars to the protagonist's battle with rats in a roach-and-rat-infested Harlem apartment. In contrast to the protagonist in *The Messenger*, Lester takes an optimistic, long-range view of life: "I touched The Wig. Yes. Security had always eluded me, but it wouldn't much longer. American until the last breath, a true believer in the Great Society, I'd turn the other cheek, cheat, steal, take the fifth amendment, walk bare-assed up Mr. Jones's ladder, and state firmly that I was too human" (p. 53). Through verbal and situational irony such as this and the chicken man episode, however, Wright repeatedly and wryly undercuts Lester's desperate yet futile attempts to make his "butterscotch-colored dreams" of success, love, and happiness a social reality. "How many people are willing to crawl on their hands and knees, ten hours a day, five and a half days a week?" Lester asks. "For me that was not difficult: I was dreaming, not of a white Christmas, I was dreaming of becoming part of The Great Society" (pp. 140–41). Even after "the necrophilic funeral director," Mr. Fishback, cuts off Lester's hair and sterilizes him, he remains an incorrigible, pathetic optimist, saying with a smile at the end of the novel, " 'I'm beginning to feel better already' " (p. 179).

Wright's novels are a unique blend of satire and ethically controlled fantasy, with *The Messenger* as the more realistic and *The Wig* as the more fantastic. Some white reviewers and critics consider the blend of satire and fantasy in the novels black humor; one reviewer of *The Wig* even proclaimed Wright "the first certified black humorist."[63] Another considers his method phenomenological. Commenting on his bold imagination and bizarre language, Charles Wright states, "I don't know; it's like when everybody is getting *on* a train, I'm going the opposite way."[64] The difficulty in classifying his major structural and stylistic concerns is largely due to the wide range of influences on his work. In addition to Hemingway and Mailer, it is apparent that he draws on the picaresque tradition, surrealistic painting, and pop culture in projecting his tragicomic vision of the outsiders in contemporary urban America. His delight in combining the bizarre with the commonplace, illuminating the more surreal, off-beat aspects of bohemian life in Greenwich Village, and experimenting with a blend of the static character, loose structure, and satire of the picaresque tradition with the soulful, self-affirming, inward quest of the blues tradition are his most important contributions to the contemporary Afro-American novel.

GEORGE "HAL" BENNETT (1930–)

Hal Bennett was born on April 21, 1930, in Buckingham, Virginia. Raised and educated in and around Newark, New Jersey, he sold his first story when he was fifteen. His pursuit of a writing career was briefly interrupted by a tour of duty in the air force during the Korean war. After his discharge, he worked as fiction editor from 1953 to 1955 for several Afro-American newspapers. He then moved to Mexico, where he attended Mexico City College and became a fellow of the Centro Mexicano de Escritores. He also won a fellowship in 1966 for *A Wilderness of Vines*, his first novel, to the Bread Loaf Writers' Conference. Called "one of the most original and gifted Black satirists to come along since Wallace Thurman,"[65] he published between 1966 and 1983 four additional novels: *The Black Wine* (1968), *Lord of Dark Places* (1970), *Wait Until Evening* (1974), and *Seventh Heaven* (1976).

Employing Christian symbolism and revealing the influence of Faulkner, each of these novels is more irreverent, obscene, and iconoclastic than its predecessor in its satirical demythicizing of American innocence and its construction of a radically new eschatology. In *A Wilderness of Vines*, about which more will be said below, Bennett introduces us to the racial madness of the pre–World War II black community of Burnside, Virginia, a snake-infested paradise where color prejudice is elevated to a religion, social hypocrisy glorified in the ritual of the Christian tableau, and sex, which is linked to death, celebrated as both the damnation and salvation of its light-skinned and dark-skinned residents. In the more loosely structured *The Black Wine*, those who escape the perverted Eden of Burnside, whose social order is in the throes of changing from a color aristocracy to a growing class of chicken raisers, extend the legacy of racial insanity to Decatur, the black community of Cousinsville, New Jersey. There David Hunter, the preadolescent protagonist, is baptized in the primal passion of racial hatred and learns that "life is the dregs, love is the dance. And the wine, the Negro wine? Well, that was a special something, a kind of powerful determination not to die, a kind of hallelujah in the spirit that kept you more or less alive and on an even keel. . . ."[66] Set in Burnside and Cousinsville, *Lord of Dark Places*, the most outrageously profane and morally ambiguous of the five novels, is a scatological attack on what one critic calls "the phallic myth, the original American folk drama in which the white female virgin and bitch goddess and the Black male as defiler and nigger stud are the two central figures."[67]

As Bennett continues to develop his elaborate personal mythology and parody of the biblical myths of innocence, carnality, and color in *Wait Until Evening* and *Seventh Heaven*, which span the years from 1944 to 1971 and 1967 to 1974 respectively, we are once again moved back and forth in time and place between Virginia and New Jersey. Kevin Brittain, the mature black protagonist of *Wait Until Evening*, looks back twenty-five years on how he came to embrace the racial and sexual madness of the Reverend Winston Cobb, a recurring symbol of insanity in each novel, and of his Grandma Cora Brittain, who had learned from a witch "how to be as evil and as cunning as white men." Both Cobb and Grandma Brittain have killed black people who threatened or irritated them. *"Isn't the black man who does violence a black hero—a Big Nigger—because he dares to imitate the tactics of the enemy?"* Kevin asks himself during the trial for murder at the end of the novel. "Isn't murder the holiest undertaking for people who have no other way to esteem themselves?" Although Kevin was responsible for the deaths of his brother and father, he was innocent of killing Janet Magee, the crippled white sister of Cop Magee. But the Newark cop was driven by the obsession that Kevin was the "Big Nigger" who killed his sister. Inspired by his grandmother's confession to him that she was responsible for Janet Magee's death and convinced that there were millions of whites like Magee who wanted simultaneously to love and destroy blacks, the protagonist concludes after his case is dismissed that "I had cut my teeth on the dead bodies of my own kin. Now it was time to turn my talents toward *them*."[68]

Despite Bennett's attempt to encourage sympathy for Kevin by filtering the events through his consciousness as a first-person narrator, many readers will still find themselves offended by this and Bennett's other novels because of the implied author's moral ambiguity, the narrators' unreliability, and the characters' grotesqueness. But for Bennett, the inversion of traditional color and religious iconography captures the truth of the perversion of contemporary American life and the truth of his vision of the ultimate destiny of black people, American society, and the world. Thus, the Cousinsville, New Jersey, housing project in *Seventh Heaven*, known ironically by its black, Puerto Rican, and Italian residents as Seventh Heaven, breeds desperate men and women who will do anything to survive the obscene American nightmare, including "toying with numbers, shooting drugs, killing each other, and blaming every good or evil act on a colorful magic known as mojo, the juju, the evil eye, la brujeriá, or the United States government, depending on who does the evaluation."[69] Like the perversions of Faulkner's Yoknapatawpha County, the madness of Alcanthia County symbolizes the madness of America and the world.

Bennett's eschatological vision is most lucidly and strongly expressed in the narrative voice, characterization, structure, and symbolism of *A Wilderness of Vines*. The third-person omniscient, disembodied narrator gives historical and philosophical expansiveness to the significance of the 1930s plantation community of Burnside, Virginia, where the masters are the light-complexioned descendants of antebellum house servants and the modern-day servants are the dark-complexioned descendants of field hands. "Trapped inside a wilderness where only the vines really prospered, and time was said to stand still underneath the talons of the hunter, the people of Burnside, Virginia, in that summer of 1939 exemplified the people of the world."[70] The narrative voice is also freighted with verbal and situational irony as it contrasts the orphanage for dark-skinned girls with that for light-skinned girls. The former, where the girls are taught domestic work, is called "Preacher's Exchange since so many of these good men have tried to insert the Holy Ghost into the black girls, to introduce them to God." The latter, where the girls "are spared this encroachment of the church," is a finishing school for mulatto child brides, providing "enough education to make them harmless, intelligent-appearing listeners" and "good daughters to primarily tobacco farmers" (pp. 9–10). The central characters in Bennett's myth of death, judgment, heaven, and hell are Neva Stapleton Manning, a light-complexioned fallen Eve, Charlie Hooker, her black farmhand and redeemer, and Ida Carlisle, "the high priestess" of the light-complexioned faithful former slaves who worshipped and imitated their antebellum masters.

Although the narrative opens with Neva, the protagonist, in the metaphorical edenic garden of the Burnside orphanage during the summer of 1920, and focuses primarily on the summer of 1939, foreshadowing the apocalypse of World War II, it flashes back to the Middle Passage of the slave trade as the probable beginning of the color insanity and social unreality of Burnside. It then projects forward to the "larger and more malicious insanity" of Nazism and the war in Europe. Thematically, the plot centers on the sexual repression, spiritual death, and redemption of Neva, the child bride who fears the pain of male domination. Her anxiety is traced back to having witnessed the rape of her mother by a black lover and the violence of a stallion pawing a mare's mattress-covered flanks doing coitus. She also suffers guilt about her sexuality because of the catechism of respectability imposed on her by the imperious old man she married. "Being woman," she wondered, "could she also be stallion and vine at the same time, servant and master twined into one" (p. 24). Throughout the novel sex is metaphorically associated with death and vitality, dark-skinned people with sex and snakes, and vines with entrapment, decay, destruction, and death.

After Neva gives birth to Gene Manning and her dreams of the death of her husband come true when he is trampled by a white mare, she realizes her fantasies about ravishing a sleeping man with Charlie Hooker. Charlie not only provides Neva's secret release from sexual inhibition but is also Bennett's symbolic Christ figure and the moral center of the novel. Before being ravished by Neva while he is semiconscious from an accident with a mare, he feverishly cries out to her, "I am the Resurrection and the life. . . . Come unto me all who labor. . . . " (p. 151). Compelled by Neva to silence about this episode, Charlie is convinced that "Neva would have to forget respectability and lose her fear of madness before she could become a real woman. . . . As long as she could not admit the truth to him, he could not preach truth to the world" (p. 231). The truth and its source are buried in Charlie's past.

Before coming to Burnside, Charlie's experiences on oil ships, in cotton fields, and at camp meetings had baptized him in the truth of American racism and insanity. If the white man's sin was slavery and his burden, the freed slave, then the black man's "sin was *accepting* slavery; his burden, to demonstrate that he is not a mule, but a man. White had nothing to do with sex. . . . Being a man wasn't all bluster and bellyfugging. It was. . . . Feelings. And fire. Fire that no water made can put out" (pp. 139–40). Charlie's marriage to a Jehovah's Witness dramatizes this truth. While traveling with his wife to sell *Watchtower* magazines to poor Alabamans who could not read, she encouraged him to believe that he was a kind of Black Messiah:

> But then, the more he saw of Alabama—God, sometimes he could cry, those poor bastards with all the life almost squeezed out of them!—and the more he saw, the less he loved Lillie, the less he witnessed for the Lord, he came to believe it was all somehow a brazen lie, it took a lot of lying to yourself to keep on witnessing for the Lord when you found out that He wasn't witnessing for you. And Lillie, in her pretty print dresses, clean as a white woman, was only interested in the three cents for that magazine, not in you or them or God or anybody else but Lillie. (P. 141)

Because of generations of moral hypocrisy, in other words, madness is the psychological norm in contemporary America.

Charlie Hooker's mission, then, is to tell the world about Burnside, to go out and preach the gospel. In preparation for this mission he must purge himself of sin and pledge himself to honesty. "Honest thought, honest action, honest feeling," on one hand, and "The World. America. The Negro" on the other, were his Trinity (p. 216). Charlie wavers in his mission, however, when he discovers that Neva, by confessing their sexual intimacy to her son, has found a more important religion than his own. She had overcome her fear of life, he realizes, whereas "his religion would only talk about the possibility of truth" (p. 276). So his departure by bus for Birmingham to tell people about "understanding" is ambiguous.

Equally ambiguous is Neva's symbolic rebirth after her sexual repression and spiritual death, confessing to the Reverend Cobb her complicity in her husband's death and leaving Burnside in a heavily painted face and a sexually provocative dress it had taken her ten years to make. Does the implied author agree with Charlie's belief that "only the frustrated are respectable and sane—ladies and virgins and weeping mothers with rape in their hearts? All real women are mad; men require this healthy madness in them" (p. 231). Or does he agree with the conclusions of white Dr. Stanhope, whose participation in the absurd baby vaccination ritual sponsored by Ida Carlisle and in the murder hearing that exposes her madness, moves him to ask himself whether it is true " 'that the human soul is callous and warlike by nature, that madness is the animal thing in us which love tries to conquer' "? Stanhope concludes " 'that the answer to the problems of Burnside—indeed, of all the world, black and white—lay in the slow conversion of the human heart and mind' " (p. 314). Perhaps, as one critic persuasively argues, what Bennett gives us in *A Wilderness of*

Vines is "the stuff of racial stereotype at that point where stereotype is transformed into archetype."[71]

Bennett's novels thus develop a frequently disturbing, occasionally offensive eschatology that derives its satirical power and symbolic meaning from the experiences, especially the double-consciousness, of black Americans. On one hand, his novels are in the comic tradition of George Schuyler and Wallace Thurman with their caustic criticism of intraracial prejudice and violence. On the other, they are in the modern tradition of William Faulkner, Richard Wright, Ralph Ellison, and James Baldwin. *A Wilderness of Vines*, for example, outlines the mythical Alcanthia County and peoples the town of Burnside, Virginia, with grotesque family lineages like the light-skinned Carlisles and the black-skinned Bartleys to introduce us to America's original sin and eternal burden, thereby providing a microcosm of the world's rituals of racial and sexual death and rebirth. Blurring the distinction between heaven and hell, *A Wilderness of Vines, The Black Wine, Lord of Dark Places, Wait Until Evening,* and *Seventh Heaven* move us from South to North and from the Civil War to the Vietnam war in tracing the search of successive generations of blacks for some place to be somebody and in telling the "good news" in apocalyptic, scatalogical terms of a new coming of Christ. Like Richard Wright, Bennett is primarily concerned with transforming the stereotype of the Big "Bad" Nigger into a modern archetypal Everyman; and like Ralph Ellison and James Baldwin he uses Christian mythology, ritual, and symbolism, although outrageously inverting and parodying them, to structure his personal vision of the world and to affirm the individual's responsibility for his own salvation. In short, Hal Bennett's unique contribution to the tradition of the Afro-American novel is a highly eclectic, irreverent satirical style and scatological mythology of black American color prejudice, sexuality, and messianic hope.

ISHMAEL REED (1938–)

Ishmael Reed is not only one of the nation's most gifted and controversial innovative artists but also the leading promoter of black postmodernist writing. Born on February 22, 1938, in Chattanooga, Tennessee, he was raised and educated in Buffalo, New York. He began writing stories in the second grade, was commissioned to write a birthday poem at the age of fourteen, baffled high school officials with a bizarre satire of the English teacher who hassled him about malapropisms, and wrote a black existential story that made him a celebrity in his English classes at the University of Buffalo. Dropping out of college in 1960 because, among other things, he "just didn't want to be a slave to somebody else's reading lists," he continued experimenting along the lines of writers like Nathanael West, whose style, especially in *The Dream Life of Balso Snell,* began influencing him in high school.[72] From 1960 to 1962 he acquired writing discipline while working as a staff correspondent for the *Empire State Weekly.* Moving to New York City in 1962 to become a writer, he wrote visionary poetry like W. B. Yeats until he began hanging out on the Lower East Side with a group of black writers in the Umbra Workshop, whose members, including Tom Dent, Calvin Hernton, and David Henderson, he claims "anticipated all of the black cultural directions that were to develop a few years later."[73]

In 1965 Reed founded the community newspaper *Advance* in Newark, New Jersey, publishing original material by many young writers, including some Umbra poets. Seeking to destroy the myth "that Afro-American or Black Writing is conformist, monolithic, and dictated by a Committee" and to demonstrate that the new generation of Afro-American writers "will not be consigned to the cultural slaves' quarters as were our geniuses of the past," his anthology *19 Necromancers from Now* showcases the originality and diversity of the contemporary Afro-American novel. In 1972–73, as principal founder of Yardbird Publishing Company and Reed, Cannon and Johnson Communications, he institutionalized his commitment to promoting artistic freedom and multicultural experimental writing. This broadening of his ethnic and artistic interests probably began in 1967 when he moved to Berkeley, California, to write a Western, but instead became embroiled in the issues of artistic and academic freedom concerning his teaching black studies at Merritt College and the University of California at Berkeley. The unconscious racism of students who would dictate to a black instructor the authors, works, and viewpoint that should be stressed in his course, says Reed,

> is sometimes as rigid as that of their elders. After all, in this country art is what White people do. All other people are "propagandists." One can see this in the methodology used by certain White and Black critics in investigating Black literature. Form, Technique, Symbology, Imagery are rarely investigated with the same care as Argument, and even here, the Argument must be one that appeals to critics' prejudices. Novels that don't have the right "message" are cast aside as "pretentious," for it is assumed that the native who goes the way of art is "uppity."[74]

Uppity, pretentious, pompous, sexist, and sophomoric are the most frequent if not the kindest names hurled by unsympathetic critics at Reed for the Neo-HooDoo aesthetic he develops between 1967 and 1983 in his four books of verse, five anthologies, and six novels.[75]

At the heart of Reed's Neo-HooDoo aesthetic, which is largely con-
structed from residual elements of syncretistic African religions (Vodun,
Pocomania, Candomblé, Macumba, and HooDoo) in the Caribbean and
the Americas, especially Haiti, Brazil, and the United States, is a belief in
the power of the unknown, particularly as expressed in artistic freedom
and originality. In the prose-poem "Neo-HooDoo Manifesto" he tells us
that "Neo-HooDoo is a Lost American Church updated," that "Neo-HooDoo
borrows from Haiti Africa and South America. Neo-HooDoo comes in all
styles and moods," and that "Neo-HooDoo believes that every man is an
artist and every artist a priest."[76] An incredibly eclectic mixture of ancient
and contemporary techniques and forms of non-Western and Western
cultures, Reed's six novels—*The Free-Lance Pallbearers* (1967), *Yellow Back
Radio Broke-Down* (1969), *Mumbo Jumbo* (1972), *The Last Days of Louisiana
Red* (1974), *Flight to Canada* (1976), and *The Terrible Twos* (1982)—challenge
the reader to be as culturally egalitarian and imaginatively bold as the
author.

As expressionistic comic satire, Reed's first novel, *The Free-Lance Pallbearers*, attacks the tragic absurdity of political, academic, religious, and
artistic bossism, opportunism, hypocrisy, and corruption in Newark, New
Jersey. Its narrator-protagonist, Bukka Doopyduk, is a signifying, black
college drop-out, Nazarene-apprentice-turned-revolutionary-leader who is
fatally and ironically betrayed by those whom he seeks to save and rule.
The Last Days of Louisiana Red, his fourth novel, is a highly innovative West
Coast thriller starring PaPa LaBas, the HooDoo detective introduced in
Mumbo Jumbo. It draws on Greek drama, old newspapers, vaudeville,
radio, film, and TV scripts to cast its spell on readers. But the dynamics
of black history and culture, especially the heroine of Cab Calloway's song,
"Minnie the Moocher," are the keys to the mystery of Louisiana Red,
symbolic of the collusion of black Americans in their own oppression and
death, which is traced back to the legendary deadly conflict between the
queen and king of HooDoo, Marie Laveau and Doctor John. *Flight to
Canada*, his fifth novel, is an intriguing parody of the slave narrative and
Uncle Tom's Cabin, as well as a demythicizing, irreverent satire on Abraham
Lincoln, Southern culture, and Canada. Interweaving fact with fiction to
illustrate that historical truth is as bizarre as imaginative truth, Reed traces
the journey of Raven Quicksill—the fugitive slave, narrator-writer—from
slavery in Virginia to freedom in Canada: "whether Canada was exile,
death, art, liberation or a woman. Each man to his own Canada."[77] In *The
Terrible Twos*, his sixth novel, Reed employs the sign of the fantasy world
of two-year-olds to satirize the selfish, heartless mood of President Reagan's America. The schemes of the Scrooges of corporate America to

monopolize Christmas are frustrated only by the bold resistance of Santa Claus, Black Peter (his servant), and the Nicolaites (the follower of Saint Nicholas). Reed's most carefully researched, innovative, and fascinating satires are *Yellow Back Radio Broke-Down* and *Mumbo Jumbo*.

The erudition and innovation of *Yellow Back Radio Broke-Down* are most fascinatingly displayed in the multileveled, discontinuous, episodic time structure Reed employs to roam at will through history, parodying popular Westerns, satirizing "Tsars, Monarchs, and their deadly and insidious flunkies," and demythologizing the American cowboy and frontier. On one level, as the title of the novel suggests, Reed draws on the once popular nineteenth-century "lurid sensational yellow kivered books" produced mainly by Eastern dudes for Western frontiersmen.[78] On another level, he has adapted the modern black oral toast to create a black cowboy tall tale: a long, oral narrative of the amazing supernatural feats of an amoral bad man. Its characters are nonrealistic types and caricatures; its language colorful, occasionally obscene, slangy, and hyperbolic; and its techniques borrowed from the black oral tradition, the interlocutor and endman dialogues of vaudeville, the abrupt scene shifts, timing, and symbolism of Western movie, radio, and TV scripts, and from the loose, episodic structure of picaresque novels. Anomalies, incongruities, and anachronisms bombard us for comic effect as radio, TV, ray guns, airplanes, and computerized busses appear in the same time frame as Thomas Jefferson, Doc John, John Wesley Hardin, Merriweather Lewis, William Clark, and Loop Garoo, the protagonist, a black HooDoo cowboy.

Having ransacked the Bancroft Library and yesteryear's newspapers for often neglected or little known Americana, Reed conjures up his irreverent, iconoclastic vision of how the West was really won. In this vision Jefferson, Lewis and Clark, and white cowboys like Drag Gibson are shown to be cultural heroes or gods with cloven feet, and the real folk heroes are the supernatural black cowboy, Loop Garoo, and the super-cool Indian, Chief Showcase, who uses the same tactics on whites that they used on his people: "Foment mischief among his tribes and they will destroy each other" (p. 40). Reed's vision, in short, shows that the perversion of individualism and freedom has its roots in Christianity, the American West and the frontier experience, and that historically oppressed American groups (blacks, Indians, children, and women) will ultimately overthrow this perverted system and replace it with a new social order in which genuine freedom and pluralism prevail. Ironically, the Seven Cities of Cibola that the mob of young and old people rush toward at the end of the novel is "a really garish smaltzy super technological anarcho-paradise" (p. 170).

The fluid, multilevel time structure is an effective technique for the colorful, retrospective introduction by the omniscient, editorializing narrator, who identifies with the norms of the Loop Garoo Kid, gradually revealed to be the apocryphal son of God. Although when we first meet him he is "a desperado so onery he made the Pope cry and the most powerful of cattlemen shed his head to the Executioner's swine," he claims to be the fallen son of God. "Booted out of his father's house after a quarrel, whores snapped at his heels and trick dogs did the fandango on his belly. Men called him brother only to cop his coin and tell malicious stories about his cleft foot" (p. 9). He was the eldest son, "according to what they call apocrypha," Loop tells the Pope. "But I've never cashed in on it like he did. I knew very early that he wasn't the only one, there were others— but his arrogance and selfishness finally got the best of him and he drove them all underground. Now they're making a strong comeback" (p. 164). For Loop, HooDoo, "an unorganized religion without ego-games or death worship," was a richer art form than Christianity. Earlier in the novel in explaining this "American version of the Ju-Ju religion that originated in Africa" to Drag Gibson, who has called for his aid to solve the mystery of Loop's power, the Pope recalls that

> when African slaves were sent to Haiti, Santo Domingo and other Latin American countries, we Catholics attempted to change their pantheon, but the natives merely placed our art alongside theirs. Our inspired and uninspiring saints were no match for theirs: Damballah, Legba and other dieties [sic] which are their Loa. This religion is so elastic that some of the women priests name Loa after their boyfriends. When Vodun arrived in America, the authorities became so paranoid they banned it for a dozen or so years, even to the extent of discontinuing the importation of slaves from Haiti and Santa Domingo. (Pp. 153–54)

Thus Loop's supernatural powers are doubly potent. And since the Pope has actually been sent by Mary to bring Loop home, at the end of the novel Loop gallops off to catch the "Pope's ship heading towards the horizon," leaving mere mortals to their heaven on earth.

Less fascinating, perhaps, but more revealing of the implied author's approval of the aesthetic values of his protagonist is the exchange early in the novel between Bo Shmo, the leader of the neosocial realist gang, and Loop, who is "always with the avant garde" (p. 165). Bo Shmo is a charismatic con man, an unoriginal confessional writer who writes about the misery of being black, and a "part time autocrat monarchist and guru."

Attacking Loop after he is driven out of town by Drag Gibson and left in the desert to die, Bo Shmo calls him a "Crazy dada nigger" who is "given to fantasy and . . . Far out esoteric bullshit. . . . " (p. 35). Loop's response is a transparent defense by Reed of his own postmodernist independence, one of the major themes of the novel: "What's your beef with me Bo Shmo, what if I write circuses? No one says a novel has to be one thing. It can be anything it wants to be, a vaudeville show, the six o'clock news, the mumblings of wild men saddled by demons" (p. 36). This satirical unmasking of black cultural nationalist ideologues who argue that "all art must be for the end of liberating the masses. A landscape is only good when it shows the oppressor hanging from a tree," and who threaten to "blast those who don't agree with us," is both comic and deadly serious as Reed closes the aesthetic distance between himself and his protagonist.[79]

Whereas *Yellow Back Radio Broke-Down*, Reed's second novel, is an intellectually provocative but far from sober or conventional Western, *Mumbo Jumbo*, his third and, perhaps, best novel, is a dazzling virtuoso performance of research and improvisation on the conventional detective narrative in the tradition of Rudolph Fisher's *Conjure-Man Dies*. Set in Harlem during the 1920s, the novel ingeniously employs cinematic techniques to juxtapose fact and fiction, ancient and modern history. It follows the cyclical path of HooDoo detectives PaPa LaBas and Black Herman in tracking down the Western conspiracy to destroy the creative spirit and vitality of man, which Reed calls Jes Grew, and to supplant it with the imitative and repressive aesthetic order of Western civilization, whose museums are Centers of Art Detention for the treasures from Africa, Asia, and South America. First expressed in the ritual dancing and singing of Osiris in Egypt, it spread through Dionysus and the Temples of Osiris and Isis to Greece and Rome, was driven underground by the Atonist (Catholic) Church, continued in the animism and pantheism of Africa, and resurfaced in Haiti, South America, and finally in the song and dance epidemic of North America. Reed ranges widely over world history, appending to the novel a partial yet impressive bibliography of six pages, to reconstruct the unorthodox tradition of his HooDoo Aesthetic, whose cyclical history began in New Orleans in about the 1890s. He satirizes the mission of the Atons, their military arm, the Wallflower Order, and their crusading agents—from the Teutonics, Knights Templars, and Hospitaliers to Hinckle Von Vampton, the Templars' librarian. Hinckle stole the sacred Book of Thoth and became their modern agent assigned to create "a 'spokesman' who would furtively work to prepare the New Negro to resist Jes Grew and not catch it."[80] At the end of the novel PaPa LaBas and Black Herman capture Hinckle Von

Vampton, but Jes Grew goes underground again with the burning of the Book of Thoth only to rise once more, we learn in the epilogue, in the 1970s.

In a lecture in the epilogue, where, as in the lengthy denouement of the last quarter of the novel, Reed's authorial presence is most intrusive, although occasionally spellbinding, PaPa LaBas expands on James Weldon Johnson's remark that, like Mrs. Stowe's Topsy in *Uncle Tom's Cabin*, the earliest ragtime songs "jes grew":

> Jes Grew, the Something or Other that led Charlie Parker to scale the Everests of the Chord. Riff fly skid dip soar and gave his Alto God-speed. Jes Grew that touched John Coltrane's Tenor; that tinged the voice of Otis Redding and compelled Black Herman to write a dictionary to Dreams that Freud would have envied. Jes Grew was the manic in the artist who would rather do glossolalia than be "neat clean or lucid". . . . Jes Grew is the lost liturgy seeking its litany. Its words, chants held in bondage by the mysterious Order "which saved the 2nd Crusade from annihilation by Islamic hordes." Those disgraced Knights. Jew Grew needed its words to tell its carriers what it was up to. Jes Grew was an influence which sought its text, and whenever it thought it knew the location of its words and Labanotations it headed in that direction. (P. 211)

The description of PaPa LaBas as "garrulous gluttonous satirical sardonic but unafraid to march up to the President's Palace and demand tribute," seems also to fit the implied author and disembodied narrator. After identifying the assistant to Osiris as the Black Birdman, for example, the author-narrator sardonically states: "(If anyone thinks this is 'mystifying the past' kindly check out your local bird book and you will find the sacred Ibis' Ornithological name to be *Threskiornis aethiopicus*)" (pp. 211 and 188).

Clearly nonrepresentational, PaPa LaBas, "noonday HooDoo, fugitive-hermit, obeah-man, botanist, animal impersonator, 2-headed man, You-Name-It," like the Loop Garoo Kid of *Yellow Back Radio Broke-Down*, is another black American incarnation of Legba:

> Some say his ancestor is the long Ju Ju of Arno in eastern Nigeria, the man who would oracle, sitting in the mouth of a cave, as his clients stood below in shallow water. Another story is that he is the reincarnation of the famed Moor of Summerland himself, the Black gypsy who according to Sufi Lit sicked the Witches on Europe. Whoever his progenitor, whatever his lineage, his grandfather it is known was

brought to America on a slave ship mixed in with other workers who were responsible for bringing African religion to the Americas where it survived to this day. (P. 23)

Because his father ran a successful mail-order root business in New Orleans, it is not surprising that PaPa LaBas was a carrier of Jes Grew, whose powers the people trusted and whose headquarters, where he helps and heals people with "jewelry, Black astrology, charts, herbs, potions, candles, talismans," was derisively called Mumbo Jumbo Kathedral by his critics. PaPa LaBas's prophecy "that before this century is out men will turn once more to mystery, to wonderment" is the Work that Reed, himself a carrier of Jes Grew, brings to the readers of his Hoodoo novels.

When he wrote *The Free-Lance Pallbearers*, Reed tells us, "I wasn't really thinking about writing a novel; I was thinking about telling a story." Storytelling or fabulation, with the emphasis on artiface rather than self-indulgence, also accurately describes the performance and power of *Yellow Back Radio Broke-Down*, *Mumbo Jumbo*, *The Last Days of Louisiana Red*, and *Flight to Canada*. "I consider myself a fetish-maker," Reed continues. "I see my books as amulets, and in ancient African cultures words were considered in this way. Words were considered to have magical meanings and were considered to be charms." In creating characters, he also tells us, he is not interested in rendering a photograph of a person but "in capturing his soul and putting it in a cauldron or in a novel."[81] Thus, despite the extraordinary original achievement of *Yellow Back Radio Broke-Down* and *Mumbo Jumto*, Reed does not consider himself an innovator. Instead, his major contributions to the tradition of the Afro-American novel are the reshaping of the ancient mythology of vodun and the redemptive power of storytelling and satirical laughter for a black audience.

Change in the Novel of the Sixties and Seventies

Of the nine authors whose novels have been closely examined in this chapter, all but one have published at least two novels, had formal training in writing, and, with the exception of Walker, Gaines, and Reed, lived outside of the United States for an extended period of time. At least six have taught or lectured at the college level, and four have worked as journalists and experienced bohemian life-styles. These various backgrounds explain, in part, the complex changes in their ethnic double-consciousness and in the range of influences that shaped their aesthetic.

Asked about the differences between white and black contemporary writers, Reed responds:

> Chester Himes has said that the black people in this country are the only new race in modern times and I think that's probably true. Nothing in history quite happened like it happened here. I think that the young black writer draws from this experience instead of looking over his shoulder to Homer or to the Latins as white writers do, at least many of them. I think that's the difference. And I don't think a white writer is likely to write a poem based on 'Curtis Mayfield and the Impressions' like David Henderson did, or write like be-bop musicians play, the way Baraka does so successfully in a book like *Tales*. I just don't see that kind of thing taking place among white writers I read . . . A black writer sitting down doesn't have all of Europe looking over his shoulder . . . I think that blacks got over that and are trying to set up their own stuff.[82]

Even when exorcising the demons of Eurocentric models, their "own stuff" is fabulously tragicomic and ironic, stressing the hybrid nature of narrative and the contemporary struggle to survive with personal integrity the bizarre disparity between American principles and practices. Despite the differences in their experiments with form and technique, sometimes parodying earlier narrative conventions and sometimes adapting those of earlier black novelists in their attack on racism, Christianity, and debilitating black traditions, Afro-American modernist and postmodernist novelists are similar in emphasizing the freedom of the individual more than the group, technique more than message, and psychological and cultural revolution more than social. Commenting both on William Buckley's perception of the black studies movement as a conflict between the barbarians and the Christians and on the commitment of Afro-American modernist and postmodernist novelists to create their own fictions, Reed states:

> So this is what we want: to sabotage history. They won't know whether we're serious or whether we are writing fiction. They made their own fiction, just like we make our own. But they can't tell whether our fictions are the real thing or whether they're merely fictional. Always keep them guessing. That'll bug them, probably drive them up the walls. What it comes down to is that you let the social realists go after the flatfoots out there on the beat and we'll go after the Pope and see which action causes a revolution. We are mystical detectives about to make an arrest.[83]

Thus the richness, diversity, and vitality of the contemporary Afro-American novel compel readers and critics alike to be as intellectually independent and imaginatively daring in their approach to black fictive worlds as the artists were in creating them.

Conclusion

I N retrospect, the Afro-American novel, like the Euro-American novel, is a hybrid form that is not the culmination of an evolutionary process in the narrative tradition, but the product of social and cultural forces that shape the author's attitude toward life and that fuel the dialectical process between romantic and mimetic narrative impulses. In contrast to the Euro-American novel, however, the Afro-American novel has its roots in the combined oral and literary traditions of Afro-American culture. It is one of the symbolic literary forms that black Americans have borrowed from western culture and adapted in their quest for status, power, and identity in a racist, capitalist, patriarchal American social arena. The Afro-American novel, in other words, is not a solipsistic, self-referential signifying system, but a symbolic sociocultural act.

In this sense, the nineteenth-century romances and novels of Brown, Delany, Harper, Wilson, and Griggs were both private and public linguistic enactments of human relationships reflecting ethical decisions inside and outside of the text. They were weapons in the struggle for freedom, literacy, dignity, and egalitarianism. Although twentieth-century novelists like Hurston, Wright, Ellison, Baldwin, Williams, Kelley, Gaines, Morrison, A. Walker, M. Walker, Wideman, and Reed also employ the novel and romance as symbolic acts to explore the disparity between American myths and American reality, they do not approach the narrative tradition from the same ideological perspective as their predecessors or each other. Among other things, social and cultural change has encouraged the movement toward more individualism in the novelists and their aesthetics. They nevertheless share in a common tradition. This is largely because as members of the largest ethnic minority group in the United States, Afro-American novelists develop their personal and national identities within and against the distinctive pattern of values, orientations to life, and shared historical memories they acquired from and contribute to Afro-American culture.

Afro-American culture, which has its historical roots in the deep South and the dynamics of sex, ethnicity, and class, means in this context the

Conclusion

symbolic and material expression by black Americans of their relationship to nature, the black community, and the white community as they seek to adapt to their environment in order first to survive and then to thrive, both individually and collectively. Culture thus signifies the constitutive social process by which people create specific, different ways of life as they adapt to environmental conditions and historical circumstances. For black Americans this process of acculturation has been shaped by a distinctive history—Africa, slavery, the South, Emancipation, Reconstruction, post-Reconstruction, Northern migration and urbanization, and, most important, racism—which has resulted in the processes of double-consciousness, socialized ambivalence, and double vision that best explain the complex, creative dynamics of black American culture and character.[1] Because the rite of passage of blacks—from their initial separation from Africa (the Middle Passage) and the denial by whites of their humanity, to the marginality imposed by ceremonial acts of segregation because of color, sex, and class, and to an ultimate reintegration with community in full recognition of their human and civil rights as Afro-Americans—is still in progress, these processes continue to be embedded in Afro-American narratives. Insofar as they are long narratives by American blacks of African ancestry that thematically, structurally, or stylistically draw on features of the Afro-American symbolic universe (the interrelated systems of language, values, beliefs, interaction rituals, and motor behavior) to reconstruct their visions of this distinctive historical, cultural, and sociopsychological experience, this interpretive history includes them in the tradition of the Afro-American novel.

Granted these assumptions and the obvious differences in background, talent, and styles of individual black novelists, how do the dominant themes, structures, and styles in the tradition of the Afro-American novel contrast with the Euro-American? On one level we have discovered that early Afro-American writers, like some of their white peers, found the freedom of the romance—its delight in rhetoric, allegorical characters, and allegiance to an idealized world—appealing. Because of their distinctive social and cultural experience, however, black writers have historically found the novel of social realism equally compelling and appropriate. "I have not attempted to give the reader a mere romance, "writes J. W. Grant in the preface to *Out of the Darkness; of Diabolism and Destiny* (1909), "but a fiction based on historical facts, written and unwritten." Given the powerful forces in their social arenas that resisted their struggle for egalitarian freedom as people and authors, Brown, Webb, Delany, Wilson, Dunbar, and Chesnutt generally found it unconscionable to ignore moral questions

Conclusion

or the spectacle of people in society. But to be published and read by their largely white editors and audiences, they were often constrained to thunderous silences in their texts or to explore with irony the moral and political issues concerning the racism, classism, and sexism of their day. In contrast, with the exception of novels like Stowe's *Uncle Tom's Cabin* and Twain's *Huckleberry Finn*, most nineteenth-century Euro-American novels reinforced the myth of white supremacy, usually defining blackness as the symbol of evil. Thus one of the major differences between American whites and blacks over the nature of reality generally centers on the designation of evil in the world. Whereas most blacks stressed the sins of slavery, most whites stressed the slavery of sin.

Like their white contemporaries, nineteenth-century black novelists tapped the roots of their culture for matter and method. But the world view of the politically and economically oppressed was and is hardly the same as that of their oppressors. Because the distinctiveness of each group's historical experience creates a different frame of reference from which it views and interprets reality, there will inevitably be corresponding differences in the meaning of the archetypal patterns they employ to reconstruct their individual and collective experiences. White and black novelists of the nineteenth and twentieth centuries, for example, may both draw on the Judeo-Christian tradition for terms to order their experiences; but because more often than not the white man's heaven is the black man's hell, blacks generally express strong ambivalence toward its values, whether by symbolic acts of silence or speech. Also, in contrast to the search for innocence and the Adamic vision that inform the Euro-American novel, we usually find the Manichean drama of white versus black, a messianic belief in freedom, an apocalyptic destiny, and the quest to reconcile the double-consciousness of Afro-American identity embedded in the texts of nineteenth- and twentieth-century Afro-American novels. Thematically and structurally, therefore, from Brown to Reed the tradition of the Afro-American novel is dominated by the struggle for freedom from all forms of oppression and by the personal odyssey to realize the full potential of one's complex bicultural identity as an Afro-American. This archetypal journey—deriving its sociocultural consciousness from the group experience of black Americans and its mythopoeic force from the interplay of Eurocentric and Afrocentric mythological systems—begins in physical or psychological bondage and ends in some ambiguous form of deliverance or vision of a new world of mutual respect and justice for peoples of color. In short, if there is an Afro-American canonical story, it is the quest, frequently with apocalyptic undertones, for freedom, literacy, and wholeness—personal and communal—grounded in social reality and ritualized in symbolic acts of Afro-American speech, music, and religion.

Prior to the 1960s, the protagonist in the Afro-American novel was generally a male who was part rebel and part victim as a result of his striving to define himself in the whirlwind of social and cultural forces of his time that denied or threatened to destroy his humanity. On a deeper level, his journey was a ritualistic reenactment on a more or less abbreviated scale of the historical experience of his people in the United States. Torn by conflicting loyalties, he ideally attained a measure of peace and fulfillment by first turning inward—drawing what strength he could from himself, his ethnic group, and his usable past—and then outward to some form of social action or vision of a new social order. Since the 1960s black protagonists such as Janie, Vyry, Miss Jane Pittman, Sula, Velma, and Celie have been resurrected, created, and recreated to illuminate the joys and sorrows of those who are poor, black, and female. Stereotypes and archetypes, idealized and realistic characters contend with each other as the novelists seek to create fictions that explore the wide range of black American character and that celebrate the humanistic values of black American life, male and female, while criticizing self-destructive values. The most distinctive character types include the preacher, the hustler, the matriarch, the messianic leader, the Bad Nigger, the liberated woman, and the blues-jazz figure, both male and female.

By examining the Afro-American novel in its holistic sociocultural context and by classifying the narratives according to their content and their most apparent structural and stylistic features, this history has sought to provide an ethnographical and formalistic approach that will enable readers and critics to understand better the interplay between the novel and romance as narrative systems, the general cyclical movement in the tradition from reality as fable to fable as reality, and the novelists' ambivalence about all systems. Whether the appeal is to white conscience or to black consciousness, whether the commitment is to traditional narrative conventions and forms or to modernist and postmodernist experimentation, the value most frequently celebrated in the tradition of the Afro-American novel is the spiritual resiliency of a people to survive, individually and collectively, with dignity and to realize fully their human potential. But the relationships between the factual and fictional worlds of the authors, especially the modernists and postmodernists, and between the authors' and readers' worlds are influenced by sociocultural changes that move authors and readers away from moral and epistemological absolutes about the nature of reality, especially good and evil. This movement encourages

Conclusion

Afro-American novelists to rediscover the viability of ritual, fable, parable, legend, romance, and satire in constructing their essentially blues visions of life, which affirm the possibilities of the human condition in the United States while struggling to overcome its limitations. Storytellers in the tradition of the Afro-American novel thus challenge us to make sense of the dancing attitudes and folk wisdom embedded in their texts, which, reduced to their propositional content, say: "You can read my writing, but you sure can't read my mind."

Notes

Introduction

1. This book is more interdisciplinary, comprehensive, and scholarly than the six books published since 1953 on the Afro-American novel. See Carl Milton Hughes, *The Negro Novelist: A Discussion of the Writing of American Negro Novelists, 1940–1950* (1953; rpt. New York: Citadel, 1979); Robert A. Bone, *The Negro Novel in America* (1958; rev. ed. New Haven: Yale University Press, 1965); Noel Schraufnagel, *From Apology to Protest: The Black American Novel* (Deland, Fla.: Everett/Edwards, 1973); Amritjit Singh, *The Novels of the Harlem Renaissance: Twelve Black Writers, 1923–1933* (University Park: Pennsylvania State University Press, 1976); Addison Gayle, Jr., *The Way of the New World: The Black Novel in America* (Garden City: Doubleday, Anchor, 1975); and Barbara Christian, *Black Women Novelists: The Development of a Tradition, 1892–1976* (Westport, Conn.: Greenwood, 1980). Useful contemporary books on black fiction include: Michael G. Cooke, *Afro-American Literature in the Twentieth Century: The Achievement of Intimacy* (New Haven: Yale University Press, 1984); Roger Rosenblatt, *Black Fiction* (Cambridge: Harvard University Press, 1974); Sherley A. Williams, *Give Birth to Brightness: A Thematic Study in Neo-Black Literature* (New York: Dial, 1972); Robert A. Bone, *Down Home: A History of Afro-American Short Fiction from Its Beginning to the End of the Harlem Renaissance* (New York: Capricorn, 1975); and Edward Margolies, *Native Sons: A Critical Study of Twentieth-Century Negro American Authors* (New York: J. B. Lippincott, 1969). The four most intriguing recent theoretical and critical studies of Afro-American literature are Robert B. Stepto, *From Behind the Veil: A Study of Afro-American Narrative* (Urbana: University of Illinois Press, 1979); Houston A. Baker, Jr., *The Journey Back: Issues in Black Literature and Criticism* (Chicago: University of Chicago Press, 1980) and *Blues, Ideology, and Afro-American Literature: A Vernacular Theory* (Chicago: University of Chicago Press, 1984); and Berndt Ostendorf, *Black Literature in White America* (Totowa, N. J.: Barnes and Noble, 1982).

2. For much of the subsequent discussion on narrative and cultural theory, I am indebted to the following: Northrop Frye, *Anatomy of Criticism: Four Essays* (Princeton: Princeton University Press, 1957); René Wellek and Austin Warren, *Theory of Literature*, 3d ed. (New York: Harvest Book, 1962); Robert Scholes and Robert Kellogg, *The Nature of Narrative* (New York: Oxford University Press, 1966); Ruth Finnegan, *Oral Literature in Africa* (London: Oxford University Press, 1970); Diana Laurenson and Alan Swingewood, *The Sociology of Literature* (London: Paladin,

344

1972); Terry Eagleton, *Literary Theory: An Introduction* (Minneapolis: University of Minnesota Press, 1983); Clifford Geertz, *The Interpretation of Cultures: Selected Essays* (New York: Basic Books, 1973); Raymond Williams, *Culture and Society, 1780–1950* (1958; rpt. New York: Harper and Row, 1966) and *Marxism and Literature* (London: Oxford University Press, 1977). For the most important modern seminal debate on the relationship of black American culture and character to white society, see Melville J. Herskovits, *The Myth of the Negro Past* (Boston: Beacon, 1941); and E. Franklin Frazier, *The Negro Family in the United States* (1939; rev. and abridged ed. Chicago: University of Chicago Press, 1948), chap. 1, and *The Negro in the United States* (1949; rev. ed. New York: Macmillan, 1957), chap. 1.

3. Fredric R. Jameson, "The Symbolic Inference; or, Kenneth Burke and Ideological Analysis," *Critical Inquiry* 4 (Spring 1978): 510. See also Kenneth Burke, *The Philosophy of Literary Form*, 3d. ed. (Berkeley: University of California Press, 1941).

4. LeRoi Jones, *Home: Social Essays* (New York: Apollo, 1966), p. 114.

5. See, for example, Ishmael Reed, ed., *19 Necromancers from Now* (Garden City: Anchor, 1979), p. xiii; and John O'Brien, ed., *Interviews with Black Writers* (New York: Liveright, 1973), p. xiii.

6. First developed in 1897 by Du Bois as a metaphor for the sociopsychological process by which the black American minority responded to the racial and cultural domination of the white American majority, double-consciousness was apparently rewritten in 1937 by anthropologist Melville J. Herskovits as socialized ambivalence to explain the existence of conflicting African and European values and behavioral alternatives in postcolonial Haitians. This trope was further developed in 1963 by Ralph Ellison as double vision to describe the ambivalence of modern black Americans toward all people and events. These interrelated terms do not signify a basic personality type or disorder. On the contrary, they signify both the complex sociopsychological process of acculturation of black Americans—the will to realize their human and civil rights—and the sociocultural relationship of colonized people of African descent to colonizers of European descent. The shifts in allegiance of black Americans between the values of the white dominant culture and those of the black subculture, in other words, are a normal survival strategy, a healthful self-protective, compensatory response to the oppression and repression fostered by institutionalized racism and economic exploitation. Double-consciousness, socialized ambivalence, and double vision should not be confused therefore with psychopathological models that, based mainly on the assumption that slaves in the United States were completely stripped of all African culture, categorize black Americans as Samboized, schizophrenic, or psychotic. For double-consciousness, see W. E. Du Bois, "Strivings of the Negro People," *Atlantic Monthly*, August 1897, pp. 194–98; and "Of Our Spiritual Strivings," *The Souls of Black Folk* (1903; rpt. Greenwich: Crest, 1965), pp. 16–17. For socialized ambivalence, see Melville J. Herskovits, *Life in a Haitian Valley* (New York: Knopf, 1937), pp. 295–96; and Norman E. Whitten, Jr., and John F. Szwed, Introduction, *Afro-American Anthropology: Contemporary Perspectives*, ed. Norman E. Whitten, Jr., and John F. Szwed (New York:

Free Press, 1970), pp. 26–27. For double vision, see Ralph W. Ellison, "The World and the Jug," *New Leader* 46, December 9, 1963: 22–26; and *Shadow and Act* (1964; rpt. New York: Signet, 1966), p. 137. For modern psychopathological theories of Afro-American personality, see, for example, Abram Kardiner and Lionel Ovesey, *The Mark of Oppression: Explorations in the Personality of the American Negro* (1951; rpt. Cleveland: Meridian, 1962); Frantz Fanon, *Black Skin, White Masks*, trans. Charles Lam Markmann (New York: Grove, 1967); William H. Grier and Price M. Cobbs, *Black Rage* (1968; rpt. New York: Bantam, 1969); and Stanley M. Elkins, *Slavery: A Problem in American Institutional and Intellectual Life* (1959; rpt. New York: Grosset and Dunlap, 1963).

7. Geertz employs this phrase to signify the process by which ethnographers seek to understand a culture, which he defines as the webs of significance or interrelated complex conceptual structures created by the symbolic action of human beings. See *Interpretation of Cultures*, chap 1.

8. Milman Parry, quoted in Scholes and Kellogg, *Nature of Narrative*, p. 18.

9. See T. S. Eliot, "Tradition and the Individual Talent," *The Sacred Wood: Essays on Poetry and Criticism* (1920; rpt. New York: University Paperbacks, 1964), pp. 47–59. See also Claudio Guillén, *Literature as System: Essays Toward the Theory of Literary History* (Princeton: Princeton University Press, 1971), pp. 17–52, 375–419.

10. Richard Wright, "Blueprint for Negro Writing," *New Challenge* (Fall 1937): 60.

11. For Bloom, poetic history involves an anxiety of influence, which he defines metaphorically as the melancholy resulting from the "battle between strong equals, father and son as mighty opposites, Lauis and Oedipus at the crossroads" (*The Anxiety of Influence: A Theory of Poetry* [New York: Oxford University Press, 1973], p. 11). Sandra M. Gilbert and Susan Gubar revise Bloom's neo-Freudian model of literary paternity for women writers, substituting anxiety of authorship for anxiety of influence (*The Madwoman in the Attic: The Woman Writer and the Nineteenth-Century Literary Imagination* [New Haven: Yale University Press, 1984], pp. 45–53). In a highly insightful essay on a black feminist literary tradition, Diane F. Sadoff revises both Bloom's and Gilbert and Gubar's psycholiterary models of influence to include race and class oppression. ("Black Matrilineage: The Case of Alice Walker and Zora Neale Hurston," *Signs: Journal of Women in Culture and Society* 9 [Autumn 1985]: 4–26).

12. "There are," R. D. Laing writes, " . . . many descriptions of depersonalization and splitting in psychopathology. However, no psychopathological theory is entirely able to surmount the distortion of the person imposed by its own premises [sic] even though it may seek to deny these very premises [sic]" (*The Divided Self: An Existential Study in Sanity and Madness* [1959; rpt. Baltimore: Penguin, 1973], pp. 23–24).

13. See, for example, Frye, *Anatomy of Criticism*, pp. 303–7; Scholes and Kellogg, *Nature of Narrative*, chap. 1; David H. Hirsch, *Reality and Idea in the Early American Novel* (The Hague: Mouton, 1971), pp. 32–48; Nicolaus Mills, *American and English Fiction in the Nineteenth Century: An Antigenre Critique and Comparison* (Bloomington: Indiana University Press, 1973), pp. 3–31; and Michael Davitt Bell, *The Development*

of American Romance: The Sacrifice of Relation (Chicago: University of Chicago, 1980), chap. 1.

14. Wellek and Warren, *Theory of Literature*, p. 216.

15. Frye, *Anatomy of Criticism*, pp. 304–5.

16. Fredric Jameson, *The Political Unconscious: Narrative as a Socially Symbolic Act* (Ithaca: Cornell University Press, 1981), p. 105.

17. See, for example, Mills, *American and English Fiction*, pp. 3–4; and David Lodge, *The Modes of Modern Writing: Metaphor, Metonomy, and the Typology of Modern Literature* (London: Edward Arnold, 1977), p. 220. For three provocative theories of Afro-American narratives, see Stepto, *From Behind the Veil*, and Baker, *Journey Back* and *Blues, Ideology, and Afro-American Literature*. None focuses sharply on the Afro-American novel nor on the relationship of culture to character, but Baker's "anthropology of art" is somewhat similar to the approach I develop here.

18. Wayne C. Booth, *The Rhetoric of Fiction* (Chicago: Phoenix, 1967), pp. 149–65.

1. The Roots of the Early Afro-American Novel

1. Pauline E. Hopkins, *Contending Forces: A Romance Illustrative of Negro Life North and South* (1900; rpt. Miami: Mnemosyne, 1969), pp. 3–4.

2. Nathan Glazer and Daniel P. Moynihan, *Beyond the Melting Pot: The Negroes, Puerto Ricans, Jews, Italians, and Irish of New York City* (Cambridge: M.I.T. Press, 1964), p. 53.

3. See, for example, Charles A. Valentine, *Culture and Poverty: Critique and Counter-Proposals* (Chicago: University of Chicago Press, 1968); Whitten and Szwed, *Afro-American Anthropology*; John W. Blassingame, *The Slave Community: Plantation Life in the Ante-Bellum South* (New York: Oxford University Press, 1972); Herbert G. Gutman, *The Black Family in Slavery and Freedom, 1750–1925* (New York: Pantheon, 1976); Lawrence W. Levine, *Black Culture and Black Consciousness: Afro-American Folk Thought from Slavery to Freedom* (New York: Oxford University Press, 1977); Alan Dundes, ed. *Mother Wit from the Laughing Barrel: Readings in the Interpretation of Afro-American Folklore* (Englewood Cliffs: Prentice-Hall, 1973); John Lovell, Jr., *Black Song: The Forge and the Flame; The Story of How the Afro-American Spiritual Was Hammered Out* (New York: Macmillan, 1972); Dell Hymes, ed. *Pidginization and Creolization of Languages: Proceedings of a Conference Held at the University of West Indies Mona, Jamaica, April 1968* (London: Cambridge University Press, 1974); J. L. Dillard, *Black English: Its History and Usage in the United States* (New York: Random House, 1972); and Ostendorf, *Black Literature in White America*.

4. Williams, *Culture and Society*, p. xiv.

5. Sidney Mintz, Foreword to Whitten and Szwed, *Afro-American Anthropology*, p. 10.

6. Valentine, *Culture and Poverty*, p. 3.

7. Herbert G. Gutman, "Work, Culture, and Society in Industrializing America, 1815–1919," *American Historical Review* 78 (1973): 542–43.

8. Mintz, Foreword to Whitten and Szwed, *Afro-American Anthropology*, p. 10.

9. Robert Blauner, "Black Culture: Myth or Reality?" Ibid., p. 352.

10. Ellison, *Shadow and Act*, pp. 136–37. I am indebted to this collection of essays for the seminal idea of this history.

11. Sidney Mintz and Richard Price, *An Anthropological Approach to the Afro-American Past: A Caribbean Perspective* (Philadelphia: Institute for the Study of Human Issues, 1977), pp. 22–24.

12. John Hope Franklin, *From Slavery to Freedom: A History of Negro Americans*, 3d ed. (New York: Knopf, 1967), p. 28.

13. Carl N. Degler, "Slavery and the Genesis of American Race Prejudice," *Comparative Studies of Society and History* 2 (October 1959): 49–66; Winthrop D. Jordan, *White Over Black: American Attitudes Toward the Negro, 1550–1812* (Chapel Hill: University of North Carolina Press, 1968), pp. 73–75. See also George M. Frederickson, "Toward a Social Interpretation of the Development of American Racism," in *Key Issues in the Afro-American Experience*, ed. Nathan I. Huggins, Martin Kilson, and Daniel M. Fox, 2 vols. (New York: Harcourt Brace Jovanovich, 1971), 1: 240–54.

14. Quoted in Franklin, *From Slavery to Freedom*, pp. 101–2.

15. Quoted in Elkins, *Slavery*, p. 40.

16. Benjamin Quarles, *The Negro in the American Revolution* (Chapel Hill: University of North Carolina Press, 1961), p. 42; and Franklin, *From Slavery to Freedom*, p. 130.

17. Max Farrand, *The Framing of the Constitution of the United States* (New Haven: Yale University Press, 1913), pp. 148–52; and Franklin, *From Slavery to Freedom*, pp. 142–44.

18. Franklin, *From Slavery to Freedom*, p. 144.

19. Although the congressional bill of March 1865 creating the Bureau of Refugees, Freedmen, and Abandoned Lands explicitly instructed General Oliver O. Howard, the head of the bureau, to " 'set apart for the loyal refugees or freedmen, such tracts of land . . . as shall have been abandoned' in lots 'not more than forty acres' and rent them, at a modest percent of their value, to freedmen and their families," President Andrew Johnson subverted this congressional plan by issuing his Amnesty Proclamation in May 1865 pardoning most former Confederates and restoring to them their abandoned lands. See William McFeely, "Unfinished Business: The Freedmen's Bureau and Federal Action in Race Relations," in Huggins, Kilson, and Fox, *Key Issues*, 2: 11–12.

20. Gunnar Myrdal, *An American Dilemma: The Negro Problem and Modern Democracy* (1944; rpt. New York: Harper and Row, 1962), pp. 927–30.

21. Peter L. Berger and Thomas Luckman, *The Social Construction of Reality: A Treatise in the Sociology of Knowledge* (Baltimore: Penguin Books, 1966), p. 86. For this and other useful insights into contemporary European perceptions of black American culture, I am indebted to Bernhard Ostendorf's criticism of an early draft of this chapter and his "Black Poetry, Blues, and Folklore: Double Consciousness in Afro-American Oral Culture," an unpublished manuscript.

22. Blauner, "Black Culture," in Whitten and Szwed, *Afro-American Anthropology*, p. 351.

23. Herskovits, *Life in a Haitian Valley*, pp. 295, 296.

24. Frazier, *Negro in the United States*, p. 21. Robert Farris Thompson, *Flash of the Spirit: African and Afro-American Art and Philosophy* (1983; rpt. New York: Vintage, 1984).

25. Ostendorf, "Black Poetry, Blues and Folklore," p. 6. See also J. Huizinga, *Homo Ludens* (London: Routledge and Kegan Paul, 1949).

26. Du Bois, *Souls of Black Folk*, pp. 16–17.

27. Sutton E. Griggs, *Imperium in Imperio: A Study of the Negro Race Problem, A Novel* (1899; rpt. Miami: Mnemosyne, 1969), p. 62.

28. William Pickens, *The New Negro: His Political, Civil, and Mental Status and Related Essays* (1916; rpt. New York: Negro Universities Press, 1969), p. 15.

29. According to the different temporal and spatial contexts in which they used it, the phrase "New Negro" obviously meant different things to Griggs, Pickens, and Locke. See Bone, *Negro Novel*, pp. 32–35. For a discussion of the ubiquitousness of the phrase, see Lawrence Levine, "The Concept of the New Negro and the Realities of Black Culture," in Huggins, Kilson, and Fox, *Key Issues*, 2: 128–29. See also Hugh Gloster, "Sutton Griggs: Novelist of the New Negro," *Phylon* 4 (1943): 335–45; rpt. in *The Black Novelist*, ed. Robert Hemenway (Columbus: Charles E. Merrill, 1970), pp. 11–23; Gloster, *Negro Voices in American Fiction* (1948; rpt. New York: Russell and Russell, 1965), pp. 56–67; and Patricia D. Watkins, "Sutton Griggs: The Evolution of a Propagandist," (Master's thesis, Howard University, 1970).

30. Hopkins, *Contending Forces*, p. 272.

31. Sutton E. Griggs, *Pointing the Way* (Nashville: Orion, 1908), p. 101.

32. According to Lawrence Levine, "at the time of emancipation at least 93 per cent of the adult Negroes in the United States were illiterate. In 1870 the number had been reduced to about 80 per cent; by 1890, 56 per cent; 1900, 44 per cent; 1950, 10 per cent. . . . When freedom first came, more than nine out of ten blacks had been illiterate; by the mid-twentieth century nine out of ten were literate." He defines literacy as "the minimal ability to read and write." (*Black Culture and Black Consciousness*, pp. 156–57).

33. Charles Keil, *Urban Blues*, (Chicago: University of Chicago Press, 1966), p. 17.

34. Richard Dorson, *American Negro Folktales* (Greenwich: Fawcett, 1967), p. 12.

35. Emmanuel Obiechina, *Culture, Tradition and Society in the West African Novel* (London: Cambridge University Press, 1975), p. 34.

36. Because the term "folklore" was first used in England in 1846 to describe the body of material and nonmaterial culture that distinguishes the intellectual from the tradition-bound classes, it is of questionable value in discussing ethnic or mythic societies in which all is oral and most is traditional. But with the emergence of African national states in the 1960s and the appearance of a Westernized African elite, the use of the term makes more sense. See Richard Dorson, "Africa and the Folklorist," *African Folklore* (Bloomington: Indiana University Press, 1972), pp. 3–67.

37. For an informative outline of the forms and functions of folklore, see William

Bascom, "The Forms of Folklore: Prose Narratives," *Journal of American Folklore* 78 (1965): 3–20, and "Folklore and Literature," *The African World* (New York: Frederick Praeger, 1965), pp. 459–90.

38. Finnegan, *Oral Literature in Africa*, pp. 315–88. See also Melville J. Herskovits and Frances S. Herskovits, *Dahomean Narrative* (Evanston: Northwestern University Press, 1958).

39. Ulli Beier, quoted in Janheinz Jahn, *Neo-African Literature: A History of Black Writing*, trans. Oliver Coburn and Ursala Lehrburger (New York: Evergreen, 1969), p. 62. This is an ambitious, provocative study of the relationship of contemporary African literature to its oral tradition. See also Janheinz Jahn, *Muntu: An Outline of the New African Culture*, trans. Marjorie Green (New York: Grove, 1961), pp. 185–216.

40. For a model study of an African writer's use of folklore, see Bernth Lindfors, "Amos Tutuola: Debts and Assets," *Cahiers d'Etudes Africaines*, 10 (1970): 306–34. See also Bernth Lindfors, "Critical Approaches to Folklore in African Literature," in Dorson, *African Folklore*, pp. 223–34. For a useful discussion of the methods for determining the presence of folklore in literature, see Richard M. Dorson, "The Identification of Folklore in American Literature," *Journal of American Folklore* 70 (1957); rpt. in Richard M. Dorson, *American Folklore and the Historian* (Chicago: University of Chicago Press, 1971), pp. 186–203. For an insightful model study of an Afro-American writer's use of folklore, see Robert Hemenway, "Are You a Flying Lark or a Setting Dove," in *Afro-American Literature: The Reconstruction of Instruction*, ed. Dexter Fisher and Robert B. Stepto (New York: Modern Language Association of America, 1979), pp. 122–52.

41. For an intriguing examination of this subject, see Gene Bluestein, *The Voice of the Folk: Folklore and American Literary Theory* (Amherst: University of Massachusetts Press, 1972); and Bernard W. Bell, *The Folk Roots of Contemporary Afro-American Poetry* (Detroit: Broadside, 1974).

42. Dorson, *American Negro Folktales*, p. 66.

43. Blassingame, *Slave Community*, p. 41. By making use of slave narratives as well as the records of white planters and travel accounts, Blassingame's study not only breaks with the tradition of American historiography but also reveals the influence of African retentions on antebellum Afro-American life and provides a more reliable account of the shaping of Afro-American identity than the Sambo thesis advanced by Stanley Elkins. Studies by several white and black social scientists and historians have uncritically applied Elkins's thesis to modern-day Afro-Americans. Glazer and Moynihan, *Beyond the Melting Pot*; Charles Silberman, *Crisis in Black and White* (New York: Vintage, 1964); Eugene D. Genovese, *The Red and the Black: Marxian Explorations in Southern and Afro-American History* (New York: Panther, 1968); Thomas Pettigrew, *A Profile of the Negro American* (Princeton: Van Nostrand, 1964); and Grier and Cobbs, *Black Rage*. See, too, the invaluable anthology of challenges to Elkins's controversial thesis in Ann J. Lane, ed. *The Debate Over Slavery: Stanley Elkins and His Critics* (Urbana: University of Illinois Press, 1971).

44. On the migration of blacks to Northern cities and the impact of urbanization, see Arna Bontemps and Jack Conroy, *Anyplace But Here* (New York: Hill and Wang, 1966); Claude McKay, *Harlem: Negro Metropolis* (1940; rpt. New York: Harvest Book, 1968); Roi Ottley and William J. Weatherby, *The Negro in New York: An Informal Social History, 1626–1640* (New York: Praeger, 1969); Richard Wright, *Twelve Million Black Voices: A Folk History of the Negro in the United States* (New York: Viking, 1941); and St. Clair Drake and Horace R. Cayton, *Black Metropolis: A Study of Negro Life in a Northern City*, rev. ed., 2 vols. (New York: Harbinger, 1962).

45. William A. Stewart, "Sociolinguistic Factors in the History of American Negro Dialects," *Florida Foreign Language Reporter* 5, no. 2 (1967): 11–29; and Dillard, *Black English*, pp. 73–185. See also Hymes, *Pidginization and Creolization of Languages*.

46. A useful recent cultural history that examines black minstrelsy in the 1920s is Nathan I. Huggins, *Harlem Renaissance* (New York: Oxford University Press, 1971). The standard works are Carl Wittke, *Tambo and Bones: A History of the American Minstrel Stage* (1930; rpt. Westport: Greenwood, 1968); Hans Nathan, *Dan Emmett and the Rise of Early Negro Minstrelsy* (Norman: University of Oklahoma Press, 1962); and Robert C. Toll, *Blacking Up: The Minstrel Show in Nineteenth-Century America* (New York: Oxford University Press, 1974). For varieties of black speech, see Thomas Kochman, ed. *Rappin' and Stylin' Out: Communication in Urban Black America* (Urbana: University of Illinois Press, 1972); Langston Hughes and Arna Bontemps, eds. *The Book of Negro Folklore* (New York: Dodd, Mead, 1958), pp. 477–97; John Dollard, "The Dozens: The Dialect of Insult," *American Imago* 1 (1939): 3–25; and Roger D. Abrahams, "Playing the Dozens," *Journal of American Folklore* 75 (1962): 209–20.

47. Ellison, "The World and the Jug," *Shadow and Act*, pp. 136–37. See, too, the exchange on the relationship of folklore to literature: Stanley E. Hyman and Ralph Ellison, "The Negro Writer in America: An Exchange," *Partisan Review* 25 (Spring 1958): 197–222. Also see Levine, *Black Culture and Black Consciousness*.

48. Ellison, *Shadow and Act*, p. 172.

49. Constance Rourke, *American Humor: A Study of the National Character* (New York: Harcourt, Brace and Co., 1931), pp. 88–89.

50. See, for example, Michael Kammen, *People of Paradox: An Inquiry Concerning the Origins of American Civilization* (New York: Knopf, 1972), esp. chap. 4. According to Kammen and Huggins, as Ostendorf notes, "everyone, white or black, was socialized into a pervasive national ambivalence, due to the 'biformity' or 'split nature' of the American 'national style.' This integrationist gesture, which forces a variety of socio-cultural conflicts into an all-American norm and which domesticates current anxieties by americanizing their genesis, belittles the 'wounds' of socialization and embezzles the 'bow' of black cultural resources. Black double consciousness is more than an existential constant; it has both a deeper historical and anthropological dimension, the first defined by slavery and segregation along a color line, the second by African cultural retentions" (*Black Literature in White America*, p. 19).

51. See Ellison, *Shadow and Act*, pp. 39–40, 42–43, and 136–37; and George E.

Kent, "Ethnic Impact in American Literature: Reflections on a Course," *College Language Association Journal* 11 (September 1967): 24–37.

52. For an exegesis of the history of the word and the tyranny of print in the Judeo-Christian tradition, see Walter J. Ong, *The Presence of the Word: Some Prolegomena for Cultural and Religious History* (New Haven: Yale University Press, 1967); and Marshall McLuhan, *The Gutenberg Galaxy: The Making of Typographic Man* (1962; rpt. New York: Signet, 1969).

53. Williams, *Marxism and Literature*, p. 122.

54. F. O. Matthiessen, *American Renaissance: Art and Expression in the Age of Emerson and Whitman* (1941; rpt. New York: Oxford University Press, 1979), p. 18.

55. Roger D. Abrahams, *Deep Down in the Jungle: Negro Narrative Folklore from the Streets of Philadelphia*, rev. ed. (Chicago: Aldine, 1979); and *Positively Black* (Englewood Cliffs: Prentice-Hall, 1970).

56. Abrahams, *Deep Down in the Jungle*, p. 97.

57. See n. 46.

58. Bruce Rosenberg, *The Art of the American Folk Preacher* (New York: Oxford University Press, 1970), pp. 5, 10, 53.

59. Henry H. Mitchell, *Black Preaching* (New York: J. B. Lippincott, 1970), p. 167.

60. According to black theologian Benjamin E. Mays, "the ideas of God in Negro literature are developed along three principal lines: (1) Ideas of God that are used to support or give adherence to traditional, compensatory patterns; (2) Ideas, whether traditional or otherwise, that are developed and interpreted to support a growing consciousness of social and psychological adjustment needed; (3) Ideas of God that show a tendency or threat to abandon the idea of God as 'a useful instrument' in perfecting social change (*The Negro's God as Reflected in His Literature* [1938; rpt. New York: Atheneum, 1968], p. 245.

61. George Pryor, *Neither Bond Nor Free* (New York: J. S. Oglive, 1902). The title of the novel is borrowed from Gal. 3:28.

62. Martin Delany, *Blake; or, the Huts of America* (Boston: Beacon, 1970), p. 21.

63. Hopkins, *Contending Forces*, p. 87; and Delany, *Blake*, p. 313.

64. Ellison, *Shadow and Act*, p. 175.

65. Charles Chesnutt, *The House Behind the Cedars*, (1900; rpt. New York: Collier, 1969), p. 163.

66. The tragedy of Nat Turner's rebellion was fictionalized by William Styron, a white Southern novelist, as a "meditation on history." Despite the criticism of many black readers that Styron manipulated history to perpetuate stereotypes of Afro-American character, the book was awarded the Pulitzer Prize in fiction in 1968. See *The Confessions of Nat Turner* (New York: Random House, 1967). For the reaction of some black scholars and critics, see *William Styron's Nat Turner: Ten Black Writers Respond*, ed. John Henrik Clark (Boston: Beacon, 1968); and Bernard W. Bell, "Styron's Confessions," *Michigan Quarterly Review* 7 (Fall 1968): 280–82.

67. Delany, *Blake*, p. 91.

68. Margaret Walker, *Jubilee* (1966; rpt. New York: Bantam, 1967), pp. 363–64.

69. See Ellison, *Shadow and Act*, pp. 78–79.

70. Hopkins, *Contending Forces*, p. 13.

71. For a useful description of the Brown and Craft lectures, see Williams E. Farrison, *William Wells Brown: Author and Reformer* (Chicago: University of Chicago Press, 1969), pp. 136–37.

72. See Frederick Douglass, *Narrative of the Life of Frederick Douglass: An American Slave*, ed. Benjamin Quarles (Cambridge: Belknap Press, 1967); Gilbert Osofsky, ed. *Puttin' on Ole Massa: The Slave Narratives of Henry Bibb, William Wells Brown, and Solomon Northup* (New York: Harper Torchbooks, 1969); Arna Bontemps, ed. *Great Slave Narratives* (Boston: Beacon, 1969); and William Loren Katz, ed. *Five Slave Narratives* (New York: Arno, 1969). See also Charles Nichols, *Many Thousand Gone: The Ex-Slaves' Account of Their Bondage and Freedom* (1963; rpt. Bloomington: Indiana University Press, 1969); George P. Rawick, *The American Slave: A Composite Autobiography*, 19 vols. *From Sundown to Sunup: The Making of the Black Community*, 1 (Westport: Greenwood, 1972); Stephen Butterfield, *Black Autobiography in America* (Amherst: University of Massachusetts Press, 1974); and Frances Smith Foster, *Witnessing Slavery: The Development of Ante-Bellum Slave Narratives* (Westport: Greenwood, 1979).

73. Charles Sumner, *The Liberator*, October 22, 1852; quoted in Osofsky, *Puttin' on Ole Massa*, p. 29.

74. Jean Toomer, *Cane* (1923; rpt. New York: Perennial Classic, 1969) p. 199.

75. The subsequent information is condensed from the following sources: James Hastings, *A Dictionary of the Bible*, 5 vols. (New York: Charles Scribner's Sons, 1908), 1: 734–57; *Encyclopedia Britannica*, (1965), 8: 694–97; John S. Mibiti, *African Religions and Philosophy* (Garden City: Anchor, 1970), pp. 1–119, 195–216, 266–81, and 299–342; E. Franklin Frazier, *The Negro Church in America* (New York: Schocken, 1964), pp. 1–19; W. E. B. Du Bois, *The Negro* (1915; rpt. New York: Oxford University Press, 1970), pp. 62–85; and Mays, *Negro's God*, pp. 245–55.

76. James H. W. Howard, *Bond and Free: A True Tale of Slave Times* (1886; rpt. Miami: Mnemosyne, 1969), pp. 24–25.

77. Paul Laurence Dunbar, *The Sport of the Gods* (1902; rpt. Miami: Mnemosyne, 1969), p. 150. Subsequent references to this novel will be in the text.

78. Ralph Ellison, *Invisible Man* (1952; rpt. New York: Signet, 1964), p. 326. Subsequent references to this novel will be in the text.

79. See Charles W. Chesnutt, "Superstitions and Folklore of the South," *Modern Culture* 13 (1901): 231–35; rpt. in Dundes, *Mother Wit*, pp. 369–76. As this article and his short stories illustrate, Chesnutt was not only a talented novelist but also, even though not formally trained in the discipline like Hurston, a serious, sensitive student of folklore.

80. William Wells Brown, *Clotel; or, The President's Daughter: A Narrative of Slave Life in the United States* (1853; rpt. New York: Collier, 1970), p. 155. Subsequent references to this novel will be in the text.

81. A notable exception is Jean Fagan Yellin, *The Intricate Knot: Black Figures in*

American Literature, 1776–1863 (New York: New York University Press, 1972), pp. 172–77.

82. David Grimstead, "Melodrama as Echo of the Historically Voiceless," *Anonymous Americans*, ed. Tamara K. Hareven (Englewood Cliffs: Prentice-Hall, 1971), pp. 82–83.

83. Ibid., p. 87.

84. Frances E. W. Harper, *Iola Leroy; or, Shadows Uplifted* (Boston: James H. Earle, 1892), p. 223. Subsequent references to this novel will be in the text.

85. Pryor, *Neither Bond Nor Free*, p. 81.

2. The Early Afro-American Novel

1. Brown wrote three revisions of *Clotel* for American publication, each time changing titles, plot details, and the names of characters. *Miralda; or, The Beautiful Quadroon: A Romance of American Slavery Founded on Fact* appeared as a serial in the Weekly Anglo-African during the winter of 1860–61. The second version, *Clotelle: A Tale of the Southern States*, was published in 1864; and the final American edition, *Clotelle; or, The Colored Heroine: A Tale of the Southern States*, in 1867. For a reprint of the 1864 edition and an excellent introduction, see J. Noel Heermance, *William Wells Brown and Clotelle: A Portrait of the Artist in the First Negro Novel* (Hamden: Archon, 1969). Less perceptive and reliable are the introductions to reprints of *Blake* and *Clotelle* in Ronald T. Takaki, *Violence in the Black Imagination: Essays and Documents* (New York: G. P. Putman's Sons, 1972).

2. Quoted in Heermance, *William Wells Brown*, p. 19.

3. Although Brown acknowledges borrowing from Lydia Maria Child's short story "The Quadroons," William E. Farrison, his chief biographer, reveals that for his main plot Brown "reproduced most of the details and most of the language verbatim of the first two-thirds of Mrs. Child's 'The Quadroons,' shifting the setting from the vicinity of Augusta, Georgia, to that of Richmond and changing the names of the characters." See Farrison, *William Wells Brown*, p. 224. Also see Yellin, *The Intricate Knot*, p. 172.

4. Also at the roots of the novel, according to one critic, is "the rumor which William Lloyd Garrison was spreading in his press to the effect that Thomas Jefferson's alleged slave-daughter had lately been sold for $1000 on the New Orleans market" (Heermance, *William Wells Brown*, p. 191).

5. Arthur P. Davis, Introduction to Frank J. Webb, *The Garies and Their Friends* (1857; rpt. New York: Arno and The New York Times, 1969), p. xii. Subsequent references to this novel will be in the text.

6. "Our Nig" [Harriet E. Wilson], *Our Nig; or, Sketches from the Life of a Free Black, In a Two-Story White House, North. Showing That Slavery's Shadows Fall Even There*, with introduction and notes by Henry Louis Gates, Jr. (1859; 2d ed. New York: Vintage, 1983), p. 3. Subsequent references to this novel will be in the text.

7. One of the most significant literary events of the 1960s was Floyd Miller's

Notes to The Early Afro-American Novel

unearthing of several missing chapters of Delany's *Blake*, the second black American novel published in America rather than England. Chapters 1–23 and 29–31 have long been available in the January and July 1859 issues of the *Anglo-African Magazine*, a black publication. The complete novel comprising approximately eighty chapters was serialized in the *Weekly Anglo-African*, also a black publication, from November 1861 through May 1862. Miller found the issues containing chapters 24–28 and 32–74, but the four issues of May have yet to be found. Consequently, the novel remains incomplete. Even so, the seventy-four chapters in the Beacon Press edition mark the first publication of the novel in book form and provide more than an adequate basis for a close examination of the text.

8. Quoted in Lerone Bennett, Jr., *Before the Mayflower: A History of the Negro in America 1619–1962* (Chicago: Johnson, 1962), p. 149.

9. Vernon Loggins, *The Negro Author: His Development in America to 1900* (1931; rpt. Port Washington: Kennikat, 1964), p. 186.

10. Delany, *Blake*, p. 20. Subsequent references to this novel will be in the text.

11. Martin R. Delany, *The Condition, Elevation, Emigration, and Destiny of the Colored People of the United States* (1852; rpt. New York: Arno and The New York Times, 1969), p. 203.

12. See David Walker's *Appeal to the Coloured Citizens of the World* and Garnet's *Address to the Slaves of the United States* in *A Documentary History of the Negro People in the United States*, ed. Herbert Aptheker (1951; 3d ed. New York: Citadel, 1965), 1: 93–97, 226–33.

13. Howard, *Bond and Free*, pp. 3–4.

14. "I have nothing to commend me to your consideration in the way of learning, nothing in the way of education to entitle me to your attention," Douglass would say in his opening remarks to white audiences. "But I will take it for granted that you know something about the degrading influences of slavery, and that you will not expect great things from me this evening, but simply facts as I may be able to advance immediately in connection with my own experience of slavery." This mock apology became an effective prefacing device for fugitive orators and early novelists. Quoted in Heermance, *William Wells Brown*, p. 44.

15. Walter H. Stowers and William H. Anderson [Sanda, pseud.], *Appointed; an American Novel* (Detroit: Detroit Law, 1894), p. 270.

16. Benjamin Brawley, *The Negro Genius: A New Appraisal of the Achievement of the American Negro in Literature and the Fine Arts* (New York: Dodd, Mead, 1937), p. 117.

17. Sterling A. Brown, Arthur P. Davis, and Ulysses Lee, eds. *The Negro Caravan: Writings by American Negroes* (1941; rpt. New York: Arno and The New York Times, 1970), p. 139; Gloster, *Negro Voices*, p. 30.

18. Sterling Brown, Hugh Gloster, Robert Bone and Arlene Elder are among the few critics who have evaluated Griggs's novels. In a highly informative study, Patricia D. Watkins comments on the controversy as to whether Griggs was "the novelist of the New Negro" (Gloster and Elder) "somewhere between 'precursor and the New Negro' and 'novelist of the New Negro incarnate' " (Bone); apologist

(Brown), militant (Gloster) or vacillator between militance and accommodationism (Bone and Elder). All four critics agree that Griggs was a propagandist, but whereas Brown and Gloster consider him a counterpropagandist to Dixon, Bone—apparently basing his thesis on Brown's observation that the first generation of black novelists "preferred the 'talented tenth' "—views him as a member of the Talented Tenth who sought acceptance from whites or the black bourgeoisie, not the black masses. Elder argues that Griggs "devoted himself to writing and publishing for the black masses," but "places his hopes for progress in representatives of the new Black bourgeoisie..." See Sterling A. Brown, *The Negro in American Fiction* (1937; rpt. New York: Atheneum, 1969), pp. 100–101, 105; and Arlene A. Elder, *The "Hindered Hand": Cultural Implications of Early African-American Fiction* (Westport: Greenwood, 1978), pp. 34, 102; see also above, chapter 1, n. 29.

19. Sutton E. Griggs, *Overshadowed: A Novel* (Nashville: Orion, 1901), p. 219.

20. Sutton E. Griggs, *The Story of My Struggles* (Memphis: National Public Welfare League, 1914), p. 11.

21. William Loren Katz, *The Black West* (Garden City: Doubleday, 1971), p. 301. Actually the novel was reviewed by J. W. Cromwell in the column "Literary Leaves," *Colored American*, April 8, 1899, p. 3.

22. Bone, *Negro Novel*, p. 33; Gloster, "Sutton E. Griggs," in Hemenway, *Black Novelist*, p. 13; and Gayle, *Way of the New World*, p. 66.

23. Bone, *Negro Novel*, p. 33.

24. Gloster, "Sutton E. Griggs," in Hemenway, *Black Novelist*, p. 14.

25. "Daily newspapers and magazines, favorable to the highest interests of the race, must be established so that the outpourings of the souls of Negro writers may have better opportunities of reaching the world. The poem, the novel, the drama must be pressed into service. The painter, the sculptor, the musical composer must plead our case in the world of aesthetics." See Sutton E. Griggs, *Unfettered* (Nashville: Orion, 1902), p. 274.

26. Griggs, *Imperium in Imperio*, p. 247.

27. The following biographical information was taken from the Chesnutt Papers at Fisk University; Helen M. Chesnutt, *Charles Waddell Chesnutt: Pioneer of the Color Line* (Chapel Hill: University of North Carolina Press, 1952); Sylvia Lyons Render, *Eagle with Clipped Wings: Form and Feeling in the Fiction of Charles Waddell Chesnutt* (Ann Arbor: University Microfilms, 1974); and William L. Andrews, *The Literary Career of Charles W. Chesnutt* (Baton Rouge: Louisiana State University Press, 1980). The Chesnutt Papers and Andrews reveal that the author was more ambivalent about his racial identity and materials than the daughter portrays in her hagiography and Render reveals in her pioneer study. It is regrettable that both H. Chesnutt and Render silently omit some unflattering, contradictory material on this topic.

28. H. Chesnutt, *Charles Waddell Chesnutt*, p. 21.

29. Charles W. Chesnutt, *The Wife of His Youth, and Other Stories of the Color Line* (1899; rpt. Ann Arbor: Ann Arbor Paperbacks, 1968), p. 7.

30. Quoted in H. Chesnutt, *Charles Waddell Chesnutt*, p. 147. Sarah Orne Jewett

Notes to The Pre-World War I Novels of the Old Guard

(1849–1909) and Mary E. Wilkins Freeman (1852–1930) were talented New England local-color and regional writers.

31. Elizabeth L. Cary, "A New Element in Fiction," *Book Buyer*, August 1901, pp. 27–28.

32. H. Chesnutt, *Charles Waddell Chesnutt*, pp. 177–79.

33. William Dean Howells, "A Psychological Counter-Current in Fiction," *North American Review* 173 (December 1901): 882.

34. Charles W. Chesnutt, *The Marrow of Tradition* (1901; rpt. Ann Arbor: Ann Arbor Paperbacks, 1969), p. 7. Subsequent references to this novel will be in the text.

35. Quoted in H. Chesnutt, *Charles Waddell Chesnutt*, p. 59.

36. For a persuasive linguistic case study of the authenticity of Chesnutt's literary dialect, see Charles W. Foster, "The Representation of Negro Dialect in Charles W. Chesnutt's *The Conjure Woman*," (Ph.D. diss., University of Alabama, 1968).

37. Quoted in Benjamin Brawley, *Paul Laurence Dunbar: Poet of His People* (Chapel Hill: University of North Carolina Press, 1936), p. 37.

38. See Paul L. Dunbar, *The Strength of Gideon and Other Stories* (New York: Dodd, Mead, 1900).

39. In collaboration with Will Marion Cook, a black composer, Dunbar wrote the lyrics for the musical, "Clorindy, or the Origin of the Cakewalk." Although the show was a hit in New York in 1898 and played successfully on the road in 1901, Dunbar soon lost interest in the theater. See Virginia Cunningham, *Paul Laurence Dunbar and His Song* (New York: Dodd Mead, 1947), pp. 166–67, 178–80.

40. Some cultural historians ascribe this phenomenon to the black middle-class's rejection of their folk heritage and imitation of white middle-class values. See LeRoi Jones, *Blues People: Negro Music in White America* (New York: Morrow Quill, 1963), pp. 122–41.

41. See Bone, *Negro Novel*, pp. 42–43.

3. The Pre-World War I Novels of the Old Guard

1. Vernon L. Parrington, *Main Currents in American Thought: The Beginnings of Critical Realism in America 1860–1920* (New York: Harbinger, 1930), 3: 346.

2. Franklin, *From Slavery to Freedom*, pp. 294–95.

3. Between 1882 and 1927, 4,951 people were lynched in the United States. Of the victims 3,513 were black and 1,438 were white; 76 black women and 16 white women are included in these numbers. "The number of victims each year has sharply decreased, but the savagery with which the smaller number of victims are tortured by American mobs is proportionately greater than at the turn of the century. From the days when one John Malcolm was 'genteely Tarr'd and Feather'd' at Pownalborough, Massachusetts, in 1773, mobbism has inevitably degenerated to the point where an uncomfortably large percentage of American citizens can read in their newspapers of the slow roasting alive of a human being in Mississippi and

turn, promptly and with little thought, to the comic strip or sporting page. Thus has lynching become an almost integral part of our national folkways" (Walter Whiter White, *Rope and Faggot: A Biography of Judge Lynch* [1929; rpt. New York: Arno and The New York Times, 1969], pp. ix–x, 227–69).

4. Quoted in Franklin, *From Slavery to Freedom*, p. 334.

5. Leslie Fiedler, *Love and Death in the American Novel*, rev. ed. (New York: Delta, 1966), p. 29.

6. See Fiedler, *Love and Death*, pp. 23–38; and Edwin M. Eigner, *The Metaphysical Novel in England and America: Dickens, Bulwer, Melville, and Hawthorne* (Berkeley: University of California Press, 1978), pp. 1–13.

7. Richard Chase, *The American Novel and Its Tradition* (Garden City: Doubleday, 1957), p. 20.

8. Fiedler, *Love and Death*, pp. 28–29.

9. George Levine, *The Realistic Imagination: English Fiction from Frankenstein to Lady Chatterly* (Chicago: University of Chicago Press, 1980), pp. 8, 20–21.

10. George Becker, "Introduction: Modern Realism as a Literary Movement," *Documents of Modern Literary Realism*, ed. George J. Becker (Princeton: Princeton University Press, 1963), p. 35.

11. Charles C. Walcutt, *American Literary Naturalism: A Divided Stream* (Minnesota: University of Minnesota Press, 1956), pp. vii–viii, 20–23.

12. Donald Pizer, *Twentieth-Century American Literary Naturalism: An Interpretation* (Carbondale: Southern Illinois University Press, 1982), pp. xi, 8–9.

13. "For the Marxist," writes Georg Lukács, "the road to socialism is identical with the movement of history itself. There is no phenomenon, objective or subjective, that has not its function in furthering, obstructing or deviating this development. A right understanding of such things is vital to the thinking socialist. Thus, *any* accurate account of reality is a contribution—whatever the author's subjective intention—to the Marxist critique of capitalism, and is a blow in the cause of socialism. In this sense, the alliance of socialism with realism may be said to have its roots in the revolutionary movement of the proletariat" (*Realism in Our Time: Literature and the Class Struggle*, trans. John and Necke Mander [1963; rpt. New York: Harper Torchbooks, 1971], p. 101). See also Becker, *Documents of Modern Literary Realism*, pp. 21–22.

14. W. E. B. Du Bois, *The Quest of the Silver Fleece* (1911; rpt. Miami: Mnemosyne, 1969), p. 184. Subsequent references to this novel will be in the text.

15. Carl Van Vechten, Introduction to James Weldon Johnson, *The Autobiography of an Ex-Coloured Man* (1912; rpt. New York: Alfred A. Knopf, 1927), p. vii. Subsequent references in the text to this novel will be from the Hill and Wang edition of 1960.

16. James Weldon Johnson, *Along This Way: The Autobiography of James Weldon Johnson* (New York: Viking Compass, 1968), pp. 9, 78, 157.

17. James Weldon Johnson, ed. *The Book of American Negro Poetry*, rev. ed. (New York: Harcourt, Brace and World, 1931), p. 9.

18. For an intriguing theory of Southern black culture as a "shame culture" and complement of the theory of Southern white culture as a "guilt culture," see Eugene D. Genovese, *Roll, Jordan, Roll: The World the Slaves Made* (New York: Random House, 1974), pp. 113–23. See also Ostendorf, *Black Literature in White America*, pp. 30–31.

4. The Harlem Renaissance and the Search for New Modes of Narrative

1. Arna Bontemps, Introduction to Toomer, *Cane*, p. x. The first flowering of Afro-American literature occurs in the antebellum slave narratives of Douglass and Brown, and culminates in the 1890s poetry, fiction, and essays of Dunbar, Chesnutt, and Du Bois. The seeds of the Harlem Renaissance, according to Bontemps, were planted in 1917 with the publication of McKay's "Harlem Dancer" and Johnson's *50 Years and Other Poems*. See "The Black Renaissance of the Twenties," *Black World*, November 1970, p. 7.

2. There were actually six international Pan-African meetings. The first was organized by Henry S. Williams, a Trinidad lawyer, in 1900, and the sixth was convened by George Padmore, also from Trinidad, and Du Bois in 1945. Because the first meeting was called a "Conference" and the subsequent meetings "Congresses," some students of pan-Africanism do not include it in their discussions. Richard B. Moore, "Du Bois and Pan Africa," *Freedomways*, First Quarter 1965, pp. 166–87.

3. See W. E. B. Du Bois, *The Negro* and *The Gift of Black Folk: The Negroes in the Making of America* (Boston: Stratford, 1924); and Carter G. Woodson, *The Negro in Our History* (Washington D.C.: Associated Publishers, 1922).

4. Robert Hayden, Preface, *The New Negro*, ed. Alain Locke (1925; rpt. New York: Atheneum, 1968), p. ix.

5. I am indebted to Professors Richard Long and Wilfred Cartey for this concept. But I have expanded and radically modified it for this study. See Richard Long, "Alain Locke: Cultural and Social Mentor," *Black World*, November 1970, pp. 87–90; and Wilfred Cartey, Introduction, *Negritude: Black Poetry from Africa and the Caribbean*, ed. and trans. Norman R. Shapiro (New York: October House, 1970), pp. 17–37.

6. Langston Hughes, "The Negro Artist and the Racial Mountain," *Nation*, 112 June 23, 1926, p. 694.

7. Locke, *New Negro*. p. 47.

8. See Frank Durham comp, *Studies in Cane* (Columbus: Charles E. Merrill, 1971); Darwin T. Turner, *In a Minor Chord: Three Afro-American Writers and Their Search for Identity* (Carbondale: Southern Illinois University Press, 1971), pp. 1–59; and Bernard W. Bell, "*Cane*: A Portrait of the Black Artist as High Priest of Soul," *Black World*, September 1974, pp. 4–19, 92–97. See also Nellie McKay, *Jean Toomer, Artist: A Study of His Literary Life and Work, 1894–1936* (Chapel Hill: University of North Carolina Press, 1984).

9. Jean Toomer, "Earth Being," Toomer Collection, Fisk University Library, p. 18.

10. Jean Toomer, "On Being American," Toomer Collection, Fisk University Library, p. 48.

11. Toomer, "Earth Being," p. 18.

12. Toomer, "On Being American," p. 45.

13. Toomer, *Cane*, p. 200. Subsequent references to this novel will be in the text.

14. Jean Toomer, "Outline of Autobiography," Toomer Collection, Fisk University Library, p. 55.

15. Arna Bontemps, Preface, *Black Thunder* (1936; rpt. Boston: Beacon, 1968), p. vii.

16. Ibid., p. 91.

17. In general, Bontemps adheres to the historical facts of the revolt. In several important instances, however, the facts were manipulated. For example, it was not a girlfriend but Gabriel's wife Nanny who participated in the conspiracy. Rather than 400, approximately 1,000 slaves met on the night of the attack, which means a far larger number were involved in the conspiracy than the 1,100 cited in the novel. And both Pharoah and Tom, the actual names of the informers, were purchased by order of the legislature and given their freedom as a reward for their loyalty (Herbert Aptheker, *American Negro Revolts* [1943; rpt. New York: New World Paperbacks, 1969], pp. 219–27). See also Ulrich B. Phillips, *American Negro Slavery: A Survey of the Supply, Employment and Control of Negro Labor as Determined by the Plantation Regime* (1918; rpt. Baton Rouge: Louisiana Paperbacks, 1969), pp. 474–75.

18. See Edmund D. Cronon, *Black Moses: The Story of Marcus Garvey and the Universal Negro Improvement Association* (1955; rpt. Madison: University of Wisconsin Press, 1968); Amy Jacques-Garvey, *Garvey and Garveyism* (New York: Collier, 1970); and *Philosophy and Opinions of Marcus Garvey*, ed. Amy Jacques-Garvey (New York: Atheneum, 1970).

19. See for example, L. S. B. Leakey, *The Progress and Evolution of Man in Africa* (New York: Oxford University Press, 1961), pp. 1–3; Robert W. July, *A History of the African People* (New York: Charles Scribner's Sons, 1970), pp. 8–10; and John G. Jackson, *Introduction to African Civilizations* (New York: University Books, 1970), pp. 40–50.

20. Locke, *New Negro* pp. 14–15, 12.

21. Silberman, *Crisis in Black and White*, p. 165.

22. Kenneth B. Clark, *Dark Ghetto: Dilemmas of Social Power* (New York: Harper Torchbooks, 1967).

23. Toomer, McKay, Hughes, Cullen, Bontemps, Hurston, Fauset, Larsen and most of the younger New Negroes attended college and their parents were "55 per cent professionals and 45 percent white collar. . . ." See Bone, *Negro Novel*, p. 56 n. 5.

24. For the revision of Fauset's birthdate from 1884 to 1882 and her place of birth from Philadelphia to Camden, see Carolyn Wedin Sylvander, *Jessie Redmon Fauset, Black American Writer* (Troy, N.Y.: Whitston, 1981), pp. 23–24.

25. Brown, *Negro in American Fiction*, p. 140.

26. Jessie Fauset, *The Chinaberry Tree: A Novel of American Life* (1931; rpt. College Park: McGrath, 1969), p. x.

27. Ibid., p. ix.

28. Jessie Fauset, *Plum Bun: A Novel Without a Moral* (New York: Frederick A. Stokes, 1929), pp. 218–19.

29. Nella Larsen, *Quicksand* (1928; rpt. New York: Collier, 1971), p. 119. Subsequent references to this novel will be in the text.

30. Nella Larsen, *Passing* (1929; rpt. New York: Collier, 1971), p. 138.

31. Ibid., p. 18.

32. Hughes, "Negro Artist and the Racial Mountain," p. 692.

33. W. E. B. Du Bois, "Review of *Nigger Heaven*," in *Nigger Heaven*, Carl Van Vechten (1926; rpt. New York: Harper Colophon, 1971), p. ix.

34. Van Vechten, *Nigger Heaven*, pp. 89–90, 281.

35. See, for example, James Weldon Johnson, "Dilemma of the Negro Author," *American Mercury* 15 (December 1928): 480.

36. Jahn, *Neo-African Literature*; pp. 15–24; and Bone, *Down Home*, pp. xiii–xxii.

37. For intriguing modern studies of this topic, see Raymond Williams, *The Country and the City* (New York: Oxford University Press, 1973); Leo Marx, *The Machine in the Garden: Technology and the Pastoral Idea in America* (1964; rpt. New York: Galaxy, 1967); and Bone, *Down Home*.

38. Senghor, quoted in Abraham Chapman, "The Harlem Renaissance in Literary History," *College Language Association Journal* 15 (September 1967): 57 n. 31.

38. Dewey P. Jones, *Chicago Defender*, March 17, 1928, quoted in Gloster, *Negro Voices*, p. 164.

40. Claude McKay, *Home to Harlem* (1928; rpt. New York: Pocket Cardinal, 1965), pp. 22, 144.

41. Claude McKay, *Banjo: A Story Without a Plot* (1929; rpt. New York: Harvest Book, 1970), pp. 321–23, 313–14.

42. Claude McKay, *Banana Bottom* (1933; rpt. New York: Harvest Book, 1970), pp. 125, 313.

43. Robert E. Hemenway, Introduction to Zora Neale Hurston, *Dust Tracks on a Road: An Autobiography*, ed. Robert E. Hemenway, 2d ed. (Urbana: University of Illinois Press, 1984), p. xi.

44. For the controversially insidious influence of white paternalism on Hurston, see her autobiography *Dust Tracks on a Road* (1942; rpt. New York: J. B. Lippincott Company, 1971); and Hemenway, *Zora Neale Hurston*, p. 27. See also, Turner, *In a Minor Chord*, pp. 89–120, and Huggins, *Harlem Renaissance*, pp. 74–75, 129–33. For a womanist perspective, see Alice Walker, "Zora Neale Hurston: A Cautionary Tale and Partisan View" and "Looking for Zora," *In Search of Our Mothers' Gardens: Womanist Prose* (New York: Harcourt Brace Jovanovich, 1983), pp. 83–92, 93–116.

45. With the exception of Darwin Turner and Robert Hemenway, most literary historians classify *Moses: Man of the Mountain* as folklore and her other long narratives

362

Notes to The Harlem Renaissance

as novels. In this study, only the final narrative is classified as a novel. See Bone, *Negro Novel*, p. 126; Turner, *In a Minor Chord*, p. 109; and Hemenway, *Zora Neale Hurston*, pp. 256–57.

46. Turner, *In a Minor Chord*, p. 100.

47. Zora Neale Hurston, *Jonah's Gourd Vine* (1934; rpt. New York: J. B. Lippincott, 1971), p. 12.

48. Zora Neale Hurston, *Their Eyes Were Watching God* (1937; rpt. Greenwich: Fawcett, 1969), pp. 5, 45. Subsequent references to this romance will be in the text.

49. See, for example, Marjorie Pryse, "Zora Neale Hurston, Alice Walker and the 'Ancient Power' of Black Women," in *Conjuring: Black Women, Fiction, and Literary Tradition*, ed. Marjorie Pryse and Hortense J. Spillers (Bloomington: Indiana University Press, 1985), pp. 13–15.

50. Walker, "Zora Neale Hurston," *In Search of Our Mothers' Gardens*, p. 88. For an excellent essay which argues, among other things, that literary critics and daughters misread Hurston "as a celebrator of liberated heterosexual love," see Sadoff, "Black Matrilineage," pp. 4–26.

51. Langston Hughes, *The Big Sea* (1940; rpt. New York: Hill and Wang, 1968), p. 228.

52. Hughes's fictional creation of a Harlem folk character, commonly known as "Simple," first appeared in the writer's regular column in the *Chicago Defender* in 1943. See, for example, *The Best of Simple* (New York: Hill and Wang, 1961).

53. Langston Hughes, *Not Without Laughter* (1930; rpt. New York: Collier, 1969), p. 75. Subsequent references to this novel will be in the text.

54. Langston Hughes, *Tambourines to Glory* (New York: Hill and Wang, 1958), p. 179.

55. Countee Cullen, *One Way to Heaven* (New York: Harper and Brothers, 1932), p. 54. Subsequent references to this novel will be in the text.

56. Bone is in error when he writes: "Satire as a literary attitude was out of the question for the early Negro novelist. The social struggle in which he was engaged was too compelling, and humor too keen a blade for his blunt needs. Self-satire, moreover, could hardly be expected of those whose first impulse was to defend their race against the slanderous attacks of white authors" (*Negro Novel*, p. 89).

57. Robert C. Elliott, *The Power of Satire: Magic, Ritual, Art* (Princeton: Princeton University Press, 1969). See also Ronald Paulsen, *Satire and the Novel in Eighteenth-Century England* (New Haven: Yale University Press, 1967), pp. 11–22.

58. Elliott, *Power of Satire*, pp. 14–15.

59. For an illuminating analysis of this controversial theory, see Gerhart Piers and Milton B. Singer, *Shame and Guilt: A Psychoanalytic and A Cultural Study* (Springfield, Ill.: Charles C. Thomas, 1953). See also Ruth Benedict, *The Chrysanthemum and the Sword* (Boston: Houghton Mifflin, 1946), pp. 222–24.

60. Rudolph Fisher, *The Walls of Jericho* (1928; rpt. New York: Arno and The New York Times, 1969), p. 37. Subsequent references to this novel will be in the text.

61. The first serialized detective novel by a black American, according to Henry

Notes to Richard Wright and the Triumph of Naturalism

Louis Gates, Jr., is J. E. Bruce's *Black Sleuth* (1907). See Angus Paul, "A Wealth of Material on Black Literature Discovered by Periodical Fiction Project," *The Chronicle of Higher Education*, October 23, 1985, pp. 5, 7.

62. S. S. Van Dine is the pen name of Willard Huntington Wright. In addition to Sam Spade, Hammett gave the world the detective team of Nick and Nora Charles. See *The Maltese Falcon* (New York: Knopf, 1930) and *The Thin Man* (New York: Knopf, 1934).

63. Rudolph Fisher, *The Conjure-Man Dies: A Mystery Tale of Dark Harlem* (1932, rpt. New York: Arno and The New York Times, 1971), p. 22. Subsequent references to this novel will be in the text.

64. George S. Schuyler, *Black No More: Being an Account of the Strange and Wonderful Workings of Science in the Land of the Free, A.D. 1933–1940* (1931; rpt. New York: Collier, 1971), p. 222. Subsequent references to this novel will be in the text.

65. See James O. Young, *Black Writers of the Thirties* (Baton Rouge: Louisiana State University Press, 1973).

66. George S. Schuyler, *Slaves Today: A Story of Liberia* (New York: Brewer, Warren and Putnam, 1931), p. 10. Subsequent references to this novel will be in the text.

67. Wallace Thurman, *The Blacker the Berry: A Novel of Negro Life* (1929; rpt. New York: Collier, 1970), p. 4. Subsequent references to this novel will be in the text.

68. Wallace Thurman, *Infants of the Spring* (1932; rpt. Plainview: Books for Libraries Press, 1972), pp. 144–45. Subsequent references to this novel will be in the text.

5. Richard Wright and the Triumph of Naturalism

1. S. P. Fullinwider, *The Mind and Mood of Black America: 20th Century Thought* (Homewood, Ill.: Dorsey, 1969), p. 172.

2. Richard Wright, Introduction to St. Clair Drake and Horace Cayton, *Black Metropolis: A Study of Negro Life in a Northern City* (New York: Harcourt, Brace and World, 1945), p. xviii.

3. Citing the work of Alfred Adler, Park was perhaps the first to develop the theory that feelings of inferiority are related to the pathological behavior that results from a disorganized community. Robert E. Park, "Community Organization and Juvenile Delinquency," in Robert E. Park, Ernest W. Burgess, and Roderick D. McKenzie, *The City* (Chicago: University of Chicago Press, 1925), pp. 99–112. According to Park's theory of "social disorganization," the impersonal, industrial life of the city breaks down the community mores of transplanted migrants and ethnic minorities. With the breakdown of the family unit, the most important social structure for controlling interpersonal relationships, the usual result is antisocial behavior on the part of the individual. Another key concept developed by Park involves the man caught between two cultures, the "marginal man." Unlike Du Bois's concept of double-consciousness, which stresses cultural fusion as well as conflict as the common fate of Afro-Americans, Park's concept of marginal man refers to the conflict of cultures and social roles of only mulattoes, racial hybrids. Drawing on

Park and others, Everett V. Stonequist defines the marginal man as "the individual who through migration, education, marriage, or some other influence leaves one social group or culture without making a satisfactory adjustment to another [and] finds himself on the margin of each but a member of neither." See Robert E. Park "Mentality of Racial Hybrids," *American Journal of Sociology* 36 (January 1931): 534–51; and Everett V. Stonequist, *The Marginal Man: A Study in Personality and Culture Conflict* (New York: Charles Scribner's Sons, 1937), pp. 2–3. See also Robert E. Park and Ernest W. Burgess, *Introduction to the Science of Sociology* (Chicago: University of Chicago Press, 1921); Robert Redfield, *Tepoztlan* (Chicago: University of Chicago Press, 1930); and Louis Wirth, *The Ghetto* (Chicago: University of Chicago Press, 1928). For a highly informative discussion of the "Chicago School," see Fullinwider, *Mind and Mood of Black America*, pp. 72–122.

4. Herbert Hill, "Reflections on Richard Wright: A Symposium on an Exiled Native Son," in *Anger, and Beyond: The Negro Writer in the United States*, ed. Herbert Hill (1966; rpt. New York: Perennial Library, 1968), p. 197.

5. Raymond Wolters, *Negroes and the Great Depression: The Problem of Economic Recovery* (Westport: Greenwood, 1970), pp. 3, 83.

6. Ibid., pp. 8, xi-xiii.

7. Wilson Record, *The Negro and the Communist Party* (1951; rpt. New York, Atheneum, 1971), pp. 25–26.

8. Michel Fabre, *The Unfinished Quest of Richard Wright*, trans. Isabel Barzun (New York: William Morrow, 1973), p. 103. Wright's early Communist affiliation was mainly responsible for the surveillance and harassment by the FBI, the CIA, and the State Department, an ordeal that Addison Gayle believes probably contributed to the anxiety and stress responsible for his sudden death in a French clinic. Gayle, *Richard Wright: Ordeal of a Native Son* (Garden City: Doubleday, Anchor Books, 1980), pp. x–xv, chaps. 16 and 17.

9. Richard Crossman, ed. *The God That Failed* (1950; rpt. New York: Bantam Matrix, 1965), pp. 106, 107–8.

10. Harvey Swados, ed. *The American Writer and the Great Depression* (New York: Bobbs-Merrill, 1966), pp. xi–xxxvi; Norman R. Yetman, ed., *Life Under the "Peculiar Institution": Selections fromm the Slave Narrative Collection* (New York: Holt, Rinehart and Winston, 1970), pp. 339–55; and Bone, *Negro Novel*, pp. 113–14.

11. Richard Wright, *Black Boy: A Record of Childhood Youth* (New York: Harper, 1945), p. 45. See also *American Hunger* (New York: Harper and Row, 1977).

12. See Richard Wright, *Black Power: A Record of Reactions in a Land of Pathos* (New York: Harper, 1954); *The Color Curtain* (New York: World, 1955); *Pagan Spain* (New York: Harper, 1956); and *White Man, Listen!* (New York: Doubleday, 1957).

13. Richard Wright, *Native Son* (1940; rpt. New York: Perennial Classic, 1966), p. 10. Subsequent references to this novel will be in the text.

14. See, for example, Gayle, *Way of the New World*, chap. 8.

15. Abraham Chapman, ed. *Black Voices: An Anthology of Afro-American Literature* (New York: Mentor, 1968), p. 542.

16. Wright, *Native Son*, pp. 46, 130, 174, 215, 274, 332, 334.

17. James Baldwin, "Many Thousands Gone," *Notes of a Native Son* (1955; rpt. Boston: Beacon, 1961), p. 37.

18. Chapman, *Black Voices*, p. 549.

19. Baldwin, *Notes of a Native Son*, pp. 42–43.

20. Chapman, *Black Voices*, p. 555. Horace Cayton calls this theory of the personality the fear-hate-fear complex. "I am convinced," he states, "that at the core of the Negro's mentality there is a 'fear-hate-fear' complex. My assumption is that all men in Western European civilization have unconscious guilt and fear of punishment for this guilt. In the case of the dominant group this guilt is to a large extent irrational. It can be shown to be false, a figment of the imagination, a holdover from early childhood experiences. Guilt can more easily be resolved by psychiatric treatment or even by rational cogitation. But in the Negro the psychological problem is ever intensified. For him, punishment in the actual environment is ever present; violence, psychological and physical, leaps at him from every side. The personality is brutalized by an unfriendly environment. This reinforces and intensifies the normal insecurity he feels as a person living in our highly complex society. Such attacks on his personality lead to resentment and hatred of the white man. However, the certain knowledge that he will be punished if his hate emotions are discovered only compound his fear. This is the Negro reaction to his own brutalization, subordination and hurt. It is this vicious cycle in which the American Negro is caught and in which his personality is pulverized by an ever-mounting self-propelling rocket of emotional conflict. The Negro has been hurt; he knows it. He wants to strike back, but he must not—there is evidence everywhere that to do so would lead to his destruction." See Horace Cayton, "Ideological Forces in the Work of Negro Writers," in Hill, *Anger, and Beyond*, pp. 43–43.

21. Calvin S. Hall. *A Primer of Freudian Psychology* (New York: Mentor, 1954), chap. 3; and Sigmund Freud, *Inhibitions, Symptoms and Anxiety* (1926; rpt. London: Hogarth, 1948).

22. Baldwin, *Notes of a Native Son*, p. 39.

23. Richard Wright, *Lawd Today* (New York: Avon, 1963), p. 142.

24. Wright, *Black Boy*, p. 274.

25. William Attaway, *Blood on the Forge* (1941; rpt. New York: Collier, 1970), p. 1. Subsequent references to this novel will be in the text.

26. Stephen F. Milliken misleadingly calls the French prize "his first significant literary award" in *Chester Himes: A Critical Appraisal* (Columbia: University of Missouri Press, 1976), pp. 207–8.

27. John A. Williams, "My Man Himes: An Interview with Chester Himes," *Amistad 1*, ed. John A. Williams and Charles F. Harris (New York: Vintage, 1970), pp. 32, 49.

28. Ibid., p. 50; and Ishmael Reed, "Chester Himes: Writer," *Shrovetide in Old New Orleans* (1978; rpt. New York: Discus, 1979), p. 115.

29. *For Love of Imabelle* (1957; 1965, *A Rage in Harlem*; rpt. New York: Dell, 1971);

The Real Cool Killers (1959; rpt. New York: Berkley, 1966); *The Crazy Kill* (1959; rpt. New York: Berkley, 1966); *The Big Gold Dream* (New York: Avon, 1960); *All Shot Up* (New York: Avon, 1960); *The Heat's On* (New York: Berkley, 1972); *Cotton Comes to Harlem* (1965; rpt. New York: Dell, 1970); and *Blind Man With a Pistol* (1969; rpt. *Hot Day, Hot Night*, New York: Dell, 1970).

30. In an interview with *Publishers Weekly*, Himes explains the origin of his detectives: "The two cops, Coffin Ed Johnson and Grave Digger Jones, are roughly based on a black lieutenant and his sergeant partner who worked the Central Avenue ghetto in L. A. back in the 1940s. My cops are just as tough, but somewhat more humane. The original pair were pitiless bastards" (*Publishers Weekly*, April 3, 1972, pp. 20–21).

31. Himes, *For Love of Imabelle*, p. 52.

32. Milliken, *Chester Himes*, pp. 238–39.

33. For a detailed, insightful analysis of the detective novels, see ibid., pp. 207–69; and James Lindquist, *Chester Himes* (New York: Frederick Ungar, 1976), pp. 106–33.

34. "Eeny, meeny, miney-mo, / Catch a nigger by his toe. / If he hollers, let him go. / Eeny, meeny, miney, no. / Out goes you." For a bowdlerized version of this children's song, see Hughes and Bontemps, *Book of Negro Folklore*, p. 422.

35. Chester Himes, *If He Hollers Let Him Go* (1945; rpt. New York: Signet, 1971), p. 84. Subsequent references to this novel will be in the text.

36. Margolies is quite perceptive on this point. "Bob himself never employs clinical language to explain the erotic implications of the psychosocial roles he knows he plays—but the meaning is never far from the surface. Not only does white society emasculate him, but it tends simultaneously to regard him as an envied symbol of sexual strength from which white women must be protected. Implicit here is Himes's view that the sexual insecurity of the white American male impels him to suppress the Negro in order to bolster his shaky masculine ego." Margolies, *Native Sons*, p. 91. See also Chester Himes, *The Quality of Hurt: The Autobiography of Chester Himes* (Garden City: Doubleday, 1976), vol. 1.

37. Milliken, *Chester Himes*, p. 95.

38. John A. Williams, ed. *Beyond the Angry Black* (1966; rpt. New York: Mentor, 1971), p. 79.

39. Ann Petry, *The Street* (1946; rpt. New York: Pyramid, 1961), p. 40. Subsequent references to this novel will be in the text.

40. See Schraufnagel, *From Apology to Protest*, p. 42; and Bone, *Negro Novel*, p. 185.

41. Ann Petry, *The Narrows* (Boston: Houghton Mifflin, 1953), p. 5. Subsequent references to this novel will be in the text.

42. William Gardner Smith, *The Stone Face* (New York: Farrar, Straus, 1963), p. 7. Subsequent references to this novel will be in the text.

43. The novels published in the forties by Micheaux and Yerby are not discussed because both authors are unique cases. Both were influenced by pulp and historical fiction, but whereas Micheaux displays more creative imagination as a filmmaker than as a novelist and published his novels through his own company, Yerby is a

367

highly talented and popular creator of historical romances with white heroes that are primarily designed for pure entertainment. His first novel with a black protagonist, *Speak Now*, was not published until 1970. See Carl Hughes, *Negro Novelist*, pp. 130–33, 149–59.

44. Ibid., p. 252.

6. Myth, Legend, and Ritual in the Novel of the Fifties

1. Franklin, *From Slavery to Freedom*, p. 464.

2. Ibid., p. 477.

3. Hughes, *Negro Novelist*, p. 20.

4. William G. Smith, *Anger at Innocence* (1950; rpt. Chatham, N.J.: Chatham Bookseller, 1973), p. 273.

5. William Demby, *Beetlecreek* (1950; rpt. New York: Avon, 1967), p. 46.

6. Ibid., p. 148.

7. Richard Wright, *The Outsider* (1953; rpt. New York: Perennial Library, 1965), pp. 128–36.

8. Gwendolyn Brooks, *Maude Martha* (1953); reprinted in *The World of Gwendolyn Brooks* (New York: Harper and Row, 1971), pp. 128, 305.

9. Ellison, *Shadow and Act*, pp. 174–75.

10. Ibid., pp. 25, xiii.

11. Ibid., pp. xvi–xvii.

12. See Kent, "Ethnic Impact in American Literature," pp. 24–37.

13. Ellison, *Shadow and Act*, p. 177.

14. Ibid., p. 105; Booker T. Washington, *Up From Slavery* in *Three Negro Classics*, ed. John H. Franklin (New York: Discus, 1968), pp. 53–56.

15. Washington, *Up From Slavery*, p. 149.

16. Bone, *Negro Novel*, p. 204.

17. See Sigmund Freud, "Totem and Taboo," in *The Basic Writings of Sigmund Freud*, trans. and ed. A. A. Brill (New York: Modern Library, 1938), pp. 807–930. Also see Selma Fraiberg, "Two Modern Incest Heroes," *Partisan Review* 28 (Fall-Winter 1961): 646–61.

18. Ellison *Shadow and Act*, pp. 58–59.

19. Ibid., pp. 189–90.

20. For an intriguing, insightful theory of repetition in black culture, see James A. Snead, "Repetition as a Figure of Black Culture," in *Black Literature and Literary Theory*, ed. Henry Louis Gates, Jr. (New York: Methuen, 1984), pp. 59–79.

21. Jordan, *White over Black*, pp. 464–65.

22. See Ex. 3:14.

23. Ellison, *Shadow and Act*, p. 172.

24. Baldwin, "Autobiographical Notes," in *Notes of a Native Son*, p. 8.

25. Fern Maria Eckman, *The Furious Passage of James Baldwin* (New York: M. Evans, 1966), pp. 27, 4.

26. Baldwin, *Notes of a Native Son*, p. 108.

27. Eckman, *Furious Passage*, pp. 46, 49, 43, 41. "Possibly the 'something' that magnetized him," Eckman unconvincingly speculates, "was that stock comedy figure, Topsy, who must have struck the boy as his feminine counterpart. She was exactly his age and, like him, a misfit, isolated, ridiculed, repugnant to those around her. She had his own round eyes, his own solemnity, his own quickness and keenness . . . his own generosity and his own misery."

28. James Baldwin, "Alas, Poor Richard," *Nobody Knows My Name: More Notes of a Native Son* (New York: Delta, 1962), p. 191.

29. Baldwin, *Notes of a Native Son*, pp. 6–7, 174.

30. Quoted in Harold R. Isaacs, *The New World of Negro Americans* (New York: Viking Compass, 1964), p. 275.

31. Baldwin, *Notes of a Native Son*, p. 87.

32. Baldwin, *Nobody Knows My Name*, p. 5.

33. Baldwin, *Notes of a Native Son*, p. 63.

34. Baldwin, *Nobody Knows My Name*, pp. 191–93.

35. Baldwin, *Notes of a Native Son*, pp. 23, 35.

36. James Baldwin, *If Beale Street Could Talk* (New York: Dial, 1974), pp. 59, 128.

37. Albert Murray, *The Hero and the Blues* (Columbia: University of Missouri Press, 1973), p. 39.

38. Eleanor Traylor, "I Hear Music in the Air: James Baldwin's *Just Above My Head*," *First World* 2, no. 3 (1979): 42.

39. James Baldwin, *Just Above My Head* (New York: Dell, 1980), p. 497. Subsequent references to this novel will be in the text.

40. James Baldwin, *Go Tell It on the Mountain* (1953; rpt. New York: Grosset's Universal Library, 1961), p. 34. Subsequent references to this novel will be in the text.

7. The Contemporary Afro-American Novel, 1: Neorealism

1. Stokeley Carmichael and Charles V. Hamilton, *Black Power: The Politics of Liberation in America* (New York: Vintage, 1967), p. 44.

2. John H. Bracey, Jr., "Black Nationalism Since Garvey," in Huggins, Kilson, and Fox, *Key Issues in the Afro-American Experience*, 2: 266–67.

3. Harold Cruse, *Rebellion or Revolution?* (New York: William Morrow, 1969), pp. 75–77.

4. Larry Neal, "The Black Arts Movement," in *The Black Aesthetic*, ed. Addison Gayle, Jr. (1971; rpt. Garden City: Anchor, 1972), p. 257.

5. Ibid.

6. Larry Neal, "And Shine Swam On," in *Black Fire: An Anthology of Afro-American Writing*, ed. LeRoi Jones and Larry Neal (New York: William Morrow, 1968), pp. 643–48.

7. Betty Friedan, *The Feminine Mystique* (New York: Dell, 1975), p. 85.

8. Gerda Lerner, ed., *Black Women in White America: A Documentary History* (New

369

Notes to The Contemporary Afro-American Novel, 1

York: Vintage, 1973), p. xxv. See also Bell Hooks, *Ain't I A Woman: Black Women and Feminism* (Boston: South End Press, 1981), pp. 119–96.

9. Toni Cade, "On the Issue of Roles," in *The Black Woman: An Anthology,* ed. Toni Cade (New York: Signet, 1970), pp. 103–4.

10. Combahee River Collective, "Black Feminist Statement," in *All the Women Are White, All the Blacks Are Men, But Some of Us Are Brave,* ed. Gloria T. Hull, Patricia Bell Scott, and Barbara Smith (Old Westbury: Feminist Press, 1982), p. 15.

11. Ibid.

12. Toni Cade Bambara, cited in *Black Women Writers at Work,* ed. Claudia Tate (New York: Continuum, 1983), p. 34.

13. Calvin Hernton, "The Sexual Mountain and Black Women Writers," *Black American Literature Forum* 18 (Winter 1984): 139.

14. Andrea Benton Rushing, "Images of Black Women in Afro-American Poetry," in *The Afro-American Woman: Struggles and Images,* ed. Sharon Harley and Rosalyn Terborg-Penn (Port Washington: Kennikat, 1978), pp. 74–84; "Images of Black Women in Modern African Poetry: An Overview," in *Sturdy Black Bridges: Visions of Black Women in Literature,* ed. Roseann P. Bell, Bettye J. Parker, and Beverly Guy-Sheftall (Garden City, N.Y.: Anchor, 1979), pp. 18–24; and "Family Resemblances: A Comparative Study of Women Protagonists in Contemporary African-American and Anglophone-African Novels" (Ph.D. diss., University of Massachusetts, Amherst, 1983).

15. Barbara Smith, "Toward a Black Feminist Criticism," in *The New Feminist Criticism: Essays on Women, Literature, and Theory,* ed. Elaine Showalter (New York: Pantheon, 1985), pp. 168–85; and Deborah E. McDowell, "New Directions for Black Feminist Criticism," ibid., pp. 186–99.

16. McDowell, "New Directions for Black Feminist Criticism," pp. 190–95.

17. Bambara cited in Tate, *Black Women Writers at Work,* pp. 19–20.

18. Mary Helen Washington, ed., *Midnight Birds: Stories of Contemporary Black Women Writers* (Garden City, N.Y.: Anchor, 1980), p. 43.

19. Georg Lukács, *Realism in Our Time,* pp. 93, 94. Lukács's emphasis.

20. John Killens, quoted in Harold Cruse, *The Crisis of the Negro Intellectual* (1967; rpt. New York: Apollo, 1968), p. 235. Cruse's critique of the failure of the Harlem Left is highly informative despite his personal attacks on individuals. On Killens, see pp. 206–52.

21. John O. Killens, "The Black Writer Vis-à-Vis His Country," *Black Man's Burden* (New York: Trident, 1965), pp. 34, 31.

22. Gayle, *Way of the New World,* p. 276.

23. John O. Killens, *Youngblood* (1954; rpt. New York: Pocket Books, 1955), p. 9.

24. John O. Killens, *And Then We Heard the Thunder* (1963; rpt. New York: Pocket Books, 1964), p. 496. Subsequent references to this novel will be in the text.

25. John O. Killens, *'Sippi* (New York: Trident, 1967), p. xiii. For an informative discussion on Killens's use of folklore, see William H. Wiggins, Jr., "Black Folktales

in the Novels of John O. Killens," *Black Scholar: Journal of Black Studies and Research*, November 1971, pp. 50–58.

26. John O. Killens, *The Cotillion; or One Good Bull Is Half the Herd* (New York: Pocket Books, 1972), p. 171. Subsequent references to this novel will be in the text.

27. John A. Williams, "Career by Accident," *Flashbacks: A Twenty-Year Diary of Article Writing* (Garden City, N.Y.: Doubleday, 1973), p. 394.

28. John Williams quoted in O'Brien, *Interviews with Black Writers*, p. 230.

29. John A. Williams, *Night Song* (1961, *Sweet Love Bitter*; rpt. New York: Pocket Books, 1970), p. 41. Subsequent references to this novel will be in the text.

30. John A. Williams, *The Man Who Cried I Am* (1967; rpt. New York: Signet, 1968), p. 308. Subsequent references to this novel will be in the text.

31. "Nobody has really influenced me," Williams tells an interviewer. "This is because I read without discrimination when I was a great deal younger. In terms of form, my single influence has been Malcolm Lowry in *Under the Volcano*. I tried to emulate him in *Sissie* and improve on what he did with the telescoping of time. But I think I did it much better in *The Man Who Cried I Am*" (O'Brien, *Interviews*, pp. 233, 230).

32. Ibid., p. 187.

33. Ibid., pp. 192, 193.

34. Alice Walker, *The Third Life of Grange Copeland* (1970; rpt. New York: Avon, 1971), p. 12. Subsequent references to this novel will be in the text.

35. Alice Walker, *Meridian* (New York: Harcourt Brace Jovanovich, 1976), pp. 40–47. Subsequent references to this novel will be in the text.

36. Alice Walker, *The Color Purple* (New York: Harcourt Brace Jovanovich, 1982), p. 167. Subsequent references to this novel will be in the text.

37. Trudier Harris, "On *The Color Purple*, Stereotypes, and Silence," *Black American Literature Forum* 18 (Winter 1984): 157.

38. Toni Cade Bambara, *The Salt Eaters* (New York: Random House, 1980), p. 8. Subsequent references to this novel will be in the text.

39. Toni Morrison, *Song of Solomon* (New York: Knopf, 1977), p. 3. Subsequent references to this novel will be in the text.

40. Toni Morrison, *The Bluest Eye* (1970; rpt. New York: Pocket Books, 1972), p. 20.

41. Toni Morrison, *Sula* (New York: Knopf, 1973), pp. 152, 65. Subsequent references to this novel will be in the text.

42. Hoyt W. Fuller, "A Survey: Black Writers' Views on Literary Lions and Values," *Negro Digest*, January 1968, p. 21.

8. The Contemporary Afro-American Novel, 2: Modernism and Postmodernism

1. Quoted in Franklin, *From Slavery to Freedom*, p. 482.

2. Albert P. Blaustein and Robert L. Zangrando, *Civil Rights and the American Negro: A Documentary History* (New York: Washington Square, 1968), pp. 559–61.

371

Notes to The Contemporary Afro-American Novel, 2

3. Gerald Graff, *Literature Against Itself: Literary Ideas in Modern Society* (Chicago: University of Chicago Press, 1979), pp. 48, 18.

4. J. Hillis Miller, quoted in ibid., p. 19.

5. Jerome Klinkowitz, *Literary Disruptions: The Making of a Post-Contemporary American Fiction*, 2d ed. (Urbana: University of Illinois Press, 1980), pp. 3–11.

6. Ibid., pp. 175–89.

7. Robert Scholes, *The Fabulators* (New York: Oxford University Press, 1967), p. 12.

8. Nikki Giovanni and Margaret Walker, *A Poetic Equation: Conversations Between Nikki Giovanni and Margaret Walker* (Washington, D.C.: Howard University Press, 1974), p. 3.

9. Most biographical sketches erroneously cite 1937 as the year she graduated from Northwestern, but she reveals that it was actually 1935. See Margaret Walker Alexander, "Richard Wright" in *Richard Wright: Impressions and Perspectives*, ed. David Ray and Robert M. Farnsworth (1971; rpt. Ann Arbor: University of Michigan Press, 1973), p. 49.

10. Ibid., pp. 91–92. Margaret Walker, *How I Wrote "Jubilee"* (Chicago: Third World Press, 1972), pp. 13–14.

11. Walker, *How I Wrote "Jubilee"*, p. 11.

12. Ibid., pp. 12, 27.

13. Walker, *Jubilee*, p. 13. Subsequent references to this novel will be in the text.

14. Charles Rowell, "Poetry, History and Humanism: An Interview with Margaret Walker," *Black World*, December 1975, p. 10.

15. Ruth Laney, "A Conversation with Ernest Gaines," *Southern Review* 10 (January 1974): 3.

16. O'Brien, *Interviews*, p. 83.

17. Some critics believe that Gaines "succumbs to the power and achievement of Hemingway and Faulkner" in *Catherine Carmier* and *Of Love and Dust*, but achieves his own distinctive style in *Bloodline* and *The Autobiography of Miss Jane Pittman*. See, for example, Jerry Bryant, "From Death to Life: The Fiction of Ernest J. Gaines," *Iowa Review*, Winter 1972, pp. 106–20.

18. Laney, "Conversation with Gaines," p. 6.

19. Ernest J. Gaines, *The Autobiography of Miss Jane Pittman* (1971; rpt. New York: Bantam, 1972), p. 228. Subsequent references to this novel will be in the text.

20. O'Brien, *Interviews*, p. 84.

21. William Melvin Kelley, *Dancers on the Shore* (1964; rpt. Chatham, N.J.: Chatham Bookseller, 1973), preface.

22. William Melvin Kelley, quoted in Hoyt W. Fuller, "The Task of the Negro Writer as Artist: A Symposium," *Negro Digest*, April 1965, p. 78.

23. For much of the following discussion of Joycean parallels, I am indebted to Grace Eckley, "The Awakening of Mr. Afrinnegan: Kelley's *Dunfords Travels Everywheres* and Joyce's *Finnegan's Wake*," *Obsidian: Black Literature in Review* 1 (Summer 1975): 27–40.

24. William Melvin Kelley, *Dunfords Travels Everywheres* (Garden City, N.Y.: Doubleday, 1970), p. 49. Subsequent references to this novel will be in the text.

25. See Edward O. G. Turville-Petrie, *Myth and Religion of the North: The Religion of Ancient Scandinavia* (New York: Holt, Rinehart and Winston, 1964); *The Poetic Edda*, 2d rev. ed., trans. Lee H. Hollander (Austin: University of Texas Press, 1962); *The Prose Edda of Snorri Sturluson; Tales from Norse Mythology*, trans. Jean I. Young (Berkeley: University of California Press, 1973); and Edith Hamilton, *Mythology* (New York: Mentor, 1969), pp. 300–315.

26. See *Prose Edda*, pp. 80–86.

27. William Melvin Kelley, *A Different Drummer* (Garden City, N.Y.: Anchor, 1969), p. 151. Subsequent references to this novel will be in the text.

28. Ronald L. Fair, *Hog Butcher* (New York: Harcourt, Brace and World, 1966), p. 161.

29. Ronald L. Fair, *Many Thousand Gone* (New York: Harcourt, Brace and World, 1965), pp. 111 and 119.

30. Ronald L. Fair, *World of Nothing: Two Novellas* (New York: Harper and Row, 1970), p. 62. Subsequent references to these novels will be in the text.

31. Leon Forrest, *The Bloodworth Orphans* (New York: Random House, 1977), pp. 185–86.

32. O'Brien, *Interviews*, pp. 216, 217.

33. Ibid., p. 214.

34. John Edgar Wideman, *A Glance Away* (1967; rpt. Chatham, N.J.: Chatham Bookseller, 1975), p. 54. For an informative analysis of Eliot's influence and the relationship between history and imagination, see Kermit Frazier, "The Novels of John Wideman," *Black World*, June 1975, pp. 18–38.

35. O'Brien, *Interviews*, p. 219.

36. John Edgar Wideman, *Hurry Home* (New York: Harcourt, Brace and World, 1970), p. 33.

37. O'Brien, *Interviews*, p. 220.

38. John Edgar Wideman, *The Lynchers* (1973; rpt. New York: Dell, 1974), pp. 114–15. Subsequent references to this novel will be in the text.

39. John Edgar Wideman, *Damballah* (New York: Bard Book, 1981), p. 7. Subsequent references to this book will be in the text.

40. John Edgar Wideman, *Sent for You Yesterday* (New York: Bard Book, 1983), p. 17. Subsequent references to this novel will be in the text.

41. O'Brien, *Interviews*, p. 218.

42. Clarence Major, *The Dark and Feeling: Black American Writers and Their Work* (New York: Third Press, 1974), p. 12.

43. O'Brien, *Interviews*, p. 138.

44. Major, *The Dark and Feeling*, p. 150.

45. O'Brien, *Interviews*, p. 127.

46. Klinkowitz, *Literary Disruptions*, pp. 183–85.

47. O'Brien, *Interviews*, p. 130.

48. Ibid., p. 126.

49. Clarence Major, *NO* (New York: Emerson Hall, 1973), p. 3.

50. Ibid., pp. 204, 205.

51. O'Brien, *Interviews*, p. 126.

52. Clarence Major, *Emergency Exit* (New York: Fiction Collective, 1979), p. 55.

53. Larry McCaffery and Linda Gregory, "Major's *Reflex and Bone Structure* and the Anti-Detective Tradition," *Black American Literature Forum*, Summer 1979, pp. 39–45.

54. Clarence Major, *Reflex and Bone Structure* (New York: Fiction Collective, 1975), p. 61. Subsequent references to this novel will be in the text.

55. McCaffery and Gregory, "Major's *Reflex and Bone Structure*," p. 40.

56. Major, *Dark and Feeling*, p. 128.

57. Ibid., pp. 24–25.

58. Frank Kermode, *The Sense of an Ending: Studies in the Theory of Fiction* (New York: Oxford University Press, 1967), p. 132.

50. Charles Wright, *The Messenger* (New York: Manor, 1974), p. 174. Subsequent references to this novel will be in the text.

60. O'Brien, *Interviews*, p. 250.

61. Charles Wright, *The Wig: A Mirror Image* (New York: Farrar, Straus and Giroux, 1966), p. 13. Subsequent references to this novel will be in the text.

62. One white critic misinterprets this black slang expression or misreads the novel, erroneously stating that "Lester even buys a wig because the salesman guarantees him that it will help" (O'Brien, *Interviews*, p. 246).

63. Victor Navasky, *New York Times*, February 27, 1966, sec. 8, p. 5. See also Max F. Schulz, *Black Humor Fiction of the Sixties: A Pluralistic Definition of Man and His World* (Athens: Ohio University Press, 1973), pp. 99–101, 108–14, 119–22.

64. O'Brien, *Interviews*, pp. 246, 257.

65. Ronald Walcott, "The Novels of Hal Bennett," Part 1, *Black World*, June 1974, p. 37.

66. Hal Bennett, *The Black Wine* (New York: Pyramid, 1968), p. 300.

67. Ronald Walcott, "The Novels of Hal Bennett," Part 2, *Black World*, July 1974, p. 79.

68. Hal Bennett, *Wait Until Evening* (Garden City, N.Y.: Doubleday, 1974), pp. 250, 256 (italics in the original), 258.

69. Hal Bennett, *Seventh Heaven* (Garden City, N.Y.: Doubleday, 1976), p. 13.

70. Hal Bennett, *A Wilderness of Vines* (New York: Pyramid, 1967), p. 85. Subsequent references to this novel will be in the text.

71. Walcott, "Novels" Part 1, p. 48.

72. O'Brien, *Interviews*, pp. 167–68.

73. Ibid., p. 167; Reed, *19 Necromancers from Now*, p. xxiv; and Tom Dent, "Umbra Days," *Black Interviews Literature Forum* 14 (Fall 1980): 107. The latter is a highly informative essay on this generally neglected, historically important group of new black artists. Besides Dent, Hernton, and Henderson, the Umbra Workshop in-

cluded Joe Johnson, Askia Muhammad Toure, Alvin Haynes, Lloyd Addison, Charles Patterson, Lorenzo Thomas, Leroy McLucas, Archie Shepp, Norman Pritchard, Ishmael Reed, Lennox Ralphael, James Thompson, Oliver Pitcher, Art Berger, and Steve Cannon.

74. Reed, *19 Necromancers from Now*, pp. xxiv, xiii.

75. See, for example, Houston Baker, Jr., review of *The Last Days of Louisiana Red*, by Ishmael Reed, *Black World*, June 1975, pp. 51–52, 89.

76. Ishmael Reed, *Conjure: Selected Poems, 1963–1970* (Amherst: University of Massachusetts Press, 1972), pp. 20–22.

77. Ishmael Reed, *Flight to Canada* (New York: Random House, 1976), p. 88.

78. Ishmael Reed, *Yellow Back Radio Broke-Down* (Garden City, N.Y.: Doubleday, 1969), p. 128. Subsequent references to this novel will be in the text. See also O'Brien, *Interviews*, p. 172; and Ishmael Reed, "Ishmael Reed on Ishmael Reed," *Black World*, June 1974, p. 25.

79. See, for example, Ron Karenga, "Black Art: A Rhythmic Reality of Revolution," *Negro Digest*, January 1968, pp. 5–9.

80. Ishmael Reed, *Mumbo Jumbo* (Garden City, N.Y.: Doubleday, 1972), p. 190. Subsequent references to this novel will be in the text.

81. O'Brien, *Interviews*, pp. 172, 177.

82. Ibid., pp. 181–82.

83. Ibid., p. 179.

Conclusion

1. Some readers will ask how I justify reducing the largest racial group in the United States to an ethnic minority. Aside from the obvious political and scientific problematics of racial classifications, I agree with sociologist William J. Wilson that "whereas racial groups are distinguished by socially selected physical traits, ethnic groups are distinguished by socially selected cultural traits." Contrary to Wilson's view, however, that "the classification of a particular group as either racial or ethnic is dependent on the perceptions and definitions of members of the larger society," I submit that people define themselves ethnically as a distinct group by their shared experiences of living with their environment, each other, and the larger society. Thus, as Wilson confirms, "certain racial minorities are also classified as ethnic groups, and some writers . . . have subsumed the concept of racial group under the general category of ethnic group (racially defined ethnic groups). If a given racial group is ethnically distinct, i.e., viewed as having a distinct subculture and as being bound by similar cultural ties, such a designation is valid." Because I have clearly demonstrated that black Americans have a distinct subculture, they are generally classified as an ethnic group in this ethnographic literary history of the Afro-American novel (*Power Racism, and Privilege: Race Relations in Theoretical and Sociohistorical Perspectives* [1973; rpt., New York: Free Press, 1976], p. 6).

Selected Bibliography

I have not attempted to list all of the primary and secondary sources that I consulted in writing this book. Instead, I list only the novels by the 112 authors that I have examined closely, beginning with the forty-one authors for whom I provide background information, and those sources that should be most useful to the reader who might want to pursue further study and research on an interdisciplinary approach to the Afro-American novel and its tradition. The most complete bibliography is *Afro-American Fiction, 1853–1976* (Detroit: Gale Research Co., 1979) by Edward Margolies and David Bakish. Other useful bibliographies are *Black American Fiction: A Bibliography* (Metuchen, N.J.: Scarecrow, 1978) by Carol Fairbanks and Eugene A. Engeldinger; *Black American Writers Past and Present: A Biographical Dictionary*, 2 vols. (Metuchen, N.J.: Scarecrow, 1975) by Theressa Gunnels Rush, Carol Fairbanks Myers, and Esther Spring Arata; *The Afro-American Novel 1965–1975: A Descriptive Bibliography of Primary and Secondary Material* (Troy: Whitston, 1977) by Helen Ruth Houston; and *Afro-American Writers* (New York: Appleton-Century-Crofts, 1970) by Darwin T. Turner.

Primary Works: Novels by Forty-one Authors

Attaway, William. *Blood on the Forge.* 1941. Reprint. New York: Collier Books, 1970.
———. *Let Me Breathe Thunder.* 1939. Reprint. Chatham, N.J.: Chatham Bookseller, 1969.
Baldwin, James. *Another Country.* 1962. Reprint. New York: Dell Book, 1963.
———. *Giovanni's Room.* 1956. Reprint. New York: Apollo Editions, 1962.
———. *Go Tell It on the Mountain.* 1953. Reprint. New York: Grosset's Universal Library, 1961.
———. *If Beale Street Could Talk.* New York: Dial Press, 1974.
———. *Just Above My Head.* 1979. New York: Dell Book, 1980.
———. *Tell Me How Long the Train's Been Gone.* 1968. Reprint. New York: Dell Book, 1969.
Bennett, Hal. *The Black Wine.* New York: Pyramid Books, 1968.
———. *Lord of Dark Places.* New York: Bantam Books, 1971.
———. *Seventh Heaven.* Garden City, N.Y.: Doubleday and Co., 1976.
———. *Wait Until Evening.* Garden City, N.Y.: Doubleday and Co., 1974.
———. *A Wilderness of Vines.* New York: Pyramid Books, 1967.

Bibliography

Bontemps, Arna. *Black Thunder*. 1936. Reprint. Boston: Beacon Press, 1968.

Brown, William Wells. *Clotel; or, The President's Daughter. A Narrative of Slave Life in the United States*. 1853. Reprint. New York: Collier Books, 1970.

———. *Clotelle: A Tale of the Southern States*. Boston: J. Redpath, 1864.

———. *Clotelle, or, The Colored Heroine. A Tale of the Southern States*. Boston: Lee and Shepard, 1867.

Chesnutt, Charles W. *The Colonel's Dream*. 1905. Reprint. Miami: Mnemosyne Publishing Co., 1969.

———. *The House Behind the Cedars*. 1900. Reprint. New York: Collier Books, 1969.

———. *The Marrow of Tradition*. 1901. Reprint. Ann Arbor: Ann Arbor Paperbacks, 1969.

Cullen, Countee. *One Way to Heaven*. New York: Harper and Brothers, 1932.

Delany, Martin. *Blake; or, the Huts of America*. Boston: Beacon Press, 1970.

Du Bois, W. E. B. *Dark Princess: A Romance*. New York: Harcourt, Brace and Co., 1928.

———. *Mansart Builds a School*. New York: Mainstream Publishers, 1959.

———. *The Ordeal of Mansart*. New York: Mainstream Publishers, 1957.

———. *The Quest of the Silver Fleece: A Novel*. 1911. Reprint. Miami: Mnemosyne Publishing Co., 1969.

———. *Worlds of Color*. New York: Mainstream Publishers, 1961.

Dunbar, Paul Laurence. *The Fanatics*. 1901. Reprint. Miami: Mnemosyne Publishing Co., 1969.

———. *The Love of Landry*. New York: Dodd, Mead and Co., 1900.

———. *The Sport of the Gods*. 1902. Reprint. Miami: Mnemosyne Publishing Co., 1969.

———. *The Uncalled: A Novel*. 1898. Reprint. New York: International Association of Newspapers and Authors, 1901.

Ellison, Ralph. *Invisible Man*. 1952. Reprint. New York: Signet Book, 1964.

Fair, Ronald L. *Hog Butcher*. New York: Harcourt, Brace and World, 1966.

———. *Many Thousand Gone*. New York: Harcourt, Brace and World, 1965.

———. *We Can't Breathe*. New York: Harper and Row, 1972.

———. *World of Nothing: Two Novellas*. New York: Harper and Row, 1970.

Fauset, Jessie. *The Chinaberry Tree: A Novel of American Life*. 1931. Reprint. College Park, Md.: McGrath Publishing Co., 1969.

———. *Comedy: American Style*. New York: Frederick A. Stokes, Co., 1933.

———. *Plum Bun: A Novel Without a Moral*. New York: Frederick A. Stokes, Co., 1929.

———. *There is Confusion*. New York: Boni and Liveright, 1924.

Fisher, Rudolph. *The Conjure-Man Dies: A Mystery Tale of Dark Harlem*. 1932. Reprint. New York: Arno Press and The New York Times, 1971.

———. *The Walls of Jericho*. 1928. Reprint. New York: Arno Press and The New York Times, 1969.

Gaines, Ernest J. *The Autobiography of Miss Jane Pittman*. 1971. Reprint. New York: Bantam Books, 1972.

————. *In My Father's House*. New York: Alfred A. Knopf, 1978.

————. *Of Love and Dust*. 1967. Reprint. New York: Bantam Books, 1969.

Griggs, Sutton E. *The Hindered Hand: or, The Reign of the Repressionist*. 1905. Reprint. Miami: Mnemosyne Publishing Co., 1969.

————. *Imperium in Imperio: A Study of the Negro Race Problem. A Novel*. 1899. Reprint. Miami: Mnemosyne Publishing Co., 1969.

————. *Overshadowed: A Novel*. Nashville: Orion Publishing Co., 1901.

————. *Pointing the Way*. Nashville: Orion Publishing Co., 1908.

————. *Unfettered*. Nashville: Orion Publishing Co., 1902.

Harper, Frances Ellen Watkins. *Iola Leroy; or, Shadows Uplifted*. Boston: James H. Earle, 1892.

Himes, Chester. *All Shot Up*. New York: Avon Books, 1960.

————. *The Big Gold Dream*. New York: Avon Books, 1960.

————. *Blind Man With a Pistol*. 1969. Reprint. *Hot Day, Hot Night*. New York: Dell Book, 1970.

————. *Cast the First Stone*. 1952. Reprint. New York: Signet Book, 1972.

————. *Cotton Comes to Harlem*. 1965. Reprint. New York: Dell Book, 1970.

————. *The Crazy Kill*. 1959. Reprint. New York: Berkley Publishing Corp., 1966.

————. *For Love of Imabelle*. 1957. *The Five-Cornered Square*. 1965. *A Rage in Harlem*. Reprint. New York: Dell Book, 1971.

————. *The Heat's On*. New York: Berkley Publishing Corp., 1972.

————. *If He Hollers Let Him Go*. 1945. Reprint. New York: Signet Book, 1971.

————. *Lonely Crusade*. 1947. Reprint. Chatham, N.J.: Chatham Bookseller, 1973.

————. *Pinktoes*. 1961. Reprint. New York: Dell-Putnam, 1966.

————. *The Primitive*. New York: Signet Book, 1955.

————. *The Real Cool Killers*. 1959. Reprint. New York: Berkley Publishing Corp., 1966.

————. *Run Man Run*. 1966. Reprint. New York: Dell Book, 1969.

————. *The Third Generation*. 1954. Reprint. New York: Signet Book, 1956.

Hughes, Langston. *Not Without Laughter*. 1930. Reprint. New York: Collier Books, 1969.

————. *Tambourines to Glory*. New York: Hill and Wang, 1958.

Hurston, Zora Neale. *Jonah's Gourd Vine*. 1934. Reprint. New York: J. B. Lippincott Co., 1971.

————. *Moses: Man of the Mountain*. 1939. Reprint. Chatham, N.J.: Chatham Bookseller, 1975.

————. *Seraph on the Suwanee*. New York: Charles Scribner's Sons, 1948.

————. *Their Eyes Were Watching God*. 1937. Reprint. Greenwich, Conn.: Fawcett Premier Book, 1971.

Johnson, James Weldon. *The Autobiography of an Ex-Coloured Man*. 1912. Reprint. New York: Hill and Wang, 1960.

Kelley, William Melvin. *dem*. 1967. Reprint. New York: Collier Books, 1969.

————. *A Different Drummer*. Garden City, N.Y.: Anchor Books, 1969.

————. *A Drop of Patience*. Garden City, N.Y.: Doubleday and Co., 1965.

————. *Dunfords Travels Everywheres*. Garden City, N.Y.: Doubleday and Co., 1970.

Killens, John O. *And Then We Heard the Thunder*. 1963. Reprint. New York: Pocket Books, 1964.

————. *The Cotillion; or, One Good Bull Is Half the Herd*. 1971. Reprint. New York: Pocket Books, 1972.

————. *'Sippi*. New York: Trident Press, 1967.

————. *Youngblood*. 1954. Reprint. New York: Pocket Books, 1955.

Larsen, Nella. *Passing*. 1929. Reprint. New York: Collier Books, 1971.

————. *Quicksand*. 1928. Reprint. New York: Collier Books, 1971.

McKay, Claude. *Banana Bottom*. 1933. Reprint. New York: Harvest Books, 1970.

————. *Banjo: A Story Without a Plot*. 1929. Reprint. New York: Harvest Books, 1970.

————. *Home to Harlem*. 1928. Reprint. New York: Pocket Cardinal, 1965.

Major, Clarence. *All-Night Visitors*. New York: Olympia Press, 1969.

————. *Emergency Exit*. New York: Fiction Collective, 1979.

————. *NO*. New York: Emerson Hall Publishers, 1973.

————. *Reflex and Bone Structure*. New York: Fiction Collective, 1975.

Morrison, Toni. *The Bluest Eye*. 1970. Reprint. New York: Pocket Books, 1972.

————. *Song of Solomon*. New York: Alfred A. Knopf, 1977.

————. *Sula*. New York: Alfred A. Knopf, 1973.

————. *Tar Baby*. New York: Alfred A. Knopf, 1981.

Petry, Ann. *Country Place*. 1947. Reprint. Chatham, N.J.: Chatham Bookseller, 1971.

————. *The Narrows*. Boston: Houghton Mifflin, 1953.

————. *The Street*. 1946. Reprint. New York: Pyramid Books, 1961.

Reed, Ishmael. *Flight to Canada*. New York: Random House, 1976.

————. *The Free-Lance Pallbearers*. 1967. Reprint. New York: Bantam Books, 1969.

————. *The Last Days of Louisiana Red*. New York: Random House, 1974.

————. *Mumbo Jumbo*. Garden City, N.Y.: Doubleday and Co., 1972.

————. *The Terrible Twos*. 1982. Reprint. New York: Bard Book, 1983.

————. *Yellow Back Radio Broke-Down*. Garden City, N.Y.: Doubleday and Co., 1969.

Schuyler, George S. *Black No More: Being an Account of the Strange and Wonderful Workings of Science in the Land of the Free, A.D. 1933–1940*. 1931. Reprint. New York: Collier Books, 1971.

————. *Slaves Today: A Story of Liberia*. New York: Brewer, Warren and Putnam, 1931.

Smith, William Gardner. *Anger at Innocence*. 1950. Reprint. Chatham, N.J.: Chatham Bookseller, 1973.

————. *Last of the Conquerors*. New York: Farrar, Straus and Co., 1948.

————. *South Street*. 1954. Reprint. Chatham, N.J.: Chatham Bookseller, 1973.

————. *The Stone Face*. New York: Farrar, Straus and Co., 1963.

Thurman, Wallace. *The Blacker the Berry: A Novel of Negro Life*. 1929. Reprint. New York: Collier Books, 1970.

————. *Infants of the Spring*. 1932. Reprint. Plainview, N.Y.: Books for Libraries Press, 1972.

Bibliography

Toomer, Jean. *Cane*. 1923. Reprint. New York: Perennial Classic, 1969.

Walker, Alice. *The Color Purple*. New York: Harcourt Brace Jovanovich, 1982.

——. *Meridian*. New York: Harcourt Brace Jovanovich, 1976.

——. *The Third Life of Grange Copeland*. 1970. Reprint. New York: Avon Books, 1971.

Walker, Margaret, *Jubilee*. 1966. Reprint. New York: Bantam Books, 1967.

Webb, Frank J. *The Garies and Their Friends*. 1857. Reprint. New York: Arno Press and The New York Times, 1969.

Wideman, John Edgar, *A Glance Away*. 1967. Reprint. Chatham, N.J.: Chatham Bookseller, 1975.

——. *Damballah*. New York: Bard Book, 1981.

——. *Hiding Place*. New York: Bard Book, 1981.

——. *Hurry Home*. New York: Harcourt, Brace and World, 1970.

——. *The Lynchers*. 1973. Reprint. New York: Dell Book, 1974.

——. *Sent for You Yesterday*. New York: Bard Book, 1983.

Williams, John A. *Captain Blackman*. 1972. Reprint. New York: Bantam Books, 1974.

——. *The Junior Bachelor Society*. Garden City, N.Y.: Doubleday and Co., 1976.

——. *The Man Who Cried I Am*. 1967. Reprint. New York: Signet Book, 1968.

——. *Mothersill and the Foxes* Garden City, N.Y.: Doubleday and Co., 1975.

——. *Night Song*. 1961. *Sweet Love Bitter*. Reprint. New York: Pocket Books, 1970.

——. *Sissie*. 1963. Reprint. Garden City, N.Y.: Anchor Books, 1969.

——. *Sons of Darkness, Sons of Light*. 1969. Reprint. New York: Pocket Books, 1970.

Wilson, Harriet E. ["Our Nig," pseud.]. *Our Nig; or, Sketches from the Life of a Free Black, In a Two-Story White House, North. Showing That Slavery's Shadows Fall Even There*. 1859. 2d ed. New York: Vintage Books, 1983.

Wright, Charles. *The Messenger*. 1963. Reprint. New York: Manor Books, 1974.

——. *The Wig: A Mirror Image*. New York: Farrar, Straus and Giroux, 1966.

Wright, Richard. *Lawd Today*. New York: Avon Books, 1963.

——. *The Long Dream*. Garden City, N.Y.: Doubleday and Co., 1958.

——. *Native Son*. 1940. Reprint. New York: Perennial Classic, 1966.

——. *The Outsider*. 1953. Reprint. New York: Perennial Library, 1965.

——. *Savage Holiday*. 1954. Reprint. New York: Award Books, 1965.

Supplementary Primary Works: Novels by Seventy-one Authors

Adams, Alger L. [Philip B. Kaye, pseud.]. *Taffy*. New York: Crown Publishers, 1950.

Bambara, Toni Cade. *The Salt Eaters*. New York: Random House, 1980.

Baraka, Amiri. [LeRoi Jones]. *The System of Dante's Hell*. New York: Grove Press, 1965.

Beckham, Barry. *My Main Mother*. 1969. Reprint. New York: Signet Book, 1971.

——. *Runner Mack*. New York: William Morrow, 1972.

Bland, Alden. *Behold a Cry*. New York: Charles Scribner's Sons, 1947.

Boles, Robert. *Curling*. Boston: Houghton Mifflin, 1968.

——. *The People One Knows*. Boston: Houghton Mifflin, 1964.

Bradley, David. *The Chaneysville Incident*. New York: Harper and Row, 1981.

Brooks, Gwendolyn. *Maud Martha*. 1953. Reprinted in *The World of Gwendolyn Brooks*. New York: Harper and Row, 1971.

Brown, Cecil. *The Life and Loves of Mr. Jiveass Nigger*. 1969. Reprint. New York: Crest Book, 1971.

Brown, Frank L. *Trumbull Park*. Chicago: Henry Regnery Co., 1959.

Brown, Lloyd. *Iron City*. New York: Masses and Mainstream, 1951.

Bullins, Ed. *The Reluctant Rapist*. New York: Harper and Row, 1973.

Cain, George. *Blueschild Baby*. 1970. Reprint. New York: Dell Book, 1972.

Childress, Alice. *A Short Walk*. 1979. Reprint. New York: Avon Books, 1981.

Colter, Cyrus. *The Hippodrome*. Chicago: Swallow Press, 1973.

——. *Rivers of Eros*. Chicago: Swallow Press, 1972.

Davis, George. *Coming Home*. New York: Random House, 1971.

Demby, William. *Beetlecreek*. 1950. Reprint. New York: Avon Books, 1967.

——. *The Catacombs*. 1965. Reprint. New York: Perennial Library, 1970.

Dodson, Owen. *Boy at the Window*. Reprint. Chatham, N.J.: Chatham Bookseller, 1972.

Downing, Henry F. *The American Cavalryman; A Liberian Romance*. New York: Neale Publishing Co., 1917.

Dreer, Herman. *The Immediate Jewel of His Soul*. 1919. Reprint. College Park, Md.: McGrath Publishing Co., 1969.

Forrest, Leon. *The Bloodworth Orphans*. New York: Random House, 1977.

——. *There Is a Tree More Ancient Than Eden*. New York: Random House, 1973.

Gilmore, F. Grant. *"The Problem": A Military Novel*. Rochester: Press of Henry Con- olly Co., 1915.

Grant, J. W. *Out of the Darkness; or Diabolism and Destiny*. Nashville: National Baptist Publishing Board, 1909.

Greenlee, Sam. *The Spook Who Sat by the Door*. 1969. Reprint. New York: Bantam Books, 1970.

Guy, Rosa. *Bird at My Window*. Philadelphia: J. B. Lippincott, 1966.

——. *A Measure of Time*. 1983. Reprint. New York: Bantam Books, 1984.

Heard, Nathan C. *Howard Street*. 1968. Reprint. New York: Signet Book, 1970.

Henderson, George W. *Ollie Miss*. New York: Frederick A. Stokes Co., 1935.

Hercules, Frank. *I Want a Black Doll*. New York: Simon and Schuster, 1967.

Hernton, Calvin. *Scarecrow*. Garden City, N.Y.: Doubleday and Co., 1974.

Hopkins, Pauline E. *Contending Forces: A Romance Illustrative of Negro Life North and South*. 1900. Reprint. Miami: Mnemosyne Publishing Co., 1969.

Howard, James H. W. *Bond and Free: A True Tale of Slave Times*. 1886. Reprint. Miami: Mnemosyne Publishing Co., 1969.

Hunter, Kristin. *God Bless the Child*. 1964. Reprint. New York: Bantam Books, 1970.

——. *The Landlord*. 1966. Reprint. New York: Avon Books, 1970.

Jones, Gayl. *Corregidora*. New York: Random House, 1975.

Bibliography

——. *Eva's Man*. 1976. Reprint. New York: Bantam Books, 1978.

Jones, J. McHenry. *Hearts of Gold*. Wheeling, W.Va.: Daily Intelligencer Steam Job Press, 1896.

Kemp, Arnold. *Eat of Me: I Am the Savior*. New York: William Morrow, 1972.

Lee, George W. *River George*. New York: Macaulay, 1937.

Lucas, Curtis. *Third Ward Newark*. New York: Ziff Davis, 1946.

Mahoney, William. *Black Jacob*. New York: Macmillan, 1969.

Marshall, Paule. *Brown Girl, Brownstones*. 1959. Reprint. New York: Avon Books, 1970.

——. *The Chosen Place, The Timeless People*. 1969. Reprint. New York: Vintage Books, 1984.

Mayfield, Julian. *The Grand Parade*. New York: Vanguard Press, 1961.

——. *The Hit*. New York: Vanguard Press, 1957.

——. *The Long Night*. New York: Vanguard Press, 1958.

Meriwether, Louise M. *Daddy Was a Number Runner*. 1970. Reprint. New York: Pyramid Books, 1971.

Micheaux, Oscar. *The Forged Note: A Romance of the Darker Races*. Lincoln, Neb.: Western Book Supply Co., 1915.

——. [Pioneer, pseud.]. *The Conquest; The Story of a Negro Pioneer*. Lincoln, Neb.: Woodruff Press, 1913.

Motley, Willard, *Knock on Any Door*. 1947. Reprint. New York: Signet Book, 1950.

——. *We Fished All Night*. New York: Appleton-Century Crofts, 1951.

Murray, Albert. *Train Whistle Guitar*. New York: McGraw-Hill Book Co., 1974.

Naylor, Gloria. *The Women of Brewster Place*. 1982. Reprint. New York: Penguin Books, 1983.

Offord, Carl. *The White Face*. New York: Robert M. McBride, 1943.

Parks, Gordon, *The Learning Tree*. 1963. Reprint. New York: Crest Book, 1964.

Pharr, Robert Dean. *The Book of Numbers*. 1969. Reprint. New York: Avon Books, 1970.

Polite, Carlene H. *The Flagellants*. New York: Farrar, Straus and Giroux, 1967.

Pryor, George. *Neither Bond Nor Free (A Plea)*. New York: J. S. Oglive Publishing Co., 1902.

Redding, Saunders. *Strangers and Alone*. 1950. Reprint. New York: J. & J. Harper, 1969.

Rhodes, Hari. *A Chosen Few*. 1965. Reprint. New York: Bantam Books, 1969.

Rogers, Joel A. *She Walks in Beauty*. Los Angeles: Western Publishers, 1963.

Savoy, Willard. *Alien Land*. New York: E. P. Dutton, 1949.

Scott-Heron, Gil. *The Nigger Factory*. New York: Dial Press, 1972.

Shackelford, Otis M. *Lillian Simmons; or The Conflict of Sections*. Kansas: R. M. Rigby Printing Co., 1915.

Shange, Ntozake. *Sassafrass, Cypress, & Indigo*. New York: St. Martin's Press, 1982.

Shockley, Ann A. *Loving Her*. 1974. Reprint. New York: Avon Books, 1978.

Simmons, Herbert A. *Corner Boy*. Boston: Houghton Mifflin, 1957.

Bibliography

Southerland, Ellease. *Let the Lion Eat Straw*. 1979. Reprint. New York: Signet Book, 1980.

Stone, Chuck. *King Strut*. Indianapolis: Bobbs-Merrill Co., 1970.

Stowers, Walter H., and William H. Anderson [Sanda, pseud.]. *Appointed; an American Novel*. Detroit: Detroit Law Printing Co., 1894.

Turpin, Waters E. *O Canaan!* New York: Doubleday, Doran, 1939.

Van Dyke, Henry. *Dead Piano*. New York: Farrar, Straus and Giroux, 1971.

———. *Ladies of the Rachmaninoff Eyes*. 1965. Reprint. New York: Manor Books, 1973.

Van Peebles, Melvin. *A Bear for the FBI*. New York: Trident Press, 1968.

Waring, Robert L. *As We See It*. Washington, D.C.: C. F. Sudwarth Press, 1910.

West, Dorothy. *The Living Is Easy*. 1948. Reprint. New York: Arno Press and The New York Times, 1969.

White, Walter F. *The Fire in the Flint*. 1924. Reprint. New York: Negro Universities Press, 1969.

———. *Flight*. 1926. Reprint. New York: Negro Universities Press, 1969.

Wright, Sarah E. *This Child's Gonna Live*. 1969. Reprint. New York: Dell Book, 1970.

Yerby, Frank. *Speak Now: A Modern Novel*. New York: Dial Press, 1969.

Young, Al. *Snakes*. New York: Holt, Rinehart and Winston, 1970.

Secondary Sources

Abrahams, Roger D. *Deep Down in the Jungle: Negro Narrative Folklore from the Streets of Philadelphia*. Rev. ed. Chicago: Aldine Publishing Co., 1979.

———. "Playing the Dozens." *Journal of American Folklore* 75 (1962): 209–20.

———. *Positively Black*. Englewood Cliffs, N.J.: Prentice-Hall, 1970.

Andrews, William L. *The Literary Career of Charles W. Chesnutt*. Baton Rouge: Louisiana State University Press, 1980.

Aptheker, Herbert. *American Negro Revolts*. 1943. Reprint. New York: New World Paperbacks, 1969.

———. ed. *A Documentary History of the Negro People in the United States*. 3d ed. Vol. 1. *From Colonial Times Through the Civil War*. New York: Citadel Press, 1965.

Baker, Houston A., Jr. *Blues, Ideology, and Afro-American Literature: A Vernacular Theory*. Chicago: University of Chicago Press, 1984.

———. *The Journey Back: Issues in Black Literature and Criticism*. Chicago: University of Chicago Press, 1980.

———. Review of *The Last Days of Louisiana Red*, by Ishmael Reed. *Black World*, June 1975, pp. 51–52, 89.

Baldwin, James. *Nobody Knows My Name: More Notes of Native Son*. New York: Delta Book, 1962.

———. *Notes of a Native Son*. 1955. Reprint. Boston: Beacon Paperback, 1961.

Bascom, William. "Folklore and Literature." In *The African World: A Survey of Social Research*, edited by Robert A. Lystod. New York: Frederick Praeger, 1965, pp. 459–90.

———. "The Forms of Folklore: Prose Narratives." *Journal of American Folklore* 78 (1965): 3–20.

Becker, George J. "Introduction: Modern Realism as a Literary Movement." In *Documents of Modern Literary Realism.* Edited by George J. Becker. Princeton: Princeton University Press, 1963.

Bell, Bernard W. "*Cane*: A Portrait of the Black Artist as High Priest of Soul." *Black World,* September 1974, pp. 4–19, 92–97.

———. *The Folk Roots of Contemporary Afro-American Poetry.* Detroit: Broadside Press, 1974.

———. "Styron's Confessions." *Michigan Quarterly Review* 7 (Fall 1968): 280–82.

Bell, Michael Davitt. *The Development of American Romance: The Sacrifice of Relation.* Chicago: University of Chicago Press, 1980.

Bell, Roseann P., Bettye J. Parker, and Beverly Guy-Sheftall, eds. *Sturdy Black Bridges: Visions of Black Women in Literature.* Garden City, N.Y.: Anchor Books, 1979.

Benedict, Ruth. *The Chrysanthemum and the Sword.* Boston: Houghton Mifflin, 1946.

Bennett, Lerone, Jr. *Before the Mayflower: A History of the Negro in America 1619–1962.* Chicago: Johnson Publishing Co., 1962.

Berger, Peter L., and Thomas Luckman. *The Social Construction of Reality: A Treatise in the Sociology of Knowledge.* Baltimore: Penguin Books, 1966.

Blassingame, John W. *The Slave Community: Plantation Life in the Ante-Bellum South.* New York: Oxford University Press, 1972.

Bloom, Harold. *The Anxiety of Influence: A Theory of Poetry.* New York: Oxford University Press, 1973.

Bluestein, Gene. *The Voice of the Folk: Folklore and American Literary Theory.* Amherst: University of Massachusetts Press, 1972.

Bone, Robert A. *Down Home: A History of Afro-American Short Fiction from Its Beginnings to the End of the Harlem Renaissance.* New York: Capricorn Books, 1975.

———. *The Negro Novel in America.* Rev. ed. New Haven: Yale University Press, 1965.

Bontemps, Arna, ed. *Great Slave Narratives.* Boston: Beacon Press, 1969.

Bontemps, Arna, and Jack Conroy. *Anyplace But Here.* New York: Hill and Wang, 1966.

Booth, Wayne C. *The Rhetoric of Fiction.* Chicago: Phoenix Books, 1967.

Brasch, Walter M. *Black English and the Mass Media.* Amherst: University of Massachusetts Press, 1981.

Brawley, Benjamin. *The Negro Genius: A New Appraisal of the Achievement of the American Negro in Literature and the Fine Arts.* New York: Dodd, Mead and Co., 1937.

———. *Paul Laurence Dunbar: Poet of His People.* Chapel Hill: University of North Carolina Press, 1936.

Brown, Sterling A. *The Negro in American Fiction.* 1937. Reprint. New York: Atheneum, 1969.

Brown, Sterling, A., Arthur P. Davis, and Ulysses Lee, eds. *The Negro Caravan:*

Bibliography

Writings by American Negroes. 1941. Reprint. New York: Arno Press and The New York Times, 1970.

Bryant, Jerry. "From Death to Life: The Fiction of Ernest J. Gaines." *Iowa Review,* Winter 1972 pp. 106–20.

Burke, Kenneth. *The Philosophy of Literary Form.* 3d ed. Berkeley: University of California Press, 1941.

Butterfield, Stephen. *Black Autobiography in America.* Amherst: University of Massachusetts Press, 1974.

Cade, Toni, ed. *The Black Woman, An Anthology.* New York: Signet Book, 1970.

Campbell, Joseph. *The Hero with a Thousand Faces.* 2d ed. 1968. Reprint. Princeton: Princeton University Press, 1972.

Carmichael, Stokeley, and Charles V. Hamilton. *Black Power: The Politics of Liberation in America.* New York: Vintage Books, 1967.

Cartey, Wilfred. Introduction to *Negritude: Black Poetry from Africa and the Caribbean.* Edited and translated by Norman R. Shapiro. New York: October House, 1970.

Chapman, Abraham, ed. *Black Voices: An Anthology of Afro-American Literature.* New York: Mentor Book, 1968.

Chase, Richard. *The American Novel and Its Tradition.* Garden City, N.Y.: Doubleday and Co., 1957.

Chesnutt, Charles W. *The Wife of His Youth and Other Stories of the Color Line.* 1899. Reprint. Ann Arbor: Ann Arbor Paperbacks, 1968.

Chesnutt, Helen M. *Charles Waddell Chesnutt: Pioneer of the Color Line.* Chapel Hill: University of North Carolina Press, 1952.

Christian, Barbara. *Black Women Novelists: The Development of a Tradition, 1892–1976.* Westport, Conn.: Greenwood Press, 1980.

Clark, John Henrik, ed. *William Styron's Nat Turner: Ten Black Writers Respond.* Boston: Beacon Press, 1968.

Clark, Kenneth B. *Dark Ghetto: Dilemmas of Social Power.* New York: Harper Torchbooks, 1967.

Cooke, Michael G. *Afro-American Literature in the Twentieth Century: The Achievement of Intimacy.* New Haven: Yale University Press, 1984.

Cromwell, J. W. Review of *Imperium in Imperio,* by Sutton E. Griggs. "Literary Leaves." *Colored American,* April 8, 1899, p. 3.

Cronon, Edmund D. *Black Moses: The Story of Marcus Garvey and the Universal Negro Improvement Association.* 1955. Reprint. Madison: University of Wisconsin Press, 1968.

Crossman, Richard, ed. *The God That Failed.* 1950. Reprint. New York: Bantam Matrix, 1965.

Cruse, Harold. *The Crisis of the Negro Intellectual.* 1967. Reprint. New York: Apollo Editions, 1968.

———. *Rebellion or Revolution?* New York: William Morrow and Co., 1969.

Cunningham, Virginia. *Paul Laurence Dunbar and His Song.* New York: Dodd, Mead, and Co., 1947.

Bibliography

Degler, Carl N. "Slavery and the Genesis of American Race Prejudice." *Comparative Studies of Society and History* 2 (October 1959): 49–66.

Delany, Martin R. *The Condition, Elevation, Emigration, and Destiny of the Colored People of the United States*. 1852. Reprint. New York: Arno Press and The New York Times, 1969.

Dent, Tom. "Umbra Days." *Black American Literature Forum*, 14 (Fall 1980): 105–8.

Dillard, J. L. *Black English: Its History and Usage in the United States*. New York: Random House, 1972.

Dollard, John. "The Dozens: The Dialect of Insult." *American Imago* 1 (1939): 3–25.

Dorson, Richard M. *African Folklore*. Bloomington: Indiana University Press, 1972.

———. *American Folklore and the Historian*. Chicago: University of Chicago Press, 1971.

———. *American Negro Folktales*. Greenwich, Conn.: Fawcett Premier Book, 1967.

Douglass, Frederick. *Narrative of the Life of Frederick Douglass: An American Slave*. Edited by Benjamin Quarles. Cambridge, Mass.: Belknap Press, 1967.

Drake, St. Clair, and Horace R. Cayton. *Black Metropolis: A Study of Negro Life in a Northern City*. Rev. ed., 2 vols. New York: Harbinger Book, 1962.

Du Bois, W. E. B. *The Gift of Black Folk: The Negroes in the Making of America*. Boston: Stratford, 1924.

———. *The Negro*. 1915. Reprint. New York: Oxford University Press, 1970.

———. *The Souls of Black Folk: Essays and Sketches*. 1903. Reprint. Greenwich, Conn.: Crest Book, 1965.

———. "Strivings of the Negro People." *Atlantic Monthly*, August 1897, pp. 194–98.

Dunbar, Paul L. *The Strength of Gideon and Other Stories*. New York: Dodd, Mead and Co., 1900.

Dundes, Alan, ed. *Mother Wit from the Laughing Barrel: Readings in the Interpretation of Afro-American Folklore*. Englewood Cliffs, N.J.: Prentice-Hall, 1973.

Durham, Frank, comp. *Studies in Cane*. Columbus, Ohio: Charles E. Merrill Publishing Co., 1971.

Eagleton, Terry. *Literary Theory: An Introduction*. Minneapolis: University of Minnesota Press, 1983.

Eckley, Grace. "The Awakening of Mr. Afrinnegan: Kelley's *Dunfords Travels Everywheres* and Joyce's *Finnegan's Wake*." *Obsidian: Black Literature in Review* 1 (Summer 1975): 27–40.

Eckman, Fern Maria. *The Furious Passage of James Baldwin*. New York: M. Evans and Co., 1966.

Eigner, Edwin M. *The Metaphysical Novel in England and America: Dickens, Bulwer, Melville, and Hawthorne*. Berkeley: University of California Press, 1978.

Elder, Arlene A. *The "Hindered Hand": Cultural Implications of Early African-American Fiction*. Westport, Conn.: Greenwood Press, 1978.

Eliot, T. S. *The Sacred Wood: Essays on Poetry and Criticism*. 1920. Reprint. New York: University Paperbacks, 1964.

Elkins, Stanley M. *Slavery: A Problem in American Institutional and Intellectual Life.* 1959. Reprint. New York: Grosset and Dunlap, 1963.

Elliott, Robert C. *The Power of Satire: Magic, Ritual, Art.* Princeton: Princeton University Press, 1969.

Ellison, Ralph W. *Shadow and Act.* 1964. Reprint. New York: Signet Book, 1966.

———. "The World and the Jug." *New Leader*, December 9, 1963, pp. 22–26.

Fabre, Michel. *The Unfinished Quest of Richard Wright.* Translated by Isabel Barzun. New York: William Morrow and Co., 1973.

Fanon, Frantz. *Black Skin, White Masks.* Translated by Charles Lam Markmann. New York: Grove Press, 1967.

Farrand, Max. *The Framing of the Constitution of the United States.* New Haven: Yale University Press, 1913.

Farrison, William E. *William Wells Brown: Author and Reformer.* Chicago: University of Chicago Press, 1969.

Fiedler, Leslie A. *Love and Death in the American Novel.* New York: Delta Book, 1966.

Finnegan, Ruth. *Oral Literature in Africa.* London: Oxford University Press, 1970.

Fisher, Dexter, and Robert B. Stepto, eds. *Afro-American Literature: The Reconstruction of Instruction.* New York: Modern Language Association of America, 1979.

Foster, Charles W. "The Representation of Negro Dialect in Charles W. Chesnutt's *The Conjure Woman.*" Ph.D. diss., University of Alabama, 1968.

Foster, Frances Smith. *Witnessing Slavery: The Development of Antebellum Slave Narratives.* Westport, Conn.: Greenwood, 1979.

Fraiberg, Selma. "Two Modern Incest Heroes." *Partisan Review* 28 (Fall–Winter 1961): 646–61.

Franklin, John Hope. *From Slavery to Freedom: A History of Negro Americans.* 3d ed. New York: Alfred A. Knopf, 1967.

———. ed. *Three Negro Classics.* New York: Discus Books, 1968.

Frazier, E. Franklin. *The Negro Church in America.* New York: Schocken Books, 1964.

———. *The Negro Family in the United States.* Revised and abridged ed. Chicago: University of Chicago Press, 1948.

———. *The Negro in the United States.* Revised ed. New York: Macmillan Co., 1957.

Frazier, George James, Sir. *The New Golden Bough.* Abridged, revised and edited by Theodor H. Gaster. 1959. Reprint. New York: Mentor Book, 1964.

Frazier, Kermit. "The Novels of John Wideman." *Black World*, June 1975, pp. 18–38.

Freud, Sigmund. *The Basic Writings of Sigmund Freud.* Edited and translated by A. A. Brill. New York: Modern Library, 1938.

———. *Inhibitions, Symptoms and Anxiety.* 1926. Reprint. London: Hogarth Press, 1948.

Friedan, Betty. *The Feminine Mystique.* New York: Dell Book, 1975.

Frye, Northrop. *Anatomy of Criticism: Four Essays.* Princeton: Princeton University Press, 1957.

Fuller, Hoyt W. "A Survey: Black Writers' Views on Literary Lions and Values." *Negro Digest*, January 1968, pp. 10–48, 81–88.

Bibliography

————, ed. "The Task of the Negro Writer as Artist: A Symposium." *Negro Digest*, April 1965, pp. 54–70, 71–83.

Fullinwider, S. P. *The Mind and Mood of Black America: 20th Century Thought*. Homewood, Ill.: Dorsey Press, 1969.

Gates, Henry Louis, Jr., ed. *Black Literature and Literary Theory*. New York: Methuen, 1984.

Gayle, Addison, Jr. *Richard Wright: Ordeal of a Native Son*. Garden City, N.Y.: Doubleday, Anchor Books, 1980.

————. *The Way of the New World: The Black Novel in America*. Garden City, N.Y.: Doubleday, Anchor Books, 1975.

————. ed. *The Black Aesthetic*. 1971. Reprint. Garden City, N.Y.: Doubleday, Anchor Books, 1972.

Geertz, Clifford. *The Interpretation of Cultures: Selected Essays*. New York: Basic Books, 1973.

Genovese, Eugene D. *The Red and the Black: Marxian Explorations in Southern and Afro-American History*. New York: Panther Books, 1968.

————. *Roll, Jordan, Roll: The World the Slaves Made*. New York: Random House, 1974.

Gilbert, Sandra M., and Susan Gubar. *The Madwoman in the Attic: The Woman Writer and the Nineteenth-Century Literary Imagination*. New Haven: Yale University Press, 1984.

Giovanni, Nikki, and Margaret Walker. *A Poetic Equation: Conversations Between Nikki Giovanni and Margaret Walker*. Washington, D. C.: Howard University Press, 1974.

Glazer, Nathan, and Daniel P. Moynihan. *Beyond the Melting Pot: The Negroes, Puerto Ricans, Jews, Italians, and Irish of New York City*. Cambridge: M.I.T. Press, 1964.

Gloster, Hugh. *Negro Voices in American Fiction*. 1948. Reprint. New York: Russell and Russell, 1965.

————. "Sutton Griggs: Novelist of the New Negro." *Phylon* 4 (1943): 335–45.

Graff, Gerald. *Literature Against Itself: Literary Ideas in Modern Society*. Chicago: University of Chicago Press, 1979.

Grier, William H., and Price M. Cobbs. *Black Rage*. New York: Bantam Books, 1968.

Griggs, Sutton E. *The Story of My Struggles*. Memphis: The National Public Welfare League, 1914.

Grimstead, David. "Melodrama as Echo of the Historically Voiceless." In *Anonymous Americans*. Edited by Tamara K. Hareven. Englewood Cliffs, N.J.: Prentice-Hall, 1971.

Guillén, Claudio. *Literature as System: Essays Toward the Theory of Literary History*. Princeton: Princeton University Press, 1971.

Gutman, Herbert G. *The Black Family in Slavery and Freedom, 1750–1925*. New York: Pantheon Books, 1976.

————. "Work, Culture, and Society in Industrializing America, 1815–1919." *American Historical Review* 78 (June 1973): 531–87.

Hall, Calvin S. *A Primer of Freudian Psychology*. New York: Mentor Book, 1954.

Hamilton, Edith. *Mythology*. New York: Mentor Book, 1969.

Harley, Sharon, and Rosalyn Terborg-Penn, eds. *The Afro-American Woman: Struggles and Images*. Port Washington, N.Y.: Kennikat Press, 1978.

Harris, Trudier. "On *The Color Purple*, Stereotypes, and Silence." *Black American Literature Forum* 18 (Winter 1984): 155–61.

Heermance, J. Noel. *William Wells Brown and Clotelle: A Portrait of the Artist in the First Negro Novel*. Hamden, Conn.: Archon Books, 1969.

Hemenway, Robert, ed. *The Black Novelist*. Columbus, Ohio: Charles E. Merrill Publishing Co., 1970.

Hemenway, Robert E. *Zora Neale Hurston: A Literary Biography*. Urbana: University of Illinois Press, 1977.

———. ed. Introduction to Zora Neale Hurston, *Dust Tracks on a Road: An Autobiography*. 2d ed. Urbana: University of Illinois Press, 1984.

Hernton, Calvin. "The Sexual Mountain and Black Women Writers." *Black American Literature Forum* 18 (Winter 1984): 139–45.

Herskovitz, Melville J. *Life in a Haitian Valley*. New York: Alfred A. Knopf, 1937.

———. *The Myth of the Negro Past*. Boston: Beacon Press, 1941.

Herskovitz, Melville J., and Frances S. Herskovits. *Dahomean Narrative*. Evanston: Northwestern University Press, 1958.

Hill, Herbert, ed. *Anger, and Beyond: The Negro Writer in the United States*. 1966. Reprint. New York: Perennial Library, 1968.

Himes, Chester B. *The Quality of Hurt*. Vol. 1 of *The Autobiography of Chester Himes*. Garden City, N.Y.: Doubleday and Co., 1972.

———. *My Life of Absurdity*. Vol. 2 of *The Autobiography of Chester Himes*. Garden City, N.Y.: Doubleday and Co., 1976.

Hirsch, David H. *Reality and Idea in the Early American Novel*. The Hague: Mouton, 1971.

Hoffman, Stanley, and Barbara Karmiller, eds. *Terms for Order*. Bloomington: Indiana University Press, 1964.

Hollander, Lee M., trans. *The Poetic Edda*. 2d rev. ed. Austin: University of Texas Press, 1962.

Hooks, Bell. *Ain't I A Woman: Black Women and Feminism*. Boston: South End Press, 1981.

Huggins, Nathan I. *Harlem Renaissance*. New York: Oxford University Press, 1971.

Huggins, Nathan I., Martin Kilson, and Daniel M. Fox, eds. *Key Issues in the Afro-American Experience*. 2 vols. New York: Harcourt Brace Jovanovich, 1971.

Hughes, Carl Milton. *The Negro Novelist: A Discussion of the Writing of American Negro Novelists, 1940–1950*. Reprint. New York: Citadel Press, 1979.

Hughes, Langston. *The Best of Simple*. New York: Hill and Wang, 1961.

———. *The Big Sea*. 1940. Reprint. New York: Hill and Wang, 1968.

———. "The Negro Artist and the Racial Mountain." *Nation*, June 23, 1926, pp. 692–94.

Hughes, Langston, and Arna Bontemps, eds. *The Book of Negro Folklore*. New York: Dodd, Mead and Co., 1958.

Hull, Gloria, Patricia Bell Scott, and Barbara Smith, eds. *All the Women Are White, All the Blacks Are Men, But Some of Us Are Brave: Black Women's Studies*. Old Westbury: Feminist Press, 1982.

Hurston, Zora Neale. *Dust Tracks on a Road*. 1942. Reprint. New York: J. B. Lippincott Co., 1971.

Huzinga, J. *Homo Ludens*. London: Routledge and Kegan Paul, 1949.

Hyman, Stanley E., and Ralph Ellison. "The Negro Writer in America: An Exchange." *Partisan Review* 25 (Spring 1958): 197–222.

Hymes, Dell, ed. *Pidginization and Creolization of Languages: Proceedings of a Conference Held at the University of the West Indies Mona, Jamaica, April 1968*. London: Cambridge University Press, 1974.

Isaacs, Harold R. *The New World of Negro Americans*. New York: Viking Compass, 1964.

Jacques-Garvey, Amy. *Garvey and Garveyism*. New York: Collier Books, 1970.

———. ed. *Philosophy and Opinions of Marcus Garvey*. New York: Atheneum, 1970.

Jahn, Janheinz. *Muntu: An Outline of the New African Culture*. Translated by Marjorie Green. New York: Grove Press, 1961.

———. *Neo-African Literature: A History of Black Writing*. Translated by Oliver Coburn and Ursula Lehrburger. 1968. Reprint. New York: Evergreen, 1969.

Jameson, Fredric. *The Political Unconscious: Narrative as a Socially Symbolic Act*. Ithaca: Cornell University Press, 1981.

———. "The Symbolic Inference; or, Kenneth Burke and Ideological Analysis." *Critical Inquiry* 4 (Spring 1978): 507–23.

Johnson, James Weldon. *Along This Way: The Autobiography of James Weldon Johnson*. New York: Viking Compass, 1968.

———. "The Dilemma of the Negro Author." *American Mercury* 15 (December 1928): 477–81.

———, ed. *The Book of American Negro Poetry*. Rev. ed. New York: Harcourt Brace and World, 1931.

Jones, LeRoi. *Blues People: Negro Music in White America*. New York: Morrow Quill Paperbacks, 1963.

———. *Home: Social Essays*. New York: Apollo Editions, 1966.

Jordan, Winthrop, D. *White Over Black: American Attitudes Toward the Negro, 1550–1812*. Chapel Hill: University of North Carolina Press, 1968.

Kammen, Michael. *People of Paradox: An Inquiry Concerning the Origins of American Civilization*. New York: Alfred A. Knopf, 1972.

Kardiner, Abram, and Lionel Ovesey. *The Mark of Oppression: Explorations in the Personality of the American Negro*. 1951. Reprint. Cleveland: Meridian Books, 1962.

Karenga, Ron. "Black Art: A Rhythmic Reality of Revolution." *Negro Digest*, January 1968, pp. 5–9.

Katz, William Loren. *The Black West*. Garden City, N.Y.: Doubleday and Co., 1971.

———, ed. *Five Slave Narratives*. New York: Arno Press and The New York Times, 1969.

Keil, Charles. *Urban Blues*. Chicago: University of Chicago Press, 1966.

Keller, Frances Richardson. *An American Crusade: The Life of Charles Waddell Chesnutt*. Provo: Brigham Young University Press, 1978.

Kelley, William Melvin. *Dancers on the Shore*. 1964. Reprint. Chatham, N.J.: Chatham Bookseller, 1973.

Kent, George. "Ethnic Impact in American Literature: Reflections on a Course," *College Language Association Journal* 11 (September 1967): 24–37.

Kermode, Frank. *The Sense of an Ending: Studies in the Theory of Fiction*. New York: Oxford University Press, 1967.

Killens, John O. *Black Man's Burden*. New York: Trident Press, 1965.

Klinkowitz, Jerome. *Literary Disruptions: The Making of a Post-Contemporary American Fiction*. 2d ed. Urbana: University of Illinois Press, 1980.

Kochman, Thomas, ed. *Rappin' and Stylin' Out: Communication in Urban Black America*. Urbana: University of Illinois Press, 1972.

Laing, R. D. *The Divided Self: An Existential Study in Sanity and Madness*. 1959. Reprint. Baltimore: Penguin Books, 1973.

Lane, Ann J., ed. *The Debate Over Slavery: Stanley Elkins and His Critics*. Urbana: University of Illinois Press, 1971.

Laney, Ruth. "A Conversation with Ernest Gaines." *Southern Review* 10 (January 1974): 1–14.

Laurenson, Diana, and Alan Swingewood. *The Sociology of Literature*. London: Paladin, 1972.

Lerner, Gerda, ed. *Black Women in White America: A Documentary History*. New York: Vintage Books, 1973.

Levine, George. *The Realistic Imagination: English Fiction from Frankenstein to Lady Chatterly*. Chicago: University of Chicago Press, 1980.

Levine, Lawrence W. *Black Culture and Black Consciousness: Afro-American Folk Thought from Slavery to Freedom*. New York: Oxford University Press, 1977.

Lindfors, Bernth. "Amos Tutuola: Debts and Assets." *Cahiers d'Etudes Africaines* 10 (1970): 306–34.

Lindquist, James. *Chester Himes*. New York: Frederick Ungar Publishing Co., 1976.

Locke, Alain, ed. *The New Negro*. 1925. Reprint. New York: Atheneum, 1968.

Lodge, David. *The Modes of Modern Writing: Metaphor, Metonymy and the Typology of Modern Literature*. London: Edward Arnold, 1977.

Loggins, Vernon. *The Negro Author: His Development in America to 1900*. 1931. Reprint. Port Washington, N.Y.: Kennikat Press, 1964.

Long, Richard. "Alain Locke: Cultural and Social Mentor." *Black World*, November 1970; pp. 87–90.

Lovell, John, Jr. *Black Song: The Forge and the Flame; The Story of How the Afro-American Spiritual Was Hammered Out*. New York: Macmillan Co., 1972.

Lukács, Georg. *Realism in Our Time: Literature and the Class Struggle*. Translated by John and Necke Mander. 1963. Reprint. New York: Harper Torchbooks, 1971.

McCaffery, Larry, and Linda Gregory. "Major's *Reflex and Bone Structure* and the

Anti-Detective Tradition." *Black American Literature Forum* 13 (Summer 1979): 39–45.

McKay, Claude. *Harlem: Negro Metropolis*. 1940. Reprint. New York: Harvest Books, 1968.

McKay, Nellie. *Jean Toomer, Artist: A Study of His Literary Life and Work, 1894–1936*. Chapel Hill: University of North Carolina Press, 1984.

McLuhan, Marshall. *The Gutenberg Galaxy: The Making of Typographic Man*. 1962. Reprint. New York: Signet Book, 1969.

Major, Clarence. *The Dark and Feeling: Black American Writers and Their Work*. New York: The Third Press, 1974.

Margolies, Edward. *Native Sons: A Critical Study of Twentieth-Century Negro American Authors*. New York: J. B. Lippincott Co., 1969.

Marx, Leo. *The Machine in the Garden: Technology and the Pastoral Idea in America*. 1964. Reprint. New York: Galaxy Book, 1967.

Matthiessen, F. O. *American Renaissance: Art and Expression in the Age of Emerson and Whitman*. 1941. Reprint. New York: Oxford University Press, 1979.

Mays, Benjamin E. *The Negro's God as Reflected in His Literature*. 1938. Reprint. New York: Atheneum, 1968.

Mibiti, John S. *African Religions and Philosophy*. Garden City, N.Y.: Doubleday, Anchor Books, 1970.

Milliken, Stephen F. *Chester Himes: A Critical Appraisal*. Columbia: University of Missouri Press, 1976.

Mills, Nicolaus. *American and English Fiction in the Nineteenth Century: An Antigenre Critique and Comparison*. Bloomington: Indiana University Press, 1973.

Mintz, Sidney, and Richard Price. *An Anthropological Approach to the Afro-American Past: A Caribbean Perspective*. Philadelphia: Institute for the Study of Human Issues, 1977.

Mitchell, Henry H. *Black Preaching*. New York: J. B. Lippincott, Co., 1970.

Moore, Richard B. "Du Bois and Pan Africa." *Freedomways*, First Quarter 1965, pp. 166–87.

Murray, Albert. *The Hero and the Blues*. Columbia: University of Missouri Press, 1973.

Myrdal, Gunnar. *An American Dilemma: The Negro Problem and Modern Democracy*. 1944. Reprint. New York: Harper and Row, 1962.

Nathan, Hans. *Dan Emmett and the Rise of Early Negro Minstrelsy*. Norman: University of Oklahoma Press, 1962.

Neal, Larry. "And Shine Swam On." In *Black Fire: An Anthology of Afro-American Writing*. Edited by LeRoi Jones and Larry Neal, pp. 638–56. New York: William Morrow and Co., 1968.

Nichols, Charles. *Many Thousand Gone: The Ex-Slaves' Account of Their Bondage and Freedom*. 1963. Reprint. Bloomington: Indiana University Press, 1969.

Obiechina, Emmanuel. *Culture, Tradition and Society in the West African Novel*. London: Cambridge University Press, 1975.

Bibliography

O'Brien, John, ed. *Interviews with Black Writers*. New York: Liveright, 1973.

Olsen, Tillie. *Silences*. New York: Dell Book, 1978.

Ong, Walter, J. *The Presence of the Word: Some Prolegomena for Cultural and Religious History*. New Haven: Yale University Press, 1967.

Osofsky, Gilbert, ed. *Puttin' on Ole Massa: The Slave Narratives of Henry Bibb, William Wells Brown, and Solomon Northup*. New York: Harper Torchbooks, 1969.

Ostendorf, Berndt. *Black Literature in White America*. Totowa, N.J.: Barnes and Noble Books, 1982.

———. "Black Poetry, Blues, and Folklore." Photocopy.

Ottley, Roi, and William J. Weatherby. *The Negro in New York: An Informal Social History, 1626–1640*. New York: Praeger Publishers, 1969.

Park, Robert E. "Community Organization and Juvenile Delinquency." In Robert E. Park, Ernest W. Burgess, and Roderick D. McKenzie, *The City*, pp. 99–112. Chicago: University of Chicago Press, 1925.

———. "Mentality of Racial Hybrids." *American Journal of Sociology* 36 (January 1931): 535–51.

Parrington, Vernon L. *Main Currents in American Thought*. Vol. 3. *The Beginnings of Critical Realism in America: 1860–1920*. New York: Harbinger Book, 1930.

Paulsen, Ronald. *Satire and the Novel in Eighteenth-Century England*. New Haven: Yale University Press, 1967.

Pettigrew, Thomas F. *A Profile of the Negro American*. Princeton: D. Van Nostrand Co., 1964.

Phillips, Ulrich B. *American Negro Slavery: A Survey of the Supply, Employment and Control of Negro Labor as Determined by the Plantation Regime*. 1918. Reprint. Baton Rouge: Louisiana Paperbacks, 1969.

Pickens, William. *The New Negro: His Political, Civil, and Mental Status and Related Essays*. 1916. Reprint. New York: Negro Universities Press, 1969.

Piers, Gerhart, and Milton B. Singer. *Shame and Guilt; A Psychoanalytic and a Cultural Study*. Springfield, Ill.: Charles C. Thomas, 1953.

Pizer, Donald. *Twentieth-Century American Literary Naturalism: An Interpretation*. Carbondale: Southern Illinois University Press, 1982.

Pryse, Marjorie, and Hortense J. Spillers, eds. *Conjuring: Black Women, Fiction, and Literary Tradition*. Bloomington: Indiana University Press, 1985.

Quarles, Benjamin. *The Negro in the American Revolution*. Chapel Hill: University of North Carolina Press, 1961.

Rank, Otto. *The Myth of the Birth of the Hero and Other Writings*. Edited by Philip Freund. 1959. Reprint. New York: Vintage Books, 1964.

Ray, David, and Robert M. Farnsworth, eds. *Richard Wright: Impressions and Perspectives*. 1971. Reprint. Ann Arbor Paperbacks, 1973.

Record, Wilson. *The Negro and the Communist Party*. 1951. Reprint. New York: Atheneum, 1971.

Reed, Ishmael. *Conjure: Selected Poems, 1963–1970*. Amherst: University of Massachusetts Press, 1972.

Bibliography

———. "Ishmael Reed on Ishmael Reed." *Black World*, June 1974, pp. 20–34.

———. *Shrovetide in Old New Orleans.* 1978. Reprint. New York: Discus Book, 1979.

———, ed. *19 Necromancers from Now.* Garden City, N.Y.: Doubleday, Anchor Books, 1979.

Render, Sylvia Lyons. *Eagle with Clipped Wings: Form and Feeling in the Fiction of Charles Waddell Chesnutt.* Ann Arbor: University Microfilms, 1974.

Robertson, James Oliver. *American Myth, American Reality.* New York: Hill and Wang, 1980.

Rosenberg, Bruce. *The Art of the American Folk Preacher.* New York: Oxford University Press, 1970.

Rosenblatt, Roger. *Black Fiction.* Cambridge: Harvard University Press, 1974.

Rourke, Constance. *American Humor: A Study of the National Character.* New York: Harcourt, Brace and Co., 1931.

Rowell, Charles. "Poetry, History and Humanism: An Interview with Margaret Walker." *Black World*, December 1975, pp. 4–17.

Rushing, Andrea Benton. "Family Resemblances: A Comparative Study of Women Protagonists in Contemporary African-American and Anglophone-African Novels." Ph.D. diss., University of Massachusetts, Amherst, 1983.

Sadoff, Diane, "Black Matrilineage: The Case of Alice Walker and Zora Neale Hurston." *Signs: Journal of Women in Culture and Society* 9 (Autumn 1985): 4–26.

Scholes, Robert. *The Fabulators.* New York: Oxford University Press, 1967.

Scholes, Robert, and Robert Kellogg. *The Nature of Narrative.* New York: Oxford University Press, 1966.

Schraufnagel, Noel. *From Apology to Protest: The Black American Novel.* Deland, Fla.: Everett/Edwards, 1973.

Schulz, Max F. *Black Humor Fiction of the Sixties: A Pluralistic Definition of Man and His World.* Athens: Ohio University Press, 1973.

Showalter, Elaine, ed. *The New Feminist Criticism: Essays on Women, Literature, and Theory.* New York: Pantheon Books, 1985.

Silberman, Charles. *Crisis in Black and White.* New York: Vintage Books, 1964.

Singh, Amritjit. *The Novels of the Harlem Renaissance: Twelve Black Writers 1923–1933.* University Park: Pennsylvania State University Press, 1976.

Soyinka, Wole. *Myth, Literature and the African World.* 1976. Reprint. New York: Cambridge University Press, 1978.

Stepto, Robert B. *From Behind the Veil: A Study of Afro-American Narrative.* Urbana: University of Illinois Press, 1979.

Stewart, William A. "Sociolinguistic Factors in the History of American Negro Dialects." *Florida Foreign Language Reporter* 5, no. 2 (1967): 11–29.

Stonequist, Everett V. *The Marginal Man: A Study in Personality and Culture Conflict.* New York: Charles Scribner's Sons, 1937.

Styron, William. *The Confessions of Nat Turner.* New York: Random House, 1967.

Swados, Harvey, ed. *The American Writer and the Great Depression.* New York: Bobbs-Merrill Co., 1966.

Sylvander, Carolyn Wedin. *Jessie Redman Fauset, Black American Writer*. Troy: Whitston Publishing Co., 1981.

Takaki, Ronald T. *Violence in the Black Imagination: Essays and Documents*. New York: G. P. Putnam's Sons, 1972.

Tate, Claudia, ed. *Black Women Writers at Work*. New York: Continuum, 1983.

Thompson, Robert Farris. *Flash of the Spirit: African and Afro-American Art and Philosophy*. 1983. Reprint. New York: Vintage Books, 1984.

Toll, Robert C. *Blacking Up: The Minstrel Show in Nineteenth-Century America*. New York: Oxford University Press, 1974.

Toomer, Jean. Toomer Collection. Fisk University Library. Nashville, Tenn.

Tourgée, Albion W. *A Fool's Errand*. 1879. Reprint. Cambridge, Mass.: Belknap Press, 1961.

Traylor, Eleanor. "I Hear Music in the Air: James Baldwin's *Just Above My Head*." *First World* 2, no. 3 (1979): 40–43.

Turner, Darwin T. *In a Minor Chord: Three Afro-American Writers and Their Search for Identity*. Carbondale: Southern Illinois University Press, 1971.

Turner, Victor W. *The Ritual Process: Structure and Anti-Structure*. 1969. Reprint. New York: Pelican Books, 1974.

Turville-Petrie, Edward O. G. *Myth and Religion of the North: The Religion of Ancient Scandinavia*. New York: Holt, Rinehart and Winston, 1964.

Valentine, Charles A. *Culture and Poverty: Critique and Counter-Proposals*. Chicago: University of Chicago Press, 1968.

Van Vechten, Carl. *Nigger Heaven*. 1926. Reprint. New York: Harper Colophon, 1971.

Walcott, Ronald. "The Novels of Hal Bennett." Part 1. *Black World*, June 1974, pp. 36–48, 89–97; Part 2. ibid., July 1974, pp. 78–96.

Walcutt, Charles C. *American Literary Naturalism: A Divided Stream*. Minneapolis: University of Minnesota Press, 1956.

Walker, Alice. *In Search of Our Mothers' Gardens: Womanist Prose*. New York: Harcourt Brace Jovanovich, 1983.

Walker, Margaret. *How I Wrote "Jubilee."* Chicago: Third World Press, 1972.

Washington, Mary Helen, ed. *Midnight Birds: Stories of Contemporary Black Women Writers*. Garden City, N.Y.: Doubleday, Anchor Books, 1980.

Watkins, Patricia D. "Sutton Griggs: The Evolution of a Propagandist." Master's thesis, Howard University, 1970.

Wellek, René, and Austin Warren. *Theory of Literature*, 3d ed. New York: Harvest Book, 1962.

Weston, Jessie L. *From Ritual to Romance*. 1920. Reprint. Garden City, N.Y.: Doubleday, Anchor Books, 1957.

White, Walter. *Rope and Faggot: A Biography of Judge Lynch*. 1929. Reprint. New York: Arno Press and The New York Times, 1969.

Whitten, Norman E., Jr., and John F. Szwed, eds. *Afro-American Anthropology: Contemporary Perspectives*. New York: The Free Press, 1970.

Bibliography

Wiggins, William H., Jr. "Black Folktales in the Novels of John O. Killens." *Black scholar: Journal of Black Studies and Research*, November 1971, pp. 50–58.

Williams, John A. *The Angry Ones*. New York: Ace Books, 1960.

———. *Flashbacks: A Twenty-Year Diary of Article Writing*. Garden City, N.Y.: Doubleday, Anchor Books, 1973.

———, ed. *Beyond the Angry Black*. 1966. Reprint. New York: Mentor Book, 1971.

Williams, John A., and Charles F. Harris, eds. *Amistad 1*. New York: Vintage Books, 1970.

Williams, Raymond. *The Country and the City*. New York: Oxford University Press, 1973.

———. *Culture and Society, 1780–1950*. 1958. Reprint. New York: Harper and Row, 1966.

———. *Marxism and Literature*. London: Oxford University Press, 1977.

Williams, Sherley A. *Give Birth to Brightness: A Thematic Study in Neo-Black Literature*. New York: Dial Press, 1972.

Wilson, William J. *Power, Racism, and Privilege: Race Relations in Theoretical and Sociohistorical Perspectives*. 1973. Reprint. New York: Free Press, 1976.

Wittke, Carl. *Tambo and Bones: A History of the American Minstrel Stage*. 1930. Reprint. Westport, Conn.: Greenwood Press, 1968.

Wolters, Raymond. *Negroes and the Great Depression: The Problem of Economic Recovery*. Westport, Conn.: Greenwood Press, 1970.

Woodson, Carter G. *The Negro in Our History*. Washington, D.C.: Associated Publishers, 1922.

Wright, Richard. *American Hunger*. New York: Harper and Row, 1977.

———. *Black Boy: A Record of Childhood Youth*. New York: Harper, 1945.

———. *Black Power: A Record of Reactions in a Land of Pathos*. New York: Harper, 1954.

———. "Blueprint for Negro Writing." *New Challenge* 2 (Fall 1937): 53–65.

———. *The Color Curtain*. New York: World Publishing Co., 1955.

———. *Pagan Spain*. New York: Harper, 1956.

———. *Twelve Million Black Voices: A Folk History of the Negro in the United States*. New York: Viking Press, 1941.

———. *White Man, Listen!* New York: Doubleday, 1957.

Yellin, Jean Fagan. *The Intricate Knot: Black Figures in American Literature, 1776–1863*. New York: New York University Press, 1972.

Yetman, Norman R., ed. *Life Under the "Peculiar Institution": Selections from the Slave Narrative Collection*. New York: Holt, Rinehart and Winston, 1970.

Young, James O. *Black Writers of the Thirties*. Baton Rouge: Louisiana State University Press, 1973.

Young, Jean I., trans. *The Prose Edda of Snorri Sturluson; Tales from Norse Mythology*. Berkeley: University of California Press, 1973.

Index

Index

306, 325; and Fisher, 140; and Hurston, 127; influence of, on black novelists, 29–30, 36
Bicultural identity, 53
Biculturalism, 105
Big "Bad" Nigger, stereotype of, 329
Big John the Conqueror, 123
Big Sea, The (Hughes), 129
Bildungsroman, 136, 245
Bird at My Window (Guy), 245
Black aesthetic, 278
Black American, as metaphor of America and the modern human condition, 215
Black American: culture and character, dynamics of, 340; culture and character, sources of, 3; culture classified, 20; culture related to white American society, 4, 9; dynamics of, 340; nationalism, 112; novelists, xiii, xiv; pastoral defined, 71, *see also* Afro-American pastoral; values, source of, 20
Black Americans: early economic exploitation of, 8; distinctive history of, 340; as metaphor of modern human condition, 215; as people with no past, 9; unique pattern of experiences of, 5
Black Art: defined, 238; renaissance in 1960s, 60
Black artist, dual responsibility of, 194
Black arts and black power, relationship of, 239
Black arts movement, 238, 246, 303
Black Arts Repertory Theatre-School, 238
Black avenger as stock character, 303
Black awareness and unity, themes of, 250
Black bourgeoisie: alienation of, 258; and Chesnutt, 69; and Ellison, 208; and Fauset, 108; goal of, 149; and

Himes, 174; and Hughes, 134; and McKay, 118; and Toomer, 98; and Wright, R., 174
Black Boy (R. Wright), 154–56, 166–67, 216
Black church: rhetoric of, 228; rhetoric, lore, and music of, 219; service as rite of passage, 262; storefront, 224; and Walker, A., 265
Black Collegian, 239
Black consciousness: historical experiences that shape, 5; and Kelley, 297; and Killens, 248–49, 252; and Wright, R., 155
Black cowboy tall tale defined, 332
"Black Criterion, A" (Major), 315
Black detective tradition, 319
Black Dialogue, 239
Black Enterprise, 239
Blacker the Berry, The (Thurman), 145, 147
Black-Eyed Susans (M.H. Washington), 242
Black experiences, cultural products of, 5
Black family and Walker, A., 265
Black female literary tradition, theory of, 242–44
Black feminism, theme of, 260–69
Black feminists, 241–43
"Black Flame Trilogy, The" (Du Bois), 81–82
Black folk humor, 149
Black folklore: and Brown, F., 191; and Brown, L., 191; and contemporary black fabulators, 285; defined, 17–20; and Du Bois, 85; and Hurston, 120; and Killens, 269; and the triumph of naturalism, 186; and Walker, A., 269; and Wideman, 307; and Williams, 269. *See also* Afro-American folklore
Black folk religion, 263

Index

Index